Basque Country,
Navarra & La Rioja

Aragón

Catalonia

Donostia
(San Sebastián)

Iruña
(Pamplona)

Zaragoza

Lleida

Barcelona

Barcelona

EASTERN
SPAIN

THE BALEARIC ISLANDS

Cuenca

Palma de
Mallorca

Valencia

Albacete

Alacant
(Alicante)

The Balearic
Islands

Murcia

Almería

The Canary Islands

THE CANARY ISLANDS

Valencia and
Murcia

Santa Cruz
de Tenerife

Las Palmas
de Gran Canaria

DK EYEWITNESS TRAVEL

Spain

Project Editor Nick Inman
Art Editors Jaki Grosvenor, Janis Utton
Editors Catherine Day, Lesley McCave,
Seán O'Connell
Designers Susan Blackburn, Dawn Davies-
Cook, Joy Fitzsimmons, Helen Westwood

Main Contributors John Ardagh, David
Baird, Mary-Ann Gallagher, Vicky Hayward,
Adam Hopkins, Lindsay Hunt, Nick Inman,
Paul Richardson, Martin Symington,
Nigel Tisdall, Roger Williams

Photographers Max Alexander, Joe Cornish,
Neil Lukas, Neil Mersh, John Miller,
Kim Sayer, Linda Whitwam, Peter Wilson

Illustrators Stephen Conlin, Gary Cross,
Richard Draper, Isidoro González-Adalid
Cabezas (Acanto Arquitectura y Urbanismo
S.l.), Claire Littlejohn, Maltings Partnership,
Chris Orr & Assocs, John Woodcock

Printed and bound in China

First American Edition, 1996

Published in the United States
by DK Publishing, 345 Hudson Street
New York, New York 10014

18 19 20 21 10 9 8 7 6 5 4 3 2 1

Reprinted with revisions 1997, 1999,
2000, 2001, 2002, 2003, 2004,
2005, 2006, 2007, 2008, 2009, 2010,
2011, 2013, 2014, 2016, 2018
Copyright 1996, 2018 © Dorling
Kindersley Limited, London
A Penguin Random House Company

Published in the UK by Dorling Kindersley
Limited.

A catalog record for this book is available
from the Library of Congress.

ISSN 1542-1554
ISBN 978-1-4654-6770-6

Floors are referred to throughout in
accordance with European usage; ie the
"first floor" is the floor above ground level.

MIX
Paper from
responsible sources
FSC
www.fsc.org   FSC™ C018179

Introducing Spain

Northern Spain

Colourful exterior of Casa Batlló, Barcelona

Barcelona

Eastern Spain

**The information in this
DK Eyewitness Travel Guide is checked regularly.**

Every effort has been made to ensure that this book is as up-to-date as possible
at the time of going to press. Some details, however, such as telephone numbers,
opening hours, prices, gallery hanging arrangements and travel information are
liable to change. The publishers cannot accept responsibility for any consequences
arising from the use of this book, nor for any material on third party websites, and
cannot guarantee that any website address in this book will be a suitable source of
travel information. We value the views and suggestions of our readers very highly.
Please write to: Publisher, DK Eyewitness Travel Guides, Dorling Kindersley,
80 Strand, London, WC2R 0RL, UK, or email: travelguides@dk.com.

◄ **Title page** Madrid's Plaza [...] [...]ella, or Old Town, in Tossa de
Mar, Catalonia **Back co[...]**

3 2895 00148 9694

Contents

Madrid

Central Spain

León Cathedral
(see pp358–9)

Crystal-clear waters in a sheltered cove along the Costa Brava

Southern Spain

Spain's Islands

Travellers' Needs

Survival Guide

HOW TO USE THIS GUIDE

This guide helps you to get the most from your visit to Spain. It provides detailed practical information and expert recommendations. Introducing Spain maps the country and sets it in its historical and cultural context. The five regional sections, plus Barcelona and Madrid, describe important sights, using maps, photographs and illustrations. Features cover topics from food and wine to fiestas and beaches. Restaurant and hotel recommendations can be found in *Travellers' Needs*. The *Survival Guide* has tips on everything from transport to using the telephone system.

Barcelona, Madrid and Seville

These cities are divided into areas, each with its own chapter. For Barcelona and Madrid, a last chapter, *Further Afield*, covers peripheral sights. Madrid Province, surrounding the capital, has its own chapter. All sights are numbered and plotted on the chapter's area map. Information on each sight is easy to locate, as it follows the numerical order on the map.

Sights at a Glance lists the chapter's sights by category: Churches and Cathedrals, Museums and Galleries, Streets and Squares, Historic Buildings, Parks and Gardens.

2 **Street-by-Street Map**
This gives a bird's-eye view of the key areas in each chapter.

Stars indicate the sights that no visitor should miss.

All pages relating to Madrid have green thumb tabs. Barcelona's are pink and Seville's are red.

A locator map shows where you are in relation to other areas of the city centre.

1 **Area Map**
For easy reference, sights are numbered and located on a map. City centre sights are also marked on Street Finders: Barcelona (*pages 183–9*); Madrid (*pages 311–19*); Seville (*pages 453–9*).

A suggested route for a walk is shown in red.

3 **Detailed information**
The sights in the three main cities are described individually. Addresses, telephone numbers, opening hours, admission charges, tours, photography and wheelchair access are also provided, as well as public transport links.

CASTILLA-LA MANCHA

Guadalajara · Cuenca · Toledo · Albacete · Ciudad Real

La Mancha's empty beauty, its windmills and medieval castles, silhouetted above the sierra plains, was immortalized by Cervantes in *Don Quixote's* epic adventures. Its brilliantly sunlit, wide horizons are one of the classic images of Spain. This scarcely visited region has great, scenic mountain ranges, dramatic gorges and the two monument-filled cities of Toledo and Cuenca.

You will always find a castle nearby in this region – as the name Castilla suggests. Most were built in the 9th–12th centuries, when the region was a battleground between Christians and Moors. Others mark the 14th- and 15th-century frontiers between the kingdoms of Aragón and Castile. Sigüenza, Belmonte, Alarcón, Molina de Aragón and Calatrava la Nueva are among the most impressive.

Toledo, which was the capital of Visigothic Spain, is an outstanding museum city. Its rich architectural and artistic heritage derives from a coexistence of Muslim, Christian and Jewish cultures with medieval and Renaissance ideas and influences.

Cuenca is another attractive city. Its Old Town is perched above converging

gorges; on two sides it spills down steep hillsides. Villanueva de los Infantes, Chinchilla, Alcaraz and Almagro are towns of character built between the 16th and 18th centuries. Ocaña and Tembleque each has a splendid *plaza mayor* (main square).

La Mancha's plains are brightened by natural features of great beauty in its two national parks – the Tablas de Daimiel, and Cabañeros, within the Montes de Toledo. Rimming the plains are beautiful upland areas: the olive groves of the Alcarria; Cuenca's limestone mountains; and the peaks of the Sierra de Alcaraz. The wine region of La Mancha is the world's largest expanse of vineyards. Around Consuegra and Albacete fields turn mauve in autumn as the valuable saffron *crocus* blooms.

Introduction

1 The landscape, history and character of each region is outlined here, showing how the area has developed over the centuries and what it has to offer to the visitor today.

Spain Area by Area

Apart from Barcelona, Madrid and Seville, the country has been divided into 12 regions, each of which has a separate chapter. The most interesting cities, towns and villages, and other places to visit, are numbered on a *Regional Map*.

Regional Map

2 This shows the road network and gives an illustrated overview of the whole region. All interesting places to visit are numbered and there are also useful tips on getting to, and around, the region by car and public transport.

Fiesta boxes highlight the best traditional fiestas in the region.

Each area of Spain can be quickly identified by its colour coding, shown on the inside front cover.

Detailed information

3 All the important towns and other places to visit are described individually. They are listed in order, following the numbering on the *Regional Map*. Within each town or city, there is detailed information on important buildings and other sights.

Toledo Cathedral

The splendour of Toledo's massive cathedral reflects its history as the spiritual heart of the Church in Spain and the seat of the Primate of all Spain. The Mozarabic Mass, which dates back to Visigothic times, is still said here today. The present cathedral was built on the site of a 7th-century church. Work began in 1226 and spanned three centuries, until the completion of the last vaults in 1493. This long period of construction explains the cathedral's mixture of styles: pure French Gothic – complete with flying buttresses – on the exterior; with Spanish decorative styles, such as Mudéjar and Plateresque work, used in the interior.

For all top sights, a Visitors' Checklist provides the practical information you will need to plan your visit.

Spain's top sights

4 These are given two or more full pages. Historic buildings are dissected to reveal their interiors. The most interesting towns or city centres are shown in a bird's-eye view, with sights picked out and described.

INTRODUCING
SPAIN

DISCOVERING SPAIN

The following tours have been designed to take in as many of Spain's highlights as possible, while keeping long-distance travel to a minimum. First come three 2-day tours exploring Spain's most enticing cities: Madrid, Barcelona and Seville. These itineraries can be combined to form a week-long tour (all three cities are linked by fast AVE trains). Extra suggestions are provided for those who want to extend their stay to 10 days.

A one-week itinerary of Bilbao and the Basque Lands and a themed 10-day tour of Northern Spain follow. Next comes a one-week itinerary of the Mediterranean coast, from Barcelona to Cartagena via Valencia. Finally, we've created a tour that combines Madrid with the three great cities of old Al Andalus: Seville, Córdoba and Granada. Pick, combine and follow your favourite tours, or simply dip in and out and be inspired.

Madrid and Moorish Spain: Granada, Córdoba and Seville

- Soak up the electric atmosphere of the Spanish capital, Madrid, admiring the world-class art museums and being spoiled for choice when it comes to shopping and eating.

- Be seduced by Seville, an enchanting city of narrow whitewashed streets, with its La Giralda bell tower and the opulent palace of the Real Alcázar.

- Explore delightfully preserved Andalucían towns like Carmona and Écija, with their fine palaces and churches.

- Marvel at the Mezquita in Córdoba and get lost in the maze of the old Jewish Quarter.

- Drive through rolling hills and olive groves to take in a string of pretty villages, from Montilla to Priego de Córdoba, enjoying fresh local wines with dinner.

- Visit Granada's extraordinary palace of Alhambra, surrounded by the scented gardens of the Generalife and the spirit of Al Andalus. Tuck into tasty tapas, and listen to flamenco in a hilltop cave.

Key

— Madrid and Moorish Spain
— Bilbao and the Basque Lands
— Wild Spain
— Barcelona and the Mediterranean Coast

MADRID · Guadalajara · Madrid · Aranjuez · Toledo · Cuenca · Tormelloso · Ciudad Real · CASTILLA-LA MANCH. · Linares · Córdoba · ANDALUCÍA · Huéscar · Écija · Montilla · Priego de Córdoba · Sevilla · Aguilar · Carmona · Montefrío · Granada · Málaga · Almería · Motril · Marbella

La Giralda
The bell tower of the Seville Cathedral, formerly a minaret, is World Heritage-listed.

◄ *Pier in the Prince's Garden at Aranjuez Castle, by Gianni Dagli Orti*

Wild Spain: Cantabria, Asturias and Galicia

- Visit enchanting fishing villages-cum-resorts, and the Cantabrian capital of Santander.

- Wander the perfectly preserved historic town of Santillana del Mar, and see prehistoric cave art at Cuevas de Altamira.

- Hike the lofty peaks and valleys of spectacular Parque Nacional de los Picos de Europa.

- Hang out in bustling Gijón, then head east along the craggy Costa Verde to discover idyllic villages and secret coves.

- Spend a day in Roman-walled Lugo, heading on to stone-and-granite Santiago de Compostela.

Bilbao and the Basque Lands

- Be dazzled in Bilbao by the spectacular Museo Guggenheim, then shop at the city's chic boutiques.

- Visit the city of Gernika-Lumo's poignant ancient oak, one of few places to survive the 1937 bombing.

- Meander the wild and beautiful Costa Vasca, sampling the day's catch at enchanting seaside towns.

- Soak up the beach glamour of San Sebastián and enjoy some of the best tapas in the world.

- Inland, visit scenic Santuario de Loiola and hilltop Santuario de Arantzazu.

- Stroll around delightful Vitoria, the Basque capital.

- Explore the historic wine-producing town of Haro, taking in a few bodegas.

Barcelona and the Mediterranean Coast by Train

- Get lost in Barcelona's Gothic Quarter, admire Gaudí's fairy-tale architecture, shop and eat to your heart's content, then relax on the fabulous city beaches.

- Stroll around Sitges, one of the prettiest (and liveliest) towns on the Med, then head to Tarragona to visit a slew of Roman remains.

- Relax in lovely Peníscola, piled up on a promontory almost completely surrounded by the sea, then head to dazzling Valencia, fusing old and new with flair.

- Spend a day in vibrant Alicante (Alacant), chock-full of fantastic art museums, and with a castle atop a crag boasting great coastal views.

- Tour traditional Murcia, taking in its Baroque architecture and old-world spirit. Then on to old Cartagena, stuffed with Punic and Roman remains.

2 Days in Madrid

Tapas, flamenco, art, monuments and museums – the capital has the lot.

- **Arriving** Barajas Airport is 13 km (8 miles) from the city centre, linked by metro, bus (local and express) and taxi.

Day 1
Morning Begin at the Plaza Mayor, the huge arcaded square in Madrid's historic heart (*p277*), then take a stroll around the surrounding cobbled streets. Head into the pretty 19th-century Mercado de San Miguel (located just off the square) for a gourmet lunch at one of the many chic tapas bars.

Afternoon Visit the Prado (*pp296–9*), Spain's biggest museum. Highlights include the superlative *Las Meninas* by Velázquez, and a host of his works for the Spanish Habsburg monarchs. The charming gardens at the sumptuous Hotel Ritz by Belmond just next door are ideal for a post-museum cocktail.

> **To extend your trip...**
> Head into the Guadarrama mountains north of Madrid, visiting ancient Segovia (*pp368–9*) and the walled city of Ávila (*pp366–7*).

Playa Mayor, Madrid's grand arcaded square

Day 2
Morning Stroll along the Gran Vía (*pp284–5*), Madrid's glittering answer to New York's Broadway, admiring the turn-of-the-20th-century theatres, as well as some of the city's first skyscrapers. The street is now a shopping mecca, packed with flagship stores. Relax at one of the arty restaurants in Malasaña (*p308*).

Afternoon Head to the Museo Nacional Centro de Arte Reina Sofía (*pp302–3*), a superb contemporary art museum, to admire Picasso's powerful *Guernica* and works by Gaudí, Miró and Dalí, among others. In the evening, take a tour of the lively tapas bars around the Plaza de Santa Ana.

2 Days in Barcelona

Be enchanted by the city's medieval quarter, Modernista monuments, gourmet cuisine and city beaches.

- **Arriving** El Prat Airport is 18 km (11 miles) south of the city centre, with regular train and bus connections.

Day 1
Morning Get lost in the beautiful stone labyrinth of Barcelona's Gothic Quarter (*Barri Gòtic, pp148–9*). Visit the remarkable ruins of the ancient Roman colony of Barcino, still visible beneath the MUHBA Plaça del Rei (home to the Barcelona History Museum, *pp150–51*). Then explore the magnificent Barcelona Cathedral (*pp152–3*), especially its enchanting cloister. There are dozens of excellent places in the area for a quick bite to eat.

Afternoon Wander down the city's most famous promenade, Las Ramblas (*pp154–5*), to the Port Vell (*p160*), now a marina full of yachts and pleasure boats. Then head to the traditional fishermen's neighbourhood of Barceloneta (*p160*), strolling through the unbelievably narrow streets packed with old-fashioned tapas bars. If you're feeling tired take a late-afternoon siesta on the

Barcelona's busy, tree-lined pedestrian thoroughfare, Las Ramblas

For practical information on travelling around Spain, see pp626–35

beach before dining on traditional paella at one of the seafront restaurants.

Day 2
Morning Spend the morning at Gaudí's spectacular (and still unfinished) Sagrada Familia (pp170–71). Admire the awesome façades, and take the lift up to the upper galleries for vertiginous city views. Stroll up to the nearby Hospital de la Santa Creu i de Sant Pau (p169), set in an enchanting complex of Modernista pavilions. Enjoy a lazy lunch in the Eixample neighbourhood.

Afternoon Wander down the fashionable Passeig de Gràcia (p161), which is lined with scores of top international designer boutiques and flag-ship stores of famous high-street brands. This street is as famous for its Modernista architecture as it is for its shopping, and is crowned by two of Gaudí's most celebrated buildings, the Casa Batlló (p168) and La Pedrera (p169), both of which must be visited. Round out the day with a tapas tour of the Eixample neighbourhood's many bars.

> **To extend your trip...**
> Visit enchanting, medieval Girona (pp218–19), then head to the glorious Costa Brava (p221) for a couple of days' hiking or simply lazing on the beach.

2 Days in Seville

The spirit of Al Andalus lives on in Seville's whitewashed lanes, intricately tiled mansions and ornate courtyards – the perfect place to enjoy authentic Spanish pleasures like flamenco and fino.

- **Arriving** San Pablo Airport is 10 km (6 miles) northeast of the city centre. Take a bus or taxi to the city. From Madrid Airport, the high-speed AVE train to Seville takes 2 hours 20 minutes.

Day 1
Morning Start with a visit to Seville's most recognizable landmark, La Giralda (pp442–3), the exquisite minaret-cum-bell tower attached to the vast cathedral. The tomb of Christopher Columbus can be found inside the cathedral, along with a wealth of lavish artworks, but the highlight is the extraordinary views from the top of La Giralda. Then head to the sumptuous Real Alcázar (pp446–7), a magnificent royal palace richly decorated with elaborate tiles and stucco work.

Afternoon Cool off with a gentle stroll in the charming Parque María Luisa (pp450–51), with its colourfully tiled benches and tinkling fountains. There are a couple of fascinating museums to explore, full of

archaeological artifacts and traditional Andalucían folk art. Enjoy a traditional dinner and perhaps some flamenco in the vibrant Triana neighbourhood (p452).

Day 2
Morning Visit the enticing Barrio Santa Cruz, an enchanting warren of narrow lanes lined with ivory houses sporting geranium-filled balconies. Spend some time in the fascinating Archivo de Indias (p445), a handsome 16th-century building that contains the historical records of Spain's colonization of the Americas. Take a look at the paintings in the Hospital de los Venerables (p115), then delight in the Casa de Pilatos (pp444–5), a breathtaking palace with a beautiful garden.

Afternoon Admire the superb art collection in the Museo de Bellas Artes (p436), housed in a handsome 17th-century convent set around a charming courtyard. Take in the fabulous shops along the nearby Calle Sierpes, some of which sell gorgeous flamenco dresses and mantilla shawls. For dinner, there is a great choice of tapas bars in the area.

> **To extend your trip...**
> Drive east, via Carmona and Écija, or travel by train to Córdoba (pp484–7) to visit the remarkable Mezquita.

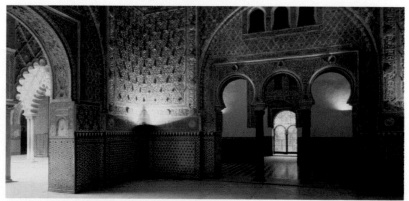

Mudéjar architecture and intricate stucco work at the Real Alcázar, Seville

Bilbao and the Basque Lands

- **Duration** 7 days.
- **Airports** Arrive and depart from Bilbao Airport.
- **Transport** This tour must be done by car.
- **Booking ahead** Bilbao: Guggenheim tickets (www.guggenheim-bilbao. es), any of the Michelin-starred restaurants.

Day 1: Bilbao

The vast, spectacular Museo Guggenheim (*pp124–5*) deserves a day to itself. Admire the gleaming curves of Frank Gehry's magnificent design from the banks of the river, and don't miss Jeff Koons' flower-covered *Puppy* at the entrance. Afterwards, stroll along the banks of the river, then enjoy an evening in the atmospheric tapas bars of the city's Old Town (*Casco Viejo, p122*).

Day 2: Bilbao and Gernika

Spend the morning at Bilbao's other fantastic art museum, the Museo de Bellas Artes (*p122*), which displays works by Basque, Spanish and inter-national artists. The museum overlooks the city's most beautiful public park, perfect for a stroll. Have lunch in a local café, and then drive to Gernika-Lumo (*pp122–3*). Bombed on the orders of General Franco in 1937, this town now contains a poignant peace museum.

Day 3: Along the Coast to San Sebastián (Donostia)

Explore the spectacular Costa Vasca (*p123*), with its plunging cliffs and beautiful bays. Stop off at a string of enchanting towns, such as Lekeitio, Zumaia, Zarautz and pretty little Getaria, barely changed in centuries. Any of these towns are ideal for a seafood lunch by the beach.

Day 4: San Sebastián

Stroll around the narrow streets surrounding the magnificent Basilica de Santa María in San Sebastián's beautiful Old Town (*pp126–7*), then visit the Museo de San Telmo, set in a 16th-century monastery. After lunch in one of the celebrated traditional tapas bars, hike up the Monte Urgell to enjoy the views, then head to the Playa de la Concha, a crescent of golden sand curving round an idyllic bay. For dinner, splash out on one of the many Michelin-starred restaurants (*see p585*).

Day 5: Oñati and the Santuario de Loiola

From San Sebastián, drive inland through verdant countryside to the Santuario de Loiola (*p128*), a lavish 18th-century complex built on the site where the founder of the Jesuits, San Ignacio de Loyola, was born in the 1490s. Continue to the elegant little university town of Oñati (*p128*), which boasts a few handsome Renaissance buildings. You could also visit the nearby Santuario de Arantzazu (*p128*),

A pretty street in San Sebastián's Old Town leads to the Basílica de Santa Maria

an unattractive modern construction from the 1950s, which nonetheless enjoys a sublime mountain setting.

Day 6: Vitoria

Explore the vibrant Basque capital of Vitoria (Gasteiz) (*p130*), beginning with the charming Plaza de la Virgen Blanca. Don't miss the older of Vitoria's two cathedrals, the handsome Gothic Catedral de Santa María. After lunch, visit the fascinating Museo de Arqueología y Naipes (BIBAT), an archaeology museum which also contains a curious collection of historic playing cards.

Day 7: Haro and back to Bilbao

Return to Bilbao, but first stop off in Haro (*p132*), capital of the Rioja Alta region, to pick up some of the area's world-famous wines and perhaps enjoy a tasting or two. It's a perfect place for lunch, with a host of lively tapas bars serving great food to match the wonderful local wines.

Frank Gehry's sleek and gleaming Museo Guggenheim, a spectacular structure of glass, titanium and limestone

For practical information on travelling around Spain, see pp626–35

Wild Spain: Cantabria, Asturias and Galicia

- **Duration** 10 days, or add this itinerary to Bilbao and the Basque Lands for a 17-day tour covering a large swathe of Northern Spain.

- **Airports** The nearest is in Santander, also a major ferry port with services from the UK. The airport is 5 km (3 miles) from the city centre, and linked by bus.

- **Transport** This tour is designed to be done by car.

The verdant valleys and majestic mountains of the Parque Nacional de los Picos de Europa

Day 1: Castro Urdiales and Lardeo

Enjoy two of Cantabria's prettiest and most popular beach resorts, Castro Urdiales (p117) and Laredo (p117). Each has a delightful Old Quarter and some spectacular beaches. Though the town beaches get busy in summer, you'll find breathtaking, emptier stretches on either side of the towns.

Day 2: Santander

Next up is the Cantabrian capital Santander (p117), which was completely rebuilt in the 1940s after a devastating fire destroyed its historic heart. Still an atmospheric port city, it has good seafood restaurants and some wonderful beaches.

Day 3: Santillana del Mar and the Cuevas de Altamira

Drive west to Santillana del Mar (p116), which, despite its name, is not on the coast but set a few kilometres inland. It is an enchanting and beautifully preserved town, replete with churches, palaces and mansions. Then visit the Cuevas de Altamira (p116), site of prehistoric cave art just a couple of kilometres from Santillana del Mar. Although you can't visit the original caves, the paintings have been re-created in the excellent museum.

Day 4: Cangas de Onís and Covadonga

Stroll around the ancient Asturian capital of Cangas de Onís (p111), which enjoys a spectacular mountain backdrop. Nearby Covadonga (p112) is also worth a visit, a charming mountain town that is the main gateway to the stunning Parque Nacional de los Picos de Europa.

Day 5: Parque Nacional de los Picos de Europa

You could spend weeks in this national park (p112). In one day you can at least enjoy a fantastic hike, some rock climbing or simply a picnic among some of the most spectacular mountain scenery Spain has to offer.

Day 6: Gijón

Continue west to Gijón (p109), a port city with a charming old town piled up on a narrow isthmus. It has some great restaurants, long beaches and a few museums, which are worth visiting.

Beachcombers soak up the sun at Playa del Camello, Santander

Day 7: Oviedo

Spend a day in handsome Oviedo (pp110–11), a historic city gathered around a splendid, Gothic cathedral. Famous across Spain for its vibrant cultural life, it has Pre-Romanesque churches located on the hills overlooking the city.

Day 8: Costa Verde

Head west along the coast road which skirts the glorious Costa Verde (pp108–9). With its cliffs and coves, verdant hills and picturesque villages, this is easily one of Spain's loveliest and least spoiled stretches of coastline. Stop off and explore charming towns like Castropol, Luarca and Cudillero.

Day 9: Lugo

Cross the border into Galicia, and aim for the ancient city of Lugo (p103). Once an important Roman settlement, Lugo is still ringed by spectacular and remarkably intact Roman walls, which you can climb to enjoy fabulous views. Within the walls, the old city is a charming jumble of narrow streets and pretty squares – perfect for a wander.

Day 10: Santiago de Compostela

End your journey in the magical city of Santiago de Compostela (pp94–7) – the goal of pilgrims for more than 1,000 years. An enchanting city built of cool grey stone, it is dominated by its magnificent cathedral, said to contain the bones of St James.

Barcelona and the Mediterranean Coast by Train

- **Duration** 7 days.
- **Airports** Arrive in Barcelona's El Prat Airport, depart from Murcia's San Javier Airport.
- **Transport** This tour is exclusively by train. There is a choice of services on this route, from the plush, expensive Talgos to inexpensive regional and local trains. Most journey times are around an hour – check timetables and prices on www.renfe.com.
- **Booking Ahead** Barcelona: Sagrada Família tickets.

Charming, balconied stone terraces in Barcelona's Gothic Quarter

Day 1: Barcelona
Choose a day from the 2 Days in Barcelona itinerary on pp12–13.

Day 2: Sitges and Tarragona
Take an early train to Sitges (p228) and spend the morning strolling around this enchanting seaside town. Enjoy a seafood lunch, then catch a train to Tarragona (pp228–9), once capital of an important Roman province and still replete with Roman monuments. Tuck into a seafood dinner by the port.

Day 3: Peníscola and Valencia
In the morning, all aboard to Benicarló-Peníscola, the station for Peníscola (p251). Take a taxi to the historic quarter,

a whitewashed maze piled up on a promontory and crowned with a castle. Have a lazy lunch by the beach, then ride the rails back to Valencia (pp254–7) in time for an evening tapas bar crawl around the charming historic quarter.

Day 4: Valencia
Spend the day sightseeing in Valencia, beginning with a visit to the cathedral (pp254–5), where you can climb the bell tower for tremendous views. In the afternoon, head to the City of Arts and Sciences (p257) to take in the interactive science museum or the Oceanografic, Europe's biggest aquarium. For dinner, enjoy a genuine paella – invented in Valencia.

Day 5: Alicante (Alacant)
Enjoy the train journey south through the hills to Alicante (pp264–5), a vibrant seaside city that offers great shopping and

nightlife as well as a lively cultural scene. Take in fabulous views from the clifftop Castillo de Santa Bárbara and wander around the winding streets of the Old Town. Tuck into some tapas in the Old Quarter.

Day 6: Murcia
Another relatively short journey brings you to Murcia (p266), the handsome capital of the Murcia region. Its centre is dominated by the vast Gothic cathedral, completed in 1467 and later given a sumptuous Baroque façade. The 19th-century casino, a sort of Spanish social club, is also worth a visit for its dazzling and eclectic decoration. Much of the city centre is pedestrianized, and Murcia's pretty squares are crammed with great tapas bars.

> **To extend your trip…**
> Reward yourself with some relaxing beach time and swimming in the warm, tranquil waters of the Mar Menor (p266).

Day 7: Cartagena
The culmination of your trip, the port city of Cartagena (p267), is an hour's train journey from Murcia. One of the oldest cities in Spain, it preserves a slew of remarkable Phoenician, Roman and Moorish monuments, including a spectacular Roman theatre and a lofty castle (now home to a history museum), which enjoys fabulous panoramic views.

Tarragona's Roman amphitheatre, overlooking the Mediterranean

For practical information on travelling around Spain, see pp626–35

Madrid and Moorish Spain: Granada, Córdoba and Seville

- **Duration** 10 days.

- **Airports** Arrive in Madrid's Barajas Airport, depart from Granada Airport.

- **Transport** High-speed AVE train from Madrid to Seville; hire car for the rest of the trip.

- **Booking Ahead** Granada: entry tickets to Alhambra.

Days 1 and 2: Madrid
See the 2 Days in Madrid itinerary on p12.

Days 3 and 4: Seville
Take the high-speed AVE train from Atocha station to Seville. *Experience the best of the city with the 2 Days in Seville itinerary on p13.*

Day 5: Carmona and Écija
Hire a car for the rest of your journey. Drive east of Seville, stopping first at Carmona (*p482*), an aristocratic town tucked behind Moorish city walls. Continue east to Écija (*p483*), famous for extreme heat and a distinctive skyline punctured by the silhouettes of 11 Baroque church spires. Spend a night here.

Day 6: Córdoba
Córdoba (*pp484–7*) is less than an hour's drive east of Écija. At its heart is the vast 8th-century

Mezquita (*pp486–7*), a masterpiece of Islamic art, where you can easily spend a couple of hours. Then head into the narrow lanes of the former Jewish Quarter, and visit the enchanting Palacio de Viana, an aristocratic mansion set around several elegant courtyards. Enjoy supper on one of Córdoba's enchanting squares.

Day 7: Córdoba
Begin your day with breakfast on the Plaza de La Corredera, a handsome 17th-century square that hosts a daily market. Visit the Alcázar de los Reyes Cristianos and its blissful gardens (*p484*). Choose one of Córdoba's many museums to visit in the afternoon, or simply explore the maze of streets, including the Callejón de las Flores, famous for its beautiful flowers. Visit the Plaza de Tendillas for dinner options.

Day 8: Montilla to Montefrío
Drive through beautiful Andalucían countryside to Granada, taking in several attractive villages. First of these is Montilla (*p488*), a celebrated wine town, followed by Aguilar de la Frontera, wrapped around an octagonal square. Continue through hills and orchards to Priego de Córdoba (*p488*), packed with breathtaking Baroque architecture, and then to Montefrío (*pp488–9*), a tumble of chalk-white buildings crowned by the remnants of a

Terracotta-and-white-striped arches top countless columns inside the Mezquita

Moorish fortress. Spend the night in either Priego de Córdoba or Montefrío.

Day 9: Granada
Press on to Granada (*pp492–8*), just a short drive from Montefrío. The spirit of old Al Andalus is strongest here, thanks to the presence of the hauntingly beautiful Alhambra Palace, which crowns the city. An old Moorish neighbourhood spills down the hill opposite the Alhambra, its narrow lanes lined with craftshops, bathhouses and cafés. Stop for lunch here, then head up to explore the vast Alhambra palace and fortress complex (*pp496–7*) and the Generalife gardens (*p498*), where the Nasrid rulers made their attempt to recreate paradise on earth. Top off the day with a tapas bar crawl – a must in Granada.

Day 10: Granada
Visit the splendid Gothic cathedral (*p492*), constructed by order of the Catholic Monarchs (Ferdinand and Isabella) after the fall of Granada in 1492. They also ordered the construction of the nearby Capilla Real (*p492*), which contains their elaborate tombs and those of their daughter and her husband. Take a look at the cultural centre in the 16th-century Corral del Carbón (*p492*), which displays local crafts. In the evening, take in a flamenco show in one of the caves in Sacromonte (*p495*).

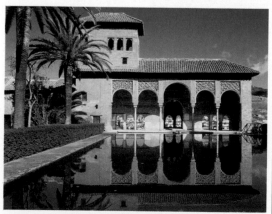
Portico and pool of the Partal, part of the Alhambra palace complex

Putting Spain on the Map

Spain, in southwestern Europe, covers the greater part of the Iberian Peninsula. The third-largest country in Europe, it includes two island groups – the Canaries in the Atlantic and the Balearics in the Mediterranean – and two small territories in North Africa. Its southernmost point faces Morocco across a strait, making Spain a bridge between continents.

Portsmouth, Plymouth

Bay of Biscay

Atlantic Ocean

ASTURIAS
CANTABRIA
GALICIA
CASTILLA Y LEÓN
PORTUGAL
EXTREMADURA
CASTILLA-LA
ANDALUCÍA
MADRID

Ortigueira
Ferrol
A Coruña
N634
Avilés
Gijón
Oviedo
Santander
Llanes
A8
A8
Santiago de Compostela
A6
AP9
Lugo
A66
Miranda de Ebr
A67
Pontevedra
AP9
AP53
Ponferrada
León
Burgos
A231
Vigo
A52
Ourense
A6
A66
A231
A1
Palencia
Braga
A52
Benavente
CASTILLA Y LEÓN
Valladolid
Peñafiel
Aranda de Duero
A7
Zamora
A11
Vila Real
A66
A62
Segovia
A1
Porto
A24
Salamanca
A6
Aveiro
A25
A62
A50
Ávila
Guadalajara
Ciudad Rodrigo
A66
MADRID
Madrid
A3
Coimbra
A23
Plasencia
Talavera de la Reina
Aranjuez
A5
Leiria
Coria
Toledo
Castelo Branco
A66
A5
Cáceres
Trujillo
N502
CASTILLA-LA
A17
A1
EXTREMADURA
N430
Tormelloso
A43
Santarem
Badajoz
A5
Mérida
Ciudad Real
Lisbon
Évora
Zafra
N502
Puertollano
Valdepeñas
A41
A4
Setúbal
A6
N432
A66
Linares
A4
A44
Úbeda
Beja
Córdoba
Jaén
A2
Sevilla
A4
ANDALUCÍA
Lagos
A22
Huelva
A49
A92
Estepa
A92
Granada
Faro
AP4
A45
Jerez de la Frontera
A45
Málaga
Motril
Cádiz
A381
A7
A48
Marbella
Algeciras
Tangier
Ceuta
Canary Islands
Melilla

Key

- Motorway
- Major road
- International border
- Regional border
- Ferry route

For keys to symbols *see back flap*

The Canary Islands

Cádiz, Huelva

Lanzarote

Arrecife

Santa Cruz de la Palma

Tenerife

Puerto del Rosario

La Palma

Fuerteventura

San Sebastián

Santa Cruz de Tenerife

Las Palmas de Gran Canaria

La Gomera

Los Cristianos

Valverde

Gran Canaria

El Hierro

Biarritz

San Sebastián

Tarbes

A64

A64

A61

Béziers

Ibao

AP8

Pau

F R A N C E

Perpignan

PAÍS

ASCO

Vitoria (Gasteiz)

Pamplona

NAVARRA

Jaca

ANDORRA

La Seu de Urgell

Figueres

Genoa, Livorno, Civitavecchia

roño

A12

A15

Huesca

CATALUÑA

Vic

Girona

A RIOJA

Tudela

A R A G Ó N

N240

Manresa

AP7

Soria

A68

Zaragoza

Lleida

A2

A54

Barcelona

Calatayud

A2

AP2

N232

N211

Sitges

A23

Alcañiz

AP7

Tarragona

N211

Tortosa

M e d i t e r r a n e a n

S e a

Teruel

N232

Benicarló

Cuenca

N320

N330

AP7

A40

Benicàssim

Ciutadella

Menorca

ANCHA

A23

Benicàssim

Alcudia

Mahón

Castellón de la Plana

36

Requena

Sagunto

Palma

Mallorca

A3

Valencia

PAÍS

VALENCIANO

ISLAS

A43

N322

Albacete

N330

A7

Gandia

BALEARES

322

Hellín

A31

Xàbia

Ibiza

Elda

AP7

Benidorm

Ibiza

A30

Alicante

MURCIA

A7

Murcia

Huéscar

AP7

Lorca

A92

A7

Cartagena

AP7

Águillas

Mojácar

Almería

0 kilometres 100

0 miles 50

Europe and North Africa

NORWAY

SWEDEN

ESTONIA

LATVIA

NORTH SEA

DENMARK

LITHUANIA

REP. OF IRELAND

UNITED KINGDOM

NETHERLANDS

POLAND

BELARUS

GERMANY

BELGIUM

CZECH REP.

UKRAINE

SLOVAKIA

ATLANTIC OCEAN

FRANCE

SWITZ.

AUSTRIA HUNGARY

ROMANIA

BOSNIA HERZ.

SERBIA

ITALY

MONTEN.

BULGARIA

MAC.

GREECE

PORTUGAL

Madrid

SPAIN

Canary Islands

MOROCCO

TUNISIA

ALGERIA

LIBYA

Melilla, Nador Ghazaouet

Regional Spain

Spain has a population of 47 million and receives more than 40 million visitors a year. It covers an area of 504,780 sq km (194,900 sq miles). Madrid is the largest city, followed by Barcelona and Valencia. The country is dominated by a central plateau drained by the Duero, Tagus (Tajo) and Guadiana rivers. This book divides Spain into 15 areas, but officially it has 17 independent regions called *comunidades autónomas*.

Getting Around

Spain's regional capitals and islands are linked by regular flights and there is a shuttle service between Madrid and Barcelona. The TALGO and AVE high-speed trains provide fast rail services and are backed up by regional and local rail networks. Some motorways have expensive tolls, but are fast. The Balearic and Canary islands are served by regular ferries.

Key

- Motorway
- Motorway under construction
- Major road
- Minor road

Key to colour coding

Northern Spain
- Galicia
- Asturias and Cantabria
- The Basque Country, Navarra and La Rioja

Eastern Spain
- Barcelona
- Catalonia
- Aragón
- Valencia and Murcia

Central Spain
- Madrid
- Castilla y León
- Castilla-La Mancha
- Extremadura

Southern Spain
- Seville
- Andalucía

Spain's Islands
- The Balearic Islands
- The Canary Islands

0 kilometres 100
0 miles 100

Sebastián (nostia)

Iruña (Pamplona)
Jaca
Tudela
Huesca
La Seu d'Urgell
Vic
Figueres
Girona
Zaragoza
Lleida
Manresa
Alcañiz
Reus
Sitges
Tortosa
Tarragona
Barcelona
Teruel
Benicarló
Castellón de la Plana
Sagunto
Valencia
Gandía
Almansa
Alcoi
Alacant (Alicante)
Benidorm
Elx
Murcia
orca
Cartagena

The Balearic Islands

Menorca
Ciutadella
Maó
Mallorca
Palma
Manacor
Ibiza
Eivissa (Ibiza)
Formentera
Cabrera

The Canary Islands

Lanzarote
Arrecife
La Palma
Santa Cruz de la Palma
Puerto de la Cruz
Tenerife
Fuerteventura
Puerto del Rosario
Santa Cruz de Tenerife
La Gomera
San Sebastián de la Gomera
Las Palmas de Gran Canaria
El Hierro
Valverde
Gran Canaria
Maspalomas

A PORTRAIT OF SPAIN

The familiar images of Spain – flamenco dancing, bullfighting, tapas bars and solemn Easter processions – do no more than hint at the diversity of this vast country. Spain boasts four official languages, two major cities of equal importance and a greater range of landscapes – from sandy beaches to mountain peaks – than any other European country. These remarkable elements contribute to making Spain an endlessly fascinating country to visit.

Separated from the rest of Europe by the Pyrenees, Spain reaches south to the coast of North Africa. It has both Atlantic and Mediterranean coastlines, and includes two archipelagos – the Balearics and the Canary Islands.

The climate and landscape vary from snowcapped peaks in the Pyrenees, through the green meadows of Galicia and the orange groves of Valencia, to the desert of Almería. Madrid is Europe's highest capital, and Spain is its most mountainous country after Switzerland and Austria. The innumerable sierras have always hindered communications. Until railways were built, it was easier to move goods from Barcelona to South America than to Madrid.

In early times, Spain was a coveted prize for foreign conquerors, including the Phoenicians and the Romans. During the Middle Ages, much of it was ruled by the Moors, who arrived from North Africa in the 8th century. Reconquered by Christian forces, the country was unified at the end of the 15th century. A succession of rulers tried to impose a common culture, but Spain remains as culturally diverse as ever. Several regions have maintained a strong sense of their own independent identities. Many Basques and Catalans, in particular, do not consider themselves to be Spanish. Madrid may be the nominal capital, but it is closely rivalled in commerce, the arts and sport by Barcelona, the capital city of Catalonia.

Landscape with a solitary cork tree near Albacete in Castilla-La Mancha

◄ Flamenco dancing in Seville

Peñafiel Castle in the Duero Valley (Castilla y León), built between the 10th and 13th centuries

The Spanish Way of Life

The inhabitants of this varied country have few things in common, except for a natural sociability and a zest for living. Spaniards commonly put as much energy into enjoying life as they do into their work. The stereo-typical "mañana" (leave every-thing until tomorrow) is a myth, but time is flexible in Spain and many people bend their work to fit the demands of their social life, rather than let themselves be ruled by the clock. The day is long in Spain, and Spanish has word, *madrugada*, for the time between midnight and dawn, when city streets are often still lively.

"Vinegar Face" in Pamplona's Los Sanfermines fiesta

Spaniards are highly gregarious. In many places people still go out in the evening for the *paseo*, when the streets are crowded with strollers. Eating is invariably communal, and big groups often meet up for tapas or dinner. Not surprisingly, Spain has more bars and restaurants per head than any other country in Europe.

Traditionally, the state in Spain has been very inefficient at providing public services. The Spanish have therefore always relied on their families and personal connections, rather than institutions, to find work or seek assistance in a crisis.

Underpinning Spanish society is the concept of the extended family. Three generations may live together under one roof, or at least see each other often. Even lifelong city-dwellers refer fondly to their *pueblo* – the town or village where their family comes from and where they return to whenever they can. Children are adored in Spain and, consequently, great importance is attached to education. The family in Spain, however, is under strain as couples increasingly opt for a higher income and better lifestyle rather than a large family. One of the most

Tables outside a café in Madrid's Plaza Mayor

striking transformations in modern Spain has been in the birth rate, from one of the highest in Europe, at 2.72 children for every woman in 1975, to 1.49 children for every woman in 2016.

Catholicism is still a pervasive influence over Spanish society, although church attendance among those under the age of 35 has been declining and now stands at below 10 per cent. The images of saints watch over some shops, bars and lorry drivers' cabs. Church feast days are marked by countless traditional fiestas, which are enthusiastically maintained in modern Spain.

The windmills and castle above Consuegra, La Mancha

Virgin of Guadalupe in Extremadura

Sport and the Arts

Spanish cultural life has been experiencing a renaissance. Spanish-made films – notably those of cult directors Pedro Almodóvar and Alejandro Amenábar – have been able to compete with Hollywood for audiences, and the actress Penélope Cruz won an Oscar in 2009. The overall level of reading has risen, and contemporary literature has steadily gained a wider readership, with a number of internationally recognised Spanish names lining bookshop shelves. The performing arts have been restricted by a lack of facilities, but major investments have provided new venues, regional arts centres and new symphony orchestras. The country has produced many remarkable opera singers, including Montserrat Caballé, Plácido Domingo and José Carreras. Spain has also excelled in design, particularly evident in the interior furnishings shops of Barcelona.

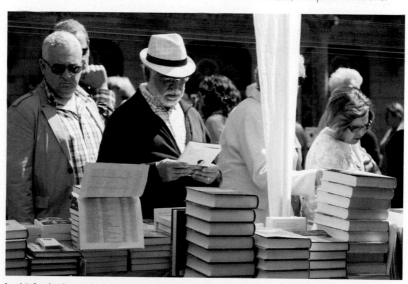

Crowds in Barcelona browsing book stalls on Sant Jordi's Day, in April, when it is customary to exchange literary gifts

Formula One driver Fernando Alonso

Spaniards are the most avid TV-watchers in Europe after the British. There are two state-owned TV channels in Spain, as well as a growing number of private channels and regional TV stations thanks to digital platforms. Sports are one of the mainstays of TV programming. Spanish sportsmen and women have been very successful – for example, tennis player Rafael Nadal and Formula 1 driver Fernando Alonso, not forgetting the

Spanish team's win in the 2010 FIFA World Cup, the country's first world title. Such role models have encouraged participation in sport and more facilities have been provided to meet this demand. Most popular are basketball and, above all, soccer.

Bullfighting remains popular with some, although it does court controversy, particularly with younger generations. For aficionados, a *corrida* provides a link to Spain's roots, and the noise, colour and crowd are as much of an attraction as the bullfight itself. In Catalonia, however, bullfighting was banned in 2012.

Spain Today

Since the mid-20th century, Spain has undergone more social change than anywhere in western Europe. Until the 1950s, Spain was predominantly a poor, rural country, in which only 37 per cent of the population lived in towns of over 10,000 people. By the 1990s, that figure was 65 per cent. As people flooded into towns and cities, many rural areas became depopulated. The 1960s saw the beginning of spectacular economic growth, partly due to a burgeoning tourist industry.

After the death of dictator General Franco in 1975, Spain became a constitutional monarchy under King Juan Carlos I, who

A farmer with his crop of maize hanging to dry on the outside of his house in the hills of Alicante

Sandy beach near the pretty town of Tossa de Mar, on Catalonia's Costa Brava

reigned until 2014 when he abdicated in favour of his son, Felipe VI. The post-Franco era, up until the mid-1990s, was dominated by Prime Minister Felipe González of the Spanish Socialist Workers' Party (PSOE). As well as presiding over major improvements in roads, education and health services, the Socialists increased Spain's international standing. The country joined the European Community in 1986, triggering a spectacular increase in national prosperity. Spain's fortunes seemed to peak in the extraordinary year of 1992, when Barcelona staged the Olympic Games and Seville hosted a world fair, Expo '92. The PSOE could not continue forever, however, and in 1996 revelations of a series of scandals lost the PSOE the election.

King Felipe VI

With the establishment of democracy, the 17 autonomous regions of Spain have acquired considerable powers. Several have their own languages, which are given equal importance to Spanish (strictly called Castilian). A number of Basques favour independence, and the Basque terrorist group ETA was a constant thorn in the side of Spanish democracy until 2011, when they declared a cessation of hostilities. The group officially disarmed in 2017, the same year that Catalonia voted for independence in a referendum deemed illegal by the Constitutional Court of Spain and the European Commission. This stand-off led to protests in Barcelona and Madrid, followed by the exile of Catalan cabinet ministers.

Spain enjoyed an economic boom in the 1980s, as service industries and manufacturing expanded. However, at the peak of the 2009 economic crisis, the unemployment rate was a staggering 27 per cent. Although this statistic dropped to 20 per cent in 2017, it remains among the highest of all EU countries. In response to the Partido Popular government's austerity policies and allegations of corruption, no party won an outright majority in the general elections of 2015. Elections were held again in 2016, and this time the Partido Popular managed to win enough seats to form a minority government under Mariano Rajoy.

Demonstration for Catalan independence

Architecture in Spain

Spain has always imported its styles of architecture: Moorish from North Africa, Romanesque and Gothic from France and Renaissance from Italy. Each style, however, was interpreted in a distinctively Spanish way, with sudden and strong contrasts between light and shady areas; façades alternating between austerity and extravagant decoration; and thick walls pierced by few windows to lessen the impact of heat and sunlight. Styles vary from region to region, reflecting the division of Spain before unification. The key design of a central patio surrounded by arcades has been a strong feature of civil buildings since Moorish times.

The 15th-century Casa de Conchas in Salamanca (see p365)

Romanesque and Earlier (8th–13th Centuries)

Romanesque churches were mainly built in Catalonia and along the pilgrim route to Santiago (see p87). Their distinctive features include round arches, massive walls and few windows. Earlier churches were built in Pre-Romanesque (see p110) or Mozarabic (see p355) style.

Round arch

Multiple apses

The Romanesque Sant Climent, Taüll (p215)

Moorish (8th–15th Centuries)

The Moors (see pp56–7) reserved the most lavish decoration for the interior of buildings, where ornate designs based on geometry, calligraphy and plant motifs were created in azulejos (tiles) or stucco. They made extensive use of the horseshoe arch, a feature inherited from the Visigoths (see pp54–5). The greatest surviving works of Moorish architecture (see pp426–7) are in Southern Spain.

The Salón de Embajadores in the Alhambra (see p496) has exquisite Moorish decoration.

Gothic (12th–16th Centuries)

Gothic arched window

Gothic was imported from France in the late 12th century. The round arch was replaced by the pointed arch which, because of its greater strength, allowed for higher vaults and taller windows. External buttresses were added to prevent the walls of the nave from leaning outwards. Carved decoration was at its most opulent in the Flamboyant Gothic style of the 15th century. After the fall of Granada, Isabelline, a late Gothic style, developed. Meanwhile, Moorish craftsmen working in reconquered areas created the highly decorative hybrid Christian-Islamic style Mudéjar (see p59).

The nave of León Cathedral (see pp358–9), built in the 13th century, is supported by rib vaulting and is illuminated by the finest display of stained glass in Spain.

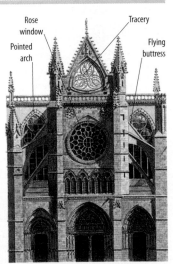

Rose window

Pointed arch

Tracery

Flying buttress

Sculptural decoration above the doorways of León Cathedral's south front depicted biblical stories for the benefit of the largely illiterate populace.

Renaissance (16th Century)

Around 1500 a new style was introduced to Spain by Italian craftsmen and Spanish artists who had studied in Italy. The Renaissance was a revival of the style of ancient Rome. It is distinguished by its sense of symmetry and the use of the round arch, and Doric, Ionic and Corinthian columns. Early Spanish Renaissance architecture is known as Plateresque because its fine detail resembles ornate silverwork (*platero* means "silversmith").

The Palacio de las Cadenas in Úbeda *(see p501)* has a severely Classical façade.

Medallions Classical columns Sculpted parapet Round arch

The Hostal de San Marcos in León *(see p357)*, one of Spain's finest Plateresque buildings

Baroque (17th–18th Centuries)

Baroque was driven by a desire for drama and movement. Decoration became extravagant, with exuberant sculpture and twisting columns. Although the excessive Baroque style of Churrigueresque is named after the Churriguera family of architects, it was their successors who were its main exponents.

The ornamentation on the Baroque façade of Valladolid University *(see p370)* is concentrated above the doorway.

Finials

Statues on parapet

The façade of the Museo de Historia in Madrid *(pp308–9)*

Modern (Late 19th Century onwards)

Modernisme *(see pp144–5)*, a Catalan interpretation of Art Nouveau, is seen at its best in Barcelona. Its architects experimented with a highly original language of ornament. In recent decades, Spain has seen an explosion of bold, functionalist architecture in which the form of a building reflects its use and decoration is used sparingly.

Curving parapet Spiral chimney Decorative ironwork

Torre de Picasso in Madrid *(p310)*

Casa Milà, in Barcelona *(see p169)*, was built in 1910 by Modernisme's most famous and best-loved architect, Antoni Gaudí, who drew much of his inspiration from nature.

Vernacular Architecture

As well as its cathedrals and palaces, Spain has a great variety of charming vernacular buildings. These have been constructed by local craftsmen to meet the practical needs of rural communities and to take account of local climate conditions, with little reference to formal architectural styles. Due to the high expense involved in transporting raw materials, builders used whatever stone or timber lay closest to hand. The three houses illustrated below incorporate the most common characteristics of village architecture seen in different parts of Spain.

A cave church in Artenara *(see p549)*, on Gran Canaria

Stone House

The climate is wet in the north and houses like this one in Carmona *(see p115)*, in Cantabria, are built with overhanging eaves to shed the rain. Wooden balconies catch the sun.

Detail of stonework

Supporting pillar

Large doors accommodate carts and animals.

The walls are built of irregularly shaped stones.

Family and farm often share rural houses. The ground floor is used to stable animals, or store tools and firewood.

Timber-Framed House

Spain, in general, has few large trees and wood is in short supply. Castilla y León is one of the few regions where timber-framed houses, such as this one in Covarrubias *(see p374)*, can be found. These houses are quick and cheap to build. The timber frame is filled in with a coarse plaster mixed from lime and sand, or adobe (bricks dried in the sun).

Half-timbered wall

Portico

Gently sloping roof

The veranda runs the length of the building.

Balcony

In town squares, upright struts of timber supporting horizontal beams were used to form porticoes. A shady space was created for people to meet, talk and trade.

The ends of the beams supporting the floorboards are visible.

Stone plinths below upright timbers provide protection from damp.

Whitewashed House

Houses in the south of Spain – often built of baked clay – are regularly whitewashed to deflect the sun's intense rays. Andalucía's famous white towns *(see pp474–5)* exemplify this attractive form of architecture.

Clay-tiled roof

Irregularly shaped houses are joined together.

Few, small windows

Shallow-pitched roof

Windows are small and few in number, and deeply recessed, in order to keep the interior cool.

Whitewashed walls

The Plaza Mayor

Almost every town in Spain centres on a main square, the *plaza mayor*, like this one in Pedraza de la Sierra *(see p369)*, near Segovia. More than a market square, it acts as a focus for local life. It is usually overlooked by the church, the town hall, shops and bars and the mansions of aristocratic families.

Town hall *(ayuntamiento)*

Medieval porticoes beneath the buildings provided shade for shops and markets.

Church

A noble family's mansion is distinguished by a coat of arms carved on the façade.

The square provides ample space for fiestas, concerts, folk dances, bullrunning and other public events.

Rural Architecture

A variety of distinctive buildings dots the countryside.

Where the rock is soft and the climate hot, subterranean dwellings have been excavated. Insulated from extremes of temperature, they provide a comfortable place to live.

Hórreos, granaries raised on stone stilts to prevent rats climbing up into the grain, are a common sight in Galicia (where they are stone-built) and Asturias (where they are made of wood). In fields you will often see shelters for livestock or for storing crops, such as the *teitos* of Asturias.

Windmills provided power in parts of Spain where there was little running water but plentiful wind, like La Mancha and the Balearic Islands.

Almost everywhere in the Spanish countryside you will come across *ermitas*, isolated chapels or shrines dedicated to a local saint. An *ermita* may be opened only on the patron saint's feast day.

Cave houses in Guadix near Granada *(see p499)*

Teito in Valle de Teverga in Asturias *(see p109)*

Hórreo, a granary, on the Rías Baixas *(see p99)* in Galicia

Windmill above Consuegra *(see p398)* in La Mancha

Farming in Spain

Spain's varied geography and climate have created a mosaic of farming patterns ranging from lush dairylands to stony hillsides where goats graze. Land can be broadly divided into *secano*, or dry cultivation (used for olives, wheat and vines), and much smaller areas of *regadío*, irrigated land (planted with citrus trees, rice and vegetables). Farming in many parts is a family affair relying on traditional, labour-intensive methods, but it is becoming increasingly mechanized.

The high rainfall and mild summers of Northern Spain make it suitable for dairy farming. Farms are often small, especially in Galicia, one of the country's most under-developed regions. Crops such as maize and wheat are grown in small quantities.

Plains of cereals make up much of the farmland of the central *meseta* of Spain. Wheat is grown in better-watered, more fertile western areas; barley is grown in the drier south.

Cork oaks thrive in Extremadura and western Andalucía.

MADRID

SEVILLA

Sheep grazed on the rough pastures of Central Spain are milked to make cheese, especially *manchego*, which is produced in La Mancha *(see p343).*

Jul–Aug Wheat harvested in Central Spain	**Sep** Rice harvest in Eastern Spain. Grape harvest at its height	**Oct** Maize harvested in Northern Spain **Oct–Nov** Table olives picked	**Dec–Mar** Olives for making oil picked
Spring	**Summer**	**Autumn**	**Winter**
Mar–Apr Orange trees in blossom on Mediterranean coast		**Nov–Dec** Oranges picked	**Feb** Almond trees in blossom
Jun–Aug Haymaking in Northern Spain	**Sep** Start of wild mushroom season	**Dec** Pigs are slaughtered when cold weather arrives	

Banana plantation in La Palma, Canary Islands

Crops from Trees

The almond, orange and olive create the three most characteristic landscapes of rural Spain, but several other trees provide important crops. Wine corks are made from the bark of the cork oak. Tropical species, such as avocado and cherimoya, a delicious creamy fruit little known outside Spain, have been introduced to the so-called Costa Tropical of Andalucía *(see p489)*; and bananas are a major crop of the Canary Islands. Elsewhere, peaches and loquats are also grown commercially. Figs and carobs – whose fruit is used for fodder and as a substitute for chocolate – grow semi wild.

Oranges, lemons and clementines are grown on the irrigated coastal plains beside the Mediterranean. The region of Valencia is the prime producer of oranges.

BARCELONA

Wine is produced in many parts of Spain *(see pp580–81)*. The country's best sparkling wine grapes are grown in Catalonia.

Rice is grown in the Ebro delta, in the Marismas del Guadalquivir around L'Albufera near Valencia and also at Calasparra in Murcia.

| 0 kilometres | 200 |
| 0 miles | 100 |

Almonds grow on dry hill-sides in many parts of Spain. The spring blossom can be spectacular. The nut, enclosed by a fleshy green skin, is used in a variety of sweetmeats, including the Christmas treat *turrón* *(see p191)*.

Olive trees grow slowly and often live to a great age. The fruit is harvested in winter and either pickled in brine, for eating as a snack, or to extract the oil, which is widely used in Spanish cuisine.

Sweet oranges are grown in dense, well-irrigated groves near the frost-free coasts. The sweet smell of orange blossom in springtime is unmistakable. Trees of the bitter orange are often planted for shade and decoration in parks and gardens.

Olive trees are planted in long, straight lines across large swathes of Andalucía, especially in the province of Jaén. Spain is the world's leading producer of olive oil.

Spain's National Parks

Few other countries in western Europe have such unspoiled scenery as Spain, or can boast tracts of wilderness where brown bears live and wolves hunt. More than 200 nature reserves protect a broad range of ecosystems. The most important areas are the 13 national parks, the first of which was established in 1918. Natural parks *(parques naturales)*, regulated by regional governments, are also vital to the task of conservation.

Clear mountain river, Ordesa

Rough terrain in the Picos de Europa

Mountains

Much of Spain's finest scenery is found in the mountains. Rivers have carved gorges between the peaks of the Picos de Europa. Ordesa and Aigüestortes share some of the most dramatic landscapes of the Pyrenees, while the Sierra Nevada has an impressive range of indigenous wildlife.

Chamois are well adapted to climbing across slopes covered in scree. They live in small groups, always alert to predators, and feed on grass and flowers.

Eagle owls are Europe's largest owl, easily identified by their large ear tufts. At night they hunt small mammals and birds.

Wetlands

Wetlands include coastal strips and freshwater marshes. Seasonal floods rejuvenate the water, providing nutrients for animal and plant growth. These areas are rich feeding grounds for birds. Spain's best-known wetland is Doñana. Catalonia's Delta de l'Ebre *(see p229)* and Tablas de Daimiel, in La Mancha, are much smaller.

Lynx, endangered by hunting and habitat loss, can occasionally be spotted in Doñana *(see pp470–71)*.

Black-winged stilts, with their long, straight legs, are adept at stalking tiny freshwater crustaceans.

Laguna del Acebuche, Parque Nacional de Doñana

Cabrera archipelago, Balearic Islands

Islands

Cabrera, off Mallorca, is home to rare plants, reptiles and seabirds, such as Eleonara's falcon. The surrounding waters are important for their marine life.

Lizards are often found in rocky terrain and on cliff faces.

National Parks

- Mountains
- Wetlands
- Islands
- Woods and Forests
- Volcanic Landscapes

Mountains

① Picos de Europa *pp112–13*
② Ordesa y Monte Perdido *pp236–7*
③ Aigüestortes y Estany de Sant Maurici *p215*
④ Sierra Nevada *p491*

Wetlands

⑤ Tablas de Daimiel *p403*
⑥ Doñana *pp470–71*

Islands

⑦ Archipiélago de Cabrera *p521*
⑧ Illa de Ons *p99*

Woods and Forests

⑨ Cabañeros *p391*
⑩ Garajonay *p537*

Volcanic Landscapes

⑪ Caldera de Taburiente *p536*
⑫ Teide *pp542–3*
⑬ Timanfaya *pp552–3*

VISITORS' CHECKLIST

All but one of the national parks are managed by the Ministerio de Medio Ambiente. **Tel** 915 46 81 11. **W** **magrama.gob.es/es/red-parques-nacionales** Parque Nacional d'Aigüestortes y Estany de Sant Maurici is administered jointly with Catalonia's Department of Environment. **Tel** 973 69 61 89. Most of Spain's national parks have visitors' centres, often called Centros de Interpretació.

Woods and Forests

Deciduous broad-leaved forests grow in the northwest of Spain, and stands of Aleppo and Scots pine cover many mountainous areas. On the central plateau there are stretches of open woodland of evergreen holm oak and cork oak in the Parque Nacional de Cabañeros. Dense, lush *laurisilva* woodland grows in the Parque Nacional de Garajonay, on La Gomera, one of the smaller Canary Islands.

Parque Nacional de Garajonay

Black vultures are the largest birds of prey in Europe, with an enormous wingspan of over 2.5 m (8 ft).

Hedgehogs, common in woodlands, root among fallen leaves and grass to find worms and slugs.

Volcanic Landscapes

Three very different parks protect parts of the Canary Islands' amazing volcanic scenery. Caldera de Taburiente on La Palma is a volcanic crater surrounded by woods. Mount Teide in Tenerife has unique alpine flora, and Lanzarote's Timanfaya is composed of barren but atmospheric lava fields.

Rabbits are highly opportunistic, quickly colonizing areas in which they can burrow. In the absence of predators, populations may increase, damaging fragile ecosystems.

Canaries belong to the finch family of songbirds. The popular canary has been bred from the wild serin, native to the Canaries.

Colonizing plant species, Mount Teide (Tenerife)

Spanish Art

Three Spanish painters stand out as milestones in the history of Western art. Diego de Velázquez was a 17th-century court portrait painter and his *Las Meninas* is a seminal work. Francisco de Goya depicted Spanish life during one of its most violent periods. The prolific 20th-century master Pablo Picasso is recognized as the founder of modern art. To these names must be added that of El Greco – who was born in Crete but who lived in Spain, where he painted religious scenes in an individualistic style. The work of these and Spain's many other great artists can be seen in world- renowned galleries, especially the Prado *(see pp296–9).*

The king and queen, reflected in a mirror behind the painter, may be posing for their portrait.

Self-portrait of Velázquez

In his series *Las Meninas* (1957), Picasso interprets the frozen gesture of the five-year-old Infanta Margarita. Altogether, Picasso produced 44 paintings based on Velázquez's canvas. Some of them are in Barcelona's Museu Picasso *(see p157).*

Religious Art in Spain

The influence of the Catholic Church on Spanish art through the ages is reflected in the predominance of religious imagery. Many churches and museums have Romanesque altarpieces or earlier icons. El Greco *(see p395)* painted from a highly personal religious vision. Baroque religious art of the 17th century, when the Inquisition *(see p278)* was at its height, often graphically depicts physical suffering and spiritual torment.

The Burial of the Count of Orgaz by El Greco *(see p394)*

Las Meninas (1656)

In Velázquez's painting of the Infanta Margarita and her courtiers, in the Prado *(see pp296–9),* the eye is drawn into the distance where the artist's patron, Felipe IV, is reflected in a mirror.

				The Resurrection *by Pedro Berruguete*		**1598–1664** Francisco de Zurbarán
1285–1348 Ferrer Bassá		**1390–1410** Pere Nicolau				
	1363–95 Jaume Serra		**1428–1460** Luis Daimau			**1591–1652** José de Ribera
1300			**1400**		**1500**	
			1388–1424 Luis Borrassa		**1474–95** Bartolomé Bermejo	**1565–1628** Francisco Ribalta
Madonna with Angels (detail) by Ferrer Bassá				**1450–1504** Pedro Berruguete		
			1427–52 Bernat Martorell		**1541–1614** El Greco	**1599–1660** Diego de Velázquez

José Nieto, the queen's chamberlain, stands in the doorway in the background of the painting.

Court jester

Modern Art

The early 20th-century artists Joan Miró (see p176), Salvador Dalí (see p219) and Pablo Picasso (see p157) all belonged to the Paris School. More recent artists of note include Antonio Saura and Antoni Tàpies (see p168). Among many great Spanish art collections, the Museo Reina Sofía in Madrid (see pp302–3) specializes in modern art. Contemporary artists are accorded great prestige in Spain. Their work is to be seen in town halls, banks and public squares, and many towns have a museum dedicated to a local painter.

Salvador Dalí's painting of the Colossus of Rhodes (1954)

Painting (1933) by Joan Miró

The Family of King Charles IV was painted in 1800 by Francisco de Goya (see p243), nearly 150 years after Las Meninas. Its debt to Velázquez's painting is evident in its frontal composition, compact grouping of figures and in the inclusion of a self-portrait.

The Holy Children with the Shell by Murillo

1893–1983 Joan Miró

1881–1973 Pablo Picasso

1904–89 Salvador Dalí

1746–1828 Francisco de Goya

1863–1923 Joaquín Sorolla

1923–2012 Antoni Tàpies

1700

1800

1900

1642–93 Claudio Coello

1887–1927 Juan Gris

1618–82 Bartolomé Esteban Murillo

Still Life with a Guitar (1913) by Juan Gris

1930–1998 Antonio Saura

Literary Spain

The best-known work of Spanish literature, *Don Quixote* is considered the first modern novel, but Spain has produced many major works over the last 2,000 years. The Roman writers Seneca, Lucan and Martial were born in Spain. Later, the Moors developed a flourishing, but now little-known, literary culture. Although Spanish (Castilian) is the national tongue, many enduring works have been written in the Galician and Catalan regional languages. Basque literature, hitherto an oral culture, is a more recent development. Many foreign writers, such as Alexandre Dumas, Ernest Hemingway and Karel Capek, have written accounts of their travels in Spain.

Middle Ages

As the Roman empire fell, Latin evolved into several Romance languages. The earliest non-Latin literature in Spain derives from an oral tradition that arose before the 10th century. It is in the form of *jarchas*, snatches of love poetry written in Mozarab, the Romance language that was spoken by Christians living under the Moors.

In the 12th century, the first poems appeared in Castilian. During the next 300 years, two separate schools of poetry developed. The best-known example of troubadour verse is the anonymous epic, *El Cantar del Mío Cid*, which tells of the heroic exploits of El Cid *(see p374)* during the Reconquest. Works of clerical poetry – for example, Gonzalo de Berceo's *Milagros de Nuestra Señora*, relating the life of the Virgin – convey a moral message.

Spanish literature evolved in the 13th century after Alfonso X the Learned *(see p59)* replaced Latin with Castilian Romance (later called Spanish) as the official language.

Under his supervision a team of Jews, Christians and Arabs wrote scholarly treatises. The king himself was a poet, writing in Galician Romance.

The first great prose works in Spanish appeared in the 14th and 15th centuries. *El Libro de Buen Amor,* by an ecclesiastic, Juan Ruiz, is a tale of the love affairs of a priest, interleaved with other stories. Fernando de Rojas uses skilful characterization in *La Celestina* to tell a tragic love story about two nobles and a scheming go-between. This was an age in which tales of chivalry were also popular.

The prolific Golden Age dramatist, Félix Lope de Vega

Golden Age

The 16th century hailed the start of Spain's Golden Age of literature. But it was also a period of domestic strife. This found expression in the picaresque novel, a Spanish genre originating with the anonymous *El Lazarillo de Tormes*, a bitter reflection on the misfortunes of a blind man's guide.

Spiritual writers flourished under the austere climate of the Counter-Reformation. St John of the Cross's *Cántico Espiritual* was influenced by Oriental erotic poetry and the Bible's *Song of Songs*.

The 17th century saw the emergence of more great talents. The life and work of Miguel de Cervantes *(see p337)* straddles the two centuries of the Golden Age. He published his master-piece, *Don Quixote*, in 1615. Other important writers of the time include Francisco de Quevedo and Luis de Góngora.

Corrales (public theatres) appeared in the 17th century, opening the way for Lope de Vega *(see p294)*, Calderón de la Barca and other dramatists.

Alfonso X the Learned (1221–84)

Don Quixote's adventures portrayed by José Moreno Carbonero

18th and 19th Centuries

Influenced by the French Enlightenment, literature in the 18th century was seen as a way to educate the people. Such was the aim, for instance, of Leandro Fernández de Moratín's comedy *El Sí de las Niñas*. This period saw the development of journalism as well as the emergence of the essay as a literary form. Romanticism had a short and late life in Spain. *Don Juan Tenorio*, a tale of the legendary irrepressible Latin lover by José Zorrilla, is the best-known Romantic play.

The satirical essayist Larra stands out from his contemporaries at the beginning of the 19th century. Towards the end of the century, the novel became a vehicle for realistic portrayals of Spanish society. Benito Pérez Galdós, regarded by many to be Spain's greatest novelist after Cervantes, studied the human condition in his *Episodios*

José Zorrilla (1817–93)

Nacionales. The heroine in Clarín's *La Regenta* is undone by the reactionary prejudices of provincial town society.

20th Century

Writers at the turn of the century, including Pío Baroja *(see p68)*, Miguel de Unamuno and Antonio Machado, described Spain as falling behind the rest of Europe. Ramón María del Valle-Inclán wrote highly satirical plays that created the foundations of modern Spanish theatre. In poetry, the Nobel Prize winner, Juan Ramón Jiménez, strived for pureness of form. The so-called "Generation of 27" combined European experimental art with Spain's traditional literary subjects. The best-known of them is the poet and playwright Federico García Lorca who was executed by a Fascist firing squad in 1936 *(see p71)*. He drew on the legends and stereotypes of his native Andalucía to make universal statements in his poems and plays, such as *Yerma*.

In the aftermath of the Civil War, many intellectuals who had backed the Republic were forced into exile. The Franco regime tried to create its own propagandist culture. Yet the finest literature of the period was written in spite of the political climate. Camilo José Cela's *La Colmena*, a description of everyday life in the hungry, postwar city of Madrid, set a mood of social realism that inspired other writers.

Since the 1960s, the novel has become increasingly popular due to the emergence of writers like Joan Benet, Julio Llamazares, Antonio Muñoz Molina, José Manuel Caballero Bonald, Juan Marsé and the best-selling Carlos Ruiz Zafón.

The 20th and 21st centuries have also witnessed a surge of great Spanish literature from Latin America. Prominent authors include Jorge Luis Borges, José Ángel Mañas, Javier Marías and Gabriel García Márquez.

Statue of García Lorca

Carlos Ruiz Zafón, author of the best-selling book *The Shadow of the Wind*

The Bullfighting Tradition

Bullfighting is a sacrificial ritual in which men (and a few women) pit themselves against a bull bred for the ring. In this "authentic religious drama", as poet García Lorca described it, spectators experience the fear and exaltation felt by the matador. Bullfights today, however, are often debased by practices that weaken the bull, such as shaving its horns. Opinion is divided on this, with a growing number of Spaniards opposing the tradition. Catalonia banned bullfighting on grounds of cruelty in 2010. The ban was reversed by Spain's constitutional court in 2016 but Catalonia's regional government continues to ignore this ruling. Many still regard the *toreo*, the art of bullfighting, as an essential part of their cultural heritage.

Plaza de Toros de la Maestranza, Seville. This ring is regarded, with Las Ventas in Madrid, as one of the top venues for bullfighting in Spain.

The matador wears a *traje de luces* (suit of light), a colourful silk outfit embroidered with gold sequins.

Well treated at the ranch, the *toro bravo* (fighting bull) is specially bred for qualities of aggressiveness and courage. As aficionados of bullfighting point out in its defence, the young bull enjoys a full life while it is being prepared for its 15 minutes in the ring. Bulls must be at least four years old before they fight.

The Bullfight

The *corrida* (bullfight) traditionally has three stages, called *tercios*. In the first stage, the *tercio de varas*, the matador and *picadores* (horsemen with lances) are aided by *peones* (assistants). In the second stage, or *tercio de banderillas*, *banderilleros*, the matador stick pairs of darts in the bull's back. In the third stage, the *tercio de muleta*, the matador makes a series of passes at the bull with a *muleta* (cape). He then executes the kill, the *estocada*, with a sword.

The matador plays the bull with a *capa* (red cape) in the *tercio de varas*. *Peones* will then draw the bull towards the *picadores*.

Horses are now padded.

Picadores goad the bull with steel-pointed lances, testing its bravery. The lances weaken the animal's shoulder muscles.

The Bullring

The *corrida* audience is seated in the *tendidos* (stalls) or in the *palcos* (balcony), where the *presidencia* (president's box) is situated. Opposite are the *puerta de cuadrillas*, through which the matador and team arrive, and the *arrastre de toros* (exit for bulls). Before entering the ring, the matadors wait in a corridor (*callejón*) behind *barreras* and *burladeros* (barriers). Horses are kept in the *patio de caballos* and the bulls in the *corrales*.

Key

- ☐ Tendidos
- ▣ Palcos
- ▣ Presidencia
- ▣ Puerta de cuadrillas
- ▣ Arrastre de toros
- ▣ Callejón
- ▣ Barreras
- ▣ Burladeros
- ☐ Patio de caballos
- ☐ Corrales

Plan of a typical bullring

Manolete is regarded by most followers of bullfighting as one of the greatest matadors ever. He was eventually gored to death by the bull Islero at Linares, Jaén, in 1947.

The passes are made with a *muleta*, a cape stiffened along one side.

The bull may go free if it shows courage spectators wave white handkerchiefs, asking the *corrida* president to let it leave the ring alive.

José Tomás is one of Spain's leading matadors today. He is famous for his purist approach and for his natural and elegant style with both the *capa* and the *muleta*.

The bull weighs about 500 kg (1,100 lbs).

Banderilleros enter to provoke the wounded bull in the *tercio de banderillas*, sticking pairs of *banderillas* in its back.

The matador makes passes with the cape in the *tercio de muleta*, then lowers it and thrusts in the sword for the kill.

The *estocada recibiendo* is a difficult kill, rarely seen. The matador awaits the bull's charge rather than moving to meet it.

The Fiestas of Spain

On any day of the year there is a fiesta happening somewhere in Spain – usually more than one. There isn't a village, town or city in the country that doesn't honour its patron saint, the Virgin or the changing seasons with processions, bullrunning, fireworks, re-enacted battles, some ancestral rite or a *romería* – a mass pilgrimage to a rural shrine. Whatever the pretext, a fiesta is a chance for everyone to take a break from normal life (most shops and offices close) and let off steam, with celebrations sometimes going on around the clock.

Many *romerías* wind through the countryside during the year

Spring Fiestas

The end of winter and the start of spring are marked by Valencia's great fire festival, Las Fallas *(see p259)*, in which huge papier-mâché sculptures are set alight in a symbolic act of burning the old in order to make way for the new.

Alcoi's mock battles between costumed armies of Moors and Christians in April *(see p259)* are the most spectacular of the countless fiestas which commemorate the battles of the Reconquest. Seville's April Fair *(see p437)*, is the biggest celebration held in Andalucía.

During the festival of Los Mayos, on 30 April and the following days, crosses are decorated with flowers in parts of Spain.

Easter

Most communities observe Easter in some form with pomp and solemnity. It is heralded by the Palm Sunday processions. The most impressive of these is in Elx, where intricate sculptures are woven from blanched leaves cropped from the most extensive forest of palm trees in Europe *(see p265)*.

The best Semana Santa (Easter Week) processions are held in Seville *(see p437)*, Granada, Málaga, Murcia and Valladolid. Brotherhoods of robed men carry *pasos*, huge sculptures depicting the Virgin, Christ or scenes of the Passion, through the streets. They are accompanied by people dressed as biblical characters or penitents, in tall conical hats. In some towns passion plays are acted out. In others, people carry heavy crosses. Sometimes the centuries-old ritual of self-flagellation can be witnessed.

Summer Fiestas

The first major fiesta of the summer is Pentecost (also known as Whitsun), in May or June, and its most famous celebration is at El Rocío *(see p469)*, where many thousands of people gather in a frenzy of religious devotion.

At Corpus Christi (in May or June) the consecrated host is carried in procession through many cities in an ornate silver monstrance. The route of the procession is often covered with a carpet of flowers. The main Corpus Christi celebrations take place in Valencia, Toledo and Granada.

On Midsummer's Eve (La Víspera de San Juan), bonfires are lit all over, especially in the areas along the Mediterranean coast, to herald the celebration of St John the Baptist on 24 June.

The Brotherhood of Candlemas, Semana Santa (Easter Week) in Seville

During Los Sanfermines *(see p136)* in Pamplona in July, young people run through the streets in front of a herd of bulls.

The Virgin of Carmen, who is revered as the patron of fishermen, is honoured in many ports on 16 July.

The important Catholic holiday of Assumption Day, 15 August, is marked by a huge number and variety of fiestas.

Autumn Fiestas

There are few fiestas in autumn, but in most wine regions the grape harvest is fêted. The annual pig slaughter has become a jubilant public event in some villages, especially in Extremadura. In Galicia it is traditional to roast chestnuts on street bonfires.

On All Saints' Day, 1 November, people remember the dead by visiting cemeteries to lay flowers, especially chrysanthemums, on graves.

Christmas and New Year

Nochebuena (Christmas Eve) is the main Christmas celebration, when families gather for an evening meal before attending Midnight Mass, known as *misa del gallo* (Mass of the rooster). During the Christmas period, *belenes* (crib scenes) of painted figurines abound. You may also see a "living crib", peopled by costumed actors. Spain's "April Fools' Day" is 28 December, when people play practical jokes on each other. Clown-like

Colourful parade at the Carnival in Santa Cruz de Tenerife *(see p540)*

characters may make fun of passers-by.

To celebrate New Year's Eve *(Noche Vieja)*, crowds gather beneath the clock in Madrid's central square, the Puerta del Sol *(see p276)*, after a midnight celebration at home with their families. Traditionally people eat 12 grapes, one on each chime of midnight, to bring good luck for the year.

Epiphany, on 6 January, is celebrated with parades of the Three Kings in villages and towns the evening before.

Winter Fiestas

Animals hold centre stage in a variety of fiestas on 17 January, the Day of St Anthony, patron saint of animals, when pets and livestock are blessed by priests. St Agatha, the patron saint of married women, is honoured

on 5 February, when women, for once, are the protagonists of many fiestas. In Zamarramala (Segovia), for example, women take over the mayor's privileges and powers for this particular day *(see p372)*.

St Anthony's Day in Villanueva de Alcolea (Castellón province)

Carnival

Carnival, in February or early March (depending on the date of Easter), brings a chance for a street party as winter comes to an end and before Lent begins. The biggest celebrations are held in Santa Cruz de Tenerife *(see p540)* – comparable with those of Rio de Janeiro – and in Cádiz *(see p469)*. Carnival was prohibited by the Franco regime because of its licentiousness and frivolity. It ends on or after Ash Wednesday with the Burial of the Sardine, a "funeral" in which a mock sardine, representing winter, is ritually burned or buried.

A spectacularly costumed choir singing during Carnival in Cádiz

SPAIN THROUGH THE YEAR

Festivals, cultural events and sports competitions crowd the calendar in Spain. Even small villages have at least one traditional fiesta, lasting a week or more, when parades, bullfights and fireworks displays replace work *(see pp42–3)*. Many rural and coastal towns celebrate the harvest or fishing catch with a gastronomic fair at which you can sample local produce.

Music, dance, drama and film festivals are held in Spain's major cities throughout the year. Meanwhile, the country's favourite outdoor sports – football, basketball, cycling, sailing, golf and tennis – culminate in several national and international championships. It is a good idea to confirm specific dates of events with the local tourist board as some vary from year to year.

Spring

Life in Spain moves outdoors with the arrival of spring, and terrace cafés begin to fill with people. The countryside is at its best as wild flowers bloom, and irrigation channels flow to bring water to the newly sown crops. The important Easter holiday is a time of solemn processions throughout the country.

March
International Vintage Car Rally *(usually first Sun)*, from Barcelona to Sitges. More than 60 vintage cars make this annual 45-km (28-mile) journey.

Las Fallas *(15–19 Mar)*, Valencia *(see p259)*. This spectacular fiesta also marks the start of the bull-fighting *(see pp40–41)* season.

Fiestas *(end Feb or mid-Mar)*, Castellón de la Plana. All in honour of Mary Magdalene.

April
Spanish Motorcycle Grand Prix *(Apr/early May)*, Jerez de la Frontera race track.

Feria del Caballo (Festival of the Horses) in Jerez de la Frontera

Religious Music Week *(Easter week, from Passion Sat)*, Cuenca.

Trofeo Conde de Godó *(mid- to late Apr)*, Barcelona. Spain's international tennis championship.

Moors and Christians *(21–24 Apr)*, Alcoi *(see p262)*. This colourful costumed event celebrates the Christian victory over the Moors in 1276.

April Fair *(2 weeks after Easter)*, Seville. Exuberant Andalucían fiesta *(see p437)*.

Feria Nacional del Queso *(late Apr/early May)*, Trujillo (Cáceres). A festival celebrating Spanish cheese *(see p411)*.

May
Dos de Mayo *(2 May)*, Madrid. Music, fireworks and dancing in the streets in remembrance of the 1808 rebellion against Napolean's occupation.

Feria del Caballo *(first week)*, Jerez de la Frontera. Horse fair showing Andalucía at its most traditional, with fine horses and beautiful women in flamenco dresses.

Fiestas de San Isidro *(8–15 May)*, Madrid *(see p294)*. Bullfights at Las Ventas bullring are the highlights of the taurine year.

Spanish Formula One Grand Prix *(May/Jun)*, Montmeló circuit, Barcelona. International motor race.

Onlookers lining the street during the Vuelta Ciclista a España *(p46)*

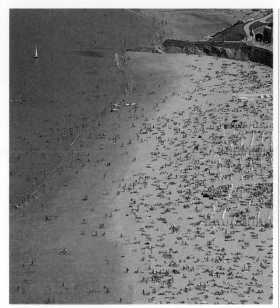

San Sebastián, one of the most popular resorts on the north coast

Summer

August is Spain's big holiday season. The cities empty as Spaniards flock to the coast or to their second homes in the hills. Their numbers are swelled by millions of foreign tourists, and beaches and camp sites are often full to bursting. As the heat starts in the centre and south, entertainment often takes place only in the evening, when the temperature has dropped. In late summer the harvest begins and there are gastronomic

The pouring and tasting of cider in Asturias's Cider Festival

fiestas everywhere to celebrate food and drink, from the fishing catches of the north coast to the sausages of the Balearic Islands.

June

International Festival of Music and Dance (Jun–Jul), Granada. Classical music and ballet staged in the Alhambra and the Generalife.
Grec Arts Festival (late Jun–Aug), Barcelona. Both Spanish and international theatre, music and dance.
A Rapa das Bestas (Jun, Jul, Aug), Pontevedra, La Coruña and Lugo provinces (Galicia). Wild horses are rounded up so that their manes and tails can be cut (see p102).
Classical Theatre Festival (end Jun–Aug), Mérida. Staged in the Roman theatre and amphitheatre (see p414).

July

Guitar Festival (timing varies), Córdoba. From classical to flamenco (see pp428–9).
International Classical Theatre Festival of Almagro (Jul). Spanish and classical repertoire in one of the oldest theatres in Europe (see p403).

Blues Cazorla (Jul), Cazorla (Jaén). Largest blues festival in Spain, held over three days.
Cider Festival (second weekend), Nava (Asturias). Includes traditional cider-pouring competitions.
International Jazz Festivals in San Sebastián (third week), Getxo (first week) and Vitoria (mid-Jul).
Pyrenean Folklore Festival (late Jul/early Aug, odd years), Jaca (Aragón). Folk costumes, music and dance.
Certamen Internacional de Habaneras y Polifonía (late Jul–early Aug), Torrevieja (Alicante). Musical competition of 19th-century seafarers' songs.

August

International Festival of Santander (Aug). Celebration of music, dance and theatre.
Copa del Rey MAPFRE (end Jul/first week Aug), Palma de Mallorca. Sailing competition, presided over by King Felipe VI.
Descent of the Río Sella (first Sat). Canoe race in Asturias from Arriondas to Ribadesella (see p111).
Assumption Day (15 Aug) The Assumption is celebrated throughout the country.

Participants in the Descent of the Río Sella canoe race

Semanas Grandes (mid-Aug), Bilbao and San Sebastián. "Great Weeks" of sporting and cultural events.
Misteri d'Elx (14–15 Aug; also 29 Oct–1 Nov during Medieval Festival), Elx (see p265). Unique liturgical drama featuring spectacular special effects.

Vines and the village of Larouco in the Valdeorras wine region of Galicia *(see p82)* in autumn

Autumn

Autumn usually brings rain after the heat of summer, and, with the tourist season over, many resorts virtually close down. Harvest festivities continue, however, and the most important celebrations are in honour of the grape. The first pressings are blessed and, in some places, wine is served for free.

In woodland areas, freshly picked wild mushrooms start to appear in various dishes on local restaurant menus. The hunting season begins in the middle of October and runs until February. Autumn is also the start of the new drama and classical music seasons in the major cities of Spain.

September

Vuelta Ciclista a España *(Sep)*. Annual bicycle race around Spain.

Grape Harvest *(mid-Sep)*, Jerez de la Frontera. Celebration of the new crop in the country's sherry capital.

San Sebastián Film Festival *(mid- to late Sep)*. Film-makers gather in this Basque city for a long-running festival and film competition *(see p127)*.

Festival de la Mercé *(17–24 Sep)*, Barcelona. Free concerts and folkloric events.

Bienal de Arte Flamenco *(early Sep–early Oct, even years only)*, Seville. Top flamenco artists perform.

October

Día de la Hispanidad *(12 Oct)*. Spain's national holiday marks Columbus's discovery of America in 1492. The biggest celebration in the country is the exuberant fiesta of Día del Pilar in Zaragoza *(see p243)*, which marks the end of the bullfighting year.

Moors and Christians *(mid-Oct)*, Callosa d'en Sarria (Alicante). Parades in honour of the local madonna.

Saffron Festival *(last weekend)*, Consuegra (Toledo). A celebration of this expensive spice, which is grown locally.

Driving down the fairway at one of Spain's golfing championships

November

All Saints' Day *(1 Nov)*. This marks the start of the *matanza* (pig slaughter) in rural Spain.

Os Magostos *(11 Nov)*. Chestnut-harvest fairs abound in Galicia.

Latin American Film Festival *(mid-Nov for one week)*, Huelva *(see p468)*.

National Flamenco Competition *(mid-Nov for two weeks)*, Córdoba. Song, dance and guitar performances.

Lana Turner on centre-stage at the San Sebastián Film Festival

Public Holidays

Besides marking the national holidays below, each region (*comunidad autónoma*) celebrates its own holiday, and every town and village has at least one other fiesta each year. If a holiday falls on a Tuesday or a Thursday, some people also choose to take holidays on the intervening Monday or Friday, making a long weekend called a *puente* (bridge).

Año Nuevo *(New Year's Day)* (1 Jan)
Día de los Tres Reyes *(Epiphany)* (6 Jan)
Jueves Santo *(Maundy Thursday)* (Mar/Apr)
Viernes Santo *(Good Friday)* (Mar/Apr)
Día de Pascua *(Easter Sunday)* (Mar/Apr)
Día del Trabajo *(Labour Day)* (1 May)
Asunción *(Assumption Day)* (15 Aug)
Día de la Hispanidad *(National Day)* (12 Oct)
Todos los Santos *(All Saints' Day)* (1 Nov)
Día de la Constitución *(Constitution Day)* (6 Dec)
Inmaculada Concepción *(Immaculate Conception)* (8 Dec)
Navidad *(Christmas Day)* (25 Dec)

Assumption Day in La Alberca (Salamanca)

Winter

Winter varies greatly from region to region. In the mountains, snowfalls bring skiers to the slopes; while in lower areas, olive and orange picking are in full swing. The higher parts of Central Spain can become very cold. Andalucía, the east coast and the Balearic Islands have cool nights but often sunny days. The winter warmth of the Canary Islands brings the high tourist season. Christmas is a special time of celebration – an occasion for families to reunite, share food and attend religious celebrations.

Skiers in the Sierra de Guadarrama, north of Madrid *(see p333)*

"El Gordo", the largest Spanish lottery prize, being drawn

December
El Gordo *(22 Dec)*. Spain's largest lottery prize, "the Fat One", is drawn.
Noche Buena *(24 Dec)* is a family Christmas Eve, followed by Midnight Mass.
Santos Inocentes *(28 Dec)*, Spain's version of April Fools' Day, when people play tricks.
Noche Vieja *(31 Dec)*. New Year's Eve is most celebrated in Madrid's Puerta del Sol.

January
Día de los Tres Reyes *(6 Jan)*. On the eve of the Epiphany, the Three Kings parade through town, throwing sweets to the children.
La Tamborrada *(19–20 Jan)*, San Sebastián. Drumming en masse in traditional costume.

Canary Islands International Music Festival *(Jan–Feb)*. Classical concerts are held on La Palma and Tenerife.

February
La Endiablada *(2–3 Feb)*, Almonacid del Marquesado (Cuenca). Townsfolk dress as devils in honour of San Blas.
ARCO *(mid-Feb)*, Madrid. International contemporary art fair.
Pasarela Cibeles (Fashion Week) *(mid-Feb)*, Madrid. Women's and men's fashion shows in the capital.
Carnival *(Feb/Mar)*. Final fiesta before Lent, with colourful costumes. Those in Santa Cruz de Tenerife and Cádiz are among the best.

The Climate of Spain

Spain's large landmass, with its extensive high plateaus and mountain ranges, and the influences of the Mediterranean and Atlantic, produce a wide range of climatic variation, especially in winter. The north is wettest year-round, the eastern and southern coasts and the islands have mild winters, while winter temperatures in the interior are often below freezing. Summers everywhere are hot, except in upland areas.

MADRID

°C				
	25	36	24	
			13	14
	3		3	
0				−5

Average monthly maximum temperature

Average monthly minimum temperature

Freezing point

☀	8 hrs	12 hrs	6.5 hrs	5 hrs
☂	48 mm	11 mm	53 mm	39 mm
month	Apr	Jul	Oct	Jan

Average daily hours of sunshine

Average monthly rainfall

ASTURIAS AND CANTABRIA

°C				
	24	29	25	
		13		18
	6		8	
0				2

☀	6 hrs	6.5 hrs	4.5 hrs	2.5 hrs
☂	83 mm	54 mm	133 mm	10 mm
month	Apr	Jul	Oct	Jan

GALICIA

°C				
	22	29	25	
		12	7	17
	5			
0				2

☀	6.5 hrs	8.5 hrs	5 hrs	3 hrs
☂	67 mm	28 mm	87 mm	118 mm
month	Apr	Jul	Oct	Jan

Oviedo · Santander · B (Bil

Santiago de Compostela

Vigo

León

Burgos

Valladolid

Salamanca

MADRID

Cáceres

Toledo

Badajoz

Ciudad Real

Córdoba

Sevilla

Granada

Cádiz · Málaga · Alme

CASTILLA Y LEÓN

°C				
	25	36	26	
		9		14
	0		1	
0				−7

☀	8 hrs	12 hrs	6.5 hrs	3.5 hrs
☂	37 mm	14 mm	36 mm	37 mm
month	Apr	Jul	Oct	Jan

EXTREMADURA

°C				
	28	41	31	
		14	7	18
	6			
0				−2

☀	9 hrs	12.5 hrs	7 hrs	5 hrs
☂	46 mm	3 mm	52 mm	61 mm
month	Apr	Jul	Oct	Jan

ANDALUCÍA

°C				
	27	38	28	
		18	12	22
	10			
0				4

☀	8 hrs	11.5 hrs	7 hrs	6 hrs
☂	46 mm	1 mm	64 mm	61 mm
month	Apr	Jul	Oct	Jan

BASQUE COUNTRY, NAVARRA & RIOJA

°C			
25	36	26	
	10		15
1		2	
0			
			−7

6 hrs	9.5 hrs	5 hrs	2.5 hrs
83 mm	46 mm	107 mm	130 mm
month	Apr	Jul	Oct	Jan

ARAGÓN

°C			
26	37	27	
4	10	5	18
0			
			−4

8 hrs	11.5 hrs	6.5 hrs	5 hrs
34 mm	15 mm	34 mm	17 mm
month	Apr	Jul	Oct	Jan

CATALONIA

°C			
28	38	28	
3	13	3	18
0			
			−5

8.5 hrs	11.5 hrs	6.5 hrs	4 hrs
46 mm	24 mm	30 mm	22 mm
month	Apr	Jul	Oct	Jan

THE BALEARIC ISLANDS

°C			
24	33	27	
6	17	9	18
0			2

7.5 hrs	11.5 hrs	6 hrs	5 hrs
32 mm	3 mm	77 mm	39 mm
month	Apr	Jul	Oct	Jan

Sebastián
(Donostia)

Iruña
(Pamplona)

Zaragoza

Lleida

Barcelona

uenca

Valencia

Palma

acete

Murcia

Alacant
(Alicante)

Santa Cruz
de Tenerife

Las Palmas
de Gran Canaria

CASTILLA-LA MANCHA

°C			
24	36	26	
	8		16
0			
−2		−1	−10

7.5 hrs	12 hrs	6 hrs	4.5 hrs
48 mm	19 mm	52 mm	43 mm
month	Apr	Jul	Oct	Jan

VALENCIA AND MURCIA

°C			
27	36	30	
7	17	9	23
0			1

8.5 hrs	11.5 hrs	7 hrs	6 hrs
40 mm	4 mm	52 mm	30 mm
month	Apr	Jul	Oct	Jan

THE CANARY ISLANDS

°C			
26	32	30	
12	17	16	25
0			11

7.5 hrs	9.5 hrs	7 hrs	6.5 hrs
13 mm	0 mm	28 mm	36 mm
month	Apr	Jul	Oct	Jan

THE HISTORY OF SPAIN

The Iberian Peninsula, first inhabited around 800,000 BC, has long been subject to foreign influences – from the Phoenicians to the Romans, the Moors to the Christians. Spain itself has a colourful, dramatic history, from the Discovery of the Americas in the 15th century to the Spanish Civil War in the 20th century. Today, tourism is a key industry and the country is the third most visited in the world.

From the 11th century BC, Iberia was colonized by eastern Mediterranean civilizations, starting with the Phoenicians, then the Greeks and Carthaginians. The Romans arrived in 218 BC to fight the Carthaginians, thus sparking off the Second Punic War. They harvested the peninsula's agricultural and mineral wealth and established cities with aqueducts, temples and theatres.

With the fall of the Roman Empire in the early 5th century AD, Visigothic invaders from the north took power but their poor political organization made them easy prey to the Moors from North Africa. In the 8th century, the peninsula came almost entirely under Moorish rule. Europe's only major Muslim territory, the civilization of Al Andalus excelled in mathematics, geography, astronomy and poetry.

From the 11th century, northern Christian kingdoms initiated a military reconquest of Al Andalus. The marriage, in 1469, of Fernando of Aragón and Isabel of Castile led to unity. They took Granada, the last Moorish kingdom in 1492, and Columbus discovered the Americas in the same year, opening the way for the Spanish conquistadors. The succeeding Habsburg dynasty spent the riches from the New World on endless foreign wars and Spain's misfortunes continued into the next century with Napoleon's invasion and the loss of American colonies. Later, the political instability of the 19th and early 20th centuries led to dictatorship in the 1920s and a republic in the 1930s, which was destroyed by the Civil War. General Franco ruled by repression until his death in 1975, and Spain has been a constitutional monarchy since.

Bullfighting in Madrid's Plaza Mayor in the 17th century

◀ *The Virgin of the Catholic Monarchs*, a 15th-century painting kept in Madrid's Museo del Prado

Prehistoric Spain

The Iberian Peninsula was first inhabited by hunter-gatherers around 800,000 BC. They were eclipsed by a Neolithic farming population from 5000 BC. First in a wave of settlers from over the Mediterranean, the Phoenicians landed in 1100 BC, to be followed by the Greeks and Carthaginians. Invading Celts mixed with native Iberian tribes (forming the Celtiberians). They proved a formidable force against the Romans, the next conquerors of Spain.

Spain in 5000 BC

☐ Neolithic farming settlements

Iron Dagger (6th century BC)
Weapons, like this Celtic dagger, represent the later Iron Age, in contrast to earlier metal objects which were for domestic use.

Small silver bottle

The 28 bracelets
have perforations and moulded decorations.

Stone Age Man
This skull belongs to a Palaeolithic man, who hunted deer and bison with tools made of wood and stone.

Incised geometric pattern

La Dama de Elche
Dating from the 4th century BC, this stone statue is a fine example of Iberian art. Her austere beauty reveals traces of Greek influence.

The Villena Treasure
Discovered in 1963 during works in Villena, near Alicante, this Bronze Age find consists of 66 dazzling objects mostly of gold, including bowls, bottles and jewellery (see p264). The treasure dates from around 1000 BC.

800,000 BC *Homo erectus* arrives in Iberian Peninsula		**35,000 BC** Cro-Magnon man evolves in Spain	**2500 BC** Los Millares (*p505*) is inhabited by early metal-workers with belief in the afterlife	**1800–1100 BC** Civilization of El Argar, an advanced agrarian society, flourishes in southeast Spain
300,000 BC Tribes of *Homo erectus* live in hunting camps in Soria and Madrid			

800,000 BC

2500

2000

500,000 BC Stones used as tools by hominids (probably *Homo erectus*)

100,000–40,000 BC Neanderthal man in Gibraltar

5000 BC Farming begins in Iberian Peninsula

18,000–14,000 BC Drawings by cave dwellers at Altamira (Cantabria), near Ribadesella (Asturias) and at Nerja (Andalucía)

Bison cave drawing, Altamira

Greek Ceramic Vase
The Greek colonizers brought new technology, including the potter's wheel, as well as refined artistic ideals. Their ceramics, such as this two-handled wine vessel, or amphora, provided sophisticated models.

Where to See Prehistoric Spain

The most famous cave paintings in Spain are at Altamira (see p116). There are dolmens in many parts of the country; among the largest are those at Antequera (see p481). The Guanches – the indigenous inhabitants of the Canary Islands – left behind more recent remains (see p551).

La Naveta d'es Tudons is one of the many prehistoric stone monuments scattered across the island of Menorca (see p531).

An excavated Celtic village, with its round huts, can be seen near A Guarda in Pontevedra (see p100).

The largest of the treasure's five bottles, made of silver, stands 22.5 cm (9 in) high.

Bowls of beaten gold may have originated in southwest Spain.

Brooches with separate clasps

The smaller pieces are of unknown use.

Astarte (8th century BC)
Worship of Phoenician deities was incorporated into local religions. One of the most popular was the fertility goddess Astarte, shown on this bronze from the kingdom of Tartessus.

Phoenician sarcophagus

1500	1000	500

1100 BC Phoenicians believed to have founded modern-day Cádiz

600 BC Greek colonists settle on northeast coast of Spain

228 BC Carthaginians occupy southeast Spain

300 BC *La Dama de Elche* is carved (p300)

1200 BC The "talaiotic" people of Menorca erect three unique types of stone building: *taulas, talaiots* and *navetas*

Taula in Menorca

775 BC Phoenicians establish colonies along the coast near Málaga

700 BC Semi-mythical kingdom of Tartessus thought to be at its height

Carthaginian sculpture

Romans and Visigoths

The Romans came to Spain to fight the Carthaginians and take possession of the region's huge mineral wealth. Later, Hispania's wheat and olive oil became mainstays of the empire. It took 200 years to subdue the peninsula, which was divided in three provinces: Tarraconensis, Lusitania and Baetica. In time, cities with Roman infrastructure developed. The fall of the empire in the 5th century left Spain in the hands of the Visigoths, invaders from the north. Politically disorganized, they fell victim to the Moors in 711.

Spain (Hispania) in 5 BC

☐ Tarraconensis
▨ Lusitania
▨ Baetica

Trajan *(AD 53–117)*
Trajan was the first Hispanic Roman emperor (AD 98–117). He improved public administration and expanded the empire.

Portico overlooking the gardens

Seneca *(4 BC–AD 65)*
Born in Córdoba, the Stoic philosopher Seneca lived in Rome as Nero's adviser.

Good acoustics at every level

A Classical façade served as a back-drop for tragedies. Additional scenery was used for comedies.

The *orchestra,* a semicircular open space for the choir

Visigothic Relief
This Visigothic stone carving depicting the sacrifice of Isaac is in the 7th-century church of San Pedro de la Nave, near Zamora (pp360–61).

The auditorium seated over 5,000. The audience was placed according to social status.

218 BC Scipio the Elder lands with a Roman army at Emporion (p220). The Second Punic War begins	**c.200 BC** Romans reach Gadir (modern Cádiz) after driving Carthaginians out of Hispania		**26 BC** Emerita Augusta (Mérida) is founded and soon becomes capital of Lusitania
	155 BC Lusitanian Wars begin. Romans invade Portugal		**19 BC** Augustus takes Cantabria and Asturias, ending 200 years of war
200 BC	**100**	**AD 1**	**AD 100**
219 BC Hannibal takes Sagunto (p253) for Carthaginians	**133 BC** Celt-Iberian Wars culminate in destruction of Numantia, Soria (p381)	**61 BC** Julius Caesar, governor of Hispania Ulterior, begins final conquest of northern Portugal and Galicia	**AD 74** Emperor Vespasian grants Latin status to all towns in Hispania, completing process of Romanization
		82–72 BC Roman Civil War. Pompey founds Pompaelo (Pamplona) in 75 BC	

Hannibal

Gladiator Mosaic
Mosaics were used as decoration both indoors and out. Themes range from mythical episodes to portrayals of daily life. This 4th-century AD mosaic shows gladiators in action and has helpful labels to name the fighters and show who is dead or alive.

Where to See Roman Spain

Like Mérida, Tarragona (see pp228–9) has extensive Roman ruins, and Itálica (see p482) is an excavated town. A magnificent Roman wall rings Lugo in Galicia (see p103). Built in Trajan's rule, the bridge over the Tagus at Alcántara (see p414) has a temple on it.

Emporion, a Roman town, was built next to a former Greek colony in the 3rd century BC. The ruins include grand villas and a forum (see p220).

The gardens were used as a foyer during intervals by the Hispanic nobility, dressed in elegant togas.

Stage building in granite and marble

Scaena, the platform on which the actors performed

Segovia's Roman aqueduct (see pp368–9), a huge monument with 163 arches, dates from the end of the 1st century AD.

Roman Theatre, Mérida
Theatre was an extremely popular form of entertainment in Hispania. This reconstruction shows the theatre at Mérida (see p414), built in 16–15 BC.

Visigothic Cross
Although Visigothic kings seldom ruled long enough to make an impact on society, the early Christian Church grew powerful. Fortunes were spent on churches and religious art.

Mosaic from Mérida

415 Visigoths establish their court at Barcelona

409 Vandals and their allies cross Pyrenees into Tarraconensis

446 Romans attempt to win back rest of Hispania

476 Overthrow of the last Roman emperor leads to end of Western Roman Empire

| 200 | 300 | 400 | 500 |

258 Franks cross Pyrenees into Tarraconensis and sack Tarragona

312 Christianity officially recognized as religion under rule of Constantine, the first Christian emperor
The Codex Vigilianus, *a Christian manuscript*

589 Visigothic King Reccared converts from Arianism to Catholicism at Third Council of Toledo

Al Andalus: Muslim Spain

The arrival of Arab and Berber invaders from North Africa, and their defeat of the Visigoths, gave rise to the most brilliant civilization of early medieval Europe. These Muslim settlers, often known as the Moors, called Spain "Al Andalus". A rich and powerful caliphate was established in Córdoba and mathematics, science, architecture and the decorative arts flourished. The caliphate eventually broke up into small kingdoms or *taifas*. Meanwhile small Christian enclaves expanded in the north.

Spain in AD 750

☐ Extent of Moorish domination

Water Wheel
Moorish irrigation techniques, such as the water wheel, revolutionized agriculture. New crops, including oranges and rice, were introduced.

The palace, dating from the 11th century, was surrounded by patios, pools and gardens.

Astrolabe
Perfected by the Moors around AD 800, the astrolabe was used by navigators and astronomers.

Remains of a Roman amphitheatre

Silver Casket of Hisham II
In the Caliphate of Córdoba, luxury objects of brilliant craftsmanship were worked in ivory, silver and bronze.

Fortified entrance gate

Curtain walls with watchtowers

711 Moors, led by Tariq, invade Spain and defeat Visigoths at battle of Guadalete

732 Moors' advance into France is halted by Charles Martel at Poitiers

778 Charlemagne's rearguard defeated by Basques at Roncesvalles (p138)

785 Building of great mosque at Córdoba begins

Charlemagne (742–814)

750

800

850

722 Led by Pelayo, Christians defeat Moors at Covadonga (p113)

Pelayo (718–37)

756 Abd al Rahman I proclaims independent emirate in Córdoba

744 Christians under Alfonso I of Asturias take León

822 Abd al Rahman II begins 30-year rule marked by patronage of the arts and culture

c.800 Tomb of St James (Santiago) is supposedly discovered at Santiago de Compostela

The East Wall of Córdoba's Mezquita

Wealth and artistic brilliance were lavished on mosques, especially in Córdoba (see pp486–7). Moorish arches were a major design element.

Where to See Moorish Spain

The finest Moorish buildings are in Andalucía, mainly in the cities of Córdoba (see pp484–5) and Granada (see pp492–8). Almería (see p505) has a large, ruined *alcazaba* (castle). In Jaén (see p499) there are Moorish baths. Further north, in Zaragoza, is the castle-palace of La Aljafería (see p241).

Medina Azahara (see p483), sacked in the 11th century but partly restored, was the final residence of Córdoba's caliphs.

Torre del Homenaje, the keep, was built by Abd al Rahman I (756–88).

Baths

Moorish Flask
A fine example of Moorish craftsmanship, this Umayyad dynasty flask dates from the 10th century.

Patio with Moorish decoration

Alcazaba at Málaga

An alcazaba was a castle built into the ramparts of a Moorish city, often protected by massive concentric walls. In Málaga (see p480) – the principal port of the Moorish kingdom of Granada – the vast Alcazaba was built in the 8–11th centuries on the site of a Roman fortress, and incorporated massive curtain walls and fortified gates.

Tariq ibn Ziyad
This Berber general, a member of the Umayyad Caliphate, was the leader of the Moorish forces that conquered Southern Spain in 711.

905 Emergent Navarra becomes Christian kingdom under Sancho I

976 Al Mansur, military dictator, usurps caliphal powers and sacks Barcelona. Córdoba Mezquita finished

1010 Medina Azahara sacked by Berbers

900

950

1000

913 Christian capital is established at León

936 Building of Medina Azahara palace starts near Córdoba

Bronze deer from Medina Azahara

1013 Caliphate of Córdoba breaks up. Emergence of *taifas*: small, independent Moorish kingdoms

The Reconquest

The infant Christian kingdoms in the north – León, Castile, Navarra, Aragón and Catalonia – advanced south gradually in the 11th century, fighting in the name of Christianity to regain land from the Moors. After the fall of Toledo in 1085, the struggle became increasingly a holy war. Militant North African Muslims – Almoravids and Almohads – rallied to the Moorish cause and ultimately took over Al Andalus in the 12th century. As the Christians pushed further south, soon only Granada remained under Moorish control.

Spain in 1173

☐ Christian kingdoms
▨ Al Andalus

Golden Goblet
The exquisite goblet (1063) of Doña Urraca, daughter of Alfonso VI, shows the quality of medieval Christian craftsmanship.

Fernando I
Fernando formed the first Christian power bloc in 1037 by uniting Léon with Castile, which was emerging as a major military force.

Armies of Castile, Aragón and Navarra

The Almohads fight until the bitter end, although many comrades lay slain.

Alhambra, Palace of the Nasrids
Moorish art and architecture of singular beauty continued to be produced in the Nasrid kingdom of Granada. Its apogee is the exquisite Alhambra *(see pp496–7).*

Las Navas de Tolosa

The Christian victory over the Almohads in the Battle of Las Navas de Tolosa (1212) led to Moorish Spain's decline. The army of Muhammad II al Nasir was no match for the forces of Sancho VII of Navarra, Pedro II of Aragón and Alfonso VIII of Castile. A stained-glass window in Roncesvalles (see p138) depicts the battle.

1037 León and Castile united for first time under Fernando I	**1065** Death of Fernando I precipitates fratricidal civil war between his sons	**1086** Almoravids respond to pleas for help from Moorish emirs by taking over *taifas* (splinter states)	**1158** Establishment of the Order of Calatrava, the first military order of knights in Spain

Fighting for the Reconquest

1050   **1100**   **1150**   **120**

1085 Toledo falls to Christians under Alfonso VI of Castile	**1137** Ramón Berenguer IV of Catalonia marries Petronila of Aragón, uniting the two kingdoms under their son, Alfonso II	**1147** Almohads arrive in Al Andalus and make Seville their capital
1094 The legendary El Cid *(see p374)* captures Valencia		**1143** Portugal becomes separate kingdom

Alfonso VI

1212 Combined Christian forces defeat Almohads at battle of Las Navas de Tolosa

Cantigas of Alfonso X (1252–84)
This detail of a manuscript by Alfonso X portrays the Moorish King of Granada preparing to invade Chincoya Castle. Alfonso the Learned encouraged his scholars to master Arab culture and translate ancient Greek manuscripts brought by the Moors.

Sancho VII of Navarra leads the Christian forces.

St James (Santiago)
Known as the Moor-slayer, St James is said to have miraculously intervened at the Battle of Clavijo in 844. This powerful figurehead is the patron saint of Spain.

Where to See Mudéjar Spain

The Mudéjares – Muslims who remained in territories under Christian occupation – created a distinctive architectural style distinguished by its ornamental work in brick, plaster and ceramics. Aragón, particularly Zaragoza (see pp240–41) and Teruel (see pp244–5), boasts some of the finest Mudéjar buildings. Seville's Reales Alcázares is an exquisitely harmonious collection of patios and halls built under Pedro I (see pp446–7).

The Tower of San Martín, in Teruel, combines both brick and colourful ceramics to highly decorative effect.

Santa María la Blanca (see p395), a former synagogue and church, shows the fusion of cultures in medieval Toledo.

---

215 Foundation of Salamanca University

1230 Fernando III reunites Castile and León

Coat of arms in Toledo's cathedral

1250 Toledo at its height as a centre of translation and learning, influenced by Alfonso X the Learned

1232 Granada becomes capital of future Nasrid kingdom. Building of the Alhambra begins

Alfonso X

1250   **1300**   **1350**   **1400**

1385 Portuguese defeat Castilians at Aljubarrota, crushing King Juan's aspirations to throne of Portugal

1386 Invasion of Galicia by the English, ended by Bayonne Treaty

1401 Work starts in Seville on what was then the world's largest Gothic cathedral

1388–9 Treaties end Spanish phase of Hundred Years' War

The Catholic Monarchs

The foundation of the Spanish nation-state was laid by Isabel I of Castile and Fernando II of Aragón (see p74). Uniting their lands in military, diplomatic and religious matters, the "Catholic Monarchs", as they are known, won back Granada, the last Moorish kingdom, from Boabdil. The Inquisition gave Spain a reputation for intolerance, yet in art and architecture brilliant progress was made and the voyages of Columbus opened up the New World.

Spain's Exploration of the New World

■ Route of Columbus's first voyage

Tomb of El Doncel (15th century)
This effigy of a page who died in the fight for Granada combines ideals of military glory and learning (see p386).

Alhambra

Boabdil, the grief-stricken king, moves forward to hand over the keys to Granada.

The Inquisition
Active from 1478, the Inquisition (see p278) persecuted those suspected of heresy with increasing vigour. This member of the Brotherhood of Death took victims to the stake.

Baptizing Jews
After the Christian reconquest of Granada, Jews were forced to convert or leave Spain. The conversos (converted Jews) were often treated badly.

The Fall of Granada (1492)
This romantic interpretation by Francisco Pradilla (1846–1921) reflects the chivalry of Boabdil, ruler of Granada, as he surrenders the keys of the last Moorish kingdom to the Catholic Monarchs, Fernando and Isabel, following ten long years of war.

1454 Enrique IV, Isabel's half-brother, accedes to throne of Castile

1465 Civil war erupts in Castile

Torquemada

1478 Papal bull authorizes Castilian Inquisition with Tomás de Torquemada as Inquisitor General

1450	1460	1470	1480

1451 Birth of Isabel of Castile

Statue of Isabel in a park near the Royal Palace

1469 Marriage of Fernando and Isabel in Valladolid unites Castile and Aragón

1474 Death of Enrique IV leads to civil war; Isabel triumphs over Juana la Beltraneja, Enrique's supposed daughter, to become queen

1479 Fernando becomes Fernando II of Aragón

Columbus Arriving in the Americas
The Catholic Monarchs financed Columbus's daring first voyage partly because they hoped for riches in return, but also because they expected him to convert infidels.

Boabdil
As the forlorn king left Granada, his mother reputedly said, "Don't cry as a child over what you could not defend as a man".

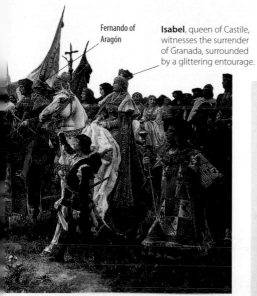

Fernando of Aragón

Isabel, queen of Castile, witnesses the surrender of Granada, surrounded by a glittering entourage.

Where to See Gothic Architecture in Spain

Spain has many great Gothic cathedrals, especially in Seville (pp442–3), Burgos (pp376–7), Barcelona (pp152–3), Toledo (pp396–7) and Palma de Mallorca (pp524–5). Secular buildings from this era include commodity exchanges like La Lonja in Valencia (p255) and castles (pp348–9).

Crown of Isabel
Worn at the surrender, Isabel's crown is now in her final resting place, the Capilla Real in Granada (see p492).

León cathedral (pp358–9) has a west front covered in statuary. Here Christ is seen presiding over the Last Judgment.

1494 Treaty of Tordesillas divides the New World territories between Portugal and Spain

1496 Foundation of Santo Domingo, on Hispaniola, first Spanish city in the Americas

1509 Cardinal Cisneros' troops attack Oran in Algeria and temporarily occupy it

Cardinal Cisneros

1490	1500	1510

1492 Fall of Granada after ten-year war. Columbus reaches America. Expulsion of Jews from Spain

Columbus's ship, the Santa María

1502 Uncon-verted Moors expelled from Spain

1504 Following death of Isabel, her daughter Juana la Loca becomes queen of Castile with Fernando as regent

1516 Death of Fernando

1512 Annexation of Navarra, leading to full unification of Spain

The Age of Discovery

Following Columbus's arrival in the Bahamas in 1492, the conquistadors went into Central and South America, conquering Mexico (1519), Peru (1532) and Chile (1541). In doing so, they destroyed Indian civilizations. In the 16th century, vast quantities of gold and silver flowed across the Atlantic to Spain. Carlos I and his son Felipe II spent some of it on battles to halt the spread of Protestantism in Europe, and in the Holy War against the Turks.

Spanish Empire in 1580
☐ Dominions of Felipe II

Mapping the World
This 16th-century German map reflects a new world, largely unknown to Europe before the era of conquistadors.

Galleons were armed with cannons as a defence against pirates and rival conquerors.

The lookout was essential for spotting enemies and making landfall.

Aztec Mask
In their great greed and ignorance, the Spanish destroyed the empires and civilizations of the Aztecs in Mexico and the Incas in Peru.

Forecastle

Seville
Granted the trading monopoly with the Americas, Seville, on the banks of the Guadalquivir, was Europe's richest port in the early 16th century.

1519 Magellan, Portuguese explorer, leaves Seville under Spanish patronage to circumnavigate the globe

1520–21 Revolt by Castilian towns when Carlos I appoints foreigner, Adrian of Utrecht, as regent

1532 Pizarro takes Peru with 180 men and destroys Inca Empire

1554 International Catholic alliance created by marriage of future king Felipe II with Mary Tudor of England

Pizarro

1520	1530	1540	1550

1519 Conquest of Mexico by Cortés. Carlos I crowned Holy Roman Emperor Charles V

1540 Father Bartolomé de las Casas writes book denouncing the oppression of Indians

Ferdinand Magellan

Bartolomé de las Casas

Defeat of the Spanish Armada
Spain's self-esteem suffered a hard blow when its "invincible" 133-ship fleet was destroyed in an attempt to invade Protestant England in 1588.

New World Crops

Not only did Spain profit from the gold and silver brought across the ocean from the Americas, but also from an amazing range of new crops. Some, including potatoes and maize, were introduced for cultivation in Spain, while others, such as tobacco and cacao, were mainly grown in native soil. Cocoa, from cacao beans, gained favour as a drink.

Cacao plant

Peruvian with exotic New World fruit

Armour of Felipe II
Felipe II (1556–98) was a cunning administrator, who claimed to rule the world with paper rather than military might.

Flag of Spain (until 1785)

Storage space for New World treasures

Spanish Galleon
Although sturdily built to carry New World treasure back to Spain, these ships were hard to manoeuvre except with the wind behind. They were often no match for smaller, swifter pirate vessels.

Carlos I (1516–56) During his tumultuous 40-year reign, Carlos I (Holy Roman Emperor Charles V) often led his troops on the battlefield.

1557 First of a series of partial bankruptcies of Spain

1561 Building of El Escorial, near Madrid, begins

El Escorial (see pp334–5)

1588 Spanish Armada fails in attack on England

1560

1570

1580

1590

1561 Madrid becomes capital of Spain

1571 Spanish victory over Turks in naval battle of Lepanto

1580 Portugal unites with Spain for the next 60 years

1568 Moriscos (converted Moors) in the Alpujarras (Granada) rebel against high taxes and persecution

1569 Bible published for first time in Castilian

The Golden Age

Spain's Golden Age was a time of great artistic and literary achievement led by the painters – El Greco and Velázquez *(see pp36–7)* – and writers *(see pp38–9)*, especially Cervantes and the prolific dramatists Lope de Vega and Calderón de la Barca. This brilliance occurred, however, against a background of economic deterioration and ruinous wars with the Low Countries and France. Spain was gradually losing its influence in Europe and the reigning house of Habsburg entered irreversible decline.

The Spanish Empire in Europe in 1647

☐ Spanish territories

Don Quixote and Sancho Panza
Cervantes' satire on chivalrous romance, *Don Quixote*, contrasts the fantasy of the main character with his servant's realism.

A clock is a reminder of the inevitable passage of time.

The knight is dressed in mid-17th-century fashion.

Money represents worldly wealth.

Duke of Lerma
This painting portrays the Duke of Lerma (c.1550–1625), a favourite of King Felipe III.

The Knight's Dream (1650)
This painting, attributed to Antonio de Pereda, is on a familiar Golden Age theme: human vanity. A young gentleman sits asleep beside a table piled with objects symbolizing power, wealth and mortality. The pleasures of life, we are told, are no more real than a dream.

Felipe III	**1609** Felipe III orders the expulsion of the Moriscos	**1621** Low Countries war resumes after 12-year truce		**1643** Fall of Count-Duke Olivares. Spain heavily defeated by France at Battle of Rocroi
1600 Capital temporarily moves to Valladolid	**1619** Construction of Plaza Mayor, Madrid	**1625** Capture of Breda, Netherlands, after one-year siege		
1600	**1610**	**1620**	**1630**	**1640**
1605 Publication of first of two parts of Cervantes' *Don Quixote*	**1609** Lope de Vega publishes poem on the art of comic drama	**1622** Velázquez moves from Seville to Madrid to become court painter the following year	**1640** Secession of Portugal, amalgamated with Spain since 1580	

Lope de Vega (1562–1635)

Fiesta in the Plaza Mayor in Madrid
This famous square *(see p277)* became the scene for pageants, royal celebrations, bullfights and executions, all overlooked from the balconies.

Seville School of Art

Seville's wealth, together with the patronage of the Church, made it a centre of the arts, second only to the royal court. Velázquez, who was born in Seville, trained under the painter Pacheco. Sculptor Juan Martínez Montañés and painters Zurbarán and Murillo created great works which are displayed in the Museo de Bellas Artes *(see p436)*.

San Diego de Alcalá Giving Food to the Poor (c.1646) by Murillo

An angel warns that death is near.

The banner says, "It [death] pierces perpetually, flies quickly and kills".

A mask symbolizes the Arts.

Expulsion of the Moriscos
Although they had converted to Christianity, the last Moors were still expelled in 1609.

Weapons represent power.

The skull on the book shows Death triumphant over Learning.

Surrender of Breda
Spain took the Dutch city of Breda on 5 June 1625 after a year-long siege. The event was later painted by Velázquez.

1652 Spanish troops regain Catalonia, following 12-year war with France

Calderón de la Barca

1669 Calderón de la Barca's last work, *La Estátua de Prometeo*, is published

1683–4 Louis XIV attacks Catalonia and Spanish Netherlands

| 1650 | 1660 | 1670 | 1680 | 1690 | 1700 |

1648 Holland achieves independence from Spain by Treaty of Westphalia, ending the Thirty Years' War

1659 Peace of the Pyrenees signed with France. Louis XIV marries Felipe IV's daughter María Teresa, leading to Bourbon succession in Spain

María Teresa, wife of France's Louis XIV

1700 Death of Carlos II brings Habsburg line to an end. Felipe V, the first Bourbon king, ascends the throne

Bourbons to First Republic

The War of the Spanish Succession ended in triumph for the Bourbons, who made Spain a centralized nation. Their power was at its height during the reign of the enlightened despot Carlos III. But the 19th century was a troubled time. An invasion by revolutionary France led to the War of Independence (Peninsular War). Later came the Carlist Wars – caused by another dispute over the succession – liberal revolts and the short-lived First Republic.

Spain in 1714
☐ Domain after Treaty of Utrecht

The Enlightenment
The Enlightenment brought new learning and novel projects. On 5 July 1784 this Montgolfier balloon rose above Madrid.

A Franciscan friar
is among the innocent victims.

Queen María Luisa
The dominating María Luisa of Parma, portrayed by Goya, forced her husband Carlos IV to appoint her lover, Manuel Godoy, prime minister in 1792.

Spanish rebel faces death in a gesture of crucifixion.

Hundreds of lives were taken in the executions, which lasted several days.

Battle of Trafalgar
The defeat of the Franco-Spanish fleet by the British admiral, Lord Nelson, off Cape Trafalgar in 1805 was the end of Spanish sea power.

1702–14 War of the Spanish Succession. Spain loses Netherlands and Gibraltar by Treaty of Utrecht

1724 Luis I (son of Felipe V) gains throne when his father abdicates, but dies within a year; Felipe V reinstated

1767 Carlos III expels Jesuits from Spain and Spanish colonies

| 1700 | 1720 | 1740 | 1760 | 178 |

1714 Siege and reduction of Barcelona by Felipe V

Felipe V, the first Bourbon king (1700–24)

Count of Floridablanca (1728–1808)

1762–3 British government declares war on Spanish over colonies in America

1782 Count of Floridablanca helps to recover Menorca from Britain

Carlos III Leaving Naples
When Fernando VI died without an heir in 1759, his half-brother Carlos VII of Naples was put on the Spanish throne as Carlos III. His enlightened reign saw the foundation of academies of science and art and the beginning of free trade.

French soldiers, operating on orders from Marshal Murat, execute Spanish patriots.

General Prim (1814–70)
General Prim was one of 19th-century Spain's most influential figures. He forced the abdication of Isabel II, and pursued liberal policies until assassinated in Madrid.

French infantry helmet

The 3rd of May in Madrid by Goya (1814)
On 2 May 1808, in reaction to Napoleon's occupation of Spain, the people of Madrid rose in vain against the occupying French forces. The next day the French army took its revenge by executing hundreds of people, both rebels and bystanders. These events sparked off the War of Independence.

Baroque Magnificence
The sacristy of the Monasterio de la Cartuja in Granada is typical of Spanish Baroque, more sumptuous than anywhere else in Europe.

1805 Battle of Trafalgar. Nelson defeats French and Spanish at sea

1809 Wellington's troops join with Spanish to triumph over French at Talavera

Duke of Wellington

1841–3 María Cristina, followed by General Espartero, acts as regent for Isabel II

1868 Revolution under General Prim forces Isabel II into exile. Amadeo I is king for three years from 1870

1800	1820	1840	1860

1808–14 Joseph Bonaparte on throne. War of Independence
1812 Promulgation of liberal constitution in Cádiz leads to military uprising

1824 Peru is the last South American country to gain independence

1833–9 First Carlist War

1836 Mendizábal seizes monastic property for the Spanish state
1847–9 Second Carlist War

First Carlist War

Republicans and Anarchists

Spain's First Republic lasted only a year (1873) and consumed four presidents. The late 19th century was a time of national decline, with Anarchism developing in reaction to rampant political corruption. The loss of Cuba, in 1898, was a low point for Spain, although there was a flurry of literary and artistic activity in the following years. The country's increasing instability was briefly checked by the dictatorship of Primo de Rivera. Spanish politics, however, were becoming polarized. Alfonso XIII was forced to abdicate and the ill-fated Second Republic was declared in 1931.

The Legacy of Spanish Colonization in 1900

☐ Spanish-speaking territories

Anarchist Propaganda
Anarchism was idealistic, though often violent. This poster states, "Anarchist books are weapons against Fascism".

Workers unite, calling for radical social reform.

Pío Baroja
Baroja (1872–1956) was one of the most gifted novelists of his day. He was too original to be grouped with the writers of the Generation of 1898, who tried to create a national renaissance after the loss of Spain's colonies.

Power to the People

Political protest was rife under the Second Republic, as shown by this Communist demonstration in the Basque Country in 1932. Industrial workers banded together, forming trade unions to demand better pay and working conditions, and staging strikes. The Spanish Communist Party developed later than the Anarchists, but eventually gained more support.

1873 Declaration of First Republic, lasting only one year

First Republic's last president, Emilio Castelar (1832–99)

1888 Universal Exhibition in Barcelona creates new buildings and parks, such as the Parc de la Ciutadella

1897 Prime Minister Cánovas del Castillo assassinated by an Italian Anarchist

1870	1880	1890	1900

1875 Second Bourbon restoration puts Alfonso XII on throne

Alfonso XII and Queen María

1893 Anarchists bomb opera-goers in the Barcelona Liceu

1898 Cuba and Philippines gain independence from Spain following the Spanish-American War

1870–75 Third Carlist War

Tragic Week
Led by Anarchists and Republicans, workers in Barcelona took to the streets in 1909 to resist a military call-up. The reprisals were brutal.

Universal Exhibitions
In 1929, Seville and Barcelona were transformed by exhibitions promoting art and industry. The fairs brought international recognition.

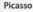

The banner appeals for working-class solidarity.

Picasso
Born in Málaga in 1881, the artist Pablo Picasso spent his formative years as a painter in the city of Barcelona *(see p157)* before moving to Paris in the 1930s.

Cuban War of Independence
Cuba began its fight for freedom in 1895, led by local patriots such as Antonio Maceo. In the disastrous campaign, Spain lost 50,000 soldiers and most of its navy.

The Garrotte
Convicted Anarchists were executed by the garrotte – an iron collar that brutally strangled the victim while crushing the neck.

Second Republic election poster

1912 Prime Minister José Canalejas murdered by Anarchists in Madrid

1921 Crushing defeat of Spanish army at Anual, Morocco

1931 Proclamation of Second Republic with a two-year coalition between Socialists and Republicans

1933 General election returns right-wing government

1910

1920

1930

1909 Semana Trágica (Tragic Week) in Barcelona. Workers' revolt against conscription for Moroccan Wars quashed by Government troops

1923 Primo de Rivera stages victorious coup to become military dictator under Alfonso XIII

1930 Primo de Rivera resigns after losing military support

1931 Republicans win local elections, causing Alfonso XIII to abdicate

1934 Revolution of Asturian miners suppressed by army under General Franco

Civil War and the Franco Era

Nationalist generals rose against the government in 1936, starting the Spanish Civil War. The Nationalists, under General Franco, were halted by the Republicans outside Madrid, but with support from Hitler and Mussolini they inched their way to victory in the north and east. Madrid finally fell in early 1939. After the war, thousands of Republicans were executed in reprisals. Spain was internationally isolated until the 1950s, when the United States brought her into the Western military alliance.

Spain on 31 July 1936
Republican-held areas
Nationalist-held areas

Franco's Ideal World
Under Franco, Church and State were united. This poster shows the strong influence of religion on education.

POR LAS ARMAS

Nationalist Poster
A Nationalist poster adorned with Fascist arrows reads "Fight for the Fatherland, Bread and Justice".

Anguished mother with dead child

Composition reflecting total chaos

Guernica (1937)

On behalf of advancing Nationalists, the Nazi Condor Legion bombed the Basque town of Gernika-Lumo (see pp122–3) on 26 April 1937 – a busy market day. This was Europe's first air raid on civilians, and it inspired Picasso's shocking Guernica *(see p303). Painted for a Republican Government exhibition in Paris, it is full of symbols of disaster.*

1936 Republican Popular Front wins the general election on 16 January. On 17 July, Nationalist generals rise against Republicans

1938 On 8 January, Republicans lose battle for Teruel in bitter cold

1939 In March, Madrid, Valencia and Alicante fall in quick succession to Franco's troops

1945 By end of World War II, Spain is diplomatically and politically isolated

1947 Spain declared monarchy with Franco as regent

| 1935 | 1940 | 1945 | 1950 |

1936 Nationalists declare Franco head of state on 29 September

1937 On 26 April, Nazi planes bomb Basque town of Guernica (Gernika-Lumo)

1939 Franco declares end of war on 1 April and demands unconditional surrender from Republicans

1938 On 23 December, Nationalists bomb Barcelona

1953 Deal with US permits American bases on Spanish soil in exchange for aid

Francisco Franco overseeing an offensive

Portrait of García Lorca taken in 1919

García Lorca

Federico García Lorca (1898–1936) was Spain's most brilliant dramatist and lyric poet of the 1920s and 1930s. His homosexuality and association with the Left, however, made him a target for Nationalist assassins. He was shot by an ad hoc firing squad near his home town of Granada.

Anarchist Poster

Anarchists fought for the Republic, forming agricultural collectives behind the lines. Their influence waned when they were discredited by the Communist Party.

A wounded horse representing the Spanish people

Witnesses to the massacre stare in wonder and disbelief.

Crucifixion gesture

The flower is a symbol of hope in the midst of despair.

The Hungry Years

Ration cards illustrate the post-war period when Spain nearly starved. Shunned by other nations, the country received aid from the US in 1953 in return for accepting military bases.

Spanish Refugees

As the Nationalists came closer to victory, thousands of artists, writers, intellectuals and other Republican supporters fled Spain into indefinite exile.

Sunbathers

1962 Tourism on the Mediterranean coast is boosted by official go-ahead

1969 Franco declares Prince Juan Carlos his successor

1973 ETA assassinates Admiral Carrero Blanco, Franco's hard-line prime minister

| 1955 | 1960 | 1965 | 1970 | 1975 |

1959 Founding of ETA, Basque separatist group

1955 Spain joins United Nations

Juan Carlos, King of Spain

1970 "Burgos trials" of the regime's opponents outrage world opinion

1975 Death of Franco results in third Bourbon restoration as Juan Carlos is proclaimed king

Modern Spain

Franco's death left Spain's political future hanging in the balance. But few people wanted to preserve the old regime and the transition from dictatorship to democracy proved surprisingly swift and painless. The previously outlawed Socialist Workers' Party, under Felipe González, won the general election in 1982 and set about modernizing Spain. Considerable power has since been devolved to the regions. For many years a major threat facing central government was the persistent violence of ETA, the Basque separatist organization. Spain's international relations have been strengthened by its membership of NATO and the European Union.

Spain Today
☐ Spain
▨ Other European Union states

Coup d'Etat, 23 February 1981
Civil Guard colonel, Antonio Tejero, held parliament at gunpoint for several hours. Democracy survived because King Juan Carlos refused to support the rebels.

Castilla y León's modern pavilion was one of EXPO's 150 pavilions built to innovative designs.

Hi-tech floodlight

Anti-NATO Protest Rally
When Spain joined NATO in 1982, some saw it as a reversal of Socialist ideals. To others it represented an improvement in Spain's international standing.

Expo '92
Over 100 countries were represented at the Universal Exposition, which focused world attention on Seville in 1992. The many pavilions displayed scientific, technological and cultural exhibits.

Spanish royal family

1981 Military officers stage attempted coup d'etat to overthrow democracy

1983 Semi-autonomous regional governments are established to appease Basque Country and Catalonia

1992 Barcelona Olympics and Seville Expo '92 place Spain firmly within community of modern European nations

1998 ETA, the Basque separatist terrorist group, announces a ceasefire that lasts a year

1980	1985	1990	1995

1977 First free elections return centrist overnment under Adolfo Suárez. Political parties, including Communists, are legalized

1982 Landslide electoral victory brings Socialist Workers' Party (PSOE), under Felipe González, to power. Football World Cup held in Spain

1986 Spain joins EC (now EU) and NATO

1992 Spain celebrates quincentenary of Columbus's voyage to America

1994/5 Corruption scandals rock the long-serving government

1996 In the gener election on 3 Marc González loses to coalition led by Az

Tourism
Spain ranks as the third most visited country in the world. A record number of visitors (in excess of 75 million) visited the country in 2016.

Felipe González Elected
In 1982 the Spanish Socialist Workers' Party (PSOE) leader was elected prime minister. González transformed Spain during his 13 years in power.

Leaning blue tower rises above Andalucía's pavilion.

Ana Belén
Spanish women enjoyed much greater freedom and opportunity upon the advent of democracy. In a 1980s opinion poll, they voted the singer and actress Ana Belén the woman they most admired.

El País
Founded in Madrid in 1976, the liberal daily *El País* is the best-selling newspaper in Spain. During the transition to democracy it had a great influence on public opinion.

A monorail carried visitors around the site.

Barcelona Olympic Games
The opening ceremony of the Barcelona Olympics included stunning displays of music, dance and colourful costumes.

...obi, Barcelona ...ympic Mascot

2004 José Luis Rodríguez Zapatero of the Spanish Socialist Party comes into power on 14 March

2008 José Luis Rodríguez Zapatero of the Spanish Socialist Party is re-elected on 9 March

2011 Mariano Rajoy of the Popular Party comes into power on 20 November

Mariano Rajoy

2005	2010	2015	2020

...Spain celebrates ...rs of democracy ...ign of Juan Carlos I

2004 Madrid is hit by the worst terrorist attacks in Spain's modern history in March. Bombs detonated on the city's trains killed 191 people

2011 ETA announces a permanent ceasefire

2014 King Juan Carlos I abdicates in favour of his son, Felipe VI

2015 No party wins a majority in the general election

2016 The Popular Party narrowly wins the general election, despite corruption scandals

Rulers of Spain

Spain became a nation-state under Isabel and Fernando, whose marriage eventually united Castile and Aragón. With their daughter Juana's marriage, the kingdom was delivered into Habsburg hands. Carlos I and Felipe II were both capable rulers, but in 1700 Carlos II died without leaving an heir. After the War of the Spanish Succession, Spain came under the French Bourbons, who have ruled ever since – apart from an interregnum, two republics and Franco's dictatorship. The current Bourbon king, Felipe VI, a constitutional monarch, is respected for his social work and his support of democracy.

1665–1700
Carlos II

1479–1516
Fernando, King
of Aragón

1474–1504 Isabel,
Queen of Castile

1516–56 Carlos I of Spain
(Holy Roman Emperor
Charles V)

1598–1621 Felipe III

1400	1475	1550	1625
Independent Kingdoms		Habsburg Dynasty	
1400	1475	1550	1625

1469 Marriage of Isabel
and Fernando leads to
unification of Spain

1504–16 Juana la
Loca (with Fernando
as regent)

1621–65
Felipe IV

Fernando and Isabel, the Catholic Monarchs

Unification of Spain

In the late 15th century the two largest kingdoms in developing Christian Spain – Castile, with its military might, and Aragón (including Barcelona and a Mediterranean empire) – were united. The marriage of Isabel of Castile and Fernando of Aragón in 1469 joined these powerful kingdoms. Together the so-called Catholic Monarchs defeated the Nasrid Kingdom of Granada, the last stronghold of the Moors (see pp60–61). With the addition of Navarra in 1512, Spain was finally unified.

1700–24 Felipe

1556–98 Felipe II

1843–68 Isabel II reigns, following the regency of her mother María Cristina (1833–41) and General Espartero (1841–3)

1724 Luis I reigns after Felipe V's abdication, but dies within a year

1871–3 Break in Bourbon rule: Amadeo I of Savoy

1939–75 General Franco Head of State

1814–33 First Bourbon restoration, following French rule: Fernando VII

1931–9 Second Republic

2014 Felipe VI

1759–88 Carlos III

1875–85 Second Bourbon restoration: Alfonso XII

700	1775	1850	1925	2000
Bourbon Dynasty		Bourbon	Bourbon	
700	1775	1850	1925	2000

1808–13 Break in Bourbon rule: Napoleon's brother, Joseph Bonaparte, rules as José I

1746–59 Fernando VI

1724–46 Felipe V reinstated as king upon the death of his son, Luis I

1902–31 Alfonso XIII

1886–1902 María Cristina of Habsburg-Lorraine as regent for Alfonso XIII

1788–1808 Carlos IV

1873–4 First Republic

1868–70 The Septembrina Revolution

1975–2014 Third Bourbon restoration: Juan Carlos I

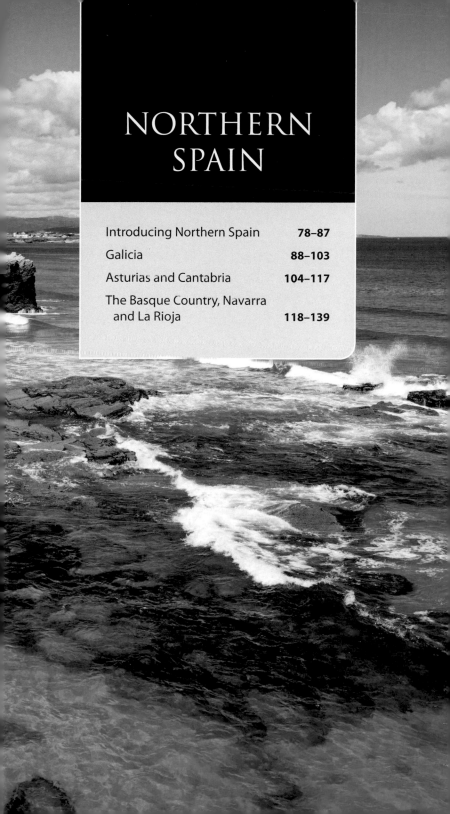

NORTHERN SPAIN

Introducing Northern Spain

Countless visitors are drawn to the magnificent landscapes of Northern Spain. The Atlantic coast, running from the Pyrenees to the Portuguese border, combines sandy beaches of intense blue waters with green mountains and valleys. All along the coast of Galicia, with its dramatic cliffs in the north and smooth beaches in the south, are attractive *rías*, or inlets. The famous medieval pilgrimage route to the city of Santiago de Compostela crosses Northern Spain, its way marked by magnificent examples of Romanesque architecture. Plentiful seafood and dairy produce, and the outstanding red wines of La Rioja, add to the pleasure of a tour through this part of Spain.

Oviedo *(see pp110–11)* has a number of Pre-Romanesque churches, most notably the graceful Santa María del Naranco, and a fine Gothic cathedral.

Ortigueira
Viveiro
Ferrol
Ribadeo
Canero
Avilés
Gijón
A Coruña
La Espina
Betanzos
Vilalba
Oviedo
Santiago de Compostela
Arzúa
Lugo

ASTURIAS AND CANTABRIA
(See pp104–117)

Padrón

GALICIA
(See pp88–103)

Pontevedra
Quiroga
Vigo
Ourense

Santiago de Compostela *(see pp94–5)* attracts thousands of pilgrims and tourists each year. Its majestic cathedral was one of the most important shrines in medieval Christendom.

The Rías Baixas *(see p99)* is one of Spain's prettiest coastlines. Scattered around its pretty towns and villages are many quaint *hórreos*, grain stores, raised on stone stilts.

0 kilometres   50
0 miles   50

The Picos de Europa mountain range *(see pp112–13)* dominates the landscape of Asturias and Cantabria. Rivers have carved deep gorges through the mountains and there are many footpaths through a variety of spectacular scenery.

◄ Dramatic stretch of the Cantabrian coastline

Santillana del Mar *(see p116)*, with its well-preserved medieval streets, is one of the most picturesque towns in Spain. The Convento de Regina Coeli houses a small museum containing a collection of painted wooden figures and other works of religious art.

San Sebastián *(see p126)*, the most elegant holiday resort in the Basque Country, is sited around a beautiful horseshoe bay of golden sandy beaches. The city hosts international arts events, including Spain's premier film festival.

nes

Panes · Santander · Laredo · Torrelavega

Reinosa · Corconte

Bilbao · Eibar · San Sebastián

Llodio · Zumárraga · Andoain

Vitoria (Gasteiz)

THE BASQUE COUNTRY, NAVARRA AND LA RIOJA
(See pp118–39)

Miranda de Ebro · Pamplona

Logroño

Torrecilla en Cameros · Calahorra

Tudela

Pamplona *(see pp136–7)*, the capital of Navarra since the 9th century, is best known for its annual fiesta, Los Sanfermines. The highlight of each day of riotous celebration is the *encierro*, in which bulls stampede through the streets of the city.

The Monasterio de Leyre *(see p139)*, founded in the early 11th century, was built in a lonely but attractive landscape. The monastery was once the burial place of the kings of Navarra and its crypt is among the finest examples of early Romanesque art in Spain.

The Flavours of Northern Spain

The wild, wet north of Spain is as famous for its rain as it is for its culinary excellence. The rain keeps the pastures lush and green – perfect dairy farming terrain – and the Atlantic provides an incredible variety of seafood. The Basques, in particular, are celebrated chefs, and the region boasts some of the finest restaurants in Europe, along with gastronomic societies (called *txokos*) in every village. Inland and in the remoter regions you'll find old-fashioned country cooking – roast lamb and tender young beef, slow-cooked stews – and traditionally made cheeses.

Idiazábal cheese

Pulpo a la gallega, Galicia's signature dish

Galicia

The westernmost tip of Spain, battered by the Atlantic into a series of plunging *rías*, is famous for its wealth of seafood – from staples like dried and salted cod *(bacalao)* to unusual delicacies like barnacles *(percebes)*, which look like tiny dinosaur feet. Every bar will serve up a plate of *pulpo a la gallega* or a dish of *pimientos del Padrón* (one in every dozen has a spicy kick). Inland, you'll find tender veal, pork specialities and delicate soft cheeses such as delicious *tetilla*.

Asturias and Cantabria

The bay-pocked coastline provides delicious fresh fish, often served simply grilled (try the fabulous sardines offered in almost every port) or slowly simmered in casseroles. Inland, the lush green pastures form Spain's dairy country – most Spanish milk, cream and some of its finest cheeses come from this region. Try Asturian Cabrales, a pungent blue cheese, best accompanied by a glass of local cider. The mountains provide succulent meat and game, often traditionally stewed with beans, as in the celebrated Asturian dish of *fabada*.

Clams Red mullet Mackerel Oysters Elvers Baby octopus
Fish and seafood from the waters of Northern Spain

Regional Dishes and Specialities

Unsurprisingly, seafood rules supreme along the coastline, from the ubiquitous octopus in a mildly piquant sauce served in Galicia, to the extraordinary spider crabs, a sought-after delicacy in the Basque Lands. The verdant pastures and rich farmland provide a wealth of fresh vegetables, including Navarra's justly famous asparagus, along with all kinds of wonderful cheeses. Slow-cooked stews, an Asturian speciality, are particularly good in the mountains, along with tender lamb and outstanding game in season. The renowned wines from La Rioja are excellent, but those of adjoining Navarra are less pricey and often equally interesting. The crisp whites of Galicia and the Basque Lands are the perfect accompaniment to the fresh seafood, and throughout the north you'll find powerful liqueurs flavoured with local herbs.

Cherries

Bacalao al Pil Pil Salted cod is slowly cooked with olive oil, chilli and garlic to create this classic Basque dish.

Array of *pintxos* laid out in a bar in the Basque Country

Basque Country

The Basque Country is a paradise for gourmets, renowned throughout Spain for the excellence of its natural produce and the creative brilliance of its chefs. Basque cuisine leans towards seafood, of which there is a dazzling variety: humble salted cod and hake (made extraordinary with delicious sauces) are most common, but sought-after delicacies include elvers (baby eels) and spider crab. Basque wines, drunk young and tart, are the perfect counterpoint. Bar counters groan with platters of *pintxos* (crusty bread with gourmet toppings), each one of them a miniature work of art, and the Basques also make wonderful cheeses, including delicate, smoky Idiazábal.

Navarra and La Rioja

The fertile farmland of landlocked Navarra produces a spectacular array of fruit and vegetables such as asparagus, artichokes, cherries, chestnuts and peppers (often hung in pretty strings to dry and used

Red peppers strung up to dry in the sun outside a house

to flavour *embutidos*, or cured meats). In the Navarrese mountains, lamb is the most popular meat and you will find *cordero al chilindrón* (lamb stew) featuring on almost every menu. In season, you'll also find richly flavoured game, including partridge, hare and pheasant.

Tiny La Rioja is Spain's most famous wine region, producing rich, oaky reds and whites *(see pp82–3)*. The cuisine of La Rioja borrows from the neighbouring Basque Country and Navarra, with lamb featuring heavily, along with seafood and top-quality local vegetables.

On the Menu

Angulas a la Bilbaína Baby eels cooked in olive oil with garlic – a Basque delicacy.

Cocido Montañes Cantabrian stew of pork, spicy sausage, vegetables – and a pig's ear.

Fabada Asturiana Asturian beans stewed with cured meats and pork.

Pimientos del Padrón A *Gallego* dish of green peppers fried in olive oil with rock salt.

Pulpo a la Gallega Octopus, cooked until tender in a mildly spicy paprika sauce.

Trucha a la Navarra Trout, stuffed with ham and quickly grilled or fried.

Empanada Gallega The perfect picnic snack, these golden pastries are stuffed with all kinds of fillings.

Chilindrón de Cordero A rich, hearty stew from the mountains of Navarra, this is made with succulent lamb.

Leche Frita "Fried milk" is a scrumptious, custardy dessert from Cantabria. Simple but utterly delicious.

Wines of Northern Spain

Spain's most renowned wine region, La Rioja, is best known for its red wines, matured to a distinctive vanilla mellowness. Some of the most prestigious bodegas were founded by émigrés from Bordeaux, and Rioja reds are similar to claret. La Rioja also produces good white and rosé wines. Navarra reds and some whites have improved dramatically, thanks to a government research programme. The Basque region produces a tiny amount of the tart *txakoli* (*chacolí*). Larger quantities of a similar wine are made further west in Galicia, whose best wines are full-bodied whites, particularly from the Albariño grape.

Repairing barrels in Haro, La Rioja

Ribeiro, a popular wine of Galicia, is slightly fizzy. It is often served in white porcelain bowls (*cuencos*).

Key

▨	Rías Baixas
▨	Ribeiro
▢	Valdeorras
▨	Txacoli de Guetaria
▢	La Rioja
▢	Navarra

0 kilometres   50

0 miles   50

Lagar de Cervera is from Rías Baixas, a region known for producing Spain's most fashionable white wines.

Wine Regions

The wine regions of Northern Spain are widely dispersed. Cradled between the Pyrenees and the Atlantic are the important regions of Rioja and Navarra. Wines from La Rioja are divided into the DOs (denominations of origin) of Rioja Alavesa, Rioja Alta and Rioja Baja, divided by the Río Ebro. The river also cuts through the wine region of Navarra. To the north are some of the vineyards of the Basque Country: the minuscule Txakoli de Guetaria region. In the far west lie the four wine regions of rugged, wet Galicia: Rías Baixas, Ribeiro, Valdeorras and Ribeira Sacra.

Wine village of El Villar de Álava in Rioja Alta

Gathering the grape harvest in the traditional way in Navarra

Remelluri, one of the single-estate "Château" Riojas, from the vineyards of Rioja Alavesa, is soft and not too oaky.

Chivite, from a family bodega in Navarra, is made entirely from Tempranillo and aged in the barrel, resulting in a style similar to Rioja.

Viña Ardanza is blended, as are most red Riojas. The best, like this reserva, are aged for two or more years in American oak casks.

Key Facts about Wines of Northern Spain

La Rioja and Navarra are influenced by both Mediterranean and Atlantic weather systems. The hillier, northwestern parts receive some Atlantic rain, while the hot Ebro plain has a Mediterranean climate. The Basque region and Galicia are both cool, Atlantic regions with high rainfall. Soils everywhere are stony and poor, except in the Ebro plain.

Grape Varieties

The great red grape of La Rioja and Navarra is Tempranillo. In Rioja it is blended with smaller quantities of Garnacha, Graciano and Mazuelo, while in Navarra Cabernet Sauvignon is permitted and blends well with Tempranillo. Garnacha, also important in Navarra, is used for the excellent *rosados* (rosés). Whites of Navarra and Rioja are made mainly from the Viura grape. Galicia has many local varieties, such as Albariño, Godello, Loureira and Treixadura.

Good Producers

Rías Baixas: Fillaboa, Palacio de Fefiñanes, Terras Gauda, Santiago Ruiz. *Ribeiro:* Viña Costeira. **La Rioja:** Baigorri, Bodegas Riojanas (Canchales, Monte Real), CVNE (Imperial, Viña Real Oro), Marqués de Cáceres, Marqués de Murrieta, Marqués de Riscal, Martínez Bujanda, Remelluri, La Rioja Alta (Barón de Oña). **Navarra:** Bodega de Sarría, Guelbenzu, Julián Chivite (Gran Feudo), Magaña, Ochoa, Príncipe de Viana.

Forests of the North

Much of Spain was once blanketed by a mantle of trees. Today, just ten per cent of the original cover remains, mostly in the mountainous north, where rainfall is high and slopes too steep for cultivation. Large areas of mixed deciduous forest – mainly beech, Pyrenean oak and chestnut, with some ash and lime – dominate the landscape, particularly in Cantabria and the Basque Country. The undergrowth of shrubs and flowering plants provides habitats for many insects, mammals and birds. The forests are also the refuge of Spain's last brown bears *(see p108).*

Forest in Northern Spain in autumn

Regeneration of the forest

Dead materials – leaves, twigs and the excrement and bodies of animals – are broken down by various organisms on the forest floor, especially fungi, bacteria and ants. This process releases nutrients which are absorbed by trees and other plants, enabling them to grow.

Fly agaric mushrooms

Lichens grow slowly and are sensitive to pollution. Their presence in a forest often indicates that it is in good health.

The stag beetle takes its name from the huge antler-like mandibles of the male. Despite their ferocious appearance, these beetles are harmless to humans.

Beech Forest

Beech, the dominant species in the Cantabrian mountains and Pyrenees, grows on well-drained soils. Some trees retain their distinctive copper-red leaves through the winter. Beech mast (nuts) are collected to feed to pigs.

Beech leaf and mast

The thick crown shuts out light, inhibiting undergrowth.

Long, thin orange buds

Male golden orioles, among the most colourful European birds, are hard to spot because they spend much of their time in the thick cover provided by old woodlands. Females and juveniles are a duller yellow-green with a brownish tail.

Beech martens are nocturnal. By day, they sleep in a hollow tree or another animal's abandoned nest. At night they feed on fruit, birds and small mammals.

Millipede on a woodland floor

Distribution of Broad-Leaved Forests

0 kilometres 100

0 miles 100

Above 1,000 mm

Below 1,000 mm

Key

- Oak
- Beech
- Chestnut
- Average annual rainfall

Dense broad-leaved forests tend to grow in areas of Northern Spain that have high precipitation.

Chestnut Forest

Chestnut trees grow on well-drained acidic soils. They have slender yellow flowers and in summer produce their fruit, which is eaten by wild boar, dormice, squirrels and mice. The wood is hard and durable but splits easily.

Leaf and chestnut

Oak Forest

Three main species of oak tree – pedunculate, Pyrenean and the evergreen holm oak – dominate the ancient woodlands of the north. Over 300 species of animal, such as wild boar, squirrels and nuthatches, feed off oaks.

Oak leaf and acorn

Large leaves have sharp, serrated edges.

Few massive, spreading branches

Grey twigs ending in numerous buds

Deep spiral ridges on trunk

The pipistrelle bat is a nocturnal species common in woodlands. It catches and eats small insects in flight. Larger insects are taken to a perch. The bat hibernates in winter in a hollow tree or cave.

The jay, a member of the crow family, is a common but somewhat shy woodland bird with a distinctively raucous cry. It can be identified in flight by its white rump, black tail and above all by its bright-blue wing patch.

Blue tits feed mainly in the tree canopy of broad-leaved woods and rarely come down to the ground. The male and female have similar, distinctive plumage. They may raise the back feathers of the crown if alarmed.

Red squirrels bury large numbers of acorns during autumn to last through winter, since these diurnal creatures do not hibernate. Many of the acorns are left to sprout into seedlings.

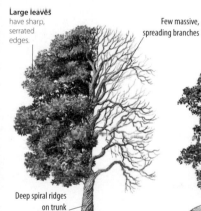

The Road to Santiago

According to legend the body of Christ's apostle James was brought to Galicia. In AD 813 the relics were supposedly discovered at Santiago de Compostela, where a cathedral was built in his honour *(see pp96–7)*. In the Middle Ages half a million pilgrims a year flocked there from all over Europe, crossing the Pyrenees at Roncesvalles *(see p138)* or via the Somport Pass *(see p234)*. They often donned the traditional garb of cape, long staff and curling felt hat adorned with scallop shells, the symbol of the saint. The various routes, marked by the cathedrals, churches and hospitals built along them, are still used by travellers today.

19th-century painting of the Pórtico da Gloria of Santiago Cathedral

Astorga *(see p356)*, once a Roman city, was an important halt on the pilgrim route in the Middle Ages. The museum within its cathedral has a collection of gold and silver plate including a 13th-century gold filigree cross.

A certificate is given to pilgrims covering 100 km (62 miles) of the route on foot, or 200 km (125 miles) on horseback.

O Cebreiro *(see p103)* has a 9th-century church and some of the ancient *pallozas* the pilgrims often used for shelter.

León was one of the main pilgrim stops. Its cathedral *(see pp358–9)* contains one of Spain's finest collections of stained glass.

Ribadeo

A Coruña

Oviedo

Maritime Route

Vilar de Donas

Santiago de Compostela

Ligonde

Villafranca del Bierzo

O Cebreiro

León

Portuguese Route

Porto
Lisboa

Ponferrada's huge Templar castle stands close to the town centre *(see p355)*.

Ponferrada

Astorga

Hospital de Órbigo

Sahagún

Vigo • Tui

Silver Route

Salamanca

0 kilometres   50

0 miles   50

Romanesque Church Architecture

Carved capital

The Romanesque style of architecture *(see p28)* was brought to Spain from France during the 10th and 11th centuries. As the pilgrimage to Santiago became more popular, many glorious religious buildings were constructed along its main routes. Massive walls, few windows, round heavy arches and barrel vaulting are typical features of Romanesque architecture.

Octagonal lantern

Twin round towers

Thick walls

Barrel vault

Round arch

Façade

Cross-section

San Martín de Frómista

(see p372), built in the 11th century, is the only complete example of the "pilgrimage" style of Romanesque. The nave and aisles are almost the same height and there are three parallel apses.

Parallel apses

Aisle

Nave

Floorplan

Pamplona's *(see pp136–7)* Gothic cathedral was one of the pilgrims' first stops after crossing the Pyrenees at Roncesvalles.

Santo Domingo de la Calzada's *(see p132)* pilgrim hospital is now a parador.

Puente la Reina

(see p135) *takes its name from the 11th-century humpbacked bridge (puente), built for pilgrims and still used by pedestrians.*

Santander

San Sebastián (Donostia)

→ Paris

Northern Route

Bilbo (Bilbao)

Orreaga (Roncesvalles)

Valcarlos

→ Le Puy Vézelay

→ Arles

Frómista preserves one of the finest Romanesque churches on the French route.

Iruña (Pamplona)

Lizarra (Estella)

Aragonese Route

San Juan de Ortega

Nájera

Puente la Reina

Sangüesa

Jaca

French Route

San Juan de la Peña

Frómista

Burgos

Santo Domingo de la Calzada

Logroño

Routes to Santiago

Several traditional pilgrimage roads converge on Santiago de Compostela. The main road from the Pyrenees is known as the French Route, with the Aragonese Route as a variation.

Burgos has a magnificent Gothic cathedral *(see pp376–7)*.

GALICIA

Lugo · A Coruña · Pontevedra · Ourense

Remotely located in the northwest corner of the peninsula, Galicia is the country's greenest region. It is also Spain's main seafaring region – three of its four provinces have an Atlantic coastline, and its cuisine is based around superb seafood. The inland villages maintain a slow and relaxed pace of life, with many locals growing their own vegetables and keeping small farmyard animals.

The Galicians, whose origins are Celtic, are fiercely proud of their culture and language. The region's official language, used on most signs, is *Gallego*. It has similarities to the language of Portugal, which borders Galicia to the south. The Celtic character of this haunting land is still evident in the Galicians' favourite traditional instrument, the bagpipes, and much of Galicia still has a medieval quality. The misty, emerald countryside abounds with old granite villages and is dotted with *pazos* – traditional stone manor houses.

The discovery of the supposed tomb of St James the Apostle, in the 9th century, confirmed medieval Santiago de Compostela as Europe's most important religious shrine after St Peter's in Rome. Every year, hundreds of pilgrims and tourists still follow this ancient route of pilgrimage across Northern Spain. The Galician coast is characterized by impressive cliffs, islands and fjord-like rías; the loveliest of these are the Rías Baixas in the west. Elsewhere it juts defiantly into the Atlantic in rocky headlands, such as Cabo Fisterra, Spain's most westerly point. Many people still make a living from the sea, whether in the fishing or ship-building industry and Vigo, in Pontevedra, is the most important fishing port in Spain.

Staple crops – maize, cabbages and potatoes – growing on the harsh land around Cabo Fisterra

◀ Grand spiral staircase in the Convento de San Domingos de Bonaval, Santiago de Compostela

Exploring Galicia

Santiago de Compostela is Galicia's major tourist attraction. This beautiful city is the centrepiece of a region with many fine old towns, especially Betanzos, Mondoñedo, Lugo and Pontevedra. The resorts along the coastline of the wild Rías Altas, with their backdrop of forest-covered hills, offer good bathing. The Rías Baixas, the southern part of Galicia's west coast, has sheltered coves and sandy beaches, and excellent seafood in abundance. Travelling through the interior, where life seems to have changed little in centuries, is an ideal way to spend a peaceful, rural holiday.

Musicians dressed in traditional costumes playing in Pontevedra

Sights at a Glance

1. Rías Altas
2. Mondoñedo
3. Betanzos
4. A Coruña
5. Costa da Morte
6. Santiago de Compostela
    pp94–7
7. Padrón
8. A Toxa
9. Pontevedra
10. Vigo
11. Baiona
12. A Guarda
13. Tui
14. Celanova
15. Verín
16. Ourense
17. Monasterio de Ribas de Sil
18. Monasterio de Oseira
19. Vilar de Donas
20. Lugo
21. O Cebreiro

The isolated monastery at Ribas de Sil

0 kilometres 25

0 miles 15

Getting Around

The region's main airports are at
A Coruña, Santiago de Compostela and
Vigo. A network of motorways connects
Verín, Vigo, A Coruña and O Cebreiro, but
traffic along the coast can be heavy. Rail
lines link Galicia's major cities, and towns
along the north coast are served by the
RENFE line (see p629). Coach services
run between the major cities.

Calvary in Pontevedra's
Praza de la Herrería

Key

━━ Motorway

━━ Major road

━━ Minor road

━━ Scenic route

══ Main railway

--- Minor railway

━━ International border

━━ Regional border

For keys to symbols see back flap

Carved coat of arms on a housefront in Mondoñedo

❶ Rías Altas

Lugo & A Coruña. 🚉 Ribadeo. 🚌 Viveiro. 🛈 Foz, 982 13 24 26. 🕭 Tue.

Deep *rías* are interspersed with coves and headlands along the beautiful north coast from Ribadeo to A Coruña. Inland are hills covered with forests of pine and eucalyptus. Many of the small resorts and fishing villages are charming.

The lovely, winding Ría de Ribadeo forms the border with Asturias. To the west of it is the small fishing port of Foz, which has two good beaches. Nearby, the medieval Iglesia de San Martín de Mondoñedo, standing alone on a hill, contains carvings of biblical scenes on its transept capitals – note the story of Lazarus. Viveiro, a summer holiday resort 37 km (23 miles) away, is a handsome old town surrounded by Renaissance walls and gateways, typically Galician glassed-in balconies or *galerías*, and a Romanesque church. Near the pretty fishing village of O Barqueiro is the headland of Estaca de Bares, with its lighthouse and wind turbines.

Westward along the coast, the lovely Ría de Ortigueira leads to the fishing port of the same name, characterized by neat white houses. Around this area there are also many wild and unspoiled beaches.

High cliffs rise out of the sea near the village of San Andrés de Teixido, whose church is the focal point for pilgrims on 8 September. According to legend, those who fail to visit the church in their lifetime will come back to it as an animal in the afterlife. The village of Cedeira, which sits on a quiet bay, is a rich summer resort with neat lawns, modern houses with *galerías*, and a long, curving beach.

❷ Mondoñedo

Lugo. 🚹 3,800. 🚌 🛈 Praza da Catedral 34, 982 50 71 77. 🕭 Thu. 🕭 As Quendas (1 May), Nuestra Señora de los Remedios (2nd Sun in Sep), San Lucas (18 Oct).

This delightful town is set in a fertile inland valley. Stately houses with carved coats of arms and *galerías* are in the main square. This is dominated by the cathedral, a building of golden stone with a Romanesque portal, a 16th-century stained-glass rose window, 17th-century cloisters and 18th-century Baroque towers. A statue in a chapel in the cathedral, Nuestra Señora la Inglesa, was rescued from St Paul's Cathedral in London. The **Museo Diocesano**, entered through the cathedral, contains works by Zurbarán and El Greco.

🏛 **Museo Diocesano**

Praza da Catedral. **Tel** 982 52 17 79. **Open** 10:30am–1pm & 4:30–6:30pm Tue–Sat, 4:30–8pm Sun. 🖉

❸ Betanzos

A Coruña. 🚹 13,000. 🚌 🚌 🛈 Praza de Galicia 1, 981 77 66 66. 🕭 Tue, Thu & Sat. 🕭 San Roque (14–25 Aug).

The handsome town of Betanzos lies in a fertile valley slightly inland. Its broad main square has a replica of the Fountain of Diana at Versailles. In its steep narrow streets are fine old houses and Gothic churches. The Iglesia de Santiago, built in the 15th century by the tailors' guild, has a statue of St James on horseback above the door. The Iglesia de San Francisco, dated 1387, has statues of wild boars and a heraldic emblem of Earl Fernán Pérez de Andrade, whose 14th-century tomb is inside the church. For centuries his family were the overlords of the region.

Ornate tomb in the Iglesia de San Francisco in Betanzos

Environs
20 km (12 miles) north is the large, though pretty, fishing village of Pontedeume, with its narrow, hilly streets. Its medieval bridge still carries the main road to the large industrial town of Ferrol, to the north. Originally a medieval port, Ferrol became an important naval base and dockyard town in the 18th century, and its Neo-Classical buildings survive from that time. General Franco *(see pp70–71)* was born in Ferrol in 1892.

Pavement cafés in Betanzos' Plaza de García Hermanos

Stone cross standing above the perilous waters of the Costa da Morte

❹ A Coruña

A Coruña. 🔼 244,000. ✈ 🚂 🚌
ℹ Praza de María Pita, 981 92 30 93.
🎉 Fiestas de María Pita (Aug).
🌐 turismocoruna.com

This proud city and busy port has played a sizable role in Spanish maritime history. Felipe II's doomed Armada sailed from here to England in 1588 *(see p63)*. Today, the sprawling industrial suburbs contrast with the elegant town centre, which is laid out on an isthmus leading to a headland. The Torre de Hércules, Europe's oldest working lighthouse, is a famous local landmark. Built by the Romans and rebuilt in the 18th century, it still flashes across the deep. Climb its 242 steps for a wide ocean view.

On the large, arcaded Praza de María Pita, the city's main square, is the handsome town hall. The sea promenade of La Marina is lined with tiers of glass-enclosed balconies or galerías. Built as protection against the strong winds, they explain why A Coruña is often referred to as the City of Glass. The peaceful, tiny Plazuela da las Bárbaras is enchanting.

A Coruña has several fine Romanesque churches, such as the Iglesia de Santiago, with a carving of its saint on horseback

situated beneath the tympanum, and the Iglesia de Santa María. This church, featuring a tympanum carved with the Adoration of the Magi, is one of the best-preserved 12th-century buildings in Galicia.

The quiet Jardín de San Carlos contains the tomb of the Scottish general Sir John Moore, who was killed in 1809 as the British army evacuated the port during Spain's War of Independence from France *(see p67)*.

The lofty Torre de Hércules lighthouse at A Coruña

❺ Costa da Morte

A Coruña. 🚌 A Coruña, Malpica.
ℹ Praza de María Pita, A Coruña, 981 92 30 93. 🎉 Fiesta de la Virgen del Carmen (16 Jul).
🌐 turismo.gal/costa-da-morte

From Malpica to Fisterra the coast is wild and remote. It is called the "Coast of Death" because of the many ships lost in storms or smashed on the rocks by gales over the centuries. The headlands are majestic. There are no coastal towns, only simple villages, where fishermen gather gastronomic percebes (barnacles), destined for the region's restaurants.

One of the most northerly points of the Costa da Morte, Malpica, has a picturesque fishing port. Laxe has good beaches and safe bathing. Camariñas, one of the most appealing places on this coast, is a fishing village where women make bobbin-lace in the streets. Beside the lighthouse on nearby Cabo Vilán, a group of futuristic wind turbines, tall and slender, swirl in graceful unison – a haunting sight.

To the south is Corcubión, exuding a faded elegance, and lastly, Cabo Fisterra "where the land ends". This cape, with its lighthouse, is a good place to watch the sun go down over the Atlantic.

❻ Street-by-Street: Santiago de Compostela

In the Middle Ages Santiago de Compostela was Christendom's third most important place of pilgrimage (see pp86–7), after Jerusalem and Rome. Around the Praza do Obradoiro is an ensemble of historic buildings that has few equals in Europe. The local granite gives a harmonious unity to the mixture of architectural styles. With its narrow streets and old squares, the city centre is compact enough to explore on foot. Two other monuments worth seeing are the Convento de San Domingos de Bonaval, to the east of the centre and the Colegiata Santa Maria la Real del Sar, a 12th-century Romanesque church, located to the east of the city.

★ **Monasterio de San Martiño Pinario**
The Baroque church of this monastery has a huge double altar and an ornate Plateresque façade with carved figures of saints and bishops.

Pazo de Xelmírez

★ **Hostal de los Reyes Católicos**
Built by the Catholic Monarchs as an inn and hospital for sick pilgrims, and now a parador, this magnificent building has an elaborate Plateresque doorway.

Praza do Obradoiro
This majestic square is one of the world's finest and the focal point for pilgrims arriving in the city. The cathedral's Baroque façade dominates the square.

The Pazo de Raxoi, with its Classical façade, was built in 1772 and houses the town hall.

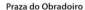

RÚA DE XERU..
RÚA DA TR..
RUELA DO VAL DE DEUS
RÚA DE SAN FRANCISCO
PRAZA DA INMACUL..
PRAZA D OBRADOI..

San Paio de Antealtares
This is one of the oldest monasteries in Santiago. It was founded in the 9th century to house the tomb of St James, now in the cathedral.

VISITORS' CHECKLIST

Practical Information
A Coruña. 🏠 96,000.
ℹ️ Calle Rúa do Vilar 63,
981 55 51 29. 🏠 Wed (cattle),
Thu. 🎭 Semana Santa (Easter
Week), Santiago Day (25 Jul).
🅦 santiagoturismo.com

Transport
✈️ 10 km (6 miles) north.
🚉 Calle Hórreo s/n, 902 32 03
20. 🚌 Praza de Camilo Díaz
Baliño s/n, 981 54 24 16.

Praza da Quintana, under the cathedral clock tower, is one of the city's most elegant squares.

Praza das Praterias
The Silversmiths' Doorway of the cathedral opens onto this charming square with a stone fountain in the centre.

Rúa Nova is a handsome arcaded old street leading from the cathedral to the newer part of the city.

To Tourist Information

Colegio de San Jerónimo

★ Cathedral
This grand towering spectacle has welcomed pilgrims to Santiago for centuries. Though the exterior has been remodelled over the years, the core of the building has remained virtually unchanged since the 11th century.

Key
— Suggested route
— Pilgrims' route

Santiago Cathedral

With its twin Baroque towers soaring high over the Praza do Obradoiro, this monument to St James is a majestic sight, as befits one of the great shrines of Christendom *(see pp86–7)*. The present building dates from the 11th–13th centuries and stands on the site of the 9th-century basilica built by Alfonso II. Through the famous Pórtico da Gloria is the same interior that met pilgrims in medieval times. The choir, designed by Maestro Mateo, has been completely restored.

"Passport" – proof of a pilgrim's journey

★ **West Façade**
The richly sculpted Baroque Obradoiro façade was added in the 18th century.

★ **Pórtico da Gloria**
The sculpted Doorway of Glory, with its statues of apostles and prophets, is 12th century.

KEY

① **Cathedral Museum** items, including a version of Goya's *The Swing*, are on display, as well as the cathedral's cloister, chapterhouse, library, reliquary chapel and crypt.

② **The Santo dos Croques** (Saint of Bumps) has greeted pilgrims since the 12th century. Touching this statue with the forehead is said to impart luck and wisdom.

③ Pazo de Xelmírez

④ **Statue of St James**

⑤ **The twin towers** are the cathedral's highest structures at 74 m (243 ft).

⑥ **The *botafumeiro***, a giant censer, is swung high above the altar by eight men during important services.

⑦ **Mondragón Chapel** (1521) contains fine wrought-iron grilles and vaulting.

⑧ **Clock Tower**

⑨ **Cloisters**

⑩ **Chapterhouse**

VISITORS' CHECKLIST

Practical Information
Praza do Obradoiro.
Tel 981 58 35 48.
Open 7am–8:30pm daily.
🕇 7:30am, 8:30am, 9am, 10am, 11am, noon, 1pm, 6pm, 7:30pm.
📷 rooftops and Pazo de Xelmírez (tickets and bookings in museum, 981 56 93 27/96 75 13).
♿ Museum: **Open** 9am–8pm daily (Nov–Mar: from 10am).
Closed 1 & 6 Jan, 25 Jul, 25 Dec.
🖥 w **catedraldesantiago.es**

High Altar
Visitors can pass behind the ornate high altar to embrace the silver mantle of the 13th-century statue of St James.

★ **Porta das Praterias**
The 12th-century Silversmiths' Doorway is rich in bas-relief sculptures of biblical scenes.

Crypt
The relics of St James and two disciples are said to lie in a tomb in the crypt, under the altar, in the original 9th-century foundations.

❼ Padrón

A Coruña. 🔼 8,500. 🚉 🚌 **ⓘ**
Avenida Compostela, 646 59 33 19.
🕖 Sun. 🎉 Santiago (24–25 Jul).

This quiet town on the Río Ulla, known for its piquant green peppers, was a major seaport until it silted up. Legend has it the boat carrying the body of St James to Galicia *(see p86)* arrived here. The supposed mooring stone, or *padrón*, lies below the altar of the church by the bridge.

The leafy avenue beside the church features in the poems of one of Galicia's greatest writers, Rosalia de Castro (1837–85). Her home, where she spent her final years, has been converted into a **museum**.

Environs

The estuary town of Noia (Noya) lies on the coast 20 km (12 miles) west. Its Gothic church has a finely carved portal. East of Padron is Pazo de Oca, a manor house, with a crenellated tower, idyllic gardens and a lake.

🏛 **Museo Rosalia de Castro**
A Matanza. **Tel** 981 81 12 04.
Open Tue–Sun. 🗓 🔾

The picturesque gardens and lake of Pazo de Oca

❽ A Toxa

Near O Grove, Pontevedra. 🚌 **ⓘ** Praza do Corgo, O Grove, 986 73 14 15. 🕖 Fri.

A tiny pine-covered island joined to the mainland by a bridge, A Toxa (La Toja) is one of the most stylish resorts in Galicia. The *belle époque* palace-hotel *(see p562)* and luxury villas add to the island's elegant atmosphere. A Toxa's best-known landmark is the small church covered with scallop shells. Across the bridge is O Grove (El Grove), a thriving family resort and fishing port on a peninsula, with holiday hotels and flats alongside glorious beaches.

❾ Pontevedra

Pontevedra. 🔼 82,500. 🚉 🚌
ⓘ Casa da Luz, Praza da Verdura s/n, 986 09 08 90. 🕖 1st, 8th, 15th & 23rd of each month. 🎉 Fiestas de la Peregrina (2nd week in Aug).
🌐 visit-pontevedra.com

Pontevedra lies inland, at the head of a long *ría* backed by green hills. The delightful old town is typically Galician and has a network of cobbled alleys and tiny squares with granite calvaries, flower-filled balconies and excellent tapas bars. On the south side of the Old Town are the Gothic Ruinas de San Domingos, now part of the **Museo de Pontevedra**, with Roman steles and Galician coats of arms and tombs. To the west, the 16th-century Iglesia de Santa María la Mayor contains a magnificent Plateresque *(see p29)* façade.

On the Praza de la Leña, two 18th-century mansions, along with two other buildings in the adjacent streets, form the Museo de Pontevedra, one of the best museums in Galicia. The Bronze Age treasures are superb. Among the paintings are 15th-century Spanish primitives, canvases by Zurbarán and Goya, and on the top floor a collection by Alfonso Castelao, a Galician artist and Nationalist who forcefully depicted the misery endured by his people during the Spanish Civil War.

🏛 **Museo de Pontevedra**
Calle Pasanteria 2–12. **Tel** 986 80 41 00. **Open** 10am–9pm Tue–Sat, 11am–2pm Sun. Ruinas de San Domingos summer: 10am–2pm Tue–Sat; call the museum for winter hours. 🌐 museo.depo.es

Scallop-covered roof of the church on A Toxa island

Rías Baixas

This southern part of Galicia's west coast consists of four large *rías* or inlets between pine-covered hills. The beaches are good, the scenery is lovely, the bathing safe and the climate much milder than on the wilder coast to the north. Though areas such as Vilagarcía de Arousa and Panxón have become popular holiday resorts, much of the Rías Baixas (Rías Bajas) coastline is unspoiled, such as the quiet stretch from Muros to Noia. This part of the coastline provides some of Spain's most fertile fishing grounds. Mussel-breeding platforms are positioned in neat rows along the *rías*, looking like half-submerged submarines. Clams are harvested in late summer.

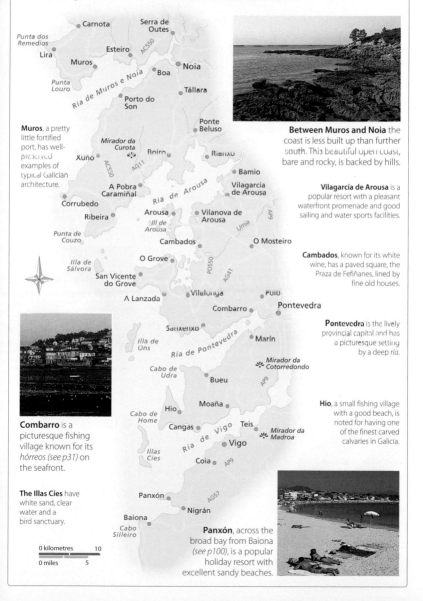

Muros, a pretty little fortified port, has well-preserved examples of typical Galician architecture.

Between Muros and Noia the coast is less built up than further south. This beautiful open coast, bare and rocky, is backed by hills.

Vilagarcía de Arousa is a popular resort with a pleasant waterfront promenade and good sailing and water sports facilities.

Cambados, known for its white wine, has a paved square, the Praza de Fefiñanes, lined by fine old houses.

Pontevedra is the lively provincial capital and has a picturesque setting by a deep *ría*.

Hio, a small fishing village with a good beach, is noted for having one of the finest carved calvaries in Galicia.

Combarro is a picturesque fishing village known for its *hórreos* (see p31) on the seafront.

The Illas Cíes have white sand, clear water and a bird sanctuary.

Panxón, across the broad bay from Baiona (see p100), is a popular holiday resort with excellent sandy beaches.

0 kilometres 10
0 miles 5

Cannons on the battlements of Monterreal fortress, Baiona

⑩ Vigo

Pontevedra. 🏔 293,000. ✈ 🚆 🚌 *i* Cánovas del Castillo 3, 986 22 47 57. 🛳 Wed, Sun. 🎭 Cristo de los Afligidos (3rd weekend in Jul), Cristo de la Victoria (1st week in Aug). **W** turismodevigo.org

Galicia's largest town is also the biggest fishing port in Spain. It is situated in an attractive setting near the mouth of a deep *ría* spanned by a high suspension bridge, and is surrounded by wooded hills. Vigo is not noted for its old buildings but does have striking modern sculptures such as Juan José Oliveira's horses statue in the Praza de España. The oldest part of the town, Barrio del Berbes, is near the port and used to be the sailors' quarter. Its cobbled alleys are full of bars and cafés where you can find some of the finest tapas. The Mercado de la Piedra, better known by its Galician name Mercado de A Pedra, is located near the port and sells reasonably priced fish and shellfish.

Bronze sculpture by Oliveira in Vigo's Praza de España

⑪ Baiona

Pontevedra. 🏔 12,100. 🚌 *i* Paseo Ribeira, 986 68 70 67. 🛳 Mon in Sabaris (nearby). 🎭 Santa Liberata (20 Jul), Virgen de la Anunciada (2nd Sun in Aug). **W** turismodebaiona.com

The *Pinta*, one of the caravels from the fleet of Christopher Columbus, arrived at this small port on 1 March 1493, bringing the first news of the discovery of the New World. Today Baiona (Bayona), which is sited on a broad bay, is a popular summer resort, its harbour a mix of pleasure and fishing boats. The 12th- to 17th-century Iglesia Antigua Colegiata de Santa María is Romanesque with Cistercian influences. Symbols on the arches indicate the local guilds that helped build the church.

A royal fortress once stood on Monterreal promontory, to the north of town. Sections of its defensive walls remain, but the interior has been converted into a smart parador *(see p562)*. A walk around the battlements offers superb views of the coast.

On the coast a short distance to the south is a huge granite and porcelain statue of the Virgen de la Roca sculpted by Antonio Palacios in 1930. Visitors can climb up inside the statue.

⑫ A Guarda

Pontevedra. 🏔 10,100. 🚌 *i* Praza do Reloxo 1, 986 61 45 46. 🛳 Sat. 🎭 Virgen del Carmen (16 Jul), Monte de Santa Tecla (2nd week Aug). **W** aguarda.es

The little fishing port of A Guarda (La Guardia) is famous for seafood and is particularly well-known for its lobsters.

On the slopes of Monte de Santa Tecla are the remains of a Celtic settlement of some 100 round stone dwellings dated around 600–200 BC. The **Museo de Monte de Santa Tecla** sits on a nearby hilltop.

Environs

About 10 km (6 miles) north, the tiny Baroque Monasterio de Santa María stands by the beach at Oia. Semi-wild horses roam the surrounding hills and, in May and June, are rounded up for branding in a series of day-long fiestas *(see p102)*.

🏛 Museo de Monte de Santa Tecla

A Guarda. **Tel** 690 017 038. **Open** Tue–Sun. **Closed** Jan. 🎟 📷 on request.

Circular foundations of Celtic dwellings at A Guarda

⑬ Tui

Pontevedra. 🏔 17,000. 🚆 🚌 *i* Praza de San Fernando, 677 418 405. 🛳 Thu. 🎭 San Telmo (first weekend after Easter).

Spain's main frontier town with Portugal, Tui (Tuy) stands on a hillside above the Río Miño. Its graceful old streets curve up to an old quarter and the 12th-century hilltop cathedral. The two countries were often at war during the Middle Ages, and as a result the church is

Unloading the catch in Spain's largest fishing port, Vigo

Fishing in Spain

The Spanish eat more seafood per head than any other European nation except Portugal. The country has Europe's largest fishing fleet in terms of catch. However, with the fishing industry in crisis, there are only about 9,500 boats that land Spain's catch of fish and shellfish. Much of this is caught offshore, where octopus, mackerel, clams and lobster are plentiful. The stocks in the seas around Spain have become depleted by overfishing and an oil spill in 2002, forcing deep-sea trawlers to travel as far as Canada and Iceland.

Gothic choir stalls. In the garden is the 10th-century Mozarabic Iglesia de San Miguel.

Environs
At Santa Comba de Bande, 26 km (16 miles) to the south, is an even older little church. The features of this 7th-century Visigothic *(see pp54–5)* church include a lantern turret and a horseshoe arch that has carved marble pillars.

⓯ Verín

Ourense. 🅜 14,000. 🚌 🛈 Rúa Irmáns La Salle s/n, 988 41 16 14. 🛍 3rd, 11th & 23rd of month. 🎭 Carnival (Feb), Santa María (15 Aug).

Though it stands amid vineyards, Verín produces more than wine. Its mineral springs have given it a thriving bottled water industry. The town has many old houses with arcades and glass balconies (galerías). The Castelo de Monterrei, built during the wars with Portugal, is 3 km (2 miles) to the west. Inside its three rings of walls are two keeps, an arcaded courtyard and a 13th-century church with a carved portal. The castle once housed a monastery and hospital. Now a *parador*, it can still be visited with a guided tour.

built in the style of a fortress, with towers and battlements. It has a cloister and choir stalls and a richly decorated west porch.

Nearby is the Iglesia de San Telmo, dedicated to the patron saint of fishermen, whose Baroque ornamentation shows a Portuguese influence. Near the cathedral is an iron bridge, the Puente Internacional, built by Gustave Eiffel in 1884 to stretch across the river to Valença do Minho in Portugal.

The Romanesque Iglesia de Santo Domingo, beside the Parque de la Alameda, has ivy-covered cloisters and tombs with carved effigies. The church overlooks the river, which is used in August for the Descent of the Río Miño, a festive canoe race.

⓮ Celanova

Ourense. 🅜 5,500. 🚌 🛈 Praza Maior 1, 988 43 22 01. 🛍 Thu. 🎭 San Roque (15 Aug).

On the main square of this little town is the massive Monasterio de San Salvador, also known as the Monasterio de San Rosendo, after its founder. Founded during the 10th century and later rebuilt, it is mainly Baroque, though one of its two lovely cloisters is Renaissance. The enormous church of this Benedictine monastery has an ornate altarpiece and

Ceramic tiled floor of the Iglesia de San Miguel

The Castelo de Monterrei, standing high above the town of Verín

The outrageous costumes of
Os Peliqueiros in Laza

Galicia's Fiestas

Os Peliqueiros *(Carnival, Feb/Mar)*, Laza (Ourense). Dressed up in grinning masks and outlandish costumes, with cowbells tied to their belts and brandishing sticks, Os Peliqueiros take to the streets on Carnival Sunday. They are licensed to lash out at onlookers, who are forbidden to retaliate. On Carnival Monday morning, a battle takes place, with flour, water and live ants used as ammunition. Laza's carnival comes to an end on the Tuesday with a reading of the satirical "Donkey's Will" and the burning of an effigy.
Flower pavements *(Corpus Christi, May/Jun)*, Ponteareas (Pontevedra). The streets of the town along which the Corpus Christi procession passes are carpeted with intricate designs made from brightly coloured flower petals.
A Rapa das Bestas *(Jun–Aug)*, Oia (Pontevedra). Semi-wild horses are rounded up by local farmers for their manes and tails to be cut. What was once a chore is now a popular fiesta.
St James's Day *(25 Jul)*, Santiago de Compostela. On the night before, there is a firework display in the Praza do Obradoiro. The celebrations are especially wild in a holy year (when 25 July falls on a Sunday).

⑯ Ourense

Ourense. 🖽 106,000. 🚇 🚌
ℹ Isabel la Católica 2, 988 36 60 64.
🗓 7th, 17th & 26th of each month.
🎉 Os Maios (1–3 May), Fiestas de Ourense (end Jun).

The old quarter of Ourense was built around the city's well-known thermal springs, Fonte das Burgas. Even today, these spout water at a temperature of 65°C (150°F) from three fountains.

This old part of the town is the most interesting, particularly the small area around the arcaded Plaza Mayor. Here the cathedral, founded in 572 and rebuilt in the 12th–13th centuries, has a vast gilded reredos by Cornelis de Holanda. On the triple-arched doorway are carved figures reminiscent of the Pórtico da Gloria at Santiago *(see p96)*. Nearby is the elegant 14th-century cloister, the Claustro de San Francisco.

Another landmark is the 13th-century Puente Romano, a seven-arched bridge which crosses the Río Miño, north of the town. Built on Roman foundations, it is now pedestrianized.

Environs
The towns of Allariz, 25 km (16 miles) south, and Ribadavia, to the west, have old Jewish quarters with narrow streets and Romanesque churches. Ribadavia is also noted for its Ribeiro wines – a dry white and a port-like red *(see pp82–3)* – and has a wine museum.

Ornate Gothic reredos in the cathedral at Ourense

⑰ Monasterio de Ribas de Sil

Ribas de Sil, Ourense. **Tel** 988 01 01 10.
Open daily.

Near its confluence with the Miño, 28 km (17 miles) from Ourense, the Río Sil carves a deep curving gorge in which dams form two reservoirs of dark-green water. A hairpin road winds to the top of the gorge, where the Romanesque Gothic Monasterio de Ribas de Sil is situated high on a crag above the chasm. Restored and converted into a charming parador, it has an enormous glass wall in one of the three cloisters, and fine views.

The Río Sil winding its way through the gorge

The grandiose Monasterio de Oseira surrounded by the forests of the Valle de Arenteiro

⑱ Monasterio de Oseira

Oseira, Ourense. **Tel** 988 28 20 04. **Open** daily. 🅿 🚻 compulsory. Tours start at 10am, 11am, noon, 3:30pm, 4:30pm & 5:30pm Mon–Sat; 12:45pm, 3:30pm, 4:30pm & 5:30pm Sun. W **mosteirodeoseira.org**

This monastery stands in a wooded valley near the hamlet of Oseira, named after the bears (*osos*) that once lived in this area. It is a grey building with a Baroque façade. On the doorway is a statue of the Virgin as nurse, with St Bernard kneeling at her feet. The interior of the 12th- to 13th-century church is typically Cistercian in its simplicity.

Fresco of a *dona* in the monastery at Vilar de Donas

⑲ Vilar de Donas

Lugo. 🏠 80. 🚹 Palas de Rei, Avenida de Compostela 47, 982 38 07 40. Church: **Open** noon–6:30pm daily. 🚻 🎉 San Antonio (13 Jun), San Salvador (6 Aug).

This hamlet on the Road to Santiago (*see pp86–7*) has a small church, San Salvador, just off the main road. Inside are tombs of some of the Knights of the Order of Santiago. Also

inside are frescoes painted by the nuns who lived here until the 15th century.

The Cistercian Monastery Sobrado de los Monjes, to the northwest, has a medieval kitchen and chapterhouse, and a church with unusual domes.

⑳ Lugo

Lugo. 🏠 98,000. ✈ 🚌 🚹 Praza do Campo 11, 982 25 16 58. 🚍 Tue & Fri. 🎉 San Froilán (4–12 Oct). W **lugo.gal**

Capital of Galicia's largest province, Lugo was also an important centre under the Romans. Attracted to the town by its thermal springs, they built what is now the finest surviving Roman wall in Spain. The wall, which encircles the city, is about 6 m (20 ft) thick and 10 m (33 ft) high, with ten gateways. Six of these give access to the top of the wall, from where there is a good view of the city.

Inside the wall, the Old Town is lively, with pretty squares. In the Praza de Santo Domingo is a black statue of a Roman eagle, built to commemorate Augustus's capture of Lugo from the Celts in the 1st century BC. The large, Romanesque cathedral is modelled on that of Santiago. It features an elegant Baroque cloister, and a chapel containing the alabaster statue of Nuestra Señora de los Ojos Grandes (Virgin of the Big Eyes). The **Museo Provincial** exhibits local Celtic and Roman finds, while the **Museo Interactivo da Historia**

Painted gourd in O Cebreiro's museum

de Lugo presents the city's history with high-tech exhibits in a striking modern building.

Environs
The stone hamlet of Santa Eulalia, to the west, conceals a curious building: a tiny temple, with lively, bright frescoes of birds and leaves. Though its exact purpose is unknown, it is thought to be an early Christian church and has been dated at around the 3rd century AD.

🏛 **Museo Provincial**
Praza da Soidade. **Tel** 982 24 21 12. **Open** Jul & Aug: Mon–Sat (am only Sat); Sep–Jun: daily (am only Sun). 🅰 W **museolugo.org**

🏛 **Museo Interactivo da Historia de Lugo**
Parque da Milagrosa. **Tel** 982 25 16 58. **Open** 11am–1:30pm & 5–7:30pm Tue Sat, 5–8pm Sun. W **lugo.es/ws/mihl**

㉑ O Cebreiro

Lugo. 🏠 1,100. 🚌 🚹 982 36 70 25. 🎉 Santa María Real (8 Sep), Santo Milagro (9 Sep).

In the hills in the east of Galicia, close to the border with León, is one of the most unusual villages on the Road to Santiago. Its 9th-century church was supposedly the scene of a miracle in 1300 when the wine was turned into blood and the bread into flesh. Nearby, there are several *pallozas*, round thatched stone huts of a Celtic design. Some have been restored, and are now part of a **folk museum**.

🏛 **Museo Etnográfico**
O Cebreiro. **Tel** 982 36 70 53. **Open** Tue–Sun.

ASTURIAS AND CANTABRIA

Asturias · Cantabria

One of the principal attractions of Asturias and Cantabria
is the spectacular Picos de Europa massif, which sits astride
the border between these two regions. Cottage crafts are still kept alive
in ancient villages located in remote mountain valleys and along the sheer
coastline. Cave paintings, such as those at Altamira, were made by people
living here about 35,000 years ago.

Asturias is proud that it resisted invasion by the Moors. The Reconquest of Spain is said to have begun in 718, when a Moorish force was defeated at Covadonga, in the Picos de Europa. The Christian kingdom of Asturias was founded in the 8th century, and in the brilliant, brief artistic period that followed, many churches were built around the capital, Oviedo. Many of these churches built in the Asturian pre-Romanesque style still stand. Today, Asturias is a province and a principality under the patronage of the heir to the Spanish throne. The unspoiled Asturian countryside is a natural paradise where cider and cheese are produced and a quaint language, known as *Bable* or *Asturiano*, is spoken.

Cantabria is a region of stunning nature, excellent gastronomy, well-preserved villages and towns – including Santillana del Mar and Carmona – and unique artistic sites, such as the Altamira Caves. It also has a rich legacy of Romanesque churches. Its capital, Santander, is an elegant resort.

Mountains cover more than half of both provinces, so mountain sports are a major attraction. Expanses of deciduous forests remain in many parts, some sheltering Spain's last wild bears. Along the coasts are pretty fishing ports and resorts, such as Castro Urdiales, Ribadesella and Comillas, and sandy coves for bathing. Both the coastal plains and uplands are ideal for quiet rural holidays.

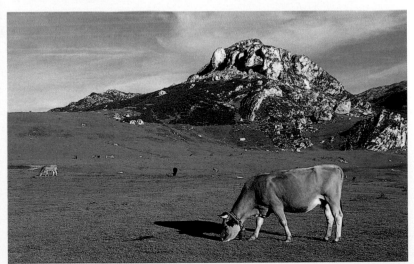

Peaceful meadow around Lago de la Ercina in the Picos de Europa massif

◀ The scenic Costa Verde, Asturias, with lush meadows reaching down to the shoreline

Exploring Asturias and Cantabria

These two provinces are straddled by the impressive Picos de Europa mountain range, which, along with several other nature reserves in the area, is home to such wildlife as golden eagles and brown bears. These jagged peaks offer excellent rock-climbing and hiking opportunities, and some parts can also be explored by car or bicycle. In addition, Asturias and Cantabria offer innumerable unspoiled villages, especially the ancient seaside town of Santillana del Mar. On the coast, there are many sandy coves for bathing, while Santander and Oviedo are busy university cities with a rich cultural life. Some of the earliest examples of art exist in Cantabria, most notably at Altamira, where the cave drawings and engravings are among the oldest to be found in Europe.

Typical flower-covered balcony in the village of Bárcena Mayor

A view along the crowded beach of Playa del Camello, Santander

Sights at a Glance

1. Taramundi
2. Castro de Coaña
3. Costa Verde
4. Teverga
5. Avilés
6. Gijón
7. Oviedo
8. Valdediós
9. Ribadesella
10. Cangas de Onís
11. *Parque Nacional de los Picos de Europa pp112–13*
12. Potes
13. Comillas
14. Valle de Cabuérniga
15. Alto Campoo
16. Cuevas de Altamira
17. Santillana del Mar
18. Puente Viesgo
19. Santander
20. Laredo
21. Castro Urdiales

Cantabrian dairy farmers loading hay onto their cart

Getting Around

The main road through the region is the A8. Most other major roads follow the directions of the valleys and run north to south. Minor roads are generally good but can be slow and winding. The private RENFE railway, which follows the coast from Bilbao to Ferrol in Galicia, is both useful and scenic. Brittany Ferries services (one to three times a week) link Santander with Plymouth and Portsmouth. Asturias has a small international airport near Avilés.

Key

━━ Motorway
= = Motorway under construction
━━ Secondary road
══ Minor road
━━ Scenic route
━━ Main railway
── Minor railway
━━ Regional border
△ Summit

Carved figure in the Convento de Regina Coeli, Santillana del Mar

For keys to symbols *see back flap*

Craftsman making knife blades in a forge at Taramundi

❶ Taramundi

Asturias. 🏛 670. 🚹 Calle Solleiro 14, 985 64 68 77. 🎉 San José (19 Mar).
🌐 **taramundi.es**

Situated in the remote Los Oscos region, this small village houses a rural tourism centre which organizes forest tours in four-wheel drive vehicles and has several hotels and holiday cottages to rent. Taramundi has a tradition of wrought-iron craftsmanship. Iron ore was first mined in the area by the Romans. There are approximately 13 forges in and around the village, where craftsmen can still be seen making traditional knives with decorated wooden handles.

Environs
About 20 km (12 miles) to the east, at San Martín de Oscos, there is an 18th-century palace. At Grandas de Salime, 10 km (6 miles) further southeast, the **Museo Etnográfico** has displays showing local crafts, traditional life and farming.

🏛 **Museo Etnográfico**
Esquios. **Tel** 985 62 72 43.
Open daily. 🌲 ♿

❷ Castro de Coaña

Asturias. 🚌 5 km (3 miles) from Navia.
Tel 985 97 84 01. **Open** Wed–Sun.

One of the best-preserved prehistoric sites of the Cantabrian area, Castro de Coaña was later occupied by the Romans. Set on a hillside in the Navia Valley are the remains of its fortifications and the stone foundations of

oval and rectangular dwellings, some of which stand head high. Inside can be found hollowed-out stones which are thought to have been used for crushing corn.

The museum on the site displays many of the finds that have been unearthed at Castro de Coaña. Among the interesting remains on display are pottery, tools and Roman coins.

Circular stone foundations of dwellings at Castro de Coaña

The Brown Bear

The population of Spain's brown bears *(Ursus arctos)* has dwindled from about 1,000 at the beginning of the 20th century to about 250 today. Hunting by man and the destruction of the bear's natural forest habitat have caused the decline. But now, protected by nature reserves such as Somiedo, where most of the bears in Asturias are found, together with new conservation laws, this magnificent omnivore is increasing in numbers again.

One of the remaining bears in the forests of Asturias

❸ Costa Verde

Asturias. ✈ 🚌 Avilés. 🚌 Oviedo, Gijón. 🚹 Avilés, Calle Ruiz Gomez 21, 985 54 43 25.

The aptly named "green coast" is a succession of attractive sandy coves and dramatic cliffs, punctuated by deep estuaries and numerous fishing villages. Inland, there are lush meadows, and pine and eucalyptus forests, backed by mountains. This stretch of coastline has been less spoiled than most in Spain; the resorts tend to be modest in size, like the hotels.

Two pretty fishing ports, Castropol and Figueras, stand by the eastern shore of the Ría de Ribadeo, forming the border with Galicia. To the east are other picturesque villages such as Tapia de Casariego and Ortiguera, in a small rocky cove. Following the coast, Luarca lies beside a church and a quiet cemetery on a headland, and has a neat little harbour packed with red, blue and white boats. The village of Cudillero is even more delightful – outdoor cafés and excellent seafood restaurants crowd the tiny plaza beside the port, all of which are squeezed into a narrow cove. Behind, white cottages are scattered over the steep hillsides.

Further along the coast is the rocky headland of Cabo de Peñas where, in the fishing village of Candás, bullfights are held on the sand at low tide on 14 September. East of Gijón, Lastres is impressively located below a cliff, and Isla has a broad open beach. Beyond Ribadesella is the

For hotels and restaurants in this region see pp562–3 and pp583–4

Church and cemetery overlooking the sea from the headland at Luarca

lively town of Llanes. Among the attractions of this old fortified seaport, with its dramatic mountain backdrop, are ruined ramparts and good beaches.

❹ Teverga

Asturias. 🚹 1,700. 🚌 La Plaza. 🛈 Dr García Miranda s/n, San Martin de Teverga, 985 76 42 93. **Open** 15 Jun–15 Sep: Tue–Sun; rest of year: Sat & Sun only. 🔳 tevergaturismo.com

This area is rich in scenery, wildlife and ancient churches. Near the southern end of the Teverga gorge is La Plaza. Its church, Iglesia de San Pedro de Teverga, is a fine example of Romanesque architecture. West of La Plaza is Villanueva, with its Romanesque Iglesia de Santa María. The 20-km (12-mile) Senda del Oso path skirts the edge of a bear enclosure.

The pretty 12th-century Iglesia de San Pedro at La Plaza

Environs
The large Parque Natural de Somiedo straddles the mountains bordering León. Its high meadows and forests are a sanctuary for wolves, brown bears and capercaillies, as well as a number of rare species of wild flowers.

The park has 4 glacial lakes, and is peppered with herdsmen's traditional thatched huts, known as *teitos (see p31)*.

❺ Avilés

Asturias. 🚹 80,100. 🛪 🚆 🚌 🛈 Calle Ruiz Gómez 21, 985 54 43 25. 🕐 Mon. 🎪 San Agustín (last week Aug).

Avilés became the capital of Asturias' steel industry in the 1800s and is still ringed by big factories. Even though it is sometimes criticized for having little to offer the visitor, the town hides a medieval heart of some character, especially around the Plaza de España. The Iglesia de San Nicolás Bari is decorated with frescoes and has a Renaissance cloister. The Iglesia de Padres Franciscanos contains a fine 14th-century chapel and holds the tomb of the first Governor of the US state of Florida. All around are arcaded streets. The international airport outside Avilés serves all Asturias.

❻ Gijón

Asturias. 🚹 273,000. 🚆 🚌 🛈 Puerto Deportivo, Espigón Central de Fomento, 985 34 17 71. 🕐 Sun. 🎪 Semana Negra (mid-Jul), La Virgen de Begoña (15 Aug). 🔳 gijon.info

The province's largest city, this industrial port has been much rebuilt since the Civil War when it was bombarded by the Nationalist navy. The city's most famous son is Gaspar Melchor de Jovellanos, an eminent 18th-century author, reformer and diplomat.

Gijón's Old Town is on a small isthmus and headland. It centres on the arcaded Plaza Mayor and the 18th-century **Palacio de Revillagigedo**, a Neo-Renaissance folly now housing a cultural centre. The beach is popular in summer.

🏛 **Palacio de Revillagigedo/ Centro Cultural Cajastur**
Plaza del Marqués 2. **Tel** 985 34 69 21. **Open** Tue–Sun for temporary exhibitions. ♿

7 Oviedo

Asturias. 220,000. Plaza de la Constitución 4, 984 49 35 63. Thu, Sat & Sun. San Mateo (14–21 Sep). turismoviedo.es

Oviedo, a university city and the cultural and commercial capital of Asturias, stands on a raised site on a fertile plain. The nearby coal mines have made it an important industrial centre since the 19th century. It retains some of the atmosphere of that time, as described by Leopoldo Alas ("Clarín") in his great novel *La Regenta (see p39)*.

In and around Oviedo are many Pre-Romanesque buildings. This style flourished in the 8th–10th centuries and was confined to a small area of the kingdom of Asturias, one of the few enclaves of Spain not invaded by the Moors.

The nucleus of the medieval city is the stately Plaza Alfonso II, bordered by a number of handsome old palaces. On this square is situated the Flamboyant Gothic cathedral *(see p28)* with its high tower and asymmetrical west façade. Inside are tombs of Asturian kings and a majestic 16th-century gilded reredos. The cathedral's supreme treasure is the Cámara Santa, a restored 9th-century chapel containing statues of Christ and the apostles. The chapel also houses many works of 9th-century Asturian

Cross of Angels in the treasury of Oviedo Cathedral

art including two crosses and a reliquary – all made of gold, silver and precious stones.

Also situated in the Plaza Alfonso II is the Iglesia de San Tirso. This church was originally constructed in the 9th century, but subsequent restorations have left the east window as the only surviving Pre-Romanesque feature.

Sited behind the cathedral is the **Museo Arqueológico**, housed in the old Benedictine monastery of San Vicente, with its fine cloisters. It contains local prehistoric, Romanesque and Pre-Romanesque treasures.

The **Museo de Bellas Artes**, in Velarde Palace, has a good range of Asturian and Spanish paintings, such as Carreño's portrait of Carlos II *(see p74)* and others by Greco, Goya, Dalí, Miró and Picasso.

Two of the most magnificent Pre-Romanesque churches are on Mount Naranco, to the

Santa María del Naranco

This church, on Mount Naranco, was originally built as a summer palace for Ramiro I in the 9th century. It is one of the finest examples of Pre-Romanesque or Asturian architecture, a style characterized by the slender proportions of its buildings and their original and graceful ornamentation.

The Hall has an unusually high ceiling.

Arcaded galleries at both ends of the building were designed to let in an enormous amount of light and were an architectural innovation.

Columns carved with *soqueado* or rope effect, were typical of the Pre-Romanesque style.

Vaultings of this size were a technical achievement and not adopted throughout Europe until the 11th century.

Exterior view of Santa María del Naranco

Church overlooking the sea at Ribadesella

north. Santa María del Naranco has a large barrel-vaulted hall on the main floor and arcaded galleries at either end. Some of the intricate reliefs on the door jambs of the nearby San Miguel de Lillo show acrobats and animal tamers in a circus.

The early 9th-century church of San Julián de los Prados stands on the road leading northeast out of Oviedo. The largest of Spain's surviving Pre-Romanesque churches, it is noted for the frescoes which cover all of its interior.

Museo Arqueológico
Calle San Vicente 3. **Tel** 985 20 89 77.
Open Wed–Sun.

Museo de Bellas Artes
Calle Santa Ana 1. **Tel** 985 21 30 61.
Open Tue–Sun.

❽ Valdediós

Asturias. 150. Monasterio de Santa María, 985 89 23 24. Monastery **Open** 11–11:45am & 1–1:45pm Tue, 11am–1pm & 4:30–6:30pm Wed–Sun.

Set alone in a field near this hamlet, the tiny 9th-century Iglesia de San Salvador is a jewel

of Pre-Romanesque art. Its ceiling has vivid Asturian frescoes, and by the portal are recesses where pilgrims slept. The church in the Monasterio de Santa María next door is 13th-century Cistercian, with cloisters from the 16th century.

Environs

To the north, the resort town of Villaviciosa lies amid apple orchards. In nearby Amandi, the hilltop Iglesia de San Juan has a 13th-century portal and delicate carvings and friezes.

Iglesia de San Salvador de Valdediós in its idyllic setting

❾ Ribadesella

Asturias. 5,800. Paseo Princesa Letizia, 985 86 00 38. Wed. Descent of the Río Sella (first Sat of Aug). **ribadesella.es**

This enchanting little seaside town bestrides a broad estuary. On one side is the lively old seaport full of tapas bars below a clifftop church. Across the estuary is a holiday resort. A multicoloured flotilla of kayaks arrives here from Arriondas (upstream) in an international regatta that is held every year on the first Saturday in August.

On the edge of town is the **Cueva de Tito Bustillo**. This cave is rich in stalactites but is best known for its many prehistoric drawings, which were discovered in 1968, some dating from around 18,000 BC. These include red and black pictures of stags and horses. To protect the paintings, only 360 visitors are allowed in per day; tickets are given out from 10am every day and should be booked in advance. There is a museum on the site.

Cueva de Tito Bustillo
Ribadesella. **Tel** 985 18 58 60.
Open Mar–Oct: Wed–Sun (free Wed).

❿ Cangas de Onís

Asturias. 6,300. Avenida Covadonga 1, 985 84 80 05. Sun. San Antonio (13 Jun), Cheese Festival (12 Oct). **cangasdeonis.com**

Cangas de Onís, one of the gateways to the Picos de Europa *(see pp112–13)*, is where Pelayo, the 8th-century Visigothic nobleman and hero of the Reconquest, set up his court. The town has a Romanesque bridge and the 8th-century chapel of Santa Cruz.

Environs

About 3 km (2 miles) east in Cardes is the **Cueva del Buxu**, which has engravings and rock-drawings over 10,000 years old. Only 25 visitors are allowed daily, and no visitors under 7.

Cueva del Buxu
Tel 608 17 54 67 (mobile). Wed–Sun. reservations essential; call 3–5pm Wed–Sun (free Wed).

⓪ Parque Nacional de los Picos de Europa

These beautiful mountains were reputedly christened the "Peaks of Europe" by returning sailors for whom this was often the first sight of their homeland. The range straddles three regions – Asturias, Cantabria and Castilla y León – and has diverse terrain. In some parts, deep winding gorges cut through craggy rocks, while elsewhere verdant valleys support orchards and dairy farming. The celebrated creamy blue cheese Cabrales *(see p80)* is made here. The Picos offer rock climbing and upland hiking as well as a profusion of flora and fauna. Tourism in the park is well organized.

Covadonga
The Neo-Romanesque basilica, built between 1877 and 1901, stands on the site of Pelayo's historic victory.

Lago de la Ercina
Together with the nearby Lago Enol, this lake lies on a wild limestone plateau above Covadonga and below the peak of Peña Santa.

Desfiladero de los Beyos
This deep, narrow gorge formed with its high limestone cliffs winds spectacularly for 10 km (6 miles) through the mountains. Tracing the route of the Río Sella below, it carries the main road from Cangas de Onís to Riaño.

KEY

① **Desfiladero del Río Cares** is a deep gorge formed by the River Cares in the heart of the Picos. A dramatic footpath follows the gorge, passing through tunnels and across high bridges up to 1,000 m (3,280 ft) above the river.

② **Bulnes**, one of the remotest villages in Spain, enjoys fine views of Naranjo de Bulnes and can now be accessed by an underground funicular railway from Puente Poncebos as well as by foot.

③ **Naranjo de Bulnes**, with its tooth-like crest, is in the heart of the massif. At 2,519 m (8,264 ft), it is one of the highest summits in the Picos de Europa.

Key

═══ Major road
─── Minor road
--- Footpath
━━━ National park boundary

A dramatic view of the mountains of the Picos de Europa

VISITORS' CHECKLIST

Practical Information
ℹ️ Casa Dago, Avenida
Covadonga 43, Cangas de Onís,
985 84 86 14. **Tel** 942 73 66 10.
🌐 infopicosdeeuropa.com
Fuente Dé cable car:
Open 10am–6pm daily.
Closed 1 & 6 Jan, 24, 25 & 31 Dec.

Transport
🚌 Oviedo to Cangas de Onís.

0 kilometres 5

0 miles 5

Panes

San Vicente De La Barquera

AS114

Arenas de Cabrales

AS264

Poncebos

②

Bulnes

③

DESFILADERO DE LA HERMIDA

Santa María de Lebeña

Deva

Parador de Fuente Dé
🅿️ 🚡

ℹ️

Monasterio de Santo Toribio de Liébana

ℹ️ **Potes**

N621

...to de Pandetrave

...243

Riaño

Puerto de San Glorio

Pelayo the Warrior

A statue of this Visigothic
nobleman who became king
of Asturias guards the basilica
at Covadonga. It was close to
this site, in 722, that
Pelayo and a band of
men – though vastly
outnumbered –
are said to have
defeated a Moorish
army. The victory
inspired Christians
in the north of
Spain to reconquer
the peninsula
(see pp58–9).
The tomb of
the warrior is
in a cave which
has become
a shrine, also
containing a
painted image
of the Virgin.

Pelayo's statue

Fuente Dé Cable Car
The 753-m (2,470-ft) ascent from
Fuente Dé takes visitors up to a
wild rocky plateau pitted with
craters. From here there is a
spectacular panorama of the
Picos' peaks and valleys.

Statue of the Virgin, San Vicente de la Barquera

Asturias and Cantabria's Fiestas

La Vijanera (first Sun of the year), Silió (Cantabria). This is a costumed parade which dates back to pre-Roman times, and celebrates the triumph of good over evil.

La Folía (second Sun after Easter), San Vicente de la Barquera (Cantabria). The statue of the Virgen de la Barquera is said to have arrived at San Vicente in a boat with no sails, oars or crew. Once a year, it is put on a decorated fishing boat, which sails at the head of a procession to bless the sea. Groups of young girls, called picayos, stand on the shore singing traditional songs. La Folía usually takes place on the second Sunday after Easter, depending on local tides.

Fiesta del Pastor (25 Jul), near Cangas de Onís (Asturias). Regional dances are performed on the shores of Lake Enol in the Picos de Europa National Park.

Battle of the Flowers (last Fri of Aug), Laredo (Cantabria). Floats adorned with flowers are paraded through this small resort. A flower-throwing free-for-all follows the procession.

Nuestra Señora de Covadonga (8 Sep), Picos de Europa (Asturias). Huge crowds converge on the shrine of Covadonga (see p112) to pay homage to the patron saint of Asturias.

⑫ Potes

Cantabria. 🅼 1,300. 🅸 Plaza de la Independencia s/n, 942 73 81 26. 🅼 Mon. 🎏 Ntra. Sra. de Valmayor (15 Aug), Santísima Cruz (14 Sep).

A small ancient town, with old balconied houses lining the river, Potes is the main centre of the eastern Picos de Europa. It is situated in the broad Valle de Liébana, whose fertile soil yields prime crops of walnuts, cherries and grapes. A potent spirit called orujo is made in the town. The Torre del Infantado, in the main square, is a defensive tower built in the 15th century.

Environs

Between Potes and the coast runs a gorge, the Desfiladero de la Hermida. Halfway up it is Santa María de Lebeña, a 10th-century Mozarabic church.

West of Potes is the monastery church of Santo Toribio de Liébana, one of the most revered spots in the Picos de Europa. Founded in the 7th century, it became known throughout Spain a century later when it received reputedly the largest fragment of the True Cross. An 8th century monk, St Beatus of Liébana, wrote the *Commentary on the Apocalypse*. The restored Romanesque monastic buildings were rebuilt in the 1200s, and are now occupied by Franciscan monks.

⑬ Comillas

Cantabria. 🅼 2,200. 🅸 Plaza Joaquín del Piélago 1, 942 72 25 91. 🅼 Fri. 🎏 El Cristo (16 Jul). Palacio Sobrellano: **Open** Apr–Oct: 9:30am–6:30pm daily (to 7:30pm mid-Jun–mid-Sep); Nov–Mar: 9:30am–3:30pm daily. 🎟 🎫 (compulsory).

This pretty resort is known for its buildings by Catalán Modernista architects (see pp144–5). Antonio López y López, the first Marquis of Comillas, hired Joan Martorell to design the Neo-Gothic Palacio Sobrellano (1881), now a museum. Comilla's best-known

Stone bridge and houses in the ancient town of Potes

Surviving Classical columns among the ruins of the Roman town of Julióbriga, near Reinosa

monument is Gaudí's *(see p168)* El Capricho, now a restaurant. It was designed from 1883 to 1889 and is a Mudéjar-inspired fantasy with a minaret-like tower covered in green and yellow tiles.

Another Modernista building is the Universidad Pontificia, on a hilltop overlooking the sea. It was designed by Joan Martorell to plans by Domènech i Montaner *(see p144)*.

Wall tile on the façade of El Capricho

Environs
The fishing port of San Vicente de la Barquera has arcaded streets, ramparts and the Gothic Romanesque church of Nuestra Señora de los Ángeles.

⑭ Valle de Cabuérniga

Cantabria. 🚌 Bárcena Mayor.
🅸 Ayuntamiento de Cabuerniga, 942 70 60 01.

Two exceptionally picturesque towns, notable for their superb examples of rural architecture, draw visitors to the Cabuérniga Valley. A good road takes you to the once-remote Bárcena Mayor. Its cobbled streets are furnished with old lamps and filled with boutiques, and restaurants serving regional dishes. The pretty houses have flower-covered balconies and cattle byres.

Carmona is an old, unspoiled village approximately 20 km (12 miles) to the northwest of Bárcena Mayor. Its solid stone houses, with pantiled roofs and wooden balconies, are typically Cantabrian *(see p30)*. Woodcarving, the traditional craft of the region, is still practised in this village, where men work outside their houses on a variety of artifacts including bowls, fiddles, *albarcas* (clogs) and chairs. The 13th-century Palacio de los Mier, a manor house in the centre of the village, is being transformed into a hotel.

The extensive, wild beech woods near Saja have been designated a nature reserve.

Traditional balconied houses in Bárcena Mayor

⑮ Alto Campoo

Cantabria. 🚠 1,900. 🚌 🚆 Reinosa.
🅸 Estación de Montaña, 942 77 92 23 (am only); Reinosa, 942 75 52 15.
🎉 San Sebastián (20 Jan, Reinosa).

Sited high in the Cantabrian mountains, this winter resort lies below the Pico de Tres Mares (2,175 m/7,000 ft), the "Peak of the Three Seas", so called because the rivers rising near it flow into the Mediterranean, the Atlantic and the Bay of Biscay. The Río Ebro, one of Spain's longest rivers, rises in this area and its source, at Fontibre, is a beauty spot. A road and a chair lift reach the summit of Tres Mares for a breathtaking panorama of the Picos de Europa and other mountain chains. The resort is small, with 22 pistes totalling 32 km (20 miles) in length, and has few facilities for après-ski.

Environs
Reinosa, some 26 km (16 miles) to the east of Alto Campoo, is a handsome market town with old stone houses. Further southeast is Retortillo, a hamlet where the remains of Julióbriga, a town built by the Romans as a bastion against the wild tribes of Cantabria, can be seen.

The main road south out of Reinosa leads to Cervatos, where the former collegiate church has erotic carvings on its façade. This novel device was meant to deter the villagers from pleasures of the flesh.

At Arroyuelo and Cadalso, to the southeast, are two churches built into rock faces in the 8th and 9th centuries.

One of the many paintings of bison at Altamira

⑯ Cuevas de Altamira

Cantabria. **Tel** 942 81 80 05. 🚌 Santillana del Mar. Caves: **Closed** to the public, check website for details. Museum: **Open** 9:30am–6pm Tue–Sat (to 8pm May–Oct), 9:30am–3pm Sun. **Closed** 1 & 6 Jan, 1 May, 28 Jun, 24, 25 & 31 Dec. 🎫 advance booking advisable, 902 24 24 24 (free every Sat from 2pm & Sun). ♿ 📷 ⓦ **museodealtamira.mcu.es**

These caves contain some of the world's finest examples of prehistoric art. The earliest engravings and drawings, discovered in 1879, date back to around 30,000 BC (see p53). Public entry to the caves is very restricted, but the on-site museum contains a replica of the caves. Similar sites that remain open to the public are found at nearby Puente Viesgo, Ribadesella (see p111) in Asturias and at Nerja (see p489) in Andalucía.

Carved figure of Christ in the Convento de Regina Coeli

⑰ Santillana del Mar

Cantabria. 🗠 4,100. 🚌 🛈 Calle Jesus Otero 20, 942 81 88 12. 🎉 Santa Juliana (28 Jun), San Roque (16 Aug). ⓦ **santillana-del-mar.com**

Set just inland, belying its name, this town is one of the prettiest in Spain. Its ensemble of 15th- to 18th-century stone houses survives largely intact.

The town grew up around a monastery, which was an important pilgrimage centre, the Romanesque La Colegiata. The church houses the tomb of the local early medieval martyr St Juliana, and contains a 17th-century painted reredos and a carved south door. In its lovely cloisters, vivid biblical scenes have been sculpted on the capitals.

On the town's two main cobbled streets there are houses built by local noblemen. These have either fine wooden galleries or iron balconies, and coats of arms inlaid into their stone façades. In the past, farmers used the open ground floors as byres for stabling their cattle.

In the enchanting Plaza Mayor, in the centre of town, is a mansion-turned-parador. The **Museo Diocesano** is housed in the restored Convento de Regina Coeli, east of the town centre, and has a collection of painted carvings of religious figures.

🏛 **Museo Diocesano**
El Cruce. **Tel** 942 84 03 17. **Open** Tue–Sun. 🎫

⑱ Puente Viesgo

Cantabria. 🗠 2,800. 🚌 🛈 Calle Manuel Pérez Mazo 2, 942 59 81 05 (town hall). 🎉 La Perolá (20 Jan), San Miguel (28–29 Sep).

This spa village is best known for **El Monte Castillo**, a complex of caves dotted around the limestone hills above the town. Decorated by prehistoric man, it is thought the late Palaeolithic cave dwellers used the deep interior as a sanctuary. They left drawings of horses, bison and other animals, and some 50 hand prints. The colours used to create the images were made from minerals in the cave.

Environs
The lush Pas valley, to the southeast, is home to transhumant dairy farmers, the Pasiegos. In the main town of Vega de Pas, you can buy two Pasiego specialities – sobaos, or sponge cakes, and quesadas, a sweet which is made from milk, butter and eggs. In Villacarriedo there is a handsome 18th-century mansion, with two Baroque façades of carved stone hiding a medieval tower.

🏠 **El Monte Castillo**
Puente Viesgo. **Tel** 942 59 84 25. **Open** Wed–Sun (mid-Jun–mid-Sep: Tue–Sun; Nov–Feb: am only). 🎫 📧

Main façade of La Colegiata in Santillana del Mar

The Palacio de la Magdalena in Santander

⓭ Santander

Cantabria. 🏛 172,500. ✈ 🚉 🚌 🚢 🛈 Jardines de Pereda s/n, 942 20 30 00. 🛒 Mon–Thu. 🎉 Santiago (25 Jul). 🌐 **turismodecantabria.com**

Cantabria's capital, a busy port, enjoys a splendid site near the mouth of a deep bay. The town centre is modern – after being ravaged by fire in 1941 it was reconstructed. The cathedral was rebuilt in Gothic style, but retains its 12th-century crypt. The **Museo de Bellas Artes** houses work by Goya as well as other artists of the 19th and 20th centuries. The town's **Museo de Prehistoria y Arqueología** displays finds from caves at Altamira and Puente Viesgo *(see opposite)*, such as Neolithic axe heads, and Roman coins, pottery and figurines. The **Museo Marítimo** has rare whale skeletons and 350 species of local fish.

The town extends along the coast around the Península de la Magdalena, a headland on which there is a park, a small zoo and the Palacio de la Magdalena – a summer palace built for Alfonso XIII in 1912, reflecting the resort's popularity at the time with the Royal Family.

The seaside suburb of El Sardinero, north of the head-land, is a smart resort with a long graceful beach, backed by gardens, elegant cafés and a majestic white casino. In July and August El Sardinero plays host to a major theatre and music festival.

🏛 **Museo de Bellas Artes**
Calle Rubio 6. **Tel** 942 20 31 20. **Open** Tue–Sun. 📷

🏛 **Museo de Prehistoria y Arqueología**
Calle Bailén s/n. **Tel** 942 20 99 22. **Open** Tue–Sun. 🦽 📷

🏛 **Museo Marítimo**
Calle Severiano Ballesteros s/n. **Tel** 942 27 49 62. **Open** daily.

⓴ Laredo

Cantabria. 🏛 11,500. 🚉 🛈 Alameda Miramar, 942 61 10 96. 🎉 Batalla de Flores (last Fri of Aug), Carlos V's last landing (3rd week in Sep).

Its long, sandy beach has made Laredo one of Cantabria's most popular bathing resorts. The attractive Old Town has narrow streets with balconied houses leading up to the 13th-century Iglesia de Santa María de la Asunción, with its Flemish altar and bronze lecterns. One of the highlights of the year in Laredo is the colourful Battle of the Flowers, which takes place in August *(see p114)*.

㉑ Castro Urdiales

Cantabria. 🏛 32,000. 🚌 🛈 Parque Amestoy Avda de la Constitución s/n, 942 87 15 12. 🛒 Thu. 🎉 San Pelayo (26 Jun), Coso Blanco (1st Fri of Jul), San Andrés (30 Nov). Iglesia: **Open** daily.

Castro Urdiales, a busy fishing town and popular holiday resort, is built around a picturesque harbour. Above the port, on a high promontory, stands the pinkish Gothic Iglesia de Santa María, as big as a cathedral. Beside it the restored castle, said to have been built by the Knights Templar, has been converted into a lighthouse. Handsome glass-fronted houses, or *galerías*, line the promenade. The small town beach often becomes crowded, but there are bigger ones to the west, such as the Playa de Ostende.

Environs
Near the village of Ramales de la Victoria, 40 km (25 miles) south, are prehistoric caves containing etchings and engravings, reached by a very steep mountain road.

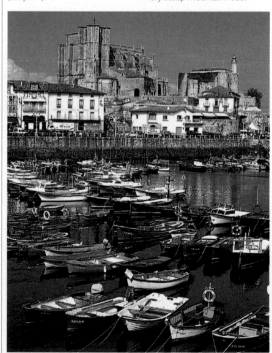

Small boats moored in the harbour at Castro Urdiales

THE BASQUE COUNTRY, NAVARRA AND LA RIOJA

Vizcaya · Guipúzcoa · Álava · La Rioja · Navarra

The landscapes of the Basque Country, land of an ancient people of controversial origin, range from green hills to Atlantic beaches. Also enjoying a remarkable setting is the former medieval kingdom of Navarra, which is partly Basque and sits across the beautiful western Pyrenees. To the south, the vineyards of La Rioja produce many of Spain's finest wines.

The Basques are a race apart – they will not let you forget that theirs is a culture different from any in Spain – and the Basque regional government enjoys considerable autonomy from Madrid.

The Basque Country (*Euskadi* is the Basque name) is an important industrial region blessed with spectacular land-scapes. The Basques are great deep-sea fishermen and fish plays a major role in their imaginative cuisine, regarded by many as the best in Spain.

Unrelated to any other tongue, the Basque language, *Euskara,* is widely used on signs and most towns have two names; the fashionable resort of San Sebastián, for example, is officially known as Donostia. *Euskara* is also spoken in parts of Navarra, which is counted as part of the wider (unofficial) Basque Country. Many of its finest sights – the towns of Olite and Estella, and the monastery of Leyre – date from the Middle Ages, when Navarra was a kingdom straddling the Pyrenees. Pamplona, its capital, is best known for its daredevil bullrunning fiesta of San Fermines, which is held in July.

As well as its vineyards and bodegas, La Rioja is a fertile region of vegetable gardens. Among its many historic sights are the cathedral of Santo Domingo de la Calzada and the monasteries of San Millán de la Cogolla and Yuso.

Basque farmhouse near Gernika-Lumo in the Basque Country

◄ Beautiful yellow fields of La Rioja in summertime

Exploring the Basque Country, Navarra and La Rioja

These green, hilly regions have diverse attractions. The Pyrenees in Navarra offer skiing in winter and climbing, caving and canoeing the rest of the year. The cliffs of the Basque Country are broken by rocky coves, *rías*, and wide bays with beaches of fine yellow sand, interspersed with fishing villages. Inland, minor roads wind through wooded hills, valleys and gorges, past lonely castles and isolated homesteads. In La Rioja, to the south, they cross vineyards, passing villages and towns clustered round venerable churches and monasteries.

The scenic Río Cárdenas valley below the village of San Millán de la Cogolla in La Rioja

Key

═══ Motorway

= = Motorway under construction

▬▬ Major road

═══ Minor road

▬▬ Scenic route

▬▬ Main railway

──── Minor railway

▬▬ International border

▬▬ Regional border

0 kilometres 25

0 miles 15

For keys to symbols *see back flap*

Sights at a Glance

Getting Around

The main road in the north is the A8 (E5). The A68 AP68 (E804) runs southwards from Bilbao via Haro and follows the Ebro Valley. Motorway spurs extend to Vitoria and Pamplona. The rail network connects the cities and the larger towns, and most towns are served by coach. Bilbao has an international airport. In the Basque Country, signs are in both Basque and Castilian.

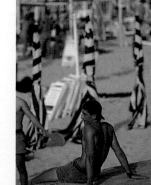

The fashionable Playa de Ondarreta, one of San Sebastián's three beaches

Buildings overlooking the Río Nervión in Bilbao

❶ Bilbao

Vizcaya. 🔼 345,000. ✈ 🚉 🚌 🚢
ℹ Plaza Ensanche 11, 944 79 57 60.
🎎 Santiago (25 Jul), La Asunción (15 Aug), Semana Grande (late Aug).
🌐 bilbao.net/bilbaoturismo

Bilbao (Bilbo) is the centre of Basque industry. An important port and the largest Basque city, it is surrounded by high, bare hills. Its suburbs spread 16 km (10 miles) along the Río Nervión (Nerbioi) to its estuary. The river between Las Arenas and the fishing port of Portugalete is crossed via the Puente Colgante, a UNESCO World Heritage Site. This iron transporter bridge, built in 1893, has a suspended cabin for cars and passengers. On the east bank of the estuary is Santurtzi (Santurce), from where ferries sail to the UK *(see p627)*.

Bilbao has flourished as an industrial city since the mid-19th century, when iron ore was first extracted from deposits northwest of the city. Soon, steelworks and chemical factories became a major part of the local landscape. In the last two decades, however, many of the old shipyards and factories have been replaced by parks, riverside walks, pavement cafés and striking new architecture.

The city's medieval heart, the *casco viejo*, was built in the 14th century. Here, amid alleys lively with *pintxos* bars, is the arcaded Plazuela de Santiago and the Catedral Basílica de Santiago. The **Museo Vasco** displays Basque art, folk artifacts and photographs of Basque life. In the cloister is the Idol of Mikeldi, an animal-like carving dating from the 3rd to 2nd century BC.

In the newer town is the large **Museo de Bellas Artes** (Museum of Fine Art), one of Spain's best art museums. It displays art ranging from 12th-century Basque and Catalan pieces to works by modern artists of international fame, including Vasarely, Kokoschka, Bacon, Delaunay and Léger. There are also paintings by Basque artists.

The jewel in the area's cultural crown is the Museo Guggenheim Bilbao (see pp124–5). The museum is part of a redevelopment of the city which includes the expansion of its port and the metro system, designed in a futuristic style by Norman Foster. Another striking building is the **Palacio de la Música y Congresos Euskalduna**, designed to resemble a ship.

The **Alhóndiga**, a century-old wine warehouse, was converted into a cultural centre in 2010. It boasts design shops and restaurants, a library, a fabulous pool and a rooftop terrace.

West of the city, a funicular railway ascends to the village of La Reineta and a panorama across the dockyards.

🏛 **Museo Vasco**
Plaza Miguel de Unamuno 4. **Tel** 94 415 54 23. **Open** Wed–Mon. **Closed** public hols. 🎫 (except Thu.). ♿

🏛 **Museo de Bellas Artes**
Plaza del Museo 2. **Tel** 94 439 60 60. **Open** Wed–Mon. 🎫 (except Wed am & Sun pm). 📷 ♿

🎭 **Palacio de la Música y Congresos Euskalduna**
Avenida Abandoibarra 4. **Tel** 94 403 50 00. **Open** for concerts. 🎫 📷 ♿

🎭 **Alhóndiga**
Plaza Arriquibar 4. **Tel** 94 401 40 14.
🌐 azkunazentroa.eus

❷ Gernika-Lumo

Vizcaya. 🔼 16,900. 🚌 🚉 ℹ Artekalea 8, 94 625 58 92. 🎎 Aniversario del Bombardeo de Guernica (26 Apr), San Roque (14–18 Aug). 🌐 gernikalumo.net

This little town is of great symbolic significance to the Basques. For centuries, Basque leaders met in democratic assembly under an oak on a hillside here. On 26 April 1937 Gernika-Lumo (Guernica) was the target of the world's first saturation bombing raid, carried out by Nazi aircraft at the request of General Franco. Picasso's powerful painting *(see pp70–71)* of this outrage can be seen in Madrid *(see p303)*.

The town has since been rebuilt and is rather dull. But in a garden, inside a pavilion and closely guarded, is the 300-year-old petrified trunk of the oak tree, the *Gernikako Arbola*, or Oak of Gernika, symbol of the ancient roots of the Basque people. Younger oaks, nurtured from its acorns, have been planted beside it. The Basque people make visits to this ancient tree as if on a pilgrimage. The **Casa de Juntas**, nearby, is a former

Zuloaga's *Condesa Mathieu de Noailles* (1913), Bilbao Museum of Fine Art

Basque fishermen depicted in the stained-glass ceiling of the Casa de Juntas in Gernika-Lumo

chapel where the parliament of the province of Vizcaya reconvened in 1979, when the Basque provinces regained their autonomy. In one room a stained-glass ceiling depicts the Oak of Gernika with Basque citizens debating their rights.

The Europa Park, next door, has peace sculptures by Henry Moore and Eduardo Chillida.

Environs

Five km (3 miles) northeast of Gernika, near Kortézubi (Cortézubl), are the **Cuevas de Santimamiñe**. On the walls of a small chamber are charcoal drawings of animals made by cave dwellers around 11,000 BC. Discovered in 1917, the drawings cannot be seen, but replicas are projected on the walls at the entrance. For conservation reasons the caves are closed to the public, but a 3D simulation in the nearby hermitage offers an impressive virtual reproduction. Guided visits last 90 minutes and must be booked in advance.

Casa de Juntas
Calle Allende Salazar. **Tel** 94 625 11 38.
Open daily. **Closed** 1 & 6 Jan, 16 Aug, 24, 25 & 31 Dec. book ahead.

Cuevas de Santimamiñe
Kortézubi. **Tel** 944 65 16 57.
Open daily (Oct–Apr: Tue–Sun). book ahead.

❸ Costa Vasca

Vizcaya & Guipúzcoa. Bilbao.
Bilbao. Getxo, 94 491 08 00.

The Basque country's 176 km (110 miles) of coastline is heavily indented: rugged cliffs alternate with inlets and coves, backed by wooded hills. Some of the fishing villages are overdeveloped, but the scenery inland is attractive.

There are good beaches north of Algorta (near Bilbao). Plentzia is a pleasant estuary town with a marina. Eastwards on the coast is Bakio, a large fishing village. Beyond it the BI3101, a dramatic corniche road, winds high above the sea past the tiny island hermitage, San Juan de Gaztelugatxe, and Matxitxaco, a headland light-

Anglers on the quayside at Lekeitio, a port on the Costa Vasca

house. It passes Bermeo, a port with a fishery museum, the **Museo del Pescador**, and Mundaka, a small surfing resort. On the serene Ría de Guernica there are two sandy beaches, Laida and Laga.

At the fishing port of Lekeitio, old Basque houses line the seafront below the 15th-century church of Santa María. One long beach, good for swimming, sweeps round the village of Saturrarán and the old port of Ondarroa. The Lekeitio–Ondarroa road is lined with pines.

Zumaia is a beach resort with an old quarter. In the **Espacio Cultural Ignacio Zuloaga**, the former home of the well-known Basque painter who lived from 1870 to 1945, colourful studies of Basque rural and maritime life are on display. Getaria, along the coast, is spread steeply around a fishing port, and has lively cafés and the 14th-century Iglesia de San Salvador. Zarautz, once a fashionable resort, has sizable beaches and elegant mansions.

Museo del Pescador
Plaza Torrontero 1. **Tel** 94 688 11 71.
Open Tue–Sun. **Closed** public hols.
(free last Thu of the month).

Espacio Cultural Ignacio Zuloaga
Santiago Etxea 4, Zumaia. **Tel** 677 07 84 45. **Open** Apr–Sep: 4–8pm Wed–Sun; other times by appt.

Bilbao: Museo Guggenheim

The Museo Guggenheim Bilbao is the jewel in the city's cultural crown. The building itself is a star attraction: a mind-boggling array of silvery curves by the American architect Frank Gehry, which are alleged to resemble a ship or a flower. The Guggenheim Bilbao's collection represents an intriguingly broad spectrum of modern and contemporary art, and includes works by Abstract Impressionists such as Willem de Kooning and Mark Rothko. The museum's programme combines temporary exhibitions with shows from the permanent collections of the Guggenheim museums in New York and Venice.

View from the City
Approaching along the Calle de Iparraguirre, the Guggenheim Bilbao stands out amid traditional buildings.

KEY

① *The Matter of Time*, by sculptor, Richard Serra, was created in hot-rolled steel. It is over 30 m (100 ft) long.

② **Nerua** is the museum's Michelin-starred restaurant.

③ **The Puente de la Salve** was incorporated into the design of the building, which extends underneath it.

④ **The tower**, on the far side of the bridge, was designed to resemble a sail. It is not an exhibition space.

⑤ **Roofscape** is reminiscent of a ship, with prow-like points and metallic material.

⑥ **Second-floor balcony**

⑦ **Puppy**, by American artist Jeff Koons, is a 13-m (43-ft) West Highland terrier with a coat of flowers watered by an internal irrigation system. It has become a favourite icon of the city.

⑧ **Café**

⑨ **Water garden beside the River Nervión**

⑩ *Tall Tree and the Eye* by Anish Kapoor.

⑪ **Yves Klein's *Fire Fountain*** consists of five fountains emitting sharp bursts of fire.

⑫ **Louise Bourgeois'** sculpture *Maman* is a 9-m (30-ft) high tribute to the artist's mother.

⑬ **Fujiko Nakaya's *F.O.G.*** sculpture is an atmospheric fog sculpture typical of this Japanese artist's work.

★ Atrium
The space in which visitors to the museum first find themselves is the extraordinary 60-m- (165-ft-) high atrium. It serves as an orientation point and its height makes it a dramatic setting for exhibiting large pieces.

VISITORS' CHECKLIST

Practical Information
Avenida Abandoibarra 2. **Tel** 944 35 90 00. **Open** 10am–8pm Tue–Sun (daily Jul & Aug). Art After Dark: 10pm–1am one Fri a month. 🔲 booking online advisable, especially during high season. 🔲 🔲 🔲 🔲 🔲 🔲
W **guggenheim-bilbao.eus**

Transport
🔲 Moyua. 🔲 1, 10, 11, 13, 18, 27, 38, 48, 71.

Main entrance

★ Titanium façade
Rarely used in buildings, titanium is more usually used for aircraft parts. In total 60 tons were used, but the layer is only 3 mm (0.1 inches) thick.

Gallery 104
Dominated by Richard Serra's *The Matter of Time*, this gallery is the museum's largest. The fish motif, seen in the flowing shape, is one of architect Frank Gehry's favourites.

San Sebastián's Playa de Ondarreta, with its view across the bay

❹ San Sebastián

Guipúzcoa. 🗺 186,000.
✈ Hondarribia (22 km). 🚊 🚌
ℹ Alameda del Bulevard 8, 943 48 11
66. 🛥 Sun. 🎭 San Sebastián (20 Jan);
Semana Grande (week of 15 Aug).
🌐 sansebastianturismo.com

Gloriously situated on a neat,
shell-shaped bay, San Sebastián
(Donostia) is the most elegant
and fashionable Spanish seaside
resort. At either end of the bay
is a tower-topped hill – Monte
Urgull in the east and Monte
Igueldo in the west. Between
the two, in the mouth of the
bay, lies a small island, the Isla
de Santa Clara.

San Sebastián became a smart
resort in the late 19th century.
It still has many luxury shops
and one of Spain's grandest
hotels, the María Cristina (see
p564), but San Sebastián is now
primarily a family resort.

The city is renowned for its
great summer arts festivals. The
theatre festival is held in May;
jazz festivals are held in July; a
classical music festival, in August;
and the San Sebastián International Film Festival, in September.
The Semana Grande in August
is the city's principal fiesta.

Cuisine plays a huge part in
local life: many Basque men
here belong to gastronomic
clubs where they gather to
cook, eat, drink and talk.
Women are invited to such
meetings, but they don't take
part in the food preparation.

The Old Town
San Sebastián's fascinating Old
Town (Parte Vieja) is wedged
between the bay and the Río
Urumea. The alleys, packed with
restaurants and tapas bars, are
intensely animated at night. In
the local fish market, stalls piled
high with delicacies testify to
the key role of fish in the town.

The heart of the Old Town is
the Plaza de la Constitución, a
handsome, arcaded square. The
numbers on the balconies date
from when the square was used
as a bullring – organizers sold a
ticket for each numbered place.
Nearby are the impressively
reverent Basílica de Santa Maria
and the 16th-century church of
Iglesia de San Vicente.

Monte Urgull rises behind the
Old Town. On the summit are a
statue of Christ and the ruined
Castillo de Santa Cruz de la Mota,
with old cannons.

Beaches
San Sebastián's two principal
beaches follow the bay round
to Monte Igueldo. The Playa
de Ondarreta is the more
fashionable of the two, while the
Playa de la Concha is the larger.
Between them is the Palacio
Miramar, built in 1889 by the
Basque architect José Goicoa,
to designs by Selden Wornum,
a British architect. The palace,
built for Queen María Cristina,
established San Sebastián
as an aristocratic resort. The
gardens are open to the public.

At the water's edge near the
Playa de Ondarreta is a striking
group of modern iron sculptures, The Comb of the Winds
by Eduardo Chillida. A road
and a funicular railway, built
in 1912, lead to the top of
Monte Igueldo, where there
is a small amusement park.

To the east of the Playa de la
Concha is the surfer's favourite,
Playa de Zurriola, with surf
schools and shops, overlooked
by the hill, Monte Ulía.

🐠 Aquarium
Plaza Carlos Blasco de Imaz 1.
Tel 943 44 00 99. **Open** Easter–Jun &
Sep: 10am–8pm daily (to 9pm Sat &
Sun); Jul–Aug: 10am–9pm daily; Oct–
Easter: 10am–7pm (to 8pm Sat & Sun).
Closed 1 & 20 Jan, 25 Dec. 🎟 📷 ♿
🌐 aquariumss.com

This remodelled aquarium
boasts a 360-degree
underwater tunnel, where
visitors can view over 5,000
fish, including four species of
shark. Tickets allow entry to
a Naval Museum, with exhibits
of Basque naval history.

The Comb of the Winds by Eduardo Chillida

Josep Maria Sert's murals of Basque life in the Museo de San Telmo

Kursaal

Avenida de Zurriola 1. **Tel** 943 00 30 00.
📷 🎬 💾 ♿ 🌐 **kursaal.org**

These giant cubes stand out as the most prominent feature on Zurriola beach, especially when lit up at night. Designed by Rafael Moneo, the cubes contain large auditoriums, for most of the year home to conferences and concerts.

🏛 Museo de San Telmo

Plaza Zuloaga 1. **Tel** 943 48 15 80.
Open 10am–8pm Tue–Sun. **Closed** 1 & 20 Jan, 25 Dec. 🎬 (free Tue). 📷 ♿

This is a large museum in a 16th-century monastery below Monte Urgull. In the cloister is a collection of Basque funerary columns dating from the 15th–17th centuries.

The museum also contains displays of furniture, tools and other artifacts, and paintings by local Basque artists: 19th-century works by Antonio Ortiz Echagüe, modern

paintings by Ignacio Zuloaga, portraits by Vicente López and masterpieces by El Greco. The chapel holds 11 murals by the Catalan artist Josep Maria Sert, depicting Basque legends, culture and the region's seafaring life.

Environs

Five kilometres (3 miles) east of San Sebastián is Pasai Donibane, a picturesque fishing village consisting of a jumble of houses built along one cobbled main street, which has some good fish restaurants.

Around 8 km (5 miles) south of San Sebastián is the interesting medieval town of Hernani, which has been awarded the status of Cultural Interest Site. The forests surrounding the town are dotted with prehistoric remains, including dolmens, megalithic monuments and burial mounds.

The waterfront of the tiny fishing village of Pasaia Donibane

Old balconied houses in the upper town, Hondarribia

❺ Hondarribia

Guipúzcoa. 🗺 17,000. 🚉 🚌 🅸
Arma Plaza 9, 943 64 36 77; Minatera, 9 Puerto Deportivo, 934 64 54 58.
🎭 La Kutxa Entrega (25 Jul), Alarde (6–8 Sep). 🌐 **bidasoaturismo.com**

Hondarribia (Fuenterrabía), the historic town at the mouth of the Río Bidasoa, was attacked by the French over many centuries. The upper town is protected by 15th-century walls and entered via their original gateway, the handsome Puerta de Santa María. They enclose alleys of old houses with carved eaves, balconies and coats of arms.

The streets cluster round the church of Nuestra Señora de la Asunción y del Manzano, with its massive buttresses, tall Baroque tower and, inside, a gold reredos. At the town's highest point is the 10th-century castle, now a parador (see p564).

Hondarribia has seafront cafés in La Marina, its lively fishermen's quarter. It is also a seaside resort, with beaches stretching to the north.

Environs

A hill road climbs westwards to the shrine of the Virgin of Guadalupe. Further along this road are panoramic views of the coast and the mountains. From the Ermita de San Marcial, which stands on a hill 9 km (6 miles) to the south, there are views of the Bidasoa plain straddling the border – the French towns are neatly white, the Spanish ones are greyer.

San Sebastián Film Festival

This festival, founded in 1953, is one of the five leading European annual film festivals. It is held in late September, drawing more than 200,000 spectators. The special Donostia Prize is awarded as a tribute to the career of a star or director: winners have included Meryl Streep, Ian McKellen and Woody Allen. Visiting celebrities have included Quentin Tarantino, Ethan Coen and Bertrand Tavernier. Prizes also go to individual new films. An early winner was Hitchcock's *Vertigo*. The festival's website is www.sansebastianfestival.com.

Benicio Del Toro receiving an award

The Renaissance façade of the former Basque university in Oñati

⑥ Santuario de Loiola

Loiola, Guipúzcoa. **Tel** 943 02 50 00.
🚌 **Open** 10am–1pm, 3:30–7pm
(to 7:30pm in summer) daily.
W santuariodeloyola.org

Saint Ignatius of Loiola (San Ignacio de Loyola), founder of the Jesuits, was born in the 1490s in the Santa Casa (holy house), a stone manor near Azpeitia. In the 1600s it was enclosed by the Basílica de San Ignacio, and the rooms in which the aristocratic Loiola family lived were converted into chapels. The Chapel of the Conversion is where Ignatius, as a young soldier, recovered from a war injury and had a profound religious experience.

A diorama depicts episodes in the saint's life: dedicating his life to Christ at the Monastery of Montserrat *(see pp222–3)*; writing his *Spiritual Exercises* in a cave at Manresa; his imprisonment by the Inquisition; and his pilgrimage to the Holy Land. The basilica, built from 1681 to 1738, has a Churrigueresque dome and a circular nave with rich carvings.

⑦ Oñati

Guipúzcoa. 🏘 11,300. 🚌 **ℹ** Calle San Juan 14, 943 78 34 53. 🖾 Sat. 🎭 Corpus Christi (May/Jun), San Miguel (29 Sep–1 Oct). W oñatiturismo.eus

This historic town in the Udana Valley has a distinguished past. In the First Carlist War, 1833–9 *(see p67)*, it was a seat of the court of Don Carlos, brother of King Fernando VII and pretender to the throne. Its former **university**, built in about 1540, was for centuries the only one in the Basque Country. It has a Renaissance façade, decorated with statues of saints, and an elegant patio.

In the Plaza de los Fueros is the Iglesia de San Miguel, a Gothic church with a stone cloister in Gothic-Flemish style. It contains the tomb of Bishop Zuázola of Ávila, the founder of the university. Opposite is the Baroque town hall (ayuntamiento).

Environs
A mountain road ascends 9 km (6 miles) to the Santuario de Arantzazu, below the peak of Aitzgorri. In 1469 it is believed a shepherd visualized the Virgin here. Over the door of the church, built in the 1950s, are sculptures of the apostles by Jorge Oteiza.

🏛 **Universidad de Sancti Spiritus**
Avenida de la Universidad Vasca.
Tel 943 78 34 53. **Open** daily for guided tours (phone Oñati tourist information in advance). 🚫

The imposing Santuario de Loiola, with its Churrigueresque cupola

The Founding of the Jesuit Order

The Society of Jesus was founded in Rome in 1539 by Saint Ignatius and a group of priests who were dedicated to helping the poor. Pope Paul III soon approved the order's establishment, with Ignatius as Superior General. The order, which grew wealthy, vowed military obedience to the pope and became his most powerful weapon against the Reformation. Today, there are approximately 20,000 Jesuits working, mainly in education, in 112 countries.

Saint Ignatius of Loiola

Basque Culture

The Basques may be Europe's oldest race. Anthropologists think they could be descended from Cro-Magnon people, who lived in the Pyrenees 40,000 years ago. The dolmens and carved stones of their ancestors are evidence of the Basques' pagan roots.

Long isolated in their mountain valleys, the Basques preserved their unique language, myths and art for millennia, almost untouched by other influences. Many families still live in the isolated, chalet-style stone *caseríos*, or farmhouses, built by their forebears. Their music and high-bounding dances are unlike those of any other culture, and their cuisine is varied and imaginative.

The *fueros*, or ancient Basque laws and rights were suppressed under General Franco, but since the arrival of democracy in 1975 the Basques have had their own parliament and police force, having won great autonomy over their own affairs.

The Basque Region

■ *Areas of Basque culture*

The national identity is symbolized by the region's flag: *La Ikurriña*. The white cross symbolizes Christianity. The green St Andrew's Cross commemorates a battle won on his feast day.

Bertsolaris are bards. They improvise witty, sometimes humorous songs, whose verses relate current events or legends. *Bertsolaris* sing, unaccompanied, to gatherings in public places, such as bars and squares, often in competition. This oral tradition has preserved Basque folklore, legends and history. No texts were written in *Euskara* (Basque) until the 16th century.

The Basque economy has always relied on fishing and associated industries, such as ship-building and agriculture. In recent history, heavy industries have made this region prosperous.

Traditional sports are highly respected in Basque culture. In pelota, teams hit a ball at a wall, then catch it with a wicker scoop or their hands. Sports involving strength, such as log-splitting and weight-lifting, are the most popular.

Vitoria City Centre

1. El Portalón
2. Museo de Arqueología y Naipes (BIBAT)
3. Catedral de Santa María
4. Palacio de Escoriaza-Esquibel
5. Iglesia de San Miguel
6. Plaza de la Virgen Blanca

0 metres   250
0 yards   250

For keys to symbols see back flap

❽ Vitoria

Álava. 🏙 244,000. ✈ 🚍 🚌
ℹ️ Plaza de España 1, 945 16 15 98.
🗓 Thu. 🎊 Romería de San
Prudencio (27–28 Apr), Fiestas
de la Virgen Blanca (4–9 Aug).
W **vitoria-gasteiz.org/turismo**

Vitoria (Gasteiz), the seat of
the Basque government,
was founded on a hill – the
province's highest point and the
site of an ancient Basque town,
Gasteiz. Vitoria's oldest part,
El Campillo, was rebuilt in 1200
after a fire. The city later grew
rich on the iron and wool trades.

The old town focuses on the
Plaza de la Virgen Blanca, with its
monument to a battle fought
nearby in 1813, when the British
Duke of Wellington defeated
the French. Around the plaza
are old houses with miradores
(glazed balconies).

On the hillside above the
plaza is the Gothic Iglesia de
San Miguel. An outside niche
contains a statue of the Virgen
Blanca (White Virgin), Vitoria's
patron saint. A big festival (see
p136) starts before her feast day,
which is on 5 August. On the wall
of San Miguel facing the Plaza
del Machete there is a recess
with a replica of the machete
on which the city's rulers swore
to uphold the laws or be slain.

The Old Town has several
Renaissance palaces, including
the 16th-century Palacio de
Escoriaza-Esquibel, with its
Plateresque (see p29) patio.
Around it is a charming area
of alleys linked by steep steps.

The city has two cathedrals.
The oldest is the Gothic Catedral
de Santa María, with a sculpted
west porch. Close by, in Calle
Correría, a street of old houses,
is El Portalón, a merchant's
house and hostel from the 15th
century. The building, which is
full of Basque country furniture
and art, is now a restaurant.

Among the city's later architectural gems are an arcaded
street, Los Arquillos, and the
adjoining Plaza de España, also
arcaded. They were built in the
late 18th century to link the Old
Town with the new quarter then
being built. South of the old town
is the Neo-Gothic Catedral Nueva
de María Inmaculada, begun in
1907 and finished in 1973.

🏛 Artium
Calle de Francia 24. **Tel** 945 20 90 00.
Open Tue–Sun. 🎫 ♿ W **artium.org**
Artium, the Basque Museum
of Contemporary Art, occupies
a striking white building and
contains one of Spain's largest
collections of modern and
contemporary art. The focus
is mainly on Spanish artists like
Dalí, Miró, Tàpies and Chillida.

The quiet Plaza de España in the centre of Vitoria

For hotels and restaurants in this region see pp563–4 and pp585–6

The Gothic west door of Vitoria's Catedral de Santa María

🏛 Museo de Arqueología y Naipes (BIBAT)

Palacio de Bendaña, C/ Cuchillería 54. **Tel** 945 20 37 00. **Open** Tue–Sun. ♿

Vitoria's archaeology museum is set in a stunning purpose-built edifice and features 1,500 pieces, including prehistory artifacts and Roman sculptures found at Álava. Visitors can experience multimedia projections and sound effects.

The grandson of Heraclio Fournier, who founded a playing cards factory in Vitoria in 1868, also displays his collection of more than 6,000 items in this museum. The oldest exhibits are late 14th-century Italian cards. Among the many sets of tarot cards are some designed by Salvador Dalí in the 1980s.

🏛 Museo de Armería

Paseo Fray Francisco 3. **Tel** 945 18 19 25. **Open** Tue–Sun. 📞 phone 945 18 19 18 for guided tours. ♿

The weapons here range from prehistoric axes to 20th-century pistols. Medieval armour and an exhibit on the 1813 battle of Vitoria are also on display.

🏛 Museo de Arte Sacro

Catedral Nueva de María Inmaculada, Calle Monseñor Cadena y Eleta s/n. **Tel** 945 15 06 31. **Open** 10am–2pm, 4–6:30pm Tue–Fri, 10am–2pm Sat, 11am–2pm Sun & public hols. 📞 call ahead. ♿

The design of this museum is considerate to the surrounding cathedral. Exhibits of religious art are displayed in sections related to their medium.

❾ Torre Palacio de los Varona

Villanañe, Álava. **Tel** 945 35 30 40. **Open** 11am–2pm, 4–7pm Tue–Sat, 11am–2pm Sun (winter: Sat & Sun only). 🅿 📷

The small town of Villanañe hosts a beautiful example of medieval civil architecture, the best-preserved 14th-century fortified military building in the region – now a museum displaying original furniture. The upper rooms are decorated with colourful 17th-century wallpaper, while some of the floors are made with traditional Manisse porcelain tiles.

Environs

On the A2622 Pobes–Tuesta road are the Salinas de Añana, a group of saltpans fed by mineral springs. The nearby village of Tuesta boasts a Romanesque church. Inside are capitals carved with historical scenes, and a medieval wood sculpture of St Sebastián.

❿ Laguardia

Álava. 🏘 1,500. 🛈 Calle Mayor 52, 945 60 08 45. 🗓 Tue. 🎉 San Juan and San Pedro (23–29 Jun).

This little wine town is the capital of La Rioja Alavesa, a part of southern Álava province where Rioja wines (see pp82–3) have been produced for centuries. It is a fertile, vine-clad plain, sheltered by high hills to the north. There are fine panoramic views from the road that climbs up to the Herrera pass. Laguardia is a medieval hill town, its encircling ramparts, towers and fortified gateways visible from afar. Along its steep, narrow cobbled streets there are many bodegas (wine cellars), offering wine tastings and tours throughout the year. It is usually necessary to make a booking in advance. The Gothic Iglesia de Santa María de los Reyes has an austere façade and a richly embellished inner portal that has retained its original colouring.

Vineyards near Laguardia, capital of La Rioja Alavesa, a wine-producing region since the Middle Ages

⓫ Haro

La Rioja. 🚆 11,300. 🚌 🚏 ℹ️ Plaza de la Paz, 941 30 35 80. 🛒 Tue & Sat. 🎉 Wine Battle (29 Jun), San Juan, San Felices, San Pedro (24–29 Jun), Virgen de la Vega (8 Sep).
🌐 haroturismo.org

A graceful town on the Río Ebro, Haro has a lively old quarter with wine taverns and mansions. It is crowned by the hilltop Iglesia de Santo Tomás, a Gothic church with a Plateresque *(see p29)* portal.

Haro is the centre for the vineyards and bodegas of the Rioja Alta wine region, which is higher and cooler than the Rioja Baja *(see pp82–3)*. The clay soil and the climate – Haro is sheltered by a sierra to the north – create the conditions in which the famous regional wines are produced. Many bodegas run tours and tastings. To join one, you need to book ahead at the bodega. There may be a small charge. The charming cafés in the Old Town offer local wines and tapas at low prices and a convivial atmosphere.

A wine-throwing orgy is the climax of the area's fiesta *(see p136)* held every June.

Tomb of St Dominic in the cathedral of Santo Domingo de la Calzada

Rows of Rioja vines on the rolling hills near Haro

⓬ Santo Domingo de la Calzada

La Rioja. 🚆 6,300. 🚌 ℹ️ Calle Mayor 33, 941 34 12 38. 🛒 Sat. 🎉 Fiestas del Santo (25 Apr–15 May), Día del Patron (12 May).

This town on the Road to Santiago de Compostela *(see pp86–7)* is named after the 11th-century saint who built bridges and roads *(calzadas)* to help pilgrims. Santo Domingo also founded a hospital, which now serves as a parador *(see p564)*. Miracles performed by the saint are recorded in carvings on his tomb in the town's part-Romanesque, part-Gothic cathedral, and in paintings on the wall of the choir. The most obvious and bizarre record is a sumptuously decorated cage set in a wall in which, for centuries, a live cock and hen have been kept. The cathedral has a carved walnut reredos at the high altar, the last work, in 1541, of the artist Damià Forment. The restored 14th-century ramparts of the town are also worth seeing.

The Cock and Hen of St Dominic

A live cock and hen are kept in the cathedral of Santo Domingo de la Calzada as a tribute to the saint's miraculous life-giving powers. Centuries ago, it is said, a German pilgrim refused the advances of a local girl, who denounced him as a thief. He was hanged as a consequence, but later his parents found him alive on the gallows. They rushed to a judge, who said, dismissively, "Nonsense, he's no more alive than this roast chicken on my plate". Whereupon, the chicken stood up on the plate and crowed.

The cock and hen in their decorated cage

⓭ San Millán de la Cogolla

La Rioja. 🚗 240. 🚌 from Logroño. ℹ Monasterio de Yuso (open Tue–Sun), Portería de Yuso, Piso de Abajo, 941 37 30 49; Monasterio de Suso, 941 37 30 82 (book ahead). 🅿 compulsory. 🎉 Traslación de las Reliquias (26 Sep), San Millán (12 Nov). 🌐 **monasteriodeyuso.org**

This village grew up around two monasteries. On a hillside above the village is the Monasterio de San Millán de Suso. It was built in the 10th century on the site of a community founded by St Emilian, a shepherd hermit, in 537. The church, hollowed out of pink sandstone, has Romanesque and Mozarabic features. It contains the carved alabaster tomb of St Emiliano.

Below it is the Monasterio de San Millán de Yuso, built between the 16th and 18th centuries. The part-Renaissance church has Baroque golden doors and a Rococo sacristy with 17th-century paintings.

In the treasury there is a collection of ivory plaques. They were once part of two 11th-century jewelled reliquaries, which were plundered by French troops in 1813.

Medieval manuscripts are also displayed in the treasury. Among them is a facsimile of one of the earliest known texts in Castilian Romance (see p38). It is a commentary by a 10th-century Suso monk on a work by San Cesáreo de Arles, the *Glosas Emilianenses*.

The Monasterio de San Millán de Yuso in the Cárdenas Valley

Cloister of the Monasterio de Santa María la Real, Nájera

⓮ Nájera

La Rioja. 🚗 8,140. 🚉 ℹ Plaza de San Miguel 10, 941 36 00 41. 🔄 Thu. 🎉 San Prudencio (28 Apr), Santa María la Real (16–19 Sep).

The Old Town of Nájera, west of Logroño, was the capital of La Rioja and Navarra until 1076, when La Rioja was incorporated into Castile. The royal families of Navarra, León and Castile are buried in the **Monasterio de Santa María la Real**. It was founded in the 11th century beside a sandstone cliff where a statue of the Virgin was found in a cave. A 13th-century Madonna can be seen in the cave, beneath the carved choir stalls of the 15th-century church.

The carved tomb of Blanca of Navarra, wife of Sancho III, is the finest of many royal sarcophagi.

🏛 Monasterio de Santa María la Real

Plaza Santa María 1, Nájera. **Tel** 941 36 10 83. **Open** Tue–Sun. 🌐 **santamarialareal.net** 🅿

⓯ Logroño

La Rioja. 🚗 151,000. 🚉 🚌 ℹ Escuelas Trevijano, C/ Portales 50, 941 29 12 60. 🎉 San Bernabé (11 Jun), San Mateo (21 Sep). 🌐 **lariojaturismo.com**

The capital of La Rioja is a tidy, modern city of wide boulevards and smart shops. It is the commercial centre of a fertile plain where quality vegetables are produced, in addition to Rioja wines. In Logroño's pleasant old quarter on the Río Ebro is the Gothic cathedral, with twin towers. Above the south portal of the nearby Iglesia de Santiago el Real, which houses an image of the patron saint Our Lady of Hope, is an equestrian statue of St James as Moorslayer (see p59).

Environs

About 50 km (30 miles) south of Logroño, the N111 winds through the dramatic Iregua Valley, through tunnels, to the Sierra de Cameros.

The ornate Baroque west door of Logroño Cathedral

⓰ Enciso

La Rioja. 🚗 100. 🚌 from Logroño. ℹ Plaza Mayor, 941 39 60 05. 🎉 San Roque (16 Aug).

Near this remote hill village west of Calahorra is Spain's "Jurassic Park". Signposts point to the *huellas de dinosaurios* (dinosaur footprints). Embedded in rocks overhanging a stream are the prints of many giant, three-toed feet, up to 30 cm (1 ft) long. They were made around 150 million years ago, when dinosaurs moved between the marshes of the Ebro Valley, at that time a sea, and these hills. Prints can also be seen at other locations in the area.

Environs

Arnedillo, 10 km (6 miles) to the north, is a spa with thermal baths once used by Fernando VI. In Autol, to the east, there are two unusual limestone peaks.

The intricately carved portal of Tudela Cathedral

⑰ Tudela

Navarra. 🗺 35,200. 🚊 🚌 ℹ Plaza Fueros 5, 948 84 80 58. 🛒 Sat. 🎉 Santa Ana (26–30 Jul).

Navarra's second city is the great commercial centre of the vast agricultural lands of the Ebro Valley in Navarra, the Ribera. Much of Tudela consists of modern developments, but its origins are ancient. Spanning the Ebro is a 13th-century bridge with 17 irregular arches. The Old Town has two well-preserved Jewish districts.

The Plaza de los Fueros is old Tudela's main square. It is surrounded by houses with wrought-iron balconies. On some of their façades are paintings of bullfights, a reminder that the plaza was formerly used as a bullring.

The cathedral, begun in 1194, exemplifies the religious toleration under which Tudela was governed after the Reconquest.

It is Early Gothic, with a carved portal depicting the Last Judgment. There is a Romanesque cloister, and beside the cathedral sits a 9th-century chapel that is thought to have once been a synagogue.

Environs
To the north is the Bárdenas Reales, an arid area of limestone cliffs and crags. About 20 km (12 miles) west of Tudela is the spa town of Fitero, with the 12th-century Monasterio de Santa María.

⑱ Monasterio de La Oliva

Carcastillo, Navarra. **Tel** 948 72 50 06. 🚌 from Pamplona. **Open** daily. 🎟 **W** monasteriodelaoliva.org

French Cistercian monks built this small monastery on a remote plain in the 1100s. The church is simple but adorned with rose windows.

One of the cloisters in the Monasterio de La Oliva

The serene cloister, dating from the 14th and 15th centuries, adjoins a 12th-century chapter-house. The church also has a 17th-century tower. Today, the monks survive by selling local honey and cheese, their own wine, and by accepting paying guests (see p561).

⑲ Ujué

Navarra. 🗺 178. ℹ Plaza Municipal, 948 73 90 23. 🎉 Virgen de Ujué (Sun after 25 April). **W** ujue.info

An unspoiled hill village, Ujué commands a high spur at the end of a winding road. It has quaint façades, cobbled alleys and steep steps. The impressive and austere Iglesia de Santa María is in Gothic style, with a Romanesque chancel and an exterior lookout gallery. The ruined fortifications around the church offer views of the Pyrenees.

On the Sunday after 25 April, pilgrims in black capes visit the Virgin of Ujué, whose Romanesque image is displayed in the church.

⑳ Olite

Navarra. 🗺 3,900. 🚊 🚌 ℹ Plaza de Teobaldos 4, 948 74 17 03. 🛒 Wed. 🎉 Medieval Markets (late Aug), Exaltación de la Santa Cruz (13–19 Sep). **W** olite.es

The historic town of Olite was founded by the Romans and later chosen as a royal residence by the kings of Navarra. Parts of the town's old walls can be seen. They enclose a delightful

---

The Kingdom of Navarra

Navarra emerged as an independent Christian kingdom in the 10th century, after Sancho I Garcés became king of Pamplona. Sancho III the Great expanded the kingdom, and at his death, in 1035, Navarra stretched all the way from Ribagorza in Aragón to Valladolid. Sancho VI the Wise, who reigned 1150–94, recognized the independent rights (fueros) of many towns. In 1234, Navarra passed by marriage to a line of French rulers. One, Carlos III, the Noble, built Olite Castle. His grandson, Carlos de Viana, wrote *The Chronicle of the Kings of Navarra* in 1455. In 1512 Navarra was annexed by Fernando II of Castile, as part of united Spain, but it kept its own laws and currency until the 1800s.

Prince Carlos de Viana, Carlos III's grandson

jumble of steep, narrow streets and little squares, churches and the Monasterio de Santa Clara, begun in the 13th century. The houses along the Rúa Cerco de Fuera and the Rúa Mayor were built between the 16th and 18th centuries.

The castle, the **Palacio Real de Olite**, was built in the early 15th century by Carlos III, and has earned Olite its nickname "the Gothic town". It was heavily fortified, but was brilliantly decorated inside by Mudéjar artists with *azulejos* (ceramic tiles) and marquetry ceilings. The walkways were planted with vines and orange trees, and there was an aviary and a lions' den.

During the War of Independence *(see pp66–7)* the castle was burned to prevent it falling into French hands. Since 1937, however, it has been restored to a semblance of its former glory. Part of it houses a parador *(see p564)*.

Today, the castle is a complex of courtyards, passages, large halls, royal chambers, battlements and turrets. From the "windy tower", monarchs could watch tournaments.

Adjoining the castle is a 13th-century former royal chapel, the Iglesia de Santa María, with its richly carved Gothic portal.

Olite is in the Navarra wine region *(see pp82–3)* and the town has several bodegas.

🏛 **Palacio Real de Olite**
Plaza de Carlos III. **Tel** 948 74 00 35.
Open daily. 📷 🔲

The battlements and towers of the Palacio Real de Olite

The five-arched, medieval pilgrims' bridge at Puente la Reina

㉑ Puente la Reina

Navarra. 🏘 2,800. 🛈 Puente de los Peregrinos 1, 948 34 13 01 (closed Jan & Feb). 🚌 Sat 🎉 Santiago (24–30 Jul).

Few towns along the Road to Santiago de Compostela *(see pp86–7)* evoke the past as vividly as Puente la Reina. The town takes its name from the graceful, humpbacked pedestrian bridge over the Río Arga. The bridge was built for pilgrims during the 11th century by royal command.

On Puente la Reina's narrow main street is the Iglesia de Santiago, which has a gilded statue by the west door showing the saint as a pilgrim. On the edge of town is the Iglesia del Crucifijo, another pilgrim church which was built in the 12th century by the Knights Templar. Contained within the church is a Y-shaped wooden crucifix of a

Distinctive crucifix in Puente la Reina

sorrowful Christ with arms upraised, which is said to have been a gift from a German pilgrim in the 14th century.

Environs
Isolated in the fields about 5 km (3 miles) to the east is the 12th-century Iglesia de Santa María de Eunate. This octagonal Romanesque church may once have been a cemetery church for pilgrims, as human bones have been unearthed here. Pilgrims would shelter beneath the church's external arcade. West of Puente la Reina is the showpiece hill village of Cirauqui. It is also charming, if rather over-restored. Chic little balconied houses line tortuously twisting alleys linked by steps. The Iglesia de San Román, built in the 13th century on top of the hill, has a sculpted west door.

Basque Country, Navarra and La Rioja's Fiestas

Los Sanfermines *(6–14 Jul)*, Pamplona (Navarra). In the famous *encierro* (bullrunning) six bulls are released at 8am each morning to run from their corral through the narrow, cobbled streets of the Old Town. On the last night of this week-long, nonstop festival, crowds with candles sing Basque songs in the main square. The event gained worldwide fame after Ernest Hemingway described it in his novel, published in 1926, *The Sun Also Rises*.

Reveller pouring wine over himself at Haro's Wine Battle

Wine Battle *(29 Jun)*, Haro (La Rioja). People dressed in white clothes squirt each other with wine from leather drinking bottles in the capital of the Rioja Alta wine region.

Danza de los Zancos *(22 Jul and last Sat of Sep)*, Anguiano (La Rioja). Dancers on stilts, wearing ornate waistcoats and yellow skirts, hurtle down the stepped alley from the church to the main square.

La Virgen Blanca *(5 Aug)*, Vitoria (Álava). A dummy holding an umbrella (the *celedón*) is lowered from San Miguel church to a house below – from which a man in similar dress emerges. The mayor fires a rocket and the crowds in the square light cigars.

Pilgrims drinking from the wine tap near the monastery at Irache

㉒ Estella

Navarra. 🖽 13,600. 🚌 ℹ️ Calle de San Nicolás 1, 948 55 63 01. 🛍 Thu. 🎎 San Andrés (first week in Aug). 🌐 turismo.navarra.es

In the Middle Ages Estella (Lizarra) was the centre of the royal court of Navarra and a major stopping point on the pilgrims' Road to Santiago de Compostela *(see pp86–7)*. The town was a stronghold of the Carlists *(see p67)* in the 19th century. A memorial rally is held here on the first Sunday of May every year.

The most important monuments in Estella are sited on the edge of town, across the bridge over the Río Ega. Steps climb steeply from the arcaded Plaza de San Martín to the remarkable Iglesia de San Pedro de la Rúa, built on top of a cliff from the 12th to 14th century. It features a Cistercian Mudéjar-influenced, sculpted doorway. The carved capitals are all that now remain of the Romanesque cloister, which was destroyed when a castle overlooking the church was blown up in 1592. The Palacio de los Reyes de Navarra (now a museum), on the other side of the Plaza de San Martín, is a rare example of civil Romanesque architecture.

In the town centre, on Plaza de los Fueros, Iglesia de San Juan Bautista has a Romanesque porch. The north portal of the Iglesia de San Miguel has Romanesque carvings of St Michael slaying a dragon.

Environs

The Monasterio de Nuestra Señora de Irache, 3 km (2 miles) southwest of Estella, was a Benedictine monastery which sheltered pilgrims on their way to Santiago. The church is mainly Transitional Gothic in style, but it has Romanesque apses and a cloister in Plateresque style. It is capped by a remarkable dome.

A bodega next to the monastery provides pilgrims with wine from a tap in a wall.

A small road branches off the NA120 north of Estella and leads to the Monasterio de Iranzu, built in the 12th–14th century. The austerity of its church and cloisters is typically Cistercian.

The Lizarraga Pass, further up the NA120, offers views of attractive beech woods.

㉓ Pamplona

Navarra. 🖽 195,600. ✈️ 🚆 🚌 ℹ️ Calle San Saturnino 2, 948 42 07 00. 🎎 Sanfermines (6–14 Jul), San Saturnino (29 Nov). 🌐 turismodepamplona.es

The old fortress city of Pamplona (Iruña) is said to have been founded by the Roman general Pompey. In the 9th century it became the capital of Navarra. This fairly busy city explodes into even more life in July during the fiesta of Los Sanfermines, with its daredevil bullrunning.

From the old city walls *(murallas)* you can get a good overview of Pamplona. The nearby cathedral, which is built in ochre-coloured stone, looks down on a

Stone tracery in the elegant cloister of Pamplona cathedral

The impressive Neo-Classical façade of the Palacio del Gobierno de Navarra

loop in the Río Arga. It was built on the foundations of its 12th-century predecessor, and is mainly Gothic in style, with twin towers and an 18th-century façade. Inside there are lovely choir stalls and the alabaster tomb of Carlos III and Queen Leonor.

The southern entrance to the cloister is the carved, medieval Puerta de la Preciosa. The cathedral priests would gather here to sing an antiphon (hymn) to La Preciosa (Precious Virgin) before the night service.

The Museo Diocesano in the cathedral's 14th-century kitchen and refectory displays Gothic altarpieces, polychrome wood statues from all over Navarra, and a French 13th-century reliquary of the Holy Sepulchre.

West of the cathedral is the Old Town, cut through with many alleys. The Neo-Classical **Palacio del Gobierno de Navarra** lies in the Plaza del Castillo and is the seat of the Navarrese government (not open to the public). Outside, a statue of 1903 shows a symbolic woman upholding the *fueros* (historic laws) of Navarra (see p134). North of the palace is the medieval Iglesia de San

Sculpture in Pamplona depicting the *encierro*

Saturnino, built on the site where St Saturninus is said to have baptized some 40,000 pagan townspeople, and the Baroque town hall (*ayuntamiento*).

Beneath the old town wall, in a 16th-century hospital with a Plateresque doorway, is the **Museo de Navarra**. This is a museum of regional archaeology, history and art. Exhibits include Roman mosaics and an 11th-century, Islam-inspired ivory casket. There are murals painted during the 14th–16th centuries, a portrait by Goya, and a collection of paintings by Basque artists.

To the southeast is the city's massive 16th-century citadel, erected in Felipe II's reign. It is designed with five bastions in a star shape. Beyond it are the spacious boulevards of the new town, and also the university's green campus.

🏛 **Palacio de Navarra**
Avenida Carlos III 2.
Tel 848 42 71 27. **Open** by appointment. ♿

🏛 **Museo de Navarra**
Cuesta de Santo Domingo s/n.
Tel 848 42 64 92.
Open Tue–Sun. 📷 ♿

Pamplona City Centre

① Museo de Navarra
② City walls
③ Cathedral
④ Town Hall
⑤ Iglesia de San Saturnino
⑥ Palacio de Navarra

Key
▬ Bullrunning route

Basque houses in the picturesque town of Etxalar, Valle de Bidasoa

㉔ Las Cinco Villas del Valle de Bidasoa

Navarra. 🚌 Pamplona, San Sebastián. **ⅈ** 948 63 12 22 (Easter week & summer; 948 59 23 86 rest of year). **Ⓦ** turismo.navarra.es; **Ⓦ** baztan-bidasoa.com

Five attractive Basque towns lie in or near this valley, the most northerly being Bera (Vera). The

houses in Lesaka have wooden balconies under deep eaves. The road south passes hills dotted with white farmsteads to reach Igantzi, (Yanci), with its red-and-white houses. Arantza is the most remote town. Since the 12th century, pigeons have been caught in huge nets strung across a pass above Etxalar (Echalar). At the summit of La Rhune on the French border is a great view of the Pyrenees.

㉕ Elizondo

Navarra. 🚹 7,700. 🚌 **ⅈ** Palacio de Arizkunenea, 948 58 12 79 (closed winter). 🛒 Thu. 🎉 Santiago (25 Jul). **Ⓦ** baztan.eus

This is the biggest of a string of typical Basque villages in the very beautiful valley of Baztán. By the river are noble houses bearing coats of arms.

Arizkun, further up the valley, has old fortified houses and a 17th-century convent. The Cueva de Brujas, in Zugarramurdi, was once a meeting place for witches.

The forested countryside around Roncesvalles

Canopy over the Virgin and Child in the Colegiata Real, Roncesvalles

㉖ Roncesvalles

Navarra. 🚹 34. **ⅈ** Antiguo Molino s/n, 948 76 03 01. 🎉 Día de la Virgen de Roncesvalles (8 Sep). **Ⓦ** roncesvalles.es

Roncesvalles (Orreaga), on the Spanish side of a pass through the Pyrenees, is a major halt on the Road to Santiago (see pp86–7). Before it became associated with the pilgrim's way, Roncesvalles was the site of a major battle in 778, in which the Basques of Navarra slaughtered the rearguard of Charlemagne's army as it marched homeward. This event is described in the 12th-century French epic poem The Song of Roland.

The 13th-century Colegiata Real, which has served travellers down the centuries, has a silver-plated Virgin and Child below a high canopy. In the graceful chapterhouse, off the cloister, is the white tomb of Sancho VII the Strong (1170–1234), looked down upon by a stained-glass window of his great victory, the battle of Las Navas de Tolosa (see pp58–9). Exhibits in the church museum include "Charlemagne's chessboard", an enamelled reliquary which is so called because of its chequered design.

㉗ Valle de Roncal

Navarra. 🚌 from Pamplona. **ⅈ** Paseo Julian Gayarre s/n, Roncal, 948 47 52 56; Isaba, 948 89 32 51. **Ⓦ** vallederoncal.es

Running perpendicular to the Pyrenees, this valley is still largely reliant on sheep, and the village of Roncal is known for its cheeses. Because of the valley's relative isolation, the inhabitants have preserved their own identity, and local costumes are worn during fiestas. The ski resort of Isaba, further up the valley, has a museum of local history and life. A spectacular road winds from Isaba to the tree-lined village of Ochagavia in the parallel Valle de Salazar. To the north, the Selva de Irati, one of Europe's largest woodlands, spreads over the Pyrenees into France, below snowy Monte Ori at 2,017 m (6,617 ft).

Colourful balconies of houses in the village of Roncal

❷❽ Monasterio de Leyre

Yesa, Navarra. **Tel** 948 88 41 50. 🚍 Yesa. **Open** daily. Chants: 7:30am, 9am, 7pm and 9:10pm daily. **Closed** 1 & 6 Jan, 25 Dec. 🅿 🌐 **monasteriodeleyre.com**

The monastery of San Salvador de Leyre is situated high above a reservoir, alone amid grand scenery, backed by limestone cliffs. The abbey has been here since the 11th century, when it was a great spiritual and political centre. Sancho III and his successors made it the royal pantheon of Navarra. The monastery began to decline in the 12th century. It was abandoned from 1836 until 1954, when it was restored by the Benedictines, who turned part of it into a hotel. To see the monastery, you must join one of the tours run every morning and afternoon.

The big 11th-century church has a Gothic vault and three lofty apses. On its west portal are weather-worn carvings of strange beasts, as well as biblical figures. The Romanesque crypt has unusually short columns with chunky capitals. The monks' Gregorian chant *(see p380)* during services is wonderful to hear.

❷❾ Castillo de Javier

Javier, Navarra. **Tel** 948 88 40 24. 🚍 from Pamplona. **Open** daily. 🌐 **santuariojaviersj.org**

St Francis Xavier, the patron saint of Navarra, a missionary and a priest of the Jesuit order *(see p128)*, was born in this 13th-century castle in 1506. It has since been restored and is now a Jesuit spiritual centre. Of interest are the saint's bedroom and a museum in the keep devoted to his life. In the oratory is a 13th-century polychrome Christ on the cross and a macabre 15th-century mural of grinning skeletons entitled *The Dance of Death*.

Crucifix in the oratory of the Castillo de Javier

❸⓪ Sangüesa

Navarra. 🅰 5,000. 🚍 🛈 Calle Mayor 2, 948 87 14 11 (closed Mon in winter). 🗓 Fri. 🎉 San Sebastián (11 Sep). 🌐 **sanguesa.es**

Since medieval times this small town beside a bridge over the Río Aragón has been a stop on the Aragonese pilgrimage route to Santiago *(see pp86–7)*.

The richly sculpted south portal of the Iglesia de Santa María la Real is a 12th- and 13th-century treasure of Romanesque art *(see p28)*. It has many figures and details depicting the Last Judgment and society in the 13th century.

The Gothic Iglesia de Santiago and the 12th- to 13th-century Gothic Iglesia de San Francisco are also worth seeing. On the main street the 16th-century town hall *(ayuntamiento)* and the square beside it stand on sites that were once part of the medieval palace of the Prince of Viana and a residence of the kings of Navarra. The library beside the square is housed in what remains of the palace and is open to the public.

Environs

To the north of Sangüesa there are two deep, narrow gorges. The most impressive is the Hoz de Arbayún, whose limestone cliffs are inhabited by colonies of vultures. It is best seen from the NA178 north of Domeño. The Hoz de Lumbier can be seen from a point on the A21.

The roughly carved columns in the crypt of the Monasterio de Leyre

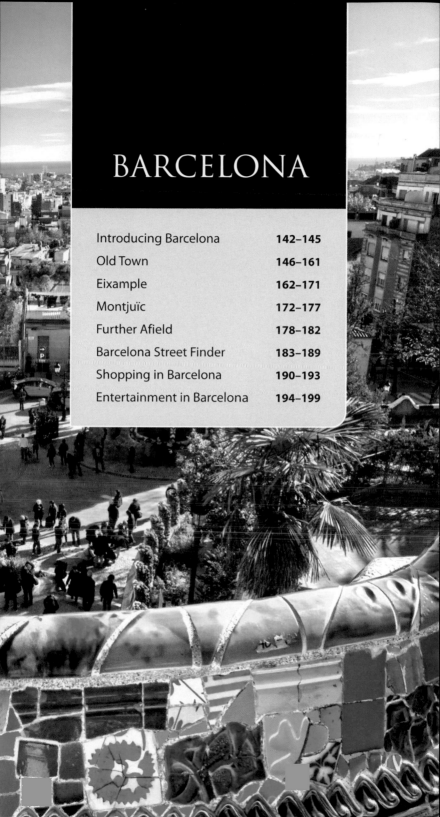

BARCELONA

Introducing Barcelona

Fringed by beaches and encircled by hills, the capital of
Catalonia is Spain's most dynamic and stylish city, and one
of the Mediterranean's busiest ports. In culture, commerce
and sport, Barcelona not only rivals Madrid, but it is itself on
a par with the greatest European cities, as confirmed by
the success of the Olympic Games in 1992. Although there
are plenty of historical monuments in the Old Town (Ciutat
Vella), Barcelona is best known for the scores of buildings in
the Eixample left by the artistic explosion of Modernisme
(see pp144–5) in the decades around 1900. Always open to
outside influences because of its location on the coast, not far
from the French border, Barcelona continues to sizzle with
creativity: its bars and the public parks speak
more of bold contemporary
design than of tradition.

Casa Milà *(see p169)*, also known
as La Pedrera, is the most avant-
garde of all the works of Antoni
Gaudí *(see p168)*. Barcelona has
more Art Nouveau buildings than
any other city in the world.

0 kilometres		1
0 miles	0.5	

Palau Nacional *(see p176)*, on the hill of
Montjuïc, dominates the fountain-filled
avenue built for the 1929 International
Exhibition. It now houses the Museu
Nacional d'Art de Catalunya, which covers
1,000 years of Catalan art and includes a
splendid Romanesque section.

La Rambla

AVINGUDA DEL PARAL·LEL

MONTJUÏC
(see pp172–77)

RONDA DEL LITORAL

Christopher Columbus
surveys the waterfront
from the top of a
60-m (200-ft) column
(see p160) in the heart
of the Port Vell (Old
Port). From the top,
visitors can look out over
the promenades and quays
that revitalized the area.

Montjuïc Castle *(see p177)* is a massive fortification
dating from the 17th century. Sited on the crest of the
hill of Montjuïc, it offers panoramic views of the city and
port, and forms a sharp contrast to the ultramodern
sports halls built nearby for the 1992 Olympic Games.

◀ Entrance to Park Güell, Barcelona, with Gaudí's mosaic balcony in foreground

The Sagrada Família *(see pp170–71)*, Gaudí's unfinished masterpiece, begun in 1882, rises above the streets of the Eixample. Its polychromatic ceramic mosaics and sculptural forms inspired by nature are typical of his work.

Casa Mila

DIAGONAL

EIXAMPLE
(see pp162–71)

PASSEIG DE SANT JOAN

PASSEIG DE GRACIA

VIA LAIETANA

OLD TOWN
(see pp146–61)

RONDA DEL LITORAL

Barcelona Cathedral *(see pp152–3)* is a magnificent 14th-century building in the heart of the Barri Gòtic (Gothic Quarter). It has 28 side chapels, which encircle the nave and contain some splendid Baroque altarpieces. The keeping of white geese in the cloisters is a centuries-old tradition.

Parc de la Ciutadella *(see p158)*, between the Old Town and the Vila Olímpica, has something for everyone. The gardens full of statuary offer relaxation, the boating lake and the zoo are fun, while the museum within its gates covers natural history.

La Rambla *(see pp154–5)* is the most famous street in Spain, alive at all hours of the day and night. A stroll down its length to the seafront, taking in its palatial buildings, shops, cafés and street vendors, makes a perfect introduction to Barcelona life.

Gaudí and Modernisme

Towards the end of the 19th century a new style of art and architecture, Modernisme, a variant of Art Nouveau, was born in Barcelona. It became a means of expression for Catalan nationalism and counted Josep Puig i Cadafalch, Lluís Domènech i Montaner and, above all, Antoni Gaudí i Cornet *(see p168)* among its major exponents. Barcelona's Eixample district *(see pp162–71)* is full of the highly original buildings that they created for their wealthy clients.

All aspects of decoration in a Modernista building, even interior design, were planned by the architect. This door and its tiled surround are in Gaudí's 1906 Casa Batlló *(see p168)*.

A dramatic cupola covers the central salon, which rises through three floors. It is pierced by small round holes, inspired by Islamic architecture, giving the illusion of stars.

Upper galleries are richly decorated with carved wood and cofferwork.

The spiral carriage ramp is an early sign of Gaudí's predilection for curved lines. He would later exploit this to the full in the wavy façade of his masterpiece, the Casa Milà (La Pedrera) *(see p169)*.

1859 Civil engineer Ildefons Cerdà i Sunyer submits proposals for expansion of Barcelona	**1900** Josep Puig i Cadafalch builds Casa Amatller *(see p168)*	**1903** Lluís Domènech i Montaner builds Hospital de la Santa Creu i de Sant Pau *(see p169)*
	1878 Gaudí graduates as an architect	*Hospital detail*

1850	1865	1880	1895	1910	1925

1883 Gaudí takes over design of Neo-Gothic Sagrada Família *(see pp170–71)*	**1888** Barcelona Universal Exhibition gives impetus to Modernisme	**1912** Casa Milà completed
Detail of Sagrada Família		**1926** Gaudí dies
		1905 Domènech i Montaner builds Casa Lleó Morera *(see p168)*. Puig i Cadafalch builds Casa Terrades *(see p169)*

izarrely decorated chimneys became one of the trademarks of Gaudí's later work. They reach a fantastic extreme on he gleaming, humpbacked roof of the Casa Batlló.

Elaborate wrought-iron lamps light the grand hall.

Ceramic tiles decorate the chimneys.

Gaudí's Materials

Gaudí designed, or collaborated on designs, for almost every known medium. He combined bare, undecorated materials – wood, roughhewn stone, rubble and brickwork – with meticulous craftwork in wrought iron and stained glass. Mosaics of ceramic tiles were used to cover his fluid, uneven forms.

Stained glass, Sagrada Família *(see pp170–71)*

Mosaic of ceramic tiles, Park Güell *(see p182)*

Detail of iron gate, Casa Vicens *(see p168)*

Ceramic tiles on El Capricho *(see p115)*

Parabolic arches, used extensively by Gaudí, show his interest in Gothic architecture *(see p28)*. These arches form a corridor in his 1890 Col·legi de les Teresianes, a convent school in the west of Barcelona.

Escutcheon alludes to the Catalan coat of arms.

Palau Güell (1889)

Gaudí's first major building in the centre of the city *(see p155)* established his international reputation for outstandingly original architecture. Built for his lifelong patron, the industrialist Eusebi Güell, the mansion stands on a small plot of land in a narrow street, making the façade difficult to view. Inside, Gaudí creates a sense of space by using carved screens, galleries and recesses. His unique furniture is also on display.

Organic forms inspired the wrought iron around the gates to the palace. Gaudí's later work teems with wildlife, such as this dragon, covered with brightly coloured tiles, which guards the steps in the Park Güell.

OLD TOWN

The Old Town, traversed by the city's most famous avenue, La Rambla, is one of the most extensive medieval city centres in Europe. The Barri Gòtic contains the cathedral and a maze of streets and squares. Across from the Via Laietana, the El Born neighbourhood is dominated by the Santa Maria del Mar church and is replete with 14th-century mansions. This area is bounded by the leafy Parc de la Ciutadella, home to the city's zoo. The revitalized seafront is a stimulating mix of old and new. Trendy shops and restaurants make up the fashionable marina, contrasted with the old maritime neighbourhood of Barceloneta and the modern Olympic port.

Sights at a Glance

Museums and Galleries
2 Museu Frederic Marès
4 MUHBA El Call
9 Museu d'Art Contemporani
14 Museu Picasso
18 Museu de la Xocolata
21 Castell dels Tres Dragons
22 Museu Martorell
29 Museu Marítim and Drassanes

Streets and Districts
8 El Raval
10 La Rambla
13 El Born
16 Carrer Montcada
25 Barceloneta

Harbour Sights
24 Port Olímpic
26 Port Vell
28 Golondrinas

Churches
7 Cathedral (pp152–3)
15 Basílica de Santa Maria del Mar

Historic Buildings
1 Casa de l'Ardiaca
3 Conjunt Monumental de la Plaça del Rei
5 Ajuntament
6 Palau de la Generalitat
11 Palau de la Música Catalana
12 La Llotja
17 El Born Centre de Cultura i Memòria

Monuments
19 Arc del Triomf
27 Monument a Colom

Parks and Gardens
20 Parc de la Ciutadella
23 Zoo de Barcelona

See also Barcelona Street Finder maps 2, 5, 6

◀ The glorious, Gothic interior of Barcelona Cathedral

For keys to symbols see back flap

Street-by-Street: Barri Gòtic

The Barri Gòtic (Gothic Quarter) is the true heart of
Barcelona. The oldest part of the city, it was the site chosen
by the Romans in the reign of Augustus (27 BC–AD 14) on
which to found a new *colonia* (town), and has been the
location of the city's administrative buildings ever since.
The Roman forum was on the Plaça de Sant Jaume, where
now stand the medieval Palau de la Generalitat, Catalonia's
parliament, and the Casa de la Ciutat, Barcelona's town
hall. Close by are the Gothic cathedral and royal
palace, where Columbus was received by
Fernando and Isabel on his return from his
voyage to the New World in 1492 *(see p61)*.

❶ Casa de l'Ardiaca
Built on the Roman city wall,
the Gothic-Renaissance archdeacon's residence now houses
Barcelona's historical archives.

To Plaça de Catalunya

SANT SEVER

❼ ★ Cathedral
The façade and spire
are 19th-century
additions to the
original Gothic
building. Among
the artistic treasures
inside are medieval
Catalan paintings.

SANT DOMÈNEC DEL CALL

CARRER DEL BISBE

SANT HONORAT

**❻ Palau de la
Generalitat**
The seat of
Catalonia's governor
has superb Gothic
features, which
include the chapel
and a stone staircase
rising to an open-air,
arcaded gallery.

CARRER DE FERRAN

PLAÇA DE
SANT
JAUME

To La Rambla

DE LA CIUTAT

❺ Ajuntament
Barcelona's town hall was built in the 14th and
15th centuries. The façade is a Neo-Classical addition.
In the entrance hall stands *Three Gypsy Boys* by Joan
Rebull (1899–1981), a 1976 copy of a sculpture he
originally created in 1946.

CARRER

❷ Museu Frederic Marès
This medieval doorway is from an extensive display of Spanish sculpture – the mainstay of this museum's extraordinarily eclectic and high-quality collections.

Roman city wall

Locator Map
See Barcelona Street Finder map 5

Saló del Tinell

❸ ★ Palau Reial
The 14th-century Capella Reial de Santa Àgata, with a 1466 altarpiece, is one of the best surviving sections of the palace.

Capella Reial de Santa Àgata

Plaça del Rei

Palau del Lloctinent

Cereria Subirà candle shop

TAPINERIA

CARRER DELS COMTES DE BARCELONA

CARRER DE JAUME I

VIA LAIETANA

M Jaume I Metro

CARRER DAGUERTA

SOTS-TINENT NAVARRA

The MUHBA (Museu d'Història de Barcelona) features the world's most extensive subterranean Roman ruins. Accessed through this 14th-century mansion, visitors can view the streets and squares of Roman Barcelona. The ruins extend underground, through to the exit at the Palau Reial.

0 metres   100
0 yards   100

The Centre Excursionista de Catalunya displays in its entrance courtyard Roman columns from the Temple of Augustus, whose site is marked by a millstone in the street outside.

Key

— Suggested route

For keys to symbols *see back flap*

Decorated marble letterbox, Casa de l'Ardiaca

❶ Casa de l'Ardiaca

Carrer de Santa Llúcia 1. **Map** 5 B2.
Tel 93 256 22 55. 🚇 Jaume I. **Open**
9am–8:45pm Mon–Fri (to 7:30pm
Jul–Sep), 9am–1pm Sat. **Closed** Sat
Jul–Sep, public hols.
🌐 **barcelona.cat/
arxiuhistoric**

Standing beside what was
originally the Bishop's
Gate, the Archdeacon's
House was built in the
12th century. Its present
appearance dates from
around 1500 when it
was remodelled and
a colonnade added.
In 1870 this was
extended to form the
Flamboyant Gothic *(see
p28)* patio around a fountain. The
Modernista architect Domènech
i Montaner (1850–1923) added
the marble letterbox, carved with
three swallows and a tortoise,
beside the Renaissance portal.
Upstairs is the Arxiu Històric de la
Ciutat (City Archives). Visitors are
only allowed into the courtyard
and the entrance hall, which
occasionally hosts art exhibitions.

Virgin, Museu
Frederic Marès

❷ Museu Frederic Marès

Plaça de Sant Iu 5. **Map** 5 B2. **Tel** 93 256
35 00. 🚇 Jaume I. **Open** 10am–7pm
Tue–Sat, 11am–8pm Sun. 🈲 (free first
Sun of each month & every Sun from
3pm). 🈶 🈂 🌐 **w110.bcn.cat/
museufredericmares**

The sculptor Frederic Marès i
Deulovol (1893–1991) was also
a traveller and collector, and this
museum is a monument to his
eclectic taste. The building is part

of the Royal Palace complex and
was occupied by 13th-century
bishops, 14th-century counts
of Barcelona, 15th-century
judges and 18th-century
nuns, who lived here until
they were expelled in
1936. Marès, who had a
small apartment in the
building, opened this
museum in 1948. It has
a notable collection
of Romanesque and
Gothic religious art. On
the ground and first
floors there are stone
sculptures and two
complete Romanesque
portals. Exhibits on the
three floors above
range from clocks,
crucifixes, costumes, antique
cameras, pipes, tobacco jars
and postcards to an amusement room full of toys.

❸ MUHBA Plaça del Rei

Plaça del Rei. **Map** 5 B2. **Tel** 93 256
21 22. 🚇 Jaume I. **Open** 10am–7pm
Tue–Sat, 10am–8pm Sun. **Closed** 1
Jan, 1 May, 24 Jun, 25 Dec. 🈲 (free
first Sun of each month & every Sun
from 3pm.) 🈂 by appointment.
🌐 **museuhistoria.bcn.cat**

MUHBA Plaça del Rei refers to
the ensemble of buildings on
the square, including the Palau
Reial (Royal Palace), which was
the residence of the count-
kings of Barcelona from its
foundation in the 13th century,
and the royal chapel. It can be
visited as part of the Museu
d'Història de Barcelona. The
complex also includes the
14th-century Gothic Saló del
Tinell, a vast room with arches
spanning 17 m (56 ft). This is
where Isabel and Fernando
(see p74) received Columbus
on his return from America.
It is also where the Holy
Inquisition sat.

On the right, built into the
Roman city wall, is the royal
chapel, the Capella Reial de
Santa Àgata, with an altarpiece
(1466) by Jaume Huguet. Its
bell tower is formed by part
of a watchtower on the Roman
wall. Stairs on the right lead
to the 16th-century tower of
Martí the Humanist (who
reigned 1396–1410), the last
of Barcelona's count-kings.

Barcelona's Early Jewish Community

Hebrew tablet

From the 11th to the 13th centuries, Jews
dominated Barcelona's commerce and culture,
providing doctors and founding the first seat
of learning. But in 1243, 354 years after they
were first documented in the city, violent anti-
Semitism led to the Jews being consigned to a
ghetto, El Call. Ostensibly to provide protection,
the ghetto had only one entrance, which led into
the Plaça de Sant Jaume. Jews were heavily taxed by the monarch,
who viewed them as "royal serfs"; but in return they also received
privileges, as they handled most of Catalonia's lucrative trade with
North Africa. However, official and popular persecution finally led
to the disappearance of the ghetto in 1401, 91 years before Judaism
was fully outlawed in Spain *(see p61)*.

Originally there were three synagogues. The main one, Sinagoga
Mayor at No. 5 Carrer de Marlet, is said to be the oldest in Europe
and can be visited. A 14th-century Hebrew tablet that reads "Holy
Foundation of Rabbi Samuel Hassardi, His soul will rest in Heaven"
is embedded in the wall.

The main draw of the Museu d'Història is underground. Entire streets of old Barcino are accessible via a lift and walkways suspended over the ruins of Roman Barcelona. The site was found when the Casa Clariana-Padellàs, the Gothic building from which you enter, was moved here stone by stone in 1931. The water and drainage systems, baths, homes with mosaic floors and the old forum are among some of the world's most extensive and complete subterranean Roman ruins.

❹ MUHBA El Call

Placeta de Manuel Ribé s/n. **Map** 5 A2. **Tel** 93 256 21 22. Jaume I, Liceu. **Open** 11am–2pm Wed & Fri, 11am–7pm Sat & Sun. (free to under-16s, from 3pm Sun & all day on the 1st Sun of month). **museu historia.bcn.cat/es/muhba-el-call**

Part of the Barcelona History Museum, this information centre occupies a modern building constructed over what was once the medieval home of Yusef Bonhiac, a Jewish weaver. The touch-screen information panels and exhibitions give an excellent overview of the Call (the former Jewish quarter) and the lives of its inhabitants.

❺ Ajuntament

Plaça de Sant Jaume 1. **Map** 5 A2. **Tel** 934 02 70 00. Jaume I, Liceu. **Open** 10am–1:30pm Sun & public hols; 10am–8pm 2nd Sat in Feb, 23 Apr & 30 May, or by appt (934 02 70 00). 10am in English. **bcn.cat**

The magnificent 14th-century city hall faces the Palau de la Generalitat. Flanking the entrance are statues of Jaime (Jaume) I, who granted the city rights to elect councillors in 1249, and Joan Fiveller, who levied taxes on court members in the 1500s.

Inside is the huge council chamber, the 14th-century Saló de Cent, built for the city's 100 councillors. The Saló de les Cròniques, on the first floor, was commissioned for the 1929 International Exhibition and decorated by Josep-Marià Sert with murals of momentous events in Catalan history.

❻ Palau de la Generalitat

Plaça de Sant Jaume 4. **Map** 5 A2. **Tel** 93 402 46 00. Jaume I. **Open** 10am–1:30pm 2nd & 4th Sun of the month; 10am–8pm 23 Apr, 11 & 24 Sep (carry your passport). Sep–Jul: by appt. **president.cat**

Since 1403, the Generalitat has been the seat of the Catalonian

The Italianate façade of the Palau de la Generalitat

Governor. Above the entrance, in its Renaissance façade, is a statue of Sant Jordi (St George) the patron saint of Catalonia – and the Dragon. The late Catalan-Gothic courtyard is by Marc Safont (1416).

Among the fine interiors are the Gothic chapel of Sant Jordi, also by Safont, and Pere Blai's Italianate Saló de Sant Jordi. At the back, one floor above street level, lies the *Pati dels Tarongers*, the Orange Tree Patio, by Pau Mateu, which has a bell tower built by Pere Ferrer in 1568.

The Catalan president has offices here as well as in the Casa dels Canonges. The two buildings are connected by a bridge across Carrer del Bisbe, built in 1928 and modelled on the famous Bridge of Sighs in Venice.

The magnificent council chamber, the Saló de Cent, in the Ajuntament

❼ Barcelona Cathedral

This compact Gothic cathedral, with a Romanesque chapel (Capella de Santa Llúcia) and beautiful cloister, was begun in 1298 under Jaime (Jaume) II, on the foundations of a site dating back to Visigothic times. It was not finished until the late 19th century, when the main façade was completed. The cathedral is dedicated to St Eulàlia, the city's patron saint, whose white marble sarcophagus is located in the crypt. Next to the font, a plaque records the baptism of six Caribbean Indians, whom Columbus brought back from the Americas in 1493.

Nave Interior
The Catalan-style Gothic interior has a single wide nave with 28 side chapels. These are set between the columns supporting the vaulted ceiling, which rises to 26 m (85 ft).

KEY

① **The Capella del Santíssim Sagrament** houses the 16th-century Christ of Lepanto crucifix.

② **The main façade** was not completed until 1889, and the central spire until 1913. It was faithfully based on the original 1408 plans of the French architect Charles Galters.

③ **The twin octagonal bell towers** date from 1386–93. The bells were installed in this tower in 1545.

④ **The Sacristy Museum** has a small treasury. Pieces include an 11th-century font, tapestries and liturgical artifacts.

⑤ **Porta de Santa Eulàlia, entrance to Cloisters**

⑥ **Capella de Santa Llúcia**

★ **Choir Stalls**
The top tier of the beautifully carved 15th-century stalls contains the coats of arms (1518) of the 12 knights of the Order of Toisón del Oro.

Capella de Sant Benet
This chapel, dedicated to the founder of the Benedictine Order and patron saint of Europe, houses a magnificent altarpiece showing *The Transfiguration* by Bernat Martorell (1452).

VISITORS' CHECKLIST

Practical Information
Plaça de la Seu. **Map** 5 A2. **Open** 8am–7:30pm daily. 🎵 choir stalls and roof terrace (cathedral free 8am–12:45pm, 5:15–7:30pm). 📷 1–5pm (2–5pm Sun). 🛗 Sacristy Museum: **Open** 9am–7pm daily. 🎧 ✝ several services daily.
🅦 catedralbcn.org

Transport
🚇 Jaume I. 🚌 17, 19, 45.

★ Crypt
In the crypt, beneath the main altar, is the alabaster sarcophagus (1339) of St Eulàlia, martyred for her beliefs by the Romans during the 4th century AD.

★ Cloisters
The fountain, set in a corner of the Gothic cloisters and decorated with a statue of St George, provided fresh water.

559 Basilica dedicated to St Eulàlia and Holy Cross

877 St Eulàlia's remains brought here from Santa Maria del Mar

1339 St Eulàlia's relics transferred to alabaster sarcophagus

1046–58 Romanesque cathedral built under Ramon Berenguer I

1913 Central spire completed

1889 Main façade completed, based on plans dating from 1408 by architect Charles Galters

400	700	1000	1300	1600	1900

4th century Original Roman (paleo-Christian) basilica built

985 Building destroyed by the Moors

1257–68 Romanesque Capella de Santa Llúcia built

1298 Gothic cathedral begun under Jaime II

1493 Indians brought back from the Americas are baptized

Plaque of the Indians' baptism

❽ El Raval

Map 2 F3. 🚇 Catalunya, Liceu.

The district of El Raval lies to the west of La Rambla and includes the old red-light area near the port, which was once known as the Barri Xinès (Chinese Quarter).

From the 14th century, the city hospital was in Carrer de l'Hospital, which still has some herbal and medicinal shops. Gaudí was brought here after being fatally hit by a tram in 1926. The buildings now house the Biblioteca de Catalunya (Catalonian Library), but the elegant former dissecting room has been fully restored.

Towards the port in Carrer Nou de la Rambla is Gaudí's Palau Güell (see p145). At the end of Sant Pau is the city's most complete Romanesque church, the 12th-century Sant Pau del Camp, with a charming cloister featuring exquisitely carved capitals.

❾ Museu d'Art Contemporani

Plaça dels Àngels 1. **Map** 2 F2. **Tel** 93 412 08 10. 🚇 Universitat, Catalunya. **Open** 11am–7:30pm Mon–Fri (to 8pm Jun–Sep), 10am–9pm Sat, 10am–3pm Sun. **Closed** 1 Jan, 25 Dec. 🚫 ♿ 📷 guided tour times change according to the exhibits; check calendar on website. 🌐 **macba.cat** Centre de Cultura Contemporània: Montalegre 5. **Tel** 93 306 41 00. 🌐 **cccb.org**

This dramatic, glass-fronted building was designed by the American architect Richard Meier. Its light, airy galleries act as the city's contemporary art mecca. The permanent collection of predominantly Spanish painting, sculpture and installation from the 1950s onwards is complemented by temporary exhibitions by foreign artists like US painter Susana Solano and South African photojournalist David Goldblatt.

Next to the MACBA, a remodelled 18th-century hospice houses the Centre de Cultura Contemporània, a lively arts centre that hosts major arts festivals and regular shows.

❿ La Rambla

The historic avenue of La Rambla (Les Rambles in Catalan) is busy around the clock, especially in the evenings and at weekends. Newsstands, caged bird and flower stalls, tarot readers, musicians and mime artists throng the wide, tree-shaded central walkway. Among its famous buildings are the Liceu Opera House, the huge Boqueria food market and some grand mansions.

Exploring La Rambla
The name of this long avenue, known as Les Rambles in Catalan, comes from the Arabic *ramla*, meaning "the dried-up bed of a seasonal river". The 13th-century city wall followed the left bank of such a river that flowed from the Collserola hills to the sea. Convents, monasteries and the university were built on the other bank in the 16th century. As time passed, the riverbed was filled in and those buildings demolished, but they are remembered in the names of the five consecutive Rambles that make up the great avenue between the Port Vell and Plaça de Catalunya.

Palau Güell: C/ Nou de la Rambla 3–5. **Map** 2 F3. **Tel** 93 472 57 75. 🚇 Liceu. **Open** 10am–8pm Tue–Sun (free Apr–Oct: 5–8pm Sun & Nov–Mar: 2:30–5:30pm Sun). **Closed** 1 & 6–13 Jan, 25 & 26 Dec. 🚫 ♿ 🌐 **palauguell.cat** Museu de Cera: Pg de la Banca 7. **Map** 2 F4. **Tel** 93 317 26 49. 🚇 Drassanes. **Open** 10am–1:30pm, 4–7:30pm Mon–Fri, 11am–2pm, 4:30–8:30pm Sat, Sun & public hols. 🚫 ♿

The monument to Columbus at the bottom of the tree-lined Rambla

For hotels and restaurants in this area see pp564–5 and pp586–8

① Font de Canaletes
Saying that someone "drinks the waters of Canaletes" – from this 19th-century fountain – indicates he or she is from Barcelona.

② Reial Acadèmia de Ciències i Arts
Converted to a theatre in 1910, this building has Barcelona's first official public clock.

④ Palau de la Virreina
The first occupant of this great palace, in 1777, was the *virreina* (viceroy's wife) of Spain in Peru.

⑤ Mercat de Sant Josep
Popularly known as "La Boquería", this is Barcelona's most colourful food market.

③ Palau Moja
This 1790 building hosts the Catalan Heritage House, with high-tech exhibits on local culture.

⑦ Gran Teatre del Liceu
The opera house has had to be restored twice after fires – in 1861 and 1994.

⑨ Palau Güell
This Neo-Gothic palace is considered to be one of Gaudí's most important works *(see p145)*.

⑩ Museu de Cera
This waxwork museum, in an atmospheric, 19th-century building, contains about 300 exhibits.

⑥ Plaça de la Boquería This square features a mosaic pavement by Miró (1976) and an Art Deco dragon designed for a former umbrella shop.

⑧ Plaça Reial
Barcelona's most lively square was built in the 1850s. The Neo-Classical lampposts were designed by Gaudí.

Monument a Colom
Plaça del Portal de la Pau

0 metres 100
0 yards 100

Glorious stained-glass dome, Palau de la Música Catalana

⓫ Palau de la Música Catalana

Carrer Palau de la Música 4–6.
Map 5 B1. **Tel** 932 95 72 00. 🚇
Urquinaona. **Open** 10am–3:30pm
daily (to 6pm Easter & Jul, 9am–6pm
Aug); and for concerts. 🚫 ♿ limited.
📷 in English on the hour, 10am–3pm.
🌐 **palaumusica.cat**

This is a real palace of music,
a Modernista celebration of
tilework, sculpture and glorious
stained glass. It is the only
concert hall in Europe lit by
natural light. Designed by Lluís
Domènech i Montaner, it was
completed in 1908. Although
a few extensions have been
added, the building still retains
its original appearance. The
elaborate red-brick façade is
hard to appreciate fully in the
confines of the narrow street.
It is lined with mosaic-covered
pillars topped by busts of the
great composers Palestrina,
Beethoven and Bach. The large
stone sculpture of St George

and other figures at the corner
of the building portrays an
allegory from Catalan folksong
by Miquel Blay.

But it is the interior of the
building that is truly inspiring.
The auditorium is lit by a huge
inverted dome of stained glass
depicting angelic choristers. The
sculptures of composers Wagner
and Clavé on the proscenium
arch that frames the stage area
were designed by Domènech
but finished by Pau Gargallo.
The stunning "Muses of the
Palau", the group of 18 highly
stylized, instrument-playing
maidens, are the stage's backdrop. Made of terracotta and
trencadís (pieces of ceramic),
the muses have become the
building's most admired feature.

The work of Josep Anselm
Clavé (1824–74) in promoting
Catalan song led to the creation
of the Orfeó Català choral
society in 1891, a focus of
Catalan nationalism and the
inspiration behind the Palau.

Although the Orfeó is now
based at the more state-of-the-
art L'Auditori on Carrer de
Lepant *(see p195)*, there is a
concert at the Palau nearly
every night; it is the main
venue for the city's jazz and
guitar festivals, and world
music, flamenco and symphony
orchestras regularly grace its
flamboyant stage.

The Palau's new era began
with the completion of the
work carried out by the top
local architect Oscar Tusquets.
An underground concert hall
and an outdoor square for
summer concerts were
added, consolidating the
Palau's reputation as Barcelona's
most loved music venue.

⓬ La Llotja

Carrer del Consolat de Mar 2. **Map** 5
B3. **Tel** 93 547 88 49. 🚇 Barceloneta,
Jaume I. **Closed** to the public (except
twice a year, days vary).

La Llotja (meaning "commodity
exchange") was built in the
1380s as the headquarters of
the Consolat de Mar. It was
remodelled in Neo-Classical style
in 1771 and housed the city's
stock exchange until 1994, the
original Gothic hall acting as
the main trading room. It can still
be seen through the windows.

The upper floors housed the
Barcelona School of Fine Arts
from 1849 to 1970, attended
by Pablo Picasso and Joan Miró.
It is now occupied by the local
chamber of commerce.

Statue of Poseidon in the courtyard of
La Llotja

⑬ El Born

Map 5 B3. 🚇 Jaume I.

Named after the jousting sessions that once took place in its central boulevard, El Born is a tiny pocket of the La Ribera district. The village-like atmosphere of the neighbourhood makes it popular with local residents and young urbanites. Trendy bars, fashion and design shops are juxtaposed with medieval architecture. The 14th-century mansions of Carrer Montcada have remained intact and now house high-calibre galleries and museums, while the tiny, pedestrianized streets and squares fanning out from the Mercat del Born are the centre of the city's café culture. The numerous bars and restaurants are a magnet for revellers, much to the annoyance of the full-time residents who voice their complaints visually through the banners hanging from El Born's balconies.

⑭ Museu Picasso

Carrer Montcada 15–23. **Map** 5 B2. **Tel** 932 56 30 00. 🚇 Jaume I. **Open** 9am–7pm Tue–Sun (to 9:30pm Thu). 🎟 (free under age 18, over 65, 1st Sun of month & every Sun after 3pm). 📷 11am Sun in English (except Aug), book in advance at 93 256 30 22. ♿
w museupicasso.bcn.cat

One of Barcelona's most popular attractions, the Picasso Museum is housed in five adjoining medieval palaces on Carrer Montcada: Berenguer d'Aguilar, Baró de Castellet, Meca, Mauri and Finestres.

It opened in 1963 showing works donated by Jaime Sabartes, a friend of Picasso. Following Sabartes' death in 1968, Picasso himself donated paintings, including early examples. These were complemented by graphic works, left in his will, and 141 ceramic pieces given by his widow, Jacqueline.

The strength of the 4,200-piece collection is Picasso's early works. These show how, even at the ages of 15 and 16, he was painting major works, such as *The First Communion* (1896) and *Science and Charity* (1897). The most famous work is his series of 44 paintings, *Las Meninas*, which was inspired by Velázquez's masterpiece.

⑮ Basílica de Santa Maria del Mar

Plaça Sta Maria 1. **Map** 5 B3. **Tel** 93 310 23 90. 🚇 Jaume I. **Open** 9am–1pm, 5–8:30pm Mon–Sat, 10am–2pm, 5–8pm Sun. 🎟 includes guided visit and access to rooftop. 📷 in English: 1:15pm (also Spanish), 2pm, 3pm & 5:15pm (also Spanish) daily.

This is the city's only example of a church entirely in the Catalan Gothic style. It took just 55 years to build, with money donated by merchants and shipbuilders. The speed gave it a unity of style both inside and out. The west front has a 15th-century rose window of the Coronation of the Virgin. More stained glass, from the 15th–18th centuries, lights the nave and aisles.

The choir and furnishings were burned in the Civil War *(see p71)*, adding to the sense of space and simplicity. The church has great acoustics for concerts

A wedding service in the Gothic interior of Santa Maria del Mar

Pablo Picasso, *Self-Portrait* in charcoal (1899–1900)

Pablo Picasso in Barcelona

Picasso (1881–1973) was born in Málaga and was almost 14 when he came to Barcelona, where his father had found a job in the city's art academy. Picasso enrolled, and was a precocious talent among his contemporaries. He was a regular visitor to Els Quatre Gats, an artists' café still in existence in Carrer Montsió, where he held his first exhibition. He also exhibited in Sala Parks, a gallery still functioning in Carrer Petritxol. The family lived in Carrer Mercé and Picasso had a studio in Carrer Nou de la Rambla. It was among the prostitutes of Carrer d'Avinyò that he found inspiration for the work that many art historians see as the wellspring of modern art, *Les Demoiselles d'Avignon* (1906–7). Picasso left Barcelona for Paris in his early twenties and initially returned several times. After the Civil War his opposition to Franco kept him in France, but he designed a frieze for Barcelona's College of Architects in 1962 and was persuaded to allow the city to open a museum of his work, which it did the following year.

Renaissance-style 17th-century façades lining Carrer Montcada

⑯ Carrer Montcada

Map 5 B3. ⚇ Jaume I. Museu dels Cultures del Món: at No. 12. **Tel** 93 256 23 00. **Open** 10am–7pm Tue–Sat, 10am–8pm Sun. ▨

The most authentic medieval street in the city is a narrow lane, overshadowed by gargoyles and roofs that almost touch overhead. The Gothic palaces that line it date back to Catalonia's expansion in the 13th century. Almost all of the buildings were modified over the years, particularly during the 17th century. Only Casa Cervelló-Guidice at No. 25 retains its original façade.

The Museu dels Cultures del Món (Museum of World Cultures), in the Nadal and Marqués de Llió 16th-century palaces at No. 12, imaginatively displays more than 700 exhibits from around the world.

At No. 22 is one of the city's best-known champagne and *cava* bars, the cheerful El Xampanyet.

The interior of El Xampanyet, decorated with colourful tiles and large barrels

⑰ El Born Centre de Cultura i Memòria

Plaça Comercial 12. **Map** 5 C3. **Tel** 93 256 68 50. ⚇ Jaume I, Barceloneta. **Open** 10am–8pm Tue–Sun (Nov–Feb: to 7pm Tue–Sat). ▨ ▨ ▨ ▨ ▨ **el bornculturaimemoria.barcelona.cat**

This covered market, with its ornate ironwork and crystal roof, was Barcelona's main wholesale market until the early 1970s, when it outgrew its location.

While the market was being remodelled, extensive ruins of the 18th-century city were discovered beneath its foundations. These ruins are now the focal point of the El Born cultural centre, complemented by exhibitions, talks and screenings.

The street names in the vicinity reflect what went on in Barcelona's former mercantile hub: L'Argenteria was lined with silversmiths, Flassaders was where you would go for a woven blanket and Vidrieria was once lit up with glass-blowers' torches. A few of these establishments remain, but they are now outnumbered by chic fashion and interiors boutiques.

Much of this area was razed after Barcelona fell to the French-Spanish forces during the War of Succession (*see p66*). This key event is remembered each year on 11 September, with activities focused on a monument dedicated to those who died in 1714, located near the market.

⑱ Museu de la Xocolata

Comerç 36. **Map** 5 C2. ⚇ Jaume I, Arc de Triomf. **Tel** 93 268 78 78. **Open** 10am–7pm Mon–Sat (to 8pm 15 Jun–15 Sep), 10am–3pm Sun & pub hols. **Closed** 1 & 6 Jan, 1 May, 25 & 26 Dec. ▨ ▨ ▨ ▨ **museuxocolata.cat**

Founded by Barcelona's chocolate- and pastry-makers' union, this museum celebrates the history of one of the most universally loved foodstuffs: from the discovery of cocoa in South America to the invention of the first chocolate machine in Barcelona. This confectionery tale is told through old posters, photographs and footage.

The real thing is displayed in a homage to the art of the *mona*. This was a traditional Easter cake that over the centuries evolved into an edible sculpture. Every year, pâtissiers compete to create the most imaginative piece, decorating their chocolate versions of well-known buildings or folk figures with jewels, feathers and other materials. The museum shop sells – you guessed it – all manner of chocolate goods.

The pink brick façade of the late 19th-century Arc del Triomf

⑲ Arc del Triomf

Passeig Lluís Companys. **Map** 5 C1. ⚇ Arc de Triomf.

The main gateway to the 1888 Universal Exhibition, which filled the Parc de la Ciutadella, was designed by Josep Vilaseca i Casanovas. It is built of brick in Mudéjar (*see p59*) style, with sculpted allegories of crafts, industry and business. The frieze by Josep Reynés on the main façade represents the city welcoming foreign visitors. Visitors can climb to the viewing terrace at the top of the arch during the 48h Open House Barcelona festival, usually held at the end of October.

⑳ Parc de la Ciutadella

Passeig de Picasso, 21. **Map** 5 D2. ⚇ Barceloneta, Ciutadella-Vila Olímpica, Arc de Triomf. **Open** 8am–dusk daily. ▨

This popular park has a boating lake, orange groves and parrots living in the palm trees. It was once the site of a massive star-shaped citadel, built for Felipe V between 1715 and 1720 after a 13-month siege of the city. The fortress was intended to house soldiers to keep law and order, but was never used for this purpose. Converted into a prison, the citadel became notorious during the Napoleonic occupation *(see p67)* and, during the 19th-century liberal repressions, it was hated as a symbol of centralized power. In 1878, under General Prim, whose statue stands in the middle of the park, it was pulled down and the park given to the city, to become, in 1888, the venue of the Universal Exhibition *(see pp68–9)*. Three buildings survived: the Governor's Palace, now a school; the chapel; and the arsenal, occupied by the Catalan parliament.

The park offers more cultural and leisure activities than any other in the city and is particularly popular on Sunday afternoons, when people gather to play instruments, dance and relax, or visit the museum and zoo. A variety of works by Catalan sculptors such as Marès, Arnau, Carbonell, Clarà, Llimona, Fuxà, Gargallo and Dunyach can be seen, alongside work by modern artists such as Tàpies and Botero.

The gardens in the Plaça de Armes were laid out by French landscape gardener Jean Forestier and centre on a cascade based around a triumphal arch. It was designed by architect Josep Fontseré, with the help of Antoni Gaudí, then still a young student.

Modernist exterior of the Castell dels Tres Dragons

㉑ Castell dels Tres Dragons

Passeig de Picasso. **Map** 5 C2.
🅜 Arc de Triomf, Jaume I.
Closed to the public.

At the entrance to the Parc de la Ciutadella is the Castell dels Tres Dragons (Castle of the Three Dragons), named after a play by Frederic Soler. A fine example of Modernista architecture *(see pp144–5)*, the combination of visible iron supports and exposed red brickwork were radical innovations at the time.

It was built by Lluís Domènech i Montaner for the 1888 Universal Exhibition and was later used as a workshop for Modernista design. Once part of the Museu de Ciències Naturals, the Castell now houses a laboratory for the museum and is open only to researchers.

㉒ Museu Martorell

Parc de la Ciutadella. **Map** 5 C3.
Tel 93 319 69 12. 🅜 Arc de Triomf, Jaume I. **Closed** for renovations.

Part of the Museu de Ciències Naturals, the Museu Martorell is Barcelona's oldest museum. It opened in 1882 and was the first building in the city to be constructed expressly for the purpose of housing a museum. Beside it is the Hivernacle, a glasshouse by Josep Amargós, and the Umbracle, a conservatory by the park's architect, Josep Fontseré. Both date from 1884 and were designed for the 1888 Universal Exhibition.

㉓ Zoo de Barcelona

Parc de la Ciutadella. **Map** 6 D3.
Tel 902 457 545. 🅜 Ciutadella-Vila Olímpica. **Open** 10am–5pm daily (Mar–mid-May & mid-Sep–Oct to 6pm; mid-May–mid-Sep: to 7pm).
🐾 🅱 🖥 🏠 🅦 zoobarcelona.cat

The animals in this zoo, laid out in the 1940s, are separated by moats instead of bars. All the aquatic creatures here will eventually move to a designated marine zoo; however, plans are currently on hold due to budget cuts. The zoo has pony rides, electric cars and a train. Roig i Soler's 1885 sculpture by the entrance, *The Lady with the Umbrella*, has become a symbol of the city.

Ornamental cascade in the Parc de la Ciutadella designed by Josep Fontseré and Antoni Gaudí

Smart boats and the twin skyscrapers at the Port Olímpic

㉔ Port Olímpic

Map 6 F4. Ⓜ Ciutadella-Vila Olímpica.

The most dramatic rebuilding for the 1992 Olympics was the demolition of the old industrial waterfront and the laying out of 4 km (2 miles) of promenade and pristine sandy beaches. Suddenly Barcelona seemed like a seaside resort. At the heart of the project was a 0.6 sq km (¼ sq mile) new estate of 2,000 apartments and parks called Nova Icària. The area is still popularly known as the Vila Olímpica because the buildings originally housed the Olympic athletes.

On the seafront there are twin 44-floor blocks, two of Barcelona's tallest skyscrapers, one occupied by offices and the other by the Hotel Arts (*see p565*). They stand beside a bustling marina, which was also built for 1992. The marina is the setting for several restaurants and bars.

㉕ Barceloneta

Map 5 B5. Ⓜ Barceloneta.

Barcelona's fishing "village", which lies on a triangular tongue of land jutting into the sea just below the city centre, is known for its fish restaurants and port-side cafés.

Barceloneta was built by the architect and military engineer Juan Martín de Cermeño in 1753 to rehouse people made homeless by the construction of the Ciutadella fortress (*see pp158–9*). Since then it has housed largely workers and fishermen. It is now

full of short-let holiday flats. Laid out on a grid system with narrow houses of two or three floors, the area has a friendly air.

In the small Plaça de la Barceloneta, is the Baroque church of Sant Miquel del Port, also by Cermeño. The large central square is dominated by a contemporary covered market.

Today, the remnants of Barceloneta's fishing fleet are based in the nearby industrial docks by a small clock tower. On the opposite side of this harbour is the Torre de Sant Sebastià, terminus of the cable car that runs across the port, via the World Trade Centre, to Montjuïc. Ricardo Bofill's sail-shaped Hotel W is a landmark on Barceloneta beach.

㉖ Port Vell

Map 5 B4. Ⓜ Barceloneta, Drassanes Aquàrium: **Tel** 93 221 74 74. **Open** Jun & Sep: 9:30am–9:30pm daily; Jul–Aug: 9:30am–11pm daily; Oct–May: 9:30am–9pm Mon–Fri, 9:30am–9:30pm Sat, Sun & public hols. 🅿 ♿ 🚻 �🆆 **aquariumbcn.com**

The city's leisure port is at the foot of La Rambla, just beyond the old customs house. This was built in 1902 at the Portal de la Pau, the former maritime entrance to the city, where steps lead into the water. To the south, the Moll de Barcelona, with a World Trade Centre, serves as the passenger pier for visiting cruise ships. In front of the customs house, La Rambla is linked to the yacht clubs on the Moll d'Espanya by a swing bridge and pedestrian

jetty. The Moll d'Espanya (*moll* meaning "quay, wharf or pier") has a shopping and restaurant complex, the Maremagnum, plus an aquarium with an underwater tunnel through an enormous shark-filled tank.

The Moll de la Fusta (Timber Wharf), with terrace cafés, has red structures inspired by van Gogh's painting of the bridge at Arles. At the end of the wharf stands *El Cap de Barcelona (Barcelona Head)*, a 20-m (66-ft) sculpture by Pop artist Roy Lichtenstein.

㉗ Monument a Colom

Plaça del Portal de la Pau. **Map** 2 F4. **Tel** 93 302 52 24. Ⓜ Drassanes. **Open** 9am–8:30pm daily (to 7:30pm Oct–Feb). **Closed** 1 & 6 Jan, 25 & 26 Dec. ♿

The Columbus Monument in the Portal de la Pau (the "Gate of Peace") was designed by Gaietà Buigas for the 1888 Universal Exhibition.

The 60-m (200-ft) cast-iron monument marks the spot where Columbus stepped ashore in 1493 after discovering America, bringing with him six Caribbean Indians. He was accorded a state welcome by the Catholic Monarchs in the Saló del Tinell (*see p150*). The Indians' conversion to Christianity is commemorated in the cathedral (*see pp152–3*).

There is a very small viewing platform at the top of the monument, where a 7-m (24-ft) bronze statue of Columbus points out to sea.

Fishing boat moored at the quayside of Barceloneta

For hotels and restaurants in this area see pp564–5 and pp586–8

A *golondrina* departing from the Plaça del Portal de la Pau

❷❽ Golondrinas

Plaça del Portal de la Pau. **Map** 2 F5.
Tel 93 442 31 06. Ⓜ Drassanes.
Open times vary – phone ahead.
Ⓦ lasgolondrinas.com

Sightseeing trips around the harbour can be made on small double-decker boats called *golondrinas* ("swallows"). They moor beside the steps of the Plaça del Portal de la Pau in front of the Columbus Monument. Tours last around half an hour. The boats go out beneath the steep, castle-topped hill of Montjuïc towards the industrial port.

An alternative one-and-a-half-hour trip in modern catamarans takes in Barcelona Harbour, the commercial port and beaches.

❷❾ Museu Marítim and Drassanes

Avinguda de les Drassanes. **Map** 2 F4.
Tel 93 342 99 20. Ⓜ Drassanes.
Open 10am–8pm daily. **Closed** 1 & 6
Jan, 25 & 26 Dec. Ⓟ free Sun after
3pm. Ⓖ Ⓦ mmb.cat

The great galleys that made Barcelona a major seafaring power were built in the sheds of the Drassanes (shipyards), which now house the maritime museum. These royal dry docks are the largest and most complete surviving medieval complex of their kind in the world. They were founded in the mid-13th century, when dynastic marriages uniting the kingdoms of Sicily and Aragón meant that

better maritime communications between the two became a priority. Three of the yards' four original corner towers survive.

Among the vessels to slip from the Drassanes' vaulted halls was the *Real*, flagship of Don Juan of Austria, Charles V's illegitimate son, who led the Christian fleet to victory against the Turks at Lepanto in 1571 *(see p63)*. The museum's showpiece is a full-scale replica decorated in red and gold.

The renovated halls now host temporary exhibitions with a maritime theme, as well as displaying some historic boats. Three times a month, you can also visit the charming Jardins de Baluard, a walled garden just behind the museum, where you can admire Barcelona's only surviving medieval city gate. The admission ticket also includes a visit to the *Santa Eulàlia*, a restored century-old schooner, which is moored a short walk away in the Port Vell.

Stained-glass window in the Museu Marítim

Barcelona's Fiestas

La Mercè *(24 Sep)*. The patroness of Barcelona, Nostra Senyora de la Mercè (Our Lady of Mercy), whose church is near the port, is honoured for a week around 24 September with Masses, concerts and dances. The biggest events are the *correfoc* – a wild procession of people dressed as devils and monsters, dancing with fireworks – and the *piro musical* – an impressive firework display with music held at the Font Màgica in Montjuïc.

Firework display during the fiesta of La Mercè

Els Tres Tombs *(17 Jan)*. Horsemen, dressed in top hats and tails, ride three times through the streets in honour of St Anthony, the patron saint of animals.
Dia de Sant Ponç *(11 May)*. Stalls along Carrer Hospital sell herbs, honey and candied fruit on the day of the patron saint of beekeepers and herbalists.
La Diada *(11 Sep)*. Catalonia's "national" day is an occasion for singing the Catalan anthem and separatist demonstrations.
Festa Major *(varies)*. Each district hosts its own *festa* in which streets compete to outdo each other in the inventiveness and beauty of their decorations. The most spectacular take place in the neighbourhood of Gràcia.

EIXAMPLE

Barcelona claims to have the greatest collection of Art Nouveau buildings of any city in Europe. The style, known in Catalonia as Modernisme, flourished after 1854, when it was decided to pull down the medieval walls to allow the city to develop into what had previously been a military zone.

The designs of the civil engineer Ildefons Cerdà i Sunyer (1815–76) were chosen for the new expansion (*eixample*) inland. These plans called for a rigid grid system of streets, but at each intersection the corners were chamfered to allow the buildings there to overlook the junctions or squares. The few exceptions to this grid system include the Diagonal, a main

avenue running from the area of Pedralbes down to the sea, and the Avinguda de Gaudí, which links the Sagrada Família to the Hospital de la Santa Creu i de Sant Pau by Modernista architect Domènech i Montaner (1850–1923). The wealth of Barcelona's commercial elite, and their passion for all things new, allowed them to give free rein to the age's most innovative architects in designing their residences as well as public buildings.

Still Barcelona's most lavish neighbourhood, Eixample's broad, tree-lined avenues are replete with designer shops and upmarket restaurants, particularly along the area's main axis, the Passeig de Gràcia.

Sights at a Glance

Museums and Galleries
❷ Fundació Antoni Tàpies

Churches
❻ Sagrada Família pp170–71

Modernista Buildings
❶ Illa de la Discòrdia
❸ La Pedrera

❹ Casa Terrades "Casa de les Punxes"
❺ Hospital de la Santa Creu i de Sant Pau

See also Barcelona Street Finder maps 3, 4, 5

◄ Aerial view of apartment block Casa Milà, designed by Gaudí

For keys to symbols *see back flap*

Street-by-Street: Quadrat d'Or

The hundred or so city blocks centring on the Passeig de Gràcia are known as the Quadrat d'Or, "Golden Square", because they contain so many of Barcelona's best Modernista buildings *(see pp144–5)*. This was the area within the Eixample favoured by the wealthy bourgeoisie, who embraced the new artistic and architectural style with enthusiasm, not only for their residences, but also for commercial buildings. Most remarkable is the Illa de la Discòrdia, a single block containing houses by Modernisme's most illustrious exponents. Many interiors can be visited by the public, revealing a feast of stained glass, ceramics and ornamental ironwork.

Diagonal Metro

Vinçon home decor store *(see pp192–3)*

Passeig de Gràcia, the Eixample's main avenue, is a showcase of highly original buildings and smart shops. The graceful street lamps are by Pere Falqués (1850–1916).

❷ Fundació Tàpies
Topped by Antoni Tàpies' wire sculpture *Cloud and Chair*, this 1879 building by Domènech i Montaner houses a wide variety of Tàpies' paintings, graphics and sculptures.

RAMBLA DE CATALUNYA

PASSEIG DE GRÀCIA

Casa Amatller

Museu del Perfum

Casa Ramon Mulleras

❶ ★ Illa de la Discòrdia
In this city block, three of Barcelona's most famous Modernista houses vie for attention. All were created between 1900 and 1910. This ornate tower graces the Casa Lleó Morera by Domènech i Montaner.

To Plaça de Catalunya

Casa Batlló

Casa Lleó Morera

Passeig de Gràcia Metro

The Palau Baró de Quadras was designed by Puig i Cadafalch in 1904. The façade, in Neo-Gothic style, is highly ornate and covered with distinctive sculptures. This carving adorns the doorway.

Locator Map
See Barcelona Street Finder map 3

❹ **Casa Terrades "Les Punxes"**
Built in red brick with carved stone ornamentation, this 1905 house by Puig i Cadafalch echoes the Gothic buildings of northern Europe, and was the Modernista architect's largest work.

Casa Thomas

To Sagrada Família

❸ ★ **Casa Milà "La Pedrera"**
Gaudí put all his architectural daring into this, his most famous house. The result is a remarkable wave-like façade and a roofscape of chimneys and vents resembling abstract sculptures.

Palau Ramon de Montaner

0 metres 100
0 yards 100

Key

— Suggested route

For keys to symbols *see back flap*

Sumptuous interior of the Casa Lleó Morera, Illa de la Discòrdia

❶ Illa de la Discòrdia

Passeig de Gràcia, between Carrer d'Aragó and Carrer del Consell de Cent. **Map** 3 A4. ⓜ Passeig de Gràcia. Casa Lleó Morera: **Closed** to the public. **w** casalleomorera.com Casa Amatller: **Tel** 93 216 01 75. **Open** 10am–6pm daily. **Closed** 2 weeks in Jan, 25 & 26 Dec. 🗺 guided tours only (no high heels), book online. **w** amatller.org Casa Batlló: **Tel** 93 216 03 06. **Open** 9am–9pm daily (last adm: 8pm). 🗺 ⓖ **w** casabatllo.es

The most famous group of Modernista *(see pp144–5)* buildings in Barcelona amply illustrates the range of styles involved in the movement. The block in which they stand has been dubbed the Illa de la Discòrdia, "Block of Discord", owing to the startling visual argument between them.

The three most famous houses, on Passeig de Gràcia, were remodelled from existing houses early in the 20th century, but named after their original owners.

No. 35 is Casa Lleó Morera (1902–6), the first residential work of Lluís Domènech i

Montaner. The ground floor was gutted to create a shop in 1943, but it is still possible to admire the Modernista façade.

At No. 41 is Casa Amatller, designed by Puig i Cadafalch in 1898. Its façade is a harmonious blend of styles, featuring Moorish and Gothic windows. The stepped gable roof is dotted with tiles. Inside the wrought-iron main doors is a fine stone staircase beneath a stained-glass roof. The Amatller family apartments have been restored to their former glory and are now open to the public. The rest of the building is occupied by the Institut Amatller d'Art Hispanic.

The third house is Gaudí's Casa Batlló (1904–6). Its façade has heavily tiled walls and curving iron balconies pierced with holes to look like masks or skulls. The humpbacked, scaly-looking roof is thought to represent a dragon, with St George (the patron saint of Catalonia) as a chimney.

❷ Fundació Antoni Tàpies

Carrer d'Aragó 255. **Map** 3 A4. **Tel** 93 487 03 15. ⓜ Passeig de Gràcia. **Open** 10am–7pm Tue–Sun & public hols. **Closed** 1 & 6 Jan, 25 Dec. 🗺 ⓖ 🏠 **w** fundaciotapies.org

Antoni Tàpies (1923–2012) was one of Spain's foremost contemporary artists. Inspired by Surrealism, his abstract work was executed in a variety of materials, including concrete and metal *(see p164)*. Only a small part of the collection can be shown at one time, and exhibits rotate regularly. There are also excellent temporary exhibitions. All are housed in the first domestic building in Barcelona to be built with iron (1880), designed by Domènech i Montaner.

Antoni Gaudí (1852–1926)

Born in Reus (Tarragona) into a family of artisans, Gaudí was the leading exponent of Catalan Modernisme. Following a stint as a blacksmith's apprentice, he studied at Barcelona's School of Architecture. Inspired by a nationalistic search for a romantic medieval past, his work was supremely original. His first major achievement was the Casa Vicens (1888) at No. 24 Carrer de les Carolines. But his most celebrated building is the extravagant church of the Sagrada Família *(see pp170–71)*, to which he devoted his life from 1914. He gave all his money to the project and often went from house to house begging for more, until his death a few days after being run over by a tram.

Decorated chimneypot, Casa Vicens

◀ Extraordinary sculptured and ceramic-encrusted chimneys of Gaudí's La Pedrera

The rippled façade of Gaudí's apartment building, La Pedrera

❸ La Pedrera

Passeig de Gràcia 92. **Map** 3 B3.
Tel 90 220 21 38. 🚇 Diagonal. **Open**
9am–8pm daily (Nov–Feb: to 6:30pm).
Pedrera Origins: from 9pm daily
(6 Nov–2 Mar: 7–9pm daily, except
26 Dec–3 Jan: 9–11pm). **Closed**
7–13 Jan, 25 Dec. 🚼 (temporary
exhibitions free.) 🅦 **lapedrera.com**

Sometimes called Casa Milà,
La Pedrera is Gaudí's greatest
contribution to Barcelona's
civic architecture, and his
last work before he devoted
himself entirely to the Sagrada
Família (see pp170–71).

Built 1906–12, La Pedrera
completely departed from
the construction principles
of the time and, as a result,
it was strongly attacked by
Barcelona's intellectuals.

Gaudí designed this corner
apartment block, eight storeys
high, around two circular
courtyards. The intricate ironwork balconies, by Josep Maria
Jujol, are like seaweed against
the wave-like walls of white
undressed stone. There are no
straight walls in the building.

The top floor now houses
the Gaudí Museum. Guided
tours take in the roof, where
the many sculpted air ducts
and chimneys are so sinister
they have been dubbed the
espanta-bruixes, the witch-
scarers. Pedrera Origins is a spectacular sound-and-light show.

❹ Casa Terrades

Avinguda Diagonal 416. **Map** 3 B3. **Tel**
930 185 242. 🚇 Diagonal. **Open**
9am–9pm daily (last adm: 8pm).
Closed 25 Dec. 🚼 🕭 🖬
🅦 **casadelespunxes.com**

This six-sided
apartment block by
Puig i Cadafalch gets
its nickname, "Casa
de les Punxes" (House
of the Points), from
the spires on its
six corner turrets,
which are
shaped like
witches' hats.
Built between
1903 and 1905 by
converting three
existing houses
on the site, it is an

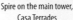

Spire on the main tower,
Casa Terrades

eclectic mixture of medieval
and Renaissance styles. The
towers and gables are
influenced by north European
Gothic architecture. However,
the deeply carved, floral stone
ornament of the exterior is
typically Modernista.

❺ Hospital de la Santa Creu i de Sant Pau

Carrer de Sant Antoni Maria Claret 167.
Map 4 F2. **Tel** 93 291 90 00. 🚇 Hospital
de Sant Pau. Grounds: **Open** 10am–
6:30pm Mon–Sat (to 4:30pm Nov–
Mar), 10am–2:30pm Sun. **Closed** 1 & 6
Jan, 25 & 26 Dec. 🕭 🚼 (free first Sun
of month). 🖬 in English at 11am.
🅦 **santpaubarcelona.org**

Lluís Domènech i Montaner
began designing a new city
hospital in 1902. Totally innovative in concept, his scheme
consisted of 26 Mudéjar-style
pavilions set in large gardens,
as he disliked huge wards and
believed that patients would
recover better amid fresh air
and trees. All the connecting
corridors and service areas
were hidden underground.
Also believing art and colour
to be therapeutic, he decorated the pavilions
profusely. The
turreted roofs were
tiled with ceramics,
and the reception
pavilion embellished
with sculptures by
Pau Gargallo and
mosaic murals.

Statue of the Virgin, Hospital de la Santa Creu i de Sant Pau

For hotels and restaurants in this area see pp564–5 and pp586–8

❻ Sagrada Família

Europe's most unconventional church, the Temple Expiatori de la Sagrada Família, is an emblem of a city that likes to think of itself as individualistic. Crammed with symbolism inspired by nature and striving for originality, it is Gaudí's *(see pp144–5)* greatest work. In 1883, a year after work had begun on a Neo-Gothic church on the site, the task of completing it was given to Gaudí, who changed everything, extemporizing as he went along. It became his life's work and he lived like a recluse on the site for 14 years. He is buried in the crypt. At his death, only one tower on the Nativity façade had been completed, but work resumed after the Civil War and several more have since been finished to his original plans. Work continues today, financed by public subscription.

Bell Towers
Eight of the 12 spires, one for each apostle, have been built. Each is topped by Venetian mosaics.

The Finished Church

Gaudí's initial ambitions have been kept over the years, using various new technologies to achieve his vision. Still to come is the central tower, which is to be encircled by four large towers representing the Evangelists. Four towers on the Glory (south) façade will match the existing four on the Passion (west) and Nativity (east) façades. An ambulatory – like an inside-out cloister – will run round the outside of the building.

★ Passion Façade
This bleak façade was completed from 1986 to 2000 by artist Josep Maria Subirachs. A controversial work, its sculpted figures are angular and often sinister.

Main entrance

Spiral Staircases
The steep stone staircases – 370 steps in each – are closed to the public. The views from the upper galleries are reachable via lift only.

VISITORS' CHECKLIST

Practical Information
C/ Sardenya. **Map** 4 E3. **Tel** 93 513 20 60. [W] **sagradafamilia.org**
Open daily. Apr–Sep: 9am–8pm; Oct–Mar: 9am–7pm; Nov–Feb: 9am–6pm (to 2pm 1 & 6 Jan, 25 & 26 Dec). timed tickets only, advance booking advisable.
in English 11am, 1pm & 3pm daily (also noon daily May–Oct).
numerous services daily.

Transport
Sagrada Família. 19, 43, 51.

★ **Nativity Façade**
The most complete part of Gaudí's church, finished in 1930, has doorways which represent Faith, Hope and Charity. Scenes of the Nativity and Christ's childhood are embellished with symbolism, such as doves representing the congregation.

★ **Crypt**
The crypt, where Gaudí is buried, was begun by the original architect, Francesc de Paula Villar i Lozano, in 1882. This is where services are held. On the lower floor a museum traces the careers of both architects and the church's history.

KEY

① **The altar canopy** was designed by Gaudí.

② **The apse** was the first part of the church Gaudí completed. Stairs lead down from here to the crypt below.

③ **Towers with lift**

④ **The nave** contains a forest of fluted pillars that support four galleries above the side aisles; a large number of skylights let in both natural and artificial light.

MONTJUÏC

The hill of Montjuïc, rising to 213 m (699 ft) above the commercial port on the south side of the city, is Barcelona's biggest recreation area. Its museums, art galleries, gardens and nightclubs make it a popular place in the evenings as well as during the day.

There was probably a Celtiberian settlement here before the Romans built a temple to Jupiter on their Mons Jovis, which may have given Montjuïc its name – though another theory suggests that a Jewish cemetery on the hill inspired the name Mount of the Jews.

The absence of a water supply meant that there were few buildings on Montjuïc until the castle was erected on the top in 1640.

The hill finally came into its own as the site of the 1929 International Fair. With great energy and flair, buildings were erected all over the north side, with the grand Avinguda de la Reina Maria Cristina, lined with huge exhibition halls, leading into it from the Plaça d'Espanya. In the middle of the avenue is the Font Màgica (Magic Fountain), which is regularly illuminated in colour. Above it is the Palau Nacional, home of the city's historic art collections. The Poble Espanyol is a crafts centre housed in copies of buildings from all over Spain. The last great surge of building on Montjuïc was for the 1992 Olympic Games, which left Barcelona with international-class sports facilities.

Sights at a Glance

Historic Buildings
8 Castell de Montjuïc

Modern Architecture
4 Pavelló Mies van der Rohe
9 Estadi Olímpic de Montjuïc

Museums and Galleries
1 Fundació Joan Miró
2 Museu Arqueològic
3 Museu Nacional d'Art de Catalunya
6 CaixaForum

Squares
7 Plaça d'Espanya

Theme Parks
5 Poble Espanyol

See also Barcelona Street Finder maps 1, 2

◀ Spectators admiring the light show at the Font Màgica (Magic Fountain)

For keys to symbols *see back flap*

Street-by-Street: Montjuïc

Montjuïc is a spectacular vantage point from
which to view the city. It has a wealth of art
galleries and museums, an amusement park
and an open-air theatre. The most interesting
buildings lie around the Palau Nacional, where
Europe's greatest Romanesque art collection
is housed. Montjuïc is approached from the
Plaça d'Espanya between brick pillars based
on the campanile of St Mark's in Venice, which
give a foretaste of the eclecticism of building
styles. The Poble Espanyol
illustrates the traditional
architecture of Spain's
regions, while the
Fundació Joan Miró
is boldly modern.

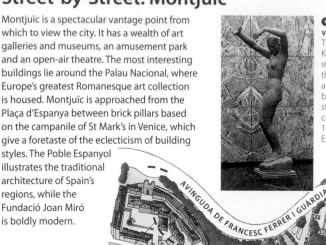

❹ **Pavelló Mies
van der Rohe**
This statue by Georg
Kolbe *(see p177)*
stands serenely in
the steel, glass, stone
and onyx pavilion
built in the Bauhaus
style as the German
contribution to the
1929 International
Exhibition.

AVINGUDA DE FRANCESC FERRER I GUARDIA

AVINGUDA DELS MONTANYANS

PASSEIG DE LES CAS

❺ ★ **Poble
Espanyol**
Containing replicas of
buildings from many
regions, this "village"
provides a fascinating
glimpse of vernacular styles.

AVINGUDA DE L'ESTADI

❸ ★ **Museu Nacional
d'Art de Catalunya**
Displayed in the
National Palace, the
main building of the
1929 International
Exhibition is Europe's
finest collection of early
medieval frescoes.
These were a great
source of inspiration for
Joan Miró *(see p176)*.

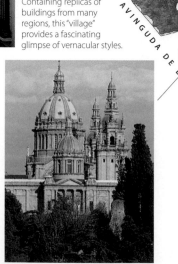

*To Montjuïc castle and
Olympic stadium*

| 0 metres | 100 |
| 0 yards | 100 |

Fountains and cascades descend in terraces from the Palau Nacional. Below them is the Font Màgica (Magic Fountain). In the evening, from Thursday to Sunday (October to April: Friday and Saturday), its jets are programmed to a multicoloured music and light show. This marvel of water-and-electrical engineering was originally built by Carles Buigas (1898–1979) for the 1929 International Exhibition.

Locator Map
See Barcelona Street Finder map 1

Museu Etnològic
displays artifacts from Oceania, Africa, Asia and Latin America.

❷ Museu Arqueològic
The museum displays important finds from prehistoric cultures in Catalonia and the Balearic Islands. The *Dama de Ibiza*, a 4th-century sculpture, was found in Ibiza's Carthaginian necropolis *(see p515)*.

ca d'Espanya

PLAÇA DE L'UNIVERS I TAULET

CARRER DE LA GUARDIA URBANA

CARRER DE LLEIDA

Mercat de les Flors theatre *(see p195)*

Teatre Grec is an open-air theatre set among gardens.

PASSEIG DE LA SANTA MADRONA

PASSEIG DE LA SANTA MADRONA

PASSEIG DE LA SANTA MADRONA

AVINGUDA DE MIRAMAR

To Montjuïc castle and cable car

❶ ★ Fundació Joan Miró
This tapestry by Joan Miró hangs in the centre he created for the study of modern art. In addition to Miró's works in various media, the modern building by Josep Lluís Sert is of architectural interest.

Key

— Suggested route

Flame in Space and Naked Woman (1932) by Joan Miró

❶ Fundació Joan Miró

Parc de Montjuïc. **Map** 1 B3. **Tel** 93 443 94 70. 🚇 Espanya, then bus 150, 55 or Paral.lel, then Montjuïc funicular. **Open** 10am–6pm Tue, Wed, Fri & Sat (Jul–Sep: to 8pm), 10am–9:30pm Thu, 10am–2:30pm Sun & public hols. **Closed** 1 Jan, 25 & 26 Dec. 🎟️ ♿ 🌐 **fmirobcn.org**

Joan Miró (1893–1983) studied at the fine art school at La Llotja *(see p156).* From 1919, he spent much of his time in Paris. Though opposed to Franco, he returned to Spain in 1940 and lived mainly in Mallorca, where he died.

An admirer of primitive Catalan art and Gaudí's Modernisme *(see pp144–5),* Miró always remained a Catalan painter but developed a Surrealistic style, with vivid colours and fantastical forms suggesting dream-like situations.

In 1975, after the return of democracy to Spain *(see p72),* his friend, the architect Josep Lluís Sert, designed the stark, white building to house a permanent collection of paintings, sculptures and tapestries lit by natural light. Miró himself donated the works and some of the best pieces on display include his *Barcelona Series* (1939–44), a set of 50 black-and-white lithographs. Periodic exhibitions of other artists' work are also held.

❷ Museu Arqueològic

Passeig Santa Madrona 39–41. **Map** 1 B3. **Tel** 93 423 21 49. 🚇 Espanya, Poble Sec. **Open** 9:30am–7pm Tue–Sat, 10am–2:30pm Sun & public hols. **Closed** 1 Jan, 25 & 26 Dec. 🎟️ (free 12 Feb, 23 Apr, 18 May, 11 & 24 Sep and for under 8s). ♿ 🌐 **mac.cat**

Housed in the Renaissance-inspired 1929 Palace of Graphic Arts, the museum shows artifacts from prehistory to the Visigothic period (AD 415–711). Highlights are finds from the Greco-Roman town of Empúries *(see p220),* Iberian silver treasure and Visigothic jewellery.

❸ Museu Nacional d'Art de Catalunya

Parc de Montjuïc, Palau Nacional. **Map** 1 B2. **Tel** 93 622 03 60. 🚇 Espanya. 🚌 55, 150. **Open** 10am–8pm Tue–Sat (to 6pm Oct–Apr), 10am–3pm Sun & pub hols. **Closed** 1 Jan, 1 May, 25 Dec. 🎟️ (free from 3pm Sat, 1st Sun of month, 12 Feb, 18 May, 11 & 24 Sep). Separate fee for roof. 📷 ♿ 🌐 by appt (93 622 03 75). 🌐 **museunacional.cat**

The austere Palau Nacional was built for the 1929 International Exhibition, but in 1934 it was used to house an art collection that has since become the most important in the city.

The museum has a great display of Romanesque *(see p28)* items, centred around a series of magnificent 12th-century frescoes taken from Catalan Pyrenean churches. The most remarkable are the wall paintings from Sant Climent de Taüll *(see p28)* and from Santa Maria de Taüll *(see p215).*

The expanding Gothic collection covers the whole of Spain but particularly Catalonia, and a collection of notable Baroque and Renaissance works hails from all over Europe.

A fine collection of modern art includes Modernista furniture by Gaudí *(see pp144–5),* and paintings by Picasso, Ramon Casas and Salvador Dalí. The museum offers a rare opportunity to view more than a millennium of Catalan artistic activity in a single location.

12th-century *Christ in Majesty*, Museu Nacional d'Art de Catalunya

Morning by Georg Kolbe (1877–1945),
Pavelló Mies van der Rohe

❹ Pavelló Mies van der Rohe

Avinguda Francesc Ferrer i Guàrdia 7.
Map 1 A2. **Tel** 93 423 40 16. 🚇
Espanya. 🚌 13, 150. **Open** 10am–
8pm daily (to 6pm in winter).
Closed 1 Jan, 25 Dec. 🎫 under 16s
free. 📷 noon Sat. 🌐 miesbcn.com

The modern, simple lines of the
glass and polished stone German
Pavilion must have shocked
visitors to the International
Exhibition in 1929. Designed
by Ludwig Mies van der Rohe
(1886–1969), director of the
avant-garde Bauhaus school,
it includes his *Barcelona Chair*,
now an icon of Modernism. The
building was demolished after
the exhibition, but a replica was
built on the centenary of his birth.

❺ Poble Espanyol

Avinguda Francesc Ferrer i Guàrdia 13.
Map 1 A2. **Tel** 93 508 63 00. 🚇 Espanya.
🚌 50, 150. **Open** 9am–midnight Tue–
Thu & Sun (to 8pm Mon, 3am Fri, 4am
Sat). 🎫 ♿ 🌐 poble-espanyol.com

The popular Poble Espanyol
(Spanish Village) was built
for the 1929 International
Exhibition to display Spanish
architectural styles and crafts.
    Building styles from all over
Spain are illustrated by 116
houses arranged on streets
radiating from a main square.
    Resident artisans produce crafts
including hand-blown glass,
ceramics, Toledo damascene
(see p394) and Catalan canvas

sandals. There are also bars,
restaurants, nightclubs and
a flamenco *tablao (see pp196–7)*.

❻ CaixaForum

Avinguda Francesc Ferrer i Guàrdia
6–8. **Map** 1 B2. **Tel** 93 476 86 00.
🚇 Espanya. 🚌 13, 50. **Open** 10am–
8pm daily (Jul & Aug: to 11pm Wed).
Closed 1 & 6 Jan, 25 Dec. 🎫 ♿
🌐 obrasocial.lacaixa.es

The Antiga Fàbrica Casaramona,
a restored Modernista textile mill
(1911), houses a glossy cultural
centre hosting talks, screenings,
performances, workshops and
high-profile temporary art
exhibitions. There is also a
permanent art collection.

❼ Plaça d'Espanya

Avinguda de la Gran Via de les Corts
Catalanes. **Map** 1 B1. 🚇 Espanya.
Fountain Show: Apr, May & Oct:
from 9pm Fri & Sat; Jun–Sep: from
9:30pm Thu–Sat; Nov–Mar: from
7pm Fri & Sat. No show 6 Jan–16 Feb.

The fountain in the middle of
this road junction is by Josep
Maria Jujol, one of Gaudí's
followers. The 1899 bullring is
by Font i Carreras. Catalans have
never taken to bullfighting, and
the arena was converted into
Las Arenas shopping centre by
British architect Richard Rogers.
    On the Montjuïc side of the
roundabout is the Avinguda de
la Reina Maria Cristina, flanked
by two brick campaniles,
modelled on the bell towers of
St Mark's in Venice. The avenue
leads up to Carles Buigas's *Font
Màgica* (Magic Fountain) in
front of the Palau Nacional.

❽ Castell de Montjuïc

Parc de Montjuïc. **Map** 1 B5. **Tel** 93 329
86 53. 🚇 Paral·lel, then funicular & cable
car. 🚌 150 from Plaça Espanya. **Open**
10am–8pm daily (to 6pm Oct–Mar).
🎫 (free Sun from 3pm & for under 16s).

The summit of Montjuïc is
occupied by an 18th-century
castle built for the Bourbon
family. During the War of
Independence the castle was
captured by the French, and
after the Civil War it became a
prison, where the Catalan leader
Lluís Companys was executed in
1940. It is now a peace museum.

❾ Estadi Olímpic de Montjuïc

Passeig Olímpic 17–19. **Map** 1 A4.
Tel 93 426 20 89. 🚇 Espanya, Poble
Sec. 🚌 50, 61, 125. Open for events.
Open Camp: **Open** times vary; see
website for details. 🎫 📱 📷
🌐 open camp.com Museum:
Open 10am–6pm Tue–Sat, 10am–
2:30pm Sun (Apr–Sep: to 8pm Tue–
Sat). 🎫 📷 ♿

The Neo-Classical façade has
been preserved from the stadium,
built by Pere Domènech i Roura
for the 1936 Olympics, cancelled
at the onset of the Civil War. It was
refitted for the 1992 Olympics.
    The stadium houses Open
Camp, a sports-themed park that
offers football simulators, the
chance to hurdle around the
main track and other activities.
    Nearby are the Palau Sant
Jordi indoor stadium, by Arata
Isozaki, swimming pools by
Ricardo Bofill and the Museu
Olímpic i de l'Esport, which
covers all aspects of sport.

View from Palau Nacional downhill towards the Plaça d'Espanya

FURTHER AFIELD

The radical redevelopment of Barcelona's outskirts in the late 1980s and early 1990s gave it a wealth of new buildings, parks and squares. The city's main station, Sants, was rebuilt and the neighbouring Parc de l'Espanya Industrial and Parc de Joan Miró were created, containing lakes, modern sculpture and futuristic architecture. The Plaça de Glòries is being remodelled to contain the design museum and a park. In the west of the city, where the streets start to climb steeply, are the historic royal palace and monastery of Pedralbes, and Gaudí's famous Park Güell, dating from 1910. Beyond is the Serra de Collserola, the city's closest rural area. Two funiculars provide an exciting way of reaching its heights, which offer superb views of the city. Tibidabo, the highest point, with a funfair, the Neo-Gothic church of the Sagrat Cor and a modern steel-and-glass communications tower, is a favourite place among Barcelonans for a day out.

Sights at a Glance

Museums and Galleries
❸ Camp Nou (Experience Tour & Museum)
❻ Museu Blau
❽ Cosmocaixa - Museu de la Ciència

Historic Buildings
❹ Monestir de Santa Maria de Pedralbes

Modern Buildings
❺ Torre de Collserola

Parks and Gardens
❶ Parc de Joan Miró
❷ Parc de l'Espanya Industrial
❾ Park Güell

Theme Parks
❼ Tibidabo

Key
▓ Barcelona city centre
═ Motorway
▬ Major road
═ Minor road

0 km   1
0 miles   1

Sights Outside the City Centre

◀ Tibidabo theme park with Barcelona in the background

For keys to symbols see back flap

Dona i Ocell (1983) by Joan Miró in the Parc de Joan Miró

❶ Parc de Joan Miró

Carrer d'Aragó 1. 🚇 Tarragona.

Barcelona's 19th-century slaughterhouse *(escorxador)* was transformed in the 1980s into this unusual park, hence its alternative name, Parc de l'Escorxador.

It is constructed on two levels, the lower of which is popular with kids because of its open areas, fringed with shady paths and palm trees. The upper level is paved and dominated by a 1983 sculpture by Joan Miró *(see p176)* entitled *Dona i Ocell* (Woman and Bird). Standing 22 m (72 ft) high in the middle of a pool, its surface is coated with colourful pieces of glazed tile. There are also several play areas for kids.

❷ Parc de l'Espanya Industrial

Plaça de Joan Peiró. 🚇 Sants-Estació.

This modern park, designed by the Basque architect Luis Peña Ganchegui, owes its name to the textile mill that used to stand on the 5-hectare (12-acre) site.

Laid out in 1986 as part of Barcelona's policy to provide more open spaces, the park has canals and a rowing lake – with a statue of Neptune at its centre. Tiers of steps rise around the lake like an amphitheatre and on one side, a row of 10 futuristic watchtowers serves as public viewing platforms and lamp standards.

Six contemporary sculptors are represented in the park, among them Andrés Nagel, whose huge metal dragon incorporates a children's slide.

❸ Camp Nou (Experience Tour & Museum)

Avda de Aristides Maillol. **Tel** 90 218 99 00. 🚇 Maria Cristina, Collblanc. **Open** late Mar–mid-Oct, Christmas & Easter hols: 9:30am–7:30pm daily; mid-Oct–late Mar: 10am–6:30pm Mon–Sat, 10am–2:30pm Sun; reduced hours on public hols & match days. **Closed** 1 & 6 Jan, 25 Dec. 🏛 📷 of the stadium. ♿ 🌐 fcbarcelona.cat

Camp Nou, Europe's largest football stadium, is home to the city's famous football club, Barcelona FC (Barça, as it is known locally). Founded in 1899, it is one of the world's richest soccer clubs, and has more than 100,000 members.

Line of watchtowers in the Parc de l'Espanya Industrial

The stadium is a magnificent, sweeping structure, built in 1957 to a design by Francesc Mitjans. An extension was added in 1982 and it can now comfortably seat 100,000 fans.

The club's popular museum is a glossy interactive experience, with touch-screen panels detailing the club's history and their many victories. There are also paintings and sculptures of famous club footballers commissioned for an exhibition held in celebration of the club in 1985 and 1987. *Blau-grana* (blue-burgundy) are the colours of Barça's strip. The club's flags were used as an expression of local nationalist feelings during the Franco dictatorship, when the Catalan flag was banned.

As well as hosting its own high-profile matches (mainly at weekends), Camp Nou also accommodates affiliated local soccer clubs and promotes a number of other sports.

Camp Nou stadium, the prestigious home of the Futbol Club Barcelona

❹ Monestir de Santa Maria de Pedralbes

Baixada del Monestir 9. **Tel** 93 256 34 34. Ⓜ Reina Elisenda or bus 22, 63, 64, 78. **Open** Apr–Sep: 10am–2pm Tue–Fri, 10am–7pm Sat, 10am–8pm Sun; Oct–Mar: 10am–2pm Tue–Fri, 10am–5pm Sat & Sun. 🎫 by appt. **Closed** 1 Jan, Good Friday, 1 May, 24 Jun, 25 Dec. 🎟 (free first Sun of month, every Sun from 3pm and for under 16s; combined ticket with the Museu d'Història de Barcelona *(see p150)* also available). ♿ ground floor only. 🌐 **monestirpedralbes.bcn.cat**

Approached through an arch in its walls, the monastery of Pedralbes still has the air of a living enclosed community. This is heightened by its furnished cells, kitchens, infirmary and refectory. But the nuns of the Order of St Clare moved to an adjoining building in 1983. The monastery was founded in 1326 by Elisenda de Montcada de Piños, fourth wife of Jaime II of Catalonia and Aragón. Her tomb lies between the church and the cloister. On the church side her effigy is dressed in royal robes; on the other, as a nun.

The monastery is built around a cloister. The rooms encircling the cloister include a dormitory, a refectory, a chapterhouse, an abbey and day cells. Artworks and liturgical ornaments, pottery and furniture are on display.

The most important room in the monastery is the Capella (chapel) de Sant Miquel, with murals of the *Passion* and the

Madonna of Humility, Monestir de Santa Maria de Pedralbes

Life of the Virgin, both painted by Ferrer Bassa in 1346, when Elisenda's niece, Francesca Saportella, was abbess.

❺ Torre de Collserola

Carretera de Vallvidrera al Tibidabo. **Tel** 93 211 79 42. Ⓜ Peu de Funicular, then Funicular de Vallvidrera & bus 111. **Open** times vary; check website for latest information. **Closed** 1 & 6 Jan, 25, 26 & 31 Dec. 🎟 ♿ 🌐 **torredecollserola.com**

In a city that enjoys thrills, the ultimate ride is offered by the communications tower

near Tibidabo mountain *(see p182)*. A glass-sided lift swiftly reaches the top of this 288-m- (944-ft-) tall structure standing on the summit of a 445-m (1,460-ft) hill.

The tower was designed by English architect Norman Foster for the 1992 Olympic Games. Needle-like in form, it is a tubular steel mast on a concrete pillar. There are 13 levels. The top one has an observatory with a powerful telescope, and a public viewing platform with a 360-degree view encompassing Barcelona, the sea and the mountains.

❻ Museu Blau

Plaça Leonardo da Vinci 4–5, Parc del Fòrum. **Tel** 93 256 22 00. Ⓜ El Maresme Fòrum. 🚌 7, 36, 43, 99, H16. **Open** 10am–7pm Tue–Sat, 10am–8pm Sun. 🎟 free first Sun of month, every Sun from 3pm, under-16s. ♿ 🌐 **museublau.bcn.cat**

Museu Blau is the city's science museum with a collection that is more than 100 years old. Exhibited across two floors are 3 million specimens in the fields of mineralogy, palaeontology, zoology and botany. Previously located in the Parc de la Ciutadella *(see pp158–9)*, the museum is now housed in the Parc del Fòrum in a modern, innovative building designed by architects Herzog & de Meuron. The same team also conceived the permanent Planet Life exhibition, which is a fascinating journey through the history of life on earth. The Biography of the Earth section illustrates the evolution of life from the first microbes to the present day, while Earth Today comprehensively details the variety of life forms sharing the planet. Independent "Islands of Science" are spaced throughout Planet Life, which focus on specific topics, such as sexuality and genetics. There are also temporary exhibitions, a Media Library and a Science Nest for children up to age 6 at weekends, where images and sound effects recreate different natural surroundings.

Barcelona v Real Madrid

FC Barcelona

Més que un club is the motto of Barcelona FC: "More than a club". More than anything else it has been a symbol of the struggle of Catalan nationalism against the central government in Madrid. To fail to win the league is one thing. To come in behind Real Madrid is a complete disaster. Each season the big question is which of the two teams will win the title. Under the Franco regime in a memorable episode in 1941, Barça won 3–0 at home. At the return match in Madrid, the crowd was so hostile that the police and referee "advised" Barça to prevent trouble. Demoralized by the intimidation, they lost 11–1. Loyalty is paramount: one Barça player who left to join Real Madrid received death threats.

Real Madrid

Merry-go-round, Tibidabo

❼ Tibidabo

Plaça del Tibidabo 3–4. **Tel** 93 211 79 42. 🚋 Avda Tibidabo, then Tramvia Blau or Bus 196 & Funicular. 🚌 111, T2A from Plaça de Catalunya. Amusement Park: **Open** variable – check website for times. **Closed** Oct–Jun: Mon–Fri. 🚻 Temple del Sagrat Cor: **Tel** 93 417 56 86. **Open** 10am–8pm daily. 🚻 🖥 **tibidabo.cat**

The heights of Tibidabo are reached by the Tramvia Blau (Blue Tram) and a funicular railway. The name, inspired by Tibidabo's views of the city, comes from the Latin *tibi dabo* (I shall give you) – a reference to the Temptation of Christ when Satan took him up a mountain and offered him the world spread at his feet.

The hugely popular Parc d'Atraccions first opened in 1908. While the old rides retain their charm, new ones have been added over the years, including the thrilling Dragon Khan rollercoaster. The hilltop location at 517 m (1,696 ft) adds to the thrill. The Museu d'Automates is a display of automated toys, jukeboxes and gaming machines.

Tibidabo is crowned by the Temple Expiatori del Sagrat Cor (Church of the Sacred Heart), built with religious zeal but little taste by Enric Sagnier between 1902 and 1911. A lift takes you up to the feet of an enormous figure of Christ.

Just a short bus ride away is another viewpoint worth visiting – the Torre de Collserola *(see p181)*.

❽ Cosmocaixa – Museu de la Ciència

Carrer Isaac Newton 196. **Tel** 93 212 60 50. 🚋 Avinguda del Tibidabo, then Tramvia Blau. 🚌 17, 22, 58, 196. **Open** 10am–8pm Tue–Sun (daily Jul–Aug & public hols). **Closed** 1 & 6 Jan, 25 Dec. 🚻 (free 5–8pm Tue–Fri, 6–8pm Sat, Sun & public hols, first Sun of every month). 🚻

This excellent science museum is located in a striking Modernista building. Exhibits include the Flooded Forest, which allows visitors to explore the Amazonian rainforest both above and below the waterline. A science lab is one of several great areas for children.

❾ Park Güell

Carrer d'Olot. **Tel** 010 (from Barcelona). 🚇 Lesseps, Vallcarca. 🚌 24, 32, 92, H6. **Tel** 90 220 03 02. **Open** Nov–Feb: 8:30am–6:30pm; Mar: 8:30am–7pm; Apr, Sep & Oct: 8am–8:30pm; May–Aug: 8am–9pm (last adm: 1 hr before closing). 🚻 timed tickets only. 🎫 🚻 Casa-Museu Gaudí: **Tel** 93 219 38 11. **Open** Apr–Sep: 10am–8pm daily (to 6pm Oct–Mar). **Closed** 1 Jan. 🚻 can be combined with the Ruta del Modernisme. 🖥 **parkguell.cat**

A UNESCO World Heritage Site, the Park Güell is Antoni Gaudí's

(see pp144–5) most colourful creation. He was commissioned in the 1890s by Count Eusebi Güell to design a garden city on 20 hectares (50 acres) of the family estate. Little of the grand design for decorative public buildings and 60 houses among landscaped gardens became reality. What we see today was completed between 1910 and 1914, and the park opened in 1922. The so-called "Monumental Area", home to most of Gaudí's surviving creations in the park, requires an admission ticket, but the green expanses around the edge of this area are free to explore.

The Room of a Hundred Columns is a cavernous hall of 84 crooked pillars that is brightened by glass and ceramic mosaics; it was intended as the marketplace for the estate. Above it is the Gran Plaça Circular, an open space with a snaking balcony of coloured mosaics that offers stunning views of the city and is said to have the world's longest bench.

Two pavilions at the entry are by Gaudí, but the Casa-Museu Gaudí, a gingerbread-style house where Gaudí lived from 1906 to 1926, was built by Francesc Berenguer.

Mosaic-encrusted chimney by Gaudí at the entrance of the Park Güell

BARCELONA STREET FINDER

The map references given with the sights, shops and entertainment venues described in the Barcelona section of the guide refer to the street maps on the following pages. Map references are also given for Barcelona hotels *(see pp564–5),* and for bars and restaurants *(see pp586–8).* The schematic map below shows the area of Barcelona covered by the *Street Finder.* The symbols used for sights and other features and services are listed in the key at the foot of the page.

Scale of Map Pages

| 0 kilometres | | 2 |
| 0 miles | | 1 |

Key to Street Finder

- ▦ Major sight
- ▢ Place of interest
- ▢ Other building
- 🚉 Main railway station
- Ⓕ Local (FGC) railway station
- ✚ Metro station
- 🚌 Coach station
- 🚠 Cable-car station
- 🚋 Funicular railway station
- 🚊 Tram station
- 🅸 Tourist information
- ➕ Hospital with casualty unit
- 🏢 Police station
- ✝ Church
- ═══ Railway line
- Pedestrianized street

Scale of Map Pages

| 0 metres | | 250 |
| 0 yards | | 250 |

SHOPPING IN BARCELONA

Barcelona is known for its style and sophistication, and can be neatly divided into distinctive shopping districts – Passeig de Gràcia for designer stores plus old shops with beautiful Modernista frontages, Barri Gòtic for eclectic antiques and boutiques, El Born for serious fashion divas, and El Raval for markets, quirky design and museum shops. These categories are not fixed, but do provide a useful rule of thumb, and help define the city when time is limited. There are many food markets as well – 44 in all – and a scattering of flea markets such as the modern Els Encants and the charming Sant Cugat antiques fair. There is something for everyone in Barcelona – from high-street fashion and unique boutiques to local shops selling traditional crafts. All shops close on Sundays, except Maremagnum.

Some of the beautifully displayed confectionery at Escribà

Markets

Barcelona has an impressive range of markets selling a wide variety of things. Everyone should explore **La Boqueria** on La Rambla, one of the most spectacular food markets in Europe. The small and lively Plaça del Pi is also home to a food market selling cheese, honey and sweets. It is held on the first and third Friday, Saturday and Sunday of each month.

On Sunday mornings, coin and stamp stalls are set up in the Plaça Reial, while antiques are sold in Plaça Nova on Thursdays. The city's main flea market, **Encants Vells**, takes place on Monday, Wednesday, Friday and Saturday. It offers a variety of goods including jewellery and clothing.

In December, a Christmas street market is held near the cathedral, where Christmas trees, figurines and other decorative items are sold.

Food and Drink

Barcelonans are proud of their culinary heritage, and rightly so. The land produces superlative vegetables and fruits, flavourful meats and a huge array of cheeses. The bountiful sea offers fresh fish and other seafood, and the wine-growing regions of the Penedès and the Priorat make some of the best vintages in the world. As if all this wasn't enough, chocolate shops, candy makers and patisseries also do their best to complete the feast.

La Boqueria food market is the obvious place to start a gastronomical journey, but Barcelona's numerous specialist food shops are not to be ignored either.

OlisOliva, in the Mercat Santa Caterina in El Born, stocks a superb selection of olive oils and a range of beauty products such as soaps and lotions. Around the corner, **La Botifarrería de Santa María** stocks wonderful artisan charcuterie and a lip-smacking selection of home-made sausages. These include inventive combinations such as pork and cuttlefish, beef and beetroot, and lamb and wild mushroom. **Casa Gispert** is the stop for top-grade dried fruit and nuts, as well as coffee toasted in-house. The fabulous **Formatgeria La Seu** is a walk-in dairy where you can choose from a great seasonal collection of cheeses made by small producers.

Xocoa is the trendiest of the many chocolate-makers in the city, with its retro packaging and fun shapes, including chocolate CDs and giant keys. **Escribà Pastisseries** is more extravagant, with magnificently sculpted cakes and life-size chocolate models of famous personalities. **Cacao Sampaka** is an innovative sweet shop that stocks amazing off-the-wall fillings such as anchovy, black olive and blue cheese, as well as more familiar herb, spice and floral flavours.

Casa Colomina is ideal for those who want to sample

Mouthwatering fruit stalls in La Boqueria market

traditional Spanish sweets such as turrón (nougat made with almonds). **Caelum**, where all the sweetmeats are made by nuns, sells lovely yemas (a sweet made with egg yolks) and mazapans (marzipan treats) and other tasty confections. **Papabubble**, a gorgeous wood-panelled shop, adds modern touches to old-fashioned sweets. You can watch the sweet chefs preparing these handmade concoctions.

For some of the best bread in town, visit **Bopan** near Rambla de Catalunya. This smart café has its own versions of many different types of bread, from Continental favourites to African specialities.

In El Born, **Vila Viniteca** sells a formidable range of Spanish and Catalan wines. Among more than 7,500 labels here you can find cheap and cheerful table wines, as well as decadently expensive Priorats and Riojas. Also remember that leaving Barcelona without a bottle of the nation's beloved Catalan champagne, cava, would be verging on the sacrilegious. The delightfully old-fashioned grocery store **Colmado Múrria** sells a wonderful range of conserves, wines, oils and other deli items.

Department Stores and Galerías

The Plaça Catalunya branch of **El Corte Inglés**, the largest department store chain in Spain, is a Barcelona landmark. It is a handy place with everything under one roof, including plug adaptors and services such as photographic development. There are other branches around the city.

The *galerías* (fashion malls), built mostly during the 1980s, are hugely popular. **Bulevard Rosa** on the Passeig de Gràcia has hundreds of stores selling clothes and accessories. On the Avinguda Diagonal is **L'Illa**, a large, lively shopping mall containing chain stores as well as specialist retailers. The **Maremagnum** shopping centre

The Loewe store, in an elegant building designed by Domènech i Montaner

has all the usual Spanish chains and is open daily, including Sundays and holidays.

High Street and Sports Fashion

Ubiquitous Spanish fashion houses Zara and Mango have stores all over the city, with both flagships on the Passeig de Gràcia. They are great for good-value basics, workwear and fashionable party dresses. Both also offer a decent menswear range.

Those looking for more upmarket buys can rely on **Massimo Dutti** and **Adolfo Domínquez**. Both labels offer classically styled, elegant and fairly affordable clothing for men and women.

For more individualized fashion, try one of the smaller, independent shops in El Born and the Barri Gòtic. Carrer Flassaders and the lanes that lead off it in El Born are a particularly good hunting ground for cutting-edge fashion boutiques.

Custo Barcelona is one of the city's most famous design labels. The three branches of this store are in the Old Town, piled high with the trademark bright prints and daringly mismatched coats and skirts.

For outlets, head to Calle Girona, where several of them are clustered.

Finally, football fans can head for FC Barcelona's official store, the **Botiga del Barça**. It stocks every conceivable item of

merchandise related to the team, including stripes, scarves, boots, balls and keychains.

Spanish and International Designer Labels

For gorgeous and original women's fashions, try **Coquette**, which features chic, slightly retro styles and includes a small but covetable range of bags, shoes and jewellery.

The Barri Gòtic has several stores that stock a range of top designer labels, and this is where you'll find seasonal collections from Vivienne Westwood, Dolce & Gabbana and many others.

Host to big designer labels such as Gucci, Chanel and Carolina Herrera, Avenida Diagonal and the Passeig de Gràcia are where fashionistas like to go shopping. Passeig de Gràcia is home to **Loewe**, which stocks sleek luxury luggage, and is also a reputed name in fashion.

Brightly coloured animal-print outfit at Custo Barcelona

Second-Hand and Vintage Fashion

The diminutive Carrer Riera Baixa in El Raval is home to many interesting second-hand stores. Once a theatre, the vintage shop **Lailo** sells whimsical collectibles such as costumes from the Liceu opera house and 1950s bathing suits. Plenty of vintage items can also be found on nearby Carrer Tallers: at **Flamingos**, which has a fabulous interior, the clothing is sold by weight, and bargains can always be found.

Jewellery, Bags and Accessories

Barcelona has plenty of tiny, Aladdin's Cave-type shops to help put together the perfect outfit. **Joi d'Art** has top-quality silver pieces at good prices, both imported and by local designers. Visit **Minu Madhu** for embroidered jackets, patchwork scarves, appliqué handbags and hand-painted silk kerchiefs in sumptuous textures and colours.

Take a bit of the city's streetlife home – literally – with a **Demano** handbag. Recycled polyester PVC from banners and placards is transformed into bags in this endeavour by three designers and the city hall. The innovative and eco-friendly range is available from stockists all over town.

La Variété has a wonderful collection of linen bags, perfect for the summer, while **Visionario** stocks ultrafashionable and surprisingly affordable sunglasses.

Hats and Shoes

Patterned leather shoes and decorative soles from the cult Mallorcan shoemaker, **Camper**, can be purchased at numerous branches around the city. **Vialis** is a home-grown Barcelona outfit selling beautifully stylish leather women's shoes and cool unisex trainers. **La Manual Alpargatera** is another cult classic, beloved by Sardana dancers *(see p229)* and celebrities alike for its exquisite, individually fitted espadrilles and straw hats. **Cherry Heel**, with several branches around town, has a fantastic selection of luxury footwear, with brands like Le Silla and Rupert Sanderson.

For the best in designer sports shoes, head to **Czar** in the Born. Their hip selection includes Puma, Paul Smith, Rizzo, Fluxa and Le Coq Sportif.

For trendily old-fashioned hats, go to **Sombrerería Obach** where you will find classics ranging from Basque berets to stetsons and hand-woven Montecristi Panamas.

Books and Music

Arguably the finest specialist travel bookshop in Spain, **Altaïr** stocks a stupendous range of maps, travel guides and coffee-table books for anyone who loves to live on the move. If you are simply looking for some holiday reading, try **Casa del Llibre**, the city's biggest bookstore for books and magazines in English.

Barcelona has also become a hot spot for music collectors, largely due to Sonár, the city's annual electronica festival. **Wah Wah Discos** and **Discos Revolver** are good for stocking up on the latest club tunes and old vinyl, while **FNAC** has a wide variety of books, CDs and DVDs.

Unusual Gifts and Knick-Knacks

Barcelona is a wonderful city for unearthing intriguing knick-knacks and one-of-a-kind gifts. **Sabater Hnos. Fábrica de Jabones** sells home-made soaps, which come in all shapes and smells, from traditional lavender to delicious chocolate.

Cereria Subirà is the city's oldest shop, and sells a phenomenal array of decorative and votive candles in a variety of beautiful designs.

Arlequí Màscares specializes in superb hand-painted, papier-mâché folk masks such as Italian Commedia dell'Arte masks, glossy French party masks, Japanese Noh masks and many others.

Arts and Antiques

Antiques aficionados will be delighted by what Barcelona has to offer. Equivalent to an antiques shopping mall, the Bulevard dels Antiquaris, in Passeig de Gràcia, is home to over 70 shops filled with vintage relics and every sort of antique imaginable. These range from ancient coins to tin drums and 19th-century candelabra.

Carrer del Call in the Barri Gòtic is another such hub with plush shops, including **L'Arca**, which sells vintage bridal gowns and antique lace. **Heritage** is a purveyor of semi-precious stone jewellery and antique silks. Also check out the several **Artur Ramón** shops on Carrer de la Palla for 18th- and 19th-century ceramics, and 14th-century paintings.

Sala Parés, the city's oldest and most prestigious gallery, exhibits Catalan artists, both past and present. For pictures that won't break the bank, try the **Boutique Galería Picasso** for prints, lithographs and posters of works by the great Spanish masters, Picasso, Dalí and Miró.

Interiors

L'Appartement is an eclectic gallery and shop that exhibits and sells furniture ranging from funky lamps to stylish folding armchairs. **Zara Home** has four basic styles in its collection: classic, ethnic, contemporary and white, all at very reason-able prices. **Siesta**, which used to be a haberdashery, is today a boutique and art gallery. It still maintains the original wood-and-glass cabinets, now filled with unique ceramics and contemporary jewellery by local artists.

The **Jaime Beriestain** concept store is full of desirable objects for the home, including furniture, linen and tableware. It also has a small but fabulous selection of plants and cut flowers, plus a stylish café-restaurant.

DIRECTORY

Markets

La Boqueria
La Rambla 101.
Map 5 A2.

Encants Vells
Plaça de les Glóries
Catalanes. **Map** 4 F5.

Food and Drink

Bopan
Rambla de Catalunya 119.
Map 3 A3.
Tel 932 37 35 23.

**La Botifarrería
de Santa María**
Carrer Santa María 4.
Map 5 B3.
Tel 933 19 97 84.

Cacao Sampaka
Carrer Consell de Cent
292. **Map** 3 A4.
Tel 932 72 08 33.

Caelum
Carrer Palla 8. **Map** 5 A2.
Tel 933 02 69 93.

Casa Colomina
Carrer de Portaferrissa, 8.
Map 5 A2.
Tel 934 12 25 11.

Casa Gispert
Carrer Sombrerers 23.
Map 5 B3.
Tel 933 19 75 35.

Colmado Múrria
Carrer Roger de Llúria 85.
Map 3 B4.
Tel 932 15 57 89.

Escribà Pastisseries
La Rambla 83. **Map** 5 A1.
Tel 933 01 60 27.

**Formatgeria
La Seu**
Carrer Daguería 16. **Map**
5 B3. **Tel** 934 12 65 48.

OlisOliva
Avenida Francesc Cambó
153–155. **Map** 5 B2.
Tel 932 68 11 47.

Papabubble
Carrer Ample 28. **Map** 5
A3. **Tel** 932 68 86 25.

Vila Viniteca
Carrer Agullers 7. **Map** 5
B3. **Tel** 902 32 77 77.

Xocoa
Carrer Vidrería 4. **Map** 5
B2. **Tel** 933 19 79 05.

Department Stores and Galerías

Bulevard Rosa
Passeig de Gràcia 55.
Map 3 A4.
Tel 932 15 83 31.

El Corte Inglés
Plaça de Catalunya 14.
Map 5 B1.
Tel 933 06 38 00.

L'Illa
Avinguda Diagonal 557.
Tel 934 44 00 00.

Maremagnum
Moll d'Espanya 5.
Map 5 A4.
Tel 932 25 81 00.

High Street and Sports Fashion

**Adolfo
Domínguez**
Passeig de Gràcia 32.
Map 3 A4.
Tel 619 660 277.

Botiga del Barça
Ronda Universitat 37.
Map 5 A1.
Tel 933 18 64 77.

Custo Barcelona
Plaça de les Olles 7.
Map 5 B3.
Tel 932 68 78 93.

Massimo Dutti
Portal de L'Angel 16.
Map 5 A1.
Tel 933 01 89 11.

Spanish and International Designer Labels

Coquette
Carrer Rec 65.
Map 5 C3.
Tel 933 19 29 76.

Loewe
Passeig de Gràcia 35.
Map 3 A4.
Tel 932 16 04 00.

Second-Hand and Vintage Fashion

Flamingos
C/ Tallers 31, El Raval. **Map**
2 F1. **Tel** 93 182 43 87.

Lailo
Carrer Riera Baixa 20. **Map**
2 F2. **Tel** 934 41 37 49.

Jewellery, Bags and Accessories

Joi d'Art
Plaça Sta. María 7. **Map** 5
B3. **Tel** 933 10 10 87.

Minu Madhu
Carrer Sta. María 18. **Map**
5 B3. **Tel** 933 10 27 85.

La Variété
Carrer Pintor Fortuny 30.
Map 5 A1.
Tel 93 270 35 15.

Visionario
Rambla Catalunya 131.
Map 3 A3.
Tel 93 541 62 04.

Hats and Shoes

Camper
Carrer Elizabets 9. **Map** 2
F2. **Tel** 933 42 41 41.

Cherry Heel
Passeig del Born 36.
Map 3 C5.
Tel 932 95 62 64.

Czar
Passeig del Born 20.
Map 5 C3.
Tel 933 10 72 22.

**La Manual
Alpargatera**
Carrer Avinyó 7. **Map** 5
A3. **Tel** 933 01 01 72.

Sombrereria Obach
Carrer del Call 2. **Map** 5
A2. **Tel** 933 18 40 94.

Vialis
Carrer Vidrieria 15. **Map** 5
B3. **Tel** 933 19 94 91.

Books and Music

Altaïr
Gran Via 616. **Map** 3 A4.
Tel 933 42 71 71.

Casa del Llibre
Passeig de Gràcia 62. **Map**
3 A4. **Tel** 932 72 34 80.

Discos Revolver
Tallers 11. **Map** 5 A1.
Tel 934 12 62 48.

FNAC
Plaça de Catalunya 4.
Map 3 A4.
Tel 933 44 18 00.

Wah Wah Discos
Carrer Riera Baixa 14. **Map**
2 F2. **Tel** 934 42 37 03.

Unusual Gifts and Knick-Knacks

Arlequí Màscares
Plaça St Josep Oriol 8. **Map**
5 A2. **Tel** 933 17 24 29.

Cereria Subirà
Baixada Llibreteria 7. **Map**
5 A2. **Tel** 933 15 26 06.

**Sabater Hnos.
Fábrica de Jabones**
Pl Sant Felip Neri 1,
Barri Gòtic. **Map** 5 B2.
Tel 933 01 98 32.

Arts and Antiques

L'Arca
C/ Banys Nous 20. **Map** 5
A2. **Tel** 933 02 15 98.

Artur Ramón
Carrer Palla 23. **Map** 5 A2.
Tel 933 02 59 70.

**Boutique Galería
Picasso**
Carrer Tapinería 10. **Map** 5
B2. **Tel** 933 10 49 57.

Heritage
C/ Banys Nous 14. **Map** 5
A2. **Tel** 933 17 85 15.

Sala Parés
Carrer Petritxol 5. **Map** 5
A2. **Tel** 933 18 70 20.

Interiors

L'Appartement
C/ Enric Granados 44. **Map**
3 A4. **Tel** 934 52 29 04.

Jaime Beriestain
Carrer Pau Claris 167. **Map**
3 B3. **Tel** 93 515 07 82.

Siesta
Ferlandina, 18. **Map** 2 F2.
Tel 933 17 80 41.

Zara Home
Rambla de Catalunya 71.
Map 3 A4.
Tel 934 87 49 72.

ENTERTAINMENT IN BARCELONA

Barcelona has one of the most colourful and alternative live arts scenes in Europe, offering a variety of entertainment, from the spectacular Modernista masterpiece the Palau de la Música and the gilded Liceu opera house, to small independent theatres hosting obscure Catalan comedies and dark Spanish dramas. But there's also much to see simply by walking around the city. Street performances you may stumble upon range from the human statues on La Rambla to excellent classical, ragtime and jazz buskers in the squares. In addition, there are a series of weekend-long musical and arts fiestas that run throughout the year, many of which now attract international performers from all over Europe and beyond.

The magnificent interior of the Palau de la Música Catalana

Entertainment Guides

The most complete guide to what's going on each week in Barcelona is the Catalan-language *Time Out*, out every Thursday. This guide also includes cinema listings. The Friday *La Vanguardia* features the entertainment supplement *Què Fem?* Barcelona's free English-language magazine, *Metropolitan*, also offers details of cultural events going on in town.

Festivals and Tickets

Theatre and concert seasons for the main venues run from September to June, with limited programmes at other times. The city's varied menu of entertainment reflects its rich, multicultural artistic heritage. In summer, the city hosts the **Grec Festival de Barcelona**, a showcase of international music, theatre and dance, held at open-air venues. There is also

a wide variety of concerts to choose from during the **Festa de la Mercè**, held in September. The **Festival del Sónar**, which takes place in June, has become Europe's biggest electronic music festival, drawing musicians from around the world. The **Música als Parcs**, held in June and July, presents classical music in serene surroundings.

The simplest way to get theatre and concert tickets is to buy them at the box office, although tickets for many theatres can also be bought from branches of Catalunya Caixa and La Caixa savings banks, or online through **Ticketmaster**. Tickets for the Grec festival are sold at **tourist offices** and at the **Palau de la Virreina**.

Theatre and Dance

Most theatre in Barcelona is performed in Catalan and English-language productions are still in short supply. However, many Catalan and

Spanish shows are well worth seeing, regardless of language constraints. There are some good independent theatre groups, such as Els Comediants and La Cubana. They offer a thrilling mélange of theatre, music, mime and elements from traditional Mediterranean fiestas. Also staged at the tiny **Cafè-Teatre LLantiol** in El Raval is a weekly repertoire of alternative shows, comedy, magic and other off-the-cuff performances designed to attract a mixed crowd, from the city's growing expatriate community to local arts lovers. Similarly, the **L'Antic Teatre** in La Ribera is a laid-back cultural centre and bar with a scruffy, but pleasant, summer roof-terrace and a small restaurant. It hosts a number of alternative production companies and also shows films outside on the terrace throughout the summer.

La Rambla and Paral.lel are the main hubs of the city's bigger and more mainstream theatres. The **Teatre Tívoli** is a

Outrageous stage show at one of Barcelona's many clubs

The façade of the modern Teatre Nacional de Catalunya

gargantuan theatre where high-quality productions, dance and musical recitals by Catalan, Spanish and international stars are held. The **Teatre Poliorama** on La Rambla, meanwhile, is known more for musicals, occasional operas and contemporary flamenco performances. The **Teatre Apolo** is good for big-bang musicals such as Queen's *We Will Rock You* and ABBA's *Mamma Mia!*

For serious theatre-lovers, the **Teatre Nacional de Catalunya** (TNC) is an imposing, columned affair designed by the Catalan architect Ricard Bofill, with state-of-the-art facilities and a weighty line-up of Spanish and Catalan directors. Good for avant-garde performances, contemporary dance and music is the **Mercat de les Flors**, a converted flower market in the Montjuïc area that is known as Barcelona's "City of Theatre". This is the same part of town that contains Barcelona's drama school and the **Teatre Lliure**, home to the most prestigious Catalan-language theatre company.

Modern dance has always been popular in Barcelona and performances can often be caught at the city's main theatres. The **Teatre Victòria** on Avinguda del Paral.lel is good for ballet and more classical dance productions, as is the **Gran Teatre del Liceu** opera house.

Opera and Classical Music

Opera and classical music are loved by Catalans who lap it up with near-religious reverence. Indeed, many of the great artists of the 20th century were locals, including the celebrated cellist Pau Casals and opera singers José Carreras and Montserrat Caballé.

The city of Barcelona is also home to some of the most spectacular venues in the world, including the glamorous, gilded **Gran Teatre del Liceu**, which first opened its doors in 1847. The opera house has been a continuing beacon of Catalan arts for more than 150 years, with a rich and dramatic history of fire and bomb attacks. It burned down for the third time in 1994, but careful renovations have restored it to its former glory. Despite its misfortunes, it has sustained a stellar line-up of the greatest composers in the world. Among them are Puccini and Tchaikovsky, as well as Catalan composers such as Felip Pedrell, Vives and Enric Granados. Sergei Diaghilev's Russian ballets were also staged here.

The whimsical fancy of the **Palau de la Música Catalana** is another of Barcelona's architectural triumphs *(see p156)*. A jewel-bright vision by the Modernista master Lluís Domènech i Montaner, this sublime concert hall has a dedicated audience, and performers who vie to play here. This is also the main venue for the city's jazz and guitar festivals, as well as national and international symphony orchestras.

Both venues, the Gran Teatre del Liceu and Palau de la Música Catalana, can be visited on interesting daytime guided tours, but booking tickets for an evening production remains by far the best way to experience the ambience.

Modern, but no less important as a shrine to the Catalan arts scene, **L'Auditori de Barcelona** was built to accommodate growing demands for better facilities and to attract ever greater numbers of world-class musicians. It began primarily as a place for classical concerts and orchestral recitals, but has since begun to embrace giants of jazz, pop and rock.

It is also worth keeping abreast of regular choral music that is performed at the city's churches and cathedrals. Most notable among these are the **Església Santa Maria del Pi**, the main cathedral on Plaça del Pi, and the **Basílica Santa Maria del Mar**, particularly around Christmas and Easter.

Packed house at the gigantic Nou Camp stadium

Sports

The undoubted kings of sport in Catalonia are **FC Barcelona**, known locally as Barça. They have the largest football stadium in Europe, Camp Nou *(see p180)*, and a fanatical following.

Tickets for Barça home matches in the national league *(La Liga)*, the King's Cup *(Copa del Rey)* and Champions League can be purchased at the FC Barcelona ticket offices (in person or by telephone) or, perhaps most conveniently, they can be bought online through the club website or Ticketmaster. Barcelona also has a high-ranking basketball team.

Amusement Park

In summer, Barcelona's giant amusement park on the summit of **Tibidabo** *(see p182)* is extremely busy and is usually open till the early hours on weekends. Getting there by tram, funicular or cable car is even more fun.

Film

Directors such as Alejandro Amenábar (*The Sea Inside* and *Agora*), Catalan writer and director Isabel Coixet (*My Life Without You* and *Elegy*) and, of course, Spain's bad boy of film, Pedro Almodóvar (*All About My Mother* and *The Skin I Live In*) have revitalized Spanish cinema. Woody Allen's *Vicky Cristina Barcelona* (2008) brought the city to an even wider audience. Today, Barcelona has become the venue for many independent film festivals. The biggest event of the year is the International Film Festival in Sitges, which is held in October.

Most cinemas dub films in Spanish or Catalan, but there are an increasing number of VO (original version) venues that screen Hollywood blockbusters as well as independent art-house movies.

The **Icària Yelmo Cineplex** is the town's biggest multiscreen VO complex, built around a US-style mall, with a variety of fast-food eateries and shops. The **Renoir Floridablanca**, on the edge of El Raval and the Eixample, screens a range of European and international movies, usually with Spanish or Catalan subtitles. In Gràcia, **Verdi** and **Verdi Park** feature good independent movies, with an interesting selection of foreign films. Escape the summer heat at outdoor film screenings held in the gardens next to the Castell de Montjuïc *(see p177)*. A band plays before the film, and there are also beer stands. You can rent deckchairs, and many people bring a picnic.

The two-screen **Méliès** is a gem showcasing art-house movies, Hollywood classics, B&W horrors and anything by Fellini or Alfred Hitchcock. At the **Phenomena** cinema, you can catch cult classics, from *Casablanca* to *The Big Lebowski*.

It's worth knowing that the prices for movie tickets are lower for weekend matinées. Some cinemas offer midnight and early-hour screenings.

Live Music: Rock, Jazz and Blues

In terms of popular music, Barcelona may not compare to London, whose endless clubs, pubs, stadiums and music emporiums make it one of the best places for live music. However, it doesn't do too badly, given its size. The city attracts a star-studded cast that ranges from pop stars such as Kylie Minogue and Madonna to contemporary jazz musicians such as the Brad Mehldau Quartet, hip-hoppers, rappers and world groove mixers, country singers and good old-fashioned rock-and-rollers.

Barcelona has a clutch of tiny, intimate venues, including the cellar-like **Jamboree**, attracting a number of jazz heavyweights as well as more experimental outfits. Later on it becomes a club.

Another good bet is the **Jazz Sí Club**, a more obscure destination but much beloved by aficionados of the genre. It doubles up as a jam session space for students from the nearby music school. The narrow, crowded and smoky **Harlem Jazz Club** is one of the city's longest surviving clubs for alternative and lesser-known jazz troupes.

One of the two major venues for pop and rock maestros is **Bikini** Barcelona's very own Studio 54. It opened in 1953, preceding the New York icon by a year. This veteran of the scene, which is open from midnight onwards, is still going strong with a robust line-up of big-name bands and a cocktail of different club nights. The other, **Razzmatazz**, arguably the city's most important live music venue, has played host to big-name pop bands such as the Arctic Monkeys, Noel Gallagher's High Flying Birds and James Morrison. Club sessions go on until dawn in some clubs, including Razz Club and The Loft, next door. This trendy venue also holds rock and jazz concerts several nights a week.

Barcelona boasts an architectural masterpiece to host visiting bands: Arata Isozaki's flying saucer, **Palau Sant Jordi**, on Montjuïc, houses extravaganzas like Disney on Ice, the Rolling Stones and Madonna.

One of the city's most popular smaller venues is **Sala BeCool**, which puts on live bands and club nights focused on electronic music.

For a touch of glamour, **Luz de Gas** is a glitzy ballroom that oozes old-fashioned atmosphere with its lamp-lit tables and chandeliers and hosts concerts and club nights. For something completely different, visit **El Cangrejo**, which has barely changed in decades and remains papered in posters and photos of the inimitable Sara Montiel, a Spanish sex symbol during the 1950s and 60s, and is popular with a curious mixture of tourists, drag queens and characters from the Raval.

Flamenco

Aside from the **Ciutat Flamenco Festival** in May, one of the best places to catch a flamenco show is **El Tablao de Carmen**, a stylish restaurant serving both Catalan and Andalucían dishes. The venue is named after Carmen Amaya, a famous dancer who performed for King Alfonso XIII in 1929, in the very spot where it now stands. Various dinner and show packages are available.

Another good place is **Tablao Cordobés**, in La Rambla since 1970 and decorated by the restorers of the Alhambra in Granada. You can have dinner o a drink while watching a show.

For a less formal ambience, **Los Tarantos** (above Jamboree) is an atmospheric nightspot with live flamenco and Latin music every night of the week.

DIRECTORY

Festivals

Festa de la Mercè
See p161.

Festival del Sónar
Palau de la Virreina.
w sonar.es

Grec Festival de Barcelona
Tel 010. Contact any tourist office.
w grec.bcn.cat

Música als Parcs
Tel 010. w bcn.es/parcsijardins

Tickets

Palau de la Virreina
La Rambla 99. **Map** 5 A1.
Tel 933 16 10 00.

Ticketmaster
w ticketmaster.es

Tourist Office
Plaça de Catalunya.
Map 5 A1.
Tel 932 85 38 34.
w barcelonaturisme.com

Theatre and Dance

L'Antic Teatre
Carrer Verdaguer i Callís 12. **Map** 5 B1.
Tel 933 15 23 54.

Café-Teatre Llantiol
Carrer Ricreta 7.
Map 2 E2.
Tel 933 29 90 09.

Mercat de les Flors
Carrer de Lleida 59. **Map** 1 B2. **Tel** 934 26 18 75.
w mercatflors.cat

Teatre Apolo
Avinguda del Paral.lel 59.
Map 1 B1.
Tel 934 41 90 07.
w teatreapolo.com

Teatre Lliure
Plaça Margarida Xirgu 1.
Tel 932 89 27 70.
w teatrelliure.com

Teatre Nacional de Catalunya (TNC)
Plaça de les Arts 1.
Tel 933 06 57 00.
w tnc.cat

Teatre Poliorama
La Rambla 115. **Map** 5 A1.
Tel 933 17 75 99.
w teatrepoliorama.com

Teatre Tívoli
Carrer Casp 8–10. **Map** 3 B5. **Tel** 934 12 20 63.
w grupbalana.com

Teatre Victòria
Avinguda del Paral.lel 67–9. **Map** 1 B1.
Tel 933 29 91 89.
w teatrevictoria.com

Opera and Classical Music

L'Auditori de Barcelona
Carrer de Lepant 150.
Map 4 E1.
Tel 932 47 93 00.
w auditori.cat

Basílica Santa Maria del Mar
Plaça de Santa Maria.
Map 5 B3.
Tel 933 10 23 90.

Església Santa Maria del Pi
Plaça del Pi. **Map** 5 A2.
Tel 933 18 47 43.

Gran Teatre del Liceu
La Rambla 51–9. **Map** 2 F3. **Tel** 934 85 99 00.
w liceubarcelona.cat

Palau de la Música Catalana
Carrer Palau de la Música 4–6. **Map** 5 B1.
Tel 902 44 28 82.
w palaumusica.org

Sports

FC Barcelona
Camp Nou, Avinguda Aristides Maillol.
Tel 934 96 36 00. w fcbarcelona.com

Amusement Park

Tibidabo
Plaça del Tibidabo, 3.
Tel 932 11 79 42.
w tibidabo.cat

Film

Icària Yelmo Cineplex
Carrer Salvador Espriu 61.
Map 6 E4.
Tel 902 22 09 22.
w yelmocines.es

Méliès
Carrer Villarroel 102.
Map 2 E1.
Tel 934 51 00 51.
w cinesmelies.net

Phenomena
Carrer de Sant Antoni Maria Claret 168.
Map 4 F1.
Tel 932 52 77 43.
w phenomena-experience.com

Renoir Floridablanca
Carrer Floridablanca 135.
Map 1 C1.
Tel 934 26 33 37.
w cinesrenoir.com

Verdi
Carrer Verdi 32.
Map 3 B1.
Tel 932 38 78 00.
w cines-verdi.com

Verdi Park
Carrer Torrijos 49.
Map 3 C2.
Tel 932 38 78 00.
w cines-verdi.com

Live Music: Rock, Jazz and Blues

Bikini
Deu i Mata 105.
Tel 933 22 08 00.
w bikinibcn.com

El Cangrejo
Carrer Montserrat 9.
Map 2 F4.
Tel 933 01 29 78.

Harlem Jazz Club
Carrer Comtessa de Sobradiel 8.
Tel 933 10 07 55.
w harlemjazzclub.es

Jamboree
Plaça Reial 17.
Map 5 A3.
Tel 933 19 17 89.
w masimas.com

Jazz Sí Club
Carrer Requesens 2.
Tel 933 29 00 20.
w tallerdemusics.com

Luz de Gas
Carrer Muntaner 246.
Map 2 F1.
Tel 932 09 77 11.
w luzdegas.com

Palau Sant Jordi
Passeig Olímpic 5–7.
Map 1 B4.
Tel 934 26 20 89.

Razzmatazz
Carrer Pamplona 88.
Map 4 F5.
Tel 933 20 82 00.
w salarazzmatazz.com

Sala BeCool
Plaça Joan Llongueras 5.
Tel 933 62 04 13.
w salabecool.com

Flamenco

Ciutat Flamenco Festival
w ciutatflamenco.com

Tablao Cordobés
La Rambla 35.
Map 5 A2.
Tel 933 17 57 11.
w tablaocordobes.com

El Tablao de Carmen
Poble Espanyol,
Avinguda da Francesc Ferrer i Guàrdia, 13.
Map 1 B1.
Tel 933 25 68 95
w tablaodecarmen.com

Los Tarantos
Plaça Reial 17.
Map 5 A3.
Tel 932 04 12 10.
w masimas.com/en/tarantos

Nightlife

Barcelona has one of the most varied nightlife scenes, with something for everybody. Old-fashioned dance halls rub shoulders with underground drum and bass clubs and trashy techno discos, and club-goers are either glammed up or grunged out. Each *barri* (neighbourhood) offers a different flavour, while clubs and bars with outdoor terraces enliven the beachfront during the summer months.

Nightlife

In the summer the beaches become party havens when the *xiringuitos* (beach bars) spring back into life. Wander from Platja de Sant Sebastià in Barceloneta, all the way to Bogatell (a few kilometres beyond the Hotel Arts) and you'll find people dancing barefoot on the sand to the tune of Barcelona's innumerable DJs. Way uptown (above the Diagonal), the city's most glamorous terraces morph into social hubs while the Barri Gòtic – lively at the best of times – becomes one massive street party throughout the summer. If you want to hang with the locals, the demolition of some of El Raval's less salubrious streets has meant that the neighbourhood has become much safer and easier to move about. The underground vibe, however, remains steadfastly intact with tiny hole-in-the-wall-style bars where folks drink and boogie till the early hours. Similarly Gràcia has a bohemian, studenty ambience. If it's an alternative scene you seek Poble Sec has a handful of "ring-to-enter" joints. The city also has a thriving and friendly gay scene, most notably within the Eixample Esquerra, also known as the Gay Eixample, boasting numerous late-night drinking holes, discotheques, saunas and cabarets.

Barri Gòtic

The Plaça Reial is overrun with tourists banging on tin drums and whooping it up, but if you're looking for more grown-up fun, check out

Marula Café. This slinky club focuses on danceable funk and R&B, and it also has a small stage for live concerts. The tiny but ultra-hip **Macarena** is one of the city's most prestigious clubs. It majors in electronica and features the city's best DJs, renowned international artists and new talent. Jazz lovers shouldn't miss the daily concerts at **Jamboree**, one of Spain's mythical jazz clubs. Later, the venue becomes one of the most popular funk and hip-hop discos in town. The **Café Royal** and **Ocaña** are both fashionable nightspots. They offer cocktails and DJs, plus tapas and food.

El Raval

Designer clubs proliferate in Barcelona these days. With slinky red, black and white decor and a specially designed underlit bar, **Zentraus** is one of the best-looking clubs in the neighbourhood. A restaurant until midnight or so, the tables are cleared away once the DJ sessions get under way. **Moog** is more extreme, with blaring, heart-pumping techno for aficionados of the genre. The stark industrial interior gives it the character of a New York nightclub in the mid-1990s. Likewise, the state-of-the-art sound system ensures a thumping, ear-bleedingly good night out. Going back in time, check out the old-school ambience of **El Cangrejo**, where in 1924 the famous *copla* singer Carmen Amaya made her debut. On Friday and Saturday nights you can see drag shows here

(the best ones are by Carmen de Mairena) followed by pop revival DJ sessions. Other nights feature a 1970s and 1980s music theme.

Port Vell and Port Olímpic

Beach parties aside, this area continues to be a hub for creatures of the night. The Port Olímpic itself is nothing but bars and boats. **Catwalk** is one of the few clubs in Barcelona playing hip-hop and R&B. **C.D.L.C.**, in front of the Hotel Arts, still draws celebrities staying nearby, while neighbouring **Shôko**, with an Oriental theme, gets the crowd overflow.

Eixample

One of the city's best-loved discos, **City Hall**, is a multiple space and terrace, where you can pick and choose your groove according to your mood. It has different themes every night from Saturday night-fever discos to Sunday chill-outs. **Sutton Club** has long been one of the smartest uptown spots and is popular with local celebrities. Salsa fans should head to **Antilla**, where live music is combined with salsa classes and exotic cocktails. **Dow Jones** is Barcelona's "drinks stock exchange", where the prices of drinks rise and fall throughout the evening according to demand.

Montjuïc

Barcelona's mega-clubs are located away from the city centre and from anyone trying to sleep. Most of them are only open on Friday and Saturday nights. The big boys are based in Poble Espanyol, where folks can party until the sunrise. **La Terrrazza** is a summer club that hosts rave-like parties under the stars. It takes its name from the giant terrace it occupies. **The One** features a state-of-the-art sound system and top international DJs. Also in Poble Espanyol is **Upload**, another mega-club, which combines club nights with burlesque dinner shows and other events.

Poble Sec

The most alternative nightlife has come to roost in the "dry village", though in name only. The bars are wet and the music is happening. **Apolo** is another old-fashioned music hall, though it attracts a more independent breed of DJ and performer. Expect anything from soulful gypsy folk singers from Marseille, to the legendary purveyor of deep funk, Keb Darge. Further into the village, **Mau Mau** is an alternative club and cultural

centre with a firm eye on what's new and happening. This could mean local DJs, Japanese musicians such as the cultish Cinema Dub Monks, alternative cinema, and multimedia art installations. If it's of the here and now, chances are Mau Mau's on it. At the other end of the spectrum, head to tiny **Tinta Roja** for low lights, romance and a tiny velvet-swathed stage that hosts concerts and cabaret shows. Milonga nights are held on the first Wednesday of the month.

Gràcia and Tibidabo

Gràcia has a laid-back, alternative vibe, and its narrow streets are packed with bars and cafés. This isn't

the neighbourhood to find big clubs, but it is the ideal place to enjoy a few drinks and watch the world go by. **Bobby Gin** is one of Gràcia's trendiest addresses and prides itself on preparing the best gin and tonics in town: speciality concoctions include the Ginfonk, with rose infusion, lime and strawberries. The friendly **Eldorado**, on the lively Plaça del Sol, manages to combine café, bar, club and games room (with table football, pool and pinball). Spanish music and 1980s pop dominate in what is just one of many relaxed "music bars". The **Mirablau** offers unparalleled views over the city from its perch near the Tramvia Blau stop, halfway up Tibidabo.

DIRECTORY

Barri Gòtic

Café Royal
Carrer Nou de Zurbano 3.
Map 5 A3.
Tel 93 318 89 56.

Jamboree
Plaça Reial 17,
Barri Gòtic. **Map** 5 A3.
Tel 93 319 17 89.
W masimas.com

Macarena
Carrer Nou de Sant
Francesc 5. **Map** 5 A3.
Tel 93 301 30 64.
W macarenaclub.com

Marula Café
Carrer Escudellers 49,
Barri Gòtic. **Map** 5 A3.
Tel 93 318 76 90.
W marulacafe.com

Ocaña
Plaça Reial 13–15.
Map 5 A3.
Tel 93 676 48 14.

El Raval

El Cangrejo
Carrer Montserrat 9. **Map**
2 F4. **Tel** 93 301 29 78.

Moog
Carrer L'Arc del Teatre 3,
El Raval. **Map** 2 F4.
Tel 93 319 1789.
W masimas.com

Zentraus
Rambla de Raval 41,
El Raval. **Map** 2 F3.
Tel 93 443 80 78.
W zentraus.cat

Port Vell and Port Olímpic

Catwalk
Carrer Ramon Trias Fargas
2–4, Port Olímpic. **Map** 6
E4. **Tel** 93 224 07 40.
W clubcatwalk.net

C.D.L.C.
Passeig Marítim 32,
Port Olímpic. **Map** 6 E4.
Tel 93 224 04 70.
W cdlcbarcelona.com

Shôko
Passeig Marítim 36, Port
Olímpic. **Map** 6 E4.
Tel 93 225 92 00.
W shoko.biz

Eixample

Antilla
Carrer d'Aragó 141–3.
Tel 93 451 45 64.
W antillasalsa.com

City Hall
Rambla de Catalunya 2–4,
Eixample. **Map** 3 A3.
Tel 93 233 33 33.
W cityhallbarcelona.
com

Dow Jones
Carrer Bruc 97. **Map** 3 B4.
Tel 93 420 35 48.

Sutton Club
Carrer Tuset 13.
Tel 667 43 27 59.
W thesuttonclub.com

Montjuïc

The One
Poble Espanyol, Avinguda
Francesc Ferrer i Guàrdia
13. **Map** 1 A2.
Tel 902 90 92 89.

La Terrrazza
Poble Espanyol, Avinguda
da Ferrer i Guàrdia 13.
Map 1 A1. **Tel** 93 272
49 80 / 687 969 825.
W laterrrazza.com

Upload
Poble Espanyol, Avinguda
Francesc Ferrer i Guàrdia
13. **Map** 1 B1.
Tel 932 28 98 08.
W uploadbarcelona.
com

Poble Sec

Apolo
Carrer Nou de la Rambla
113, Poble Sec. **Map** 2 D4.
Tel 93 441 40 01.
W sala-apolo.com

Mau Mau
Carrer d'en Fontrodona
35, Poble Sec.
Map 2 D3.
Tel 93 441 80 15.
W maumaunder
ground.com

Tinta Roja
Carrer Creu dels Molers
17. Poble Sec.
Map 2 D3.
Tel 93 443 32 43.
W tintaroja.cat

Gràcia and Tibidabo

Bobby Gin
Carrer Francisco
Giner 47, Gràcia.
Map 3 B2.
Tel 93 368 18 92.
W bobbygin.com

Eldorado
Plaça del Sol 4,
Gràcia. **Map** 3 B1.

Mirablau
Plaça Doctor
Andreu, Tibidabo.
Tel 93 418 58 79.
W mirablaubcn.com

EASTERN
SPAIN

Introducing Eastern Spain

Eastern Spain covers an extraordinary range of climates and landscapes, from the snowbound peaks of the Pyrenees in Aragón to the beaches of the Costa Blanca and Costa Cálida, popular for their winter warmth and sunshine. The region has a wealth of historical sights including ancient monasteries near Barcelona, magnificent Roman ruins in Tarragona, Mudéjar churches and towers in Aragón and the great cathedrals of Valencia and Murcia. Away from the busy coasts, the countryside is often attractive but little visited.

Ordesa National Park *(see pp236–7)* in the Pyrenees has some of the most dramatic mountain scenery in Spain. It makes excellent walking country.

Zaragoza *(see pp240–41)* has many striking churches, especially the cathedral, the Basílica de Nuestra Señora del Pilar, and the Mudéjar-style Iglesia de la Magdalena.

Valencia *(see pp254–7)* is Spain's third-largest city. It has an old centre of narrow streets overlooked by venerable houses and monuments, such as the Miguelete, the cathedral's conspicuous bell tower. The city hosts a spectacular festival, Las Fallas, in March.

Jaca

Almudévar

Gallur

Zaragoz

Calatayud

ARAGÓN
(See pp230–45)

Calamocha

Montalbán

Alfambra

Teruel

Chelva

Requena

V

VALENCI
AND MURC
(See pp246–6

Jumilla

Elda

Cieza

Elche

Caravaca de La Cruz

Murcia

Alhama de Murcia

San Javier

Lorca

Mazarrón

Cartagena

Águillas

Murcia Cathedral *(see p266)*, built in the 14th century, has a Baroque façade and belfry, and two ornate side chapels – one in Late Gothic style and the other Renaissance. The cathedral museum houses Gothic altarpieces and other fascinating exhibits.

0 kilometres   50
0 miles   50

◀ Picturesque town of Albarracín, surrounded by stony hills, Teruel province

Ordesa National Park

ampo

Pont de Suert

Puigcerdà

La Seu
de Urgell

Benabarre

Berga

Girona

Monzón

CATALONIA
(See pp210–29)

Vic

Tàrrega

Manresa

Lleida

oz

Montblanc

Barcelona

Poblet

Sitges

Móra d'Ebre

Tarragona

Tortosa

lla

Benicarló

m

tellón
a
na

idorm

ia

ia

The Costa Brava *(see pp220–21)*, stretching south from the French border, is a mix of cliffs, wooded coves and pretty beaches. Lloret de Mar is the busiest, most popular tourist resort on the coast.

Poblet *(see pp226–7)*, enclosed by triple walls, is one of the most interesting medieval Cistercian monasteries in Catalonia. It contains a royal pantheon with the carved tombs of six of the kings of Aragón.

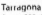

Tarragona
(see pp228–9) was one of the most important cities in Roman Spain. Among its remains are an amphitheatre and an aqueduct. A statue of Roger de Llúria, the great 13th-century Catalan naval commander, overlooks the beach.

The Costa Blanca *(see pp262–5)* is an attractive coast, as well as a popular holiday destination. Calp is overshadowed by a huge rock, the Penyal d'Ifach. In La Vila Joiosa, a line of houses has been painted in striking colours to make them visible to sailors at sea.

The Flavours of Eastern Spain

The current stars of Spain's culinary firmament are Catalans like Ferran Adriá or Carme Ruscalleda, whose creativity and innovation have brought them international acclaim. Fashionable new eateries and traditional country inns alike still place the emphasis firmly on fresh local ingredients. Along with adjoining Murcia and Catalonia, Valencia produces a huge array of fruit, vegetables, seafood, meat and game, all heaped colourfully in local markets. Rice is the key ingredient in paella and its many local variations. In landlocked Aragón, country cooking includes dishes that recall the Arabic occupation more than 1,000 years ago.

Valencian rice

Fresh octopus lie on the ice of a fish-seller's stall

Catalonia

The incredible variety of fresh produce in Catalonia is a reflection of the varied landscape – the Mediterranean provides all manner of fish and shellfish, the inland plains offer a wealth of vegetables and fields of golden rice, and the mountains contribute meat, game and wild mushrooms (a Catalan obsession). Spain's finest chefs create culinary fireworks in their celebrated restaurants, but Catalan cuisine, even at its most experimental, is essentially simple and relies on the wonderful freshness of its produce.

Aragón

In landlocked, mountainous Aragón, the emphasis is firmly on meat – particularly lamb, but also beef, rabbit and free-range chicken, often served simply grilled or slowly simmered in earthenware pots. There is also much excellent charcuterie, including hams and cured sausages, some flavoured with spices, which are often used to flavour the hearty stews popular in the mountainous north. River trout and eels are regularly found on local menus and, perhaps unusually so far

Artichokes   Onions   Aubergines (eggplants)
Celery
Capers
Tomatoes
Green beans
A range of fresh vegetables grown in eastern Spain

Regional Dishes and Specialities

The lush Mediterranean coastline, backed by fertile plains and cool mountains, offers an extraordinary abundance of fresh produce here. From the sturdy stews of land-locked Aragón and the traditional cured meats of inland Murcia, to the celebrated seafood paellas and other rice dishes of Valencia, this is a region that dazzles with the variety of its cuisine. Spring and summer bring tiny broad beans, asparagus, and all manner of other vegetables and fruits. In autumn and winter, the annual pig slaughter is followed by the preparation of hams and cured meats, mushrooms proliferate on shady hills, and gamey stews keep out the winter cold. Seafood remains a constant, whether in *zarzuela de mariscos* (a rich shellfish stew) or the Murcian favourite of sea bream baked in a salty crust.

Candied fruits

Suquet de peix A Catalan stew of fresh, firm-fleshed fish, flavoured with tomatoes, garlic and toasted almonds.

Spectacular harvest of wild autumn mushrooms in a local market

north, the ancient Arabic heritage can still be tasted in exquisite local sweets and desserts, from candied fruits to heavenly *guirlache*, made from almonds and sugar.

Valencia

Valencia, the "Orchard of Spain", is magnificently lush and fertile. Most famous for its oranges, it also produces countless other fruits and vegetables, partnered in local recipes with Mediterranean seafood and mountain lamb, rabbit and pork. In spring, hillsides blaze with cherry and almond blossom and, in autumn, the golden rice fields are spectacular. Spain's signature dish, paella, is a Valencian invention – the local plump *bomba* rice is perfect for soaking up juices.

Murcia

Tiny, arid Murcia is almost a desert in parts but, thanks to irrigation methods introduced by the Arabs more than 1,000 years ago, it has become one of the largest fruit- and vege- table-growing regions in Europe.

An *embutidos* (cured meats) producer shows off his wares

The mountainous hinterland is famous for its flavoursome *embutidos* (cured meats), especially *morcilla* (black pudding/blood sausage) and *chorizo* (spicy, paprika- flavoured cured sausage), along with its excellent rice, which has earned its own DO *(denominación de origen)*. Along the coast, you can enjoy a wide range of fresh Mediterranean seafood, including sea bream baked in a salt crust, or lobster stew from the Mar Menor. The area's Arabic heritage lingers particularly in the desserts, flavoured with saffron, pine nuts and delicate spices.

ON THE MENU

Arroz Negro A Valencian rice dish; squid ink gives the distinctive dark colour.

Caldero Murciano Fishermen's stew, flavoured with saffron and plenty of garlic.

Dorada a la Sal Sea bream baked in a salty crust to keep the fish moist and succulent.

Fideuá A paella made with shellfish and tiny noodles instead of rice.

Guirlache An Aragonese sweet, made of toasted whole almonds and buttery caramel.

Migas con Tropezones Crusty breadcrumbs fried with garlic, pork and spicy cured sausage.

Paella In Spain's best-known dish, ingredients include saffron, round *bomba* rice, and meat, fish and shellfish.

Lentejas al estilo del Alto Aragón Lentils are slowly cooked with garlic, chunks of ham and black sausage.

Crema Catalana This hugely popular dessert is an eggy custard topped with a flambéed sugar crust.

Wines of Eastern Spain

Spain's eastern seaboard offers a wide spread of wines of different styles. Catalonia deserves pride of place, and here the most important region is Penedès, home of *cava* (traditional-method sparkling wine) and some high-quality still wine. In Aragón, Cariñena reds can be good, and Somontano, in the Pyrenees, has fine, international-style varietals. Valencia and Murcia provide large quantities of easy-drinking reds, whites and *rosados* (rosés). Most notable among these are the rosés of Utiel-Requena, the Valencian Moscatels and the strong, full-bodied reds made in Jumilla.

Cabernet Sauvignon vines

Monastery of Poblet and Las Murallas vineyards in Catalonia

Somontano has had remarkable success due to the cultivation of international grape varieties such as Chardonnay and Pinot Noir.

0 kilometres — 100
0 miles — 50

Key Facts about Wines of Eastern Spain

Location and Climate
The climate of Eastern Spain varies mainly with altitude – low-lying parts are hot and dry; it also gets hotter the further south you go. The wine regions of Catalonia have a Mediterranean climate along the coast, which becomes drier further inland. The middle Penedès is a favoured location with a range of climates which suits many grape varieties. Somontano has a cooler, altitude-tempered climate. Valencia and Murcia can be, in contrast, unrelentingly hot.

Grape Varieties
The most common native red grape varieties planted in much of Eastern Spain are Garnacha, Tempranillo – which is called Ull de Llebre in Catalonia – Monastrell and Cariñena. Bobal makes both reds and, to a greater extent, rosés in Utiel-Requena. For whites,

Catalonia has Parellada, Macabeo and Xarel·lo (the trio most commonly used for *cava*), while in Valencia, Merseguera and Moscatel predominate. In the regions furthest to the southeast, Airén and Pedro Ximénez are sometimes found. French grape varieties, such as Chardonnay, Merlot, Cabernet Sauvignon and Sauvignon Blanc, flourish in the regions of Penedès, Costers del Segre and Somontano.

Good Producers
Somontano: Viñas del Vero, Viñedos del Altoaragón. ***Alella***: Marqués de Alella, Parxet. **Penedès**: Codorníu, Conde de Caralt, Freixenet, Juvé y Camps, Masía Bach, Mont-Marçal, René Barbier, Miguel Torres. **Costers del Segre**: Castell del Remei, Raimat. **Priorat**: Cellers Scala Dei, Masía Barril. **Valencia**: Vicente Gandia. **Utiel-Requena**: C. Augusto Egli. **Alicante**: Gutiérrez de la Vega. **Jumilla**: Asensio Carcelén (Sol y Luna), Bodegas Vitivino.

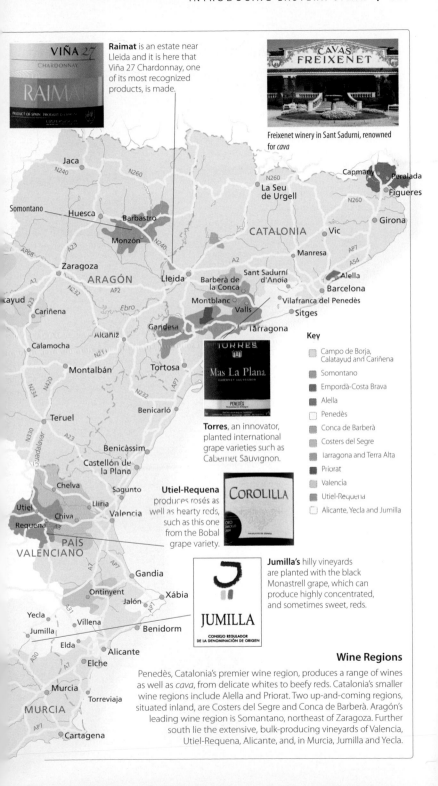

Raimat is an estate near Lleida and it is here that Viña 27 Chardonnay, one of its most recognized products, is made.

Freixenet winery in Sant Sadurni, renowned for *cava*

Key

- Campo de Borja, Calatayud and Cariñena
- Somontano
- Empordà-Costa Brava
- Alella
- Penedès
- Conca de Barberà
- Costers del Segre
- Tarragona and Terra Alta
- Priorat
- Valencia
- Utiel-Requena
- Alicante, Yecla and Jumilla

Torres, an innovator, planted international grape varieties such as Cabernet Sauvignon.

Utiel-Requena produces rosés as well as hearty reds, such as this one from the Bobal grape variety.

Jumilla's hilly vineyards are planted with the black Monastrell grape, which can produce highly concentrated, and sometimes sweet, reds.

Wine Regions

Penedès, Catalonia's premier wine region, produces a range of wines as well as *cava*, from delicate whites to beefy reds. Catalonia's smaller wine regions include Alella and Priorat. Two up-and-coming regions, situated inland, are Costers del Segre and Conca de Barberà. Aragón's leading wine region is Somontano, northeast of Zaragoza. Further south lie the extensive, bulk-producing vineyards of Valencia, Utiel-Requena, Alicante, and, in Murcia, Jumilla and Yecla.

Flowers of the Matorral

The *matorral*, a scrubland rich in wild flowers, is the distinctive landscape of Spain's eastern Mediterranean coast. It is the result of centuries of woodland clearance, during which the native holm oak was felled for timber and to provide land for grazing and cultivation. Many colourful plants have adapted to the extremes of climate here. Most flower in spring, when hillsides are daubed with pink and white cistuses and yellow broom, and the air is perfumed by aromatic herbs such as rosemary, lavender and thyme. Buzzing insects feed on the abundance of nectar and pollen.

Spanish broom is a small bush with yellow flowers on slender branches. The black seed pods split when dry, scattering the seeds on the ground.

The century plant's flower stalk can reach 10 m (32 ft).

Aleppo pine   Rosemary

Jerusalem sage, an attractive shrub which is often grown in gardens, has tall stems surrounded by bunches of showy yellow flowers. Its leaves are greyish-white and woolly.

Rose garlic has round clusters of violet or pink flowers at the end of a single stalk. It survives the summer as the bulb familiar to all cooks.

Foreign Invaders

Several plants from the New World have managed to colonize the bare ground of the *matorral*. The prickly pear, thought to have been brought back by Christopher Columbus, produces a delicious fruit which can be picked only with thickly gloved hands. The rapidly growing century plant, a native of Mexico which has tough spiny leaves, sends up a tall flower shoot only when it is 10–15 years old, after which it dies.

Prickly pear in fruit

Flowering shoots of the century plant

Common thyme is a low-growing aromatic herb, which is widely cultivated for use in the kitchen.

The mirror orchid, a small plant that grows on grassy sites, is easily distinguished from other orchids by the brilliant metallic blue patch inside the lip, fringed by brown hairs.

Most plants found in the *matorral* come into bloom in the warm, moist spring. The plants protect themselves from losing water during the dry summer heat with thick leaves or waxy secretions, or by storing moisture in bulbs or tubers.

— Temperature   ▪ Rainfall

Wildlife of the Matorral

The animals that live in the *matorral* are most often seen early in the morning, before the temperature is high. Countless insects fly from flower to flower, providing a source of food for birds. Smaller mammals, such as mice and voles, are active only at night, when it is cooler and there are few predators around.

Holm oaks are very common in Eastern Spain. The leaves are tough and rubbery to prevent water loss.

The strawberry tree is an evergreen shrub with glossy serrated leaves. Its edible, strawberry-like fruit turns red when ripe.

Ladder snakes feed on small mammals, birds and insects. The young are identified by a black pattern like the rungs of a ladder, but adults are marked with two simple stripes.

Scorpions hide under rocks or wood by day. When disturbed, the tail is curled quickly over the body in a threatening gesture. The sting, lethal to small animals, can cause some irritation to humans.

Tree heather

The Dartford warbler, a skulking bird that has dark plumage and a cocked tail, sings melodiously during its mating display. Males are more vividly coloured than females.

The swallow-tail butterfly is one of the most conspicuous of the great many insects living in the *matorral*. Bees, ants and grasshoppers are also extremely common.

Grey-leaved cistus, growing on sunny sites, has crumpled petals and bright yellow anthers.

Narrow-leaved cistus exudes a sticky aromatic gum used in perfumes.

Star clover is a low-growing annual whose fruit develops into a star-shaped seed head. Its flowers are often pale pink.

CATALONIA

Lleida · Andorra · Girona · Barcelona province · Tarragona

Catalonia is a proud nation-within-a-nation, which was once, under the count-kings of Barcelona-Aragón, one of the Mediterranean's great sea powers. It has its own semi-autonomous regional government and its own language, Catalan, which is used in place names, menus and on road signs throughout the region.

The Romans first set foot on the Iberian Peninsula at Empúries on Catalonia's Costa Brava ("wild coast"). They left behind them great monuments, especially in and around Tarragona, the capital of their vast province of Tarraconensis. Later, Barcelona emerged as the region's capital, economically and culturally important enough to rival Madrid.

In the 1960s the Costa Brava became one of Europe's first mass package-holiday destinations. Although resorts such as Lloret de Mar continue to draw the crowds, former fishing villages such as Cadaqués remain relatively unspoiled on this naturally attractive coast.

Inland, there is a rich artistic heritage to be explored. Catalonia has several spectacular monasteries, especially Montserrat, its spiritual heart, and Poblet. There are also many medieval towns, such as Montblanc, Besalú and Girona – which contain a wealth of monuments and museums.

In the countryside there is a lot to seek out, from the wetland wildlife of the Delta de l'Ebre area to the vineyards of Penedès (where most of Spain's sparkling wine is made). In the high Pyrenees rare butterflies brighten remote mountain valleys, and little hidden villages encircle exquisite Romanesque churches.

Aigüestortes i Estany Sant Maurici National Park in the central Pyrenees, in the province of Lleida

◀ Boats shelter in Tossa de Mar's horseshoe bay on the Costa Brava

Exploring Catalonia

Catalonia includes a long stretch of the Spanish Pyrenees, whose green, flower-filled valleys hide picturesque villages with Romanesque churches. The Parc Nacional d'Aigüestortes and Vall d'Aran are paradises for naturalists, while Baqueira-Beret offers skiers reliable snow. Sun-lovers can choose between the rugged Costa Brava or the long sandy stretches of the Costa Daurada. Tarragona is rich in Roman monuments while the inland monasteries of Poblet and Santes Creus, and the well-known vineyards of Penedès, provide idyllic scenery.

Isolated houses in the countryside around La Seu d'Urgell

Key

═══ Motorway (highway)

═══ Other highway

▬▬ Main road

···· Minor road

▬▬ Scenic route

▬·▬ Main railway

─── Minor railway

▬▬ International border

▬▬ Regional border

△ Summit

Getting Around

A tunnel near Puigcerdà has made the central Catalan Pyrenees easily accessible. Buses, more frequent in summer, connect most towns. The main north–south railway hugs the coast from Blanes southwards. Other lines run from Barcelona through Vic, Lleida and Tortosa.

Church on the seafront of Sitges

Vineyards outside Gandesa, west of Tarragona

Sights at a Glance

The Vall d'Aran, surrounded by the snowcapped mountains of the Pyrenees

Butterflies of the Vall d'Aran

A huge variety of butterflies and moths is found high in the mountains and valleys of the Pyrenees. In particular, the isolated Vall d'Aran is the home of several unique and rare subspecies. The best time of year to see the butterflies is between May and July.

Grizzled Skipper *(Pyrgus malvae)*

Clouded Apollo
(Parnassius mnemosyne)

Checkered Skipper
(Carterocephalus palaemon)

❶ Vall d'Aran

Lleida. 🚌 Vielha. 🚹 Carrer Sarriulèra 10, Vielha, 973 64 01 10.
🌐 visitvaldaran.com

This Valley of Valleys – *aran* means "valley" – is a beautiful haven of forests and flower-filled meadows, surrounded by towering mountain peaks.

The Vall d'Aran was formed by the Riu Garona, which rises in the area and flows out to France as the Garonne. With no proper link to the outside world until 1924, when a road was built over the Bonaigua Pass, the valley was cut off from the rest of Spain for most of the winter. Snow still blocks the narrow pass from November to April, but today access is easy through the Túnel de Vielha from El Pont de Suert.

The fact that the Vall d'Aran faces north means that it has a climate similar to that found on the Atlantic coast. Many rare wild flowers and butterflies flourish in the perfect conditions created by the damp breezes and shady slopes. It is also a noted habitat for many species of narcissus.

Tiny villages have grown up beside the Riu Garona, often around Romanesque churches, notably at Bossòst, Salardú, Escunhau and Arties. The valley is also ideal for outdoor sports such as skiing and is popular with walkers.

❷ Vielha

Lleida. 🏔 5,400. 🚌 🚹 Carrer Sarriulèra 10, 973 64 01 10. 🗓 Thu.
🎉 Fiesta de Vielha (8 Sep), Feria de Vielha (8 Oct).

The capital of the Vall d'Aran preserves relics of its medieval past. The Romanesque church of Sant Miquel has an octagonal bell tower, a tall, pointed roof and a superb wooden 12th-century crucifix, the *Mig Aran Christ*. It once formed part of a larger carving, since lost, which represented the Descent from the Cross. The **Musèu dera Vall d'Aran** is a museum devoted to Aranese history and folklore.

🏛 **Musèu dera Vall d'Aran**
Carrer Major 26. **Tel** 973 64 18 15. **Open** Tue–Sun. **Closed** public hols.

Mig Aran Christ (12th-century), Sant Miquel church, Vielha

❸ Baqueira-Beret

Lleida. 🏔 100. 🚌 ℹ️ Baqueira-Beret, 973 63 90 25. 🎿 Romería de Nuestra Señora de Montgarri (2 Jul).
🌐 **baqueira.es**

This ski resort, one of Spain's best, is popular with both the public and the Spanish royal family. There is reliable winter snow cover and a choice of over 100 pistes at altitudes from 1,520 m to 2,470 m (4,987 ft to 8,104 ft).

Baqueira and Beret were separate mountain villages before skiing became popular, but now form a single resort. The Romans took full advantage of the thermal springs located here; nowadays they are appreciated by tired skiers.

❹ Vall de Boí

Lleida. 🚉 La Pobla de Segur. 🚌 Pont de Suert. ℹ️ Barruera, 973 69 40 00. 🌐 **vallboi.com**

This small valley on the edge of the Parc Nacional d'Aigüestortes is dotted with tiny villages, many of which are built around Catalan Romanesque churches.

Dating from the 11th and 12th centuries, these churches are distinguished by their tall belfries, such as the Església de Santa Eulàlia at Erill-la-Vall, which has six floors.

The two churches at Taüll, Sant Climent (see p28) and Santa Maria, have superb frescoes. Between 1919 and 1923 the originals were taken for safekeeping to the Museu Nacional d'Art de Catalunya in Barcelona (see p176) and replicas now stand in their place. You can climb the towers of Sant Climent for superb views of the surrounding countryside.

Other churches in the area worth visiting include those at Coll, for its fine ironwork, Barruera, and Durro, which has another massive bell tower.

At the head of the valley is the hamlet of Caldes de Boí, popular for its thermal springs and the nearby ski station, Boí-Taüll. It is also a good base for exploring the Parc Nacional d'Aigüestortes, the entrance to which is only 5 km (3 miles) from here.

The tall belfry of Sant Climent church at Taüll in the Vall de Boí

❺ Parc Nacional d'Aigüestortes

Lleida. 🚉 La Pobla de Segur. 🚌 Pont de Suert, La Pobla de Segur. ℹ️ Boí, 973 69 61 89; Espot, 973 62 40 36.
🌐 **parcsnaturals.gencat.cat/en/ aiguestortes**

The pristine mountain scenery of Catalonia's only national park (see pp34–5) is among the most spectacular to be seen in the Pyrenees.

Established in 1955, the park covers an area of 102 sq km (40 sq miles). Its full title is Parc Nacional d'Aigüestortes i Estany de Sant Maurici, named after the lake (estany) of Sant Maurici in the east and the Aigüestortes (literally, "twisted waters") area in the west. The main access towns

are Espot, to the east, and Boí, to the west. Dotted around the park are waterfalls and the sparkling, clear waters of around 150 lakes and tarns which, in an earlier era, were scoured by glaciers to depths of up to 50 m (164 ft).

The finest scenery is around Sant Maurici lake, which lies beneath the twin shards of the Serra dels Encantats (Mountains of the Enchanted). From here, there is a variety of walks, particularly along the string of lakes that lead north to the towering peaks of Agulles d'Amitges. To the south is the dramatic vista of Estany Negre, the highest and deepest tarn in the park

Early summer in the lower valleys is marked by a mass of pink and red rhododendrons, while later in the year wild lilies bloom in the forests of fir, beech and silver birch.

The park is also home to a variety of wildlife. Chamois (also known as izards) live on mountain screes and in the meadows, while beavers and otters can be spotted by the lakes. Golden eagles nest on mountain ledges, and grouse and capercaillie are found in the woods.

During the summer the park is popular with walkers, while in winter, the snow-covered mountains are ideal for cross-country skiing.

Picturesque landscape in the Parc Nacional d'Aigüestortes

The Catalan Language

Catalan has now fully recovered from the ban it suffered under Franco's dictatorship and has supplanted Castilian (Spanish) as the language in everyday use all over Catalonia. Spoken by more than 9.5 million people, it is a Romance language akin to the Provençal of France. Previously it was suppressed by Felipe V in 1717 and only officially resurfaced in the 19th century, when the Jocs Florals (medieval poetry contests) were revived during the rebirth of Catalan literature. A leading figure of the movement was the poet Jacint Verdaguer (1845–1902).

Catalonia's national emblem

---

❻ Andorra

Principality of Andorra. 🏔 78,000. 🚌 Andorra la Vella. 🛈 Plaça de la Rotonda, Andorra la Vella, 376 73 00 03. 🌐 visitandorra.com

Andorra occupies 464 sq km (179 sq miles) of the Pyrenees between France and Spain. In 1993, it became fully independent and held its first ever democratic elections. Since 1278, it had been an autonomous feudal state under the jurisdiction of the Spanish bishop of La Seu d'Urgell and the French Count of Foix (a title adopted by the President of France). These are still the ceremonial joint heads of state.

Andorra's official language is Catalan, though French and Castilian are also spoken. The currency changed from the peseta to the euro in 2002.

For many years Andorra has been a tax-free paradise for shoppers, reflected in the crowded shops of the capital, Andorra la Vella. Les Escaldes (near the capital), as well as Sant Julià de Lòria and El Pas de la Casa (near the Spanish and French borders), have also become shopping centres.

Most visitors never see Andorra's rural charms, which match those of other parts of the Pyrenees. The region is excellent for walkers. One of the main routes leads to the Cercle de Pessons, a bowl of lakes in the east, and past Romanesque chapels such as Sant Martí at La Cortinada. In the north is the picturesque Sorteny Valley, where traditional farmhouses have been converted into snug restaurants.

---

❼ La Seu d'Urgell

Lleida. 🏔 12,300. 🚌 🛈 Carrer Major 8, 973 35 15 11. 🛒 Tue & Sat. 🎉 Festa Major (Aug).

This ancient Pyrenean town was made a bishopric by the Visigoths in the 6th century. Feuds between the bishops of Urgell and the Counts of Foix over land ownership led to the emergence of Andorra in the 13th century.

The 12th-century cathedral has a much-venerated Romanesque statue of Santa Maria d'Urgell. The **Museu Diocesà** contains medieval works of art and manuscripts, including a 10th-century copy of St Beatus of Liébana's *Commentary on the Apocalypse (see p114)*.

🏛 Museu Diocesà
Plaça del Deganat. **Tel** 973 35 32 42. **Open** daily. **Closed** public hols. 🎨 ♿

Carving, La Seu d'Urgell cathedral

---

❽ Puigcerdà

Girona. 🏔 9,000. 🚉 🚌 🛈 Plaça Santa Maria, 972 88 05 42. 🛒 Sun. 🎉 Festa de l'Estany (third Sun of Aug). 🌐 puigcerda.cat

Puig is Catalan for "hill". Although Puigcerdà sits on a relatively small hill compared with the encircling mountains, which rise to 2,900 m (9,500 ft), it nevertheless has a fine view

right down the beautiful Cerdanya Valley, watered by the trout-filled Riu Segre.

Puigcerdà, very close to the French border, was founded in 1177 by Alfonso II as the capital of Cerdanya, which shares a past and its culture with the French Cerdagne. The Spanish enclave of Llívia, an attractive little town with a medieval pharmacy, lies 6 km (4 miles) inside France.

Cerdanya is the largest valley in the Pyrenees. At its edge is the nature reserve of Cadí-Moixeró, which has a population of alpine choughs.

Portal of Monestir de Santa Maria, Ripoll

❾ Ripoll

Girona. 🏔 11,000. 🚉 🚌 🛈 Plaça Abat Oliba, 972 70 23 51. 🛒 Sat. 🎉 Festa Major (11–12 May). 🌐 ripoll.cat/turisme

Once a tiny mountain base from which raids against the Moors were made, Ripoll is now best known for the Monestir de Santa Maria, built in AD 888. The town has been called "the cradle of Catalonia", as the monastery was both the power base and cultural centre of Guifré el Pélos (Wilfred the Hairy), founder of the 500-year dynasty of the House of Barcelona. He is buried in the monastery.

In the later 12th century, the huge west portal gained a series of intricate carvings, which are perhaps the finest Romanesque carvings in Spain. They depict historical and biblical scenes. The two-storey cloister is the only other part of the original monastery to have survived wars and anti-clerical purges. The rest is a 19th-century reconstruction.

The medieval town of Besalú on the banks of the Riu Fluvià

⑩ Sant Joan de les Abadesses

Girona. 🏔 3,600. 🚌 ℹ️ Plaça de l'Abadia 9, 972 72 05 99. 🚍 Sun. 🎪 Festa Major (second Sun of Sep). 🌐 santjoandelesabadesses.cat

A fine, 12th-century Gothic bridge arches over the Riu Ter to this unassuming market town, whose main attraction is its monastery.

Founded in AD 885, it was a gift from Guifré, first count of Barcelona, to his daughter, the first abbess. The church is unadorned except for a superb wooden calvary, *The Descent from the Cross*. Made in 1150, it looks modern; part of it, a thief, was burned in the Civil War and replaced with such skill that it is hard to tell which is new. The monastery's museum has Baroque and Renaissance altarpieces.

12th-century calvary, Sant Joan de les Abadesses monastery

Environs

To the north is Camprodon, a small town full of grand houses, and shops selling local produce. The region is especially noted for its *embutits* (charcuterie).

⑪ Olot

Girona. 🏔 34,000. 🚌 ℹ️ Carrer Francesc Fàbregas 6, 972 26 01 41. 🚍 Mon. 🎪 Corpus Christi (Jun), Festa del Tura (8 Sep). 🌐 turismeolot.com

This small market town is at the centre of a landscape pockmarked with the conical hills of extinct volcanoes. But it was an earthquake in 1474 which last disturbed the town, destroying its medieval past.

During the 18th century the town's textile industry spawned the "Olot School" of art: finished cotton fabrics were printed with drawings, and in 1783 the Public School of Drawing was founded.

Much of the school's work, which includes sculpted saints and paintings such as Joaquim Vayreda's *Les Falgueres*, is in the **Museu Comarcal de la Garrotxa**, housed in an 18th-century hospice. There are also pieces by Modernista sculptor Miquel Blay, whose damsels support the balcony at No. 38 Passeig Miquel Blay.

🏛 **Museu Comarcal de la Garrotxa**
Carrer Hospici 8. **Tel** 972 27 11 66.
Closed for renovation. 📷 ♿

⑫ Besalú

Girona. 🏔 2,400. 🚌 ℹ️ Carrer del Pont 1, 972 59 12 40. 🚍 Tue. 🎪 Sant Vicenç (22 Jan), Festa Major (last weekend of Sep). 📷 🌐 besalu.cat

A magnificent medieval town, with a striking approach across a fortified bridge over the Riu Fluvià, Besalú has two fine churches. These are the Romanesque Sant Vicenç and Sant Pere, the sole remnant of Besalú's Benedictine monastery. It was founded in AD 948, but pulled down in 1835.

In 1964 a mikvah, a ritual Jewish bath, was discovered. It was built in 1264 and is one of only three of that period to survive in Europe. The tourist office organizes guided visits to all the town's attractions.

To the south, the sky-blue lake of Banyoles, where the 1992 Olympic rowing contests were held, is ideal for picnics.

Sausage shop in the mountain town of Camprodon

Girona Old Town

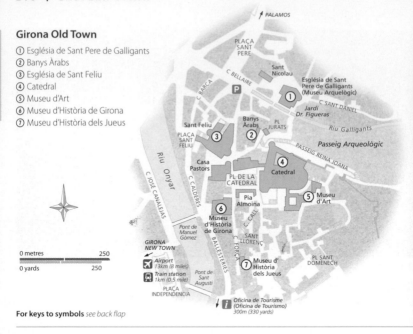

For keys to symbols *see back flap*

⓭ Girona

Girona. 🏘 98,000. ✈ 🚇 🚌
ℹ Rambla de la Llibertat 1, 972 01
00 01. 🛒 Tue, Sat. 🎉 Sant Narcís
(late Oct). **W** girona.cat/turisme

This handsome town puts on its best face beside the Riu Onyar, where tall, pastel-coloured buildings rise above the water. Behind them, in the Old Town, the Rambla de la Llibertat is lined with busy shops and street cafés.

The houses were built in the 19th century to replace sections of the city wall damaged during a seven-month siege by French troops in 1809. Most of the rest of the ramparts, first raised by the Romans, are still intact and have

been turned into the Passeig Arqueològic (Archaeological Walk), which runs around the city.

The walk starts on the north side of the town, near the Església de Sant Pere de Galligants (St Peter of the Cock Crows). The church now holds the city's archaeological collection.

From here a narrow street into the old part of town passes through the north gate, where huge Roman foundation stones are still visible. They mark the route of the Via Augusta, the road that originally ran from Tarragona to Rome. The most popular place of devotion for the people of Girona is the Església de Sant

Feliu. The church, begun in the 14th century, was built over the tombs of St Felix and St Narcissus, both patrons of the city. Next to the high altar are eight Roman sarcophagi embedded in the apse wall.

Despite their name, the nearby Banys Àrabs (Arab Baths), lit by a fine octagonal lantern, were built in the late 12th century, about 300 years after the Moors had left.

🏛 Museu d'Història dels Jueus

Carrer de la Força 8. **Tel** 972 21 67 61.
Open 10am–6pm Tue–Sat (Jul & Aug: to 8pm; Sep–Jun: to 2pm). **Closed** 1 & 6 Jan, 25 & 26 Dec. 🎫 🎩 ♿
W girona.cat/call

Amid the maze of alleyways and steps in the Old Town is the former, partially restored, Jewish quarter of El Call. The Museu d'Història dels Jueus gives a history of Girona's Jews, who were expelled in the late 15th century.

⓵ Cathedral

Open 10am–6:30pm daily (Jul–Aug: to 7:30pm; Nov–Mar: to 5:30pm). 🎫 free Sun. **W** catedraldegirona.cat

The style of Girona Cathedral's solid west face is pure Catalan Baroque, but the rest of the building is Gothic. The single nave, built in 1416 by Guillem

Painted houses crowded along the bank of the Riu Onyar in Girona

Bofill, is the widest Gothic span in Christendom. Behind the altar is a marble throne known as "Charlemagne's Chair" after the Frankish king whose troops took Girona in 785. In the chancel is a 14th-century jewel-encrusted silver and enamel altarpiece. In the museum are Romanesque paintings and statues such as a 14th-century statue of the Catalan king, Pere the Ceremonious, and a 10th-century illuminated copy of St Beatus of Liébana's *Commentary on the Apocalypse*.

The collection's most famous item is a large, well-preserved 11th- to 12th-century tapestry, called *The Creation*.

Tapestry of *The Creation*

🏛 Museu d'Art

Pujada de la Catedral 12. **Tel** 972 41 27 77. **Open** Tue–Sun. **Closed** 1 & 6 Jan, 25 & 26 Dec. 🅿 ♿ 📷 by appt.
w museuart.com

This former episcopal palace is one of Catalonia's best art galleries, with works ranging from the Romanesque period to the 20th century. Items from churches destroyed through war or neglect give an idea of church interiors long ago. Highlights are 10th-century carvings, a silver-clad altar from the church at Sant Pere de Rodes and a 12th-century beam from Cruïlles.

🏛 Museu d'Història de Girona

Carrer de la Força 27. **Tel** 972 22 22 29. **Open** 10:30am–6:30pm Tue–Sat (to 6:30pm Oct–Apr), 10:30am–1:30pm Sun. 🅿

This museum is housed in a former convent. Parts of the cemetery are preserved, including the recesses where the bodies of members of the Capuchin Order were placed while decomposing. The collection includes old *sardana (see p229)* instruments.

⑭ Figueres

Girona. 🅰 45,000. 🚉 🚌 ℹ Plaça de l'Escorxador 2, 972 50 31 55. 🗓 Thu. 🎉 Santa Creu (3 May), Sant Pere (29 Jun). **w** visitfigueres.cat

Figueres is in the north of the Empordà (Ampurdán) region, the fertile plain that sweeps inland from the Gulf of Roses. Every Thursday, the market here fills with fruit and vegetables from the area.

The **Museu del Joguet** (Toy Museum) is housed on the top floor of the old Hotel de Paris, on the Rambla, Figueres' main street. Inside are exhibits from all over Catalonia. At the lower end of the Rambla is a statue of Narcís Monturiol i Estarriol (1819–85), claimed to be the inventor of the submarine.

A much better known son of the town is Salvador Dalí, who founded the **Teatre-Museu Dalí** in 1974. The most visited museum in Spain after the Prado, the galleries occupy Figueres' old main theatre. Its roof has an eye-catching glass dome. Not all the work shown is by Dalí, and none of his best-known works are here. But the

Rainy Taxi, a monument in the garden of the Teatre-Museu Dalí

displays, including *Rainy Taxi* – a black Cadillac being sprayed by a fountain – are a monument to the man who, fittingly, is buried here.

🏛 Museu del Joguet

Carrer Sant Pere 1. **Tel** 972 50 45 85. **Open** daily. 🅿 ♿

🏛 Teatre-Museu Dalí

Plaça Gala-Salvador Dalí. **Tel** 972 67 75 00. **Open** Jun–Sep: daily; Oct–May: Tue–Sun. **Closed** Mon Oct–May, 1 Jan, 25 Dec. 🅿 **w** salvador-dali.org

The Art of Dalí

Salvador Dalí i Domènech was born in Figueres in 1904 and mounted his first exhibition at the age of 15. After studying at the Escuela de Bellas Artes in Madrid, and dabbling with Cubism, Futurism and Metaphysical painting, the young artist embraced Surrealism in 1929, becoming the movement's best-known painter. Never far from controversy, the self-publicist Dalí became famous for his hallucinatory images – such as *Woman – Animal Symbiosis* – which he described as "hand-painted dream photographs". Dalí's career also included writing and film-making, and established him as one of the 20th century's greatest artists. He died in his home town in 1989.

Ceiling fresco in the Wind Palace Room, Teatre-Museu Dalí

⓯ Cadaqués

Girona. 🏔 3,000. 🚌 🛈 Carrer Cotxe 1, 972 25 83 15. 🛡 Mon. 🎉 Festa Major de Verano (first week of Sep), Santa Esperança (18 Dec). **W** visitcadaques.org

This whitewashed town is overlooked by the Baroque Església de Santa Maria. Perched at the tip of the remote Cap de Creus headland, in the 1960s Cadaqués was dubbed the "St Tropez of Spain", due to the young crowd that sought out Salvador Dalí in nearby Port Lligat. The house where he lived from 1930 until his death in 1989 is known as the **Casa-Museu Salvador Dalí**. Visitors can see the painter's workshop, the library, private bedrooms, garden area and swimming pool. Advanced booking is required.

🏛 **Casa-Museu Salvador Dalí**
Port Lligat. **Tel** 972 25 10 15. Reservations required, email pll@fundacio dali.org **Open** Tue–Sun (mid-Jun–mid-Sep: daily). **Closed** 1 Jan, 7 Jan–early Feb, 25 Dec. 🚫 **W** salvador-dali.org

⓰ Empúries

Girona. 🚌 L'Escala. **Tel** 972 77 59 76. **Open** from 10am, closing time varies with season; check website. 🚫 ruins. 🎉 25 Jun–15 Sep: 11:30am daily. **W** mac.cat

The ruins of this Greco-Roman town *(see p55)* are dramatically located overlooking the sea. Three settlements were built between the 7th and 3rd centuries BC: the old town (Palaiapolis);

An excavated Roman pillar in the ruins of Empúries

the new town (Neapolis); and the Roman town. The **old town** was founded by the Greeks in 600 BC as a trading port. It was built on what was a small island, and is now the site of the hamlet of Sant Martí de Empúries. In 550 BC this was replaced by a town on the shore which the Greeks named Emporion, meaning "trading place". In 218 BC, the Romans landed at Empúries and built a city next to the new town.

A nearby museum exhibits some of the site's finds, but the best are in Barcelona's Museu Arqueològic *(see p176)*.

⓱ Peratallada

Girona. 🏔 188. 🛈 Plaça del Castell 3 (872 98 70 30). 🎉 Fira de les Herbes (last weekend in Apr or first in May), Festa Major (6 & 7 Aug), Medieval Market (first weekend in Oct). **W** forallac.cat

This tiny village is stunning and only a short inland trip from the Costa Brava. With Pals and Palau Sator it forms part of the "Golden Triangle" of medieval villages. Its mountaintop position gives some dramatic views of the area. A labyrinth of cobbled streets wind up to the well-conserved castle and lookout tower, whose written records date from the 11th century. Both counts and kings made doubly sure of fending off any attackers by constructing a sturdy wall enclosing the entire village that even today limits the nucleus from further expansion, ensuring it retains its medieval character.

Looking south along the Costa Brava from Tossa de Mar

⓲ Tossa de Mar

Girona. 🏔 5,500. 🚌 🛈 Avinguda Pelegrí 25, 972 34 01 08. 🛡 Thu. 🎉 Festa Major d'Hivern (22 Jan), Festa Major d'Estiu (29 Jun–2 Jul). **W** infotossa.com

At the end of a corniche, the Roman town of Turissa is one of the prettiest along the Costa Brava. Above the New Town is the Vila Vella (Old Town), a protected national monument. In the old town, the **Museu Municipal** has a collection of local archaeological finds and modern art including *The Celestial Violinist*, by the artist Marc Chagall.

🏛 **Museu Municipal**
Plaça Pintor Roig i Soler 1. **Tel** 972 34 07 09. **Open** Jun–Sep: daily. 🚫

⓳ Blanes

Girona. 🏔 40,000. 🚊 🚌 🛈 Plaça de Catalunya s/n, 972 33 03 48. 🛡 Mon. 🎉 El Bilar (6 Apr), Sta Ana (late Jul). **W** visitblanes.net

The working port of Blanes has one of the longest beaches on the Costa Brava, but the highlight of the town is the **Jardí Botànic Marimurtra**. These fine gardens, designed by Karl Faust in 1928, are spectacularly sited above cliffs. There are 7,000 species of Mediterranean and tropical plants.

🌿 **Jardí Botànic Marimurtra**
Passeig Carles Faust 9. **Tel** 972 33 08 2 **Open** daily. **Closed** 1 & 6 Jan, 24 & 25 Dec. 🚫 🛗 **W** marimurtra.cat

The Costa Brava

The Costa Brava ("wild coast") runs for some 200 km (125 miles) from Blanes northwards to the region of Empordà (Ampurdán), which borders France. It is a mix of pine-backed sandy coves, golden beaches and crowded, modern resorts. The busiest resorts – Lloret de Mar, Tossa de Mar and La Platja d'Aro – are to the south. Sant Feliu de Guíxols and Palamós are still working towns behind the summer rush. Just inland there are medieval villages to explore, such as Peralada, Peratallada and Pals. Wine, olives and fishing were the mainstays of the area before the tourists came in the 1960s.

Cadaqués retains an air of seclusion, as it is accessible only by a steep road. It has an arty atmosphere and its small, stony beaches remain unspoiled and less crowded than others.

L'Estartit is a good base for the Illes Medes, a former pirates' lair, which now form a marine reserve with clear waters perfect for skin diving.

Palamós is a working port with modern hotels to the south, and secluded beaches and coves lapped by clear water to the north.

La Platja d'Aro's long and sandy beach is lined with modern hotel blocks. It is one of the most popular resorts on the coast.

Tossa de Mar has a golden beach and a small cove beneath the fortified Old Town.

Roses lies at the head of a sweeping bay. Its sandy beach, the longest on the Costa Brava, has become a mecca for lovers of water sports.

L'Escala is a small resort, popular mainly with local tourists. It has fine beaches and a small port where fishing nets dry in the sun.

Begur is a hilltop town just inland. It has good views of the coast, and small coves are tucked at its feet.

Llafranc, a white-washed resort, with a promenade leading to neighbouring Calella, is one of the coast's most pleasant resorts.

Lloret de Mar has more hotels than anywhere else on the coast. But there are unspoiled beaches nearby, such as Santa Cristina.

Llançà
Port de la Selva — Cap de Creus
Peralada
Parc Natural del Cap de Creus
Cadaqués
Castelló d'Empúries
Roses
Fortià
Empuriabrava
Parc Natural dels Aiguamolls de l'Empordà
L'Escala
Punta del Milà
L'Estartit
Illes Medes
Riu Ter
Torroella de Montgrí
Peratallada
Pals
Begur
Palafrugell
Llafranc
Calella de Palafrugell
Palamós
Platja d'Aro
S'Agaró
Sant Feliu de Guíxols
Llagostera
Tossa de Mar
Lloret de Mar
Tordera
Blanes
Malgrat de Mar

0 kilometres 10
0 miles 10

⑳ Monestir de Montserrat

The "Serrated Mountain" *(mont serrat)*, its highest peak rising to 1,236 m (4,055 ft), is a magnificent setting for Catalonia's holiest place, the Monastery of Montserrat, which is surrounded by chapels and hermits' caves. A chapel was first mentioned in the 9th century, the monastery was founded in the 11th century and in 1811, when the French attacked Catalonia in the War of Independence *(see p67)*, it was destroyed and the monks killed. Rebuilt and repopulated in 1844, it was a beacon of Catalan culture during the Franco years. Today Benedictine monks live here. Visitors can hear the Escolania singing the *Salve Regina* and the *Virolai* (Marian and Montserrat hymns) in the basilica at 1pm and 7pm Monday to Friday, 6:45pm Monday to Thursday and noon and 6:45pm on Sundays, except in the summer and during the Christmas period.

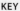

The Way of the Cross
This path passes 11 statues representing the Stations of the Cross. It begins near the Plaça de l'Abat Oliba.

KEY

① **Funicular to the holy site of Santa Cova**

② **The Museum** has a collection of 19th- and 20th-century Catalan paintings and many Italian and French works. It also displays liturgical items from the Holy Land.

③ **Plaça de Santa Maria's** focal points are two wings of Gothic cloister built in 1476. The modern monastery façade is by Françesc Folguera.

④ **Gothic cloister**

⑤ **The Black Virgin** *(La Moreneta)* looks down from behind the altar. Protected behind glass, her wooden orb protrudes for pilgrims to touch.

⑥ **The rack railway** *(La Cremallera)*, follows the course of a historic rail line built in 1880.

⑦ **Cable car to Aeri de Montserrat station**

View of Montserrat
The complex includes cafés and a hotel. A second funicular transports visitors to nature trails above the monastery.

★ Basilica Façade
Agapit Vallmitjana sculpted Christ and the apostles on the basilica's Neo-Renaissance façade. It was built in 1900 to replace the Renaissance façade of the original church, consecrated in 1592.

VISITORS' CHECKLIST

Practical Information
Montserrat, Barcelona province.
Tel 938 77 77 77.
W **montserratvisita.com**
Basilica: **Open** 7:30am–8pm daily.
from 7:30am daily.
Museum: **Open** 10am–5:45pm daily.

Transport
Aeri de Montserrat, then cable car; Monistrol-Enllaç, then La Cremallera rack railway.
from Barcelona.

Basilica Interior
The sanctuary in the domed basilica is adorned by a richly enamelled altar and paintings by Catalan artists.

★ The Virgin of Montserrat
The small wooden statue of La Moreneta (the dark one) is the soul of Montserrat. It is said to have been made by St Luke and brought here by St Peter in AD 50. Centuries later, the statue is believed to have been hidden from the Moors in the nearby Santa Cova (Holy Cave). Carbon dating suggests, however, that the statue was carved around the 12th century. In 1881 Montserrat's Black Virgin became patroness of Catalonia.

The blackened Virgin of Montserrat

Inner Courtyard
On one side of the courtyard is the baptistry (1958), with sculptures by Carles Collet. Pilgrims may approach the Virgin through a door to the right.

㉑ Vic

Barcelona. 🏛 43,200. 🚍 🚌
ℹ Plaça del Pes, 93 886 20 91.
🛒 Tue, Sat & Sun. 🎉 Mercat del
Ram (Sat before Easter), Sant Miquel
(28 Jun–7 Jul), Música Viva (mid-Sep),
Mercat Medieval (early Dec).
🔳 **victurisme.cat**

Market days are the best time to
go to this small country town.
This is when the renowned local
sausages *(embotits)* are piled
high in the large Gothic Plaça
Major, along with other produce
from the surrounding plains.
    In the 3rd century BC Vic was
the capital of an ancient Iberian
tribe, the Ausetans. The town was
then colonized by the Romans –
the remains of a Roman temple
survive today. Since the 6th
century the town has been a
bishop's see. In the 11th century,
Abbot Oliva commissioned the
El Cloquer tower, around which
the cathedral was built in the
18th century. The interior of the
cathedral is covered with vast
murals by Josep Maria Sert
(1876–1945). They are painted
in reds and golds, and represent
scenes from the Bible.
    Adjacent to the cathedral is
the **Museu Episcopal de Vic**,
which has one of the best
collections of Romanesque
artifacts in Catalonia. Its large
display of mainly religious art
and relics includes bright,
simple murals and wooden
sculptures from rural churches.
Also on display are 11th- and
12th-century frescoes.

Cardona dominating the surrounding area from its hilltop site

🏛 **Museu Episcopal**
Plaça Bisbe Oliba. **Tel** 938 86 93 60.
Open Tue–Sun. **Closed** 1 & 6 Jan,
Easter Sun, 25 & 26 Dec. ♿ 📷 📷
🔳 **museuepiscopalvic.com**

㉒ Cardona

Barcelona. 🏛 4,800. 🚌 ℹ Avinguda
Rastrillo, 93 869 27 98. 🛒 Sun.
🎉 Festa Major (2nd last Sun of Sep).
🔳 **cardonaturisme.cat**

The 13th-century castle of the
dukes of Cardona, constables to
the crown of Aragón, is set on
the top of a hill. The castle was
rebuilt in the 18th century and is
now a parador. Beside the castle
is an early 11th-century church,
the Església de Sant Vicenç,
where the dukes are buried.
    The castle gives views of the
town below and of the Mon-
tanya de Sal (Salt Mountain),
a huge salt deposit beside the
Riu Cardener which has been
mined since Roman times.

㉓ Solsona

Lleida. 🏛 9,200. 🚌 ℹ Carretera de
Bassella 1, 973 48 23 10. 🛒 Tue & Fri.
🎉 Carnival (Feb); Corpus Christi
(May/Jun), Festa Major (early Sep).
🔳 **solsonaturisme.com**

Nine towers and three gateways
remain of Solsona's fortifications.
Inside the walls is an ancient
town of noble mansions. The
cathedral has a black stone
Virgin. The **Museu Diocesà
i Comarcal** contains
Romanesque paintings
and archaeological finds.

🏛 **Museu Diocesà i Comarcal**
Plaça Palau 1. **Tel** 973 48 21 01. **Open**
Tue–Sun. **Closed** 1 Jan, 25 & 26 Dec. ♿

㉔ Lleida

Lleida. 🏛 138,400. 🚍 🚌 ℹ Carrer
Major 31 bis, 973 70 03 19. 🛒 Thu &
Sat. 🎉 Sant Anastasi (11 May), Sant
Miquel (29 Sep). 🔳 **lleidaturisme.cat**

Dominating Lleida (Lérida),
the capital of Catalonia's only
landlocked province, is La Suda,
a large fort taken from the
Moors in 1149. Within its walls is
the old cathedral, La Seu Vella,
founded in 1203, which was
transformed into barracks by
Felipe V in 1707 but still retains
its beautiful cloister and Gothic
rose window. After years of
neglect, the fort complex has
been restored and now offers
panoramic viewpoints.
    A lift descends from the Seu
Vella to the Plaça de Sant Joan
in the town below. This square is
at the midpoint of a busy street
sweeping round the foot of the

Twelfth-century altar frontal, Museu Episcopal de Vic

For hotels and restaurants in this region see pp565–7 and pp588–90

hill. The new cathedral is here, as are manorial buildings such as the rebuilt 13th-century town hall, the Paeria.

㉕ Poblet

See pp226–7.

㉖ Montblanc

Tarragona. 🚗 7,300. 🚌 🚆 ℹ️ Antiga Església de Sant Francesc, 977 86 17 33. 🗓️ Tue, Fri. 🎭 Setmana Medieval (2 weeks in Apr), Festa Major (8–9 Sep).
Ⓦ montblancmedieval.org

The medieval grandeur of Montblanc lives on within its walls, said to be Catalonia's finest piece of military architecture. At the Sant Jordi gate, St George allegedly slew the dragon. The **Museu Comarcal de la Conca de Barberà** has displays on local crafts.

🏛️ **Museu Comarcal de la Conca de Barberà**
Carrer Josa 6. **Tel** 977 86 03 49.
Open Tue–Sun & public hols. 📷

㉗ Santes Creus

Tarragona. 🚗 150. 🚆 ℹ️ Plaça Jaume el Just (Monestir) s/n, 977 63 81 41. 🗓️ Sat & Sun. 🎭 Sta Llúcia (13 Dec). Ⓦ larutadelcister.info

Home to the prettiest of the "Cistercian triangle" monasteries is the tiny village of Santes Creus. The other two, Vallbona

de les Monges and Poblet *(see pp226–7)*, are nearby. The **Monestir de Santes Creus** was founded in 1150 by Ramón Berenguer IV *(see p58)* during his reconquest of Catalonia. The Gothic cloisters are decorated with figurative sculptures, a style first permitted by Jaime II, who ruled from 1291 to 1327. His finely carved tomb, along with that of other nobles, is in the 12th-century church.

🏰 **Monestir de Santes Creus**
Tel 977 63 83 29. **Open** Tue–Sun.
Closed 1 & 6 Jan, 25 & 26 Dec.
📷 🎥 ♿

㉘ Vilafranca del Penedès

Barcelona. 🚗 38,700. 🚆 🚌 ℹ️ Carrer Cort 14, 93 818 12 54. 🗓️ Sat. 🎭 Festa Major (29 Aug– 2 Sep). Ⓦ turismevilafranca.cat

This busy market town is set in Catalonia's main wine-producing region *(see pp206–7)*. The **Vinseum** (Wine Museum), in a 14th-century palace, documents the history of the area's wine trade. Local *bodegas* can be visited for wine tasting.

Eight km (5 miles) to the north is Sant Sadurní, the capital of Spain's sparkling wine, *cava (see pp580–81)*.

🏛️ **Vinseum**
Plaça Jaume I. **Tel** 93 890 05 82.
Open Tue–Sun & public hols. 📷

Anxaneta climbing to the top of a tower of castellers

Catalonia's Festes

Human Towers *(various dates and locations)*. The province of Tarragona is famous for its *castellers* festivals, where teams of men stand on each other's shoulders in an effort to build the highest human tower. Each tower, which can be up to seven people high, is topped by a small child called the *anxaneta*. *Castellers* can be seen in action in many towns, especially Vilafranca del Penedès and Valls.
Dance of Death *(Maundy Thu)*, Verges (Girona). Men dressed as skeletons perform a macabre dance.
St George's Day *(23 Apr)*. Lovers give each other a rose and a book on the day of Catalonia's patron saint. The book is in memory of Cervantes, who died on this day in 1616.
La Patum *(Corpus Christi, May/Jun)*, Berga (Barcelona province). Giants, devils and bizarre monsters parade through the town.
Midsummer's Eve *(23 Jun)*. Celebrated all over Catalonia with bonfires and fireworks.

Monestir de Santes Creus, surrounded by poplar and hazel trees

㉕ Monestir de Poblet

The Monastery of Santa Maria de Poblet is a haven of tranquillity and a resting place of kings. It was the first and most important of three Cistercian monasteries, known as the "Cistercian triangle" *(see p225)*, that helped to consolidate power in Catalonia after it had been recaptured from the Moors by Ramon Berenguer IV. The monastery was abandoned and fell into disrepair as a result of the Ecclesiastical Confiscations Act of 1835. Restoration, now largely complete, began in 1930 and monks returned in 1940.

Library
The Gothic scriptorium was converted into a library in the 17th century, when the Cardona family donated its book collection.

KEY

① **Royal doorway**

② ④ **Museum**

③ **Wine cellar**

⑤ **Former kitchen**

⑥ **The 12th-century refectory** is a vaulted hall with an octagonal fountain and a pulpit.

⑦ **The dormitory** is reached by stairs from the church. The vast 87-m (285-ft) gallery dates from the 13th century.

⑧ **San Esteve cloister**

⑨ **Parlour cloister**

⑩ **New sacristy**

⑪ **The Abbey Church**, large and unadorned, with three naves, is a typical Cistercian building.

⑫ **Baroque church façade**

1150 Santes Creus founded – the third abbey in the "Cistercian triangle"

1156 Founding of monastery at Vallbona de les Monges

Royal tombs

14th century Main cloister finished

1479 Juan II, last king of Aragón, buried here

1940 Monks return

1100	1300	1500	1700	1900

1196 Alfonso II is the first king to be buried here

1336–87 Reign of Pere the Ceremonious, who designates Poblet a royal pantheon

1952 Tombs reconstructed. Royal remains returned

1150 Poblet monastery founded by Ramón Berenguer IV

1835 Disentailment of monasteries. Poblet ravaged

Chapterhouse
This perfectly square room, with slender columns, has tiers of benches for the monks. It is paved with the tombstones of 11 abbots who died between 1312 and 1623.

★ **Altarpiece**
Behind the stone altar, supported by Romanesque columns, an impressive alabaster reredos fills the apse. It was carved by Damià Forment in 1527.

★ **Royal Tombs**
The tombs in the pantheon of kings were begun in 1359. In 1950 the sculptures were restored by Frederic Marès.

★ **Cloisters**
The evocative, vaulted cloisters were built in the 12th and 13th centuries and were the centre of monastic life. The capitals are beautifully decorated with carved scrollwork.

Palm trees lining the waterfront at Sitges

㉙ Sitges

Barcelona. 👥 28,500. 🚗 🚌 ℹ️ Plaça
Eduard Maristany 2, 93 894 42 51. 📧
Thu. 🎭 Carnival (Feb–Mar), Festa
Major (22–27 Aug). 🆆 sitgestur.cat

There are no less than nine
beaches to choose from at this
seaside town. It has a reputation
as a gay resort but is just as
popular with all. Lively bars and
restaurants line its main boulevard, the Passeig Marítim, and
there are many examples of
Modernista architecture among
the 1970s apartment blocks.
Modernista artist Santiago
Rusiñol (1861–1931) spent much
time here and bequeathed his
quirky collection of ceramics,
sculptures, painting and ornate
ironwork to the **Museu Cau
Ferrat**. It lies next to Sitges's
landmark, the 17th-century
church of Sant Bartomeu i Santa
Tecla, which juts out proudly
on a promontory.

🏛️ **Museu Cau Ferrat**
Carrer Fonollar. **Tel** 938 94 03 64.
Open Tue–Sun. 🎫 📷

㉚ Costa Daurada

Tarragona. 🚗 🚌 Calafell, Sant Vicenç
de Calders, Salou. ℹ️ Tarragona, 977
23 03 12. 🆆 costadaurada.info

The long, sandy beaches of the
Costa Daurada (Golden Coast)
run along the shores of Tarragona
province. El Vendrell is one of the
area's active ports. The **Museu
Pau Casals** in Sant Salvador
(El Vendrell) is dedicated to the

famous cellist. **Port Aventura**,
south of Tarragona, is one of
Europe's largest theme parks
and has many exotically themed
attractions, such as Polynesia and
Wild West. Cambrils and Salou
are the liveliest resorts – the rest
are low-key, family holiday spots.

🏛️ **Museu Pau Casals**
Avinguda Palfuriana 67.
Tel 977 68 42 76. **Open** Tue–Sun. 🎫

🎢 **Port Aventura**
Avinguda de l'Alcalde Pere Molas,
km 2, Vila-seca. **Tel** 902 20 22 20.
Open spring–6 Jan. 🎫 ♿

㉛ Tarragona

Tarragona. 👥 131,000. ✈️ 🚗 🚌
ℹ️ Carrer Major 39, 977 25 07 95.
📧 Tue, Thu & Sun. 🎭 Sant Magí
(19 Aug), Santa Tecla (23 Sep).
🆆 tarragonaturisme.cat

Tarragona is now a major
industrial port, but it has
preserved many remnants of its
Roman past. As the capital of
Tarraconensis, the Romans used
it as a base for the conquest
of the peninsula in the 3rd
century BC *(see pp54–5)*.

The avenue of Rambla Nova
ends on the clifftop Balcó de
Europa, in sight of the ruins
of the Amfiteatre Romà and
the ruined 12th-century church
of Santa Maria del Miracle.

Nearby is the Praetorium,
a Roman tower that was
converted into a palace in
medieval times. It now houses
the **Pretori i Circ Romans**. This
displays Roman and medieval
finds, and gives access to the
cavernous passageways of the
excavated Roman circus, built
in the 1st century AD. Next to
the Praetorium is the **Museu
Nacional Arqueològic**,
containing the most important
collection of Roman artifacts in
Catalonia. It has an extensive
collection of bronze tools and
beautiful mosaics, including a

The remains of the Roman amphitheatre, Tarragona

Head of Medusa. Among the most impressive remains are the huge Pre-Roman stones on which the Roman wall is built. An archaeological walk stretches 1 km (half a mile) along the wall.

Behind the wall lies the 12th-century cathedral, built on the site of a Roman temple. This evolved over many centuries, as seen from the blend of styles of the exterior. Inside is an alabaster altarpiece of St Tecla, carved by Pere Joan in 1434. The 13th-century cloister has Gothic vaulting, but the doorway is Romanesque.

To the west of town is a 3rd- to 6th-century Christian cemetery, the Necròpolis Paleocristiana i Conjunt Paleocristià del Francolí.

Ruins of the Necropolis Paleocristiana, Tarragona

Environs

The Aqüeducte de les Ferreres lies just outside the city, next to the A7 motorway. This 2nd-century aqueduct was built to bring water to the city from the Riu Gaià, 30 km (19 miles) to the north. The Arc de Berà, a 1st-century triumphal arch on the Via Augusta, is 20 km (12 miles) northeast on the N340.

The bustling, provincial town of Reus lies inland from Tarragona. Although its airport serves the Costa Daurada, it is often overlooked by holiday-makers. However there is some fine Modernista architecture to be seen here, notably some early work by Antoni Gaudí who was born in Reus. The Pere Mata Psychiatric Institute was designed by Domènech i Montaner before his master-piece, the Hospital de la Santa Creu i de Sant Pau *(see p169).*

🏛 **Pretori i Circ Romans**
Plaça del Rei. **Tel** 977 22 17 36.
Open Tue–Sun. 🐾

🏛 **Museu Nacional Arqueològic de Tarragona**
Plaça del Rei 5. **Tel** 977 23 62 09.
Open Tue–Sun. 🐾 (senior citizens and under 18s free). ♿ 🔲 **mnat.es**

ⓜ Tortosa

Tarragona. 📊 33,700. 🚊 Rambla Felip Pedrell 3, 977 44 96 48. 🚌 Mon. 📅 Nostra Senyora de la Cinta (Aug/Sep). 🔲 **tortosaturisme.cat**

A ruined castle and medieval walls are clues to Tortosa's historical importance. Sited at the lowest crossing point on the Riu Ebre (Río Ebro), it has been strategi-cally significant since Iberian times. The Moors held the city from the 8th century until 1148. The old Moorish castle, known as La Zuda, is all that remains of their defences. It has been renovated as a parador. The Moors also built a mosque in 914. Its foundations were used for the cathedral, on which work began in 1347. Although not completed for 200 years, the style is Gothic.

Tortosa was badly damaged in 1938–9 during one of the fiercest battles of the Civil War *(see pp68–71)*, when the Ebre formed the front line between the opposing forces.

ⓜ Delta de L'Ebre

Tarragona. 🚊 Aldea. 🚌 Deltebre, Aldea. ℹ Deltebre, 977 48 93 09. 🔲 **turismedeltebre.com**

The delta of the Riu Ebre is a prosperous rice-growing region and wildlife haven. Some 70 sq km (27 sq miles) have been turned into a nature reserve, the Parc Natural del Delta de L'Ebre. In Deltebre there is an information centre and an interesting **Eco-Museu**, with an aquarium containing species found in the delta.

The main towns in the area are Amposta and Sant Carles de la Ràpita, both of which serve as good bases for exploring the reserve.

The best sites for seeing wildlife are along the shore, from the Punta del Fangar in the north to the Punta de la Banya in the south. Everywhere is accessible by car except Illa de Buda. Flamingoes breed on this island, and other waterbirds, such as avocets, can be seen from tourist boats that leave from Riumar and Deltebre.

🏛 **Eco-Museu**
Carrer Doctor Martí Buera 22. **Tel** 977 48 96 79. **Open** Tue–Sun. **Closed** 1 & 6 Jan, 25 & 26 Dec. 🐾 ♿ 🔲

The Sardana

Catalonia's national dance is more complicated than it appears. The success of the Sardana depends on all of the dancers accurately counting the complicated short- and long-step skips and jumps, which accounts for their serious faces. Music is provided by a *cobla,* an 11-person band consisting of a leader playing a three-holed flute *(flabiol)* and a little drum *(tabal),* five woodwind players and five brass players. When the music starts, dancers join hands and form circles. The Sardana is performed during most local fiestas *(see p225)* and at special day-long gatherings called *aplecs.*

A group of Sardana dancers captured in stone

ARAGÓN

Zaragoza · Huesca · Teruel

Stretching almost half the length of Spain, and bisected by the Ebro, one of the country's longest rivers, Aragón takes in a wide variety of scenery, from the snowcapped summits of Ordesa National Park in the Pyrenees to the dry plains of the Spanish interior. This largely unsung and undervisited region contains magnificent Mudéjar architecture and many unspoiled medieval towns.

From the 12th to 15th centuries Aragón was a powerful kingdom, or (more accurately) a federation of states, including Catalonia. In its heyday, in the 13th century, its dominions stretched across the Mediterranean as far as Sicily. By his marriage to Isabel of Castile and León in 1469, Fernando II of Aragón paved the way for the unification of Spain.

After the Reconquest, Muslim architects and craftsmen were treated more tolerantly here than elsewhere, and they continued their work in the distinctive Mudéjar style, building with elaborate brickwork and patterned ceramic decoration. Their work can be seen in churches all over Aragón and there are outstanding examples in the cities of Teruel and the capital, Zaragoza, Spain's fifth-largest city, which stands on the banks of the Ebro.

The highest peaks of the Pyrenees lie in Huesca province. Some of the region's finest sights are in the Pyrenean foothills, which are crossed by the Aragonese variation of the pilgrims' route to Santiago de Compostela. Probably the most spectacular of them is the monastery of San Juan de la Peña – half-concealed beneath a rock overhang – which was founded in the 9th century.

The climate of the region varies as much as the landscape: winters can be long and harsh and summers hot.

A view of the rooftops and medieval walls of Daroca

◀ Moorish arches inside the Aljafería Palace, Zaragoza

Exploring Aragón

The landscapes of Aragón range from the high Pyrenees, north of Huesca, through the desiccated terrain around Zaragoza to the forested hills of Teruel province. The cities of Teruel and Zaragoza have some of the most striking Mudéjar monuments in Spain and there are many small, picturesque preserved towns in the region. Ordesa National Park contains stunning mountain scenery, but it can only be visited fully after the snow melts in spring, and even then much of it has to be explored on foot. Pretty Los Valles offers less dramatic but equally enjoyable landscapes and is a popular tourist destination. Other attractive places include the impressively sited Castillo de Loarre and Monasterio de San Juan de la Peña, and the waterfalls of Monasterio de Piedra.

The Puerto de Somport, near Panticosa

Sights at a Glance

For keys to symbols *see back flap*

Getting Around

Zaragoza is linked by motorway to the Basque Country, Navarra, Madrid and Barcelona. Major roads link the region's main cities with each other, and Teruel with Valencia. Many minor roads have been improved and may be fast and uncongested in the flatter, central areas. The principal railway lines run from Zaragoza to Madrid and Barcelona, both of which are linked by high-speed AVE trains, and to Valencia. Coaches are infrequent, except between the main population centres. Zaragoza has a small international airport.

Key

- ▬ Motorway
- ▪▪ Motorway under construction
- ▬ Major road
- ▬ Minor road
- ▬ Scenic route
- ▭▭ Main railway
- ---- Minor railway
- ▬ International border
- ▬ Regional border
- △ Summit

*Map labels:*

Lourdes

3 PUERTO DE SOMPORT

N330

Monte Perdido 3355m

Torla-Ordesa

Bielsa

Pico de Aneto 3404m △

4 PARQUE NAC. DE ORDESA

5 BENASQUE

JACA **7**

Sabiñánigo

N260

Castejón de Sos

N260

MONASTERIO DE SAN JUAN DE LA PEÑA

Boltaña

6 AÍNSA

Campo

N230

Arguís

Roda de Isábena

10 CASTILLO LOARRE N330

Sierra de Guara

SANTUARIO DE TORRECIUDAD

13 **14** GRAUS

HUESCA **11**

ALQUÉZAR **12**

N123

Angüés

Benabarre

A22

Barbastro

Granén

Huerto

Cinca

N230

Tardienta

Monzón

N240

Tamarite de Litera

Alcubierre

Sariñena

Binéfar

ARAGÓN

Onthiena

Lleida Barcelona

AP2

Fraga

NII

232 Pina de Ebro

Bujaraloz

Ebro

Mequinenza

Quinto

Embalse de Mequinenza

N211

Chite

Escatrón

Fayón

Azaila

Caspe

Martín

Híjar

Maella

N232

22 ALCAÑIZ

Andorra

Valjunquera

Oliete

Cálanda

N211

VALDERROBRES **23**

Iban

Castellote

Monroyo

Culve

Guadalope

N232

Aliaga

Mirambel

Arillas

Cantavieja

SIERRA DE GUDAR

Peñarroya 2019m

RA DE RUBIELOS

Rubielos de Mora

0 kilometres 20
0 miles 20

Mudéjar tower of Iglesia de Santa Magdalena, Tarazona

The town hall, Sos del Rey Católico

❶ Sos del Rey Católico

Zaragoza. 🏔 650. 🚌 ℹ️ Palacio de Sada, Plaza Hispanidad s/n, 948 88 85 24 (closed Mon). 🗓 Fri. 🎉 Fiesta Mayor (third week of Aug). 🎫 to Palacio de Sada. 🌐 oficinaturismo sosdelreycatolico.com

Fernando of Aragón – the so-called "Catholic King" who married Isabel of Castile, thereby uniting Spain (see pp60–61) – was born in this small town in 1452, thus its distinguished royal name.

The Palacio de Sada, the king's reputed birthplace, with a beautiful inner courtyard, is among the town's grandest stone mansions. It stands in a small square amid a maze of narrow cobbled streets. At the top of the town are the remnants of a castle and the Iglesia de San Esteban. The church's font and carved capitals are noteworthy, as are the 13th-century frescoes in two of the crypt's apses. From here there are fine views over the surrounding hills.

The Gothic-arched Lonja (commodities exchange) and the 16th-century town hall (ayuntamiento) are located on the adjacent main square.

Environs

The "Cinco Villas" are five towns recognized by Felipe V for their loyalty during the War of the Spanish Succession (see p66). Sos del Rey Católico is the most appealing of these. The others are Ejea de los Caballeros, Tauste, Sádaba and Uncastillo. The latter, 20 km (12 miles) to the southeast, has a fortress and a Romanesque church, the Iglesia de Santa María.

❷ Los Valles

Huesca. 🚉 Jaca. 🚌 from Jaca to Hecho. ℹ️ Museo de Arte Contemporáneo al aire libre, Pallar d'Agustín, Hecho (Jun–Sep), 974 37 55 05.

The delightful valleys of Ansó and Hecho, formed by the Veral and Aragón Subordán rivers respectively, were once isolated due to poor road links, enabling their villages to retain traditional customs and a local dialect called Cheso. Now the area's crafts and costumes have made it popular with tourists. The Pyrenean foothills and forests above the valleys are good for walking, fishing and cross-country skiing.

Ansó lies in the prettiest valley, which becomes a shadowy gorge where the Río Veral and the road next to it squeeze between vertical crags and through rock tunnels. Many of its buildings have stone façades and steep, tiled roofs. The Gothic church (16th century) has a museum dedicated to local costume. Pieces of modern sculpture lie scattered beside the tourist information office of Hecho, from an open-air festival previously held in the village. The bucolic village of Siresa, which contains the 11th-century church of San Pedro, lies to the north of Hecho.

❸ Puerto de Somport

Huesca. 🚌 Somport, Astun or Jaca. ℹ️ Pl Ayuntamiento 1, Canfranc, 974 37 31 41 (closed Sep–Jun: Sun & Mon).

Just inside the border with France, the Somport Pass was for centuries a strategic crossing point for the Romans and Moors, and for medieval pilgrims en route to Santiago de Compostela (see pp86–7). Today the austere scenery is specked with holiday apartments built for skiing. Astún is modern and well organized, while El Formigal, to the east, is a stylish, purpose-built resort. Non-skiers can enjoy the scenery around the Panticosa gorge. Sallent de Gállego is popular for rock climbing and fishing.

Steep, tiled roofs of Hecho, with a typical pepper-pot chimney

Rough and craggy landscape around Benasque

❹ Parque Nacional de Ordesa

See pp236–7.

❺ Benasque

Huesca. 🗻 2,000. 🚹 Calle de San Pedro s/n, 974 55 12 89. 🚌 Tue. 📅 San Pedro (29 Jun), San Marcial (30 Jun). 🌐 turismobenasque.com

Tucked away in the northeast corner of Aragón, at the head of the Esera Valley, the village of Benasque presides over a ruggedly beautiful stretch of Pyrenean scenery. Although the village has expanded greatly to meet the holiday trade, a sympathetic use of wood and stone has resulted in buildings which complement the existing older houses. A stroll through the old centre filled with aristocratic mansions is a delight.

The most striking buildings in Benasque are the 13th-century Iglesia de Santa María Mayor, and the Palacio de los Condes de Ribagorza. The latter has a Renaissance façade.

Above the village rises the Maladeta massif. There are magnificent views from its ski slopes and hiking trails. Several local mountain peaks, including Posets and Aneto, exceed 3,000 m (9,800 ft).

Environs

For walkers, skiers and climbers, the area around Benasque has a great deal to offer. The neighbouring resort of Aramón Cerler was developed with care from a rustic village into a popular base for skiing and other winter sports.

At Castejón de Sos, 14 km (9 miles) south of Benasque, the road passes through the Congosto de Ventamillo, a scenic rocky gorge.

❻ Aínsa

Huesca. 🗻 2,200. 🚌 🚹 Plaza Castillo 1, 974 50 05 12. 🚌 Tue. 📅 San Sebastián (20 Jan), Fiesta Mayor (14 Sep).

The capital of the kingdom of Sobrarbe in medieval times, Aínsa has retained its charm. The Plaza Mayor, a broad cobbled square, is surrounded by neat terraced arcades of brown stone. On one side stands the belfry of the Iglesia de Santa María – consecrated in 1181 – and on the other the restored castle.

❼ Jaca

Huesca. 🗻 13,000. 🚉 🚌 🚹 Plaza de San Pedro 11, 974 36 00 98. 🚌 Fri. 📅 La Victoria (first Fri of May), Santa Orosia y San Pedro (25–29 Jun). 🌐 jaca.es

Jaca dates back as far as the 2nd century AD. In the 8th century the town bravely repulsed the Moors – an act which is commemorated in the festival of La Victoria – and in 1035 became the first capital of the kingdom of Aragón. Jaca's 11th-century cathedral, one of Spain's oldest, is much altered inside. Traces of its original splendour can be seen on the restored south porch and doorway, where carvings depict biblical scenes. The dim nave and chapels are decorated with ornate vaulting and sculpture. A museum of sacred art, in the cloisters, contains a collection of Romanesque and Gothic frescoes and sculptures from local churches. The streets that surround the cathedral form an attractive quarter.

Sculpture in Jaca Cathedral

Jaca's only other significant tourist sight is its 16th-century citadel, a fort decorated with corner turrets, on the edge of town. Today the town serves as a principal base for the Aragonese Pyrenees.

The arcaded main square of Aínsa with the Iglesia de Santa María

❹ Parque Nacional de Ordesa

Within its borders the Parque Nacional de Ordesa y Monte Perdido combines all the most dramatic elements of Spain's Pyrenean scenery. At the heart of the park are four glacial canyons – the Ordesa, Añisclo, Pineta and Escuain valleys – which carve the great upland limestone massifs into spectacular cliffs and chasms. Most of the park is accessible only on foot: even then, snow during autumn and winter makes it inaccessible to all except those with specialist climbing equipment. In high summer, however, the crowds testify to the park's well-earned reputation as a paradise for walkers and nature lovers alike.

Valle de Ordesa
The Río Arazas cuts through forested limestone escarpments, providing some of Ordesa's most popular walks.

Brecha de Rolando
EL TAILLON

3,144 M
(10,315 FT) Gruta de Casteret

MONDARRUEGO
2,848 M
(9,344 FT)

VALLE DE ORDESA

ℹ

Cascada Torro botera

Torla-Ordesa

Biescas

Broto

Oto

Fa

Sarvisé

Ara

Jalle

Ainsa

d

Torla-Ordesa
This village, at the gateway to the park, huddles beneath the forbidding slopes of Mondarruego. With its core of cobbled streets and slate-roofed houses around the church, Torla is a popular base for visitors to Ordesa.

Pyrenean Wildlife

Ordesa is a spectacle of flora and fauna, with many of its species unique to the region. Trout streams rush along the valley floor, where slopes provide a mantle of various woodland harbouring creatures such as otters, marmots and capercaillies (large grouse). On the slopes, flowers burst out before the snow melts, with gentians and orchids sheltering in crevices and edelweiss braving the most hostile crags. Higher up, the Pyrenean chamois is still fairly common; but the Ordesa ibex, or mountain goat, became extinct in 2000. Attempts to resurrect it by cloning have had little success so far. The rocky pinnacles above the valley are the domain of birds of prey, among them the huge bearded vulture.

Spring gentian *(Gentiana verna)*

0 kilometres | 2
0 miles | 2

Key

═══ Major road
═══ Minor road
- - - Footpath
▬▬▬ Spanish/French border
━━━ National park boundary

View from Parador de Bielsa
The parador, at the foot of Monte Perdido, looks out at stunning sheer rock faces streaked by waterfalls.

VISITORS' CHECKLIST

Practical Information
🛈 Visitors' centre open all year (exhibition area closed in winter), Avenida Ordesa s/n, Torla-Ordesa, 974 48 64 72. 🆆 **ordesa.net**

Transport
🚌 change at Sabiñánigo for Torla. 🚋 Sabiñánigo.

Parador de Biesla

Ⓟ

VALLE DE PINETA

DIDO

Cinca

io de Góriz

Bielsa

Sierra de Las Tucas

ada
de Caballo

Vellos

Cañón de Añisclo

Revilla

Escuaín

Garganta de Escuaín

Bielsa

☀ Tella

• Nerin

Vellos

Bestué •

Puértolas •

Hikers in Ordesa National Park

Cola de Caballo
The 70-m (230-ft) "Horse's Tail" waterfall makes a scenic stopping point near the northern end of the long hike around the Circo Soaso. It provides a taste of the spectacular scenery found along the route.

Tips for Walkers

Several well-marked trails follow the valleys and can be easily tackled by anyone reasonably fit, though walking boots are a must. The mountain routes may require climbing gear, so check first with the visitors' centre and get a detailed map. Pyrenean weather changes rapidly – beware of ice and snow early and late in the season. Overnight camping is permitted, but only for a single night above certain altitudes.

Cañón or Garganta de Añisclo
A wide path leads along this beautiful, steep-sided gorge, following the wooded course of the turbulent Río Vellos through dramatic limestone scenery.

Royal pantheon

Lower church

Capilla de San Victorián

Cloister

Residential quarters

Upper church

Capilla de San Voto

❽ Monasterio de San Juan de la Peña

Huesca. **Tel** 974 35 51 19. **Open** Nov–Feb: 10am–2pm daily (to 5pm Sat); Mar–Oct: 10am–2pm, 3:30–7pm daily (to 8pm Jun–Aug). **Closed** 1 Jan, 25 Dec. 🎫 🖻 🖥 🖳 **w monasterio sanjuan.com**

Set under a bulging rock, this monastery was an early guardian of the Holy Grail *(see p255)*. In the 11th century it underwent reformation in Cluniac style, and was the first monastery to introduce the Latin Mass in Spain. After a fire in the 1600s, the building was abandoned in favour of a newer one further up the hillside. This was later sacked by Napoleon's troops. It now houses a hotel and interpretation centre.

The church of the old monastery is on two floors. The lower one is a primitive rock-hewn crypt built in the early 10th century. The upper floor contains an 11th-century church with a simple triple apse hollowed out of the side of the cliff. The Romanesque pantheon contains the stacked tombs of the early Aragonese kings. The exterior cloister is San Juan de la Peña's *pièce de résistance*, the capitals of its columns carved with biblical scenes.

❾ Agüero

Huesca. 🏠 150. 🎭 San Blas (3 Feb), San Roque (16 Aug). **w aytoaguero.es**

The picturesque setting of this attractive village, clustered against a dramatic crag of eroded pudding stone, amply rewards a brief detour from the main road. The most important reason for visiting Agüero, however, is to see the 12th-century Iglesia de Santiago. This Romanesque church is reached by a long stony track leading uphill just before the village.

The capitals of the columns in this unusual triple-naved building are carved with fantastical beasts as well as scenes from the life of Jesus and the Virgin Mary. The beautiful carvings on the doorway display biblical events, including scenes from the Epiphany and Salome dancing ecstatically. The lively, large-eyed figures are attributed to the mason responsible for the superb carvings in the monastery at San Juan de la Peña.

❿ Castillo de Loarre

Loarre, Huesca. **Tel** 974 34 21 61. 🚉 Ayerbe. 🚌 from Huesca. **Open** daily. **Closed** Nov–Feb: Mon, 1 Jan, 25 Dec. 🎫 🖻 🖳 **w castillodeloarre.es**

The ramparts of this fortress stand majestically above the road from Ayerbe. The fortress is so closely moulded around the contours of a rock that in poor visibility it could be easily mistaken for a natural outcrop. It was used as a set for Ridley Scott's film *Kingdom of Heaven* (2005). On a clear day, the hilltop setting is stupendous, with clear views of the surrounding orchards and reservoirs of the Ebro plain.

Village of Agüero, situated under a rocky crag

Inside the curtain walls lies a complex founded in the 11th century on the site of what had originally been a Roman settlement. It was later remodelled under Sancho I (Sancho Ramírez) of Aragón, who established a religious community here, placing the complex under the rule of the Order of St Augustine.

Within the castle walls is a Romanesque church with carved capitals, a chequered frieze and alabaster windows.

Sentry paths, iron ladders and flights of steps ramble precariously around the castle's towers, dungeons and keep.

The formidable Castillo de Loarre looming above the surrounding area

Altarpiece by Damià Forment, in Huesca Cathedral

⓫ Huesca

Huesca. 52,000. Plaza López Allué, 974 29 21 70. Tue, Thu & Sat. San Vicente (22 Jan), San Lorenzo (9–15 Aug).
w huescaturismo.com

Founded in the 1st century BC, the independent state of Osca (present-day Huesca) had a senate and an advanced education system. From the 8th century, the area grew into a Moorish stronghold. In 1096 it was captured by Peter of Aragón and was the region's capital until 1118, when the title passed to Zaragoza.

Huesca is now the provincial capital. The pleasant old town has a Gothic cathedral. The eroded west front is surmounted by an unusual wooden gallery in Mudéjar style. Above the nave is slender-ribbed star vaulting studded with golden bosses. There is an alabaster altarpiece by the master

sculptor, Damià Forment. On the altarpiece, a series of Crucifixion scenes in relief are highlighted by illumination.

Opposite the cathedral is the Renaissance town hall (ayuntamiento). Inside hangs La Campana de Huesca, a gory 19th-century painting depicting the town's most memorable event: the beheading of a group of troublesome nobles in the 12th century by order of King Ramiro II. The massacre occurred in the former Palacio de los Reyes de Aragón, later the university and now the superb **Museo de Huesca**, containing archaeological finds and a collection of art.

Museo de Huesca
Plaza de la Universidad 1. Tel 974 22 05 86. Open 10am–2pm, 5–8pm Tue–Sat, 10am–2pm Sun & pub hols. Closed 1 & 6 Jan, 24, 25 & 31 Dec.

⓬ Alquézar

Huesca. 300. Calle Arrabal s/n, 974 31 89 40. San Sebastián (20 Jan), San Ipolito (12 Aug).

This Moorish village attracts much attention because of its spectacular setting. Its main monument, the stately 16th-century collegiate church, dominates a hill jutting above the strange rock formations of the canyon of the Río Vero. Inside, the church's cloisters have capitals carved with biblical scenes. Next to it is the chapel built after Sancho I recaptured Alquézar from the Moors. Nearby are the ruined walls of the original alcázar, which gives the village its name.

⓭ Santuario de Torreciudad

Huesca. Tel 974 30 40 25. to El Grado from Barbastro. Open daily. w torreciudad.org

This shrine was built to honour the devotion of the founder of the Catholic lay order of Opus Dei – San Jose María Escrivá de Balaguer – to the Virgin. It occupies a promontory with picturesque views over the waters of the Embalse de El Grado at Torreciudad. The huge church is made of angular red brick in a stark, modern design.

Inside, the elaborate modern altarpiece of alabaster, sheltering a glittering Romanesque Virgin, is in contrast to the bleak, functional nave.

Environs
The town of Barbastro, 30 km (18 miles) to the south, has an arcaded plaza mayor and a 16th-century cathedral with an altar by Damià Forment.

The ruins of Alquézar Castle, rising above the village

Houses with frescoed façades on the Plaza de España, Graus

⑭ Graus

Huesca. 🚇 3,400. 🚌 ℹ️ Plaza Mayor 15, 974 54 08 74. 🚍 Mon. 🎉 San Antonio (19 Jan), Santa Agneda (5 Feb), San Miguel (29 Sep–1 Oct). 🌐 **turismograus.com**

In the heart of Graus's old town is the unusual Plaza de España, surrounded by stone arcades and columns. It has brightly frescoed half-timbered houses and a 16th-century city hall. The home of the infamous Tomás de Torquemada *(see p60)* is in the narrow streets of the old quarter. At fiesta time, Graus is a good spot to see Aragonese dancing.

Environs

About 20 km (12 miles) north-east, the hill village of Roda de Isábena is the smallest village in Spain to boast a cathedral. Dating from 1067, this striking building has a 12th-century cloister off which is a chapel with 13th-century frescoes. North of the village is the picturesque Isábena valley.

⑮ Tarazona

Zaragoza. 🚇 10,700. 🚌 ℹ️ Plaza San Francisco 1, 976 64 00 74. 🚍 every other Thu. 🎉 San Atilano (27 Aug–1 Sep). 🌐 **tarazona.es**

Mudéjar towers stand high above the earth-coloured, mottled pantiles of this ancient bishopric. On the outskirts of the Old Town is the cathedral, all turreted finials and pierced brickwork with Moorish cloister tracery and Gothic tombs. In the upper town on the other side of the river, more churches, in typical Mudéjar

style, can be found amid the maze of narrow hilly streets. More unusual perhaps are the former bullring, now a circular plaza enclosed by houses, and the splendid Renaissance town hall *(ayuntamiento)*. The town hall, built of golden stone, has a façade carved with mythical giants and a frieze showing Carlos V's homage to Tarazona.

⑯ Monasterio de Veruela

Vera de Moncayo, Zaragoza. **Tel** 976 64 90 25. 🚌 Vera de Moncayo. **Open** Wed–Mon. 🎟️ 📷 by appt. ♿ 🌐 **turismodeborja.com**

This Cistercian retreat, set in the green Huecha Valley near the Sierra de Moncayo, is one of the greatest monasteries in Aragón. Founded in the 12th century by French monks, the huge abbey church has a mixture of Roman-esque and Gothic features. Worn green and blue Aragonese tiles line the floor of its handsomely

vaulted triple nave. The well-preserved cloisters sprout exuberantly decorated beasts, heads of human beings and foliage in the Gothic style *(see p28)*. The plain, dignified chambers make a suitable venue for art exhibitions in the summer.

Environs

In the hills to the west the small Parque Natural de Moncayo rises to a height of 2,315 m (7,600 ft). Streams race through the woodland of this nature reserve, abound with birdlife. A tortuous potholed road leads to a chapel at 1,600 m (5,250 ft).

⑰ Zaragoza

Zaragoza. 🚇 666,000. ✈️ 🚃 🚌 ℹ️ Plaza del Pilar, 976 20 12 00. 🚍 Wed & Sun. 🎉 San Valero (29 Jan), Cincomarzada (5 Mar), San Jorge (23 Apr), Virgen del Pilar (12 Oct). 🌐 **turismodezaragoza.es/ciudad/turismo**

A Celtiberian settlement called Salduba existed on the site of the present city; but it is from the Roman settlement of Cesaraugusta that Zaragoza takes its name. Its location on the fertile banks of the Río Ebro ensured its ascendancy, now Spain's fifth-largest city and the capital of Aragón.

Damaged during the War of Independence *(see p66)*, the city was largely rebuilt, but the old centre retains some interesting buildings. Most of the main sights are grouped around Plaza del Pilar. The most impressive of them is the Basílica de Nuestra

Entrance and tower of the Monasterio de Veruela

Señora del Pilar, with its huge church sporting 11 brightly tiled cupolas. Inside, the Santa Capilla (Lady Chapel) by Ventura Rodríguez contains a small statue of the Virgin on a pillar amid a blaze of silver and flowers. Her skirt-like *manta* is changed every day, and pilgrims pass behind the chapel to kiss an exposed part of the pillar. The basílica also has frescoes by Goya.

Nearby, on the square, stand the town hall *(ayuntamiento)*, the 16th-century Renaissance Lonja (commodities exchange) and the Palacio Arzobispal.

Occupying the east end of the square is Zaragoza's cathedral, La Seo, displaying a great mix of styles. Part of the exterior is faced with typical Mudéjar brick and ceramic decoration, and inside are a fine Gothic reredos and splendid Flemish tapestries.

Close by is the flamboyant Mudéjar bell tower of the Iglesia de la Magdalena, and remains of the Roman forum. Parts of the Roman walls can also be seen at the opposite side of the Plaza del Pilar, near the Mercado de Lanuza, a market with sinuous ironwork in Art Nouveau style.

The **Museo Goya** in the Pardo's Palace exhibits the eclectic

Some of the cupolas of the Basílica de Nuestra Señora del Pilar

collection of a wealthy local art historian, whose special interest was Goya. The top floor contains a collection of his etchings. Minor works by artists of other periods can be seen, as well as contemporary art. The **Museo de Zaragoza** has a Goya room and archaeological artifacts.

The **Museo Pablo Gargallo** is a showroom for the Aragonese sculptor after whom it is named, who was active at the beginning of the 20th century. One of the most important monuments in Zaragoza lies on the busy road to Bilbao. The Aljafería is an enormous Moorish palace built in the 11th century. A courtyard of lacy arches surrounds a sunken

garden and a small mosque. The **CaixaForum**, a cultural centre set in a contemporary building, hosts Spain's best touring exhibitions as well as talks, screenings and family activities.

Museo Goya
Calle Espoz y Mina 23. **Tel** 976 39 73 87. **Open** Tue–Sun.

Museo de Zaragoza
Plaza de los Sitios 6.
Tel 976 22 21 81. **Open** Tue–Sun.

Museo Pablo Gargallo
Plaza de San Felipe 3.
Tel 976 72 49 22. **Open** Tue–Sun.

CaixaForum
Avenida Anselmo Clavé 4.
Tel 976 76 82 00. **Open** daily.

Zaragoza City Centre

1. Roman walls
2. Mercado de Lanuza
3. Museo Pablo Gargallo
4. Basílica de Nuestra
   Señora del Pilar
5. Museo Goya
6. Lonja
7. La Seo (Cathedral)
8. Palacio Arzobispal

0 metres   150
0 yards   150

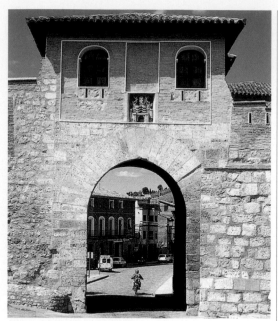

Gateway through the medieval walls of Daroca

⑱ Calatayud

Zaragoza. 🗺 20,200. 🚆 🚌 🛈 Plaza
España 1, 976 88 63 22. 🖰 Tue.
🎊 San Roque (14–17 Aug), Virgen
de la Peña (6–10 Sep). 🌐 **catalayud.
es/turismo**

The huge Moorish fortress and
minaret-like church towers are
visible from miles around. Only
ruins are left of the 8th-century
Arab castle of the ruler, Ayub,
which gave the town its name.
The church of Santa María la
Mayor has a Mudéjar tower
and an elaborate façade in
the Plateresque style. The
17th-century church of San
Juan Real holds Goya paintings.
    The ruins of the Roman set-
tlement of Bílbilis are east of
Calatayud, near Huérmeda.

⑲ Monasterio de Piedra

3 km (2 miles) south of Nuévalos,
Zaragoza. **Tel** 976 87 07 00.
🚆 Calatayud. 🚌 from Zaragoza.
Open daily. 🎫 ✏ 🅿 ♿
🌐 **monasteriopiedra.com**

Built on the site of a Moorish
castle conquered by Alfonso II
of Aragón and given to

Cistercian monks in the 12th
century, this monastery was
damaged in the 19th century
and subsequently rebuilt. Some
of the 12th-century buildings
remain, including the chapterhouse, refectory and hostel.
    In the damp cellars, the monks
once distilled strong potions of
herbal liqueur. This was allegedly
the first place in Europe where
drinking chocolate, from Mexico,
was made *(see p63)*, and there is
now a chocolate exhibition.
    The park in which the mon-
astery stands is a nature reserve
full of grottoes and waterfalls.
A hotel is now located in the
old monastery buildings.

⑳ Daroca

Zaragoza. 🗺 2,100. 🛈 Calle Mayor
44, 976 80 01 29. 🖰 Thu. 🎊 Santo
Tomás (7 Mar). 🎫 (of village).

An impressive array of battlemented medieval walls stretches
approximately 4 km (2 miles)
around this old Moorish stronghold. Although parts of the walls
have decayed, some of the 114
towers and gateways are still a
remarkable sight, particularly
from the main road to Zaragoza.
    The Colegial de Santa María,
a church in the Plaza España,
houses the Holy Cloths from the
Reconquest *(see pp58–9)*. After a
surprise attack by the Moors in
1239, priests celebrating Mass
bundled the consecrated bread
into the linen sheets used for
the altar. Upon being unwrapped,
the cloths were miraculously
stained with blood.

Environs
The agricultural town of
Monreal del Campo, 42 km
(26 miles) south of Daroca, has
a saffron museum. Towards
Molina de Aragón, 20 km
(12 miles) from Daroca, is the
Laguna de Gallocanta, a lake
and wildlife refuge.

㉑ Fuendetodos

Zaragoza. 🗺 126. 🛈 Calle Cortes
de Aragón 7, 976 14 38 67. 🎊 San
Roque (last Sat of May), San Bartolomé
(24 Aug). 🌐 **fuendetodos.org**

This small village was the
birthplace of one of Spain's
best-known artists of the late
18th and early 19th centuries,
Francisco de Goya. The

Interior of Goya's cottage in Fuendetodos

Castle-parador above Alcañiz

Casa-Museo de Goya is a neat cottage said to have been the painter's home. It has been restored and furnished in a style appropriate for the period.

Environs

Lying 14 km (9 miles) east of Fuendetodos is Belchite, the site of one of the most horrific battles of the Spanish Civil War *(see pp70–71)*, for control of the strategic Ebro Valley. Remains of the old, shell-torn town have been left tottering as a monument to the horrors of war.

In Cariñena, 25 km (16 miles) west of Fuendetodos, bodegas offer the opportunity to sample and buy the excellent, full-bodied red wine for which the region is justly renowned *(see pp206–7)*.

🏛 Casa-Museo de Goya
Calle Zuloaga 3. **Tel** 976 14 38 30. **Open** 11am–2pm, 4–7pm Tue–Sun. 🎨

㉒ Alcañiz

Teruel. 🚆 16,000. 🚌 ℹ Calle Mayor 1, 978 83 12 13. 🗓 Tue. 🎉 Fiestas Patronales (8–13 Sep). 🌐 **alcaniz.es**

Two buildings rise above the town of Alcañiz. One is the castle, once the head-quarters of the Order of Calatrava. This historic building has been converted into a parador. The keep, the Torre del Homenaje, has a collection of 14th-century frescoes depicting the conquest of Valencia by Jaime I.

The other building is the Iglesia de Santa María. This church, on the sloping Plaza de España, has a Gothic tower and a Baroque façade.

On the same square are the elegantly galleried Lonja (commodities exchange), with its lacy Gothic arches, and the town hall *(ayuntamiento)*, with one Mudéjar and one Renaissance façade.

Francisco de Goya

Self-Portrait by Goya

Born in Fuendetodos in 1746, Francisco de Goya specialized in designing cartoons for the tapestry industry *(see p310)* in his early life, and in decorating churches such as Zaragoza's Basílica del Pilar with vivacious frescoes. In 1799 he became painter to Carlos IV, and depicted the king and his wife María Luisa with unflattering accuracy *(see p37)*. The invasion of Madrid by Napoleon's troops in 1808 *(see pp66–7)* and its attendant horrors had a profound and lasting effect on Goya's temperament, and his later works are imbued with cynical despair and isolation. He died in Bordeaux in 1828.

Aragón's Fiestas

Las Tamboradas *(Maundy Thursday and Good Friday)*, Teruel province. During Easter Week, brotherhoods of men wearing long black robes beat drums in mourning for Christ. Las Tamboradas begins with "the breaking of the hour" at midnight on Thursday in Híjar. The Tamborada in Calanda begins the following day at midday. The solemn drum rolls continue for several hours. Aching arms and bleeding hands are considered to be signs of religious devotion.

Young drummer in Las Tamboradas, Alcorija

Carnival *(Feb/Mar)*, Bielsa (Huesca). The protagonists of this fiesta, known as *Trangas*, have rams' horns on their heads, blackened faces and teeth made of potatoes. They are said to represent fertility.

Romería de Santa Orosia *(25 Jun)*, Yebra de Basa (Huesca). Pilgrims in folk costume carry St Orosia's skull to her shrine.

Día del Pilar *(12 Oct)*, Zaragoza. Aragón's distinctive folk dance, the *jota*, is performed everywhere during the city's festivities in honour of its patroness, the Virgin of the Pillar *(see pp240–41)*. On the Día del Pilar there is a procession with cardboard giants, and a spectacular display of flowers dedicated to the Virgin.

Alcalá de la Selva Castle, overlooking the town

㉓ Valderrobres

Teruel. 📊 2,300. 🚌 *ℹ* Avenida Cortes de Aragón 7, 978 89 08 86. 🚐 Sat. 🎪 San Roque (mid-Aug). **W** valderrobres.es

Just inside Aragón's border with Catalonia, the town of Valderrobres overlooks the trout-filled Río Matarraña. Dominating the town is the **castle**, formerly a palace for Aragonese royalty. Below it stands the imposing Gothic Iglesia de Santa María la Mayor, with a huge rose window in Catalan Gothic style. The arcaded plaza has a pleasing late 16th-century town hall *(ayuntamiento)*.

Environs
Near Valderrobres is the mountain peak of La Caixa. At 14 km (9 miles) are the mountain passes of Beceite.

🏰 **Castillo de Valderrobres**
Tel 679 63 44 38. **Open** Tue–Sun (Oct–Jun: Fri–Sun & public hols). 🅿 🎫

㉔ Sierra de Gúdar

Teruel. 🚉 Mora de Rubielos. 🚌 Alcalá de la Selva. *ℹ* Calle Diputación 2, Mora de Rubielos, 978 80 05 29. **W** sierradegudar.com

This range of hills, northeast of Teruel, is a region of pine woods, jagged limestone outcrops and scrub-covered slopes. At 2,028 m (6,653 ft), Peñarroya is the highest point. Nearby Valdelinares, Spain's highest village, is a ski station. From the access roads there are panoramic views of the hills. Especially noteworthy are the views from the towns of Linares

de Mora and Alcalá de la Selva, which has a castle set against a backdrop of rock faces. Its Gothic-Renaissance church, with shell motifs and twisted columns, shelters the shrine of the Virgen de la Vega.

㉕ Mora de Rubielos

Teruel. 📊 1,650. *ℹ* Calle Diputación 2, 978 80 05 29. 🚐 Mon & Fri. 🎪 San Miguel (28 Sep–1 Oct).

Dominated by one of the best-preserved castles in Aragón, Mora de Rubielos displays the remains of the old walled city with its bridges and a medieval old town. There is a fine 17th-century town hall as well as the collegiate church of Santa María.

Environs
Rubielos de Mora, lying 14 km (9 miles) to the southeast, is worth exploring simply for its well-preserved stone and timber buildings. Among the balconied houses is an Augustinian convent with a Gothic reredos.

㉖ Teruel

Teruel. 📊 34,200. 🚉 🚌 *ℹ* Plaza de los Amantes 6, 978 62 41 05. 🚐 Thu. 🎪 Día del Sermón de las Tortillas (Tue of Easter week), La Vaquilla del Ángel (mid-Jul), Feria del Jamón (mid-Sep). **W** turismo.teruel.es

This industrial town has been the scene of much desperate fighting throughout the centuries. It began with the Romans, the first to capture and civilize Celtiberian Turba.

During the Reconquest the town became a strategic frontier prize. In 1171 Alfonso II recaptured Teruel for Christian Spain, but many Muslims continued to live peacefully in the city, which they embellished with beautiful Mudéjar towers. The last mosque was closed only at the height of the Inquisition *(see p278)*, in 1502. More recently, during the terrible, freezing winter of 1937, the bitterest battle of the Civil War *(see pp70–71)* was fought here. There were many thousands of casualties.

The old quarter is home to the wedge-shaped Plaza del Torico, with a monument of a small bull,

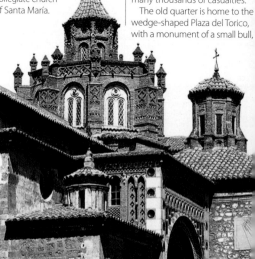

Tiled towers and rooftops of Teruel Cathedral

Balconied café above Albarracín's main square

the city's emblem. Within walking distance lie the five remaining Mudéjar towers. Most striking are those of San Salvador and San Martín, both dating back to the 12th century. The latter has multi-patterned brickwork studded with blue and green ceramics.

Beside the Iglesia de San Pedro are the tombs of the famous Lovers of Teruel. The cathedral has more colourful Mudéjar work, including a lantern dome of glazed tiles, and a tower completed in the 17th century. The dazzling coffered ceiling is painted with lively scenes of medieval life.

The **Museo Provincial**, one of Aragón's best museums, is housed in an elegant mansion. It has a large collection of ceramics, testifying to an industry for which Teruel has long been known. North of the centre is the Acueducto de los Arcos, a 16th-century aqueduct.

▥ Museo Provincial
Plaza Fray Anselmo Polanco 3.
Tel 978 60 01 50. **Open** Tue–Sun. ♿

㉗ Albarracín

Teruel. ⚄ 1,100. ▦ *i* Calle San Antonio 2, 978 71 02 62. ⌂ Wed. ⚄ Los Mayos (30 Apr–1 May), Fiestas Patronales (8–17 Sep).
w albarracin.es

It is easy to see why this picturesque town earned an international award for historical preservation. A dramatic cliff above the Río Guadalaviar is the perfect setting for this attractive cluster of mellow pink buildings.

Standing on a ridge behind the town are defensive walls and towers dating from Muslim times.

There is a good view of the town from below the Palacio Episcopal (Bishop's Palace). Inside the neighbouring 16th-century cathedral, which is topped by a belfry, there is a Renaissance carved wooden altarpiece depicting scenes from the life of St Peter. The treasury museum contains 16th-century Brussels tapestries and enamelled chalices.

Some of Albarracín's sturdy beamed and galleried houses have an unusual two-tier structure. The ground floor is limestone, and the overhanging upper storey is covered in rough coral-pink plasterwork. Many have been restored to their medieval form. Just outside the town are the caves of Navazo and Callejón, with their prehistoric rock paintings. Reproductions can be seen in Teruel's Museo Provincial.

Environs
In the surrounding Montes Universales, which rise to 1,935 m (6,348 ft), is the source of the Tagus, one of Spain's longest rivers. From fertile cereal plains to crumbling rocks, this area is a colourful mixture of poplars, junipers and thick pine woods, with poppies in spring. At Cella, northeast of Albarracín, the Río Jiloca has its source.

㉘ Rincón de Ademuz

Valencia. ⚄ 2,400. ▦ Ademuz. *i* Fuente Vieja 10, Ademuz, 978 78 22 67. ⌂ Wed. ⚄ Fiestas de Agosto (15 Aug), Fiestas de la Virgen del Rosario (early Oct). **w rincondeademuz.es**

This remote enclave south of Teruel belongs to the Comunidad Valenciana *(see p247)*, but is effectively an island of territory, stranded between the borders of Aragón and Castilla-La Mancha. The area has not prospered in modern times, but still has an austere charm and some peaceful tracts of country scattered with red rocks.

The Lovers of Teruel

According to legend, in 13th-century Teruel two young people, Diego de Marcilla and Isabel de Segura, fell in love and wished to marry. However, her wealthy family forbade the match because he was poor. Diego was given five years in which to make his fortune. When he returned to Teruel, laden with wealth, he found Isabel already married. Diego died of a broken heart and Isabel, full of despair, died the following day. The Bodas de Isabel de Segura, a festival held in mid-February, includes a re-enactment of the events.

Isabel de Segura   Diego de Marcilla

VALENCIA AND MURCIA

Castellón · Valencia · Alicante · Murcia

Centuries ago, Muslim settlers planted up the central region of Spain's eastern Mediterranean coast, and the fertile fields and citrus groves of the coastal plains are still the country's market garden today. This region of Spain's eastern Mediterranean coast is also an attractive holiday destination – the beaches of the Costa Blanca, the Costa del Azahar and the Costa Cálida draw millions of tourists annually.

These productive lands have been occupied for over 50,000 years. The Greeks, Phoenicians, Carthaginians and Romans all settled here before the Moors arrived, trading fish and local produce.

The provinces of Castellón, Valencia and Alicante (which make up the Comunidad Valenciana) were reconquered from the Moors by a Catalan army. The language these troops left behind them developed into a dialect, *Valenciano*, which is widely spoken and increasingly seen on signposts. Murcia, to the south, is one of Spain's smallest autonomous regions.

The population is concentrated on the coast where the historic towns and cities of Valencia, Alicante and Cartagena have been joined by modern package holiday resorts, such as Benidorm and La Manga del Mar Menor. Inland, where tourism has barely reached, the landscape rises into the chains of mountains that stand between the coast and the plateau of Central Spain. The scenery here ranges from picturesque valleys and hills in the Maestrat, in the north of Castellón, to the semi-desert terrain around Lorca in southern Murcia.

The warm climate encourages outdoor life and exuberant fiestas. Most famous of these are Las Fallas of Valencia; the mock battles between Moors and Christians staged in Alcoi; and the lavish, costumed Easter processions in Murcia and Lorca.

ill terraces of olive and almond trees ascending the hillsides near Alcoi

◀ Gulls on the beach at Peñíscola, Costa del Azahar

Exploring Valencia and Murcia

The coasts of Valencia and Murcia offer popular seaside holidays and water sports almost all year round. Principal resorts include Benidorm, Benicàssim, La Manga del Mar Menor and Oropesa. Some coastal towns such as Peníscola, Gandia, Dénia, Alicante (Alacant) and Cartagena have charming old quarters, castles and other sites well worth visiting. Close to the sea are several scenic nature reserves: the freshwater lagoon of L'Albufera, and, on the Costa Blanca, the saltpans of Santa Pola and the striking limestone crag of the Penyal d'Ifach. Inland, the region offers excursions to such undiscovered beauty spots as El Maestrat and the mountains around Alcoi, as well as the undervisited historic towns of Xàtiva and Lorca. The two regional capitals, Valencia and Murcia, are both lively university cities with fine cathedrals and numerous museums.

Fishing nets strung out in the lagoon of L'Albufera

Getting Around

The region's principal roads are the A7/AP7/E15 motorway and the N332 along the coast. Other motorways connect Valencia with Madrid, A3 (E901), and Alicante with Madrid, N330 A31. There are main rail lines from Alicante, Valencia and Murcia to Madrid and Barcelona, but the rest of the rail network is rather fragmented and buses are often quicker than trains. A scenic narrow-gauge railway line along the Costa Blanca connects Dénia to Alicante via Benidorm. The region's international airports are at Alicante and Valencia.

Key

━━ Motorway

━━ Major road

══ Minor road

━━ Scenic route

━━ Main railway

--- Minor railway

━━ Regional border

△ Summit

For keys to symbols *see back flap*

La Balma
Forcall
La Poble de
Benifassà
La Sènia
N232
2 MORELLA
Mirambel
Barcelona
1
EL MAESTRAT
Sant
Mateu
tavieja
Ares del
Maestre
Vinarós
franca del Cid
Benicarló
3
Albocàcer
PENÍSCOLA
AP7
nagolosa
1813m
Cabanes
Alcossebre
Torreblanca
5 VILLAFAMÉS
Oropesa
4
za
Alcora
CV10
N340
Benicàssim
III H ONDA 7
6 CASTELLÓ
DE LA PLANA
La Val
d'Uixo
Burriana
A23
8 COVES DE SANT JOSEP
Pucol
10 SAGUNT
V35
A7
11 MONASTERIO
DE EL PUIG
erna
12 VALENCIA
nte
Catarroja
13 L'ALBUFERA
Alginet
ueca
Cullera
Alzira
Tavernes de
la Valldigna
14 XÀTIVA 15 GANDIA
Oliva
ntinyent
Pego
16 DÉNIA
Agres
17 XÀBIA
20
19 GUADALEST
Callosa
d'en Sarrià
Calp
Altea
18 PENYAL D'IFACH
CV800
Xixona
21 BENIDORM
N332
La Vila Joiosa
El Campello
23 ALICANTE
(ALACANT)
(ELCHE)
Santa Pola
24 ILLA DE TABARCA
rdamar del Segura
REVIEJA
NOR

Lemon groves outside Dénia

Sights at a Glance

1. El Maestrat
2. Morella
3. Peníscola
4. Costa del Azahar
5. Vilafamés
6. Castelló de la Plana
7. Onda
8. Coves de Sant Josep
9. Alto Turia
10. Sagunt
11. Monasterio de El Puig
12. *Valencia pp254–7*
13. L'Albufera
14. Xàtiva
15. Gandia
16. Dénia
17. Xàbia

18. Penyal d'Ifac
19. Guadalest
20. Alcoi
21. Benidorm
22. Novelda
23. Alicante (Alacant)
24. Illa de Tabarca
25. Elx (Elche)
26. Orihuela
27. Torrevieja
28. Murcia
29. Mar Menor
30. Cartagena
31. Costa Cálida
32. Lorca
33. Caravaca de la Cruz

0 kilometres   25
0 miles   20

One of the many coves on Xàbia's rugged coast

The unbroken medieval wall surrounding the historic hilltop town of Morella in El Maestrat

❶ El Maestrat

Castellón & Teruel. 🚌 Morella.
ℹ️ Calle Mayor 15, Cantavieja, 964 18
54 14. 🌐 **comarcamaestrazgo.es**

Crusading warlords of the Knights Templar and the Knights of Montesa – known as *maestres* (masters) – gave their name to this lonely upland region. To rule over this frontier land, which straddles the border between Valencia and Aragón, they built fortified settlements in dramatic defensive positions, often on rocky crags. The best preserved of them is Morella, the principal town. Forcall, not far from Morella, has two 16th-century mansions on its porticoed

The Torre de la Sacristía, in the restored village of Mirambel

square. To the south, the village of Ares del Maestre is spectacularly sited beneath a 1,318-m- (4,300-ft-) high rock.

Cantavieja is the main town in the Aragonese part of El Maestrat (where it is known as El Maestrazgo). It has a pretty arcaded square. The walled village of Mirambel, nearby, has been restored to its medieval condition.

There are several spooky but fascinating shrines to the Virgin in El Maestrat, notably the cave of La Balma at Zorita, which is reached via a rocky ledge.

The scenery in most parts is striking: fertile valleys alternate with breathtaking cliffs and bare, flat-topped mountains overflown by eagles and vultures. Tourism is developing very slowly here: there are few places to stay and the roads can be windy and slow.

❷ Morella

Castellón. 🏠 2,600. 🚌 ℹ️ Plaza de San Miguel, 964 17 30 32. 🚪 Sun.
🎏 Fiestas Patronales (mid–late Aug).
🌐 **morellaturistica.com**

Built on a high, isolated outcrop and crowned by a ruined castle, Morella cuts a dramatic profile. Its unbroken medieval walls retain six gates, which lead into a fan-shaped maze

of streets and steep, tapering alleys, many of which are shaded by the eaves of ancient houses. The main street is lined with shady porticoes. In the upper part of town is the Basílica de Santa María la Mayor. Its unique raised choir loft is reached by a finely carved spiral staircase.

EN ESTA CASA OBRO SAN VICENTE FERRER EL PRODIGIOS
ILA GRODE LA RESURECCION DE UN NIÑO QUE SU MADRE
NAJENADA HABIA DESCUARTIZADO Y GUISADO E
RESEQUIO AL SANTO (1414)

Morella's Miracle

A plaque on the wall of Morella's Calle de la Virgen marks the house in which St Vincent Ferrer is said to have performed a bizarre miracle in the early 15th century. A housewife, distraught at having no meat to offer the saint, cut up her son and put him in the cooking pot. When St Vincent discovered this, he reconstituted the boy – except for one of his little fingers, which his mother had eaten to see if the dish was sufficiently salted.

❸ Peníscola

Castellón. 🚠 7,000. 🚌 ℹ️ Paseo Marítimo, 964 48 02 08. 🗓 Mon. 🎪 Fiestas Patronales (2nd week Sep). 🌐 **peniscola.es**

The fortified Old Town of Peníscola clusters around the base of a castle built on a rocky promontory, surrounded on three sides by the sea. This labyrinth of narrow winding streets and white houses is enclosed by massive ramparts. These are entered by either the Fosch Gate – reached by a ramp from the Plaza del Caudillo – or through the San Pedro Gate, from the harbour. Some visitors are drawn to the town because the 1961 Hollywood blockbuster *El Cid* was filmed there.

The Castell del Papa Luna was built on the foundations of an Arab fortress in the late 13th century by the Knights Templar. Their cross is carved above the door. It later became the residence of the papal pretender Pedro de Luna, cardinal of Aragón. He was elected Pope Benedict XIII during the Great Schism that split the Catholic Church at the end of the 14th century. Although he was deposed by the Council of Constance in 1414, he continued to proclaim his right to the papacy until his death as a nonagenarian in 1423.

🏰 **Castell del Papa Luna**
Calle Castillo. **Tel** 964 48 00 21. **Open** daily. **Closed** 1 & 6 Jan, 9 Sep, 9 Oct, 25 Dec. 🎟 📷

Sunset view of the beach and old town of Peníscola

❹ Costa del Azahar

Castellón. 🚉 Castelló de la Plana. 🚌 Castelló de la Plana. ℹ️ Plaza de la Hierba s/n, Castelló de la Plana, 964 35 86 88. 🌐 **turismodecastellon.com**

The "Orange Blossom Coast" of Castellón province is named after the dense citrus groves of the coastal plain. The three principal resorts are Oropesa, Peníscola and Benicàssim, where handsome old villas stand beside modern hotels and other tourist amenities. Alcossebre also has a popular beach. Vinaròs – the most northerly point – and Benicarló are key fishing ports supplying prawns and date mussels to local restaurants.

Sculpture in the Casa del Batle

❺ Vilafamés

Castellón. 🚠 2,000. 🚌 ℹ️ Plaza del Ayuntamiento 2, 964 32 99 70. 🗓 Fri. 🎪 San Miguel (late Mar), Patronales (mid-Aug).

This medieval town climbs from a plain along a rocky ridge to the restored round keep of its castle. The older, upper part of the town is a warren of sloping streets.

A 15th-century mansion houses the **Museo de Arte Contemporáneo de Vilafamés**. The artworks on display date from 1959 to the present.

🏛 **Museo de Arte Contemporáneo de Vilafamés**
Casa del Batle, Calle Diputación 20. **Tel** 964 32 91 52. **Open** Tue–Sun. 📷 🌐 **macvac.vilafames.es**

Castelló de la Plana's planetarium, close to the beach

❻ Castelló de la Plana

Castellón. 🚠 180,000. 🚉 🚌 ℹ️ Plaza de la Hierba s/n, 964 35 86 88. 🗓 Mon. 🎪 Fiesta de la Magdalena (3rd Sun of Lent). 🌐 **castellonturismo.com**

Originally founded on high ground inland, the capital of Castellón province was relocated nearer to the coast in the 13th century.

The city centre, the Plaza Mayor, is bordered by the market, the cathedral, the town hall and El Fadrí, a 58-m- (190-ft-) high octagonal bell tower begun in 1590 and finished in 1604.

The **Museo de Bellas Artes** contains a collection of artifacts dating from the middle Palaeolithic era, paintings from the 14th to the 19th centuries and modern ceramics from the region. Most of the older works come from the nearby convents, because the government seized many church possessions in the 19th century. An important collection of paintings attributed to Francisco de Zurbarán is also on display here.

In **El Planetari** there are demonstrations of the night sky, the solar system and the nearest stars, plus temporary exhibits.

🏛 **Museo de Bellas Artes**
Avda Hermanos Bou 28. **Tel** 964 72 75 00. **Open** 10am–2pm & 4–8pm Tue–Sat, 10am–2pm Sun. 📷 by appt. 🚻 📷

🔭 **El Planetari**
Paseo Marítimo 1, Grao. **Tel** 964 28 29 68. **Open** Oct–Jun: 9:30am–2:45pm Tue–Fri; 10:30am–2pm & 4:30–8pm Sat; 10:30am–2pm Sun (Mar–Jun & Oct: also 4:30–8pm Tue–Fri); Jul–Sep: 9:30am–2:30pm & 4:30–9pm daily. 📷 🚻

❼ Onda

Castellón. 🏛 25,700. 🚌 ℹ Calle
Ceramista Peyró, 964 60 28 55.
🛍 Thu. 🎑 Feria del Santísimo
Salvador (5 & 6 Aug). 🌐 onda.es

Onda, home to a thriving
ceramics industry, is overlooked
by a ruined castle, which was
known to its Moorish founders
as the "Castle of the Three
Hundred Towers". The castle
houses a museum of local history.

However, the main reason
to visit Onda is to take a look
at the **Museo de Ciencias
Naturales El Carmen**, a natural
history museum belonging to
a Carmelite monastery.

The collection was begun in
1952 by the monks for their own
private scientific study. It was
opened to the public a decade
later. The clever use of subdued
lighting lends dramatic effect to
the 10,000 plant and animal
specimens which are exhibited
over three floors. Objects include
large stuffed animals placed in
naturalistic settings, butterflies
and other insects, shells, fossils,
minerals and grisly, preserved
anatomical specimens.

🏛 Museo de Ciencias Naturales El Carmen

Carretera de Tales. **Tel** 964 60 07 30.
Open daily (winter: Fri–Sun only). See
website for details. **Closed** 20 Dec–7
Jan. 🎫 museodelcarmen.com

Two butterfly exhibits in the
Museo El Carmen

Boat ride through the winding Coves de
Sant Josep

❽ Coves de Sant Josep

Vall d'Uixó, Castellón. **Tel** 964 69 05 76.
🚌 Vall d'Uixó. **Open** daily. **Closed** 1 &
6 Jan, 25 Dec. 🎫 🎦 compulsory.
🌐 **riosubterraneo.com**

The caves of St Joseph were first
explored in 1902. The subterranean river that formed them
and that still flows through
them, has been charted for
almost 3 km (2 miles). However,
only part of this distance can be
explored on a visit.

Boats take visitors along the
serpentine course of the river.
You may have to duck to avoid
projections of rock on the way.
Sometimes the narrow caves
open out into large chambers
such as the *Sala de los Murcié-
lagos* (Hall of the Bats – the bats
left when the floodlights were
installed). The water is at its
deepest – 12 m (39 ft) – in the
Lago Azul (Blue Lake). You can
explore a further 250 m (820 ft)
along the *Galería Seca* (Dry
Gallery) on foot. The caves are
often closed after heavy rain.

❾ Alto Turia

Valencia. 🚌 Chelva. ℹ Plaza Mayor 1,
Chelva, 96 210 01 65.

The attractive wooded hills of
the upper reaches of the Río
Turia in Valencia (Alto Turia) are
popular with hikers and day-
trippers. **Chelva**, the main town,
has an unusual clock on its
church, which shows not only
the hour but the day and month

as well. The town is overlooked
by the Pico del Remedio
(1,054 m /3,458 ft), from the
summit of which there is a fine
panoramic view of the region. In
a valley near Chelva, at the end
of an unsurfaced but drivable
track, are the remains of a Roman
aqueduct, Peña Cortada.

The most attractive and
interesting village in Alto Turia is
Alpuente, situated above a dry
gorge. Between 1031 and 1089,
when it was captured by El Cid
(see p374), Alpuente was the
capital of a small *taifa*, a Moorish
kingdom. In the 14th century
it was still important enough
for the kingdom of Valencia's
parliament to meet here. The
town hall is confined to a small
tower over a 14th-century
gateway, which was later
extended in the 16th century
by the addition of a rectangular
council chamber.

Requena, to the south is
Valencia's main wine town.
Further south, Valencia's other
principal river, the Xúquer
(Júcar), carves tremendous
gorges near Cortes de Pallas
on its way past the Muela de
Cortes. This massive, wild
plateau and nature reserve is
crossed by one small road and
a lonely dirt track.

La Tomatina

The highpoint of the annual
fiesta in Buñol (Valencia) is a
sticky food fight on the last
Wednesday of August, which
attracts thousands of visitors
dressed in their worst clothes.
Lorry loads of ripe tomatoes are
provided by the town council at
11am for participants to hurl at
each other. No one in range of
the combatants is spared:
foreigners and photographers
are prized targets.

The battle originated in
1944. Some say it began
with a fight between friends.
Others say irreverent locals
pelted civic dignitaries with
tomatoes during a procession.
Increasing national and
international press coverage
means that more people
attend, and more tomatoes
are thrown, every year.

For hotels and restaurants in this region see pp567–8 and p591

Sagunt's ruined fortifications, added to by successive rulers of the town

➓ Sagunt

Valencia. 🚠 66,000. 🚉 🚌 ℹ️ Plaza Cronista Chabret, 962 65 58 59. 🚃 Wed. 🎆 Fallas (15–19 Mar), Fiestas (Jul–Aug). 🅦 **turismo.sagunto.es**

Sited near the junction of two Roman roads, Sagunt (Sagunto) played a crucial role in Spain's ancient history.

In 219 BC, Hannibal, the Carthaginian commander in southern Spain, stormed and sacked Rome's ally Saguntum. All the inhabitants of the town were said to have died in the assault, the last throwing themselves on to bonfires rather than fall into the hands of Hannibal's troops. The incident sparked off the Second Punic War, a disaster for the Carthaginians, which ended with Rome's occupation of the peninsula *(see pp54–5)*.

The town still contains several reminders of the Roman occupation, including the 1st-century-AD Roman theatre. Built out of limestone in a natural depression on the hillside above the town, it has been controversially restored using modern materials. The theatre is now used as a venue for music, plays and Sagunt's annual theatre festival.

The ruins of the **castle**, sprawling along the crest of the hill above the modern-day town, mark the original site of Saguntum. Superimposed on each other are the excavated remains of various civilisations, including the Iberians, the Carthaginians, the Romans and the Moors. The ruins of the castle are divided into seven divisions, the highest being La Ciudadella, and the most important Armas.

🏯 **Castillo de Sagunt**
Open Tue–Sun. **Tel** 962 66 62 01.

⓫ Monasterio de El Puig

El Puig, Valencia. **Tel** 961 47 02 00. 🚉 🚌 El Puig. **Open** Tue–Sat. 🎆 🕐 only, 10am, 11am, noon, 4pm, 5pm. 🅦 **monasteriodelpuig.es.tl**

This Mercedarian monastery was founded by King Jaime I of Aragón, who conquered Valencia from the Moors in the 13th century. The monastery is now home to a collection of paintings from between the 16th and 18th centuries and the Museo de la Imprenta y de la Obra Gráfica (Museum of Printing and Graphic Art). The museum commemorates the printing of the first book in Spain – thought to have been in Valencia in 1474 – and illustrates the development of the printing press. Exhibits include printers' blocks and a copy of the smallest printed book in the world.

Revellers throwing tomatoes at each other in the annual fiesta of La Tomatina

⑫ Valencia

Spain's third-largest city is sited in the middle of the *huerta*: a fertile plain of orange groves and market gardens, which is one of Europe's most intensively farmed regions. With its warm coastal climate, Valencia is known for its exuberant outdoor living and nightlife. In March the city stages one of Spain's most spectacular fiestas, Las Fallas *(see p259)*, in which giant papier-mâché sculptures are burned in the streets. Modern Valencia is a centre for trade and manufacturing, notably ceramics. A ferry service connects the city with the Balearic Islands.

Flowers in honour of Valencia's patroness, Virgen de los Desamparados

Exploring Valencia

Valencia stands on the course of the Río Turia. The city centre and the crumbling old quarter of El Carmen are on the right bank. Most of the monuments are within walking distance of the Plaza del Ayuntamiento, the triangular main square, which is presided over by the town hall.

The city was founded by the Romans in 138 BC and later conquered by the Moors. It was captured by El Cid *(see p374)* in 1096, retaken by the Moors, and finally recaptured by Jaime I, the Conqueror, in 1238, to become absorbed into the kingdom of Aragón. The three finest

buildings in Valencia were built during its economic and cultural heyday in the 14th and 15th centuries: the Torres de Serranos, a gateway that survived the demolition of the medieval walls in the 19th century, La Lonja and the cathedral.

🏛 Palau de la Generalitat
Plaza de Manises. **Tel** 963 86 34 61. **Open** 9am–2pm Mon–Fri and by appt only.

This palace, which is now used by the Valencian regional government, was built in Gothic style between 1482 and 1579 but added to in the 17th and 20th centuries. It surrounds an enclosed stone patio from which two staircases ascend to splendidly decorated rooms.

The larger of the two Salas Doradas (Golden Chambers), on the mezzanine level, has a multicoloured coffered ceiling and tiled floor. The walls of the parliament chamber are decorated with frescoes.

🏛 Basílica de la Virgen de los Desamparados
Plaza de la Virgen. **Tel** 963 91 92 14. **Open** 11am–2pm & 5–8pm Mon–Thu; 10:30am–2pm Sun & public hols.

The statue of Valencia's patroness, the Virgin of the Helpless, stands above an altar in this 17th-century church, lavishly adorned with flowers and candles. She is honoured during Las Fallas by La Ofrenda ("the Offering"), a display of flowers in the square outside the church.

🏛 Cathedral
Plaza de la Reina. **Tel** 963 91 81 27. **Open** 10am–6:30pm Mon–Sat, 2–6:30pm Sun & public hols (Nov–19 Mar: 10am–5:30pm Mon–Sat). 🎫 includes entry to the museum. Museo: **Open** as above. Miguelete: **Open** daily. 🎫 📷

Built originally in 1262, the cathedral has been added to over the ages, and its three doorways are all in different styles. The oldest is the Romanesque Puerta del Palau, but the main entrance is the 18th-century Baroque portal, the Puerta de los Hierros.

A unique court meets on Thursdays at noon in front of the Gothic Puerta de los Apóstoles. For about 1,000 years,

The Miguelete, the cathedral's bell tower on Plaza de la Reina

the Water Tribunal has settled disputes between farmers over irrigation in the *huerta*.

Inside the cathedral, a chapel holds an agate cup, claimed to be the Holy Grail and formerly kept in the San Juan de la Peña *(see p238)*. Behind the main altar are some 15th-century frescoes.

The cathedral's bell tower, the Miguelete, is Valencia's main landmark and popular for the views it offers from the top. The cathedral also houses a museum.

🏛 La Lonja

Plaza del Mercado. **Tel** 962 08 41 53. **Open** Tue–Sun (daily mid-Mar–mid-Oct). 🎫

An exquisite Late Gothic hall, built between 1482 and 1498 as a commodities exchange, La Lonja now hosts cultural events. The outside walls are decorated with gargoyles and other grotesque figures. The ceiling of the transactions hall features star-patterned vaulting, supported by spiral columns.

🏛 Mercado Central

Plaza del Mercado 6. **Tel** 963 82 91 00. **Open** 7am–3pm Mon–Sat.
This huge iron, glass and tile Art Nouveau building, with its

Ornate toilet sign outside Valencia's Mercado Central

parrot and swordfish weathervanes, opened in 1928 and is one of the largest and most attractive markets in Europe. Every morning its 350 or so stalls are filled with a bewildering variety of food.

🏛 Museo Nacional de Cerámica Gonzalez Martí

Poeta Querol 2. **Tel** 963 08 54 29. **Open** Tue–Sun, **Closed** 1, 6 & 22 Jan, 1 May, 24, 25 & 31 Dec. 🎫 (free Sat pm & Sun). ♿

Spain's Ceramics Museum is housed in the mansion of Marqués de Dos Aguas, an 18th-century fantasy of coloured plasterwork. The doorway is edged by a carving

VISITORS' CHECKLIST

Practical Information
Valencia. 🔢 786,400. ℹ️ Plaza del Ayuntamiento 1, 963 52 49 08. 📅 Mon–Sat. 🎉 Las Fallas (15–19 Mar). 🌐 visitvalencia.com

Transport
✈️ 8 km (5 miles) SW. 🚃 Calle Játiva 24, 902 320 320. 🚌 Avda Menéndez Pidal 13, 963 46 62 66. 🚍 963 93 95 00.

by Ignacio Vergara. The exhibits include prehistoric, Greek and Roman ceramics and pieces by Picasso.

🏛 Colegio del Patriarca

Calle Nave 1. **Tel** 692 49 17 69. **Open** Mon–Sat. **Closed** Aug. 🎫 📷 10am, 11am, noon, 12:30pm, 5pm & 6pm (compulsory).

This seminary was built in 1584. The walls and ceiling of the church are covered with frescoes by Bartolomé Matarana. During Friday morning Mass, the painting above the altar, *The Last Supper* by Francisco Ribalta, is lowered to reveal a sculpture of the Crucifixion by an anonymous 15th-century German artist.

Valencia City Centre

① Palau de la Generalitat
② Basílica de la Virgen de los Desamparados
③ Cathedral
④ La Lonja
⑤ Mercado Central
⑥ Museo Nacional de Cerámica Gonzalez Martí
⑦ Colegio del Patriarca
⑧ Jardines del Río Turia
⑨ Museo de Bellas Artes
⑩ Torres de Serranos
⑪ Instituto Valenciano de Arte Moderno (IVAM)
⑫ Estación del Norte

| 0 metres | 250 |
| 0 yards | 250 |

The Palau de la Música, Valencia's prestigious concert hall

Beyond the Centre

The centre of the city is bordered by the Gran Vía Marqués del Túria and the Gran Vía Ramón y Cajal. Beyond these lie the 19th-century suburbs laid out on a grid plan.

The best way to get around beyond the centre is by the metro, one line of which is a tramway to the beaches of El Cabañal and La Malvarrosa. The port area, redeveloped for the 2007 America's Cup, is full of bars and restaurants.

🟢 Jardines del Río Túria

Where once there was a river there is now a 10-km- (6-mile-) long strip of gardens, sports fields and playgrounds crossed by 19 bridges. In a prominent position above the riverbed stands the Palau de la Música, a concert hall built in the 1980s. The centrepiece of the nearby children's playground is the giant figure of Gulliver pinned to the ground and covered with steps and slides. Jardín de Cabecera aims to recreate the

A light-filled room in Valencia's Museo de Bellas Artes

Túria River's original landscape, with a lake, beach, waterwheel, waterfall and riverside wood.

The best of Valencia's other public gardens stand near the banks of the river. The largest of them, the Jardines del Real – known locally as Los Viveros – occupy the site of a royal palace which was torn down in the Peninsular War. The Jardín Botánico, created in 1802, is planted with 7,000 species of shrubs and trees.

🏛 Museo de Bellas Artes

Calle San Pío V 9. **Tel** 963 87 03 00. **Open** 10am–8pm Tue–Sun. **Closed** 1 Jan, Good Fri, 25 Dec. 🚻 🛒 by appt.

An important collection of 2,000 paintings and statues dating from the 14th to the 19th centuries is housed in this former seminary, which was built between 1683 and 1744.

Valencian art dating from the 14th and 15th centuries is represented by a series of golden altarpieces by Alcanyis, Pere Nicolau and Maestro de Bonastre. Velázquez's self-portrait and works by Bosch, El Greco, Murillo, Ribalta, Van Dyck and the local Renaissance painter Juan de Juanes hang on the first floor. On the top floor there are six paintings by Goya and others by important 19th- and 20th-century Valencian artists: Ignacio Pinazo, Joaquín Sorolla and Antonio Muñoz Degrain. A large collection of the latter's hallucinatory coloured paintings are gathered together in one room, among them the disturbing *Amor de Madre*.

🏯 Torres de Serranos

Plaza de los Fueros. **Tel** 963 91 90 70. **Open** 9:30am–7pm daily (to 3pm Sun). **Closed** 1 Jan, 1 May, 25 Dec. 🏛 (free Sun).

Erected in 1391 as a triumphal arch in the city's walls, this gateway combines defensive and decorative features. Its two towers combine battlements and delicate Gothic tracery.

🏛 Instituto Valenciano de Arte Moderno (IVAM)

Calle Guillem de Castro 118. **Tel** 963 17 66 00. **Open** 11am–7:30pm Tue–Sun. 🏛 (free Sun). 🛒 by appt. 🖥 🏯 ⚙ 🖥 **ivam.es**

The Valencian Institute of Modern Art is one of Spain's most highly respected spaces for displaying contemporary art. The core of its permanent collection is formed of work by the 20th-century sculptor Julio Gonzalez. All art forms are represented in its temporary exhibitions, with emphasis on photography and photomontage. One of the eight galleries, Sala Muralles, incorporates a stretch of the old city walls.

Art Nouveau-style column in the Estación del Norte

🚉 Estación del Norte

Calle Xátiva 24. **Tel** 902 32 03 20 (RENFE). **Open** daily.

Valencia's local railway station was built from 1906 to 1917 in a style inspired by Austrian Art Nouveau. The exterior is decorated with orange and orange-blossom flower motifs, while, inside, ceramic murals and stained glass in the foyer and cafeteria depict the life and crops of the *huerta* and L'Albufera (see p258).

The hemispherical IMAX cinema at the Ciutat de les Arts i de les Ciències

🏛 Ciutat de les Arts i de les Ciències

Avenida Autovia del Saler 1–7. **Tel** 961 97 46 86, Museum **Open** 10am–6pm or 7pm daily (to 9pm 1 Jul–15 Sep). 📷 ✏ 🖥 🏠 ♿ 🌐 cac.es

The futuristic complex of the City of Arts and Sciences stands at the seaward end of the Río Túria gardens. It is made up of five stunning buildings, four of them designed by Valencian architect Santiago Calatrava.

The Palau de les Arts, the final building to be added to the complex, has a concert hall with four performance spaces including an open-air theatre. On the other side of the Puente de Monteolivete is l'Hermisfèric, an architectural pun by Calatrava on the theme of vision, consisting of a blinking eye. The "eyeball" is an auditorium equipped as an IMAX cinema and planetarium. Next to this is the Museu de les Ciències Príncipe Felipe, a science museum contained within a structure of glass and gleaming white steel arches. The displays inside are mainly geared towards visiting school parties. Opposite the museum is L'Umbracle, a giant pergola of parabolic arches covering the complex's car park.

The last part of the "city" is an aquarium, the Oceanografic, designed by architect Felix Candela as a series of lagoons and pavillions linked up by bridges and tunnels.

🏛 Museo de Historia de Valencia

Carrer Valencia 42, Mislata. **Tel** 963 70 11 05. **Open** Tue–Sun. 🏠 (free Sat & Sun). ♿ 🌐 mhv.valencia.es

Valencia's history museum is housed in the 19th-century cistern that used to supply the city with water, now an atmospheric labyrinth of pillars and arches. The displays tell the story of the city's development, from its foundations by the Romans to the present day. In each section there is a "time machine", a full-sized screen on which a typical scene of daily life is reproduced in the language of the visitor's choice.

El Cabañal and La Malvarrosa Beaches

To the east of the city, the beaches of El Cabañal and La Malvarrosa are bordered by a broad and lively esplanade about 2 km (1 mile) long. Although these two former fishermen's districts were carelessly developed in the 1960s and 1970s, they retain some quaint, traditional houses tiled on the outside to keep them cool in summer. The light of La Malvarrosa inspired the Impressionist painter Joaquín Sorolla (see p309). The Paseo de Neptuno, near the port, is lined with restaurants, many of which specialize in paella. The revamped port district and marina feature many modern hotels.

Environs

The farmed plain of the *huerta* is a maze of fields planted with artichokes and *chufas*, the raw ingredient of *horchata*.

Manises, near the airport, is famous for its ceramics, which are sold in shops and factories. There is also a ceramics museum.

Horchata, Valencia's Speciality

In summer, the bars and cafés of Valencia offer a thirst-quenching drink unique to the area. *Horchata*, a sweet, milky drink produced mainly in the nearby town of Alboraia, is made from *chufas* (earth almonds). It is served semi-frozen or in liquid form and usually eaten with *fartons* – soft, sweet breadsticks – or *rosquilletas* – crunchy biscuit sticks. The oldest *horchatería* in the city centre is Santa Catalina, off the Plaza de la Virgen.

Painted tiles showing woman serving *horchata*

Fishing boats on the shore of the freshwater lake, L'Albufera

⑬ L'Albufera

Valencia. 🚌 ℹ️ Carretera del Palmar, Racó de l'Olla, 963 86 80 50. 🖥 **citma. gva.es/va/web/pn-l-albufera**

A freshwater lake on the coast just south of Valencia, L'Albufera is one of the prime wetland habitats for birds in Eastern Spain.

It is cut off from the sea by a wooded sandbar, the Dehesa, and fringed by a network of paddy fields, which produce a third of Spain's rice.

L'Albufera is fed by the Río Turia and connected to the sea by three channels, which are fitted with sluice gates to control the water level. The lake reaches a maximum depth of 2.5 m (8 ft), and is gradually shrinking because of natural silting and the reclamation of land. In the Middle Ages the lake encompassed an area over ten times its present size.

Over 250 species of birds – including large numbers of egrets and herons – have been recorded in the lake's reedbeds and marshy islands, the *matas*. L'Albufera was declared a nature reserve in 1986. Many birds can be seen with binoculars from the shores of the lake.

A visitors' centre at Racó de l'Olla provides information on the ecology of lake, the paddy fields and the Dehesa.

⑭ Xàtiva

Valencia. 🚹 29,300. 🚉 🚌 ℹ️ Alameda de Jaime I 50, 962 27 33 46. 🛍 Tue & Fri. 🎉 Las Fallas (16–19 Mar); Fira de Agosto (14–20 Aug).

Along the narrow ridge of Mount Vernissa, above Xàtiva, run the ruins of a once-grand **castle** of 30 towers. It was largely destroyed by Felipe V in the War of the Spanish Succession *(see p66)*. Felipe also set fire to the town, which continues to wreak its revenge in an extraordinary way – by hanging Felipe's full-length portrait upside down in the **Museo de Bellas Artes**.

Until the attack, Xàtiva was the second town of the kingdom of Valencia. It is thought to have been founded by the

Felipe V's full-length portrait hanging upside down in Xàtiva

Iberians. Under the Moors it became prosperous, and in the 12th century it was the first European city to make paper.

Among the sights in the streets and squares of the Old Town are a former hospital with a Gothic-Renaissance façade, and a Gothic fountain in the Plaça de la Trinidad.

The oldest church in Xàtiva is the Ermita de San Feliú (Chapel of St Felix) on the road up to the fortress. It dates from around 1262 and is hung with a number of 14th- to 16th-century icons.

🏰 **Castillo de Xàtiva**
Subida del Castillo. **Tel** 962 27 42 74.
Open Tue–Sun. 🚻

🏛 **Museo de Bellas Artes**
Plaza Arzobispo Mayoral 2. **Tel** 962 28 24 55. **Open** Tue–Sun. 🚻 ♿

⑮ Gandia

Valencia. 🚹 78,000. 🚉 🚌 ℹ️ Avinguda Marqués de Campo, 962 87 77 88. 🛍 Thu, Sat. 🎉 Las Fallas (16–19 Mar). 🖥 **visitgandia.com**

In 1485, Rodrigo Borja (who became Pope Alexander VI) was granted the title of Duchy of Gandia. He founded the Borgia clan and, together with his children, was later implicated in murder and debauchery. Rodrigo's great-grandson later redeemed the family name by joining the Jesuit order. He was canonized as St Francis Borja by Pope Clement X in 1671.

The house in which he was born, the **Palau Ducal** (Duke's Palace), is now owned by the Jesuits. Its simple Gothic courtyard belies the ornate chambers within, especially the Baroque Golden Gallery. The small patio's tiled floor depicts the elements of earth, air, fire and water.

🏛 Palau Ducal
Carrer Duc Alfons el Vell 1. **Tel** 962 87 14 65. **Open** daily. 🅿 📷
W palauducal.com

The ornate and gilded interior of the Palau Ducal, Gandia

🔵 Dénia

Alicante. 🚶 41,600. 🚗 🚌 🚉
i Plaza Oculista Baigues 9, 966 42 23 67. 🗓 Mon & Fri. 🎉 Fiestas Patronales (early Jul). **W** denia.net

This town was founded as a Greek colony. It takes its name from the Roman goddess Diana – a temple in her honour was excavated here. In the 11th century it became the capital of a short-lived Muslim kingdom, whose dominion extended from Andalucía to the Balearic Islands.

It is now a fishing port and holiday resort. The town centre spreads around the base of a low hill. A large **castle**, once an Arab fortress, on its summit overlooks the harbour. The entrance gate, the Portal de la Vila, survives, but it was altered in the 17th century. The Palacio del Gobernador

(Governor's House), within the castle, contains an archaeological museum, which shows the development of Dénia from 200 BC to the 18th century.

North of the harbour is the sandy beach of Las Marinas. To the south is the rocky and less-developed Las Rotas beach, which is good for snorkelling.

🏛 Castillo de Dénia
Carrer Sant Francesc. **Tel** 966 42 06 56. **Open** daily. **Closed** 1 Jan, 25 Dec.
📷 ♿

🔵 Xàbia

Alicante. 🚶 31,000. 🚌 **i** Plaza de la Iglesia 4, 965 79 43 56. 🗓 Thu. 🎉 San Juan (24 Jun), Moros Y Cristianos (third weekend of Jul), Bous a la Mar (first week of Sep). **W** xabia.org

Pirates and smugglers once took advantage of the hiding places afforded by the cliffs, caves, inlets and two rocky islands along the coastline of Xàbia (also known as Jávea).

The town centre is perched on a hill on the site of an Iberian settlement. Many buildings here are made from the local Tosca sandstone. The 16th-century Iglesia de San Bartolomé was fortified to serve as a refuge in times of invasion. Missiles could be dropped on to attackers via openings over the door.

The seafront at Cabo de San Antonio is overlooked by ruined 17th- and 18th-century windmills. The bay is filled with modern developments, but the beaches are free of high-rise apartment blocks.

Entrance to the Gothic Iglesia de San Bartolomé in Xàbia

The ceremonial burning of Las Fallas on St Joseph's Day

Valencia and Murcia's Fiestas

Las Fallas *(15–19 Mar)*. Huge papier-mâché monuments *(fallas)* are erected in the crossroads and squares of Valencia around 15 March and ceremonially set alight on the night of the 19th, St Joseph's Day. Costing thousands of euros each, the *fallas* depict satirical scenes. During the fiesta, known as Les Falles in Valencian, the city echoes to the sound of firecrackers.
Good Friday, Lorca (Murcia). The "blue" and "white" brotherhoods compete to outdo each other in pomp and finery during a grand procession of biblical characters.
Moors and Christians *(21–24 Apr)*, Alcoi (Alicante). Two costumed armies march into the city, where they perform ceremonies and fight mock battles in commemoration of the Reconquest.
Bous a la Mar *(early Jul)*, Dénia (Alicante). People dodge bulls on the quay until one or the other falls into the sea *(see p43)*.
Misteri d'Elx *(11–15 Aug)*, Elx (Alicante). This choral play, in the Iglesia de Santa María, has spectacular special effects.
La Tomatina *(last Wed of Aug)*, Buñol (Valencia). Thousands of participants pelt each other with ripe tomatoes *(see pp252–3)*.

The Costa Blanca

Less hectic than the Costa del Sol *(see pp478–9)* and with warmer winters than the Costa Brava *(see p221)*, the Costa Blanca occupies a prime stretch of Spain's Mediterranean coastline. Alicante, with its airport and mainline railway station, is the arrival and departure point for most tourists. Between Alicante and Altea there are long stretches of sandy beach, which have been heavily built up with apartment blocks and hotels. North of Altea there are more fine beaches, but they are broken by cliffs and coves. South from Alicante, as far as the resort of Torrevieja, the scenery is drier and more barren, relieved only by the wooded sand dunes of Guardamar del Segura.

Gandia marks the southern end of the Costa de Valencia, whose extensive beaches of fine sand and shallow water are popular with the Spanish.

Dénia's Las Marinas beach is a flat, sandy strip lined by hotels. The rocky Les Rotes beach is good for snorkelling.

El Grau

Gandia

Platja d'Oliva

Oliva

N332

Xàbia's busiest beach is El Arenal. Most of the resort's coastline is punctuated by cliffs and coves.

Pego

AP7

Ondara

Dénia

Cap de Sant Antoni

Gata de Gorgos

Xàbia

Cap Martí

Altea is a resort with an unspoiled, whitewashed old town on a hilltop. Beneath it is a long, shingle beach.

Benissa

Cap de la Nau

AP7

N332

Moraira

Calp

Polop

Altea

Finestrat

l'Albir

Benidorm's liveliest beach, Levante, has been voted one of the ten best beaches in the world. Poniente is further from the town centre.

AP7

N332

Benidorm

Santa Pola is still a working fishing port, but its long, sandy beaches are very popular.

Busot

La Vila Joiosa

CV800

AP7

Coveta Fumà

El Campello

Platja de Sant Joan has a long strip of seamless sand bordered by a road and a narrow-gauge railway, which gives easy access to the beach.

Mutxamel

Sant Joan d'Alacant

Platja de Sant Joan

A31

A70

Cap de las Huertas

Alicante

Torrellano

N332

Elx

Els Arenals del Sol

0 kilometres   20
0 miles   10

The Illa de Tabarca attracts day-trippers for its natural beauty and clear waters, good for snorkelling.

Santa Pola

Platja del Pinet   *Illa de Tabarca*

Guardamar del Segura has one of the coast's least busy beaches. It is bordered by windswept sand dunes covered with aromatic pine woods.

Guardamar del Segura

N332

La Mata

Torrevieja is a very popular package holiday resort with sweeping, sandy beaches to the south. It has been highly developed in recent years.

Torrevieja

Alicante's city centre is served by the popular Postiguet beach. Nearby are vast, sandy beaches, such as La Albufereta and Sant Joan.

◀ Burning papier-mâché dragon at Las Fallas festival, Valencia

⓲ Penyal d'Ifac

Calp, Alicante. 🚉 Calp. 🚌 Calp.
ℹ Avenida de los Ejércitos Españoles,
30, Calp, 965 83 69 20. Limited access
in Jul & Aug.

When viewed from afar, the rocky
outcrop of the Penyal d'Ifac
seems to rise vertically out of the
sea. One of the Costa Blanca's
most dramatic sights, this 332-m-
(1,089-ft-) tall block of limestone
looks virtually unclimbable.
However, a short tunnel, built in
1918, allows walkers access to the
gentler slopes on its seaward side.

Allow about 2 hours for the
round trip, which starts at the
visitors' centre above Calp
harbour. It takes you up gentle
slopes covered with juniper
and fan palm, with the waves
crashing below. As you climb,
and at the exposed summit,
there are spectacular views of a
large stretch of the Costa Blanca.
On a clear day you can see the
hills of Ibiza (see pp514–17).

The Penyal d'Ifac is also home
to 300 types of wild plant, including several rare species. Migrating
birds use it as a landmark, and
the salt flats below it are an
important habitat for them.
The rock was privately owned
until 1987, when the regional
government acquired it and
turned it into a nature reserve.

Situated below the rock
is the Iberian town of Calp,
renowned for its beaches.

⓳ Guadalest

Alicante. 🚹 226. **ℹ** Avenida de
Alicante, 96 588 52 98. 🎉 Fiestas
de San Gregorio (1st week of Jun),
Virgen de la Asunción (14–17 Aug).
W guadalest.es

Despite drawing coach loads
of day-trippers from Benidorm,
this pretty mountain village
remains relatively unspoiled.
This is largely because its older
part is accessible only on foot
by a single entrance: a sloping
tunnel cut into the rock on
which the castle ruins and the
church's distinctive belfry are
precariously perched.

Guadalest was founded by
the Moors, who carved the
surrounding hillsides into

The magnificent limestone rock Penyal d'Ifac

terraces and planted them with
crops. These are still irrigated by
the original ditches constructed
by the Moors.

From the castle there are
fine views of the surrounding
mountains. Access to the castle
is through the Casa Orduña.

The intriguing **Museo de
Microminiaturas**, displays a
microscopic version of Goya's
Fusilamiento 3 de Mayo painted
on a grain of rice, his The Naked
Maja (see p297), painted on the
wing of a fly; and a sculpture
of a camel passing through
the eye of a needle.

🏛 Museo de Microminiaturas
Plaza San Gregorio 14. **Tel** 965 88 50 62.
Open 10am–9pm daily (winter: 6pm).
🅿 **W** miniaturasguadalest.com

The belfry of Guadalest, perched on
top of a rock

⓴ Alcoi

Alicante. 🚹 59,600. 🚉 🚌 **ℹ** Plaça
de España, 14, 965 53 /1 55. 🔲 Wed
& Sat. 🎉 Mercado Medieval (mid-
to late Mar), Moors and Christians
(23 Apr). **W** alcoiturisme.com

Sited at the confluence of three
rivers and surrounded by high
mountains, Alcoi is an industrial
city. But it is best known for its
mock battles between Moors and
Christians (see p259) and its pela-
dillas – almonds coated in sugar.

On the slopes above it is Font
Roja, a nature reserve offering
pleasant walks, and a shrine
marked by a towering statue
of the Virgin Mary.

Environs

To the north of Alcoi is the Sierra
de Mariola, a mountain range
famed for its herbs. The best
point of access is the village of
Agres. A scenic route runs from
here to the summit of Mont
Cabrer at 1,390 m (4,560 ft). It
passes two ruined neveras –
pits once used to store ice for
preserving fish and meat.

The bullring of Bocairent,
10 km (6 miles) west of Agres,
was carved out of rock in 1813.
A nearby cliff is pockmarked
with Les Covetes dels Moros
("The Moors' Caves"), but their
origin remains a mystery.

㉑ Benidorm

Alicante. 🗺 69,100. 🚍 🚌 *i* Plaza
Canalejas, El Torrejó, 965 85 13 11.
🛒 Wed & Sun. 🎉 Las Fallas (16–19
Mar), Virgen del Carmen (16 Jul),
Moros y Cristianos (late Sep, early Oct),
Fiestas Patronales (second weekend in
Nov). 🖵 visitbenidorm.es

With forests of skyscrapers
overshadowing its two long
beaches, Benidorm is far
removed from the obscure
fishing village it once was in the
early 1950s.

Benidorm boasts more
accommodation than any other
resort on the Mediterranean,
but its clientele has changed
since the 1980s, when its name
was synonymous with "lager
louts". A huge public park and
open-air auditorium used for
cultural events, the Parque de
l'Aigüera, is emblematic of the
face-lift Benidorm has gone
through. The town attracts
elderly holiday-makers from
the north of Spain and English
expats, the latter coming for
splendid sandy beaches, reliable
sunshine, nightclubs and
knock off "English" pubs.

A park on a promontory
between the Levante and
Poniente beaches, the Balcón del
Mediterráneo, ends in a giant
waterspout – a single-jet fountain.
From here there is a panoramic
view of the town. A short way out

Main staircase with floral lamp in the Casa
Modernista, Novelda

to sea is the Illa de Benidorm,
a wedge-shaped island served
by ferries from the harbour. The
island has been converted into
a nature reserve for seabirds.

Environs
La Vila Joiosa (Villajoyosa), to
the south, is much older than
Benidorm. Its principal sight is
a line of brightly painted houses
that overhang the riverbed.
They were painted in such vivid
colours, it is said, so that their
fishermen owners would be
able to identify their homes
when they were out at sea.

The older part of Altea, to the
north of Benidorm, stands on a
hill above modern beachfront
developments. It is a delightful
jumble of white houses, narrow
streets and long flights of steps
around a blue-domed church.

The old town of Altea, dominated by its domed church

㉒ Novelda

Alicante. 🗺 27,000. 🚍 🚌 *i* Carrer
Mayor 6, 965 60 92 28. 🛒 Wed & Sat.
🎉 Santa María Magdalena (19–25
Jul). 🖵 novelda.es

The industrial town of Novelda is
dominated by marble factories.
But it is the exquisitely preserved
Art Nouveau house, the **Casa
Modernista**, that is of special
interest. It was built in 1903 and
and rescued from demolition in
1970. The building's three floors
are furnished in period style.
There are few straight lines or
functional shapes and almost
every inch of wall space has
some floral or playful motif.

Environs
Villena's museum has a collection
of Bronze Age gold objects, the
Tesoro de Villena (see pp52–3).

🏛 **Casa Modernista**
Calle Mayor 24. **Tel** 965 60 02 37. **Open**
10am–2pm Tue–Fri. 🎟 by appt.

🏛 **Tesoro de Villena**
Plaza de Santiago 1. **Tel** 965 80 11 50.
Open Tue–Sun am. 🅿 ♿
🖵 museovillena.com

㉓ Alicante

Alicante. 🗺 332,000. ✈ 🚍 🚌 🚢
i Rambla Méndez Núñez 41, 965
20 00 00. 🛒 Thu & Sat. 🎉 Hogueras
(20–24 Jun). 🖵 alicanteturismo.com

A port and seaside resort built
around a natural harbour,
Alicante (Alacant) is the principal city of the Costa Blanca.
Both the Greeks and Romans
established settlements here.
In the 8th century the Moors
refounded the city under the
shadow of Mount Benacantil.
Its summit is now occupied by
the **Castillo de Santa Bárbara**,
which dates from the 16th
century. Its top battlements
offer a view over the whole city.

The focus of the city is the
Explanada de España, a palm-
lined promenade along the
waterfront. The 18th-century
ayuntamiento (town hall) is
worth seeing for the Salón Azul
(Blue Room). A metal disc on
the marble staircase is used as a
reference point in measuring the
sea level all around Spain. A fine

Yachts moored in Alicante harbour, beside the Explanada de España

collection of 20th-century art can be seen at the **Museo de Arte Contemporáneo (MACA)**. Local artist Eusebio Sempere (1924–85) assembled works by Dalí, Miró, Picasso *(see pp36–7)* and others.

🏰 **Castillo de Santa Bárbara**
Playa del Postiguet. **Tel** 965 92 77 15. **Open** daily. 🦽 (for elevator only). 🎫
w castillodesantabarbara.com

🏛 **Ayuntamiento**
Plaza del Ayuntamiento 1. **Tel** 965 14 91 00. **Open** 9am–2pm Mon–Fri.

🏛 **Museo de Arte Contemporáneo (MACA)**
Plaza de Santa María 3. **Tel** 965 21 31 56. **Open** 10am–8pm Tue–Sat, 10am–2pm Sun. **Closed** 1 & 6 Jan, 1 May, 25 Dec & local hols. 🦽
v maca-alicante.es

㉔ Illa de Tabarca

Alicante. 🚢 from Santa Pola/Alicante. 🚢 Santa Pola, 966 69 22 76.

The best point of departure for the Illa de Tabarca is Santa Pola. This small, flat island is divided into two parts: a stony, treeless area of level ground known as *el campo* (the countryside), and a walled settlement, which is entered through three gateways. The settlement was laid out on a grid plan in the 18th century, on the orders of Carlos III, to deter pirates. Tabarca is a popular place to swim or snorkel and it can get crowded in the summer.
Fish and salt have long been important to the economy of Santa Pola. A Roman fish salting works has been excavated here, and outside the town are some modern saltpans.

㉕ Elx

Alicante. �︎ 230,000. 🚉 🚌 🛈 Plaza Parque 3, 966 65 81 96. 🚆 Mon & Sat. 🎭 Misteri d'Elx (14–15 Aug).
w visitelche.com

The forest of over 300,000 palm trees that surrounds Elx (Elche) on three sides is said to have been planted by the Phoenicians around 300 BC. Part of it has been enclosed as a private garden called the **Huerto del Cura**. Some of the palms – one with a trunk which has divided into eight branches – are dedicated to notable people, like the Empress Elizabeth of Austria, who visited here in 1894.
The first settlement in the area, around 5000 BC, was at La Alcudia, where a 5th-century BC Iberian stone bust of a priestess, *La Dama de Elche (see p52)*, was discovered in 1897. The original is in Madrid, but there are several replicas scattered around Elx.
The blue-domed Baroque church, the Basílica de Santa María, was built in the 17th century to house the Misteri d'Elx *(see p45)*. Next to it is **La Calahorra**, a Gothic tower, which is a surviving part of the city's defences.
A clock on the roof next to the town hall has two 16th-century mechanical figures, which strike the hours on bells.

🌳 **Huerto del Cura**
Porta de la Morera 49. **Tel** 965 45 19 36. **Open** daily. 🦽🎫 **w** jardin. huertodelcura.com

🏛 **La Calahorra**
Calle Uberna. **Open** Tue–Sun.

㉖ Orihuela

Alicante. 🚫 83,400. 🚉 🚌 🛈 Plaza Teniente Linares, 965 30 46 45. 🚆 Tue. 🎭 Moros y Cristianos (10–17 Jul).
w orihuelaturistica.es

In the 15th century Orihuela was prosperous enough for Fernando and Isabel to stop and collect men and money on their way to do battle against the Moors at Granada. The Gothic cathedral houses Velázquez's *The Temptation of St Thomas Aquinas* in its museum. Among the exhibits in the **Museo San Juan de Dios** archaeological museum is a processional float bearing a 17th-century statue of a she-devil, *La Diablesa*.

🏛 **Museo San Juan de Dios**
Calle del Hospital. **Tel** 966 74 31 54. **Open** Tue–Sun. 🦽🎫

La Diablesa, Orihuela

㉗ Torrevieja

Alicante. 🚫 91,400. 🛈 Paseo Vista Alegre, 965 70 34 33. 🚆 Fri. 🎭 Habaneras (22–30 Jul).
w turismodetorrevieja.com

During the 1980s, Torrevieja grew at a prodigious rate as thousands of Europeans purchased homes here. Before tourism, the town's source of income was sea salt. The salt-works are the most productive in Europe and the second most important in the world.
The *habaneras* festival cele-brates Cuban music brought back by salt exporters.

Capilla del Junterón, Murcia

㉘ Murcia

Murcia. 🗻 439,700. 🚊 🚌 ℹ️ Plaza Cardenal Belluga, Ayuntamiento Building, 968 35 87 49. 🗓️ Thu. 🎭 Semana Santa (Easter Week). 🌐 **turismodemurcia.es**

A regional capital and university city on the River Segura, Murcia was founded in 825 by the Moors, following successful irrigation of the surrounding fertile plain.

The pedestrianized Calle de la Trapería, linking the cathedral and the former marketplace (now the Plaza Santo Domingo), is the city's main street.

On it stands the **Casino**, a gentlemen's club founded in 1847. It is entered through an Arab-style patio, fashioned on the royal chambers of the Alhambra. The huge ballroom has a polished parquet floor and is illuminated by five crystal chandeliers. Visitors can take a tour of the interior and splash out on a meal in the fine restaurant.

Work on the cathedral began in 1394 over the foundations of Murcia's central mosque, and it was finally consecrated in 1467. The large tower was added much later and constructed in stages from the 16th to the 18th centuries. The architect Jaime Bort built the main, Baroque façade between 1739 and 1754.

The cathedral's finest features are two exquisitely ornate side chapels. The first, the Capilla de los Vélez, is in Late Gothic style and was built between 1490 and 1507. The second, the Renaissance Capilla del Junterón, dates from the early 16th century.

The cathedral museum displays grand Gothic altarpieces, a frieze from a Roman sarcophagus and the third-largest monstrance in Spain.

Francisco Salzillo (1707–83), one of Spain's greatest sculptors, was born in Murcia, and a museum in the Iglesia de Jesús (Church of Jesus) exhibits nine of his *pasos* – sculptures on platforms. These are carried through the streets on Good Friday morning. The figures are so lifelike that a fellow sculptor is said to have told the men carrying a paso: "Put it down, it will walk by itself."

The **Museo Etnológico de la Huerta de Murcia**, 7 km (4.5 miles) out of Murcia, stands beside a large waterwheel – a 1955 copy in iron of the original 15th-century wooden wheel. The galleries display agricultural and domestic items, some of them 300 years old. A traditional, thatched Murcian farmhouse forms part of the museum.

🎰 Casino

C/ Trapería 18. **Tel** 968 21 53 99. **Open** 10:30am–7:30pm daily. 🍽️ ♿ 📷

🏛️ Museo Etnológico de la Huerta de Murcia

Avda Principe, Alcantarilla. **Tel** 968 89 38 66. **Open** Museum & Gardens: Tue–Sun. **Closed** Aug & public hols. ♿

㉙ Mar Menor

Murcia. ✈️ San Javier. 🚊 to Cartagena, then bus. 🚌 La Manga. ℹ️ La Manga, 968 14 61 36. 🌐 **marmenor.es**

The elongated, high-rise holiday resort of La Manga,

Arab-style patio, Murcia Casino

built on a long, thin, sandy strip, separates the Mediterranean and the Mar Menor, literally the "Smaller Sea".

Really a large lagoon, the sheltered Mar Menor can be 5°C (9°F) warmer than the Mediterranean in summer. Its high mineral concentrations first drew rest-cure tourists in the early 20th century. They stayed at the older resorts of Santiago de la Ribera and Los Alcázares, which still have pretty wooden jetties.

From either La Manga or Santiago de la Ribera you can make a ferry trip to the Isla Perdiguera, one of the five islands in the Mar Menor.

These days the region is very built-up, but to escape the crowds head to the Parque Regional de Calblanque. Its dunes and beaches are wild and unspoilt.

The resort of Los Alcázares on the edge of the Mar Menor

View of the domes and spires of Cartagena's town hall from the seafront

㉚ Cartagena

Murcia. 218,200. ✈ San Javier. 🚌 🚢 ℹ Palacio Consistorial, Plaza del Ayuntamiento 1, 968 12 89 55. 🕐 Wed. 🎎 Semana Santa (Easter Week), Carthaginians and Romans (last two weeks Sep). 🆆 cartagenaturismo.es

The first settlement founded in the natural harbour of Cartagena was constructed in 223 BC by the Carthaginians, who called it *Quart Hadas* (New City). After conquering the city in 209 BC, the Romans renamed it *Carthago Nova* (New Carthage). Although the city declined in importance in the Middle Ages, its prestige increased in the 18th century when it became a naval base.

The park surrounding the ruins of the Castillo de la Concepción, Cartagena's castle, has views over the impressive Roman theatre and its museum, the **Museo del Teatro Romano**. The city hall is at the end of the Calle Mayor, a street with handsome buildings and balconies. Excavations in the city include a Roman street and the **Muralla Bizantina** (Byzantine Wall), built between 589 and 590. The **Museo Nacional de Arqueología Marítima** has treasures from Greek and Roman wrecks.

▥ Museo del Teatro Romano
Plaza del Ayuntamiento 9.
Tel 968 52 51 49. 🅿 🆑 🦽
🆆 teatroromanocartagena.org

▥ Muralla Bizantina
Calle Doctor Tapia Martínez.
Tel 968 50 79 66. **Open** Tue–Sat.

▥ Museo Nacional de Arqueología Marítima
Paseo Alfonso XII. **Tel** 968 12 11 66.
Open Tue–Sun. 🎎 free Sat pm & Sun.

㉛ Costa Cálida

Murcia. 🚌 Murcia. 🚆 Murcia. ℹ Plaza Antonio Cortijos, Águilas, 968 49 32 85. 🆆 murciaturistica.es

The most popular resorts of Murcia's "Warm Coast" are around the Mar Menor. Between Cabo de Palos and Cabo Tinoso the few small beaches are dwarfed by cliffs. The resorts of the southern part of the coast are relatively quiet. There are several fine beaches at Puerto de Mazarrón; and at nearby Bolnuevo the wind has eroded soft rocks into strange shapes. The growing resort of Águilas marks the southern limit of the coast, at the border with Andalucía.

㉜ Lorca

Murcia. 🚍 91,700. 🚌 🚆 ℹ Plaza de España 7, 968 44 19 14. 🕐 Thu. 🎎 Semana Santa (Easter Week), Feria (3rd week of Sep), Día de San Clemente (23 Nov).
🆆 lorcaturismo.es

The farmland around Lorca is a fertile oasis in one of Europe's most arid areas. Lorca was an important staging post on the Via Heraclea, as witnessed by the Roman milepost standing in a corner of the Plaza San Vicente. During the wars between Moors and Christians in the 13th to 15th centuries, Lorca became a frontier town between Al Andalus and the Castilian territory of Murcia. Its castle dates

from this era, although only two of its original 35 towers remain. In 2011, the city was hit by Spain's worst earthquake for more than 50 years. The castle was badly damaged but it has since been repaired – there is now a parador inside. After Granada fell the town lost its importance and, except for one surviving gateway, its walls were demolished.

The central Plaza de España is lined with handsome stone buildings. One side of the square is occupied by the Colegiata de San Patricio (Church of St Patrick), built between 1533 and 1704, the only church in Spain dedicated to the Irish saint.

㉝ Caravaca de la Cruz

Murcia. 🚍 26,400. ℹ Calle de las Monjas 17, 968 70 24 24. 🕐 Mon, 3rd Sun of month (crafts). 🎎 Vera Cruz (1–5 May). 🆆 caravaca.org

A town of ancient churches, Caravaca de la Cruz's fame lies in its castle, which houses the Santuario de la Vera Cruz (Sanctuary of the True Cross). This is where a double-armed cross is said to have appeared miraculously in 1231 – 12 years before the town was seized by Christians. The highlight of the Vera Cruz fiesta is the Race of the Wine Horses, which commemorates the lifting of a Moorish siege of the castle and the appearance of the cross. The cross was dipped in wine, which the thirsty defenders then drank and recovered their fighting strength.

Environs
Just to the north, among the foothills on Murcia's western border, is the village of Moratalla, a jumble of steep streets and stone houses lying beneath a 15th-century castle. Cehegín, east of Caravaca, is a partially preserved 16th- and 17th-century town.

Roman milepost topped by a statue of St Vincent, Lorca

INTRODUCING MADRID

Introducing Madrid

Spain's capital, a city of over three million people, is situated close to the geographical centre of the country, at the hub of both road and rail networks. Because of its distance from the sea and its altitude – 660 m (2,150 ft) – the city endures cold winters and hot summers, making spring and autumn the best times to visit. Madrid's attractions include three internationally famous art galleries, a royal palace, grand public squares and many museums filled with the treasures of Spain's history. The city is surrounded by its own small province, the Comunidad de Madrid, which takes in the Sierra de Guadarrama and one of Spain's most famous monuments, the palace of El Escorial.

The Palacio Real *(see pp280–81)*, the royal palace built by Spain's first Bourbon kings, dominates the western part of Old Madrid. Its lavishly decorated chambers include the throne room.

The Plaza Mayor *(see p277),* Old Madrid's great 17th-century square, has been a focal point of the city since the days when it was used as a public arena for bullfights, trials by the Inquisition and executions *(see p278).* An equestrian statue of Felipe III stands in the middle of the square.

PLAZA DE ESPAÑA

GRAN VIA

PLAZA DEL CALLAO

GRA

CALLE DE BAILEN

OLD MADRID
(See pp272–85)

PUERTA DEL SOL

PLAZA MAYOR

CALLE DE SEGOVIA

CA

Madrid Province
(see pp330–37)

Buitrago del Lozoya

El Escorial

Torrelodones

Alcobendas

MADRID
(See main map)

Alcalá de Henares

Alcorcón

Getafe

Aranjuez

0 kilometres   25
0 miles   25

El Escorial *(see pp334–5),* the massive, architecturally austere monastery-palace built by Felipe II, has some sumptuous apartments decorated with great works of art. Marble sarcophagi in the octagonal Royal Pantheon contain the mortal remains of many Spanish monarchs.

The **Museo Thyssen-Bornemisza** *(see pp292–3)*, one of the most important privately assembled art collections in the world, was sold to Spain in 1993. The early 19th-century palace houses works by Titian, Rubens, Goya, van Gogh and Picasso.

0 metres   500
0 yards   500

PLAZA DE COLÓN

PASEO DE RECOLETOS

PLAZA DE CIBELES   CALLE DE   ALCALÁ

BOURBON MADRID
(See pp286–303)

PLAZA DE CÁNOVAS DEL CASTILLO

PASEO DEL PRADO

ATOCHA

The **Plaza de Cibeles** *(see p290)*, one of the city's most impressive squares, is ringed by distinctive buildings, including Madrid's former main post office. The building, with sculptures on its white façade, is now a cultural centre and the headquarters of the city council.

The **Parque del Retiro** *(see p301)* has leafy paths and avenues, and a boating lake overlooked by a majestic colonnade. It is an ideal place in which to relax between visits to the great art galleries and museums of Bourbon Madrid.

The **Museo del Prado** *(see pp296–9)* is one of the world's greatest art galleries. It has important collections of paintings by Velázquez and Goya, whose statues stand outside the main entrances.

The **Museo Nacional Centro de Arte Reina Sofía** *(see pp302–3)*, an outstanding museum of 20th-century art, is entered by highly original exterior glass lifts. Inside, the star exhibit is *Guernica*, Picasso's famous painting *(see p303)*.

OLD MADRID

When Felipe II chose Madrid as his capital in 1561, it was a small Castilian town of little real significance. In the following years, it was to grow into the nerve centre of a mighty empire.

According to tradition, it was the Moorish chieftain Muhammad ben Abd al Rahman who established a fortress above the Río Manzanares. Magerit, as it was called in Arabic, fell to Alfonso VI of Castile between 1083 and 1086. Narrow streets with houses and medieval churches began to grow up on the higher ground behind the old Arab *alcázar* (fortress), which was replaced by a Gothic palace in the 15th century.

When this burned down in 1734, it was replaced by the present Bourbon palace, the Palacio Real.

The population had scarcely reached 20,000 when Madrid was chosen as capital, but by the end of the century it had more than trebled. The 16th-century city is known as the "Madrid de los Austrias", after the reigning Habsburg dynasty. During this period royal monasteries were endowed and churches and private palaces were built. In the 17th century, the Plaza Mayor was added and the Puerta del Sol, the "Gate of the Sun", became the spiritual and geographical heart not only of Madrid but of all Spain.

Sights at a Glance

Historic Buildings
9 Palacio Real pp280–81

Museums and Galleries
14 Real Academia de Bellas Artes de San Fernando

Churches and Convents
2 Colegiata de San Isidro
5 Iglesia de San Nicolás de Bari
7 Catedral de la Almudena
10 Monasterio de la Encarnación
13 Monasterio de las Descalzas Reales

Streets, Squares and Parks
1 Puerta del Sol
3 Plaza de la Villa
4 Plaza Mayor
6 Plaza de Oriente
8 Campo del Moro
11 Plaza de España
12 Gran Vía

See also Madrid Street Finder, maps 1, 2, 3, 4, 7

| 0 metres | 500 |
| 0 yards | 500 |

Street-by-Street: Old Madrid

Stretching from the charming Plaza de la Villa to the busy Puerta del Sol, the compact heart of Old Madrid is steeped in history and full of interesting sights. Trials by the Inquisition *(see p278)* and executions were once held in the Plaza Mayor. This porticoed square is Old Madrid's finest piece of architecture, a legacy of the Habsburgs *(see pp64–5)*. Other buildings of note are the Colegiata de San Isidro and the Palacio de Santa Cruz. For a more relaxing way of enjoying Old Madrid, sit in one of the area's numerous cafés or browse among the stalls of the Mercado de San Miguel.

④ ★ Plaza Mayor
This beautiful 17th-century square competes with the Puerta del Sol as the focus of Old Madrid. The arcades at the base of the three-storey buildings are filled with cafés and craft shops.

The Mercado de San Miguel is housed in a 19th-century building with wrought-iron columns. The market has several excellent places to stop for a snack.

CALLE MAYOR
PLAZA COMMANDANTE MORENAS
PLAZA DE LA VILLA

To Palacio Real

Old Town Hall *(ayuntamiento)*

Casa de Cisneros

CORDÓN

PUÑONROSTRO

Arco de Cuchilleros

❸ ★ Plaza de la Villa
The 15th-century Torre de los Lujanes is the oldest of several historic buildings standing on this square.

0 metres		100
0 yards		100

The Basílica Pontificia de San Miguel is an imposing 18th-century church with a beautiful façade and a graceful interior. It is one of very few churches in Spain inspired by the Italian Baroque style.

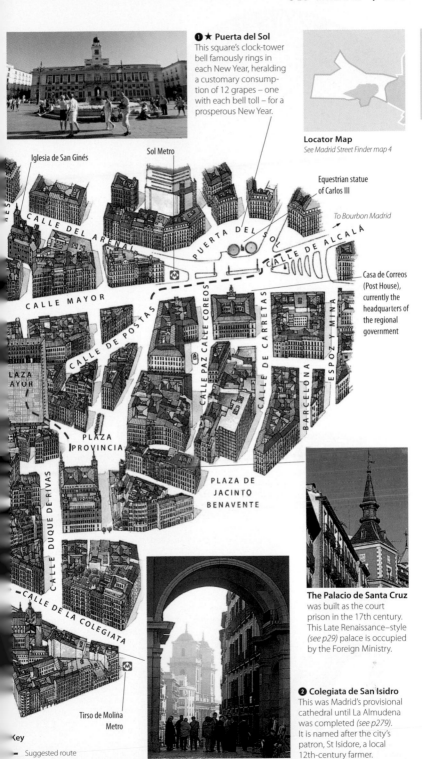

❶ ★ Puerta del Sol
This square's clock-tower bell famously rings in each New Year, heralding a customary consumption of 12 grapes – one with each bell toll – for a prosperous New Year.

Locator Map
See Madrid Street Finder map 4

Iglesia de San Ginés

Sol Metro

Equestrian statue of Carlos III

To Bourbon Madrid

CALLE DEL ARENAL

PUERTA DEL SOL

CALLE DE ALCALÁ

Casa de Correos (Post House), currently the headquarters of the regional government

CALLE MAYOR

CALLE DE POSTAS

CALLE PAZ

CALLE COREOS

CALLE DE CARRETAS

ESPOZ Y MINA

BARCELONA

PLAZA MAYOR

PLAZA PROVINCIA

CALLE DUQUE DE RIVAS

PLAZA DE JACINTO BENAVENTE

The Palacio de Santa Cruz
was built as the court prison in the 17th century. This Late Renaissance–style (see p29) palace is occupied by the Foreign Ministry.

CALLE DE LA COLEGIATA

Tirso de Molina Metro

❷ Colegiata de San Isidro
This was Madrid's provisional cathedral until La Almudena was completed (see p279). It is named after the city's patron, St Isidore, a local 12th-century farmer.

Key

— Suggested route

Kilometre Zero, the centre of Spain's road network, Puerta del Sol

❶ Puerta del Sol

Map 4 F2. Ⓜ Sol.

Crowded and noisy with chatter and policemen's whistles, the Puerta del Sol makes a fitting centre for Madrid. This is one of the city's most popular meeting places, and huge crowds converge here on their way to the shops and sights in the old part of the city.

The square marks the site of the original eastern entrance to the city, once occupied by a gatehouse and castle. These disappeared long ago and in their place came a succession of churches. In the late 19th century the area was turned into a square and became the centre of café society.

Today the "square" is shaped like a half-moon. A recent addition is the modern glass train station in front of the statue of Carlos III. The southern side of the square is edged by an austere red-brick building, originally the city's post office, built in the 1760s under

The bronze bear and strawberry tree of Madrid, Puerta del Sol

Carlos III. In 1847 it became the headquarters of the Ministry of the Interior. The clock tower, which gives the building much of its identity, was added in 1866. During the Franco regime (see pp70–71), the police cells beneath the building were the site of many human rights abuses. In 1963, Julián Grimau, a member of the underground Communist Party, allegedly fell from an upstairs window and miraculously survived, only to be executed soon afterwards.

The building is now home to the regional government and is the focus of many festive events. At midnight on New Year's Eve crowds fill the square to eat a grape on each stroke of the clock, a tradition supposed to bring good luck for the year. Outside a symbol on the ground marks Kilometre Zero, considered the centre of Spain's huge road network.

The buildings opposite are arranged in a semicircle and contain modern shops and cafés. At the start of Calle Alcalá is a bronze statue of the symbol of Madrid – a bear reaching for the fruit of a madroño (strawberry tree).

The Puerta del Sol has witnessed many important historical events. On 2 May 1808 the uprising against the occupying French forces began here, but the crowd, pitted against the well-armed French troops, was crushed (see p67). In 1912 the liberal prime minister José Canalejas was assassinated in the square and, in 1931, the Second Republic (see p69) was proclaimed from the balcony of the Ministry of the Interior.

❷ Colegiata de San Isidro

Calle Toledo 37. Map 4 E3. Tel: 91 369 20 37. Ⓜ La Latina, Tirso de Molina. Open 7:30am–1pm & 6–9pm daily.

The Colegiata de San Isidro was built in the Baroque style (see p29) for the Jesuits in the mid-17th century. This twin-towered church served as Madrid's cathedral until La Almudena (see p279) was completed in 1993.

After Carlos III expelled the Jesuits from Spain in 1767 (see p66), Ventura Rodríguez was commissioned to redesign the interior of the church. It was then rededicated to Madrid's patron saint, St Isidore, and two years later the saint's remains were moved here from the Iglesia de San Andrés. San Isidro was returned to the Jesuits during the reign of Fernando VII (1814–33).

Altar in the Colegiata de San Isidro

❸ Plaza de la Villa

Map 4 D3. Ⓜ Ópera, Sol.

The much-restored Plaza de la Villa is one of the most atmospheric spots in Madrid. Some of the city's most historic secular buildings are situated around this square.

The oldest building is the early 15th-century Torre de los Lujanes, with its Gothic portal and Mudéjar-style horseshoe arches. François I of France was allegedly imprisoned in it following his defeat at the Battle of Pavia in 1525. The Casa de Cisneros was built in 1537 for the nephew of Cardinal Cisneros

Portal of the Torre de los Lujanes

founder of the historic University of Alcalá (see pp336–7). The main façade, on the Calle de Sacramento, is an excellent example of the Plateresque style (see p29).

Linked to this building, by an enclosed bridge, is the Old Town Hall (ayuntamiento). Designed in the 1640s by Juan Gómez de Mora, architect of the Plaza Mayor, it exhibits the same combination of steep roofs with dormer windows, steeple-like towers at the corners and an austere façade of brick and stone. Before construction was finished – more than 30 years later – the building had acquired handsome Baroque doorways. A balcony was later added by Juan de Villanueva, the architect of the Prado (see pp296–9), so that the royal family could watch Corpus Christi processions passing by.

❹ Plaza Mayor

Map 4 E3. 🚇 Opera, Sol, Tirso de Molina.

The Plaza Mayor forms a splendid rectangular square, all balconies and pinnacles, dormer windows and steep slate roofs. The square, with its theatrical atmosphere, is very Castilian in character. Much was expected to happen here and a great deal did – bullfights, executions, pageants and trials by the Inquisition (see p278) – all watched by crowds, often in the presence of the reigning king and queen. The canonization of Madrid's patron, St Isidore, took

place here in 1622. One year earlier, in 1621, the execution of Rodrigo Calderón, secretary to Felipe III, was held here. Although hated by the Madrid populace, Calderón bore himself with such dignity on the day of his death that the phrase "proud as Rodrigo on the scaffold" survives to this day. Perhaps the greatest occasion of all, however, was the arrival here – from Italy – of Carlos III in 1760.

The square was started in 1617 and built in just two years, replacing slum houses. Its architect, Juan Gómez de Mora, was successor to Juan de Herrera, designer of Felipe II's austere monastery-palace, El Escorial (see pp334–5). Gómez de Mora echoed the style of his master, softening it slightly. The square was later reformed by Juan de Villanueva. The fanciest part of the arcaded construction

is the Casa de la Panadería (bakery). Its façade, now crudely reinvented, is decorated with allegorical paintings. Madrid's main tourist office is sited here.

The equestrian statue in the centre is of Felipe III, who ordered the square's construction. Started by the Italian Giovanni de Bologna and finished by his pupil Pietro Tacca in 1616, the statue was moved here in 1848 from the Casa de Campo (see p306). Today the square is lined with cafés, and hosts a collectors' market on Sundays (see pp320–21). The square's southern exit leads into Calle de Toledo towards the streets where the Rastro, Madrid's flea market (see p306), is held. A flight of steps in the southwest corner takes you under the Arco de Cuchilleros to the Calle de Cuchilleros, and some mesones, traditional restaurants.

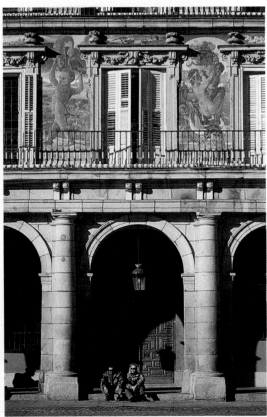

Allegorical paintings on the Casa de la Panadería, Plaza Mayor

The Spanish Inquisition

The Spanish Inquisition was set up by Fernando and Isabel in 1478 to create a single, monolithic Catholic ideology in Spain. Protestant heretics and alleged "false converts" to Catholicism from the Jewish and Muslim faiths were tried, to ensure the religious unity of the country. Beginning with a papal bull, the Inquisition was run like a court, presided over by the Inquisitor-General. However, the defendants were denied counsel, not told the charges facing them and tortured to obtain confessions. Punishment ranged from imprisonment to beheading, hanging or burning at the stake. A formidable system of control, it gave Spain's Protestant enemies a major propaganda weapon by contributing to the *Leyenda Negra* (Black Legend) which lasted, along with the Inquisition, into the 18th century.

A Protestant heretic appears before the royal family, his last chance to repent and convert.

A convicted defendant, forced to wear a red *sanbenito* robe, is led away to prison.

Those who have refused to confess are sentenced in public by day, and then executed before nightfall.

Auto-da-Fé in the Plaza Mayor

This painting by Francisco de Ricci (1683) depicts a trial, or auto-da-fé – literally, "show of faith" – held in Madrid's main square on 30 June 1680. Unlike papal inquisitions elsewhere in Europe, it was presided over by the reigning monarch, Carlos II, accompanied by his queen.

Torture was widely used by the Inquisitors and their assistants to extract confessions from their victims. This early 19th-century German engraving shows a man being roasted on a wheel.

The Procession of the Flagellants (c.1812) by Goya shows the abiding influence of the Inquisition on the popular imagination. The penitents in the picture are wearing the tall conical hats of heretics tried by the Inquisition. These hats can still be seen in Easter Week processions (see p42) throughout Spain.

❺ Iglesia de San Nicolás de Bari

Plaza de San Nicolás 1. **Map** 3 C2. **Tel** 91 559 40 64. 🚇 Ópera. **Open** 8:30am–1pm, 5:30–8:30pm Mon, 8:30–9:30am, 6:30–8:30pm Tue–Sat, 10am–1:45pm, 6:30–8:45pm Sun & public hols. Groups should call in advance.

The first mention of the church of San Nicolás is in a document of 1202. Its brick tower, with horseshoe arches, is the oldest surviving ecclesiastical structure in Madrid. It is thought to be 12th-century Mudéjar in style, and may have originally been the minaret of a Moorish mosque.

❻ Plaza de Oriente

Map 3 C2. 🚇 Ópera.

During his days as king of Spain, Joseph Bonaparte *(see p67)* carved out this stirrup-shaped space from the jumble of buildings to the east of the Palacio Real *(see pp280–81)*, providing the view of the palace enjoyed today.

The square was once an important meeting place for state occasions; kings, queens and dictators all made public appearances on the palace balcony. The statues of early kings that stand here were originally intended for the palace roof, but proved too heavy. The equestrian statue of Felipe IV in the centre of the square is by Italian sculptor Pietro Tacca,

Equestrian statue of Felipe IV, by Pietro Tacca, Plaza de Oriente

View of the Catedral de la Almudena and the Royal Palace

and is based on drawings by Velázquez. Across the square is the imposing Teatro Real, or Teatro de la Ópera, inaugurated in 1850 by Isabel II.

❼ Catedral de la Almudena

C/ Bailén 8–10. **Map** 3 C2. **Tel** 91 542 22 00. 🚇 Ópera. **Open** 9am–8:30pm daily (10am–9pm Jul & Aug); Museum & Dome: 10am–2:30pm Mon–Sat. 🅰️ 🚻 🆆 **catedraldelaalmudena.es**

Dedicated to the city's patron, the cathedral was begun in 1883 and completed over a century later. The Neo-Gothic grey and white façade is similar to that of the Palacio Real, which stands opposite. The crypt houses a 16th-century image of the Virgen de la Almudena. The dome offers grand views of the city.

Further along the Calle Mayor is the site of archaeological excavations of the remains of Moorish and medieval city walls.

The first royal wedding took place here between Prince Felipe (now King Philip VI) and Letizia Ortiz in May 2004.

❽ Campo del Moro

Paseo Virgen del Puerto s/n. **Map** 3 A2. **Tel** 91 454 87 00. 🚇 Ópera, Príncipe Pío. **Open** Oct–Mar: 10am–6pm daily; Apr–Sep: 10am–8pm daily. **Closed** 1 & 6 Jan, 1 & 15 May, 12 Oct, 9 Nov, 24, 25 & 31 Dec and for official functions. 🆆 **patrimonionacional.es**

The Campo del Moro (the "Field of the Moor") is a pleasing park, rising steeply from the Río Manzanares to offer one of the finest views of the Palacio Real *(see pp280–81)*.

The park has a varied history. In 1109 a Moorish army led by Ali ben Yusuf camped here, hence the name. It went on to become a jousting ground for Christian knights. In the late 19th century it was used as a lavish playground for royal children. Around the same time it was landscaped in what is described as English style, with winding paths, grass and woodland, fountains and statues. It was reopened to the public in 1931 under the Second Republic *(see p69)*, closed again under Franco, and not reopened until 1978.

❾ Palacio Real

Madrid's vast and lavish Royal Palace was built to impress. The site, on a high bluff over the Río Manzanares, had been occupied for centuries by a royal fortress, but after a fire in 1734, Felipe V commissioned a truly palatial replacement. Construction lasted 17 years, spanning the reign of two Bourbon monarchs, and much of the exuberant decor reflects the tastes of Carlos III and Carlos IV *(see p75)*. The palace was used as a residence by the royal family until the abdication of Alfonso XIII in 1931 and is still used today for state occasions. A new museum of royal collections, being built next to the palace, is due to open in 2019.

★ Dining Room
This gallery was decorated in 1879. With its chandeliers, ceiling paintings and tapestries, it evokes the grandeur of regal Bourbon entertaining.

★ Porcelain Room
The walls and ceiling of this room, built on the orders of Carlos III, are entirely covered in royal porcelain from the Buen Retiro factory. Most of the porcelain is green and white, and depicts cherubs and wreaths.

First floor

The Hall of Columns, once used for royal banquets, is decorated with 16th-century bronzes and Roman imperial busts.

★ Gasparini Room
Named after its Neapolitan designer, the Gasparini Room is decorated with lavish Rococo chinoiserie. The adjacent antechamber, with painted ceiling and ornate chandelier, houses Goya's portrait of Carlos IV.

Key to Floorplan

☐ Exhibition rooms
☐ Entrance rooms
☐ Carlos III rooms
☐ Chapel rooms
☐ Carlos IV rooms

VISITORS' CHECKLIST

Practical Information
Calle de Bailén. **Map** 3 C2.
Tel 91 454 88 00.
Open 10am–8pm daily (Oct–Mar: to 6pm). Changing of the Guard: 11am–2pm Wed. (The Changing of the Guard takes place every 30 min). **Closed** for official functions, some public hols.
(free for EU citizens; Apr–Sep: Wed & Thu after 6pm); Oct–Mar: Wed & Thu after 4pm.
W patrimonionacional.es

Transport
Ópera, Principe Pío. 3, 25, 39, 148.

Plaza de la Armería
The square in front of the main entrance also gives access to the Royal Armoury. The outstanding collection of weaponry includes the suits of armour belonging to Charles V and Felipe II.

Entrance Hall
A marble staircase by Sabatini, next to the statue of Carlos III as a Roman emperor, leads to the main floor. The painted Rococo ceiling by Giaquinto vividly depicts allegorical scenes.

Billiards room

Hall of the Halberdiers

Entrance

Pharmacy
This unique collection includes decorated Talavera pottery storage jars and herb drawers. The Pharmacy Museum has recipe books detailing medications prescribed for the royal family.

Visitors' centre

Plaza de la Armería

★ Throne Room
This room maintains the original decor of Carlos III. There are two gold and scarlet thrones and mirrors made in the royal glass factory of La Granja.

Royal Armoury

Entrance to the Convento de la Encarnación

⓾ Monasterio de la Encarnación

Plaza de la Encarnación 1. **Map** 4 D1.
Tel 91 454 88 00. Ópera, Santo
Domingo. **Open** 10am–2pm,
4–6:30pm Tue–Sat, 10am–3pm Sun &
public hols. **Closed** 1 & 6 Jan, Easter,
1 & 15 May, 27 Jul, 9 Nov, 24, 25 &
31 Dec. (free Wed and Thu after
4pm for EU residents).
w patrimonionacional.es

Standing in a delightful tree-shaded square, this tranquil Augustinian convent was founded in 1611 for Margaret of Austria, wife of Felipe III. The architect, Juan Gómez de Mora, also built the Plaza Mayor *(see p277)* and the façade clearly reveals his work.

Still inhabited by nuns, the convent has the atmosphere of old Castile, with its blue and white Talavera tiles, wooden doors, exposed beams and portraits of royal benefactors. Inside is a collection of 17th-century art, with paintings by José de Ribera and Vincente Carducho lining the walls. Polychromatic wooden statues include *Cristo Yacente* (*Lying Christ*), by Gregorio Fernández.

The convent's main attraction is the reliquary chamber with a ceiling painted by Carducho. It is used to store the skulls and bones of saints. There is also a phial containing the dried blood of St Pantaleon. According to a popular myth, the blood liquefies each year on 27 July, the anniversary of the saint's death. Should the blood

fail to liquefy, it is said that disaster will befall Madrid. The church was rebuilt by Ventura Rodríguez after a fire in 1767.

⓫ Plaza de España

Map 1 C5. Plaza de España.

One of Madrid's busiest traffic intersections and most popular meeting places is the Plaza de España, which slopes down towards the Palacio Real *(see pp280–81)* and the Sabatini Gardens. In the 18th and 19th centuries the square was occupied by military barracks, built here because of the square's close proximity to the palace. However, further expansion of Madrid resulted in its becoming a public space.

The square acquired its present appearance during the Franco period *(see pp70–71)*, with the construction, on the northern side, of the massive Edificio España between 1947 and 1953. Across the square is the Torre de Madrid (1957), known as *La Jirafa* (The Giraffe),

which, for a while, was the tallest concrete structure in the world. The most attractive part of the square is its centre, occupied by a massive stone obelisk built in 1928. In front of it is a statue of the author Cervantes *(see p337)*. Below him, Don Quixote *(see pp398–9)* rides his horse Rocinante while the plump Sancho Panza trots alongside on his donkey. On the left-hand side is Dulcinea, Don Quixote's sweetheart.

⓬ Gran Vía

Map 2 D5. Plaza de España, Santo Domingo, Callao, Gran Vía.

A main traffic artery of the modern city, the Gran Vía was inaugurated in 1910. Its construction was executed in three phases, spanned several decades and required the demolition of large numbers of run-down buildings and small lanes between the Calle de Alcalá and the Plaza de España. This road-building scheme soon became the subject of a

Stone obelisk with statue of Miguel de Cervantes, Plaza de España

◀ Night-time traffic on the Gran Vía, seen from the Plaza de España

One of the many 1930s buildings lining the Gran Vía

zarzuela – a comic opera – that most madrileño of art forms (see p326). Nowadays, the Gran Vía is at the centre of city life and, following a restoration programme, has become an architectural showpiece.

The most interesting buildings are clustered at the Alcalá end, starting with the Corinthian columns, high-level statuary and tiled dome of the Edificio Metrópolis (see p288).

A temple with Art Nouveau mosaics on its upper levels crowns No. 1 Gran Vía. One striking feature of buildings at this end of the street is colonnaded galleries on the upper floors, imitating medieval Aragonese and Catalan architecture. Another is the fine wrought-iron balconies and carved stone details, such as the gargoyle-like caryatids at No. 12. This part of the Gran Vía has a couple of old-world Spanish shops.

On the Red de San Luis, an intersection of four major roads, is the Telefónica building. The first skyscraper to be erected in the capital, built between 1926 and 1929, it caused a sensation. Beyond here, the Gran Vía becomes much more American in character, with cinemas, tourist shops and many cafés.

Opposite Callao metro station, on the corner of the Calle Jacometrezo, is another well-known building, the Art Deco Capitol cinema, built in the 1930s.

⓲ Monasterio de las Descalzas Reales

Plaza de las Descalzas 3. **Map** 4 E2. **Tel** 91 454 88 00. 🚇 Sol, Callao. **Open** 10am–2pm, 4–6:30pm Tue–Sat, 10am–3pm Sun & public hols. **Closed** 1 & 6 Jan, Easter, 1 & 15 May, 9 Nov, 24, 25 & 31 Dec. 🔲 🔲 (free Wed & Thu after 4pm for EU residents). 🔳 patrimonionacional.es

Madrid's most notable religious building has a fine exterior in red brick and granite, and one of the few surviving examples of 16th-century architecture.

Around 1560, Felipe II's sister, Doña Juana, decided to convert the original medieval palace which stood here into a convent for nuns and women of the royal household. Her high rank, and that of her fellow nuns, accounts for the massive store of art and wealth of the Descalzas Reales (Royal Barefoot Sisters).

The stairway has a fresco of Felipe IV's family looking down, as if from a balcony, and a fine ceiling by Claudio Coello and his pupils. It leads up to a first-floor cloister, ringed with chapels containing works of art relating to the lives of the former nuns. The main chapel houses Doña Juana's tomb. The Sala de Tapices has a series of tapestries, one woven in 1627 for Felipe II's daughter, Isabel Clara Eugenia. Another,

Decorated chapel, Monasterio de las Descalzas Reales

The Triumph of the Eucharist, is based on cartoons by Rubens. The tapestries hang in the cloister on Good Friday and Corpus Christi. Major paintings on show include works by Brueghel the Elder, Titian and Zurbarán.

Fray Pedro Machado by Zurbarán

⓳ Real Academia de Bellas Artes de San Fernando

Calle Alcalá 13. **Map** 7 A2. **Tel** 91 524 08 64. 🚇 Banco de España, Gran Vía, Sevilla, Sol. **Open** 10am–3pm Tue–Sun. **Closed** some pub hols. 🔲 (free Wed). 🔲 by appt. 🔲 🔳 realacademia bellasartessanfernando.com/en

Famous former students of this arts academy, housed in an 18th-century building by Churriguera (see p29), include Dalí and Picasso. Its art gallery's collection includes works such as drawings by Raphael and Titian. Among the old masters are paintings by Rubens and Van Dyck. Spanish artists from the 16th to the 19th centuries are well represented, with works by Ribera, Murillo, El Greco and Velázquez. One of the highlights is Zurbarán's Fray Pedro Machado, typical of the artist's paintings of monks.

An entire room is devoted to Goya, a former director of the academy. On show here are his painting of a relaxed Manuel Godoy (see p66), the Burial of the Sardine (see p43), the grim Madhouse, and a self-portrait painted in 1815.

For hotels and restaurants in this area see pp568–9 and pp591–3

BOURBON MADRID

To the east of Old Madrid, there once lay an idyllic district of market gardens known as the Prado, the "Meadow". In the 16th century a monastery was built and later the Habsburgs extended it to form a palace, of which only fragments now remain; the palace gardens are now the popular Parque del Retiro (see p301). The Bourbon monarchs chose this area to expand and embellish the city in the 18th century. They built grand squares with fountains, a triumphal gateway, and what was to become the Museo del Prado, one of the world's greatest art galleries. Also in the area is the Museo Nacional Centro de Arte Reina Sofía, a collection of modern Spanish and international art.

Sights at a Glance

Historic Buildings
1. Hotel Ritz by Belmond
12. Real Academia de la Historia
13. Teatro Español
14. Ateneo de Madrid
15. Congreso de los Diputados
16. Café Gijón
22. Estación de Atocha

Museums and Galleries
3. Museo Thyssen-Bornemisza pp292–3
6. Biblioteca Nacional de España
7. Museo Nacional de Artes Decorativas
8. Salón de Reinos
10. Museo del Prado pp296–9
11. Casa-Museo de Lope de Vega
19. Museo Arqueológico Nacional
23. Museo Nacional Centro de Arte Reina Sofía pp302–3

Monuments
5. Puerta de Alcalá

Churches
9. Iglesia de San Jerónimo el Real

Streets, Squares and Parks
2. Plaza Cánovas del Castillo
4. Plaza de Cibeles
17. Plaza de Colón
18. Calle de Serrano
20. Parque del Retiro
21. Real Jardín Botánico

See also Madrid Street Finder, maps 5, 6, 7, 8

◄ Memorial to the victims of the 2004 terrorist attacks, Parque del Retiro

For keys to symbols see back flap

Street-by-Street: Paseo del Prado

In the late 18th century, before the museums and lavish hotels of Bourbon Madrid took shape, the Paseo del Prado was laid out and soon became a fashionable spot for strolling. Today the Paseo's main attraction lies in its museums and art galleries. Most notable are the Museo del Prado (just south of the Plaza Cánovas del Castillo) and the Museo Thyssen-Bornemisza, both displaying world-famous collections. Among the grand monuments built under Carlos III are the Puerta de Alcalá, the Fuente de Neptuno and the Fuente de Cibeles, which stand in the middle of busy roundabouts.

The Paseo del Prado, based on the Piazza Navona in Rome, was built by Carlos III as a centre for the arts and sciences in Madrid.

Banco de España Metro

The Edificio Metrópolis
(see p285), on the corner of Gran Vía and Calle de Alcalá, was built in 1910. Its façade is distinctively Parisian.

Banco de España

❸ ★ **Museo Thyssen-Bornemisza**
This excellent art collection occupies the Neo-Classical Villahermosa Palace, completed in 1806.

| 0 metres | 100 |
| 0 yards | 100 |

❶ **Congreso de los Diputados**
Spain's parliament witnessed the transition from dictatorship to democracy *(see pp72–3)*.

❷ **Plaza de Cánovas del Castillo**
In the middle of this large square stands a sculpted fountain of the god Neptune in his chariot.

PLAZA DE LAS CORTES

PLAZA CÁNOVAS DEL CASTILLO

To Museo del Prado

Hotel Palace

5 ★ Puerta de Alcalá
Sculpted from granite, this former gateway into the city is especially beautiful when floodlit at night.

Locator Map
See Madrid Street Finder maps 7, 8

Palacio de Linares

Palacio de Comunicaciones and City Hall

PLAZA DE LA INDEPENDENCIA

CALLE DE ALCALÁ

ALFONSO XI

CALLE DE ALFONSO XII

CALLE DE MONTALBAN

CALLE DE

CALLE ANTONIO MAURA

DE LA LEALTAD

RUIZ DE ALARCON

CALLE FELIPE IV

MORETO

4 ★ Plaza de Cibeles
A fountain with a statue of the Roman goddess Cybele stands in this square.

7 The Museo Nacional de Artes Decorativas
This museum, near the Retiro, was founded in 1912 as a showcase for the Spanish manufacturing industry.

8 Salón de Reinos
The former army museum, this section of the Palacio del Buen Retiro will form part of the Prado Museum.

Casón del Buen Retiro *(see p296)*

Hotel Ritz by Belmond
With its *belle époque* interior, this is one of the most elegant hotels in Spain.

The Monumento del Dos de Mayo commemorates the War of Independence against the French *(see p67)*.

Key

— Suggested route

For keys to symbols *see back flap*

❶ Hotel Ritz by Belmond

Plaza de la Lealtad 5. **Map** 7 C2.
Tel 91 701 67 67. ⓜ Banco de España.
☒ ♿ ⓦ **ritz.es** *See also p569.*

A few minutes' walk from the Prado, this hotel is said to be Spain's most extravagant. It was part of the new breed of hotels constructed as luxury accommo-dation for the wedding guests of Alfonso XIII in 1906.

There is a dress code in the hotel's public areas. Each room is beautifully decorated in a different style, with carpets made by hand at the Real Fábrica de Tapices *(see p310)*.

At the start of the Civil War *(see pp70–71)* the hotel was converted into a hospital, and it was here that the Anarchist leader Buenaventura Durruti died of his wounds in 1936.

The Fuente de Neptuno

❷ Plaza Cánovas del Castillo

Map 7 C3. ⓜ Banco de España.

This busy roundabout is named after Antonio Cánovas del Castillo, one of the leading statesmen of 19th-century Spain *(see p68)*, who was assassinated in 1897.

Dominating the plaza is the Fuente de Neptuno – a fountain with a statue depicting Neptune in his chariot, being pulled by two horses. The statue was designed in 1777 by Ventura Rodríguez as part of Carlos III's scheme to beautify eastern Madrid.

Visitors admiring the works of art in the Museo Thyssen-Bornemisza

❸ Museo Thyssen-Bornemisza

See pp292–3.

❹ Plaza de Cibeles

Map 7 C1. ⓜ Banco de España.
Casa de América exhibition room:
Tel 91 595 48 00. **Open** 9am–3pm & 4–8pm Mon–Fri. **Closed** Aug & public hols. 🎟 11am, noon, 1pm Sat & Sun.
ⓦ **casamerica.es**

The Plaza de Cibeles is one of Madrid's best-known and most beautiful landmarks.

The Fuente de Cibeles stands in the middle of the busy traffic island at the junction of the Paseo del Prado and the Calle de Alcalá. This sculpted fountain is named after Cybele, the Greco-Roman goddess of nature, and shows her sitting in her lion-drawn chariot. Designed by José Hermosilla and Ventura Rodríguez in the late 18th century, it is considered

a symbol of Madrid. Around the square rise four important buildings. The most impressive are the town hall, where the mayor has his office, and the main post office, the Palacio de Comunicaciones, also home to a cultural centre, CentroCentro. Its appearance – white, with high pinnacles – is often likened to a wedding cake. It was built between 1905 and 1917 on the site of former gardens.

On the northeast side is the stone façade of the Palacio de Linares, built by the Marquis of Linares at the time of the second Bourbon restoration of 1875 *(see p68)*. Once threatened with demolition, the palace was reprieved and converted into the Casa de América, and now hosts art exhibitions by Latin American artists as well as theatrical performances and lectures. Take a break in the palace gardens and try one of Le Cabrera's excellent cocktails *(see p593)*.

In the northwest corner of the Plaza de Cibeles, surrounded by attractive gardens, is the heavily guarded Army Headquarters, which is housed in the buildings of the former Palacio de Buena-vista. Commissioned by the Duchess of Alba in 1777, const-ruction was twice delayed by fire

On the opposite corner is the Banco de España, constructed between 1884 and 1891. Its design was inspired by the Venetian Renaissance style, with delicate ironwork adorning the roof and windows. Much-needed renovation work has returned the bank to its late 19th-century magnificence.

The Fuente de Cibeles, with the Palacio de Linares in the background

central arch of the Puerta de Alcalá

❺ Puerta de Alcalá

Map 8 D1. 🚇 Retiro.

This ceremonial gateway is the grandest of the monuments erected by Carlos III in his attempt to improve the looks of eastern Madrid. It was designed by Francesco Sabatini to replace a smaller Baroque gateway, which had been built by Felipe III for the entry into Madrid of his wife, Margarita de Austria.

Construction of the gate began in 1769 and lasted nine years. It was built from granite in Neo-Classical style, with a lofty pediment and sculpted angels. It has five arches – three central and two outer rectangular ones.

Until the mid-19th century the gateway marked the city's easternmost boundary. It now stands in the busy Plaza de la Independencia, and is best seen when floodlit at night.

❻ Biblioteca Nacional de España

Paseo de Recoletos 20–22. **Map** 6 D5, **Tel** 91 580 78 00. **Open** 9am–9pm Mon–Fri, 9am–2pm Sat. Open for exhibitions only Sun. **Closed** public hols. 📷 5pm Tue & Fri, noon Sat. 🚹 🆆 bne.es

King Philip V of Spain founded the National Library in 1712. Since then, it has been mandatory for printers to submit a copy of every book printed in Spain. Currently it holds some 28 million publications, plus a large number of maps, musical scores and audiovisual records. Jewels include a first-edition *Don Quixote* and two handwritten codes by da Vinci.

A museum looks at the history of the library as well as the evolution of writing, reading and media systems. The library also holds regular exhibitions, talks and concerts.

❼ Museo Nacional de Artes Decorativas

Calle Montalbán 12. **Map** 8 D2. **Tel** 91 532 64 99. 🚇 Retiro, Banco de España. **Open** 9:30am–3pm Tue–Sat (Thu also 5–8pm, except Jul & Aug), 10am–3pm Sun. **Closed** public hols. 🎟 (free Thu pm & Sun). 📷 Sun (except Jul & Aug). 🆆 mnartesdecorativas.mecd.es

Housed in the 19th-century Palacio de Santoña near the Parque del Retiro, the National Museum of Decorative Arts contains an interesting collection of furniture and objets d'art. The exhibits are mainly from Spain and date back as far as Phoenician times. There are also some excellent ceramics from Talavera de la Reina (*see p390*), and ornaments from the Far East.

Refurbishment work may affect some rooms.

❽ Salón de Reinos

Calle Méndez Núñez 1. **Map** 8 D2. 🚇 Retiro, Banco de España. **Closed** for refurbishment.

The Salón de Reinos (Hall of Kingdoms) is one of the two remaining parts of the 17th-century Palacio del Buen Retiro and gets its name from the shields of the 24 kingdoms of the Spanish monarchy, part of the decor supervised by court painter Velázquez (*see p36*). In the time of Felipe IV, the Salón was used for diplomatic receptions and official ceremonies.

Impressive façade of the Salón de Reinos

❾ Museo Thyssen-Bornemisza

This magnificent museum is based on the collection assembled by Baron Heinrich Thyssen-Bornemisza and his son, Hans Heinrich, the preceding baron. In 1992 it was installed in Madrid's 18th-century Villahermosa Palace, and was sold to the nation the following year. From its beginnings in the 1920s, the collection was intended to illustrate the history of Western art, from Italian and Flemish primitives, through to 20th-century Expressionism and Pop Art. The museum's collection, consisting of more than 1,000 paintings, includes masterpieces by Titian, Goya, van Gogh and Picasso. Carmen Thyssen's collection of mainly Impressionist art opened to the public in 2004. It is regarded by many critics as the most important private art collection in the world.

★ **The Virgin of the Dry Tree** (c.1465)
This tiny painted panel is by Bruges master Petrus Christus. The letter A hanging from the tree stands for "Ave Maria".

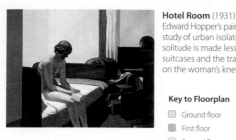

Hotel Room (1931)
Edward Hopper's painting is a study of urban isolation. The solitude is made less static by the suitcases and the train timetable on the woman's knee.

Key to Floorplan

- ⬜ Ground floor
- ⬜ First floor
- ⬜ Second floor
- ⬜ Temporary exhibitions
- ⬜ Non-exhibition space

Gallery Guide

The galleries are arranged around a covered central courtyard, which rises the full height of the building. The top floor starts with early Italian art and goes through to the 17th century. The first floor continues the story with 17th-century Dutch works and ends with German Expressionism. The ground floor is dedicated to 20th-century paintings.

★ **Harlequin with a Mirror**
The figure of the harlequin was a frequent subject of Picasso's. The careful composition in this 1923 canvas, which is thought by some to represent the artist himself, is typical of Picasso's "Classical" period.

Portrait of Baron Thyssen-Bornemisza
This informal portrait of the previous baron, against the background of a Watteau painting, was painted by Lucian Freud.

For hotels and restaurants in this area see pp568–9 and pp591–3

★ Venus and Cupid
This reflection of ideal beauty was painted by the Flemish master Rubens between 1606 and 1611. The picture illustrates his luscious use of colour and form.

Second floor

VISITORS' CHECKLIST

Practical Information
Paseo del Prado 8. **Map** 7 C2.
Tel 902 760 511. **Open** noon–4pm Mon, 10am–7pm Tue–Sun; Jun–mid-Sep: to 10pm Tue–Sat, to 7pm Sun & Mon for temp exhibs. **Closed** 1 Jan, 1 May & 25 Dec. 🎫 advance bookings online or by phone. 🦽 🍽 (free Mon). 🛗 ▲ 📷 ✏
W museothyssen.org

Transport
🚇 Banco de España, Sevilla. 🚌 1, 2, 5, 9, 10, 14 and many others.

St Casilda (c.1630–35)
Francisco de Zurbarán is known for his depictions of monks and saints. In this work, St Casilda's brightly coloured robe stands out against the plain background.

First floor

Ground floor

Main entrance

Autumn Landscape in Oldenburg
Karl Schmidt-Rottluff was a member of the Brücke Expressionist group, founded in Dresden in 1905. He painted this north German landscape two years later.

Mata Mua
Painted in 1892, during a stay on the Marquesas Islands, Gauguin's colourful depiction of a Tahitian paradise is one of his most highly regarded works of this period.

❾ Iglesia de San Jerónimo el Real

Calle del Moreto 4. **Map** 8 D3.
Tel 91 420 30 78. Banco de España.
Open 9:30am–2:30pm & 5:30–8pm
Mon–Sat (Apr–Sep: 6–8pm);
weekends: open for ceremonies.

Built in the 16th century for
Queen Isabel, but since
remodelled, San Jerónimo is
Madrid's royal church. From the
17th century it became virtually
a part of the Retiro palace which
once stood here (see p301). The

Castizos during San Isidro

Madrid's Fiestas

San Isidro (15 May). Madrid's
great party around 15 May
is in honour of St Isidore,
the humble 12th-century
farmworker who became
the city's patron. With a
corrida every day, this is
Spain's biggest bullfighting
event. Throughout the city
there are also art exhibitions,
open-air concerts and fireworks. Many people dress
in *castizo* (see p306) folk
costume for the occasion.
The Passion (Easter Saturday),
Chinchón. A passion play
is performed in the town's
atmospheric arcaded
Plaza Mayor.
Dos de Mayo (2 May). This
holiday marks the city's
uprising against Napoleon's
troops in 1808 (see p67).
New Year's Eve. The nation
focuses on the Puerta del
Sol (see p276) at midnight
as crowds gather to swallow
a grape on each chime of
the clock.

church was originally attached
to the Hieronymite monastery.
The cloister and part of the
atrium now form part of a
building at the Prado Museum.
 The marriage of Alfonso XIII
and Victoria Eugenia of Batten-
berg took place here in 1906,
as did King Juan Carlos I's
coronation in 1975.

❿ Museo del Prado

See pp296–9.

⓫ Casa-Museo de Lope de Vega

Calle Cervantes 11. **Map** 7 B3.
Tel 91 429 92 16. Antón Martín,
Sevilla. **Open** 10am–6pm Tue–Sun.
Closed some public hols. only
(available in English). **w casamuseo
lopedevega.org**

Félix Lope de Vega, a leading
Golden Age writer (see p38),
moved into this house in 1610.
Here he wrote over two-thirds
of his plays, thought to total

Portrait of the writer Félix Lope de Vega

almost 1,000. Meticulously
restored in 1935 using some of
Lope de Vega's own furniture,
the house gives a great feeling
of Castilian life in the early 17th
century. A dark chapel with no
external windows occupies the
centre, separated from the
writer's bedroom by only a
barred window. The small
garden at the rear is planted
with the flowers and fruit trees
mentioned by the writer in his
works. He died here in 1635.

Statue of Goya in front of the Prado

Sunlit balcony of the magnificent Teatro Español

⑫ Real Academia de la Historia

Calle León 21. **Map** 7 A3.
Tel 91 429 06 11. Antón Martín.
✉ **Closed** to the public. 🌐 **rah.es**

The Royal Academy of History is an austere brick building built by Juan de Villanueva in 1788. Its location, in the so-called Barrio de las Letras (Writers' Quarter), is apt.

In 1898, the intellectual and bibliophile, Marcelino Menéndez Pelayo, became director of the academy, living here until his death in 1912. The library holds more than 200,000 books.

The building is closed to the public and can only be viewed from the outside.

⑬ Teatro Español

Calle del Príncipe 25. **Map** 7 A3.
Tel 91 360 14 80. Sol, Sevilla.
Open performances from 7pm Tue–Sun. 🌐 **teatroespanol.es**

Dominating the Plaza Santa Ana is the Teatro Español, one of Madrid's oldest and most beautiful theatres. From 1583 many of Spain's finest plays, by leading dramatists of the time such as Lope de Rueda, were first performed in the Corral del Príncipe, which originally stood on this site. In 1802 this was replaced by the Teatro Español. The Neoclassical façade, with pilasters and medallions, is by Juan de

Villanueva. Engraved on it are the names of great Spanish dramatists, including that of celebrated writer Federico García Lorca (see p39).

⑭ Ateneo de Madrid

Calle del Prado 21. **Map** 7 B3.
Tel 91 429 17 50. Antón Martín, Sevilla. **Open** by appt 10am–1pm Mon–Fri. 📷 only.
🌐 **ateneodemadrid.com**

Formally founded in 1835, this learned association is similar to a gentlemen's club in atmosphere, with a grand stairway and panelled hall hung with the portraits of famous fellows Closed down during past periods of repression and dictatorship, it is a mainstay of liberal thought in Spain. Many leading Socialists are members, along with writers and other Spanish intellectuals.

Carving on the façade of the Ateneo de Madrid

⑮ Congreso de los Diputados

Plaza de las Cortes. **Map** 7 B2.
Tel 91 390 65 25. Sevilla.
Open by appt only. 9am–2:30pm & 4–6:30pm Mon–Thu, 9am–1:30pm Fri. ✉ ♿ 🌐 **congreso.es**

This imposing yet attractive building is home to the Spanish parliament, the Cortes. Built in the mid-19th century, it is characterized by Classical columns, heavy pediments and guardian bronze lions. It was here, in 1981, that Colonel Tejero of the Civil Guard held the deputies at gunpoint on national television, as he tried to spark off a military coup (see p72). His failure was seen as an indication that democracy was now firmly established in Spain.

Bronze lion guarding the Cortes

⑯ Café Gijón

Paseo de Recoletos 21. **Map** 5 C5.
Tel 91 521 54 25. Banco de España.
Open 7:30am–1:30am daily. ♿
🌐 **cafegijon.com**

Madrid's bustling café life (see pp324–5) was one of the most attractive features of the city from the turn of the 20th century, right up to the outbreak of the Civil War. Of the many intellectuals' cafés which once thrived, only the Gijón survives. Today the café continues to attract a lively crowd of literati. With its cream-painted wrought-iron columns and black and white tabletops, it is perhaps better known for its atmosphere and emanating history than for its appearance.

❿ Museo del Prado

The Prado Museum contains the world's
greatest assembly of Spanish painting –
especially works by Velázquez and Goya –
ranging from the 12th to 19th centuries.
It also houses impressive foreign collections,
particularly of Italian and Flemish works.
The Neo-Classical building was designed in
1785 by Juan de Villanueva on the orders of
Carlos III, and it opened as a museum in
1819. The Spanish architect Rafael Moneo
has constructed a new building, over the
adjacent church's cloister, where the temporary exhibitions are located. The Casón
del Buen Retiro, now the Prado library, can
be visited with a guided tour on Sundays.

★ Velázquez Collection
The Triumph of Bacchus
(1629), Velázquez's
first portrayal of a
mythological subject,
shows the god of
wine (Bacchus) with
a group of drunkards.

Second floor

**The Martyrdom of
St Philip**
(c.1639) José de Ribera
was influenced by
Caravaggio's dramatic
use of light and shadow,
known as chiaroscuro,
as seen in this work.

**The Adoration of the
Shepherds** (1612–14)
This dramatic work shows the
elongated figures and swirling
garments typical of El Greco's
style. It was painted during his
late Mannerist period for his
own funerary chapel.

First floor

Ticket office

The Garden of Delights (c.1505) Hieronymus Bosch
(El Bosco in Spanish), one of Felipe II's favourite artists,
is especially well represented in the Prado. This
enigmatic painting depicts Paradise and Hell.

Key to Floorplan

- Spanish painting
- Flemish and Dutch painting
- Italian painting
- French painting
- German painting
- British painting
- Sculpture
- Decorative arts
- Non-exhibition space

Goya entrance
(upstairs)

The Three Graces (c.1635)
This was one of the last paintings by the Flemish master Rubens, and was part of his own collection. The women dancing in a ring the Graces – are the daughters of Zeus, and represent Love, Joy and Revelry.

VISITORS' CHECKLIST

Practical Information
Paseo del Prado. **Map** 7 C3.
Tel 902 10 70 77.
Open 10am–8pm Mon–Sat, 10am–7pm Sun & public hols, last entry 30 min before closing.
Closed 1 Jan, 1 May, 25 Dec.
(free entry last 2 hours of day).
W museodelprado.es

Transport
Atocha, Banco de España.
10, 14, 19, 27, 34, 37, 45.

Ground floor

Murillo entrance

The Dolphin's Treasure is a spectacular collection of decorative objects from the 16th and 17th centuries.

Velázquez entrance

★ Goya Collection
In *The Clothed Maja* and *The Naked Maja* (both c.1800), Goya tackled the taboo subject of nudity, for which he was later accused of obscenity.

Gallery Guide

The museum's permanent collection is arranged chronologically over three main floors. Classical sculpture is on the ground floor, Velázquez on the first floor, and the extensive Goya collection across the Murillo side of all three floors. The permanent collection is accessed via the Velázquez and Goya entrances. Visitors to the temporary exhibitions should use the Jerónimos entrance.

The Annunciation
Fra Angelico's work of c.1425–8 is a high point of Italy's early Renaissance, as illustrated by the detailed architectural setting.

Casón del Buen Retiro — Jerónimos Building — Underground link — Villanueva Building

CALLE DE MORETO

Jerónimos entrance

CALLE DE FELIPE IV

PASEO DEL PRADO

Changes at the Prado

The Jerónimos Building houses temporary exhibitions and Renaissance sculptures, as well as a shop, restaurant, café, auditorium and cloakroom. In the future the Salón de Reinos *(see p291)* may also become part of the Prado.

▪ Museum buildings

Exploring the Prado's Collection

The importance of the Prado is founded on its royal collections. The wealth of foreign art, including many of Europe's finest works, reflects the historical power of the Spanish crown. The Low Countries and parts of Italy were under Spanish domination for centuries. The 18th century was an era of French influence, following the Bourbon accession to the Spanish throne. The Prado is worthy of repeated visits, but if you go only once, see the Spanish works of the 17th century.

Saturn Devouring One of his Sons (1820–23) by Francisco de Goya

St Dominic of Silos Enthroned as Abbot (1474–7) by Bermejo

Spanish Painting

Right up to the 19th century, Spanish painting focused on religious and royal themes. Although the limited subject matter was in some ways a restriction, it also offered a sharp focus that seems to have suited Spanish painters.

Spain's early medieval art is represented somewhat sketchily in the Prado, but there are some examples, such as the anonymous mural paintings from the Holy Cross hermitage in Maderuelo, which show a Romanesque heaviness of line and forceful characterization.

Spanish Gothic art can be seen in the Prado in the works of Bartolomé Bermejo and Fernando Gallego. The sense of realism in their paintings was borrowed from Flemish masters of the time.

Renaissance features began to emerge in the works of painters such as Pedro de Berruguete, whose auto-da-fé is both chilling and lively. St Catherine, by Fernando Yáñez de la Almedina, shows the influence of Leonardo da Vinci, for whom Yáñez probably worked while training in Italy.

What is often considered as a truly Spanish style – with its highly wrought emotion and deepening sombreness – first started to emerge in the 16th century in the paintings of the Mannerists. This is evident in Pedro Machuca's fierce *Descent from the Cross* and in the *Madonnas* of Luis de Morales, "the Divine". The elongation of the human figure in Morales' work is carried to a greater extreme by Domenikos Theotocopoulos, who is better known as El Greco *(see p395)*. Although many of his masterpieces remain in his adopted town of Toledo, the Prado has an impressive collection, including *The Nobleman with his Hand on his Chest*.

The Golden Age of the 17th century was a productive time for Spanish art. José de Ribera, who lived in (Spanish) Naples, followed Caravaggio in combining realism of character with the techniques of chiaroscuro (use of light and dark) and tenebrism (large areas of dark colours, with a shaft of light). Another master who used this method was Francisco Ribalta, whose *Christ Embracing St Bernard* is here. Zurbarán, known for still lifes and portraits of saints and monks, is also represented in the Prado.

This period, however, is best represented by the work of Diego de Velázquez. As Spain's leading court painter from his late twenties until his death, he produced scenes of heightened realism, royal portraits, and religious and mythological paintings. Examples of his art are displayed in the Prado. His greatest work is perhaps *Las Meninas (see p36)*, in Room 12.

Another great Spanish painter, Goya, revived Spanish art in the 18th century. He first specialized in cartoons for tapestries, then became a court painter. His work went on to embrace the horrors of war, as seen in *The 3rd of May in Madrid (see p67)*, and culminated in a sombre series known as *The Black Paintings*.

Still Life with Four Vessels (c.1658–64) by Francisco de Zurbarán

Flemish and Dutch Painting

Spain's long connection with the Low Countries naturally resulted in an intense admiration for the so-called Flemish primitives. Many exceptional examples of Flemish and Dutch art now hang in the Prado. *St Barbara*, by Robert Campin, has a quirky intimacy, while Rogier van der Weyden's *The Descent from the Cross* is an unquestioned masterpiece. Most notable of all, however, are Hieronymus Bosch's weird and eloquent inventions. The Prado has some of his major paintings, including *The Temptation of St Anthony* and *The Haywain*. Works from the 16th century include *The Triumph of Death* by Bruegel the Elder. There are nearly 100 canvases by the 17th-century Flemish painter Peter Paul Rubens, including *The Adoration of the Magi*. The most notable Dutch painting on display is Rembrandt's *Artemisia*, a portrait of the artist's wife. Other Flemish and Dutch artists featured at the Prado are Antonis Moor, Anton Van Dyck and Jacob Jordaens, considered one of the finest portrait painters of the 17th century.

Italian Painting

The Prado is the envy of many museums, not least for its vast collection of Italian paintings. Botticelli's dramatic wooden panels telling *The Story of Nastagio degli Onesti*, a vision of a knight forever condemned to hunt down and kill his own beloved, were

David Victorious over Goliath (c.1600) by Caravaggio

commissioned by two rich Florentine families and are a sinister high point.

Raphael contributes the superb *Christ Falls on the Way to Calvary* and the sentimental *The Holy Family of the Lamb*. *Christ Washing the Disciples' Feet*, an early work by Tintoretto, is a profound masterpiece and reveals the painter's brilliant handling of perspective.

Caravaggio had a profound impact on Spanish artists, who admired his characteristic handling of light, as seen in *David Victorious over Goliath*. Venetian masters Veronese and Titian are also very well represented. Titian served as court painter to Charles V, and few works express the drama of Habsburg rule so deeply as his sombre painting *The Emperor Charles V at Mühlberg*. Also on display are works by Giordano and Tiepolo, the master of Italian Rococo, who painted *The Immaculate Conception* as part of a series intended for a church in Aranjuez.

French Painting

Marriages between French and Spanish royalty in the 17th century, culminating in the Bourbon accession to the throne in the 18th century, brought French art to Spain. The Prado has eight works attributed to Poussin, among them his serene *St Cecilia* and *Landscape with St Jerome*. The magnificent *Landscape with the Embarkation of St Paula Romana at Ostia* is the best work here by Claude Lorrain. Among the 18th-century artists featured are Antoine Watteau and Jean Ranc. *Felipe V* is the work of the royal portraitist Louis-Michel van Loo.

St Cecilia (c.1635) by the French artist Nicolas Poussin

German Painting

Although German art is not especially well represented in the Prado, there are a number of paintings by Albrecht Dürer, including his classical depictions of Adam and Eve. His lively *Self-Portrait* of 1498, painted at the age of 26, is undoubtedly the highlight of the small but valuable German collection in the museum. Lucas Cranach is also featured and works by the late 18th-century painter Anton Raffael Mengs include some magnificent portraits of Carlos III.

The Descent from the Cross (c.1430) by Rogier van der Weyden

One of the many Roman mosaics at the Museo Arqueológico Nacional

⑰ Plaza de Colón

Map 6 D5. 🔳 Serrano, Colón.
Teatro Fernán Gómez Centro
de Arte: **Tel** 91 436 25 40.
🔳 teatrofernangomez.com

This large square, one of
Madrid's undisputed focal
points, is dedicated to 15th-
century explorer Christopher
Columbus (Colón in Spanish).

It is overlooked by huge
tower blocks, built in the 1970s
to replace the 19th-century
mansions which stood here.

On the south side of the
square is a palace housing
the National Library and
Archaeological Museum.
The Post-Modernist
skyscraper of the Heron
Corporation towers over
the Plaza de Colón from
the far side of the Paseo
de la Castellana.

The real feature of the
square, however, is the pair
of monuments dedicated
to the discoverer of the
Americas. The prettiest,
and oldest, is the Neo-Gothic
spire erected in 1885, with
Columbus at its top, pointing west. Carved reliefs on
the plinth give highlights of
his discoveries. Across the
square is the second, more
modern monument –
a cluster of four large
concrete shapes
inscribed with
quotations about
Columbus's journey
to America (see p61).

Constantly busy with
traffic, the plaza may
seem an unlikely venue
for cultural events.

Statue of Columbus,
Plaza de Colón

Beneath it, however, is
an extensive complex,
the Teatro Fernán Gómez
Centro de Arte. Formerly
known as the Centro
Cultural de la Villa, this
centre is now named after
the Spanish cinema and
theatre actor, director and
writer Fernando Fernán
Gómez, who died in
Madrid in 2007. Exhibitions
are held in its prestigious
halls. The complex also
includes lecture rooms,
a theatre and a café.

⑱ Calle de Serrano

Map 8 D1. 🔳 Serrano.

Named after the 19th-century
politician Francisco Serrano y
Domínguez, Madrid's smartest
shopping street runs north
from the Plaza de la
Independencia, in the district
of Salamanca, to the Plaza del
Ecuador, in the district of El
Viso. Calle de Serrano is lined
with attractive shops (p320) –
many specializing in expensive
luxury items – housed in old-
fashioned mansion blocks.
Several of the country's top
designers, including
Adolfo Domínguez and
Purificación García, have
boutiques towards the
north, near the ABC Serrano
(see p321) and the Museo
Lázaro Galdiano (see p309).
Branches of the Italian
shops Versace, Gucci and
Armani, as well as the
French Chanel, can be
found on the Calle de
José Ortega y Gasset.
Lower down the Calle de
Serrano, towards Serrano
metro station, are two
branches of Spain's famous
department store El Corte
Inglés. On the Calle de
Claudio Coello, which
runs parallel with
Serrano, there are
several lavish antique
shops, in keeping
with the area's
upmarket atmos-
phere. Under Juan
Bravo's bridge is the
Museo de Arte Público

de Madrid, an open-air
sculpture museum (Paseo
de la Castellana 40).

⑲ Museo Arqueológico Nacional

Calle Serrano 13. **Map** 6 D5.
Tel 91 577 79 12. 🔳 Serrano.
🚌 1, 9, 19, 51, 74. **Open** 9:30am–
8pm Tue–Sat, 9:30am–3pm Sun.
🔳 man.es

Founded by Isabel II in 1867,
Madrid's archaeological
museum, which has reopened
after extensive and impressive
restoration work, houses a
collection that consists mainly
of material uncovered during
excavations all over Spain, as
well as important pieces from
Egypt, ancient Greece and the
Etruscan civilization.

Highlights of the earliest finds
include an exhibition on the
ancient civilization of El Argar
in Andalucía (see p52), and a
display of jewellery uncovered
at the Roman settlement of
Numantia, near Soria (see p381).

Other exhibited pieces are
devoted to the period between
Roman and Mudéjar Spain.
Iberian culture is also represented, with two notable funerary
sculptures – La Dama de Elche
(see p52) and La Dama de Baza.
The Roman period is illustrated
with some impressive mosaics,
including one from the 3rd
century. The underside of
this 1,800-year-old work
shows a combat between two
gladiators, Simmachius and
Maternus; the upper register
displays Simmachius' victory.

Outstanding pieces from the
Visigothic period include several
splendid 7th-century gold votive
crowns from Toledo province.

On show from the Islamic
era is well-preserved pottery
uncovered from Medina
Azahara in Andalucía (see
p481) and metal objects.

Romanesque exhibits at
the museum include an ivory
crucifix carved in 1063 for
Fernando I of Castilla-León,
and the Madonna and Child
from Sahagún, considered
a masterpiece of Spanish art.

⑳ Parque del Retiro

Map 8 E3. **Tel** 91 530 00 41. 🚇 Retiro, Ibiza, Atocha. **Open** 6am–10pm (Apr–Oct: 6am–midnight). ♿

The Retiro Park, in Madrid's smart Jerónimos district, takes its name from Felipe IV's royal palace complex, which once stood here. Today, all that is left of the palace is the Casón del Buen Retiro (see p296) and the Salón de Reinos (see p291).

Used privately by the royal family from 1632, the park became the scene of elaborate pageants, bullfights and mock naval battles. In the 18th century it was partially opened to the public, provided visitors were formally dressed, and in 1869 it was fully opened. Today, the Retiro remains one of the most popular places for relaxing in Madrid.

A short stroll from the park's northern entrance down the tree-lined avenue leads to the pleasure lake, where rowing boats can be hired. On one side of the lake is a half-moon colonnade in front of which an equestrian statue of Alfonso XII rides high on a column. Opposite, portrait painters and fortune-tellers ply their trade.

To the south of the lake are two palaces. The Neo-Classical Palacio de Velázquez and the Palacio de Cristal (Crystal Palace) were built by Velázquez Bosco in 1883 and 1887 respectively and regularly hold contemporary art exhibitions.

Statue of Bourbon King Carlos III in the Real Jardín Botánico

㉑ Real Jardín Botánico

Plaza de Murillo 2. **Map** 8 D4. **Tel** 91 420 30 17. 🚇 Atocha, Banco de Espana. **Open** 10am–dusk daily. **Closed** 1 Jan, 25 Dec. 📷 ♿ 🌐 rjb.csic.es

South of the Prado (see pp296–9), and a suitable place for resting after visiting the gallery, are the Royal Botanical Gardens. Inspired by Carlos III, they were designed in 1781 by Gómez Ortega, Francesco Sabatini and Juan de Villanueva, architect of the Prado.

Interest in the plants of South America and the Philippines took hold during the Spanish Enlightenment (see p66), and the neatly laid out beds offer a huge variety of flora, ranging from trees to herbs.

㉒ Estación de Atocha

Plaza del Emperador Carlos V. **Map** 8 D5. **Tel** 902 32 03 20. 🚇 Atocha RENFE. **Open** 5am–1am daily. ♿ 🌐 renfe.com

Madrid's first railway service, from Atocha to Aranjuez, was inaugurated in 1851. Forty years later Atocha station was replaced by a new building, which was extended in the 1980s. The older part, built of glass and wrought iron, now houses an indoor palm garden. Next to it is the terminus for high-speed AVE trains to Seville, Toledo, Córdoba, Zaragoza, Lleida, Barcelona, Málaga, Valencia, Valladollid and France (see p628).

The Ministerio de Agricultura, opposite, is a splendid late 19th-century building.

Entrance of Madrid's Estación de Atocha, busy with travellers

Monument of Alfonso XII (1901), facing the Retiro's boating lake

㉓ Museo Nacional Centro de Arte Reina Sofía

The highlight of this museum, commonly referred to as the Museo Reina Sofía, of 20th-century art is Picasso's *Guernica*. There are, however, other major works by influential artists, including Miró and Dalí. The collection is housed in Madrid's former General Hospital, built in the late 18th century. Major extensions, designed by Jean Nouvel, were inaugurated in 2005. The Nouvel Building includes the *Collection 3: From Revolt to Postmodernity*, a library, a bookshop, a café and auditoriums that host various events such as film screenings, lectures and concerts.

Portrait II (1938)
Joan Miró's huge work shows elements of Surrealism, but was painted more than 10 years after his true Surrealist period ended.

Nouvel building

★ **Woman in Blue** (1901)
Picasso disowned this work after it won only an honourable mention in a national competition. Decades later it was located and acquired by the Spanish state.

Landscape at Cadaqués
Salvador Dalí was born in Figueres in Catalonia. He became a frequent visitor to the town of Cadaqués, on the Costa Brava *(see p220–21)*, where he painted this landscape in the summer of 1923.

Key to Floorplan

☐ Exhibition space
▨ Non-exhibition space

Self-Portrait (Accident)
Alfonso Ponce de León's disturbing work, painted in 1936, prefigured his death in a car crash later that same year.

★ **The Gathering at Pombo Café** (1920)
José Gutiérrez Solana depicts a gathering
of intellectuals *(tertulia)* in a famous café
in Madrid, which no longer exists.

VISITORS' CHECKLIST

Practical Information
Calle Santa Isabel 52. **Map** 7 C5.
Tel 91 774 10 00.
Open 10am–9pm Mon, Wed–Sat,
10am–7pm Sun. **Closed** 1 & 6 Jan,
1 & 15 May, 9 Nov, 24, 25 & 31 Dec,
some pub hols. 🎟 (free after 7pm
Mon, Wed–Sat & after 1:30pm
Sun). 🅿 ♿ 📷 🖊 🛗 🖥 📷 📷
w museoreinasofia.es

Transport
🚇 Atocha. 🚌 6, 14, 19, 27,
45, 55, 86.

Gallery Guide

*The permanent collection is in
the Sabatini Building. Collection 1
on the second floor displays
works dating from 1900 to 1945,
and includes rooms dedicated
to important movements such
as Cubism and Surrealism;
Collection 2 on the fourth floor
has works dating from 1945 to
1968, including representatives
of Pop Art, Minimalism and
more recent tendencies.
Collection 3: From Revolt to
Postmodernity (1962–1982) is
located in the Nouvel Building.*

Glass lift

Entrance

Visitors admiring *Guernica*

★ Picasso's Guernica

The most famous single work of the 20th
century, this Civil War protest painting *(see
pp70–71)* was commissioned by the Spanish
Republican government in 1937 for a Paris
exhibition. The artist found his inspiration
in the mass air attack of the same year on
the Basque town of Gernika-Lumo *(see
pp122–3)*, by German pilots flying for the
Nationalist air force. The painting hung in
a New York gallery until 1981, reflecting
the artist's wish that it should not return to
Spain until democracy was re-established.
It was moved here from the Prado in 1992.

oki-Egin (Homenaje a San Juan de la Cruz) (1990)
n his abstract sculptures, Eduardo Chillida used a variety of
materials, such as wood, iron and steel, to convey strength.

FURTHER AFIELD

Several of Madrid's best sights, including some interesting but little-known museums, lie outside the city centre. The axis of modern Madrid is the Paseo de la Castellana, a long, wide avenue lined by skyscraper offices and busy with traffic. A journey along it gives a glimpse of Madrid as Spain's commercial and administrative capital. La Castellana skirts the Barrio de Salamanca, an upmarket district of stylish boutiques, named after the 19th-century aristocrat who built it, the Marquis de Salamanca. The districts around Old Madrid, especially Malasaña and La Latina, offer a more typically authentic *madrileño* atmosphere. On Sundays, some of the old streets are crowded with bargain hunters at the sprawling second-hand market, El Rastro. If you need to escape from the bustle of the city for a while, west of Old Madrid, across the Río Manzanares, is Madrid's vast, green recreation ground, the Casa de Campo, with its pleasant pine woods, boating lake, amusement park and zoo.

Sights at a Glance

Historic Buildings
6 Templo de Debod
9 Palacio de Liria
16 Real Fábrica de Tapices

Churches and Convents
5 Ermita de San Antonio de la Florida

Museums and Galleries
7 Museo de América
8 Museo Cerralbo
11 Museo de Historia de Madrid
12 Museo Sorolla
13 Museo Lázaro Galdiano

Streets, Squares and Parks
1 El Rastro
2 La Latina
3 Plaza de la Paja
4 Casa de Campo
10 Malasaña
14 Paseo de la Castellana
15 Plaza de Toros de Las Ventas
17 Parque de El Capricho

Key
Madrid city centre
Parks and open spaces
Motorway
Major road
Minor road

0 kilometres 2
0 miles 1

◀ Detail of the Plaza de Toros, with its ornate tilework decoration   **For keys to symbols** *see back flap*

❶ El Rastro

Calle Ribera de Curtidores. **Map** 4 E4.
🚇 La Latina, Tirso de Molina.
Open 10am–3pm Sun & public hols.

Madrid's celebrated flea market
(see p321), established in the
Middle Ages, has its hub in
the Plaza de Cascorro and
sprawls downhill towards the
Río Manzanares. The main street
is the Calle Ribera de Curtidores,
or "Tanners' Riverbank", once the
centre of the slaughterhouse
and tanning industry.

Although some people claim
that the Rastro has changed
a great deal since its heyday
during the 19th century, there
are still plenty of madrileños, as
well as tourists, who shop here.
They come in search of a bargain
from the stalls which sell a huge
range of wares – anything from
new furniture to second-hand
clothes. The wide range of
goods and the lively crowds in
the Rastro make it an ideal way
to spend a Sunday morning.
It is also worth making a stop
at the Galerías Piquer (Calle
Ribera de Curtidores 29) and
the Plaza General Vara del Rey.

The Calle de Embajadores is
the market's other main street.
It runs down past the Baroque
façade of the Iglesia de San
Cayetano, designed by José
Churriguera and Pedro de
Ribera. Its interior has been
restored since fire destroyed
it during the Civil War.

Further along the street is the
former Real Fábrica de Tabacos
(the Royal Tobacco Factory), begun
as a state enterprise in 1809. It is

Some of the curios on display at the Rastro
flea market

partly occupied by an unofficial
and alternative cultural centre.

❷ La Latina

Map 4 D4. 🚇 La Latina.

The district of La Latina, together
with the adjacent Lavapiés, is
considered to be the heart of
castizo Madrid. This term is used
to describe the culture of the traditional working classes of Madrid
– that of the true madrileño.

La Latina runs along the city's
southern hillside from the Plaza
Puerta de Moros, southwards
through the streets where the
Rastro is held. To the east it
merges with Lavapiés. La Latina's
steep streets are lined with tall,
narrow houses, renovated to
form an attractive neighbourhood. There are old-fashioned
and trendy bars around the
Plaza del Humilladero as well
as in the Lavapiés district.

Bottles of wine for sale in an old-style bar
in Lavapiés

❸ Plaza de la Paja

Map 4 D3. 🚇 La Latina.

Once the focus of medieval
Madrid, the area around the
Plaza de la Paja – literally
Straw Square – is extremely
atmospheric and many
interesting buildings are
located on the square.

Climbing upwards from the
Calle de Segovia, a glimpse
left along the Calle Príncipe
Anglona yields a view of the
Mudéjar-style brick tower
of the Iglesia de San Pedro,
dating from the 14th century.

Interior of San Francisco el Grande

Up past the fountain, the Plaza
de la Paja ends with the harsh
stone walls of the Capilla del
Obispo, or Bishop's Chapel,
belonging originally to the
adjoining Palacio Vargas. The
superb Plateresque altarpiece
is by Francisco Giralte. Up to
the left, the Baroque, cherub-
covered dome of the Iglesia
de San Andrés stands out.

Nearby is a small cluster of
interlinked squares, ending in
the Plaza Puerta de Moros, a
reminder of the Muslim community which once occupied
the area. From here, a right turn
leads to the domed bulk of
San Francisco el Grande, an
impressive landmark. Inside the
church is a painting by Goya
and his brother-in-law Francisco
Bayeu. The choirstalls were
moved here from the monastery
of El Paular (see pp332–3).

❹ Casa de Campo

Paseo Puerta del Angel 1. **Tel** 91 479 60
02. 🚇 Batán, Lago, Príncipe Pío, Casa
de Campo. **Open** 9am–9pm daily.
Closed to cars. 🌐 esmadrid.com

This former royal hunting
ground, stretching over 1,740 ha
(4,300 acres), lies in southwestern Madrid. Its wide range of
amenities make it a popular
daytime recreation area. Attractions include a boating lake, a
zoo, and an amusement park –
the Parque de Atracciones.
Sports enthusiasts can make
use of the swimming pool and
jogging track. In the summer
the park is also used as a venue
for rock concerts.

Egyptian temple of Debod, with two of its original gateways

❺ Ermita de San Antonio de la Florida

Glorieta San Antonio de la Florida 5.
Tel 91 547 79 37. 🚇 Príncipe Pío.
Open 9:30am–8pm Tue–Sun.
Closed public hols. 🚫 ♿
W esmadrid.com

Goya enthusiasts should not miss a visit to the Neo-Classical Ermita de San Antonio de la Florida, built during the reign of Carlos IV. The present church stands on the site of two previous ones and is dedicated to St Anthony. It is named after the pastureland of la Florida, on which the first church was built.

Goya took four months, in 1798, to paint the cupola. It depicts the resurrection of a murdered man who rises in order to prove the innocence of the falsely accused father of St Anthony. The characters in it are everyday people of the late 18th century: lurking, low-life types and lively *majas (see p297)* – shrewd but elegant

women. The fresco is considered by many art critics to be among Goya's finest works.

Goya's tomb is housed in the chapel. His remains were brought here from Bordeaux, where he died in exile in 1828 *(see p243)*.

❻ Templo de Debod

Paseo de Pintor Rosales. **Map** 1 B5.
Tel 91 366 74 15. 🚇 Ventura Rodríguez, Plaza de España.
Open 9:30am–8pm Sat & Sun; Apr–Sep: 10am–2pm, 6–8pm Tue–Fri; Oct–Mar: 10am–2pm, 4–6pm Tue–Fri. **Closed** public hols & afternoons in Aug.
W esmadrid.com

The Egyptian temple of Debod, built in the 2nd century BC, was rescued from the area flooded by the Aswan Dam and given to Spain as a tribute to Spanish engineers involved in

the project. The temple is carved with shallow reliefs, and stands in a line with two of its original three gates on high ground above the Río Manzanares, in the gardens of the Parque del Oeste. From the park there are views over the Casa de Campo to the Guadarrama mountains.

The park is the site of the former Montaña barracks, which were stormed by the populace at the start of the Civil War in 1936. Further west, below the brow of the hill, is an attractive rose garden.

❼ Museo de América

Avenida de los Reyes Católicos 6.
Tel 91 549 26 41. 🚇 Moncloa. **Open** 9:30am–3pm Tue–Sat (to 7pm Thu), 10am–3pm Sun. **Closed** some public hols. 🚫 (free Sun). ♿ 💻 by appt.
W museodeamerica.mcu.es

This museum houses artifacts related to Spain's colonization of parts of the Americas. Many of the exhibits, which range from prehistoric times to the present, were brought back to Europe by early explorers of the New World *(see pp62–3)*.

The collection is arranged on the first and second floors, and individual rooms are given a cultural theme such as society, communication and religion. There is documentation of the Atlantic voyages by the first explorers, and examples of the objects which they found. The highlight of the museum is perhaps a war helmet belonging to the Tlingit people of North America. It depicts a wolf, the lineage motif and protector spirit, and was worn as a symbol of power and strength during battle. Also worth seeing are the solid gold funereal ornaments from Colombia, the Treasure of the Quimbayas (AD 500–1000), and the collection of contemporary folk art from some of Spain's former American colonies.

Flask from the Treasure of the Quimbayas

❽ Museo Cerralbo

Calle Ventura Rodríguez 17. **Map** 1 C5.
Tel 91 547 36 46. 🚇 Plaza de España,
Ventura Rodríguez. **Open** 9:30am–3pm
Tue–Sat (also 5–8pm Thu), 10am–3pm
Sun. **Closed** some public hols. 🖼
(free Sun, after 5pm Thu & 2pm Sat).
🖼 🎥 ⓦ enmuseocerralbo.mcu.es

This 19th-century mansion
near the Plaza de España is a
monument to Enrique de
Aguilera y Gamboa, the 17th
Marquis of Cerralbo. A com-
pulsive collector of art and
artifacts, he bequeathed his
lifetime's collection to the
nation in 1922, stipulating
that the exhibits be arranged
exactly as he left them. They
range from Iberian pottery to
18th-century marble busts.

One of the star exhibits is
El Greco's magnificent *The
Ecstasy of Saint Francis of Assisi*.
There are also paintings by
Ribera, Zurbarán, Alonso Cano
and Goya.

The focal point of the main
floor is the ballroom, lavishly
decorated with mirrors. A large
collection of weaponry is on
display on this floor.

❾ Palacio de Liria

Calle la Princesa 20. **Tel** 91 547 53 02.
🚇 Ventura Rodríguez. **Open** 10am–
noon Fri. 🎥 obligatory. 🖼

The lavish but much-restored
Palacio de Liria was completed
by Ventura Rodríguez in 1780.
Once the residence of the Alba
family, and still owned by the
Duke, it can be visited by a
maximum of 15 people at one
time and by appointment only.

The palace houses the Albas'
outstanding collection of art,
and Flemish tapestries. There
are paintings by Titian, Rubens
and Rembrandt. Spanish art is
particularly well represented,
with major works by Goya,
such as his 1795 portrait of
the Duchess of Alba, as well as
examples of work by El Greco,
Zurbarán and Velázquez.

Behind the palace is the
Cuartel del Conde-Duque, the
former barracks of the Count-
Duke Olivares, Felipe IV's
minister. They were built in
1720 by Pedro de Ribera, who
adorned them with a Baroque
façade. The barracks now house
a cultural centre.

Rooftops in the Malasaña district

❿ Malasaña

Map 2 F5. 🚇 Tribunal, Bilbao.

A feeling of the authentic old
Madrid pervades this district of
narrow, sloping streets and tall
houses. For some years it was
the centre of the *movida*, the
frenzied nightlife which began
after the death of Franco.

A walk along the Calle San
Andrés leads to the fashionable
area, Plaza del Dos de Mayo.
In the centre is a monument
to artillery officers Daoíz and
Velarde, who defended the
barracks which stood here at
the time of the uprising against
the French in 1808 *(see p67)*.

On Calle de la Puebla is the
Iglesia de San Antonio de los
Alemanes. The church was
founded by Felipe III in the
17th century as a hospital for
Portuguese immigrants, and
was later given over for use by
German émigrés. Inside, the
walls are decorated with 18th-
century frescoes by Giordano.

Nearby is the neighbourhood
of Conde Duque, a lively area
with a great cultural scene.

⓫ Museo de Historia de Madrid

Calle de Fuencarral 78. **Map** 5 A4.
Tel 91 701 18 63. 🚇 Tribunal.
Open 10am–8pm Tue–Sun. ♿
ⓦ madrid.es/museodehistoria

The History Museum is worth
visiting just for its Baroque
doorway *(see p29)* by Pedro
de Ribera, arguably the finest

Main staircase of the exuberant Museo Cerralbo

in Madrid. Housed in the former hospice of St Ferdinand, the museum was inaugurated in 1929.

It holds a series of bird's-eye views and maps of Madrid. Among them is Pedro Teixeira's map of 1656, thought to be the oldest of the city. There is also a model of Madrid, made in 1830 by León Gil de Palacio.

Modern exhibits include a reconstruction of the collage-filled study of Ramón Gómez de la Serna, a key figure of the literary gatherings in the Café de Pombo (see p303).

Baroque façade of the Museo de Historia, by Pedro de Ribera

⑫ Museo Sorolla

Paseo del General Martínez Campos 37. **Map** 5 C1. **Tel** 91 310 15 84. 🚇 Rubén Darío, Iglesia, Gregorio Marañón. **Open** 9:30am–8pm Tue–Sat, 10am–3pm Sun. **Closed** some public hols. 🎟 (free Sat after 2pm, Sun). 🌐 **museosorolla.mcu.es**

The former studio-mansion of Valencian Impressionist painter Joaquín Sorolla has been left virtually as it was when he died in 1923.

Although Sorolla is perhaps best known for his brilliantly lit Mediterranean beach scenes, the changing styles of his paintings are well represented in the museum, with examples of his gentle portraiture and a series of works representing people from different parts of Spain. Also on display are objects amassed during Sorolla's lifetime, including Spanish tiles and

Sorolla's former studio in the Museo Sorolla

ceramics. The house, built in 1910, has an Andalucían-style garden designed by Sorolla himself.

⑬ Museo Lázaro Galdiano

Calle Serrano 122. **Map** 6 E1. **Tel** 91 561 60 84. 🚇 Rubén Darío, Gregorio Marañón. **Open** 10am–4:30pm Tue–Sat, 10am 3pm Sun. **Closed** public hols. 🎟 (free for last hour). 📷 by appt. 🌐 **flg.es**

This art museum is housed in the former mansion-home of the editor and financier José Lázaro Galdiano, and consists of his private collection of fine and applied art, bequeathed to the nation in 1947.

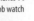

Charles V's fob watch

The collection ranges from the 6th to the 20th century and contains items of exceptional quality, ranging from less familiar Goya portraits to a mass of fob watches, including a cross-shaped pocket watch worn by Charles V. Among the most beautiful objects are a series of Limoges enamels, miniature sculptures, and *The Saviour*, a portrait attributed to a student of Leonardo da Vinci. The museum features paintings by English artists Constable, Turner, Gainsborough and Reynolds, as well as 17th-century paintings by the likes of Spanish painters Madrazo, Zurbarán, Ribera, Murillo and El Greco.

La Movida

With Franco's death in 1975 came a new period of personal and artistic liberty that lasted until the mid-1980s. For some, this translated into the freedom to stay out late, drinking and sometimes sampling drugs. The phenomenon was known as *la movida*, "the action", and it was at its most intense in Madrid. Analysts at the time saw it as having serious intellectual content, and *la movida* has had many lasting cultural effects on art, music and literature, like the emergence of satirical film director Pedro Almodóvar.

Poster for Almodóvar's *Women on the Verge of a Nervous Breakdown*

Torre de Picasso towering over the Paseo de la Castellana

⑭ Paseo de la Castellana

Map 6 D3. 🚇 Santiago Bernabéu, Cuzco, Plaza de Castilla, Gregorio Marañón, Colón.

The busy traffic artery which cuts through eastern Madrid has several parts. Its southernmost portion – the Paseo del Prado *(see pp288–9)* – starts just north of the Estación de Atocha *(see p301)*. The oldest section, it dates from the reign of Carlos III, who built it as part of his embellishment of eastern Madrid. At the Plaza de Cibeles, the avenue becomes the Paseo de Recoletos, which boasts stylish cafés, including the Café Gijón *(see p295)*.

The Plaza de Colón marks the start of the Paseo de la Castellana. This northernmost section has several examples of modern architecture, including the huge grey Nuevos Ministerios building. East of the square is the Estadio Bernabéu, home of Real Madrid Football Club *(see p181)*. At the north end, in Plaza de Castilla, you can find the two Puerta de Europa buildings, built at an angle as if leaning toward each other.

⑮ Plaza de Toros de Las Ventas

Calle Alcalá 237. **Tel** 913 54 22 00. 🚇 Ventas. **Open** for bullfights & concerts. 🎟️ 📷 by appt. (910 24 28 44). Museo Taurino: **Tel** 917 25 18 57. **Open** 10am–5:30pm daily. 🌐 **lasventastour.com**

Whatever your opinion of bullfighting, Las Ventas is undoubtedly one of the most beautiful bullrings in Spain. Built in 1929 in Neo-Mudéjar

style, it replaced the city's original bullring which stood near the Puerta de Alcalá. With its horseshoe arches around the outer galleries and the elaborate tilework decoration, it makes a lovely venue for the *corridas* held during the bull-fighting season, from May to October. The statues outside are monuments to two renowned Spanish bullfighters: Antonio Bienvenida and José Cubero.

Adjoining the bullring is the Museo Taurino. Memorabilia includes portraits and sculptures of famous matadors, as well as the heads of several bulls killed during fights at Las Ventas. Visitors can view close up the tools of the bullfighter's trade: capes and *banderillas* – sharp darts used to wound the bull *(see pp40–41)*. For some people, the gory highlight of the exhibition is the blood-drenched *traje de luces* worn by the legendary Manolete during his fateful bullfight at Linares in Andalucía in 1947.

⑯ Real Fábrica de Tapices

Calle Fuenterrabía 2. **Map** 8 F5. **Tel** 914 34 05 50. 🚇 Menéndez Pelayo. **Open** 10am–2pm Mon–Fri, last entry 30 minutes before closing. **Closed** public hols & Aug. 🎟️ 📷 only. 🌐 **realfabricadetapices.com**

Founded by Felipe V in 1721, the Royal Tapestry Factory is the sole survivor of several factories which were opened by the Bourbons *(see pp66–7)* during the 18th century. In 1889 the factory was relocated to this building just south of the Parque del Retiro.

Visitors can see the making of the carpets and tapestries by hand, a process which has changed little. Goya and his brother-in-law Francisco Bayeu created drawings, or cartoons, which were the models for tapestries made for the royal family. A number of the cartoons are displayed here; others can be seen in the Museo del Prado *(see pp296–9)*. Some of the tapestries can be seen at El Pardo *(see p336)* and at El Escorial *(see pp334–5)*. Nowadays one of the factory's main tasks is making and repairing the carpets decorating Hotel Ritz by Belmond *(see p290)*.

⑰ Parque de El Capricho

Paseo de la Alameda de Osuna s/n. **Tel** 915 88 01 14. 🚇 El Capricho. **Open** Apr–Sep: 9am–9pm Sat (to 6:30pm Oct–Mar).

This lesser-known, remote park is one of the most unique and charming examples of a land-scape garden in Spain. Built in the Romantic style on the whim of a duchess in the late 18th century, it displays both Italian and French influences. The plantlife is abundant, particularly in spring, when the garden comes to life with the groves of lilacs and cascading roses. Other interesting places include an artificial canal that leads to a lake with ducks and swans, the reed-covered boathouse known as the Casa de Cañas, the Casino del Baile (Dance Casino), a small temple, a modest palace with a beautiful ballroom, an unusual beehouse and underground bunkers dating back to the Civil War.

Plaza de Toros de Las Ventas, Madrid's beautiful bullring

MADRID STREET FINDER

The map references given with the sights, shops and entertainment venues described in the Madrid section of the guide refer to the street maps on the following pages. Map references are also given for Madrid hotels (*see pp568–9*), and

for bars and restaurants (*pp591–3*). The schematic map below shows the area of Madrid covered by the *Street Finder*. The symbols used for sights and other features are listed in the key at the foot of the page.

Key to Street Finder

- Major sight
- Place of interest
- Other building
- Main railway station
- Metro station
- Tourist information
- Hospital with casualty unit
- Police station
- Church

- 🔺 Convent or monastery
- Pedestrianized street
- Railway line

0 kilometres   1
0 miles   0.5

Scale of Map Pages

0 metres   250
0 yards   250

SHOPPING IN MADRID

Madrid is a shoppers' paradise, with well-known designer stores competing for attention with small, creative shops. Madrid still has more independent and family-run shops than most European capitals, so it should not be hard to pick up some truly original gifts. There are two main shopping hearts in the city – the crowded and popular streets around the pedestrianized Preciados and the Puerta del Sol, and Calle de la Princesa and adjacent streets. The Salamanca district is host to designer brands as well as upmarket antiques, while for the latest streetware visit the Chueca district. The colourful food markets dotted around the city are well worth a visit.

Opening Hours

Most shops in Madrid are open from 10am to 2pm and 5pm to 8:30pm Monday–Friday, though larger stores tend to stay open during lunch and close at 10pm. Small shops often close on Saturday afternoon. Shopping centres, department stores and big shops are permitted to open on Sundays, and the downtown shops around Sol open on Sundays, too. Many small shops close for a month (usually August) in the summer.

Food and Drink

Madrid is a paradise for gourmet food shopping. Strongly scented saffron, matured ewe's cheese or a fruity extra-virgin olive oil all make ideal gifts. Spain has a deep-rooted tradition of pork products, ranging from whole hams to sausages of every shape and size. The best and most expensive ham is Ibérico, from the small, black-hoofed Iberian pig. In Old Madrid, branches of **Museo del Jamón** have an enormous range of Spanish hams, cheeses and cured sausages. **La Chinata** is famous for its selection of olive oils and gourmet products. The department store El Corte Inglés has its own department dedicated to gourmet delicacies, as well as a supermarket for more general groceries. There are smaller delicatessens in nearly every district. In the Salamanca area, visit **Mantequerías Bravo**, famous for its excellent cheeses, preserves and sweets, and **Gold Gourmet**, with its selection of fresh produce including edible flowers.

If you are looking for good wine, head to **Bodega Santa Cecilia**, an outlet with a long history of selling Spanish and international wines. It also organizes tasting sessions. **Lavinia**, in the Salamanca district, is said to be Europe's biggest wine shop, with more than 1,500 brands available. For a truly authentic *madrileño* souvenir, try **La Violeta**, famous for its fragrant violet sweets.

Markets

A favourite local activity is shopping at the street, or flea, markets, where you can spend a pleasant few hours browsing for antiques, second-hand clothes, pottery, handicrafts and furniture. Some markets are focused on only one item, such as the Sunday-morning stamp, postcard and coin market under the arches of Plaza Mayor, or the Cuesta de Moyano at the Atocha end of Paseo de Prado, where stalls selling second-hand books are set up daily. The legendary El Rastro Sunday flea market *(see p306).* is a must for any visitor to Madrid, not only for the variety of goods to be found, from antiques to trendy

The enticing frontage of the Museo del Jamón

Inside one of the many antique shops in the streets around El Rastro

garments, but also for its lively atmosphere. It gets really crowded from noon onwards, with bargain hunters rubbing shoulders with those out to enjoy a pre-lunch apéritif at the numerous bars of the La Latina area. Be careful, however, as pickpockets frequent the market.

The best place for paintings is the street market in Plaza del Conde de Barajas, near Plaza Mayor on Sunday mornings, organized by the art association Taller Abierto.

The colourful Mercado de San Miguel in Plaza San Miguel offers an array of produce and delicious delicatessen items, including traditional cured meats and Spanish cheeses. Mercado de San Antón in Chueca, Mercado de San Ildefonso in Malasaña or the trendy Platea in Plaza de Colón are other renovated markets with the same mix of stalls and bars.

Annual Fairs

February has become the "art month" in Madrid, with contemporary art fairs such as ARCO, Just Mad and Art Madrid. Whether you want to buy or simply browse, these and other events provide a great opportunity to catch up on the latest trends in the art world.

In the week prior to Madrid's Fiesta de San Isidro (see p44) which begins on 15 May, you can buy earthen cookware and wine jugs at the Feria de la Cerámica held in the Plaza de las Comendadoras in the colourful district of Malasaña. The Feria del Libro, held in May–

June, is an impressive outdoor bookfair. Hundreds of stalls are set up in the Parque del Retiro, and publishers and bookshop owners exhibit their wares for two weeks, with book signings taking place as well.

On the Plaza de España, the Feria de Artesanos takes place every December, selling all kinds of crafts, making it ideal for Christmas shopping. Throughout December, the Plaza Mayor is the venue for a traditional Christmas fair – the Mercado de Artículos Navideños, where festive bric-a-brac can be picked up.

Antiques and Arts

The commercial galleries and antiques shops of Madrid are all conveniently located along the streets of Serrano, Velázquez, Jorge Juán and Claudio Coello; in the Salamanca area, around Alonso Martínez; and on Doctor Fourquet street behind the Museo Reina Sofía. For cutting-edge Spanish art, head to the **Juana de Aizpuru** gallery, considered to be one of Madrid's top galleries for contemporary art.

Antique shops can also be found in El Rastro flea market, mainly along Calle de la Ribera de Curtidores. **Antigüedades Palacios** sells collectors' items such as furniture, paintings and European ceramics. Also in El Rastro, **La Turmix** is an artists' cooperative with workshops and galleries (open weekends only).

For specialist antique outlets – ranging from 18th-century lacquered furniture to Spanish paintings from the 16th to 18th centuries – visit **Coll & Cortés**,

Portuondo, Cotanda, Codosero and **Theotokopoulos**. There are also opportunities for pricier antique shopping along the streets of the Prado, Santa Catalina (**Alcocer Anticuarios**) and Cervantes, near Plaza de Santa Ana. In Madrid, art and antiques auctions are held by both Spanish and international firms, including Durán, Goya, Segre, Ansorena and Alcalá.

Shopping Centres and Department Stores

Among the best shopping centres, or centros comerciales, are the tempting and expensive malls of the elegant Salamanca neighbourhood. **El Jardín de Serrano** is a high-quality galleria, housed in two restored 19th-century palaces that stocks fashion, jewellery, gifts and accessories. **ABC Serrano** has a range of shops that includes home furniture as well as designer fashions and gifts.

If you want more variety at a cheaper price, visit the huge **La Vaguada** in the north, or **El Corte Inglés**, a national institution with branches throughout the city. The latter also has a travel agency and offers services such as photo development and shoe repairs. Also good value for money are the shops in the **Príncipe Pío** shopping centre, located in the former Northern Railway Station. Shops, restaurants and cinemas sit under the original glass and iron roof.

Stall selling vintage posters in the busy Rastro flea market

Fashion

The Spanish chain stores **Zara**, **Mango** and **Bimba y Lola** have become international phenomena, offering easy-to-wear clothes for women at very good prices. Zara also caters to men and children. Both stores have branches all over the city. For upmarket fashion there are many well-known Spanish designers, such as **Purificacion Garcia**, who have their own shops in Madrid, mainly in the elegant Salamanca district or on the Calle de Jorge Juan.

Those in favour of a more unusual or original look should try **Ágatha Ruiz de la Prada's** creations (for kids and adults).

For high-quality designer menswear, check out **Roberto Verino**, **Custo Barcelona** or **Adolfo Domínguez**. These shops also offer women's clothes. Another popular, reasonably priced Spanish chain store for men is **Springfield**. At the top end of the market is the **Loewe** store for men, where a silk tie with a Spanish art motif makes a stylish gift.

The lively Chueca and Malasaña districts are the best places for the latest in streetwear, with offbeat local designers and second-hand shops on almost every corner. Some outlets also sell international brands at reduced prices. If your taste runs to vintage, do not miss the quirky **Magpie** store.

Shoes and Leather Goods

Madrid is a haven for those with a shoe fetish. You will find every type of shoe here, from the traditional espadrille sold at **Antigua Casa Crespo** to the popular Majorcan Camper shoes. Try **Pretty Ballerinas** for beautiful ballerina shoes and pumps, while for sophistication, opt for the elegant **Farrutx**. If you are looking for trendy leather goods, head to **Malabaska**. Make a trip to **Bravo** for some of the best national and international labels. Chic shoes, sandals and handbags with an innovative touch are available at **Cristina Castañer**. For a classical look, try **Carmina** or the Majorcan

Meermin. For trainers or other budget buys, visit the shops along Calle de Fuencarral. The well-heeled will also want to check out the range of shoe outlets in the Chueca area, along Calle Augusto Figueroa.

Spain undoubtedly produces some of the best-quality leather in the world. The ultimate in bags and leather goes under the prestigious label of **Loewe**, whose products are sold all over the world. Another impressive (and perhaps more budget-friendly) national brand is **Salvador Bachiller**, where you will discover quality leather and exclusively designed bags, suitcases, wallets and other accessories.

Jewellery

In Calle Serrano and Gran Vía you will find both small shops, stacked with trays of gold studs, chains and bracelets, and grand, more exclusive jewellers. Man-made "Majorica" pearls, as well as the cultivated variety, can be found all over the city, including at the high-end department store El Corte Inglés.

The innovative Catalan **Tous** on Calle Serrano is popular among the young for its ubiquitous teddy-bear logo. If you are interested in original, simple designs, visit the acclaimed jeweller **Joaquín Berao** on Calle Lagasca. His shop resembles an art gallery devoted to tastefully designed pieces. For Spanish designs, visit **Aristocrazy** and the beautiful atelier of **Andrés Gallardo**. Museum shops are also a good place to shop for designer jewellery. Look out for original pieces from Verili, sold at the main museums in the city. **Uno de 50** sells unique silver and leather jewellery.

Crafts and Design

Traditional crafts such as woven baskets or embroidered linen are hard to find in Madrid and those that are available often tend to be Asian imports. However, lovely and inexpensive ceramics

are widely available, though sometimes the more colourful pieces are from Morocco. A wide choice of ceramics can be found at **Cántaro**, near the Plaza de España. Well stocked in regional styles, the shop also carries so-called "extinct" ceramics – traditional styles of pottery no longer regularly produced. Many shops around Puerta del Sol stock embroidered tablecloths and shawls, but be aware that the authentic pieces can be quite expensive. The Spanish firm **PeSeta** makes artisanal fabric goods in their atelier.

In the Plaza Mayor, adjoining the Arco de Cuchilleros, is **El Arco Artesanías**, which sells handmade modern Spanish crafts, such as pottery, glassware and ironwork.

For unique household decorations made by local and European designers, head to **El Moderno**.

Books and Music

The giant French-owned **FNAC** book and video store has an extensive selection of books and magazines in English and other languages, as do **Machado** and the **Casa del Libro**. A little further afield, **Booksellers** stocks English classics, though only a limited selection of new books. The second-hand bookstalls of the Mercado del Libro near the Parque del Retiro are good for cheap paperbacks and, some-times, rare volumes. The libraries of the Círculo de Bellas Artes (see p327) and the Museo Reina Sofía (see pp302–3) have a great collection of books as well. Art books can be found at one of the best specialist art book-shops, **Gaudí**, near Chueca.

For all types of music, go to the FNAC or one of the El Corte Inglés branches, either in Calle de Preciados or Paseo de la Castellana.

For flamenco enthusiasts, the specialist **El Flamenco Vive** store on Calle del Conde de Lemos stocks a fantastic range of flamenco kit, including the widest selection of books, guitars and CDs in the world.

DIRECTORY

Food and Drink

Bodega Santa Cecilia
Calle Blasco de Garay 74.
Map 2 D1.
Tel 914 45 52 83.

La Chinata
Calle Mayor 44. **Map** 4 D2.
Tel 911 52 20 08.

Gold Gourmet
Calle de José Ortega y
Gasset 85–89. **Map** 6 F3.
Tel 914 02 03 63.

Lavinia
Calle de José Ortega y
Gasset 16. **Map** 6 F3.
Tel 914 26 06 04.

Mantequerías Bravo
Calle de Ayala 24. **Map** 6
E4. **Tel** 915 75 80 72.

Museo del Jamón
Carrera de San
Jerónimo 6. **Map** 7 A2.
Tel 915 21 03 46.

La Violeta
Plaza Canalejas 6. **Map** 7
A2. **Tel** 915 22 55 22.

Antiques and Arts

Alcocer Anticuarios
Calle de Santa Catalina 5.
Map 7 B2.
Tel 914 29 79 19.

Antigüedades Palacios
Plaza General Vara del
Rey 14. **Map** 4 E4.
Tel 915 27 31 70.

Codosero
Calle de Lagasca 36. **Map**
6 F5. **Tel** 914 31 58 11.

Coll & Cortés
Calle de Justiniano 3.
Map 5 B4.
Tel 913 10 05 82.

Cotanda
Calle de Lagasca 96. **Map**
6 F2. **Tel** 917 81 30 01.

Juana de Aizpuru
Calle Barquillo 44. **Map** 5
B5. **Tel** 913 10 55 61.

Portuondo
Calle Castelló 85.
Tel 616 79 22 95.

Theotokopoulos
Calle Alcalá 97. **Map** 8 F1.
Tel 915 75 84 66.

La Turmix
Calle López Silva 4. **Map** 4
D4. **Tel** 687 93 29 19.

Shopping Centres and Malls

ABC Serrano
Calle Serrano 61. **Map** 6
E2. **Tel** 915 77 50 31.
w **abcserrano.com**

El Corte Inglés
Calle Preciados 1–3. **Map**
4 F2. **Tel** 913 79 80 00.
w **elcorteingles.es**
One of several branches.

El Jardín de Serrano
Calle Goya 6–8. **Map** 6 E4.
Tel 915 77 00 12.
w **jardindeserrano.es**

Príncipe Pío
Paseo de la Florida 2. **Map**
3 A1. **Tel** 917 58 00 40.
w **ccprincipepio.com**

La Vaguada
Avda Monforte de Lemos
36. **Tel** 917 30 10 00.
w **enlavaguada.com**

Fashion

Adolfo Domínguez
Calle Serrano 96. **Map** 6
E2. **Tel** 915 76 70 53.
One of several branches.

Ágatha Ruiz de la Prada
Calle Serrano 27. **Map** 6
E4. **Tel** 913 19 05 01.

Bimba y Lola
Calle Serrano 22. **Map**
6 E5. **Tel** 915 76 11 03.
One of several branches.

Custo Barcelona
Fuencarral 29. **Map** 5 A5.
Tel 913 60 46 36.
w **custo-barcelona.com**

Loewe
Calle Serrano 34.
Map 6 E4.
Tel 915 77 60 56.

Magpie
Calle Velarde 3.
Map 2 F1.
Tel 914 48 31 04.

Mango
Calle de Goya 23.
Map 6 E4.
Tel 914 35 40 28.
One of several branches.

Purificacion Garcia
Calle Serrano 28. **Map** 6
E5. **Tel** 914 35 80 13.

Roberto Verino
Calle Serrano 33. **Map** 6
E4. **Tel** 914 26 04 75.

Springfield
Calle Fuencarral 107. **Map**
2 F3. **Tel** 914 47 59 94.
One of several branches.

Zara
Gran Vía 34. **Map** 4 F1.
Tel 915 21 12 83.

Shoes and Leather Goods

Antigua Casa Crespo
C/ del Divino Pastor 29.
Map 2 F4. **Tel** 915 21 56 54.

Bravo
Calle Serrano 42. **Map** 6
E4. **Tel** 914 35 27 29.
One of several branches.

Camper
Calle Fuencarral 42,
Map 5 A5. **Tel** 915 31
23 47. w **camper.es**

Carmina
Calle de Claudio
Coello 73. **Map** 6 E3.
Tel 915 76 40 90.

Cristina Castañer
C/ de Claudio Coello 51
Map 6 E3. **Tel** 915 78 18 90.

Farrutx
Calle de Claudio Coello
22. **Map** 6 E3.
Tel 916 40 20 11.

Malababa
Calle Santa Teresa 5. **Map**
5 B4. **Tel** 912 03 59 51.

Meermin
Calle de Claudio Coello
20. **Map** 6 E5.
Tel 914 31 21 17.

Pretty Ballerinas
Calle de Lagasca 30. **Map**
6 F4. **Tel** 914 31 95 09.

Salvador Bachiller
Gran Vía 65. **Map** 2 D5.
Tel 915 59 83 21.

Jewellery

Andrés Gallardo
Conde de Romanones 5,
Patio. **Tel** 911 56 91 10.
w **andresgallardo.es**

Aristocrazy
Calle Serrano 46.
Map 6 E4.
Tel 914 35 11 38.
w **aristocrazy.com**

Joaquín Berao
Calle Lagasca 44.
Map 6 E5.
Tel 915 77 28 28.

Tous
Calle Serrano 50.
Map 6 E4.
Tel 914 31 92 42.

Uno de 50
Calle Fuencarral 17. **Map**
5 A5. **Tel** 915 23 99 75.

Crafts and Design

El Arco Artesanías
Plaza Mayor 9. **Map** 4 E3.
Tel 913 65 26 80.
w **artesaniaelarco.com**

Cántaro
Calle de la Flor Baja 8.
Map 2 D5.
Tel 915 47 95 14.

El Moderno
La Corredera Baja de
San Pablo 19. **Map** 2 F5.
Tel 913 48 39 94.

PeSeta
Calle Huertas 37. **Map** 7
B3. **Tel** 910 52 59 71.

Books and Music

Booksellers
Calle Fernández de la Hoz
40. **Tel** 914 42 79 59.

Casa del Libro
Gran Vía 29. **Map** 4 F1.
Tel 902 02 64 02.
w **casadellibro.com**

El Flamenco Vive
Calle del Conde de
Lemos 7. **Map** 4 D2.
Tel 915 47 39 17.

FNAC
Calle Preciados 28. **Map** 4
E1. **Tel** 902 10 06 32.
w **fnac.es**

Gaudí
Calle Argensola 13. **Map** 5
C4. **Tel** 913 08 18 29.

Machado
Calle Marqués de Casa
Riera 2. **Map** 7 B2.
Tel 913 10 17 05.

ENTERTAINMENT IN MADRID

As a major European capital, Madrid takes its arts and entertainment very seriously, hosting the finest and most diverse dance, music and theatre productions from around the world. Vibrant art, music and film festivals are held around the year, supplemented by a pulsating nightlife, raucous street parties and lively cafés.

Even traditional art forms, such as flamenco, bullfighting and Madrid's version of the operetta, *zarzuela*, are characterized by flamboyance and spectacle. Football is also a major draw, and Real Madrid is a hugely celebrated team. Between fiestas, flamenco, football and much more, the revelry never stops in Madrid.

Madrid's Teatro Real *(see p326)*

Entertainment Guides

Madrid's entertainment guides are mostly in Spanish. *Guía del Ocio*, a handy weekly guide to what's on in the city, comes out every Thursday and can be bought from kiosks. Three daily newspapers have entertainment supplements on Friday: *El Mundo, ABC* and *El País*.

The English-language monthly, *InMadrid* (www. inmadrid.com), publishes cultural listings and reviews of the latest bars and clubs. It is available in bookshops, record stores and Barajas Airport information office.

Information on forthcoming events can also be obtained from one of the **tourist information offices** in the city, where English will be spoken. The tourist board also publishes *Es Madrid*, a free, bilingual brochure.

Seasons and Tickets

There is always something going on in Madrid's theatres and stadiums, but the cultural season is at its peak from September to June. May's Fiesta de San Isidro, Madrid's patron saint festival, and the Festival de Otoño a Primavera, a music, theatre and dance festival held from October to June, attract many big Spanish and international names. Tickets can be bought from **Entradas.com** or **Ticketea.com**.

In July and August, Madrid hosts Veranos de la Villa (book through tourist offices), a special programme that includes art exhibitions, jazz, opera, flamenco, cinema and drama at various venues.

Tickets for a number of events can be bought at **FNAC** and **El Corte Inglés** stores and websites. Many other reliable internet sites also sell tickets. Check the websites of venues too, since many of them offer online booking services.

Cafés, Bars and Terraces

Madrid's social life revolves around an endless array of cafés, bars and summer terraces.

These venues are perfect places to relax and people-watch. Especially popular areas for *terraceo* (doing the rounds of various terraces) are Plaza de Santa Ana, Paja, Chueca and Dos de Mayo. The glamorous crowd often spend evenings strolling down avenues, such as Paseo de Recoletos and Rosales, stopping now and then to nip into a terrace bar or café.

Madrid has retained many of its old grand cafés. **El Espejo**, a city landmark, is an excellent meeting place with its Art Nouveau ambience. **Café del Círculo de Bellas Artes**, housed in a cultural foundation, is an institution in itself. It is ideal for coffee or lunch after spending a day pursuing cultural interests. Of the literary cafés, the famous **Café Gijón** *(see p295)* should not be missed. For delicious tea and cakes, visit **Mamá Framboise** and **Pomme Sucre** near Alonso Martínez.

In the evening, it is almost essential to head to a *taberna*, where you can order a *ración*,

Elegant Café Gijón, one of Madrid's foremost literary salons

Exterior of the historic Café Gijón

the more substantial version of tapas, and accompany it with a good local wine. Go for a *taberna* crawl and visit the the older and most interesting establishments, such as **Taberna Antonio Sánchez**, which is well-known for its history and the quality of its tapas. **Bodega La Ardosa** is popular with both tourists and locals, and **Taberna Maceiras** is favoured for its Galician wines and other specialities.

Bullfighting

Although bullfighting *(see pp40–41)* remains controversial, it continues to thrive in Madrid. The **Plaza de Toros de las Ventas** is the most important ring in the world, holding *corridas* every Sunday from March to October. In May, during the Fiesta de San Isidro, there are *corridas* every day, with some of the biggest names participating in the spectacle.

The Las Ventas box office is open on Fridays from 10am to 2pm and from 5pm to 7pm. You can also purchase tickets from abroad through the **Taquilla Toros** website, and collect them at the box office up to two hours before the fight.

Football

Madrid is very proud of its team, **Real Madrid** *(see p181)*, and the players are celebrities in Spain. With a capacity of 80,000, their home stadium Santiago Bernabéu is one of the greatest theatres of the game. Tickets can be bought on the phone, or through the team's official website.

For those wishing to visit the stadium, guided tours are conducted on Mondays and Saturdays between 10am and 7pm (10:30am to 6:30pm on Sundays and holidays); on days when there are matches, times vary. Tickets can be bought at the box office and online with no need to book in advance.

Real Madrid's rivals, **Atlético de Madrid**, are based at the Vicente Calderón stadium.

Dance

Madrid's dance scene has come a long way in recent years, with international companies and local talent performing regularly around the city. Madrid is the home of Spain's prestigious Ballet Nacional de España and the more contemporary Compañía Nacional de Danza, for many years directed by the world-famous dancer and choreographer Nacho Duato. Víctor Ullate's Ballet de la Comunidad de Madrid presents a more avantgarde mix of classical and contemporary dance.

A good time to experience Madrid's rich dance tradition is around April, when the annual En Danza festival takes place. Both Spanish and international dancers perform at this time in various theatres and other venues in and around Madrid.

Two major venues hosting dance are the **Teatros del Canal** and the **Teatro Real** (where opera is usually performed). Smaller venues such as **La Casa Encendida** and **Cuarta Pared** present alternative dance performances.

Details can usually be found in the entertainment listings or on the individual venue's website.

Flamenco

Although flamenco originated in Andalucía *(see pp428–9)*, Madrid is often seen as its spiritual home and some of the best flamenco dancers and musicians regularly perform here. The scene is sparklingly vibrant, and interpretations of the art range from the traditional to the daringly innovative, inspired by dancers such as Joaquín Cortés. The big Suma Flamenca festival is held every year in June.

Most *tablaos* (flamenco venues) offer drinks and dinner with the show. Sometimes, however, the show may feature only singing and not the familar rhythmic dancing.

Café de Chinitas and **Corral de la Moreria** are among the older and better tablaos in town, but are somewhat touristy. Also well worth a visit are **La Taberna de Mister Pinkleton** and **Casa Patas**.

Mixed flamenco and pop bars such as **Cardamomo** are full of boisterous young people, but are a fun way of experiencing the sound and feel of flamenco. Two bars that feature regular, spontaneous performances are the atmospheric **Candela** and **Las Tablas**. Note that as these places are frequented by local flamenco aficionados, visitors should be respectful of the art.

Take into account that although bars are fun and a good introduction to the art of flamenco, some of the best dance troupes, singers and players usually perform at the city's theatres.

A male flamenco dancer performing at Casa Patas

Classical Music, Opera and Zarzuela

Madrid's Auditorio Nacional de Música is home to Spain's national orchestra, Orquesta Nacional, as well as its national choir, Coro Nacional de España. With two concert halls, the auditorium also hosts many high-profile performances.

The illustrious **Teatro Real** is best known as the home of the city's opera company. It also houses Orquesta Sinfónica de Madrid, Spain's oldest orchestra with a rich history dating back to more than a century. The magnificent Real is the best place to watch top-class international and national opera performances. Tickets for a show can be bought at a maximum of two weeks in advance by phone or from the website and can be collected at the box office up to half an hour before the show begins.

The **Teatro Monumental** is the main venue for the excellent Orquesta Sinfónica y Coro de RTVE, the orchestra and choir of Spain's state television and radio company. The **Centro Cultural Conde Duque** hosts classical concerts among many other art events. **Fundación Juan March** holds free classical concerts every Saturday morning (book online).

Those who want to experience a Spanish, especially a *madrileño*, take on the operetta, should definitely make time to see a *zarzuela* being performed. The origins of this lively form of musical-drama-cum-social-satire can be traced back to early 17th-century Madrid, and the tradition is still going strong. With both spoken and sung parts as well as dancing, the *zarzuela* can be comic, ribald and even romantic. It is always enjoyable to watch.

The best productions are usually staged at the **Teatro de la Zarzuela**. Other theatres also host *zarzuela* performances occasionally. Check listings for details.

Look our for details on free, outdoor concerts in the papers. The Teatro Real normally opens the opera season with a live transmission of the first show on massive video screens in Plaza de Oriente.

Rock, Jazz and World Music

Madrid's music scene is eclectic and energetic, mixing top international pop stars with independent local bands performing at a variety of venues. Madrid's increasingly multicultural mix has ensured an explosion of Latin American and African sounds recently, as well as interesting fusions of both with more familiar Spanish sounds. In the 1980s, the heady days of *la movida (see p309)* gave birth to Spanish pop, and the momentum continues to this day with Madrid remaining the centre of the country's music scene.

For rock music, **Sala la Riviera**, located next to the Manzanares river, has an excellent and well-deserved reputation. It has hosted major international stars such as Bob Dylan, Patti Smith, the Cranberries and guitarist Joe Satriani, among countless others. **Honky Tonk**, in the Chamberí district, often has performances from local bands, so keep an eye out for posters advertising events, some of which are free.

Siroco has devoted itself to discovering new alternative and indie bands, and also doubles as a club with live music performances.

One of Europe's best jazz clubs, **Café Central**, with its Art Deco elegance, is one place that should not be missed. Also popular is the lively **El Junco** jazz and blues venue.

Musicians from all over the world and of a range of musical genres can be heard at **El Sol**. One of the most important clubs of the Movida Madrileña *(see p309)*, El Sol is the only one that continues to promote the underground style of music of the 1980s.

There are plenty of other well-reputed live-music venues in the city. The best way to keep abreast of the latest events is to check out weekly listings and to keep an eye out for adverts on the street.

Theatre

Madrid has a theatrical tradition that stretches back to the Golden Age of the 17th century, with writers such as Lope de Vega and Calderón de la Barca creating a canon of work that is still performed today.

One of the most prestigious theatres in the city, the **Teatro de la Comedia** is traditionally home to the Compañía Nacional de Teatro Clásico, which stages classic works by Spanish playwrights. Alternatively, take in a repertory performance at **El Pavón Teatro Kamikaze**.

Another one of the most highly regarded theatres is the **Teatro María Guerrero**, which presents Spanish modern drama, as well as foreign plays.

For contemporary and alternative theatre, Madrid has a thriving network of fringe venues such as **Cuarta Pared**. **Teatro Español** also puts on excellent productions.

For musicals, try **Teatro Nuevo Apolo**, **Teatro Lope de Vega** or **Teatro Calderón**. Other venues such as **Teatro la Latina** and **Teatro Muñoz Seca** do comedy productions.

A wide range of Spanish and international theatrical talent take part in the annual Festival de Otoño a Primavera from October to June.

Cinema

Spanish cinema *(see p196)* has earned great international acclaim in recent years. For those with a grasp of the language, Spanish film is a rewarding experience, especially enjoyed at one of the grand film theatres along Gran Vía, such as **Capitol**, which has screened films since the early 1900s.

Non-Spanish movies can be seen in their original-language versions at **Verdi**, **Ideal**, **Golem** and **Renoir**. Screenings will be found listed in newspapers and listings magazines. Note that tickets cost less on the *día del espectador*, which is usually on Mondays or Wednesday.

DIRECTORY

Tourist Offices

Comunidad de Madrid Tourist Office
Calle Duque de Medinacelli 2. **Map** 7 B3.
Tel 914 29 49 51.

Municipal Tourist Office
Pl Mayor 27. **Map** 4 E3.
Tel 914 54 44 10.

Tickets

El Corte Inglés
Tel 902 40 02 22.
w elcorteingles.com

Entradas.com
Tel 902 48 84 88.

FNAC
Tel 902 10 06 32.
w fnac.es

Ticketea
w ticketea.com

Cafés, Bars and Terraces

Bodega La Ardosa
Calle Colón 13. **Map** 5 A5.
Tel 915 21 49 79.

Café del Círculo de Bellas Artes
Calle Alcalá 42. **Map** 7 B2.
Tel 677 45 84 48.

Café Gijón
Paseo de Recoletos 21.
Map 7 C1.
Tel 915 21 54 25.

El Espejo
Paseo Recoletos 31. **Map** 6 D5. **Tel** 913 08 23 47.

Mamá Framboise
Calle de Fernando VI 23.
Map 5 B5.
Tel 913 91 43 64.

Pomme Sucre
Calle Barquillo 49. **Map** 5 B5. **Tel** 913 08 31 85.

Taberna Antonio Sánchez
Calle de Mesón de Paredes 13. **Map** 4 F5.
Tel 915 39 78 26.

Taberna Maceiras
Calle Huertas 66. **Map** 7 B3. **Tel** 914 29 58 18.

Bullfighting

Taquilla Toros
w taquillatoros.com

Las Ventas
Calle Alcalá 237.
Tel 913 56 22 00.
w las-ventas.com

Football

Atlético de Madrid
Estadio Vicente Calderón, Paseo de la Virgen del Puerto 67.
Tel 902 26 04 03.
w atleticodemadrid.com

Real Madrid
Estadio Santiago Bernabéu, Calle Concha Espina 1. **Tel** 913 98 43 00.
w realmadrid.com

Dance

La Casa Encendida
Ronda de Valencia 2.
Tel 902 43 03 22.

Teatros del Canal
Calle Cea Bermúdez 1.
Map 3 B1.
Tel 913 08 99 99.

Flamenco

Café de Chinitas
Calle Torija 7. **Map** 4 D1.
Tel 915 47 15 02.

Candela
Calle Olmo 2. **Map** 7 A4.
Tel 914 67 33 82.

Cardamomo
Calle Echegaray 15. **Map** 7 A2. **Tel** 918 05 10 38.

Casa Patas
Calle Cañizares 10. **Map** 7 A3. **Tel** 913 69 04 96.

Corral de la Morería
Calle de la Morería 17.
Map 3 C3.
Tel 913 65 11 37.

La Taberna de Mister Pinkleton
Calle de los Cuchilleros 7.
Map 4 E3. **Tel** 913 64 02 63. w latabernade misterpinkleton.com

Las Tablas
Plaza de España 9. **Map** 1 C5. **Tel** 915 42 05 20.

Classical Music Opera and Zarzuela

Auditorio Nacional de Música
Calle del Príncipe de Vergara 146.
Tel 913 37 01 40.
w auditorionacional. mcu.es

Centro Cultural Conde Duque
Calle del Conde Duque 11. **Map** 2 D4.
Tel 913 18 47 00.

Fundación Juan March
Calle de Castelló 77.
Tel 914 35 42 40.
w march.es

Teatro Calderón
Calle Atocha 18. **Map** 4 F3. **Tel** 914 29 40 85.

Teatro de la Zarzuela
Calle de los Jovellanos 4.
Map 7 B2. **Tel** 915 24 54 00. w teatrodela zarzuela.mcu.es

Teatro Monumental
Calle Atocha 65. **Map** 7 A3. **Tel** 914 29 12 81.

Teatro Real
Plaza de Isabel II. **Map** 4 D2. **Tel** 902 24 48 48.
w teatro-real.com

Rock, Jazz and World Music

Café Central
Plaza del Ángel 10. **Map** 7 A3. **Tel** 913 69 41 43.
w cafecentral madrid.com

Honky Tonk
Calle de Covarrubias 24.
Map 5 B3.
Tel 914 45 61 91.

El Junco
Plaza Santa Barbara 10.
Map 5 B4.
w en.eljunco.com

Sala La Riviera
Paseo Virgen del Puerto s/n. **Tel** 913 65 24 15.

Siroco
Calle de San Dimas 3.
Map 2 E4.
Tel 915 93 30 70.

El Sol

Calle Jardínes 3. **Map** 7 A1. **Tel** 915 32 64 90.
w salaelsol.com

Theatre

Cuarta Pared
Calle del Ercilla 17.
Tel 915 17 23 17.
w cuartapared.es

El Pavón Teatro Kamikaze
Calle de Embajadores 9.
Map 4 E4.
Tel 910 51 33 31.

Teatro de la Comedia
Calle del Príncipe 14. **Map** 7 A2. **Tel** 915 21 49 31.

Teatro Español
Calle Príncipe 25. **Map** 7 A2. **Tel** 913 60 14 84.

Teatro la Latina
Pl de la Cebada 2. **Map** 4 D4. **Tel** 913 65 28 35.

Teatro Lope de Vega
Gran Vía 57. **Map** 4 E1.
Tel 915 47 20 11.

Teatro María Guerrero
Calle de Tamayo y Baus 4.
Map 5 C5.
Tel 913 10 29 49.

Teatro Muñoz Seca
Plaza del Carmen 1. **Map** 4 F1 **Tel** 915 23 21 28.

Teatro Nuevo Apolo
Pl Tirso de Molina 1. **Map** 4 F3. **Tel** 913 69 06 37.

Cinema

Capitol
Gran Vía 41. **Map** 4 E1.
Tel 915 22 22 29.

Golem
Calle de Martín de los Heros 14. **Map** 1 A1.
Tel 915 59 38 36.

Ideal
C/ del Doctor Cortezo 6.
Map 4 F3. **Tel** 913 69 10 53.

Renoir
Calle de Martín de los Heros 12. **Map** 1 C5.
Tel 915 42 27 02.

Verdi
Calle Bravo Murillo 28.
Tel 914 47 39 30.

Nightlife

Madrid's reputation as the city that never sleeps persists, despite political measures for earlier closing times. In fact, people from Madrid are known as *gatos* (cats) around Spain because of their nocturnal habits. The best nightlife is concentrated around specific districts, each with its own unique atmosphere and a wealth of places for people to get down to one of Madrid's best talents: *la marcha* (partying). Things hot up first in the Huertas area, moving on to Malasaña, Bilbao, Lavapiés and Chueca into the early hours of the morning. You don't need to go to a club for dancing as *madrileños* also dance to DJs and live music in smaller clubs, called *pubs* – all sorts of musical tastes are catered to more than amply *(see p326)*. Expect to find places crowded from Thursday to Sunday. Also prepare for late nights because things don't get going for *gatos* until midnight.

Santa Ana and Huertas

With many tapas bars, cafés and terraces, the Huertas area is the perfect place to begin preparing for the wild night ahead. The atmosphere is made by the crowd, which is a heady amalgam of ages, looks and origins. If you want to stay in one area, this is a good choice.

There are several little bars overlooking the lively Plaza de Santa Ana. Pop into any one of them to begin the night. **Viva Madrid** attracts a vivacious crowd of locals and foreigners. **Cardamomo**, a famous club, is a mandatory stop for any bar crawl. There is live flamenco at least once a week.

For late-night dancing, try the house DJs at **Joy Madrid Discoteque**. Near Atocha, you will find the spectacular seven-floor **Kapital**, which features every kind of music, and a rooftop bar that allows drinkers to gaze at the starlit sky. **Sol y Sombra** is a posh nightclub, so dress to impress the bouncers, and you can get your groove on to live soul and R&B.

It is a local tradition to end the night with hot chocolate and *churros* (dough sticks) in one of the cafés around Plaza del Sol. The **Chocolatería San Ginés** is a great place for chocolate gorging: it's open 24 hours.

If the chocolate fix leaves you buzzing, check out **Independance Club**, which plays indie and pop rock on Friday and Saturday nights, taking the straight/gay mix of clubbers through to 6am the next day.

Alonso Martínez and Bilbao

This is one of the city's most animated areas. You will find hundreds of great haunts that play music ranging from R&B to Spanish pop.

To begin with, try some of the local bars around Plaza de Santa Bárbara, such as the **Cervecería Santa Bárbara**, the perfect place to start the night with a *caña* (beer). Later on (if you can get past the queues), try the glamorous club **Alegoría**, with its eclectic decor and pop music, where you can dance until late with the beautiful people, or **El Junco**, a dance and concert venue with the best jazz, funk and soul music in the capital. Alternatively, you can head for **Teatro Barceló**, formerly known as Pacha, one of Madrid's most famous discotheques. There are also plenty of live-music venues around, such as **Clamores**, one of Madrid's many temples of jazz music. However, note that areas such as Huertas are more active during weekdays.

Argüelles and Moncloa

This area is a favourite haunt of students, thanks to its proximity to the halls of residence of one of Madrid's major universities.

The "basements of Argüelles" are huge double-storeyed patios with several bars and discotheques. The atmosphere is fresh and young.

Another popular district is Moncloa, which has a more mature crowd, as well as several places where you can listen to local Spanish pop and dance tunes, such as nightclub **Lasal**, which is also a venue for concerts.

Chueca

The Chueca district dominates Madrid's gay scene. As well as having a large resident gay community, there are plenty of trendy late-night bars and clubs where gays and non-gays party together. In fact, what sets Chueca apart from other gay neighbourhoods in the world is the *mezcla*, the tolerant gay/straight mix.

The heart of the area is the Plaza de Chueca, packed with crowds visiting the terraces in the summer. Close by are mixed bars such as **Acuarela**, with its camp, religious-artifact decor. The Gay Pride Week in late June or July focuses around this area, though there are also plenty of well-established gay bars elsewhere in the city.

Malasaña

Malasaña was the centre of *la movida* in the Madrid of the 1980s *(see p309)*, and still has an alternative flavour that attracts many young bohemian types. The hub of this cosmopolitan district is the Dos de Mayo square, where you can have a *caña* on the terrace of the **El 2D** bar. However, the characteristic atmosphere of the area is changing rapidly into a more design-driven space. Some examples are the **La Huida**, **El Circo de las Tapas** and **Kike Keller** bars, which have cultivated a revolutionary, arty atmosphere. **Bar & Co** is a typical Malasaña venue, where local bands play weekly. You can relax there after 3am if you don't feel like clubbing.

Tupperware, a fusion of past and present, is a rock bar with an ultra pop decor, where you can also listen to garage, indie and pop music.

Lavapiés

Once the Jewish quarter of Madrid, the narrow streets of Lavapiés are rich with an eclectic mix of races and cultures. One of the most fascinating and diverse districts in town, the locals' old habit of sitting outside their doors on summer nights continues, as does the multiracial crowd on the terraces of Calle de Argumosa. A vibrant fusion of artists, immigrants, hipsters and squatters results in some of the most brilliant music, art, food, alternative theatre and nightlife in the city.

La Escalera de Jacob and **La Victoria** hold concerts, theatre performances and intercultural workshops. The endearingly eccentric bar **El Gato Verde** offers exhibitions and, on occasion, live music.

La Latina

Still the best district in town for cosy little hideaways and tapas bars, La Latina is an especially good place to go on Sundays after wandering around the Rastro flea market *(see p306)*. For an excellent cocktail, or coffee and cake in the morning, head to **Delic**, and for a cultural experience try **Anti Café**, where you can listen to unique DJs, poetry and drama. For a taste of the traditional, visit **Taberna Almendro 13**, a classic from before La Latina became a fashionable nightlife area. Another worthwhile bar is **Taberna del Tempranillo**, which also serves a variety of Spanish wines, cheeses and ham. In the exquisite **María Pandora** bar, you can try a selection of champagnes and *cavas*, surrounded by books and antiques. Afterwards, you can dance until late at **Berlín Cabaret**, a modern nightclub that runs a 1930s cabaret every night.

Azca

With a skyline punctuated by the highest buildings, this is one of the most modern areas in town. Near the Paseo de la Castellana and the Santiago Bernabéu stadium, this financial district has a multitude of clubs and bars doing brisk business in basements.

If visitors feel the urge to dance, Avenida de Brasil is the stretch to head for, full of large clubs, though they tend to be a little overcrowded.

Nearby, in the Chamartín area, you will find another hardcore clubbing scene, which vibrantly unfolds late at night.

DIRECTORY

Nightlife Venues

El 2D
Calle Velarde 24.
Map 2 F4.
Tel 914 48 64 72.

Acuarela
Calle Gravina 10.
Map 5 B5.
Tel 915 22 21 43.

Alegoría
Calle Villanueva 2.
Map 6 D5.
Tel 915 77 27 85.

Anti Café
Calle Unión 2.
Map 4 D2.
Tel 915 41 76 57.

Bar & Co
Calle Barco 34.
Map 2 F5. **Tel** 915 31 77 54.

Berlín Cabaret
Costanilla de San Pedro 11.
Tel 913 66 20 34.

Cardamomo
Calle De Echegaray 15.
Map 7 A3.
Tel 918 05 10 38.

Cervecería Santa Bárbara
Plaza Santa Bárbara 8.
Tel 913 19 04 49.

Chocolatería San Ginés
Pasadizo de San Ginés,
Calle Arenal 11.
Map 4 E2.
Tel 913 65 65 46.

Clamores
Calle Alburquerque 14.
Map 5 A3.
Tel 914 45 54 80.

Circo
Calle Corredera Baja de San Pablo 21.
Map 2 F5.

Delic
Plaza De La Paja s/n.
Map 4 D3.
Tel 913 64 54 50.

La Escalera de Jacob
Calle de Lavapíes 11.
Map 4 F4.
Tel 625 72 17 45.

El Gato Verde
Calle Torrecilla del Leál 15.
Map 7 A4.
Tel 693 82 98 97.

La Huida
Calle Colón 11. **Map** 5 A5.
Tel 600 87 05 09.

Independance Club
Plaza de Callao 4. **Map** 4
F1. W **independance club.com**

Joy Madrid Discoteque
Calle Arenal 11. **Map** 4 E2.
Tel 913 66 54 39.

El Junco
Plaza de Santa Bárbara 10.
Map 5 B4.
Tel 913 19 20 81.

Kapital
Calle Atocha 125. **Map** 7
C4. **Tel** 914 20 29 06.

Kike Keller
Calle Corredera Baja de San Pablo 17.
Tel 915 22 87 67.
Map 2 F5.

Lasal
Calle Guzmán el Bueno 98. **Tel** 686 41 09 90.

María Pandora
Plaza Gabriel Miró 1.
Map 3 B3.
Tel 910 42 82 13.

Sol y Sombra
Calle de Echegaray 18.
Map 7 A3.
Tel 619 23 58 02.

Taberna Almendro 13
Calle Almendro 13.
Map 4 D3.
Tel 913 65 42 52.

Taberna del Tempranillo
Calle de la Cava Baja 38.
Tel 913 64 15 32.

Teatro Barceló
Calle de Barceló 11.
Map 5 A4.
Tel 914 47 01 28.

Tupperware
Calle Corredera Alta de San Pablo 26.
Tel 625 52 35 61.

La Victoria
Calle Santa Isabel 40.
Map 7 B4.
Tel 915 28 64 57.

Viva Madrid
Calle Manuel Fernández González 7.
Tel 914 20 35 96.

MADRID PROVINCE

Madrid province (the Comunidad de Madrid) sits high on Spain's central plateau. There is plenty of superb scenery and good walking country in the sierras to the north, which are a refuge for city dwellers who go there to ski in winter or cool down during the torrid summers. In the western foothills of these mountains stands El Escorial, the royal palace-cum-monastery built by Felipe II, from which he ruled his empire.

Close by is the Valle de los Caídos, the war monument erected by Franco. The smaller royal palace of El Pardo is on the outskirts of Madrid, and south of the city is the 18th-century summer palace of Aranjuez, set in lush parkland. Historic towns include Alcalá de Henares, which has a Renaissance university building, and Chinchón, where taverns cluster around a picturesque arcaded market square.

Sights at a Glance

Towns and Cities
2 Buitrago del Lozoya
7 Manzanares el Real
9 Alcalá de Henares
10 Chinchón

Historic Buildings
3 Monasterio de Santa María de El Paular
5 Santa Cruz del Valle de los Caídos
6 *El Escorial pp334–5*
8 Palacio de El Pardo
11 Palacio Real de Aranjuez

Mountain Ranges
1 Sierra Norte
4 Sierra Centro de Guadarrama

Key
- Madrid city
- Madrid province
- Motorway
- Major road
- Minor road

0 kilometres 25

0 miles 20

Sights in Madrid Province

The village of Montejo de la Sierra in the Sierra Norte

❶ Sierra Norte

Madrid. 🚌 Montejo de la Sierra.
ℹ Calle Real 64, Montejo, 91 869
70 58. 🌐 sierradelrincon.org

The black slate hamlets of the Sierra Norte, which were once known as the Sierra Pobre (Poor Sierra), are located in the most attractively rural part of Madrid province.

At Montejo de la Sierra, the largest village in the area, an information centre organizes riding, the rental of traditional houses *(see p559)*, and visits to the nearby nature reserve of the Hayedo de Montejo de la Sierra. This is one of the most southern beech woods *(see p84)* in Europe, and a relic of a previous era, when climatic conditions here were more suitable for the beech. From Montejo, you can drive on to picturesque hamlets such as La Hiruela or Puebla de la Sierra, both in lovely walking country.

The drier southern hills slope down to the Embalse de Puentes Viejas, a reservoir where summer chalets cluster around artificial beaches. On the eastern edge

of the sierra is the village of Patones, which is thought to have escaped invasion by the Moors and Napoleon's troops because of its isolated location.

❷ Buitrago del Lozoya

Madrid. 👥 2,000. 🚌 ℹ Calle Tahona 19, 91 868 16 15. **Open** Castle: 10am–1pm & 4–6pm Tue–Fri, 10am–2pm Sat–Sun, 4–7pm Sat. 🛒 Sat. 🎉 La Asunción and San Roque (15–16 Aug), Cristo de los Esclavos (14–15 Sep).

Picturesquely sited above a meander in the Río Lozoya is the walled town of Buitrago del Lozoya. Founded by the Romans, it was fortified by the Arabs, and became an important market town in medieval times. The 14th-century Gothic-Mudéjar castle is in ruins, although the gatehouse, arches and stretches of the original Arab wall have survived. The castle is open to the public.

The town walls retain a charming atmosphere and can be visited for a fee.

The church of Santa María del Castillo, dating from the 14th–15th century, has a Mudéjar tower and ceilings which were moved here from the old hospital. The town hall *(ayuntamiento)*, in the newer part of Buitrago, preserves a 16th-century processional cross. In the basement is the Museo Picasso. The prints, drawings and ceramics were collected by the artist's friend, Eugenio Arias.

🏛 **Museo Picasso**
Plaza de Picasso 1. **Tel** 91 868 00 56. **Closed** Mon, Sun pm. 🌐 madrid. org/museopicasso

Altarpiece in the Monasterio de Santa María de El Paular

❸ Monasterio de Santa María de El Paular

Southwest of Rascafría on M604. **Tel** 918 69 19 58. 🚌 Rascafría. **Open** 11am–1:30pm & 4–7pm daily (Nov–mid-Apr: to 6pm). 📷 obligatory. **Closed** some public hols. 🌐 monasteriopaular.com

Founded in 1390 as Castile's first Carthusian monastery, Santa María de El Paular stands on the site of a medieval royal hunting lodge. Although it is mainly Gothic in style, Plateresque and Renaissance features were added later. The monastery was abandoned in 1836, when government minister Mendizábal ordered the sale of church goods *(see p67)*. It fell into disrepair until its restoration in the 1950s. Today the complex comprises a working Benedictine monastery church and private hotel.

The church's delicate alabaster altarpiece, attributed to Flemish

Buitrago del Lozoya, standing next to the river

craftsmen, dates from the 15th century. Its panels depict scenes from the life of Jesus. The lavish Baroque *camarín* (chamber), behind the altar, was designed by Francisco de Hurtado in 1718. The cloister has impressive paintings by Vicente Carducho.

Every Sunday, the monks sing an hour-long Gregorian chant. If they are not busy, they will show you the cloister's Mudéjar brick vaulting and double sun-clock.

The monastery is a good starting point for exploring the towns of Rascafría and Lozoya. To the southwest is the nature reserve Lagunas de Peñalara.

❹ Sierra Centro de Guadarrama

Madrid. 🚉 Puerto de Navacerrada, Cercedilla. 🚌 Navacerrada, Cercedilla. 🛈 Cuartel 1, Navacerrada, Cercedilla, 918 42 85 04.
Ⓦ sierraguadarrama.info

The central section of the Sierra de Guadarrama was little visited until the 1920s, when the area was linked by train to Madrid. Today, the granite slopes are planted with pines and specked by holiday chalets. Villages such as Navacerrada and Cercedilla have grown into popular resorts for skiing, mountain biking, rock climbing and horse riding. Walkers wanting to enjoy the mountain air can follow marked routes from Navacerrada.

The Valle de la Fuenfría, a nature reserve of wild forests, is best reached via Cercedilla. It has a well-preserved stretch of the original Roman road, as well as several picnic spots and marked walking routes.

The gigantic cross at Valle de los Caídos

❺ Santa Cruz del Valle de los Caídos

North of El Escorial on M600.
Tel 91 890 54 11. 🚌 from El Escorial.
Open Crypt: 10am–6pm Tue–Sun; (Apr–Sep: 10am–7pm). **Closed** some pub hols. 🎫 (free from 3pm Wed & Thu for EU citizens; from 4pm Apr–Sep).

General Franco had the Holy Cross of the Valley of the Fallen built as a memorial to those who died in the Civil War

(see pp70–71). The vast cross is located some 13 km (8 miles) north of El Escorial (see pp334–5), and dominates the surrounding countryside. Some Spanish people find it too chilling a symbol of the dictatorship to be enjoyable, while for others its sheer size is rewarding.

The cross is 150 m (490 ft) high and rises above a basilica carved 250 m (820 ft) deep into the rock by prisoners. A number of them died during the 20-year-plus project. Access to the cross is currently closed to visitors for safety reasons.

Next to the basilica's high altar is the plain white tombstone of Franco, and, opposite, that of José Antonio Primo de Rivera, founder of the Falange Española Party. A further 40,000 coffins of soldiers from both sides in the Civil War lie here out of sight, including those of two unidentified victims.

Navacerrada pass in the Sierra de Guadarrama

o El Escorial

Felipe II's imposing grey palace of San Lorenzo de El Escorial stands out against the foothills of the Sierra de Guadarrama to the northwest of Madrid. It was built between 1563 and 1584 in honour of St Lawrence, and its unornamented severity set a new architectural style, known as Herreriano, which became one of the most influential in Spain. The interior was conceived as a mausoleum and contemplative retreat rather than a splendid residence. Its artistic wealth, which includes some of the most important works of art of the royal Habsburg collections, is concentrated in the museums, chapterhouses, church, royal pantheon and library. In contrast, the royal apartments are sober, with incongruous interiors.

★ **Royal Pantheon**
The funerary urns of Spanish monarchs line the marble mausoleum.

KEY

① **Patio de los Reyes**

② **The Alfonso XII College** was founded by monks in 1875 as a boarding school.

③ **Bourbon Palace**

④ **Architectural Museum**

⑤ **Sala de Batallas**

⑥ **The Basílica's altarpiece** is the highlight of this huge decorated church. The chapel houses a superb marble sculpture of the Crucifixion by Cellini.

⑦ **The Royal Apartments**, on the second floor of the palace, consist of Felipe II's modestly decorated living quarters. His bedroom opens directly onto the high altar of the basilica.

⑧ **The Patio de los Evangelistas** is a temple by Herrera. The Jardín de los Frailes makes a nice walk.

⑨ **The Monastery** was founded in 1567, and has been run by Augustinian monks since 1885.

Main entrance

Entrance to Basílica only

★ **Library**
This impressive array of 40,000 books incorporates Felipe II's personal collection. On display are precious manuscripts, including a poem by Alfonso X the Learned. The 16th-century ceiling frescoes are by Tibaldi.

★ Museum of Art
One of the highlights here is *The Calvary*, by 15th-century Flemish artist Rogier van der Weyden, which has been restored by the Prado museum.

The Glory of the Spanish Monarchy by Luca Giordano
This beautiful fresco, above the main staircase, depicts Charles V and Felipe II, and scenes of the building of the monastery.

Chapterhouses
On display here is Charles V's portable altar. The ceiling frescoes depict monarchs and angels.

The Building of El Escorial
When chief architect Juan Bautista de Toledo died in 1567, he was replaced by Juan de Herrera, royal inspector of monuments. The plain architectural style of El Escorial is called *desornamentado*, literally, "unadorned".

Climber resting on a rock face of La Pedriza, near Manzanares el Real

❼ Manzanares el Real

Madrid. 🚊 7,200. 🚌 ℹ️ Calle del Cura, 918 53 00 09. 🏛 Tue & Fri. 🎉 Fiesta de Verano (early Aug), Cristo de la Nave (14 Sep). 🌐 manzanareselreal.org

The skyline of Manzanares el Real is dominated by its restored 15th-century castle. Although the castle has some traditionally military features, such as double machicolations and turrets, it was used mainly as a residence by the Dukes of Infantado. Below the castle is a 16th-century church, a Renaissance portico and fine capitals. Behind the town, bordering the foothills of the Sierra de Guadarrama, is La Pedriza, a mass of granite screes and ravines, very popular with climbers. It now forms part of an attractive nature reserve.

Environs
Colmenar Viejo, 12 km (7.5 miles) southeast of Manzanares, has a Gothic-Mudéjar church.

❽ Palacio de El Pardo

El Pardo, northwest of Madrid off the A6. **Tel** 91 376 15 00. 🚌 601 from Moncloa. **Open** Oct–Mar: 10am–6pm daily; Apr–Sep: 10am–8pm daily **Closed** for royal visits & public hols. 🎟 (free from 3pm Wed & Thu for EU residents; from 5pm Apr–Sep). 🌐 patrimonionacional.es

This royal hunting lodge and palace, set in parkland just outside Madrid's city limits, lists General Franco among its former residents. A tour takes visitors round the moated palace's Habsburg wing and the identical 18th-century extension, designed by Francesco Sabatini. The Bourbon interior is heavy with frescoes, gilt mouldings and tapestries, many made to designs by Goya (see p310). Today the palace hosts visiting heads of state and royal guests. Surrounding the palace and the 18th-century village of El Pardo is a vast forest of holm oak. The area is popular for picnicking, and game animals still run free.

Façade of Colegio de San Ildefonso in Alcalá de Henares

❾ Alcalá de Henares

Madrid. 🚊 204,000. 🚃 🚌 ℹ️ Plaza de los Santos Niños s/n, 918 81 06 34. 🏛 Mon, Wed. 🎉 Feria de Alcalá (late Aug). 🎫 weekend city tours. 🌐 turismoalcala.es

At the heart of a modern industrial town is one of Spain's most renowned university quarters. Founded in 1499 by

Lavish 18th-century tapestry inside the Palacio de El Pardo

Cardinal Cisneros, Alcalá's university became one of the foremost places of learning in 16th-century Europe. The most historic college, San Ildefonso, survives. Former students include Golden Age playwright Lope de Vega (see p294). In 1517 the university produced Europe's first polyglot bible, with text in Latin, Greek, Hebrew and Chaldean.

Alcalá's other sights are the cathedral, the **Casa-Museo de Cervantes**, birthplace of the Golden Age author, and the restored 19th-century neo-Moorish Palacio de Laredo.

🏛 **Casa-Museo de Cervantes**
Calle Mayor 48. **Tel** 91 889 96 54. **Open** 10am–6pm Tue–Sun. **Closed** some public hols.

❿ Chinchón

Madrid. 🚗 5,300. 🚌 ℹ Plaza Mayor 6, 91 893 53 23. 🛍 Sat. 🎉 Semana Santa (Easter Week), San Roque (12–18 Aug). 🚗 🌐 ciudad-chinchon.com

Chinchón is arguably Madrid province's most picturesque town. The 15th- to 16th-century, typically Castilian, porticoed Plaza Mayor has a splendidly theatrical air. It comes alive for the Easter passion play, acted out by the townspeople (see p294), and during the August bullfights. The 16th-century church, perched above the square, has an altar painting by Goya, whose brother was a priest here. Just off the square is the 18th-century Augustinian

Chinchón's unique porticoed Plaza Mayor

monastery, which has been converted into a parador with a peaceful patio garden. A ruined 15th-century castle is on a hill to the west of town. Although it is closed to the public, there are views of Chinchón and the countryside from outside it.

Chinchón is a popular weekend destination for madrileños, who come here to sample the excellent chorizo and locally produced anís (see p581) in the town's many taverns.

⓫ Palacio Real de Aranjuez

Plaza de Parejas, Aranjuez. **Tel** 91 891 07 40. 🚉 🚌 **Open** Tue–Sun. **Closed** some public hols. 🎫 (free from 3pm Wed & Thu for EU residents; from 5pm Apr–Sep). 🚹 🚗 🌐 patrimonio nacional.es

The Royal Summer Palace and Gardens of Aranjuez grew up around a medieval hunting lodge standing beside a natural weir, the meeting point of the Tagus and Jarama rivers.

Today's palace of brick and white stone was built in the 18th century and later redecorated by the Bourbons. A guided tour takes you through numerous Baroque rooms, among them the Chinese Porcelain Room, the Hall of Mirrors and the Smoking Room, modelled on the Alhambra in Granada. It is worth visiting Aranjuez to walk in the 3 sq km (1 sq mile) of shady royal gardens which inspired Joaquín Rodrigo's Concierto de Aranjuez. The Parterre Garden and the Island Garden survive from the original 16th-century palace.

Between the palace and the River Tagus is the 18th-century Prince's Garden, decorated with sculptures, fountains and lofty trees from the Americas. In the garden is the Casa de Marinos (Sailors' House), a museum housing the launches once used by the royal family for trips along the river. At the far end of the garden is the Casa del Labrador (Labourer's Cottage), a decorative royal pavilion built by Carlos IV.

The town's restaurants are popular for the exceptional quality of their asparagus and strawberries. In summer, a 19th-century steam train, built to carry strawberries, runs between here and the capital.

Miguel de Cervantes

Miguel de Cervantes Saavedra, Spain's greatest literary figure (see p38), was born in Alcalá de Henares in 1547. After fighting in the naval Battle of Lepanto (1571), he was held captive by the Turks for more than five years. In 1605, when he was almost 60 years old, the first of two parts of his comic masterpiece Don Quixote (see p399) was published to popular acclaim. He continued writing novels and plays until his death in Madrid on 23 April 1616, the same date that Shakespeare died.

Gardens surrounding the Royal Palace at Aranjuez

CENTRAL SPAIN

Introducing Central Spain

Much of Spain's vast central plateau, the *meseta*, is covered with wheat fields or dry, dusty plains, but there are many attractive places to explore. Central Spain's mountains, gorges, forests and lakes are filled with wildlife. A deep sense of history permeates the towns and cities of the tableland, reflected in some stunning architecture: the Roman ruins of Mérida, the medieval mansions of Cáceres, the Gothic cathedrals of Burgos, León and Toledo, the Renaissance grandeur of Salamanca, and castles almost everywhere.

León Cathedral *(see pp358–9)*, an outstanding Gothic building, was completed during the 14th century. As well as many glorious windows of medieval glass, it has superb carved choir stalls depicting biblical scenes and everyday life.

Salamanca *(see pp362–5)* is the site of some of the finest Renaissance and Plateresque architecture in Spain. Among the city's most notable buildings are the university, its façade a mass of carved detail; the old and new cathedrals (built side by side); and the handsome Plaza Mayor, built in warm golden sandstone.

Museo Nacional de Arte Romano in Mérida *(see pp414–15)* houses Roman treasures. The city has a well-preserved Roman theatre still in use.

Cistier

Ponferrada

León

S

Astorga

CASTILLA Y LE
(See pp350–81)

Puebla de Sanabria

Benavente

Zamora

Tordes

Salamanca

Ciudad Rodrigo

Béjar

Plasencia

Ta de l

Navalmoral de la Mata

Cáceres

Trujillo

EXTREMADURA
(See pp404–17)

Herrera Du

Badajoz

Mérida

Zafra

Llerena

0 kilometres   50

0 miles   50

◀ Historic city of Toledo, Castilla-La Mancha

Burgos Cathedral *(see pp376–7)* is the work of some of the great medieval architects and artists, and it is full of treasures from all periods. This Baroque fresco of the coronation of the Virgin covers the domed ceiling of the sacristy.

Segovia *(see pp368–9)* extends along a rocky spur that divides two rivers. The city's landmarks are the Alcázar *(see pp348–9)* – a castle with distinctive fairy-tale towers – and the Roman aqueduct, built in the 1st century AD, which towers 29 m (95 ft) above a busy urban square.

Oña

Burgos

lencia

Peñafiel
d

Aranda de
Duero

Soria

Medinaceli
Sigüenza
Maranchón

Segovia

MADRID   Guadalajara

Madrid

Getafe

Cañaveras

Aranjuez

Tarancón   Cuenca

Toledo

CASTILLA-LA MANCHA
(See pp382–403)
Alarcón

Consuegra   San Clemente

Tormelloso

udad
Real   Manzanares   Albacete

Almagro

Valdepeñas

Puertollano

Hellín

Cuenca's Old Town *(see pp388–9)* was built on a ridge high above two gorges. One of the picturesque but precariously sited "Hanging Houses" is now home to a museum of abstract art.

Toledo Cathedral
(see pp396–7), with its exuberant sculptured decoration, is a great medieval building in a city of monuments. Toledo's architectural wealth stems from a fusion of Jewish, Christian and Muslim cultures.

The Flavours of Central Spain

Madrid is famous for its extremes of temperature – a climate that has given rise to the rueful local saying "nine months of winter and three months of hell". The surrounding regions suffer the same extremes, and their traditional cuisines reflect both the wintry cold and the dusty, scorched terrain. Meat predominates as roasts and stews and in warming soups, thickened with beans and pulses, which thrive despite the weather. Cured hams, spicy sausages and pungent cheeses are excellent accompaniments to the strong local wine. The finest ham is from Extremadura, where black-footed (*pata negra*) pigs forage freely among the oaks.

Manchego cheese

A chef preparing *gambas al ajillo*, a popular tapas dish

Madrid

Restaurants in Madrid, as befits the Spanish capital, offer cuisine from every corner of the country. Curiously, considering its distance from the ocean, the capital is famed for its seafood, flown in freshly every day. *Madrileños* appreciate every part of an animal,

particularly when it comes to pork, and Madrid menus may feature brains, ears, pigs' trotters, and *callos a la madrileña* (tripe) is a classic local dish. Sturdy stews, such as the celebrated *cocido madrileño*, keep out the bitter winter cold. The *tapeo* – a bar crawl between tapas bars – is an institution in the city, and each bar has its own speciality dish.

Castilla y Leon

Spread out high on a plain, searingly hot in summer, and bitingly cold in winter, Castilla y León is famous for its roasted meats, served in *asadores* (grillhouses). The most celebrated local dish is *cochinillo* (suckling pig), but pork, chicken, game in season and lamb are also popular. These are often combined with local pulses and lentils in hearty

Beans and pulses, key ingredients in the cooking of Central Spain

Pinto beans — White (butter) beans — Castillian garbanzos (chickpeas) — Red (kidney beans) — Black beans — Armuña lent[il] —

Regional Dishes and Specialities

The cuisine of Spain's often wild and remote interior is characterized by warming soups and stews; traditionally made hams, cured meats and cheeses; plenty of filling beans and pulses; and flavourful fruit and vegetables. On the high plains of Castilla y León, locals keep out the winter cold with succulent roasted meats, and Extremaduran ham is the best you'll taste. In Don Quixote country, a glass of robust local wine and a chunk of Manchegan cheese is sheer delight. Fancy restaurants with fashionable food are few and far between, but welcoming, old-fashioned inns offer simple and tasty home cooking. Madrid, of course, is the exception: here you'll find every possible cuisine, along with excellent seafood, which is harder to find anywhere else in this landlocked region.

Fresh figs

Cocido Madrileño This rich stew is traditionally eaten in stages: first the broth, then vegetables and finally the meat.

Plucking the stamens from crocus flowers to make saffron

soups and stews, which are given extra flavour with local *embutidos* (cured meats). The region also produces delicious cheeses such as soft Burgos, often served with honey, *membrillo* (quince jelly) or nuts for dessert. Local wines are robust and simple, a good accompaniment to the strong flavours of the regional cuisine of Castilla y León.

Castilla-La Mancha

This is Don Quixote country: empty, flat, dusty and scattered with windmills. Local inns and taverns serve traditional country cooking, with plenty of hearty soups, substantial casseroles and simply grilled local meat, poultry and seasonal game. Manchegan *gazpacho*, unlike its cold, vegetable-soup *andaluz* namesake, is a hefty stew made with whatever meat is available. A common accompaniment to it is *pisto*,

a ratatouille-like dish made with a range of tasty, fresh local vegetables. The Arabs brought with them saffron, which is still grown around Consuegra, and their influence also lingers on in Toledo's famous marzipan sweets and the fragrant Alajú almond soup from Cuenca.

Cured hams hanging in an *embutidos* shop

Extremadura

Wild, beautiful Extremadura sees few visitors and, in many places, life continues virtually untouched by the 21st century. Endless rolling fields dotted with holm oak shelter the acorn-fed, black-footed pigs that make Spain's most highly prized hams (*jamón Ibérico*). Thanks to the deeply rooted hunting tradition, partridge, hare and wild boar regularly feature on local menus along with river fish such as tench and trout. There are some delicious cheeses, as well as perfumed local honey and wonderful fruit, particularly cherries, peaches and figs.

On the Menu

Chocolate con Churros The typical Spanish breakfast – thick hot chocolate with sugary strips of fried batter for dipping, originated in Madrid.

Cochinillo The speciality of Segovia: 21-day-old suckling pig, roasted until so tender it can be cut with a plate.

Gazpacho Manchego Sometimes called a *galiano*, this is a rich stew traditionally made with hare and partridge.

Macarraca Extremaduran salad of chopped ripe tomatoes with peppers, onion and garlic.

Tortilla de Patata A simple potato omelette, now a staple in restaurants all over Spain.

Albóndigas Meatballs – sturdy and comforting country fare from the high plain of Castilla y León.

Migas Extremeñas Crumbs of country bread are fried up with peppers, pork and chorizo or cured sausage.

Yemas A delicious treat from Ávila, these lemony, custardy cakes are made with egg yolks and sugar.

Wines of Central Spain

The wines of Central Spain originate in either the small, high-quality regions of northwest Castilla y León or in the vast wine-producing plains of La Mancha and Valdepeñas. Ribera del Duero has become Spain's most fashionable red wine region, with its aromatic, rich yet fine reds made from Tinto Fino grapes (the local name for Tempranillo) and, more recently, lighter, fruity wines. Rueda makes a good white wine, made from the Verdejo grape. La Mancha and Valdepeñas both produce lots of simple white wine, and reds which can be mellow and fruity.

Harvesting Viura grapes at Rueda

Artesian well for irrigating vines in La Mancha

Toro makes the most powerful and fiery of all red wines from the ubiquitous Tempranillo grape.

Villafranca del Bierzo
Cacabelos
Ponferrada
A6
A52
Benaven
Zamora
Duero
Salaman
A62
Ciudad Rodrigo
Coria
Plas
A66
EXTREMADUR
Cáceres
T

Key Facts about Wines of Central Spain

Location and Climate
Ribera del Duero, Rueda and Toro are all high-lying areas with extreme climates – very hot summer days combined with cool nights, and cold winters. The marked difference of temperature between day and night helps to preserve the acidity in the grapes. Both La Mancha and Valdepeñas are extremely hot and dry areas. In recent years, droughts have caused a severe shortage of grapes, though 2013 saw more rain and a better yield.

Grape Varieties
The Tempranillo grape – also known as Tinto Fino, Tinto del Toro and Cencibel – produces nearly all the best red wines of Central Spain. Cabernet Sauvignon is permitted in some regions; it is used in some Ribera

del Duero wines and occasionally surfaces as a single varietal, as at the estate of the Marquis of Griñón in Méntrida. Verdejo, Viura and Sauvignon Blanc are used for white Rueda. The white Airén grape predominates in the vineyards of Valdepeñas and La Mancha.

Good Producers
Toro: Fariña (Gran Colegiata). **Rueda:** Álvarez y Diez, Los Curros, Marqués de Riscal, Sanz. **Ribera del Duero:** Alejandro Fernández (Pesquera), Boada, Hermanos Pérez Pascuas (Viña Pedrosa), Ismael Arroyo (Valsotillo), Vega Sicilia, Victor Balbás. **Méntrida:** Marqués de Griñón. **La Mancha:** Fermín Ayuso Roig (Estola), Vinícola de Castilla (Castillo de Alhambra). **Valdepeñas:** Casa de la Viña, Félix Solís, Luis Megía (Marqués de Gastañaga), Los Llanos.

Traditional earthenware *tinaja*, still used for fermenting wine

0 kilometres   100
0 miles   50

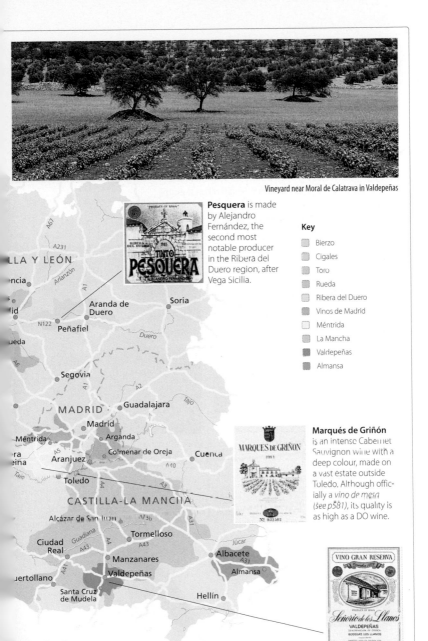

Vineyard near Moral de Calatrava in Valdepeñas

Pesquera is made by Alejandro Fernández, the second most notable producer in the Ribera del Duero region, after Vega Sicilia.

Key

- Bierzo
- Cigales
- Toro
- Rueda
- Ribera del Duero
- Vinos de Madrid
- Méntrida
- La Mancha
- Valdepeñas
- Almansa

Marqués de Griñón is an intense Cabernet Sauvignon wine with a deep colour, made on a vast estate outside Toledo. Although officially a *vino de mesa* (see p581), its quality is as high as a DO wine.

Señorío de los Llanos is produced in Valdepeñas. Its fine reds – made from Cencibel (Tempranillo) and aged in oak – are of excellent value.

Wine Regions

The wine regions of Ribera del Duero, Toro and Rueda are situated on remote, high plateaus, straddling the Río Duero. To the northwest lies the isolated region of Bierzo, whose wines have more in common with neighbouring Valdeorras in Galicia. Some wine is produced around Madrid, and southwest of the capital is the largely undistinguished region of Méntrida. Most of Central Spain's wine is produced in La Mancha – the world's largest single wine region – and in the smaller enclave of Valdepeñas, which produces a great deal of *vino de mesa*.

Birds of Central Spain

The vast and varied wild habitats of Central Spain are home to the richest avifauna in the peninsula. White storks' nests are a common sight on the church towers and chimneypots of towns. Grebes, herons and shovelers can be seen in the marshlands; the distinctive hoopoe is often spotted in woods; and grasslands are the nesting grounds of bustards and cranes. The mountains and high plains are the domain of birds of prey such as the imperial eagle, peregrine falcon and vultures. Deforestation, changing agricultural practices and hunting have all taken their toll in recent decades. Today, almost 160 bird species are the subject of conservation initiatives.

Migration Routes

— Cranes
— Storks
— Raptors
— Wildfowl

Marshland and Wet Meadow

Wetlands, such as Lagunas de Ruidera *(see p401)*, on the edge of the plains of La Mancha, are vital feeding grounds for a wide range of waterfowl, some of which may remain in Spain throughout the year. Other migratory species use such sites as stopover points to feed, rest and build up enough energy to enable them to complete their journeys.

Woodland and Scrub

Habitats in areas of woodland, such as the Parque Nacional de Cabañeros *(see p391)*, and scrub support many species, such as rollers and woodpeckers, throughout the year. Food is plentiful and there are many places to roost and nest. Early in the morning is the best time for spotting some of the rarer species, such as the bluethroat.

Little egrets are recognized by their snow-white plumage and graceful slow flight. They feed largely on frogs, snails and small fish.

Rollers are commonly found in woodland, often nesting in tree stumps or holes left by woodpeckers. Their food includes grasshoppers, crickets and beetles.

Shovellers feed on the water surface with a characteristic shovelling motion. The male has brightly coloured plumage but the female is a dull brown.

Hoopoes can be easily identified by their striking plumage and by the crest which can be raised if the bird is alarmed. They feed on ground insects.

Storks

Both the white and the (much rarer) black stork breed in Spain. They can be recognized in flight by their slow, steady wingbeats and may occasionally be seen soaring on thermals, usually during migrations. During the breeding season they put on elaborate courtship displays, which involve "dancing", wing-beating and bill-clapping. Their large nests, made of branches and twigs and lined with grasses, are constructed on roofs, towers, spires and chimneypots, where they are easy to watch. They feed on insects, fish and amphibians. Stork populations are threatened by wetland reclamation and the use of pesticides.

The endangered black stork

Nesting on a monastery roof

Grassland and Field

Many of Spain's natural grasslands have been ploughed over to plant cereals and other crops. Remaining vestiges are rich in wild grasses and flowers and are vital habitats for species such as bustards and larks.

Cranes perform elegant courtship dances and are also stately birds in flight, their long necks extended to the limit. They are omnivores, feeding on amphibians, crustaceans, plants and insects.

Great bustards nest in shallow depressions formed in open grassland and cultivated fields. Spain is home to half of the world's population.

Mountain and High Plain

Some of Spain's most spectacular birds of prey live in mountain ranges, such as the Sierra de Gredos (see p366), and the high plains of Central Spain. The broad wingspans of eagles and vultures allow them to soar on currents of warm air as they scan the ground below for prey and carrion.

Imperial eagles, with their vast wingspan of 2.25 m (7 ft), are extremely rare – only around 300 pairs are left in the whole of Spain.

Griffon vultures, a gregarious species, nest in trees and on rocky crags, often using the same place from year to year. Their broad wingspans can exceed 2 m (6 ft).

The Castles of Castile

The greatest concentration of Spain's 2,000 castles is in Castilla y León (now part of Castile), which derived its name from the word *castillo*, or castle. In the 10th and 11th centuries this region was the battleground between Moors and Christians. Villages and towns were fortified as protection against one side or the other. Most of the surviving castles in Castile, however, were built as noble residences after the area had been reconquered and there was no longer a military purpose for them. Fernando and Isabel *(see pp60–61)* banned the building of new castles at the end of the 15th century; many existing ones were converted to domestic use.

Coca Castle *(see p369)*, a classic Mudéjar design in brick

La Mota Castle *(see p370)*, at Medina del Campo, near Valladolid, was originally a Moorish castle but was rebuilt after 1440 and later became the property of Fernando and Isabel. The square-shaped Torre del Homenaje has twin bartizan turrets at its corners and machicolations beneath its battlements. Great curtain walls surround the castle.

Patio de armas (courtyard)

Bartizan turrets

The Torre de Juan II contained the dungeons.

The barbican, with the coat of arms of the Catholic Monarchs carved over the gate, contains the portcullis and guards' watchrooms.

Belmonte Castle *(see p398)* was built in the 15th century as the stronghold of the quarrelsome Marquis of Villena, Juan Pacheco. Late Gothic in style, it has a sophisticated, hexagonal ground plan, with a triangular bailey.

The Alcázar, Segovia

The plan of the royal castle of Segovia (see p368) is determined by the contours of the rocky outcrop on which it stands. Although first records date from the 12th century, it was mostly built between 1410 and 1455 and had to be largely rebuilt following a fire in 1862. The fortress's walls conceal several sumptuous apartments.

Torre del Homenaje has pointed turrets, atypical of Spanish castles.

Curtain wall

The King's Room, the most important room in the castle, is Gothic in style.

The Pine Cone Room gets its name from the golden pine cones on the ceiling.

The Galley Room

The Throne Room has ornate plasterwork and a Mudéjar ceiling.

Peñafiel Castle *(see p371)* has been compared to a battleship because of its long, narrow shape. The site above the Duero Valley has been defended since the 10th century, but the present castle is 15th century.

Terms used in this Guide

Alcázar: Castle or palace used as a royal residence.

Bartizan: A small turret which projects from the battlements of a tower above attackers.

Cross and orb loophole: Narrow slit, shaped to allow archers to shoot at various angles.

Curtain wall: Outer, window-less wall, often low enough for archers to fire over it from the keep and other towers.

Machicolation: A projection overhanging the wall beneath a battlement to allow boiling oil, missiles or human waste to be dropped on to the enemy.

Torre del Homenaje: The fortified tower or keep at the heart of a castle, often built to a square plan, in which the nobleman's family lived.

The Castles of Castilla y León

Some of Central Spain's finest surviving castles can be visited today. A few, such as Ciudad Rodrigo *(see p361)*, have been turned into luxurious paradors.

CASTILLA Y LEÓN

*León · Zamora · Salamanca · Ávila · Segovia
Valladolid · Palencia · Burgos · Soria*

Awesome expanses of ochre plains stretch to hills crowned with the castles that cover this vast region. Through Spain's history, these central provinces have had a major influence on its language, religion and culture. Their many historic cities preserve some of the country's most magnificent architectural sights.

The territories of the two rival medieval kingdoms of Castile and León, occupying the northern half of the great plateau in the centre of Spain, now form the country's largest region, or *comunidad autónoma*.

Castile and León were first brought together under one crown in 1037 by Fernando I, but the union was not consolidated until the early 13th century. The kingdom of Castile and León was one of the driving forces of the Reconquest. El Cid, the legendary hero, was born near Burgos.

Wealth pouring in from the wool trade and the New World, reaching a peak in the 16th century, financed the many great artistic and architectural treasures that can be seen today in the cities of Castilla y León. Burgos has an exuberantly decorated Gothic cathedral. León Cathedral is famous for its wonderful stained glass. At the heart of the monumental city of Salamanca is the oldest university in the peninsula. Segovia's aqueduct is the largest Roman structure in Spain and its Alcázar is the country's most photographed castle. Ávila is surrounded by an unbroken wall, built by Christian forces against the Moors. In Valladolid, the regional capital, a superb collection of multicoloured sculpture is displayed in a magnificent 15th-century building.

Beyond the cities, in Castilla y León's varied countryside, there are many attractive small towns which preserve outstanding examples of the region's vernacular architecture.

Cereal fields and vineyards covering the fertile Tierra de Campos in Palencia province

◀ View of the Old Town of Segovia, dominated by the tower of the Gothic cathedral

Exploring Castilla y León

Covering the northern part of Central Spain's vast tableland, Castilla y León has a huge variety of sights. Many are well known, like the great cathedrals of Burgos and León, the Alcázar and aqueduct of Segovia, the medieval walls of Ávila and the monastery at Santo Domingo de Silos. Other historic towns and villages worthy of a detour include Ciudad Rodrigo, Covarrubias, Pedraza de la Sierra and Zamora. This region also has beautiful mountainous countryside in the Sierra de Francia, Sierra de Bejar and Sierra de Gredos.

Sights at a Glance

① El Bierzo
② Villafranca del Bierzo
③ Ponferrada
④ Puebla de Sanabria
⑤ Astorga
⑥ Cueva de Valporquero
⑦ León pp357–9
⑧ Zamora
⑨ Ciudad Rodrigo
⑪ Salamanca pp362–5
⑫ Sierra de Gredos
⑬ Ávila
⑭ La Granja de San Ildefonso
⑮ Segovia
⑯ Pedraza de la Sierra
⑰ Sepúlveda
⑱ Castillo de Coca
⑲ Medina del Campo
⑳ Tordesillas
㉑ Valladolid
㉒ Medina de Rioseco
㉓ Palencia
㉔ Frómista
㉕ Aguilar de Campoo
㉖ Briviesca
㉗ Covarrubias
㉘ Burgos pp374–7
㉙ Lerma
㉚ Monasterio de Santo Domingo de Silos
㉛ Peñaranda de Duero
㉜ El Burgo de Osma
㉝ Soria
㉞ Medinaceli

Tours

⑩ Sierra de Francia and Sierra de Bejar

Getting Around

Madrid makes a convenient springboard for touring in Castilla y León. The major cities of the region are connected by rail, but the coach is often a quicker alternative. If you intend on exploring rural areas or small towns, it is advisable to hire a car.

Sunflowers growing in Burgos province

Key

━━ Motorway

= = Motorway under construction

▬ Major road

═ Secondary road

▭ Scenic route

▭▬ Main railway

— Minor railway

▬ International border

▬ Regional border

△ Summit

Peñaranda de Duero castle

❶ El Bierzo

León. 🚉 Ponferrada. 🚌 Ponferrada.
ℹ️ C/ Gil y Carrasco, Ponferrada, 987
42 42 36. 🅦 **turismodelbierzo.es**

This northwestern region of
León province was at one time
the bed of an ancient lake.
Sheltered by hills from the
worst extremes of Central
Spain's climate, its sun-soaked,
alluvial soils make for fertile
orchards and vineyards. Over
the centuries, the area has also
yielded rich mineral pickings
including coal, iron and gold.
Many hiking routes and picnic
spots are within reach of the
main towns of Ponferrada and
Villafranca del Bierzo.

In the eastern section, you
can trace the course of the old
Road to Santiago *(see pp86–7)*
through the Montes de León,
past the pilgrim church and
medieval bridge of Molinaseca.
Turning off the road at the
remote village of El Acebo,
you pass through a deep valley
where there are signs pointing
to the **Herrería de Compludo**,
a water-powered 7th-century
ironworks. The equipment still
works and is demonstrated
regularly, although the site is
currently closed for restoration.

The Lago de Carucedo, to the
southwest of Ponferrada, is an
ancient artificial lake. It acted
as a reservoir in Roman times, a
by-product of a vast gold-mining

A *palloza* in the Sierra de Ancares

operation. Using slave labour,
millions of tonnes of alluvium
were washed from the hills of
Las Médulas by a complex
system of canals and sluice
gates. The ore was then panned,
and the gold dust collected
on sheep's wool. It is estimated
that more than 500 tonnes of
precious metal were extracted
between the 1st and 4th
centuries AD. These ancient
workings lie within a memorable landscape of wind-eroded
crags, and hills pierced by
tunnels and colonized by
gnarled chestnut trees. You can
best appreciate the area from
a viewpoint at Orellán, which is
reached via a rough, steep track.
Las Médulas, a village south
of Carucedo, is another place
to go for a fine view.

To the north of the A6 highway
lies the Sierra de Ancares, a
wild region of rounded, slate
mountains marking the borders
of Galicia and Asturias. Part of it
now forms the Reserva Nacional
de los Ancares Leoneses, an
attractive nature reserve. The
heathland is home to deer, wolves,
brown bears and capercaillies.

Several villages high in the
hills contain *pallozas* – primitive,
pre-Roman stone dwellings.
One of the most striking collections can be found in isolated
Campo del Agua, in the west.

🏛️ **Herrería de Compludo**
Compludo. **Tel** 661 250 756.
Open Wed–Sun & public hols. ♿

🏞️ **Las Médulas**
Tel 987 42 07 08. **Open** 11am–2pm,
4–8pm daily (Oct–Mar: to 6pm).
Closed public hols. ♿ 📷
🅦 **fundacionlasmedulas.org**

❷ Villafranca del Bierzo

León. 🏘️ 3,500. ℹ️ Avenida Díez
Ovelar 10, 987 54 00 28. 🗓️ Tue.
🎉 Santo Tirso (28 Jan), Spring Fiesta
(1 May), Fiesta del Cristo (14 Sep).
🅦 **villafrancadelbierzo.org**

Emblazoned mansions line the
ancient streets of this delightful
town. The solid, early 16th-
century, drum-towered castle
is still inhabited. Near the Plaza
Mayor a number of imposing

Craggy, tree-clad hills around the ancient gold workings near the village of Las Médulas churches and convents compete for attention. Particularly worth seeing are the fine sculptures adorning the north portal of the simple, Romanesque Iglesia de Santiago (open Jul–mid-Sep). At the church's Puerta del Perdón (Door of Mercy), pilgrims who were too weak to make the final gruelling hike across the hills of Galicia could obtain dispensation. Also sample the local speciality, cherries in *aguardiente*, a spirit.

Environs

One of the finest views over El Bierzo is from Corullón, to the south. This village with grey stone houses is set in a sunny location above the broad, fertile basin of the Río Burbia where the vines of the Bierzo wine region flourish (*see pp82–3*). Two churches, the late 11th-century San Miguel and the Romanesque San Esteban, are worth a visit. Down in the valley, the Benedictine monastery at Carracedo del Monasterio stands in splendour. Founded in 990, it was once the most powerful religious community in El Bierzo.

Puerta del Perdón of Villafranca's Iglesia de Santiago

❸ Ponferrada

León. 🗺 68,700. 🚌 🚍 ℹ Calle Gil y Carrasco 4, 987 42 42 36. 🏪 Wed & Sat. 🎉 Virgen de la Encina (8 Sep).
🌐 ponferrada.org/turismo/en

A medieval bridge reinforced with iron (*pons ferrata*), erected for the benefit of pilgrims on their way to Santiago de Compostela, gave this town its name. Today, prosperous from

The imposing Templar castle of Ponferrada

both iron and coal deposits, Ponferrada has expanded into a sizable town.

Most of its attractions are confined to the small old quarter. Ponferrada's majestic castle was constructed between the 12th and 14th centuries by the Knights Templar to protect pilgrims. During the Middle Ages it was one of the largest fortresses in northwest Spain.

Standing on the main square is the Baroque town hall (*ayuntamiento*). One entrance to the square, one of the gateways of the medieval wall, is straddled by a tall clock tower. Nearby is the Renaissance Basílica de la Virgen de la Encina. The older Iglesia de Santo Tomás de las Ollas is hidden away in the town's village-like northern suburbs. Mozarabic, Romanesque and Baroque elements combine in the architecture of this simple church. The 10th-century apse has beautiful horseshoe arches. Ask at the nearest house for the key. The neighbour will open it for you.

Environs

A drive through the idyllic Valle de Silencio (Valley of Silence), south of Ponferrada, follows a poplar-lined stream past several bucolic villages. The last and most beautiful of these is Peñalba de Santiago. Its

10th-century Mozarabic church has horseshoe arches above its double portal.

❹ Puebla de Sanabria

Zamora. 🗺 1,500. 🚌 🚍 ℹ Muralla Mariquillo, 980 62 07 34. 🏪 Fri. 🎉 Candelas (Feb), Las Victorias (8–9 Sep). 🌐 pueblasanabria.com

This attractive old village lies beyond the undulating broom and oak scrub of the Sierra de la Culebra. A steep cobbled street leads past stone and slate houses with huge, overhanging eaves and walls bearing coats of arms, to a hilltop church and castle.

The village has become the centre of a popular inland holiday resort based around the largest glacial lake in Spain, the Lago de Sanabria, now a nature park. Among the many activities available are fishing, walking and water sports.

Most routes beckon visitors to Ribadelago, but the road to the quaint hill village of San Martín de Castañeda gives better views. There's a small visitors' centre for the nature reserve in San Martín's restored monastery. The village is very traditional – you may see cattle yoked to carts, and women dressed completely in black.

The 12th-century church and 15th-century castle of Puebla de Sanabria

The nave of Astorga Cathedral

❺ Astorga

León. 🚊 11,900. 🚉 🚌 **ℹ** Plaza Eduardo de Castro 5. **Tel** 987 61 82 22. 🗓 Tue. 🎉 Roman Festival (end Jun), Santa Marta (late Aug). **w** aytoastorga.es

The Roman town of Asturica Augusta was a strategic halt on the Vía de la Plata (Silver Road), a Roman road linking Andalucía and northwest Spain. Later it came to form a stage on the pilgrimage route to Santiago (see pp86–7).

Soaring above the ramparts in the upper town are Astorga's two principal monuments, the cathedral and the Palacio Episcopal. The cathedral was built between the 15th and the 18th centuries and displays a variety of architectural styles ranging from its Gothic apse to the effusive Baroque of its two towers, which are carved with various biblical scenes. The gilt altarpiece by Gaspar Becerra is a masterpiece of the Spanish Renaissance. Among the many fine exhibits in the cathedral's museum are the 10th-century carved casket of Alfonso III the Great, the jewelled Reliquary of the True Cross and a lavish silver monstrance studded with enormous emeralds.

Opposite the cathedral is a fairy-tale building of multiple turrets and quasi-Gothic windows. The unconventional **Palacio Episcopal** (Bishop's Palace) was designed at the end of the 19th century by Antoni Gaudí, the highly original Modernista architect (see p168), for the incumbent bishop, a fellow Catalan, after a fire in 1887 had destroyed the previous building. Its bizarre appearance as well as its phenomenal cost so horrified the diocese that no subsequent bishops ever lived in it. Today it houses an assembly of medieval religious art devoted to the history of Astorga and the pilgrimage to Santiago. Roman relics, including coins unearthed in the Plaza Romana, are evidence of Astorga's importance as a Roman settlement. The palace's interior is decorated with Gaudí's ceramic tiles and stained glass.

Reliquary of the True Cross

🏛 Palacio Episcopal
Plaza Eduardo de Castro. **Tel** 987 61 68 82. **Open** Tue–Sun. **Closed** Mon, Sun pm, public hols. 📷

❻ Cueva de Valporquero

León. **Tel** 987 57 64 08. **Open** mid-Oct–Dec & Mar–mid-May: 10am–5pm Thu–Sun, public hols; mid-May–mid-Oct: 10am–6pm daily. 📷 **w** cuevadevalporquero.es

This complex of limestone caves – technically a single cave with three separate entrances – is directly beneath the village of Valporquero de Torío. The caves were formed in the Miocene period between 5 and 25 million years ago. Severe weather conditions in the surrounding mountains make the caverns inaccessible between December and Easter. Less than half of the huge system, which stretches 3,100 m (10,200 ft) under the ground, is open to the public. Guided tours take parties through an impressive series of galleries in which lighting picks out the beautiful limestone concretions. Iron and sulphur oxides have tinted the rocks many subtle shades of red, grey and black. The vast Gran Rotonda, covering an area of 5,600 sq m (18,350 sq ft) and reaching a height of 20 m (65 ft), is the most stunning.

As the interior is cold, and the surface often slippery, it is advisable to wear warm clothes and sturdy shoes.

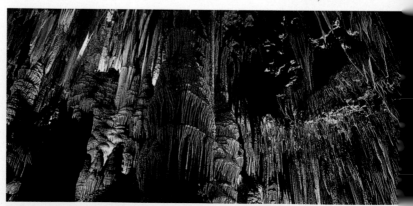

Illuminated stalactites hanging from the roof of one of the chambers in the Cueva de Valporquero

❼ León

León. 🏠 131,700. 🚉 🚌 ℹ Plaza
Regla 2, 987 23 70 82. 🛒 Wed & Sat.
🎉 San Juan and San Pedro (21–29
Jun), San Froilán (5 Oct).
w turismoleon.org

Founded as a camp for the
Romans' Seventh Legion,
León became the capital of a
kingdom in the Middle Ages.
As such it played a central
role in the early years of the
Reconquest *(see pp58–9)*.

The city's most important
building – apart from its great
cathedral *(see pp358–9)* – is the
Colegiata de San Isidoro, built
into the Roman walls which
encircle the city. A separate
entrance leads through to the
Romanesque Panteón Real
(Royal Pantheon), the last resting
place of more than 20 monarchs.
It is superbly decorated with
carved capitals and 12th-century
frescoes illustrating a variety of
biblical and mythical subjects, as
well as scenes of medieval life.

The alleyways in the picturesque old quarter around the
Plaza Mayor are dotted with
bars and cafés, decrepit mansions
and churches. Two well-
preserved palaces stand near
to the Plaza de Santo Domingo:
the Palacio de los Guzmanes,
with its elegantly arcaded
Renaissance patio, and Antoni
Gaudí's unusually restrained
Casa de Botines.

The Hostal de San Marcos is a
fine example of Spanish

Frescoes in Colegiata de San Isidoro showing medieval seasonal tasks

Renaissance architecture *(see p29)*.
Founded in the 12th century as
a monastery lodging pilgrims
going to Santiago, the present
building was begun in 1513 as
the headquarters of the Knights
of Santiago. The main hall has
a fine 16th-century coffered
ceiling. A parador now occupies
the main part of the Hostal.
The Museo de León has many
treasures, including a haunting
little ivory crucifix, the *Cristo de*

Carrizo. The MUSAC, Museo de
Arte Contemporáneo de Castilla
y León, has a radical, interactive
approach to exhibiting
contemporary art.

Environs

Around 30 km (20 miles) east
of León is the Iglesia de San
Miguel de Escalada. Dating from
the 10th century, it is one of the
finest surviving churches built
by the Mozarabs – Christians
influenced by the Moors. It has
Visigothic panels and stately
horseshoe arches resting on
carved capitals. At Sahagún,
70 km (40 miles) southeast of
León, are the Mudéjar churches
of San Tirso and San Lorenzo,
with triple apses and belfries.
A colossal ruined castle
overlooks the Río Esla beside
Valencia de Don Juan, 40 km
(25 miles) south of León.

🏛 **Museo de León**
Plaza Santo Domingo 8. **Tel** 987 23
64 05. **Open** Tue–Sun. **Closed** Mon,
Sun pm. 🎫 (free Sat & Sun).

🏛 **MUSAC**
Avenida de los Reyes Leoneses 24.
Tel 987 09 00 00. **Open** Tue–Sun. ♿
🎫 🅿 (free 6pm Sun). **w** musac.es

The Maragatos

Astorga is the principal town of
the Maragatos, an ethnic group
of unknown origin, thought to
be descended from 8th-century
Berber invaders. By marrying
only among themselves,
they managed to preserve
their customs through the
centuries and keep them-
selves apart from the rest of
society. The demise of their
traditional trade of mule-
driving, however, changed
their way of life and the
Maragatos have adapted to
contemporary life, although
their typical gastronomy and
craftwork still survive.

Maragatos dressed in
traditional costume

León Cathedral

The master builders of this Spanish Gothic cathedral *par excellence (see p28)* were inspired by French techniques of vaulting and buttressing. The present structure of golden sandstone, built on the site of King Ordoño II's 10th-century palace, was begun in the mid-13th century and completed less than 100 years later. It combines a slender but very high nave with the huge panels of stained glass which are its most magnificent feature. Although the cathedral has survived for 700 years, today there is concern about air pollution attacking the soft stone.

Cathedral Museum
Pedro de Campaña's panel, *The Adoration of the Magi*, is one of the many magnificent treasures displayed in the museum.

KEY

① **The West Rose Window** is largely 14th-century and depicts the Virgin and Child, surrounded by 12 trumpet-blowing angels.

② **The silver reliquary** is an ornate chest dating from the 16th century.

③ **The 13th- to 14th-century** cloister galleries are decorated with Gothic frescoes by Nicolás Francés.

④ **The altarpiece** includes five original panels created by Gothic master Nicolás Francés.

⑤ **The choir** has two tiers of 15th-century stalls. Behind it is the carved and gilded retrochoir, in the shape of a triumphal arch.

Entrance

★ **13th-Century Carvings**
Among the Gothic carvings on the front of León's cathedral, above the Puerta de la Virgen Blanca, is one depicting a scene from the Last Judgment.

Inside the Cathedral
The plan of the building is a Latin cross. The tall nave is slender but long, measuring 90 m (295 ft) by 40 m (130 ft) at its widest. To appreciate the dazzling colours of the stained glass it is best to visit on a sunny day.

VISITORS' CHECKLIST

Practical Information
Plaza de Regla.
Tel 987 87 57 70.
Open Oct–Apr: 9:30am–1:30pm & 4–7pm Mon–Sat, 9:30am–2pm Sun; May–Sep: hours vary, check website for details. 🕐 9am, noon, 1pm & 6pm daily, plus 11am & 2pm Sun. 🚻 ♿
Museum: **Open** Mon–Sat, check website for details. 📷 📧
Ⓦ catedraldeleon.org

The *Virgen Blanca* is a Gothic sculpture of a smiling Virgin. The original is kept in this chapel. A copy stands by the west door.

León's Stained Glass

León Cathedral's great glory is its magnificent glasswork. The 125 large windows and 57 smaller, round ones date from every century from the 13th to the 20th. They cover an enormous range of subjects. Some reveal fascinating details about medieval life: *La Cacería*, in the north wall, depicts a typical hunting scene, while the rose window in the Capilla del Nacimiento shows pilgrims worshipping at the tomb of St James in Santiago de Compostela in Galicia (*see pp96–7*). Restoration work can be viewed from an elevated platform on a guided tour.

A large window in León Cathedral

★ **Stained Glass**
The windows, covering an area of 1,900 sq m (20,400 sq ft), are the outstanding feature of the cathedral.

❽ Zamora

Zamora. 🔼 65,300. 🚌 🚐 **i** Plaza de Arias Gonzalo, 980 53 36 94. 🔔 Tue. 🎭 Semana Santa (Easter Week), San Pedro (23–29 Jun). **W** zamora-turismo.com

Little remains of Zamora's past as an important strategic frontier town. In Roman times, it was on the Vía de la Plata (see p356), and during the Reconquest was fought over fiercely. The city has now expanded far beyond its original boundaries, but the old quarter contains a wealth of Romanesque churches.

The ruins of the city walls, built by Alfonso III in 893, are pierced by the Portillo de la Traición (Traitor's Gate), through which the murderer of Sancho II passed in 1072. The 16th-century parador (see p570) is in an old palace with a Renaissance courtyard adorned with coats of arms.

Two other palaces, the Palacio de los Momos and the Palacio del Cordón, have ornately carved façades and windows. Zamora's most important monument is its unique cathedral, a 12th-century structure built in Romanesque style but with a number of later Gothic additions. The building's most eye-catching feature is its striking, scaly, hemispherical dome. Inside, there are superb iron grilles and Mudéjar pulpits surround Juan de Bruselas' 15th-century choir stalls.

Peaceful gardens of the Colegiata de Santa María in Toro

The allegorical carvings of nuns and monks on the misericords and armrests were once considered risqué. The museum, off the cloisters, has a collection of 15th- and 16th-century Flemish tapestries. These illustrate biblical passages and classical and military scenes.

Nearby, several churches exhibit features characteristic of Zamora's architectural style, notably multi-lobed arches and heavily carved portals. The best are the 12th-century Iglesia de San Ildefonso and the Iglesia de la Magdalena.

Another reason for visiting Zamora is for its lively Easter Week celebrations, when elaborate pasos (sculpted floats) are paraded in the streets. Otherwise they can be admired in the Museo de Semana Santa.

Environs
The 7th-century Visigothic church of San Pedro de la Nave, 23 km (14 miles) northwest of Zamora, is Spain's oldest church. Carvings

❿ Sierra de Francia and Sierra de Béjar

These attractive schist hills buttress the western edges of the Sierra de Gredos (see p366). Narrow roads wind their way through picturesque chestnut, olive and almond groves, and quaint rural villages of wood and stone. The highest point of the range is La Peña de Francia, which, at 1,732 m (5,700 ft), is easily recognizable from miles around. The views from the peak, and from the roads leading up to it, offer a breathtaking panorama of the surrounding empty plains and rolling hills.

① La Peña de Francia
Atop the windswept peak is a 15th-century Dominican monastery sheltering a blackened statue of the Virgin and Child dating from 1890.

② La Alberca
This pretty and much-visited village sells local honey, hams and handicrafts. On 15 August each year it celebrates the Assumption with a traditional mystery play performed in costume.

③ Las Batuecas
The road from La Alberca careers down into a green valley, past the monastery where Luis Buñuel made his film Tierra sin Pan (Land without Bread).

Key
▬▬ Tour route
═══ Other roads

The unmistakable peak of La Peña de Francia

Fish-scale tiling on dome of Zamora Cathedral

adorn its capitals and friezes. Toro, 30 km (18 miles) east of Zamora, is at the heart of a wine region (*see pp344–5*). The highlights of its Colegiata de Santa María are the Gothic west portal and a fine 16th-century Hispano-Flemish painting, *La Virgen de la Mosca*. In 1476, the forces of Isabel I (*see pp60–61*) secured a victory over the Portuguese at Toro, confirming her succession to the Castile throne.

⑨ Ciudad Rodrigo

Salamanca. 🚗 13,600. 🚉 🚌
ℹ️ Plaza Mayor 27, 923 49 84 00.
🗓️ Tue, Sat. 🎭 San Sebastián (20 Jan), Carnaval del Toro (before Lent), Easter week, Charrada (mid-Jul).

Despite its lonely setting – stranded on the country's western marches miles from anywhere – this lovely old town is well worth a detour. Its frontier location inevitably gave

rise to fortification, and its robust 14th-century castle is now an atmospheric parador. The prosperous 15th and 16th centuries were Ciudad Rodrigo's heyday. During the War of Independence (*see pp66–7*), the city, then occupied by the French, was besieged for two years before falling to the Duke of Wellington's forces.

The golden stone buildings within the ramparts are delightful. The main monument is the cathedral (closed Mon pm), whose belfry still bears the marks of shellfire from the siege. The exterior has a shapely curved balustrade and accomplished portal carvings. Inside, it is worth seeing the cloisters and the choir stalls, carved with lively scenes by Rodrigo Alemán. In the adjacent 16th-century Capilla de Cerralbo (Cerralbo Chapel; *only open to tourists in the summer*) is a 17th-century altarpiece. Off the chapel's south side is the arcaded Plaza del Buen Alcalde.

④ Miranda del Castañar
The narrow streets of this pretty, fortified village are lined with ancient houses with wide eaves.

0 kilometres 5
0 miles 5

SA205 ↗ *Salamanca*

Santibáñez de la Sierra

• **Cristóbal**

SA225

Cepeda

Sotoserrano

Alagón

Sangusín

SA220

La Calzada de Béjar

⑤ Béjar
This textile town is strung out along a ridge at the foot of the Sierra de Béjar. From the approach road, 19th-century factories and mills can be seen.

Tips for Drivers

Tour length: 72 km (45 miles).
Stopping-off points: Candelario, Miranda del Castañar and La Alberca all have good eating places, and are renowned for their hams and sausages. In summer, refreshments are available from the *hospedería* (inn) in La Peña's monastery.

⑥ Candelario
The steep, cobbled streets are lined with deep channels and stormgates to cope with the spring meltwater from the surrounding mountains and flash floods.

A66 (E803)

↗ *Salamanca*

⑪ Street-by-Street: Salamanca

The great university city of Salamanca is Spain's finest showcase of Renaissance and Plateresque architecture. Founded as an Iberian settlement in pre-Roman times, the city fell to Hannibal in 217 BC. Pre-eminent among its artists and master craftsmen of later years were the Churriguera brothers *(see p29)*. Their work can be seen in many of Salamanca's golden stone buildings, notably in the Plaza Mayor. Other major sights are the two cathedrals and the 13th-century university, one of Europe's oldest and most distinguished.

The Casa de las Conchas is easily identifiable from the stone scallop shells that stud its walls. It is now a library.

The Palacio de Monterrey is a Renaissance mansion.

Casa de las Muertes

Convento de las Ursulas

Palacio de Fonseca

CALLE DE LA COMPAÑIA

★ **Universidad**
In the centre of the university's elaborate façade is this medallion, carved in relief, which depicts the Catholic Monarchs.

★ **Catedral Vieja and Catedral Nueva**
Despite being in different architectural styles, the adjoining old and new cathedrals blend well together. This richly coloured altarpiece painted in 1445 is in the old cathedral.

CALLE DE SERRANOS

CALLE DE LOS LIBREROS

Puente Romano
The Roman bridge across the Río Tormes, built in the 1st century AD, retains 15 of its original 26 arches. It provides an excellent view of the city.

CALLE VERACRUZ

PASE

| 0 metres | 100 |
| 0 yards | 100 |

Casa Lis, Museo de Art Decó y Art Nouveau

★ Plaza Mayor
This 18th-century square is one of Spain's largest and grandest. On the east side is the Royal Pavilion, decorated with a bust of Felipe V, who built the square.

VISITORS' CHECKLIST

Practical Information
Salamanca. 🅼 152,000.
ℹ️ Plaza Mayor 32, 923 21 83 42.
🚌 Sun. 🎉 San Juan de Sahagún (10–12 Jun), Virgen de la Vega (8–15 Sep).
🌐 salamanca.es

Transport
✈️ 15 km (9 miles) east.
🚆 Paseo de la Estación, 902 32 03 20. 🚌 Avenida de Filiberto Villalobos 71, 923 23 67 17.

Key

— Suggested route

Torre del Clavero
This 15th-century tower still has its original turrets. They are adorned with the coats of arms of its founders, and Mudéjar trelliswork.

Iglesia-Convento de San Esteban
The Plateresque façade of the church is carved with delicate relief. Above the door is a frieze decorated with medallions and coats of arms.

Convento de las Dueñas
Sculptures on the capitals of the beautiful two-storey cloister show demons, skulls and tormented faces, which contrast with serene carvings of the Virgin.

For keys to symbols *see back flap*

Exploring Salamanca

The majority of Salamanca's monuments are located inside the city centre, which is compact enough to explore on foot. The university, the Plaza Mayor, and the old and new cathedrals are all unmissable.

⚘ Catedral Vieja and Catedral Nueva

Tel 923 28 11 23. **Open** 10am–8pm daily (Oct–Mar: to 6pm).
W catedralsalamanca.org

The new cathedral (built during the 16th–18th centuries) did not replace the old, but was built beside it. It combines a mix of styles, being mainly Gothic, with Renaissance and Baroque additions. The west front has elaborate Late Gothic stonework.

The 12th- to 13th-century Romanesque old cathedral is entered through the new one. The highlight is a 53-panel altarpiece, painted in lustrous colours by Nicolás Florentino. It frames a statue of Salamanca's patron saint, the 12th-century Virgen de la Vega, crafted in Limoges enamel. In the vault above is a fresco depicting scenes from the Last Judgment, also by Florentino.

The 15th-century Capilla de Anaya (Anaya Chapel) contains the superb 15th-century alabaster tomb of Diego de Anaya, an archbishop of Salamanca.

Façade of Salamanca University, on the Patio de las Escuelas

⊞ Universidad

Calle Libreros. **Tel** 923 29 44 00.
Open daily. **Closed** 1 & 6 Jan, 25 Dec and for official functions.
W usal.es

The university was founded by Alfonso IX of León in 1218, making it the oldest in Spain. The 16th-century façade of the Patio de las Escuelas (Schools Square) is a perfect example of the Plateresque style *(see p29)*. Opposite is a statue of Fray Luis de León, who taught theology here. His former lecture room is preserved in its original style. The Escuelas Menores building houses a huge zodiac fresco, *The Salamanca Sky*.

⊞ Plaza Mayor

This magnificent square was built by Felipe V to thank the city for its support during the War of the Spanish Succession *(see p66)*. Designed by the Churriguera brothers *(see p29)* in 1729 and completed in 1755, it was once used for bullfights, but nowadays is a delightful place to stroll or shop. Within the harmonious blend of arcaded buildings and cafés are the Baroque town hall and, opposite, the Royal Pavilion, from where the royal family used to watch events in the square. The Plaza Mayor is built of warm golden sandstone, and is especially resplendent at dusk.

Royal Pavilion in Salamanca's beautiful Plaza Mayor

⚘ Iglesia-Convento de San Esteban

Plaza del Concilio de Trento s/n.
Tel 923 21 50 00. **Open** 10am–2pm, 4–6pm daily. **Closed** public hols.

The 16th-century church of this Dominican monastery has an ornamented façade. The relief on the central panel, completed by Juan Antonio Ceroni in 1610, depicts the stoning of St Stephen, to whom the monastery is dedicated. Above is a frieze with figures of children and horses.

The interior is equally stunning. The ornate altarpiece, of twisted gilt columns decorated with vines, is the work of José Churriguera and dates from 1693. Below it is one of Claudio Coello's last paintings, another representation of the martyrdom of St Stephen.

The double-galleried Claustro de los Reyes, completed in Plateresque style in 1591, has capitals that are carved with the heads of the prophets.

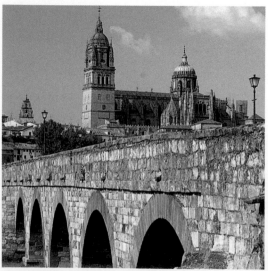

Salamanca's double cathedral, towering over the city

Sculpted shells on the walls of the Casa de las Conchas

Casa de las Conchas
Calle de la Compañía 2. **Tel** 923 26 93 17. **Open** Mon–Sat. Library: **Open** 9am–9pm Mon–Fri, 9am–2pm Sat.

This mansion's name – House of the Shells – derives from the stone scallop shells that cover its walls. They are a symbol of the Order of Santiago, one of whose knights, Rodrigo Arias Maldonado, built the mansion in the early 1500s. He also adorned it with his family's coat of arms. It now houses a public library.

Convento de las Dueñas
Pl del Concilio de Trento 1. **Tel** 923 21 54 42. **Open** 10:30am–12:45pm, 4:30–6:45pm Mon–Sat. **Closed** pub hols.

The main feature of this Dominican convent, beside San Esteban, is its Renaissance double cloister, whose tranquil gardens seem strangely at odds with the grotesques carved on the capitals. The cloister also preserves tiled Moorish arches.

Casa Lis Museo Art Nouveau y Art Deco
Calle Gibraltar 14. **Tel** 923 12 14 25. **Open** Tue–Sun. (free Thu am).

This important art collection, housed in a 19th-century building, includes paintings, jewellery and furniture from all over Europe. Individual rooms are devoted to porcelain and Limoges enamel, and stained-glass work by Lalique.

Colegio de Fonseca or de los Irlandeses
Calle de Fonseca 4. **Tel** 923 29 45 70. **Open** daily.

The Archbishop of Toledo, Alfonso de Fonseca, built this Renaissance palace in 1521, and the coat of arms of the Fonseca family appears over the main entrance. Its name arises from the fact that it became a seminary for Irish priests at the end of the 19th century. The interior Italianate courtyard has a first-floor gallery and a chapel. Today it is used as a hotel, restaurant and university premises

Convento de las Úrsulas
Calle de las Úrsulas 2. **Tel** 923 21 98 77. **Open** Tue–Sun. **Closed** last Sun of month.

In the church of this convent is the carved tomb of its founder, Alonso de Fonseca, the powerful 16th-century Archbishop of Santiago. The museum includes fine paintings by Luis de Morales.

Casa de las Muertes
Calle Bordadores. **Closed** to the public.
The House of the Dead takes its name from the small skulls that embellish its façade. Grotesques and other figures also feature, and there is a cornice decorated with cherubs. The façade is a

Skull carving on the façade of the Casa de las Muertes

wonderfully accomplished example of the early Plateresque style.

The adjacent house is where author and philosopher Miguel de Unamuno died in 1936. The Casa-Museo de Unamuno, next door to the university, contains information about his life.

Torre del Clavero
Plaza de Colón. **Closed** to the public.
The tower is the last vestige of a palace that once stood here. It was built around 1480 and is named after a former resident, the key warden (clavero) of the Order of Alcántara.

Tower opposite Casa de las Muertes

Environs
Northwest of the city, the Río Tormes leads through the fortified old town of Ledesma, across lonely countryside to the Arribes del Duero, a series of massive reservoirs near to the Portuguese border.

Dominating the town of Alba de Tormes, 20 km (12 miles) east of Salamanca, is the Torre de la Armería, the only remaining part of the castle of the Dukes of Alba. The Iglesia de San Juan was built in the 12th century in Romanesque style. The Iglesia-Convento de las Madres Carmelitas was founded by St Teresa de Ávila in 1571, and is where her remains are now kept.

The castle of Buen Amor, 24 km (15 miles) to the north, was founded in 1227. Later, it was used by the Catholic Monarchs while fighting Juana la Beltraneja (see p60). Today it is a hotel but can still be visited.

⑫ Sierra de Gredos

Ávila. 🚌 Navarrendonda. 🛈
Navarrendonda, Calle del Río s/n, 920
34 80 01. 🖳 **gredosturismo.com**

This great mountain range, west of Madrid, has abundant wildlife, especially ibex and birds of prey. Some parts have been developed to cater for week-enders who come skiing, fishing, hunting or hiking. Tourism here isn't a recent phenomenon – Spain's first parador opened in Gredos in 1928. Despite this, there are many traditional villages off the beaten track.

The slopes on the south side of the range, extending into Extremadura, are fertile and sheltered, with pinewoods, and apple and olive trees. The northern slopes, in contrast, have a covering of scrub and a scattering of granite boulders.

A single main road, the N502, crosses the centre of the range via the Puerto del Pico, a pass at 1,352 m (4,435 ft), leading to Arenas de San Pedro, the largest town of the Sierra de Gredos. On this road is the castle of Mombeltrán, built at the end of the 14th century.

Near Ramacastañas, south of the town of Arenas de San Pedro, are the limestone caverns of the Cuevas del Águila.

The sierra's highest summit, the Pico Almanzor (2,592 m/ 8,500 ft) dominates the west. Around it lies the Reserva Nacional de Gredos, protecting the mountain's wildlife. Near

The Toros de Guisando near El Tiemblo in the Sierra de Gredos

El Tiemblo, in the east, stand the Toros de Guisando, four stone statues resembling bulls, believed to be of Celtiberian origin (see pp52–3).

⑬ Ávila

Ávila. 🏙 59,000. 🚉 🚌 🛈 Avenida de Madrid 39, 920 35 40 00. Walls: **Open** Tue–Sun (also Mon in summer). 🎨 🎭 Fri. 🎊 San Segundo (2 May); Sta Teresa (15 Oct). 🖳 **avilaturismo.com**

At 1,131 m (3,710 ft) above sea level, Ávila de los Caballeros ("of the Knights") is the highest provincial capital in Spain. In winter access roads can be blocked with snow. The centre of the city is encircled by the finest-preserved medieval walls in Europe. The walls are open to visitors (except Monday and in low season). One of the best views of the walls is from Los Cuatro Postes (Four Posts) on the road

Tuna in Ávila

to Salamanca. Built in the 11th century, the walls are over 2 km (1 mile) long. They are punctuated by 88 sturdy turrets, on which storks can be seen nesting in season. The ground falls away very steeply from the walls on three sides, making the city practically impregnable. The east side, however, is relatively flat, and therefore had to be fortified more heavily. The oldest sections of the wall are here. They are guarded by the most impressive of the city's nine gateways, the Puerta de San Vicente. The apse of the cathedral also forms part of the walls. The cathedral's war-like (and unfinished) exterior, decorated with beasts and scaly wild men, is an unusual design. The interior is a mixture of Romanesque and Gothic styles using an unusual mottled red and white stone. Finer points

The superbly preserved 11th-century walls, punctuated with 88 cylindrical towers, which encircle Ávila

to note are the carvings on the retrochoir and, in the apse, the tomb of a 15th-century bishop known as El Tostado, "the Tanned One", because of his dark complexion.

Many churches and convents in Ávila are linked to St Teresa, who was born in the city. The Convento de Santa Teresa was built on the site of her home within the walls and she also lived for more than 20 years in the Monasterio de la Encarnación outside the walls. There is even a local sweetmeat, *yemas de Santa Teresa*, named after the saint.

The Basílica de San Vicente, also located just outside the eastern walls, is Ávila's most important Romanesque church, distinguished by its ornamented belfry. It was begun in the 11th century but has some Gothic features which were added later. The west doorway is often compared to the Pórtico

Cloisters of the Real Monasterio de Santo Tomás in Ávila

da Gloria of Santiago Cathedral (*see pp96–7*). Inside, the carved tomb of St Vincent and his sisters depicts their hideous martyrdom in detail. Another Romanesque-Gothic church worth seeing is the Iglesia de San Pedro.

Some way from the centre is the Real Monasterio de Santo Tomás, with three cloisters. The middle one, carved with the yoke and arrow emblem of the Catholic Monarchs, is the most beautiful. The last cloister leads to a museum displaying chalices and processional crosses. The church contains the tomb of Prince Juan, the only son of Fernando and Isabel. In the sacristy lies another historic figure: Tomás de Torquemada, head of the Inquisition (*see p60*).

In Ávila, you may see groups of *tunas* – students dressed in traditional costume walking the town's streets while singing songs and playing guitars.

Beautiful gardens and palace of La Granja de San Ildefonso

⑭ La Granja de San Ildefonso

Segovia. **Tel** 921 47 00 19. 🚌 from Madrid or Segovia. **Open** 10am–8pm Tue–Sun (to 6pm Oct–Mar); gardens open until dusk. **Closed** 1, 6 & 23 Jan, 1 May, 24, 25 & 31 Dec. 🎫 (free from 3pm Wed & Thu for EU residents; from 5pm Apr–Sep). 📷
W webdelagranja.com

This royal pleasure palace, a project launched by Felipe V in 1720, is set against the backdrop of the Sierra de Guadarrama mountains, on the site of the old Convento de Jerónimos.

A guided tour meanders through countless impressive salons decorated with ornate objets d'art and Classical frescoes against settings of marble, gilt and velvet. Huge glittering chandeliers, produced locally, hang from the ceiling. In the private apartments there are superb tapestries. The church is adorned in lavish high Baroque style, and the Royal Mausoleum contains the tomb of Felipe V and his queen.

In the gardens, stately chestnut trees, clipped hedges and statues frame a complex series of pools. On 30 May, 25 July and 25 August each year all of the spectacular fountains are set in motion. Between May and July, four fountains run every Wednesday and Saturday at 5:30pm, and Sunday at 1pm.

The Real Fábrica de Cristales de La Granja (Royal Glass Manufacture) is also worth a visit. Founded in 1727, it still produces high-quality pieces, and it includes a glass museum.

St Teresa of Jesus

Teresa de Cepeda y Ahumada (1515–82) was one of the Catholic Church's greatest mystics and reformers. When aged just 7, she ran away from home in the hope of achieving martyrdom at the hands of the Moors, only to be recaptured by her uncle on the outskirts of the city. She became a nun at 19 but rebelled against her order. From 1562, when she founded her first convent, she travelled around Spain with her disciple, St John of the Cross, founding more convents for the followers of her order, the Barefoot Carmelites. Her remains are in Alba de Tormes near Salamanca (*see p365*).

Statue of St Teresa of Jesus in the city of Ávila

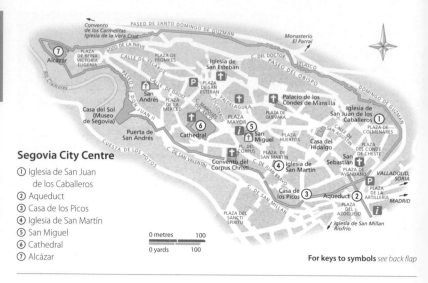

Segovia City Centre

① Iglesia de San Juan
   de los Caballeros
② Aqueduct
③ Casa de los Picos
④ Iglesia de San Martín
⑤ San Miguel
⑥ Cathedral
⑦ Alcázar

For keys to symbols *see back flap*

⓯ Segovia

Segovia. ⚑ 54,900. 🚊 🚌
ℹ️ Plaza del Azoguejo 1, 921 46
67 20. 🛍️ Thu & Sat. 🎉 San Pedro
(29 Jun), San Frutos (25 Oct).
🌐 **turismodesegovia.com**

Segovia is the most spectacularly sited city in Spain. The old
town is set high on a rocky
spur and surrounded by the
Río Eresma and Río Clamores.
It is often compared to a ship –
the Alcázar on its sharp crag
forming the prow, the pinnacles
of the cathedral rising like
masts, and the aqueduct trailing
behind like a rudder. The view
of it from the valley below at
sunset is magical.

The aqueduct, in use until the
late 19th century, was built at
the end of the 1st century AD
by the Romans, who turned
the ancient town into an
important military base.

The cathedral, dating from
1525 and consecrated in 1678,
is the last great Gothic church
in Spain. It was built to replace
the old cathedral, which was
destroyed in 1520 during the
revolt of the Castilian towns
(*see p62*). The cloister, however,
survived and was rebuilt on the
new site. The pinnacles, flying
buttresses, tower and dome
form an impressive silhouette,
while the interior is light and
elegantly vaulted. Ironwork

grilles enclose the side chapels.
The chapterhouse museum,
with a coffered ceiling, houses
17th-century Brussels tapestries.

At the city's western end is
the **Alcázar** (*see pp348–9*).
Rising sheer above crags with
a multitude of gabled roofs,
turrets and crenellations, it
appears like the archetypal
fairy-tale castle. The present
building is mostly a fanciful
reconstruction following a fire
in 1862. It contains a museum
of weaponry and a series of
elaborately decorated rooms.
Climb the keep for great views.

Notable churches include
the Romanesque San Juan

de los Caballeros, which
features an outstanding
sculptured portico, San Martín
with its beautiful arcades
and capitals, and San Miguel,
where Isabel the Catholic was
crowned Queen of Castile.
Just inside the city walls, Casa
de los Picos has a unique
façade adorned with diamond-
shaped stones.

Environs

The vast palace of **Riofrío**,
11 km (7 miles) to the southwest, is located in a deer
park. It was built as a hunting
lodge in 1752, and has richly
decorated rooms.

The imposing Gothic cathedral of Segovia

Segovia's Aqueduct

Water channel

Slots used to support blocks of ashlar

Arches reach a maximum height of 29 m (95 ft).

Water from the Río Frío flowed into the city, filtered through a series of tanks along the way.

Two tiers of arches – a total of 728 m (2,400 ft) in length – were needed to cope with the ground's gradient.

In this niche a statue of the Virgin Mary replaces an earlier inscription relating to the founding of the aqueduct.

Segovia's distinctive Alcázar, towering over the city

🏠 Alcázar de Segovia
Plaza de la Reina Victoria Eugenia. **Tel** 921 46 07 59. **Open** daily. **Closed** 1 & 6 Jan, 24 & 25 Dec. 🎫 (free for EU residents 3rd Tue of each month). ♿ 🎥 🖥 alcazardesegovia.com

🏛 Palacio de Riofrío
Tel 921 47 00 19. **Open** Tue–Sun 🎫 (free for EU res Wed pm & Thu pm). 🖥 patrimonionacional.es

⑯ Pedraza de la Sierra
Segovia. 🔼 500. 🚹 C/ Real 3, 921 50 86 66 (closed Mon & Tue). 🎭 Nuestra Señora la Virgen del Carrascal (8 Sep).

The aristocratic little town of Pedraza de la Sierra is perched high over rolling countryside. Within its medieval walls, old streets lead to the porticoed Plaza Mayor (see p31). The huge castle, standing on a rocky outcrop, was owned by Basque artist Ignacio Zuloaga (1870–1945). The castle museum shows some of his works. On the first and second Saturdays in July, concerts are held in Plaza Mayor.

Environs
The main sight at Turégano, 30 km (19 miles) west, is a large hilltop castle with the 15th-century Iglesia de San Miguel.

⑰ Sepúlveda
Segovia. 🔼 1,300. 🚹 C/ Santos Justo y Pastor 8, 921 54 04 25 (closed Mon Jul–Sep; Mon, Tue Oct–Jun). 🛒 Wed. 🎭 Los Toros (last week of Aug).

On a slope above the Río Duratón, this picturesque town offers views of the Sierra de Guadarrama. Parts of its medieval walls and castle survive. Of its several Romanesque churches, the Iglesia del Salvador, behind the main square, is notable for possessing one of the oldest atria in Spain (1093).

Environs
Winding through a canyon haunted by griffon vultures is the Río Duratón, 7 km (4 miles) west of Sepúlveda. This area of striking beauty has been designated the Parque Natural de las Hoces del Duratón.
Ayllón, 45 km (28 miles) northeast of Sepúlveda, has an arcaded main square and the Plateresque (see p29) Palacio de Juan de Contreras of 1497.
The Iberian and Roman ruins at Tiermes, 28 km (17 miles) further southeast, have been partially excavated, and finds can be seen in Soria's Museo Numantino (see p381).

⑱ Castillo de Coca
Coca, Segovia. **Tel** 617 57 35 54. **Open** daily. **Closed** 15 days in Jan, 1st Tue of each month. 🎫 📷

Built in the late 15th century for the influential Fonseca family, Coca castle is one of Castilla y León's most memorable fortresses. It was used more as a residential palace than a defensive castle, although its turrets and battlements are a fine example of Mudéjar military architecture. The complex moated structure comprises three concentric walls around a massive keep. It is now a forestry school, with a display of Romanesque woodcarvings.

Environs
The 14th-century castle of Arévalo in Avila, 26 km (16 miles) southwest, is where Isabel I spent her childhood. The porticoed Plaza de la Villa is surrounded by some attractive half-timbered houses.

Massive keep of the 15th-century Castillo de Coca

⑲ Medina del Campo

Valladolid. 🏠 21,600. 🚃 🚌
ⓘ Plaza Mayor 48, 983 81 13 57.
🍴 Sun. 🎉 San Antolín (1–8 Sep).
🌐 **medinadelcampo.es**

Medina became wealthy in medieval times on the proceeds of huge sheep fairs and is still an important agricultural centre today. The vast brick Gothic-Mudéjar **Castillo de la Mota** *(see p348)*, on its outskirts, began as a Moorish castle but was rebuilt in 1440. The town transferred the castle's ownership to the Crown in 1475. Isabel I and her daughter Juana "la Loca" ("the Mad") both stayed here. Later, it served as a prison – Cesare Borja was incarcerated here from 1506 to 1508. In a corner of the Plaza Mayor stands the modest house where Isabel died in 1504.

Environs
Towering over the plains, some 25 km (16 miles) to the south of Medina del Campo, are the walls of Madrigal de las Altas Torres, which owes its name to the hundreds of bastions that marked the old wall; only 23 remain. In 1451 Isabel was born here in a palace that later became the Monasterio de las Agustinas in 1527.

🏰 **Castillo de la Mota**
Tel 983 81 00 63. **Open** Tue–Sun pm. **Closed** public hols. 📷 only.
🌐 **castillodelamota.es**

⑳ Tordesillas

Valladolid. 🏠 9,000. 🚌 ⓘ Casas del Tratado, 983 77 10 67 (closed Mon).
🍴 Tue. 🎉 Fiestas de la Peña (mid-Sep). 🌐 **tordesillas.net**

This pleasant town is where the historic treaty between Spain and Portugal was signed in 1494, dividing the lands of the New World *(see p60)*. A fateful oversight by the Spanish mapmakers left the immense prize of Brazil to Portugal.

The town's main place to visit is the **Monasterio de Santa Clara**. It was constructed by

Castillo de la Mota at Medina del Campo

Alfonso XI around 1340 and then converted by his son Pedro the Cruel into a stunning residence for his mistress, María de Padilla. Pining for her native Andalucía, she had the convent decorated with fine Moorish arches, baths and tiles. Most impressive are the beautiful patio and the main chapel. There is a fantastic display of royal musical instruments, including the portable organ of Juana "la Loca".

In the old quarter, the **Iglesia de San Antolín** now houses a fascinating religious art museum, which displays paintings as well as a collection of liturgical objects.

🏛 **Monasterio de Santa Clara**
Tel 983 77 00 71. **Open** Tue–Sun. 🎟 (free Wed pm & Thu pm for EU citizens). 🌐 **patrimonionacional.es**

🏛 **Iglesia de San Antolín**
Calle Postigo. **Tel** 983 77 09 80.
Open Tue–Sun. 🎟

Moorish patio in the Monasterio de Santa Clara, Tordesillas

㉑ Valladolid

Valladolid. 🏠 311,500. 🚃 🚌 ⓘ Glass Pavilion, Acera de Recoletos, 983 21 93 10. 🍴 Wed, Sat, Sun.
🎉 Easter week, San Pedro Regalado (13 May), Virgen de San Lorenzo (8 Sep). 🌐 **info.valladolid.es**

The Arabic city of Belad-Walid (meaning "Land of the Governor") is located at the confluence of the Río Esgueva and Río Pisuerga. Although it has become sprawling and industrialized, Valladolid has some of Spain's best Renaissance art and architecture.

Fernando and Isabel *(see pp60–61)* were married in the Palacio Vivero in 1469 and, following the completion of the Reconquest in 1492, they made Valladolid their capital. Less spectacularly, Columbus died here, alone and forgotten, in 1506. In 1527 Felipe II was born in the Palacio de los Pimentel. José Zorrilla, who popularized the legendary Don Juan in his 1844 play *(see p39)*, was also born in the city.

The Baroque façade *(see p29)* of the city's 15th-century university was begun in 1715 by Narciso Tomé. He later created the Transparente of Toledo Cathedral *(see p397)*.

The Iglesia de San Pablo has a spectacular façade, embellished with angels and coats of arms in Plateresque style. Among the other noteworthy churches are Santa María la Antigua, with its Romanesque belfry, and the Iglesia de Las Angustias, where Juan de Juni's fine sculpture of the Virgen de los Cuchillos (Virgin of the Knives) is on display.

🏠 Casa de Cervantes

Calle Rastro s/n. **Tel** 983 30 88 10. **Open** Tue–Sun. **Closed** pub hols. 📷 (free Sun am). 🌐 **museocasacervantes.mcu.es**

The author of *Don Quixote* (*see p38*) lived in this simple house with whitewashed walls from 1603 to 1606. The rooms contain some of Cervantes' original furnishings.

🏛 Cathedral

Calle Arribas 1. **Tel** 983 30 43 62. **Closed** Mon. 📷 (Oct–Jun: free Thu). 🕐 by appt. 🌐 **catedral-valladolid.com**

Work started on the unfinished cathedral in 1580 by Felipe II's favourite architect, Juan de Herrera, but lost momentum over the centuries. Churri-gueresque (*see p29*) flourishes on the façade are in contrast to the sombre, square-pillared interior, whose only redeeming flamboyance is a Juan de Juni altarpiece. The Museo Diocesano inside, however, contains some fine religious art and sculpture.

🏛 Museo Nacional de Escultura

Cadenas de S Gregorio 1, 2 & 3. **Tel** 983 25 03 75. **Open** Tue–Sun. **Closed** Sun pm, public hols. 📷 (free Sat pm & Sun). 🌐 **museoescultura.mcu.es**

This permanent art collection in the 15th-century Colegio de San Gregorio consists mainly of wooden religious sculptures from the 13th to 18th centuries.

Façade of Colegio de San Gregorio, Valladolid

Antonio Moro's *Calvary*, in the Museo Nacional de Escultura, Valladolid

They include Juan de Juni's emotive depiction of the burial of Christ and *Recumbent Christ* by Gregorio Fernández. An Alonso Berruguete altarpiece, and walnut choir stalls by Diego de Siloé and other artists, are among the other fine works to be found here.

The building itself is worthy of attention, particularly the Plateresque staircase, the chapel by Juan Güas, and the patio of twisted columns and delicate basket arches. The façade is a fine example of Isabelline (*see p28*) sculpture, portraying a melee of naked children scrambling about in thorn trees and strange beasts.

The nearby 16th-century Palacio de Villena displays the valuable Belén Napolitano (Naples Christmas crib).

🏛 Patio Herreriano Museo de Arte Contemporáneo Español

Calle Jorge Guillén 6. **Tel** 983 36 27 71. **Open** Tue–Sun. **Closed** Sun pm. 📷 ♿ 🌐 **museopatioherreriano.org**

This private collection of contemporary Spanish art opened in 2002, housed in the former Monastery of San Benito with its fine cloisters. More than 800 works by 200 Spanish artists are displayed, including work by Joan Miró, Eduardo Chillida, Antoni Tàpies and Miquel Barceló.

Environs

The moated grey castle that dominates the village of Simancas, 11 km (7 miles) southwest of Valladolid, was converted by Charles V into Spain's national archive. The Visigothic church in the village of Wamba, 15 km (9 miles) to the west, contains the tomb of King Recceswinth.

An unusual long, narrow 15th-century castle on a ridge overlooks the wine town of Peñafiel, 60 km (40 miles) east of Valladolid (*see p349*).

㉒ Medina de Rioseco

Valladolid. 🚗 5,000. 🚌 ℹ️ Paseo de San Francisco, 983 72 03 19 (closed Mon). 🚆 Wed. 🎭 Easter week; San Juan (24 Jun), Virgen del Castillviejo (8 Sep). 🌐 **medinaderioseco.com**

During the Middle Ages this town grew wealthy from the profitable wool trade, enabling it to commission leading artists, mainly of the Valladolid school, to decorate its churches. The dazzling star vaulting and superb woodwork of the Iglesia de Santa María de Mediavilla, in the centre of town, are evidence of this. Inside, the Los Benavente Chapel is a tour de force, with a colourful stucco ceiling by Jerónimo del Corral (1554), and an altarpiece by Juan de Juni.

The interior of the Iglesia de Santiago is stunning, with a triple altarpiece designed by the Churriguera brothers of Salamanca (*see p29*).

The ancient buildings on Medina de Rioseco's main street, the Calle de la Rúa, are supported on wooden pillars, forming shady porticoes.

Altarpiece by Juan de Juni, Iglesia de Santa María de Mediavilla

Castilla y León's Fiestas

El Colacho *(Sun after Corpus Christi, May/Jun)*, Castrillo de Murcia (Burgos). Babies born during the previous 12 months are dressed in their best Sunday clothes and laid on mattresses in the streets. Crowds of people, including the anxious parents, watch as *El Colacho* – a man dressed in a bright red and yellow costume – jumps over the babies in order to free them from illnesses, especially hernias. He is said to represent the Devil fleeing from the sight of the Eucharist. This ritual is thought to have originated in 1621.

El Colacho jumping over babies in Castrillo de Murcia

St Agatha's Day *(Sun closest to 5 Feb)*, Zamarramala (Segovia). Every year two women are elected as mayoresses to run the village on the day of St Agatha, patron saint of married women. They ceremonially burn a stuffed figure representing a man.

Good Friday, Valladolid. The procession of 28 multi-coloured sculptures, which depict various scenes of the Passion, is one of the most spectacular in Spain.

Fire-walking *(23 Jun)*, San Pedro Manrique (Soria). Men, some carrying people on their backs, walk barefoot over burning embers. It is said that only local people can do this without being burned.

The beautiful carved retrochoir of Palencia Cathedral

❷❸ Palencia

Palencia. 🅼 81,200. 🚆 🚌 ℹ️ Calle Mayor 31, 979 70 65 23. 🗓️ Tue, Wed. 🎉 Virgen de la Calle (2 Feb). 📷
🌐 **palenciaturismo.es**

In medieval times, Palencia was a royal residence and the site of Spain's first university, founded in 1208. The city gradually diminished in importance following its involvement in the failed revolt of the Castilian towns of 1520 *(see p62)*.

Although Palencia has since expanded considerably on profits from coal and wheat, its centre, by the old stone bridge over the Río Carrión, remains almost village-like.

The city's main sight is the cathedral, known as *La Bella Desconocida* (the Unknown Beauty). It is especially worth a visit for its superb works of art, many the result of Bishop Fonseca's generous patronage. The retrochoir, exquisitely sculpted by Gil de Siloé and Simon of Cologne, and the two altarpieces, are also noteworthy. The altarpiece above the high altar was carved by Philippe de Bigarny early in the 16th century. The inset panels are by Juan de Flandes, Isabel I's court painter. Behind the high altar is the Chapel of the Holy Sacrament, with an altarpiece dating from 1529 by Valmaseda. In this chapel, high on a ledge to the left, is the colourful tomb of Doña Urraca of Navarra. Below the retrochoir, a Plateresque *(see p29)* staircase leads down to the fine Visigothic crypt.

Environs

Baños de Cerrato, 12 km (7 miles) to the south, boasts the tiny Visigothic Iglesia de San Juan Bautista, founded in 661. It is alleged to be the oldest intact church in Spain. Carved capitals and horseshoe arches decorate the interior.

❷❹ Frómista

Palencia. 🅼 820. 🚆 🚌 ℹ️ Barrio del Canal s/n, 672 14 69 94. 🗓️ Fri. 🎉 San Telmo (week after Easter).
🌐 **fromista.es**

This town on the Road to Santiago de Compostela *(see pp86–7)* is the site of one of Spain's purest Romanesque churches. The Iglesia de San Martín is the highlight of the town, partly due to a restoration in 1904, leaving the church, dating from 1066, entirely Romanesque in style. The presence of Pagan and Roman motifs suggest it may have pre-Christian origins. Nearby, the Iglesia de San Pedro has notable Renaissance and Gothic sculptures.

Environs

Carrión de los Condes, 20 km (12 miles) to the northwest, is also on the Road to Santiago. The frieze on the door of the Iglesia de Santiago depicts not religious figures but local artisans. There are carvings of bulls on the façade of the 12th-century Iglesia de Santa María del Camino. The Monasterio de San Zoilo has a Gothic cloister and now operates as a hotel.

Interior of the Iglesia de San Juan Bautista at Baños de Cerrato

Posada of the Monasterio de Santa María la Real, Aguilar de Campoo

Located at Gañinas, 20 km (12 miles) to the northwest (just south of Saldaña), is the Roman villa, **La Olmeda**. It has a number of mosaics, including a hunting scene. Finds are shown in the archaeological museum in the Iglesia de San Pedro in Saldaña.

🏛 Villa Romana La Olmeda

Pedrosa de la Vega. **Tel** 979 11 99 97. **Open** Tue–Sun. **Closed** 1 & 6 Jan, 24, 25 & 31 Dec. 📷 Includes museum. 📷

㉕ Aguilar de Campoo

Palencia. 🔼 7,300. 🚉 🚌 **ℹ** Paseo de la Cascajera, 10, 979 12 36 41 (closed Mon, Tue & Sun pm). 🚌 Tue. 📷 San Juan y San Pedro (23–29 Jun), Virgen del Llano (1st Sun in Sep). **w** aguilardecampoo.com

Situated between the parched plains of Central Spain and the lush foothills of the Cantabrian Mountains is the old fortified town of Aguilar de Campoo. In the centre of its ancient porticoed main square is the bell tower of the Colegiata de San Miguel. In this church is a mausoleum containing the tomb of the Marquises of Aguilar. Ask at the priest's house for the key.

Among the other places of interest are the Ermita de Santa Cecilia, and the restored Romanesque-Gothic Monasterio de Santa María la Real, which has a friendly *posada* (inn).

Environs
Six km (4 miles) south, at Olleros de Pisuerga, is a church built in a cave. From the parador at Cervera de Pisuerga, 25 km (15 miles) northwest of Aguilar, there are stunning views, and tours of the Reserva Nacional de Fuentes Carrionas. This is a rugged region overlooked by Curavacas, a 2,540-m (8,333-ft) peak.

㉖ Briviesca

Burgos. 🔼 7,700. 🚉 🚌 **ℹ** Calle Santa María Encimera 1, 947 59 39 39. 🚌 first Sat of month. 📷 Feria de San José (19 Mar), Santa Casilda (9 May). **w** turismo-briviesca.com

This walled town, in the northeast of Burgos province, has an arcaded main square and several mansions. The best known of its churches is the Convento de Santa Clara, with its 16th-century walnut reredos carved with religious scenes. In 1387 Juan I of Aragón created the title Príncipe de Asturias for his son, Enrique, in the town. The Santuario de Santa Casilda, situated outside Briviesca, has a collection of votive objects.

Environs
Oña, 25 km (15 miles) north, is an attractive town. A Benedictine monastery was founded here in 1011.

Overlooking a fertile valley, 20 km (12 miles) further northeast, is the little hilltop town of Frías. Its castle overlooks cobbled streets and pretty old houses. Crossing the Río Ebro is a fortified medieval bridge, still with its central gate tower.

At Medina de Pomar, 30 km (20 miles) north of Oña, there is a 15th-century castle, once the seat of the Velasco family. Inside are the ruins of a palace with fine Mudéjar stucco decoration and Arabic inscriptions.

The medieval bridge over the Río Ebro at Frías, with its central gate tower

Flemish triptych inside the collegiate church in Covarrubias

㉗ Covarrubias

Burgos. 🚇 630. 🚌 ℹ️ Calle Monseñor Vargas, 947 40 64 61 (closed Sun pm; Mon–Wed in winter). 🎪 Tue. 🎉 San Cosme and San Damián (26–27 Sep).

Named after the reddish caves on its outskirts, Covarrubias stands on the banks of the Río Arlanza. Medieval walls surround the charming old centre with its arcaded half-timbered houses (see p30). The distinguished collegiate church (closed Tue) shows the historical importance of Covarrubias: here is the tomb of Fernán González, first independent Count of Castile, and one of the great figures in Castilian history. By uniting several fiefs against the Moors in the 10th century, he started the rise in Castilian power that ensured the resulting kingdom of Castile would play a leading role in the unification of Spain. The church museum contains a Flemish triptych of the Adoration of the Magi, attributed to the school of Gil de Siloé, and a 17th-century organ.

Environs
A short distance east along the Río Arlanza lies the ruins of the 11th-century Romanesque monastery of San Pedro de Arlanza. At Quintanilla de las Viñas, 24 km (15 miles) north of Covarrubias, is a ruined 7th-century Visigothic church. The reliefs on the columns of the triumphal arch are remarkable, depicting sun and moon symbols that may be pagan.

㉘ Burgos

Burgos. 🚇 180,000. ✈️ 🚌 ℹ️ Plaza de Alonso Martínez 7, 947 20 31 25. 🎪 Wed, Fri, Sat & Sun. 🎉 San Lesmes (30 Jan); Pedro and San Pablo (29 Jun). 🌐 **turismoburgos.org**

Founded in 884, Burgos has played a significant political and military role in Spanish history. It was the capital of the united kingdoms of Castile and León from 1073 until losing that honour to Valladolid after the fall of Granada in 1492 (see pp60–61). During the 15th and 16th centuries, Burgos grew rich from the wool trade and used its riches to finance most of the great art and architecture which can be seen in the city today. Less auspiciously, Franco chose Burgos as his Civil War headquarters (see pp70–71).

The city's strategic location on the main Madrid–France highway and on the route to Santiago (see pp86–7) ensure many visitors; but even without this Burgos would justify a long detour. Despite its size and extremes of climate, it is one of most agreeable provincial capitals in Castilla y León.

Approach via the bridge of Santa María, which leads into the old quarter through the restored Arco de Santa María, a gateway carved with statues of various local worthies. The main bridge into the city, however, is the Puente de San Pablo, where a statue commemorates the city's hero, El Cid. Not far from the bridge stands the Casa del Cordón, a 15th-century palace (now a bank) which has a Franciscan cord motif carved over the portal. A plaque declares that this is where the Catholic Monarchs welcomed Columbus on his return, in 1497, from the second of his famous voyages to the Americas.

The lacy, steel-grey spires of the cathedral (see pp376–7) are a prominent landmark from almost anywhere in the city. On the rising ground behind it stands the restored Iglesia de San Nicolás, whose main feature is a superb altarpiece by Simon of Cologne (1505). Other churches worth visiting are the Iglesia de San Lorenzo, with its superb Baroque ceiling, and the Iglesia de San Esteban, which houses the Museo del Retablo, open to the public during summer. The Iglesia de Santa Águeda is the place where El Cid made King Alfonso VI swear that he played no part in the murder of his elder brother, King Sancho II (see p360).

The Arco de Santa María in Burgos, adorned with statues and turrets

El Cid (1043–99)

Rodrigo Díaz de Vivar was born into a noble family in Vivar del Cid, north of Burgos, in 1043. He served Fernando I, but was banished from Castile after becoming embroiled in the fratricidal squabbles of the king's sons, Sancho II and Alfonso VI. He switched allegiance to fight for the Moors, then changed side again, capturing Valencia for the Christians in 1094, ruling the city until his death. For his heroism he was named El Cid, from the Arabic *Sidi* (Lord). He was a charismatic man of great courage, but it was an anonymous poem, *El Cantar de Mío Cid*, in 1180, that immortalized him as a romantic hero of the Reconquest (see pp58–9). The tombs of El Cid and his wife, Jimena, are in Burgos Cathedral.

Equestrian statue of El Cid

Burgos City Centre

① Iglesia de San Esteban
② Iglesia de San Nicolás
③ Iglesia de Santa Águeda
④ Cathedral
⑤ Iglesia de San Lorenzo
⑥ Arco de Santa María
⑦ Casa del Cordón
⑧ Museo de Burgos
⑨ Museo de la
   Evolución Humana

0 metres   150
0 yards   150

For keys to symbols *see back flap*

Across the river, the palace of the Casa de Miranda houses the archaeological section of the **Museo de Burgos**, with finds from the Roman city of Clunia. Nearby, the Casa de Angulo contains the Fine Arts section, whose prize exhibits are Juan de Padilla's tomb by Gil de Siloé, and a Moorish casket in enamelled ivory. Also nearby is the **Museo de la Evolución Humana**, which exhibits fossils from the site of the Sierra de Atapuerca, dating from some 780,000 years ago. A combined entrance ticket includes the museum, the Yacimientos de

Sculpted tomb of Juan de Padilla by Gil de Siloé, in Museo de Burgos

Atapuerca, the site of Europe's earliest settlement (on the outskirts of Burgos), and a bus to the site.

Two religious houses, on the outskirts of Burgos, are worth visiting. Just west of the city is the **Real Monasterio de Huelgas**, a late 12th-century Cistercian convent founded by Alfonso VIII. One of the most interesting parts is the Museo de Ricas Telas, a textile museum of ancient fabrics from the convent's royal tombs. In the Capilla de Santiago is a curious wooden figure of St James holding a sword, with which, according to tradition, royal princes were dubbed Knights of Santiago.

To the east of Burgos is the **Cartuja de Miraflores**, a Carthusian monastery founded during the 15th century. The church includes two of Spain's most notable tombs, attributed to Gil de Siloé. One holds the bodies of Juan II and Isabel of Portugal; the other contains that of their son, Prince Alfonso. The altarpiece by Gil de Siloé, allegedly gilded with the first consignment of gold brought back to Spain from the New World, is spectacular.

Polychrome altarpiece by Gil de Siloé, in Cartuja de Miraflores

🏛 **Museo de Burgos**
Calle Miranda, 13. **Tel** 947 26 58 75.
Open Tue–Sun. 🖼 (free Sat & Sun).
♿ partial. 🌐 museodeburgos.com

🏛 **Museo de la Evolución Humana**
Paseo Sierra de Atapuerca. **Tel** 902 02 42 46. **Open** Tue–Sun. 🖼 (ticket offers combined entry to Yacimientos de Atapuerca and transport).

🏛 **Real Monasterio de Huelgas**
Calle de los Compases. **Tel** 947 20 16 30. **Open** Tue–Sun. **Closed** some public hols. 🖼 📷 (free Wed & Thu pm).

🏛 **Cartuja de Miraflores**
Carretera Burgos–Cardeña, km 3.
Tel 947 26 34 25. **Open** daily.

Burgos Cathedral

Spain's third-largest cathedral was founded in 1221 by Bishop Don Mauricio under Fernando III. The ground plan – a Latin cross – measures 84 m (92 yards) by 59 m (65 yards). Its construction was carried out in stages over three centuries and involved many of the greatest artists and architects in Europe. The style is almost entirely Gothic, and shows influences from Germany, France and the Low Countries. First to be built were the nave and cloisters, while the intricate, crocketed spires and the richly decorated side chapels are mostly later work. The architects cleverly adapted the cathedral to its sloping site, incorporating stairways inside and out.

West Front
The lacy, steel-grey spires soar above a sculpted balustrade depicting Castile's early kings.

★ Golden Staircase
This elegant Renaissance staircase by Diego de Siloé (1519–22) links the nave with a tall door (kept locked) at street level.

Puerta de Santa María

KEY

① **Capilla de la Presentación** (1519–24) is a funerary chapel with a star-shaped, traceried vault.

② **Capilla de Santa Tecla**

③ **Tomb of El Cid**

④ **Capilla de Santa Ana** features an altarpiece (1490) by the sculptor Gil de Siloé. The central panel shows St Anne with St Joachim.

⑤ **Lantern**

⑥ **Capilla de San Juan Bautista and museum**

⑦ **Interpretation Centre**

⑧ **Capilla de la Visitación**

⑨ **Reception and Information Centre**

⑩ **Capilla del Santísimo Cristo**

For hotels and restaurants in this region see pp569–70 and pp594–5

Retrochoir
Several of the reliefs around the chancel were carved by Philippe de Bigarny. This expressive scene, which was completed in 1499, depicts the road to Calvary.

VISITORS' CHECKLIST

Practical Information
Plaza de Santa María. **Tel** 947 20 47 12. **Open** 9:30am–7:30pm daily (Nov–Mar: 10am–7pm). 🕙 9am, 10am, 11am, 7:30pm daily; noon, 1pm, 2pm Sun. 🅿 ♿
Ⓦ catedraldeburgos.info

★ **Constables' Chapel**
The tomb of the High Constable of Castile and his wife lies beneath the openwork vault of this chapel of 1496.

Sacristy (1765) The sacristy was rebuilt in Baroque style, with an exuberant plasterwork vault and Rococo altars.

Puerta del Sarmental
The tympanum of this portal of 1240 shows Christ flanked by the Evangelists. This is the main entrance for tourists.

★ **The Crossing**
The magnificent star-ribbed central dome, begun in 1539, rises on four huge pillars. It is decorated with effigies of prophets and saints. Beneath it is the tomb of El Cid and his wife.

㉙ Lerma

Burgos. 🚟 2,900. 🚌 🚍 ℹ️ Calle
Audiencia 6, 947 17 70 02 (closed
Mon, except Aug). 🛎️ Wed.
🎎 Nuestra Señora de la Natividad
(8 Sep). 🅦 citlerma.com

The grandiose appearance of
this town is largely due to the
ambition of the notorious first
Duke of Lerma (see p64), Felipe
III's corrupt favourite and
minister from 1598 to 1618.
He misused vast quantities of
Spain's new-found wealth on
new buildings in his home town
– all strictly Classical in style,
in accordance with prevailing
fashion. At the top of the town,
the Palacio Ducal, built in 1605
as his residence, has been
transformed into a parador.

There are good views over
the Río Arlanza from the archways near to the Convento de
Santa Clara and also from the
Colegiata de San Pedro church,
which has a bronze statue of
the Duke's uncle.

The narrow, sloping streets of the Old Town
of Lerma

Cloisters of the Monasterio de Santo
Domingo de Silos

㉚ Monasterio de Santo Domingo de Silos

Santo Domingo de Silos (Burgos).
Tel 947 39 00 49. 🚍 from Burgos.
Open 10am–1pm, 4:30–6pm Tue–
Sun. **Closed** pub hols. 🎎 ✝️ 9am,
7pm Mon–Sat, 11am & 7pm Sun.
🅦 abadiadesilos.es

St Dominic gave his name to
the monastery he built in 1041
over the ruins of an abbey
destroyed by the Moors. It is
a place of spiritual and artistic
pilgrimage – its tranquil setting
has inspired countless poets.

Others come to admire the
beautiful Romanesque cloisters,
whose capitals are sculpted in a
variety of designs, both symbol-
istic and realistic. The carvings on
the corner piers depict various
scenes from the Bible and the
ceilings are coffered in Moorish
style. The body of St Dominic
rests in a silver urn, supported
by three Romanesque lions, in

a chapel in the north gallery.
The old pharmacy, just off the
cloister, has a display of jars from
Talavera de la Reina (see p390).

The Benedictine community
holds regular services in Gregorian chant in the Neo-Classical
church by Ventura Rodríguez.
The monastery offers accommodation for male guests.

Environs
To the southwest lies the
Garganta de la Yecla (Yecla
Gorge), where a path leads to
a narrow fissure cut by the river.
To the northeast, the peaks
and wildlife reserve of the
Sierra de la Demanda extend
over into La Rioja.

The 15th-century castle of Peñaranda
de Duero

㉛ Peñaranda de Duero

Burgos. 🚟 580. 🚍 ℹ️ Calle
Trinquete 7. **Tel** 947 55 20 63
(closed Mon, Sun pm). 🛎️ Fri.
🎎 Santiago (25 Jul), Santa Ana
(26 Jul), Virgen de los Remedios
(8 Sep). 🅦 penarandadeduero.es

The castle of Peñaranda was
built during the Reconquest (see
pp58–9) by the Castilians, who
had driven the Moors back
south of the Río Duero. From
its hilltop site, there are views
down to one of the most
charming villages in old Castile,
where pantiled houses cluster
around a huge church. The
main square is lined with porticoed, timber-framed buildings
and the superb Renaissance
Palacio de Avellaneda. Framing
its main doorway are various

Gregorian Plainchant

At regular intervals throughout the
day, the monks of Santo Domingo
de Silos sing services in plainchant,
an unaccompanied singing of Latin
texts in unison. The origins of chant
date back to the beginnings of
Christianity, but it was Pope Gregory
I (590–604) who codified this
manner of worship. It is an ancient
and austere form of music which
has found a new appeal with
modern audiences. In 1994 a
recording of the monks became
a surprise hit all over the world.

Manuscript for an 11th-century
Gregorian chant

Curtain walls and drum towers of Berlanga de Duero castle

heraldic devices, and inside is a patio with fine decorated ceilings. On Calle de la Botica is a 17th-century pharmacy.

Environs

In Aranda de Duero, 18 km (10 miles) to the west, the Iglesia de Santa María, has an Isabelline façade (see p28).

🏛 **Palacio de Avellaneda**
Plaza Condes de Miranda 1. **Tel** 947 55 20 13. **Open** 10am–2pm, 4–8pm Tue–Sun. 📷 only (every 30 min).

㉜ El Burgo de Osma

Soria. 🗺 5,250. 🚌 ℹ Plaza Mayor 9, 975 36 01 16 (closed Wed except in high season). 🛍 Sat. 🎉 Virgen del Espino and San Roque (14–19 Aug). 🌐 burgodeosma.com

The most interesting sight in this attractive village is the cathedral. Although it is mostly Gothic (dating from 1232), with Renaissance additions, the tower is Baroque (1739). Its treasures include a Juan de Juni altarpiece and the tomb of its founder, San Pedro de Osma. The museum has a valuable collection of illuminated manuscripts and codices.

Porticoed buildings line the streets and the Plaza Mayor, and storks nest on the Baroque Hospital de San Agustín.

Environs

Overlooking the Río Duero at Gormaz, 12 km (7 miles) south, is a massive castle with 28 towers. There are also medieval fortresses at Berlanga de Duero,

20 km (12 miles) further south-east, and at Calatañazor, 25 km (16 miles) northeast of El Burgo de Osma, near to where the Moorish leader al Mansur was killed in 1002 (see p57).

㉝ Soria

Soria. 🗺 40,150. 🚌 🚆 ℹ Calle Medinaceli 2, 975 21 20 52. 🛍 Thu. 🎉 San Juan (24 Jun). 🌐 sorianitelaimaginas.com

Castilla y León's smallest provincial capital stands on the banks of the Río Duero. Soria's stylish, modern parador is named after the poet Antonio Machado (1875–1939, see p39), who wrote in praise of the town and the surrounding plains. Many of the older buildings are gone, but among those remaining are the imposing Palacio de los Condes de Gómara, and the Concatedral de San Pedro, both built in the 16th century.

The **Museo Numantino**, opposite the municipal gardens, displays a variety of finds from the nearby Roman ruins of Numantia and Tiermes (see p369).

Across the Duero is the ruined monastery of San Juan de Duero, with a 13th-century cloister of interlacing arches.

Environs

North of Soria are the ruins of Numantia, whose inhabitants endured a year-long Roman siege in 133 BC before defiantly burning the town and themselves (see p54). To the northwest is the Sierra de Urbión, a range of pine-clad hills with a lake, the Laguna Negra de Urbión.

🏛 **Museo Numantino**
Paseo del Espolón 8. **Tel** 975 22 13 97. **Open** Tue–Sun. 🎟 (free Sat & Sun). ♿

㉞ Medinaceli

Soria. 🗺 820. 🚌 🚆 ℹ Campo San Nicolás, 975 32 63 47. 🎉 Beato Julián de San Agustín (28 Aug), Cuerpos Santos (13 Nov). 🌐 **medinaceli.es**

Only a triumphal arch remains of Roman Ocilis, perched on a high ridge over the Río Jalón. Built in the 1st century AD, it is the only one in Spain with three arches. It has been adopted as the symbol for ancient monuments on Spanish road signs.

Environs

Just to the east are the red cliffs of the Jalón gorges. On the Madrid–Zaragoza road is the 12th-century Cistercian monastery of **Santa María de Huerta**. It includes a 13th-century Gothic cloister and the superb, crypt-like Monks' Refectory.

🏛 **Monasterio de Santa María de Huerta**
Tel 975 32 70 02. **Open** daily. **Closed** 24 Aug. 🎟 ♿ 🌐 monasteriohuerta.org

Decorative arches in the cloister of the monastery of San Juan de Duero

CASTILLA-LA MANCHA

*Guadalajara · Cuenca · Toledo ·
Albacete · Ciudad Real*

La Mancha's empty beauty, its windmills and medieval
castles, silhouetted above the sienna plains, was
immortalized by Cervantes in Don Quixote's epic
adventures. Its brilliantly sunlit, wide horizons are among
the classic images of Spain. This scarcely visited region has
great, scenic mountain ranges, dramatic gorges and the two
monument-filled cities of Toledo and Cuenca.

As the name Castilla suggests you will
always find a castle nearby in this region.
Most were built in the 9th–12th centuries,
when the region was a battleground
between Christians and Moors, while
others mark the 14th- and 15th-century
frontiers between the kingdoms of Aragón
and Castile. Sigüenza, Belmonte, Alarcón,
Molina de Aragón and Calatrava la
Nueva are among the most impressive.

Toledo, which was the capital of
Visigothic Spain, is an outstanding
museum city. Its rich architectural and
artistic heritage derives from a coa-
lescence of Muslim, Christian and Jewish
cultures with medieval and Renaissance
ideas and influences.

Cuenca is another attractive city. Its
Old Town is perched above converging
gorges; on two sides it spills down
steep hillsides. Villanueva de los Infantes,
Chinchilla, Alcaraz and Almagro are
towns of character built between the
16th and 18th centuries. Ocaña and
Tembleque each has a splendid
plaza mayor (main square).

La Mancha's plains are brightened by
natural features of great beauty in its two
national parks – the Tablas de Daimiel, and
Cabañeros, within the Montes de Toledo.
Rimming the plains are beautiful upland
areas: the olive groves of the Alcarria;
Cuenca's limestone mountains; and the
peaks of the Sierra de Alcaraz. The wine
region of La Mancha is the world's largest
expanse of vineyards. Around Consuegra
and Albacete fields turn mauve in autumn
as the valuable saffron crocus blooms.

Windmills above Campo de Criptana on the plains of La Mancha

◀ Hanging Houses over the Huécar ravine in Cuenca, Castilla-La Mancha

Exploring Castilla-La Mancha

The historic city of Toledo is Castilla-La Mancha's major
tourist destination. Less crowded towns with historical
charm include Almagro, Oropesa, Alcaraz and Guadalajara.
At Sigüenza, Calatrava, Belmonte and Alarcón there are
medieval castles, reminders of the region's eventful past.
Some towns on the plains of La Mancha, such as El Toboso
and Campo de Criptana, are associated with the adventures
of Don Quixote *(see p399)*. The wooded uplands of the
Serranía de Cuenca, the Alcarria and the Sierra de Alcaraz
provide picturesque scenic routes, and the wetland nature
reserve of the Tablas de Daimiel is a haven for bird lovers.

0 kilometres   50

0 miles   30

Sights at a Glance

The tranquil Montes de Toledo

Cattle grazing on the isolated plains of La Mancha

Key

- 🚗 Motorway
- Major road
- Secondary road
- Scenic route
- Main railway
- Minor railway
- Regional border
- △ Summit

The village of Alcalá del Júcar

Getting Around

Castilla-La Mancha is best explored by car as it is well endowed with a network of motorways radiating outwards from Madrid. The region is also served by high-speed AVE trains which run between Madrid, Seville, Toledo and Albacete (via Cuenca). Otherwise, public transport is infrequent and slow.

For keys to symbols see back flap

❶ Atienza

Guadalajara. 🏔 500. 🅸 Héctor Vázquez 2, 949 39 92 93 (closed Mon–Fri). 🚌 Fri. 🎉 La Caballada (Pentecost Sun). 🆆 **turismo castillalamancha.es**

Rising high above the valley it once protected, Atienza contains vestiges of its medieval past. Crowning the hill is a ruined 12th-century castle. The arcaded Plaza Mayor and the Plaza del Trigo are joined by an original gateway. The **Museo de San Gil**, a religious art museum, is in the church of the same name. The Iglesia de Santa María del Rey, at the foot of the hill, displays a Baroque altarpiece.

Environs
Campisábalos, to the west, has a 12th-century Romanesque church. The Hayedo de Tejera Negra, further west, is a nature reserve of beech woods.

🏛 Museo de San Gil
Calle San Gil. **Tel** 949 39 90 41. **Open** Sat & Sun; by appt weekdays. 📷

❷ Sigüenza

Guadalajara. 🏔 5,000. 🚉 🚌 🅸 Calle Serrano Sanz 9, 949 34 70 07. 🚌 Sat. 🎉 San Vicente (22 Jan), San Juan (24 Jun), Fiestas Patronales (mid-Aug). 🆆 **siguenza.es**

Dominating the hillside town of Sigüenza is its impressive castle-parador. The cathedral is Romanesque, with later additions such as the Gothic-Plateresque cloisters. In one of the chapels is the Tomb of El

Semi-recumbent figure of El Doncel on his tomb in Sigüenza Cathedral

Doncel, built for Martín Vázquez de Arce, Isabel of Castile's page *(see p60)*. He was killed in battle against the Moors in 1486. The sacristy has a ceiling carved with flowers and cherubs.

❸ Molina de Aragón

Guadalajara. 🏔 4,000 🚌 🅸 Calle de las Tiendas 62, 949 83 20 98. 🚌 Thu. 🎉 Día del Carmen (16 Jul), Ferias (30 Aug–5 Sep). 🆆 **turismomolinaaltotajo.com**

Molina's attractive medieval quarter is at the foot of a hill next to the Río Gallo. The town was disputed during the Reconquest and captured from the Moors by Alfonso I of Aragón in 1129. Many monuments were destroyed during the War of Independence *(see p67)*, but the 11th-century hilltop castle preserves seven original towers. It is possible to visit the Romanesque-Gothic Iglesia de Santa Clara.

Environs
West of Molina is the Virgen de la Hoz chapel, set in a rust-red ravine. Further southwest is a nature reserve, the Parque Natural del Alto Tajo.

Arab ramparts above Molina de Aragón's Old Town

❹ La Alcarria

Guadalajara. 🚌 Guadalajara. 🅸 Palacio Ducal, Plaza de la Hora, Pastrana, 949 37 06 72. 🆆 **turismo castillalamancha.es**

This vast stretch of undulating olive groves and fields east of Guadalajara is still evocative of Camilo José Cela's *(see p39)* book *Journey to the Alcarria*. Driving through the rolling hills, it seems that little has changed since this account of Spanish rural life was written in the 1940s.
Towards the centre of the Alcarria are three immense, adjoining reservoirs called the Mar de Castilla (Sea of Castile). The first reservoir was built in

Olive groves in La Alcarria in the province of Guadalajara

1946, and holiday homes have subsequently sprung up close to the shores and on the outskirts of villages.

In the historic ducal town of Pastrana, 45 km (28 miles) southeast of Guadalajara, is one of the prettiest towns in the Alcarria. The town developed alongside the Palacio Mendoza, and by the 17th century was larger and more affluent than Guadalajara. The Iglesia Colegiata de la Asunción contains four 15th-century Flemish tapestries and paintings from El Greco's school.

Brihuega, 30 km (19 miles) northeast of Guadalajara, has a pleasant old centre.

❺ Guadalajara

Guadalajara. 🏢 84,800. 🚆 🚌 ℹ️ Plaza Aviación Militar Española, 949 88 70 99. 📅 Tue, Sat. 🎭 Virgen de la Antigua (Sep). 🌐 **guadalajara.es**

Guadalajara's history is largely lost within the modern city, although traces of its Renaissance splendour survive. The **Palacio de los Duques del Infantado**, built between the 14th and 17th centuries by the powerful Mendoza dynasty, is an outstanding example of Gothic-Mudéjar architecture *(see p28)*. The main façade and patio are adorned with carving. The restored palace now houses the Museo Provincial. Among the churches in the town is the Iglesia de Santiago, with a Gothic-Plateresque chapel by Alonso de Covarrubias.

Detail of the façade of the Palacio de los Duques del Infantado

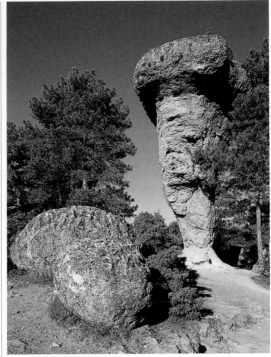

Sculpted rock figures in Ciudad Encantada

The 15th-century Iglesia de San Francisco is home to the mausoleum of the Mendoza family; it cannot, however, be visited. The cathedral is built on the site of a mosque.

Environs

At Lupiana, 11 km (7 miles) east of Guadalajara, is the two-storey Monasterio de San Bartolomé, founded in the 14th century.

🏛️ **Palacio de los Duques del Infantado**
Plaza de los Caídos en la Guerra Civil 13. **Tel** 949 21 33 01. **Open** daily; museum: Tue–Sun. ♿

❻ Serranía de Cuenca

Cuenca. 🚌 Cuenca. ℹ️ Calle Alfonso VIII 2, Cuenca, 969 24 10 51. 🌐 **serraniaaltadecuenca.es**

To the north and east of Cuenca stretches the vast *serranía*, a mountainous area of forests and pastures dissected by deep gorges. Its two most popular beauty spots are the Ciudad Encantada (Enchanted City), where the limestone has been eroded into spectacular shapes, and the moss-clad waterfalls and rock pools of the Nacimiento del Río Cuervo (Source of the River Cuervo).

The main river flowing through the area, the Júcar, carves a gorge near Villalba de la Sierra. The viewpoint of the Ventano del Diablo gives the best view of the gorge.

Between Beteta and Priego, to the north, is another spectacular river canyon, the Hoz de Beteta, where the Río Guadiela has cut its way through the surrounding cliffs. There are good views from the convent of San Miguel de las Victorias. A small road leads to the 18th-century royal spa of Solán de Cabras.

In the emptier eastern and southern tracts is Cañete, a pretty, fortified old town with a parish church displaying 16th-century paintings. To the south-east of Cañete are the eerie ruins of the abandoned town of Moya.

❼ Street-by-Street: Cuenca

Cuenca's picturesque Old Town sits astride a steeply sided spur which, drops precipitously on either side to the deep gorges of the Júcar and Huécar rivers. Around the Moorish town's narrow, winding streets grew the Gothic and Renaissance city, its monuments built with with the profits of the wool and textile trade. The main sight is the cathedral, one of the most original works of Spanish Gothic, with Anglo-Norman influences. One of the picturesque Hanging Houses, which jut out over the Huécar ravine, has been converted into the excellent Museum of Abstract Art.

The Plaza de la Merced
buildings contrast with the modern Museo de las Ciencias (Science Museum).

Museo de las Ciencias

CALLE DE SANTA MARIA

CALLE MOSEN DIEGO DE VALERA

CALLE DE ALFONSO VIII

Torre Mangana
This ruined lookout tower at the top of the town is all that remains of an Arab fortress. There are wonderful panoramic views from the top.

Ayuntamiento

Museo de Cuenca
The collection, covering prehistory up to the 17th century, includes an excellent exhibition on Roman Cuenca.

Key

— Suggested route

★ Museo de Arte Abstracto
Spain's abstract art museum is inside one of the Hanging Houses. It contains works by the movement's leading artists, including Antoni Tàpies and Eduardo Chillida.

For hotels and restaurants in this region see pp570–71 and pp595–7

Plaza Mayor
This café-lined, arcaded square is in the heart of the Old Town. The 18th-century Baroque town hall (*ayuntamiento*), built with arches, stands at the south end.

VISITORS' CHECKLIST

Practical Information
Cuenca. 🅰 57,000.
W **cuenca.es**
ℹ Calle Alfonso VIII 2, 969 24 10 51. 🚌 Tue. Museo Diocesano: **Open** Tue–Sun. 🎨 Museo de Arte Abstracto: **Open** Tue–Sun. 🏛 Museo de las Ciencias: **Open** Tue–Sun. 🎫 🎟 Museo de Cuenca: **Open** Tue–Sat, Sun am. 🎨

Transport
🚆 Calle Mariano Catalina, 902 32 03 20. 🚌 Calle Fermín Caballero 20, 969 22 70 87.

0 metres 50
0 yards 50

The Iglesia de San Miguel, perched over the Júcar gorge, was built in the Romanic style.

SEVERO CATALINA

PLAZA MAYOR

CALLE DE SAN PEDRO

VALERO

CALIF DE JULIÁN ROMERO

To Parador de Cuenca

Museo Diocesano
The cathedral's treasures, which are housed in the Palacio Episcopal, include paintings by El Greco.

★ **Cathedral**
Highlights of the 12th- to 18th-century building are the decorated altar, chapterhouse and the side chapels.

★ **Hanging Houses**
The 14th-century beamed Casas Colgadas were once used as a summer residence for the royal family.

For keys to symbols *see back flap*

Remains of a Roman building in Segóbriga

❽ Segóbriga

Saelices, Cuenca, CM-310, km 58.
Tel 629 75 22 57. **Open** Tue–Sun.
Museum: **Closed** some public hols.
🅿️ 🎫 by appt. **W** segobriga.org

The small ruined Roman city of Segóbriga, near the town of Saelices, is located in open, unspoiled countryside close to the Madrid–Valencia motorway. The Romans who lived here exploited the surrounding area, growing cereals, felling timber and mining minerals.

Many parts of the city can be explored. The 1st-century theatre – which has a capacity of 2,000 people – is sometimes used for performances today. Segóbriga also had a necropolis, an amphi-theatre, a temple to Diana and public baths. The quarries which supplied the stone to build the city can also be seen.

Nearby, a small museum has some of the site's finds, although the best statues are in Cuenca's Museo Arqueológico (see p388).

❾ Monasterio de Uclés

Uclés, Cuenca. **Tel** 969 13 50 58.
Open 10am–6pm daily (till 8pm Jul & Aug). **Closed** 1 & 6 Jan, 25 Dec.
🅿️ **W** monasteriouclés.com

The small village of Uclés, to the south of the Alcarria, is domi-nated by its impressive castle-monastery, nicknamed "El Escorial de La Mancha" for the similarity of its church's profile to that of El Escorial (see pp334–5). Originally an impregnable medieval fortress, Uclés became the monastery seat of the Order of Santiago

from 1174, because of its central location. The austere building you see today is mainly Renaissance but overlaid with Baroque detail. It has a magnificent carved wooden ceiling and staircase.

❿ Illescas

Toledo. 🚇 23,500. 🚌 🚍 🛈 Plaza Mercado 14, 925 51 10 51. 🛒 Thu. 🎪 Fiesta de Milagro (11 Mar), Virgen de la Caridad (31 Aug). **W** illescas.es

Illescas was the summer location for Felipe II's court. While there is little to see of its Old Town, the 16th-century **Hospital de la Caridad**, near the Iglesia de Santa María (12th–13th century and renovated in the 15th), has an important art collec-tion, including five late El Grecos (see p395). The subjects of three of these are the Nativity, the Annunciation and the Coronation of the Virgin.

Ceramics in Talavera workshop

🏛 **Hospital de la Caridad**
Calle Cardenal Cisneros 2. **Tel** 925 54 00 35. **Open** Mon–Sat. 🅿️ ♿

⓫ Talavera de la Reina

Toledo. 🚇 89,000. 🚌 🚍 🛈 Calle Ronda del Cañillo 22, 925 82 63 22. 🛒 Wed & 1st Sat of month. 🎪 Las Mondas (Sat after Easter), Feria de San Isidro (15–18 May), Virgen del Prado (8 Sep), Feria de San Mateo (20–23 Sep). **W** talavera.org

A ruined 15th-century bridge across the Tagus marks the entrance to the old part of this busy market town. From the bridge you can walk past the surviving part of the Moorish and medieval wall to the 12th-century collegiate church. It has a small but beautiful Gothic cloister, and 18th-century belfry.

Talavera's ceramic workshops still produce the blue and yellow azulejos (tiles) which have been a trademark of the town since the 16th century; but nowadays they also make domestic and decorative objects.

A good selection of azulejos can be seen in the large Ermita de la Virgen del Prado by the river. Many of the interior walls have superb 16th- to 20th-century tile friezes of religious scenes.

Housed in a 17th-century convent, the Museo Ruiz de Luna houses the private Talavera pottery collection and personal works of ceramist Juan Ruiz de Luna.

Part of a frieze of tiles in Talavera's Ermita del Virgen del Prado

Traditional embroidery work in Lagartera, near Oropesa

⑫ Oropesa

Toledo. 🏘 2,900. 🚍 ℹ️ Calle Hospital 10, 925 43 02 01. 🚌 Mon & Thu. 🎉 Virgen de Peñitas (8–10 Sep), Beato Alonso de Orozco (19 Sep). ⓦ oropesadetoledo.org

Oropesa's medieval and Renaissance splendour as one of Toledo's satellite communities has left a charming old quarter at the centre of today's small farming town. A circular Ruta Monumental starts from the massive, mainly 15th-century castle on the top of the hill. A Renaissance extension – thought to be the work of Juan de Herrera, co-architect of El Escorial (see pp334–5) – was added to the castle in the 16th century by the wealthy and influential Álvarez family. Part of the castle has been converted into a parador.

The Ruta Monumental continues around the town, taking in a number of churches, convents, a small ceramics museum and the town hall which presides over the main square.

Environs

The area around Oropesa is excellent for buying handicrafts. Lagartera, just to the west of the town, is famous for the embroidery and lacework by the women in the village, and at Puente del Arzobispo, 12 km (7 miles) south of Oropesa, is a good source of painted ceramics and esparto (grass-weaving) work. Ciudad de Vascos, further southeast, is a ruined 10th-century Arab city in splendid countryside around Azután.

⑬ Montes de Toledo

Toledo. 🚍 Pueblo Nuevo del Bullaque. ℹ️ Parque Nacional de Cabañeros, 926 78 32 97. 🌐 ⓦ turismocabaneros.com

To the southwest of Toledo a range of low mountains sweeps towards Extremadura. In medieval times the Montes de Toledo were owned by bishops and the kings. They cover some 1,000 sq km (386 sq miles).

The attractive nature reserve of the Parque Nacional de Cabañeros (see pp34–5) encloses a sizable area of woodland and pastures used for grazing sheep. The easiest access to the park is from Pueblo Nuevo del Bullaque. From here it is possible to make four-hour guided trips in Land Rovers, during which you may spot wild boar, deer and imperial eagles. In the pasturelands stand chozos, conical refuges for shepherds.

In the eastern foothills of the Montes de Toledo is Orgaz, with a parish church which contains works by El Greco. Nearby villages, such as Los Yébenes and Ventas con Peña Aguilera, are known for their leather goods and restaurants serving game.

On the plains stands the small church of Santa María de Melque, believed to date back to the 8th century. Close by is the Templar castle of Montalbán, a vast but ruined 12th-century fortress. Nearer to Toledo, at Guadamur, there is another handsome castle.

A chozo (shepherd's cabin) in the Parque Nacional de Cabañeros

Castilla-la Mancha's Fiestas

La Endiablada (2–3 Feb) Almonacid del Marquesado (Cuenca). At the start of the two-day-long "Fiesta of the Bewitched", men and boys, gaudily dressed as "devils", with cowbells strapped to their backs, gather in the house of their leader, the Diablo Mayor. They accompany the images of the Virgen de la Candelaria (Virgin of Candlemas) and St Blaise in procession. As the devils dance alongside the floats bearing the saints' images, they ring their bells loudly and incessantly.

One of the so-called "devils" in La Endiablada fiesta

Romería del Cristo del Sahúco (Whit Monday, May/Jun), Peñas de San Pedro (Albacete). A cross-shaped coffin bearing a figure of Christ is carried 15 km (9 miles) here from its shrine by men dressed in white.

La Caballada (Whit Sunday, early Jun), Atienza (Guadalajara). Horsemen follow the route across country taken by the 12th-century muleteers of Atienza, who are said to have saved the boy King Alfonso VIII of Castile from his uncle, Fernando II.

Corpus Christi (May/Jun), Toledo. One of Spain's most dramatic Corpus Christi (see p42) processions. The cathedral monstrance (see p396) is paraded in the streets, whose walls are adorned with 48 17th-century Flemish tapestries.

⑭ Street-by-Street: Toledo

Picturesquely sited on a hill above the River Tagus is the historic centre of Toledo. Behind the old walls lies much evidence of the city's rich history. The Romans built a fortress on the site of the present-day Alcázar. The Visigoths made Toledo their capital in the 6th century AD, and left behind several churches. In the Middle Ages, Toledo was a melting pot of Christian, Muslim and Jewish cultures, and it was during this period that the city's most outstanding monument – its cathedral – was built. In the 16th century the painter El Greco came to live in Toledo, and today the city is home to many of his works.

Puerta Cristo de la Luz

The Iglesia de San Román, of Visigothic origin, now contains a museum relating the city's past under the Visigoths.

CARDENAL LORENZANA

CALLE DE SAN ROMÁN

CALLE DE ALFONSO X

★ **Iglesia de Santo Tomé**
This church, with a beautiful Mudéjar tower, houses El Greco's masterpiece, *The Burial of the Count of Orgaz (see p36)*.

To Sinagoga de Santa María la Blanca and Monasterio de San Juan de los Reyes →

CALLE DE ALFONSO XII

CALLE DE LA TRINIDAD

To Sinagoga del Tránsito and Casa-Museo de El Greco ↙

Archbishop's Palace
Spread over a large block, with façades on three streets, this 16th-century palace features an austere Renaissance design.

0 metres		100
0 yards		100

The Puerta de Sol has a double Moorish arch and two towers.

Mezquita del Cristo de la Luz
This mosque, one of the city's two remaining Muslim buildings, dates from around AD 1000.

To Estación de Autobuses and Estación de RENFE

VISITORS' CHECKLIST

Practical Information
Toledo. 84,000.
toledo-turismo.com
Plaza del Consistorio 1, 925 25 40 30. Tue. Easter, Corpus Christi (May/Jun), Virgen del Sagrario (15 Aug). Iglesia de San Román: **Open** Tue–Sun am.

Transport
Paseo de la Rosa, 902 32 03 20. Avenida de Castilla-La Mancha, 925 21 58 50.

PLAZA DE ZOCODOVER

★ **Museo de Santa Cruz**
The museum's fine arts collection includes among its exhibits this 15th-century zodiac tapestry from Flanders.

The Plaza de Zocodover is named after the market which was held here in Moorish times. It is still the city's main square, with many cafés and shops.

Key
— Suggested route

★ **Cathedral**
Built on the site of a Visigothic cathedral and a mosque, this impressive structure is one of the largest cathedrals in Christendom (see pp396–7). The Flamboyant Gothic high-altar reredos (1504) is the work of several artists.

Alcázar
The National Army Museum is housed here. In the central patio is a replica of the statue Carlos V y el Furor.

For keys to symbols *see back flap*

Toledo Cathedral rising above the rooftops of the medieval part of the city

Exploring Toledo

Toledo is easily reached from Madrid by rail, bus or car, and is then best explored on foot. To visit all the main sights you need at least two days, but it is possible to walk around the medieval and Jewish quarters in a long morning. To avoid the heavy crowds, go midweek and stay for a night, when the city is at its most atmospheric.

Alcázar

Calle Unión s/n. **Tel** 925 23 88 00. **Open** Thu–Tue. (free Sun).

Charles V's fortified palace stands on the site of former Roman, Visigothic and Muslim fortresses. Its severe square profile suffered damage by fire three times before being almost completely destroyed in 1936, when the Nationalists survived a 70-day siege by the Republicans. Restoration followed the original plans and the siege headquarters have been preserved as a monument to Nationalist heroism. The former National Museo del Ejército was transferred from Madrid to this building, making the Alcázar the main army museum in Spain.

The Borbón-Lorenzana Library (open to the public) contains 100,000 books and manuscripts from the 16th to 19th centuries.

Museo de Santa Cruz

Calle Miguel de Cervantes 3. **Tel** 925 22 14 02. **Open** 10am–6:30pm Mon–Sat, 10am–2pm Sun. **patrimonio historicoclm.es**

This museum is housed in a 16th-century hospital founded by Cardinal Mendoza. The building has some Renaissance architectural features, including the main doorway, staircase and cloister. The four main wings, laid out in the shape of a Greek cross, are dedicated to the fine arts. The collection is especially strong in medieval and Renaissance tapestries, paintings and sculptures. There are also works by El Greco, including one of his last paintings, *The Virgin of the*

The Virgin of the Immaculate Conception by El Greco (1613) in the Museo de Santa Cruz

Immaculate Conception (1613), still in its original altarpiece. Decorative arts on display include two typically Toledan crafts: armour and damascened swords, made by inlaying blackened steel with gold wire. Damascene work, such as plates and jewellery (as well as swords), is still produced in the city.

Iglesia de Santo Tomé

Plaza del Conde 4. **Tel** 925 25 60 98. **Open** daily. **santotome.org**

Visitors come here mainly for El Greco's masterpiece, *The Burial of the Count of Orgaz (see p36)*. The Count paid for much of the 14th-century building that stands today. The painting, commissioned in his memory by a parish priest, depicts the miraculous appearance of St Augustine and St Stephen at his burial, to raise his body to heaven. It has never been moved from the setting for which it was painted, nor restored. Nevertheless, it is remarkable for its contrast of glowing and sombre colours. In the foreground, allegedly, are the artist and his son (both looking out), as well as Cervantes. The church is thought to date back to the 11th century, and its tower is a fine example of Mudéjar architecture.

Nearby is the Pastelería Santo Tomé, a good place to buy locally made marzipan.

Sinagoga de Santa María la Blanca

Calle de los Reyes Católicos 4.
Tel 925 22 72 57. **Open** daily.
Closed 1 Jan, 25 Dec.

The oldest and largest of the city's original synagogues, this monument dates back to the 12th–13th century. In 1405 it was taken over as a church by San Vincente Ferrer after the expulsion of the Jews. Restoration has returned it to its original beauty – carved stone capitals and wall panels stand out against white horseshoe arches and plasterwork. In the main chapel is a Plateresque altarpiece. In 1391 a massacre of Jews took place on this site, a turning point after years of religious tolerance in the city.

Mudéjar arches in the Sinagoga de Santa María la Blanca

Sinagoga del Tránsito, Museo Sefardí

Calle Samuel Leví. **Tel** 925 22 36 65.
Open Tue–Sun (Sun am only).
Closed public hols. (free Sat pm & Sun). **W** museosefardi.mcu.es

The most elaborate Mudéjar interior in the city is hidden behind the humble façade of this former synagogue, built in the 14th century by Samuel Haleví, the Jewish treasurer to Pedro the Cruel. The interlaced frieze of the lofty prayer hall fuses Islamic, Gothic and Hebrew geometric motifs below a wonderful coffered ceiling.

The synagogue houses a museum of Sephardi (Spanish Jewish) culture. The items on display date from both before and after the Jews' expulsion from Spain in the late 15th century (see p61).

Ornate ceiling in the Monasterio de San Juan de los Reyes

Monasterio de San Juan de los Reyes

Calle de los Reyes Católicos 17. **Tel** 925 22 38 02. **Open** daily. **Closed** 1 Jan, 25 Dec. (ground floor only).
W sanjuandelosreyes.org

A wonderful mixture of architectural styles, this monastery was commissioned by the Catholic Monarchs in honour of their victory at the battle of Toro in 1476 (see p361). It was originally intended to be their burial place, but they were actually laid to rest in Granada (see p492). Largely the work of Juan Guas, the church's main Isabelline structure was completed in 1496. Although it was badly damaged by Napoleon's troops in 1808 (see p67), it has been restored to its original splendour with features such as a Gothic cloister (1510), which has a multicoloured Mudéjar ceiling. Near to the church is a stretch of the Jewish quarter's original wall.

Museo del Greco

Paseo del Tránsito. **Tel** 925 22 36 65.
Open Tue–Sun. **Closed** Mon, Sun pm. (free Sat pm, Sun).
W museodelgreco.mcu.es

This museum is located in the heart of the Jewish quarter, in a house near to the one in which El Greco lived. It has a wide collection of his works. Canvases on display include *View of Toledo*, a detailed depiction of the city at the time, and the superb series *Christ and the Apostles*. Underneath the museum, on the ground floor, is a domestic chapel with a fine Mudéjar ceiling and a collection of art by painters of the Toledan School.

Iglesia de Santiago del Arrabal

Calle Real del Arrabal. **Tel** 925 22 06 36. **Open** for mass.

Close to the Puerta Antigua de Bisagra, this is one of Toledo's most beautiful Mudéjar monuments. It can be easily identified by its tower, which dates from the 12th-century Reconquest (see pp58–9). The church, which was built slightly later, has a beautiful woodwork ceiling and an ornate Mudéjar pulpit, but only the exterior of the building can be visited.

Puerta Antigua de Bisagra

When Alfonso VI conquered Toledo in 1085, he entered it through this gateway, alongside El Cid. It is the only gateway in the city to have kept its original 10th-century military architecture. The huge towers are topped by a 12th-century Arab gatehouse.

El Greco

Born in Crete in 1541, El Greco ("the Greek") came to Toledo in 1577 to paint the altarpiece in the convent of Santo Domingo el Antiguo. Enchanted by the city, he stayed here, painting religious portraits and altarpieces for other churches. Although El Greco was trained in Italy and influenced by masters such as Tintoretto, his works are closely identified with the city where he settled. He died in Toledo in 1614.

Domenikos Theotocopoulos, better known as El Greco

Toledo Cathedral

The splendour of Toledo's massive cathedral reflects its history as the spiritual heart of the Church in Spain and the seat of the Primate of all Spain. The Mozarabic Mass, which dates back to Visigothic times, is still said here today. The present cathedral was built on the site of a 7th-century church. Work began in 1226 and spanned three centuries, until the completion of the last vaults in 1493. This long period of construction explains the cathedral's mixture of styles: pure French Gothic – complete with flying buttresses – on the exterior; with Spanish decorative styles, such as Mudéjar and Plateresque work, used in the interior.

★ Sacristy
El Greco's *The Denuding of Christ*, above the marble altar, was painted especially for the cathedral. Also here are works by Titian, Van Dyck and Goya.

View of Toledo Cathedral
Dominating the city sky-line is the Gothic tower at the west end of the nave. The best view of the cathe-dral, and the city, is from the parador (see p571).

KEY

① **The Puerta del Mollete**, on the west façade, is the main entrance to the cathedral. From this door, *mollete*, or soft bread, was distributed to the poor.

② **The belfry** in the tower contains a heavy bell known as *La Gorda* ("the Fat One").

③ **The Cloister**, on two floors, was built in the 14th century on the site of the old Jewish market.

④ **Capilla de Santiago**

⑤ **The Capilla de San Ildefonso** contains the superb Plateresque tomb of Cardinal Alonso Carrillo de Albornoz.

⑥ **Puerta de los Leones**

⑦ **The Puerta del Perdón**, or Door of Mercy, has a tympanum decorated with religious characters.

⑧ **The Capilla Mozárabe** has a beautiful Renaissance ironwork grille, carved by Juan Francés in 1524.

Monstrance
In the Treasury is the 16th-century Gothic silver and gold mon-strance. It is carried through the streets of Toledo during the Corpus Christi cele-brations (see p391).

★ Transparente
This Baroque altarpiece of marble, jasper and bronze, by Narciso Tomé, is illuminated by an ornate skylight. It stands out from the mainly Gothic interior.

VISITORS' CHECKLIST

Practical Information
Calle Cardenal Cisneros 1.
Tel 925 22 22 41.
🌐 **catedralprimada.es**
Open 10am–6:30pm daily (from 2pm Sun), last entry 1 hr before closing.
🕇 8am, 10am, 10:30am, 5:30pm, 6:30pm Mon–Sat, 8am, 9am, 11am, noon, 1pm, 5:30pm, 6:30pm Sun (Catholic); 9am Mon–Sat, 9:45am Sun (Mozarabic).
Choir, Treasury, Sacristy and Chapterhouse: **Open** as above.
♿ 🚻 ⛔ 🔊

Chapterhouse
Above 16th-century frescoes by Juan de Borgoña is this multicoloured Mudéjar ceiling, unique in the city.

★ High Altar Reredos
The polychrome reredos, one of the most beautiful in Spain, depicts scenes from Christ's life.

Entrance via Puerta Llana

★ Choir
The carvings on the wooden lower stalls depict scenes of the fall of Granada. The alabaster upper ones show figures from the Old Testament.

Windmills on the ridge above Consuegra, overlooking the plains of La Mancha

⑮ Tembleque

Toledo. 🚹 2,300. ℹ️ Plaza Mayor 1, 925 14 55 53. 🚌 Wed. 🎭 Jesús de Nazareno (23–27 Aug).
🌐 turismocastillalamancha.es

The stone Plaza Mayor *(see p31)* at Tembleque dates from the 17th century. It is decorated with the red cross of the Knights Hospitallers, the military order which once ruled the town.

Environs

Ocaña, 30 km (20 miles) north of Tembleque, centres on the huge yet elegant, late 18th-century *plaza mayor*, one of the largest town squares in Spain, after Madrid and Salamanca.

⑯ Consuegra

Toledo. 🚹 11,000. 🚍 ℹ️ Avenida Castilla-La Mancha, 925 59 31 18. 🚌 Sat. 🎭 Consuegra Medieval (mid-Aug), La Rosa de Azafrán (last weekend Oct).

Consuegra's 11 windmills *(see p31)* and restored castle stand on a ridge, overlooking the plains of La Mancha. One windmill is set in motion every year during the town's festival to celebrate the autumn harvest of saffron *(see p342)*. During the fiesta, pickers compete to see who can strip petals from the saffron crocus the fastest.

Environs

About 4 km (2 miles) from Consuegra, on the road to Urda, is a Roman dam. An old restaurant at Puerto Lápice, off the A4 20 km (13 miles) south of Consuegra, claims to be the inn in which Don Quixote was "knighted" by the landlord.

⑰ Campo de Criptana

Ciudad Real. 🚹 14,800. 🚉 ℹ️ Calle Rocinante 39, 926 56 22 31 (closed Mon & Sun pm). 🚌 Tue. 🎭 Virgen de Criptana (Easter Mon), Cristos de Villejos (first Thu in Aug), Ferias (23–28 Aug). 🌐 campodecriptana.es

Ten windmills stand on a hillcrest in the town. Three are 16th-century and have their original machinery intact. One is the tourist information office, and three others are museums.

Environs

More windmills stand above Alcázar de San Juan and Mota del Cuervo, a good place to buy *queso manchego*, local sheep's cheese *(see p343)*.

⑱ El Toboso

Toledo. 🚹 2,200. ℹ️ Calle Daoíz y Velarde s/n, 925 56 82 26 (closed Mon). 🚌 Wed. 🎭 Carnival (17–20 Jan), Cervantes Day (23 Apr), San Agustín (27–30 Aug). 🌐 eltoboso.es

Of all the villages of La Mancha claiming links to Don Quixote, El Toboso has the clearest ties. It was chosen by Cervantes as

the birthplace of Dulcinea, Don Quixote's sweetheart. The **Casa de Dulcinea**, the home of Doña Ana Martínez Zarco, on whom Dulcinea was allegedly based, has been refurbished in its original 16th-century style.

The French army allegedly refused to attack the village during the War of Independence *(see pp66–7)*.

🏛 **Casa de Dulcinea**
Tel 925 19 72 88. **Open** Tue–Sun. 🎟 (free Sat & Sun). ♿

⑲ Belmonte

Cuenca. 🚹 2,200. 🚍 ℹ️ Avenida Luis Pinedo, 627 406 680. 🚌 Mon. 🎭 San Bartolomé (24 Aug), Virgen de Gracia (Sep). 🌐 turismocastilla lamancha.es

Belmonte's magnificent 15th-century **castle** *(see p348)* is one of the best preserved in the region. It was built by Juan Pacheco, Marquis of Villena, after Enrique IV gave him the town in 1456. Inside it has decorative carved coffered ceilings, and Mudéjar plasterwork. The collegiate church is especially remarkable for its richly

Belmonte's splendid 15th-century castle

decorated chapels and Gothic choirstalls, which were brought here from Cuenca Cathedral *(see p389)*. There is also outstanding ironwork, a Renaissance reredos and the font at which the Golden Age poet Fray Luis de León (1527–91) was baptized.

Environs

Two villages near Belmonte also flourished under the Marquis of Villena. The church at Villaescusa de Haro, 6 km (4 miles) to the northeast, has an outstanding 16th-century reredos. San Clemente, some 40 km (25 miles) further southeast, clusters around two near-perfect Renaissance squares. There is a Gothic alabaster cross in the Iglesia de Santiago Apóstol.

Castillo de Belmonte
Tel 967 81 00 40. **Open** Tue–Sun.

The castle of Alarcón, which has been converted into a state-run parador

⑳ Alarcón

Cuenca. 200. *i* Calle Posadas 6, 969 33 03 01. San Sebastián (20 Jan), Fiesta del Emigrante (Aug), Cristo de la Fe (14 Sep). **W** descubre alarcon.es

Perfectly preserved, the fortified village of Alarcón guards a narrow loop of the Río Júcar from on top of a rock. As you drive through its defences, you may have the impression of entering a film set for a medieval epic.

The village dates back to the 8th century. It became a key military base for the Reconquest *(see pp58–9)* and was recaptured from the Moors by Alfonso VIII in 1184 following a nine-month

The chalk cliffs of Alcalá del Júcar, honeycombed with tunnels

siege. It was later acquired by the Marquis of Villena. Alarcón has dramatic walls and three defensive precincts. The small, triangular castle, high above the river, has been turned into a parador, preserving much of its medieval atmosphere.

The Iglesia de Santa María is a Renaissance church with a fine portico and an altarpiece attributed to the Berruguete school. The nearby Iglesia de Santísima Trinidad is in Gothic-Plateresque style *(see p29)*.

㉑ Alcalá del Júcar

Albacete. 1,350. *i* Avenida de los Robles 1, 96/ 47 30 90 (Sat & Sun only). Sun. San Lorenzo (7–15 Aug). **W** alcaladeljucar.net

Where the Río Júcar runs through the chalk hills to the northeast of Albacete, it cuts a deep, winding gorge, the Hoz

de Júcar, along which you can drive for a stretch of 40 km (25 miles). Alcalá del Júcar is dramatically sited on the side of a spur of rock jutting out into the gorge. The town is a warren of steep alleys and flights of steps. At the top of the town, below the castle, houses have been extended by digging caves into the soft rock. Some of these have been transformed into tunnels cut from one side of the spur to the other.

Environs

To the west, the gorge runs past fertile orchards to the Baroque Ermita de San Lorenzo. Further on is the picturesque village of Jorquera, which was an independent state for a brief period during the Middle Ages, refusing to be ruled by the Crown. It retains its Arab walls. A collection of shields is on display in the Casa del Corregidor.

Don Quixote's La Mancha

Cervantes *(see p337)* doesn't specify where his hero was born, but several places are mentioned in the novel. Don Quixote is knighted in an inn in Puerto Lápice, believing it to be a castle. His sweetheart, Dulcinea, lives in El Toboso. The windmills he tilts at, imagining them to be giants, are thought to be those at Campo de Criptana. Another adventure takes place in the Cueva de Montesinos *(see p401)*.

Illustration from a 19th-century edition of *Don Quixote*

㉒ Albacete

Albacete. 172,500. 🚉 🚌
🛈 Plaza del Altozano, 967 63
00 04 (closed Sun pm). 🛍 Tue.
🎉 Virgen de los Llanos (8 Sep).
W albaceteturistico.es

This provincial capital is not
without its attractions. The
excellent **Museo de Albacete**
is located in a pleasant park
and has exhibits ranging
from Iberian sculptures and
unique Roman amber and
ivory dolls to 20th-century
paintings. The cathedral, begun
in 1515 and devoted to San
Juan Bautista, has Renaissance
altarpieces.

Albacete, also known for its
daggers and jackknives, crafted
here since Muslim times, holds
an agricultural fair, every year.

🏛 Museo de Albacete

Parque Abelardo Sánchez. **Tel**: 967 22
83 07. **Open** Tue–Sun (Jul–mid-Sep:
am only). 🎟 (free Sat & Sun). ♿

Environs
Chinchilla de Monte Aragón,
12 km (7 miles) to the southeast,
has a well-preserved old quarter.
Above the town is the shell of
its 15th-century castle (closed
to the public).

Almansa, 70 km (43 miles)
further east, is dominated by
another imposing castle, which
is of Moorish origin.

㉔ Alcaraz

Albacete. 1,600. 🛈 Calle Mayor 3,
967 38 09 60 (closed Mon). 🛍 Wed.
🎉 Canto de Los Mayos (30 Apr–1
May), La Romería de la Virgen (26 Aug,
8 Sep), Feria (4–9 Sep). **W** alcaraz.es

An important Arab and Christian
stronghold, Alcaraz's military
power waned after the
Reconquest but its economy
flourished around its (now
defunct) carpet-making industry.

Standing in the attractive
Renaissance Plaza Mayor are the

The castle of Chinchilla de Monte Aragón, overlooking the town

㉓ Sierra de Alcaraz

Where the Sierras of Segura and Alcaraz push
northwards into the southeastern plains of
La Mancha, they form spectacular mountains,
broken up by dramatic gorges and fertile
valleys. The source of the Río Mundo is a
favourite beauty spot. Nearby Riópar is perched
on the side of the mountain and has a charming
15th-century parish church. Among the less-
explored villages, Letur, Ayna, Yeste and Liétor
are especially picturesque. Their narrow,
winding streets and craft traditions clearly
reflect their Muslim origins.

⑤ **Source of the Río Mundo**
The river begins as a waterfall, inside
the Cueva de Los Chorros, and
tumbles down a dramatic cliff face
into a bubbling spring at the bottom.

```
0 kilometres    5
0 miles         5
```

Key

▬ Tour route

═ Other roads

④ **Yeste**
The village of Yeste, which stands
at the foot of the Sierra de Ardal, is
crowned by a hilltop Arab castle. It was
reconquered under Fernando III, and
was later ruled by the Order of Santiago.

"twin towers" of Tardón and Trinidad, and an 18th-century commodity exchange, the Lonja del Corregidor, with Plateresque decoration. The square is surrounded by lively, narrow streets. On the outskirts of the town are the castle ruins and surviving arch of a Gothic aqueduct. Alcaraz makes a good base for touring the sierras of Alcaraz and Segura.

The "twin towers" of Tardón and Trinidad on Alcaraz's main square

㉕ Lagunas de Ruidera

Ciudad Real. 🚌 Ruidera. 🛈 Avenida Castilla la Mancha 47, Ruidera (Sep–Jun: Wed–Sun, Jul–Aug: daily), 926 52 81 16. 🕸 **lagunasderuidera.es**

Once nicknamed "The Mirrors of La Mancha", the 15 inter-connected lakes which make up the Parque Natural de las Lagunas de Ruidera stretch for 39 km (24 miles) through a valley. They allegedly take their name from a story in *Don Quixote (see p399)* in which a certain Mistress Ruidera, her daughters and her nieces are said to have been turned into lakes by a magician.

La Mancha's lakes have recovered well from the recent years' falling water table, and are especially worth visiting for their wealth of wildlife, which includes great and little bustards, herons and many types of duck. The wild-life has increasingly come under

One of the lakes in the Parque Natural de las Lagunas de Ruidera

threat due to the number of tourists, and the development of holiday chalets on the lakes' shores. Near one of the lakes, the Laguna de San Pedro, is the Cueva de Montesinos, a deep, explor-able cave which was also used as the setting for an episode in *Don Quixote.*

To the northwest, the lakes link up with the Embalse de Peñarroya reservoir.

① Ayna
The village of Ayna is set deep in a gorge of the Río Mundo. There are spectacular views over the countryside from the Mirador del Diablo.

Foothills of the Sierra de Alcaraz

② Liétor Worth visiting in this
small hillside village are the Gothic Ermita de Belén and the Iglesia de Santiago, with a *trompe l'oeil* altarpiece.

Tips for Drivers

Tour length: 280 km (175 miles).
Stopping-off points: All of these villages have bars and restaurants. Alternatively, there are numerous places along the way to stop for a picnic.

③ Letur
With its pretty whitewashed Jewish quarter, this is perhaps the most picturesque village in the area.

㉖ Villanueva de los Infantes

Ciudad Real. 🏠 5,800. 🚌 ℹ️ Calle Cervantes 16, 926 36 13 21. 🔔 Fri. 🎉 Cruz de Mayo (2–3 May), Ferias (late Aug), Fiesta del Pimiento (1st week of Sep). 🖥️ villanuevadelosinfantes.es

Villanueva's Old Town, which centres on the graceful Neo-Classical Plaza Mayor, is one of the most attractive in La Mancha. Many buildings on the square have wooden balconies and arcades. Also on the square is the Iglesia de San Andrés, which has a Renaissance façade. Inside are a Baroque altarpiece and organ, as well as the (now empty) tomb of the Golden Age author Francisco de Quevedo. He lived and died in the Convento de los Domínicos.

Environs
The village of San Carlos del Valle, 25 km (15 miles) to the northwest, has an 18th-century square and galleried houses of rust-red stone.

㉗ Valdepeñas

Ciudad Real. 🏠 31,200. 🚃 🚌 ℹ️ Plaza de España, 926 31 25 52. 🔔 Thu. 🎉 Grape Harvest (1–8 Sep). 🖥️ valdepenas.es

Valdepeñas is the capital of La Mancha's vast wine region, the world's largest expanse of vineyards, producing vast quantities of red wine (see pp344–5). This largely modern town comes alive for its wine festival in September. In the network of older streets around the café-lined Plaza de España are the Iglesia de la Asunción and the municipal museum.

Valdepeñas has over 30 bodegas, 10 of which can be visited. One of them has been converted into the **Museo del Vino**, illustrating the various stages of wine production.

🏛️ Museo del Vino
Calle Princesa 39. **Tel** 926 32 11 11. **Open** Tue–Sat & Sun am. 🎫

Courtyard of the Palacio del Viso in Viso del Marqués

㉘ Viso del Marqués

Ciudad Real. 🏠 2,750. 🚌 ℹ️ Calle Real 39, 926 33 68 15 (closed Sun pm & Mon). 🔔 Tue. 🎉 San Andrés (second Sun of May), Feria (24–28 Jul). 🖥️ visodelmarques.es

The small village of Viso del Marqués in La Mancha is the unlikely setting of the **Palacio del Viso**, a grand Renaissance mansion commissioned in 1564 by the Marquis of Santa Cruz, the admiral of the fleet that defeated the Turks at Lepanto in 1571 (see p63). One of the main features of the house is a Classical patio. Inside, the main rooms are decorated with Italian frescoes.

Environs
About 25 km (16 miles) northeast is Spain's oldest bullring at Las Virtudes. It was built in 1641 next to a 14th-century church, which has a Churrigueresque altarpiece.

🏛️ Palacio del Viso
Plaza del Pradillo 12. **Tel** 926 33 75 18. **Open** Tue–Sun am. **Closed** some public hols. 🎫 📷

㉙ Calatrava la Nueva

Ciudad Real. Aldea del Rey. **Tel** 926 69 31 19. **Open** Tue–Sun. 🎫 🖥️ castillodecalatrava.com

Magnificent in its isolated hilltop setting, the ruined castle-monastery of Calatrava la Nueva is reached by a stretch of original medieval road.

It was founded in 1217 by the Knights of Calatrava, Spain's first military-religious order (see p58), to be their headquarters. The complex is of huge proportions, with a double patio and a church with a triple nave. The church has been restored and is illuminated by a beautiful rose window above the entrance. After the Reconquest,

Expanse of vineyards near Valdepeñas

Calatrava la Nueva castle-monastery, dominating the plains of La Mancha

the building continued to be used as a monastery until it was abandoned in 1802 following fire damage.

Opposite the castle are the ruins of a Muslim frontier fortress, Salvatierra, which was captured from the Moors by the Order of Calatrava in the 12th century.

⑳ Almagro

Ciudad Real. 🏠 9,100. 🚉 🚌
ℹ️ Ejido de Calatrava 1, 926 86 07 17.
🚪 Wed. 🎭 Virgen de las Nieves (5 Aug), San Bartolomé (23–24 Aug).
🌐 ciudad-almagro.com

Almagro was disputed during the Reconquest, until the Order of Calatrava captured it and built the castle of Calatrava la Nueva to the southwest of the town. The rich architectural heritage of the atmospheric Old Town is partly the legacy of the Fugger brothers, the Habsburgs' bankers who settled in nearby Almadén during the 16th century.

The town's main attraction is its colonnaded stone plaza, with enclosed, green balconies. On one side is a 17th-century courtyard-theatre the Corral de Comedias – where a drama festival is held for the Festival de Teatro Clásico every summer.

Other monuments worth seeing include the Fuggers' Renaissance warehouse and former university, and also the castle, which has been converted into a parador.

Environs

To the northwest is Ciudad Real, founded by Alfonso X the Learned in 1255. Its sights include the Iglesia de San Pedro and the Mudéjar gateway, the Puerta de Toledo.

Raised walkway in the Parque Nacional de Las Tablas de Daimiel

㉛ Tablas de Daimiel

Ciudad Real. 🚌 Daimiel. ℹ️ Daimiel, Calle Santa Teresa s/n, 926 26 06 39 (closed Mon). 📷 book in advance.
🌐 lastablasdedaimiel.com

The marshy wetlands of the Tablas de Daimiel, northeast of Ciudad Real, are the feeding and nesting grounds of a huge range of aquatic and migratory birds. Despite being national parkland since 1973, in recent years they became an ecological *cause célèbre* due to the growing threat from the area's lowering water table. They are now fully recovered.

One corner of the park is open to the public, with walking routes to islets and observation towers. Breeding birds here include great crested grebes and mallards. Otters and red foxes are also found in the park.

㉜ Valle de Alcudia

Ciudad Real. 🚌 Fuencaliente 🛈 Plaza Mayor 41, 926 47 02 88 (closed Mon).

Alcudia's lush lowlands, which border the Sierra Morena foothills to the south, are among Central Spain's most unspoiled countryside. The area is used largely as pastureland. In late autumn it is filled with sheep, whose milk makes the farmhouse cheese for which the valley is known.

The mountain village of Fuencaliente has thermal baths that open in the summer. Further north, Almadén is the site of a large mercury mine with a museum. Chillón, to the north-west, has a Late Gothic church.

Small isolated farmhouse in the fertile Valle de Alcudia

EXTREMADURA

Cáceres · Badajoz

Of all the Spanish regions, far-flung Extremadura – "the land beyond the River Douro" – is the most unspoiled. Green sierras run southwards through rolling hills strewn with boulders, while forests and reservoirs shelter rare wildlife. Even the towns, with their atmospheric old quarters and storks nesting on spires and bell towers, exude a romantic, slow-paced charm.

Extremadura was the birthplace of many conquistadors and emigrants to the New World; the riches they found there financed a surge of building. Guadalupe monastery, in the eastern hills, is the most splendid monument to the region's New World ties.

The region has three UNESCO World Heritage sites, including the towns of Mérida and Cáceres. The former is home to some of Spain's finest Roman architecture, including an aqueduct and a magnificent theatre. The old town of Cáceres, with its ancient walls, winding streets and nobles' mansions, is still marvellously intact. Other Classical remains dot the country-side – notably a Tartessan temple at Cancho Roano and a Roman bridge at Alcántara. Trujillo, Zafra and Jerez de los Caballeros have medieval and Renaissance quarters; and there are small, splendidly decorated cathedrals in Plasencia, Coria and Badajoz. The castles and stout walls of Alburquerque and Olivenza mark frontiers embattled through history.

Whether you visit for its architecture, gastronomy, history or nature, Extremadura makes the perfect off-the-beaten-track destination. Charming villages are scattered throughout the valleys of the north, where small rivers and streams create natural pools that provide swimming oppor-tunities during the region's notoriously hot summers.

iew over the rooftops of the historic town of Cáceres

◀ Typical pastures of the Extremadura region

Exploring Extremadura

Extremadura is ideal for nature lovers and those who want to get off the beaten track to discover the old Spain. It offers beautiful driving and walking country in its northern sierras and valleys, and exceptional wildlife in Monfragüe National Park. Some of the best Roman ruins in Spain can be found throughout Extremadura, especially in the regional capital, Mérida. The walled old town of Cáceres, with its well-preserved Jewish quarter, and the monasteries of Guadalupe and Yuste, boasts historic sights that are not to be missed. To the south, the Templar towns in the Sierra Morena, such as Jerez de los Caballeros, have fine old buildings, while the small, historic towns of Coria, Zafra and Llerena all make charming bases for excursions.

Sights at a Glance

1 Las Hurdes
2 Sierra de Gata
3 Hervás
4 Coria
5 Plasencia
6 Monasterio de Yuste
7 Parque Nacional de Monfragüe
8 Guadalupe
9 Trujillo
10 Cáceres pp412–13
11 Arroyo de la Luz
12 Alcántara
13 Valencia de Alcántara
14 Mérida
15 Badajoz
16 Olivenza
17 Cancho Roano
18 Zafra
19 Jerez de los Caballeros
20 Llerena
21 Tentudía

Typical Extremaduran landscape, near Albuquerque

Panoramic view of the small village of Garganta la Olla

Key

═══ Motorway

▬▬ Major road

═══ Secondary road

▬▬ Scenic route

═══ Main railway

──── Minor railway

▬▬ International border

▬▬ Regional border

△ Summit

Getting Around

Extremadura is not very well connected by air or rail services. Badajoz has the only (domestic) airport in the region, while the main rail link is the line from Madrid to Cáceres, Mérida and Badajoz. Coach services are infrequent in many areas, such as the northern sierras and, sometimes, even nonexistent. It is generally much more convenient to travel by car.

0 kilometres 25

0 miles 15

Roman bridge crossing the Río Guadiana at Mérida

For keys to symbols *see back flap*

The Melero Meander of the Alagón River, in Las Hurdes

❶ Las Hurdes

Cáceres. 🚌 Pinofranqueado, Caminomorisco, Nuñomoral. 🛈 Caminomorisco, 927 43 53 29 or 927 43 52 12. 🆆 todohurdes.com

Las Hurdes' slate mountains and goats were memorably caught in the 1932 Luis Buñuel film *Tierra sin Pan (Land without Bread)*. The area's poverty disappeared with the arrival of roads in the 1950s, but the black slopes, riverbeds and hill terraces remain.

A rural gem, this area is great for trekking, with mountain viewpoints and the Melero Meander formed by the Alagón River. From Pinofranqueado, roads climb past picturesque "black" villages like Batuequilla, Fragosa and El Gasco, which sits under an extinct volcano. The Lower Hurdes area, crossed by the Río Hurdano and the main access route (EX204), is dotted with camp sites and restaurants.

❷ Sierra de Gata

Cáceres. 🚌 Cáceres. 🛈 San Martín de Trevejo, 927 51 45 85. 🆆 sierradegata.org

There are 21 hamlets in the Sierra de Gata, scattered between olive groves, orchards and fields. The area has retained its charm by conserving hunters' paths for woodland walking, and its local crafts, most notably lace-making. In Valverde del Fresno, Eljas and San Martín de Trevejo, the local dialect, *a fala*, is still spoken. On the higher slopes, Gata and Villamiel have remains of medieval fortresses. The old granite houses have family crests on the front and distinctive outside staircases.

Coat of arms on a house front in Acebo

❸ Hervás

Cáceres. 🚏 4,200. 🛈 Calle Braulio Navas 6, 927 47 36 18. 🚌 Sat. 🎉 Las Ferias Cristo de la Salud (14–16 Sep). 🆆 turismodehervas.com

Sitting at the top of the Valle del Ambroz, Hervás is known for its medieval Jewish quarter, with its whitewashed, half-timbered houses. The tiny streets, dotted with taverns and craft work-shops, slope down towards the Río Ambroz. Just off the main plaza is the **Museo Pérez Comendador-Leroux**, named after the town's noted 20th-century sculptor and his wife, whose work is exhibited here.

The next town up towards the Béjar pass is Baños de Montemayor, whose name comes from its sulphurous baths, which date back to Roman times. These were revived in the early 1900s and are open to the public. At Cáparra, southwest of Hervás, four triumphal arches stand on the Roman road, the Vía de la Plata (*see p356*).

🏛 **Museo Pérez Comendador-Leroux**
Calle Asensio Neila 5. **Tel** 927 48 16 55. **Open** Tue–Fri; am only Sat & Sun. 🎫

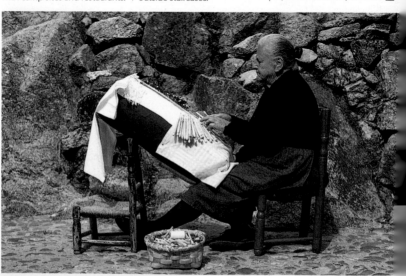

Traditional lace-making in one of the villages of the Sierra de Gata

Ancient wall and olive groves in the Valle del Ambroz

❹ Coria

Cáceres. 🅰 13,000. 🚌 ❼ Plaza de San Pedro 1, 927 50 80 00. 🗓 Thu. 🎉 Día de la Virgen (2nd Mon in May), San Juan (23–29 Jun). 🖥 turismo. coria.org

Coria's walled old town, perched above the Río Alagón, boasts a Gothic-Renaissance cathedral with rich Plateresque carving, and the 16th-century Convento de la Madre de Dios, which has a fine Renaissance cloister.

Forming part of the town walls, which are a Muslim and medieval patchwork, are an imposing castle tower, and four gates, two of which date back to Roman times. The gates are closed for the fiesta of San Juan in June for night-time bull-running. Situated below the old town is the Puente Seco, or Puente Viejo, a Roman bridge.

❺ Plasencia

Cáceres. 🅰 41,000. 🚊 🚌 ❼ Santa Clara 4, 927 42 38 43. 🗓 Tue. 🎉 Ferias (6–8 Jun). 🖥 plasencia.es

Plasencia's golden-grey walls, rising above a curve in the banks of the Río Jerte, tell of the town's past as a military bastion. Nowadays Plasencia is best known for its Tuesday market, dating back to the 12th century.

A short walk away are the town's two cathedrals, which are built back-to-back. The 15th- to 16th-century Catedral Nueva has a Baroque organ and

carved wooden choir stalls. The Romanesque Catedral Vieja, next to it, has a museum with works by Ribera, and a late 14th-century Bible.

The **Museo Etnográfico y Textil Pérez Enciso**, housed in a 14th-century hospital, has displays of crafts and costumes.

The rest of the Jerte Valley has pockets of outstanding beauty, such as the Garganta de los Infiernos, a nature reserve with dramatic, rushing waterfalls.

🏛 **Museo Etnográfico y Textil Pérez Enciso**
Plaza del Marqués de la Puebla.
Tel 927 42 18 43. **Open** Mon–Sat (winter: Wed–Sun).

❻ Monasterio de Yuste

Cuacos de Yuste (Cáceres). **Tel** 927 17 21 97. **Open** Tue–Sun. **Closed** some pub hols. 🎫 (free from 3pm Wed & Thu for EU res; from 5pm Apr–Sep). 🖥 patrimonionacional.es

Yuste's Hieronymite monastery, where Charles V (see p63) retired from public life in 1557 and died a year later, is remarkable for its simplicity and its setting in the wooded valley of La Vera. The church's Gothic and Plateresque cloisters and the austere palace are open to visitors.

From here, a single-track road leads to the village of Garganta la Olla, with its half-timbered architecture and the bright-blue Casa de las Muñecas building.

The Casa de las Muñecas (House of the Dolls), a former brothel in Garganta la Olla

A Carantoña, during the fiesta of St Sebastian, Acehuche

Extremadura's Fiestas

Carantoñas (20–21 Jan), Acehúche (Cáceres). During the fiesta of St Sebastian, the Carantoñas take to the streets of the town dressed up in animal skins, with their faces covered by grotesque masks designed to make them look terrifying. They represent the wild beasts which are said to have left the saint unharmed.

Pero Palo (Carnival Feb/Mar), Villanueva de la Vera (Cáceres). In this ancient ritual a wooden figure dressed in a suit and representing the devil is paraded around the streets and then destroyed – except for the head, which is reused the year after.

Los Empalaos (Maundy Thursday), Valverde de la Vera (Cáceres). Men do penance by walking in procession through the town with their arms outstretched and bound to wooden plough beams.

La Encamisá (7–8 Dec), Torrejoncillo (Cáceres). Riders on horseback, covered in white cloth, parade around town, where bonfires are set alight for the occasion.

Los Escobazos (7 Dec), Jarandilla de la Vera (Cáceres). At night, the town is illuminated by bonfires in the streets, and torches are made from burning brooms.

❼ Parque Nacional de Monfragüe

Cáceres. 🚌 Villarreal de San Carlos.
ℹ️ Villarreal de San Carlos, 927 19
91 34. **Open** daily. 🌐 **turismo
extremadura.com**

To the south of Plasencia, rolling
hills drop from scrubby peaks
through wild olive and cork
woods to the dammed Tagus
and Tiétar river valleys;
Monfragüe has outstandingly
varied wildlife, including a large
proportion of Spain's bird
species *(see pp346–7)*.

The many species of bird which
breed here include the black-
winged kite, black vulture and,
most notably, the black stork, as
well as more common aquatic
species on and near the water.

Birdwatchers in the Parque Nacional de Monfragüe

Mammals living here include
the lynx, red deer and wild boar.
At Villarreal de San Carlos, a
hamlet founded in the 18th
century, there is parking and an
information centre. An ideal
time to visit the park is September, when many migrating birds
stop off here. Monfragüe was
granted UNESCO Biosphere
Reserve status in 2003 and
became a National Park in 2007.

❽ Guadalupe

Cáceres. 🔼 2,000. 🚌 ℹ️ Plaza Santa
María de Guadalupe, 927 15 41 28.
Monasterio: **Tel** 927 36 70 00. **Open**
daily. 🔲 🔲 only. 🔲 Wed. 🔲 Cruz
de Mayo (3 May), La Virgen y Día de
la Comunidad (8 Sep).
🌐 **monasterioguadalupe.com**

This village grew around the
magnificent Hieronymite
Monasterio de Guadalupe,
founded in 1340. The main
square has shops that sell handmade ceramics and beaten
copper cauldrons, both traditional monastic crafts.

The turreted towers of the
monastery, which is set in a deep
wooded valley, help give it a
fairy-tale air. According to legend,
a shepherd found a wooden
image of the Virgin Mary here
in the early 14th century. The
monastery grew to splendour
under royal patronage, acquiring
schools of grammar and
medicine, three hospitals, an
important pharmacy and one
of the largest libraries in Spain.

The 16th-century *hospedería*
where royalty once stayed was
destroyed by fire; the 20th-
century reconstruction is now a
hotel run by the monks. The old
hospital has been converted
into a parador. In the car park
is a plaque commemorating
Spain's first human dissection,
which took place here in 1402.

By the time the New World
was discovered, the monastery
was very important and in 1496
was the site of the baptism of
some of the first native
Caribbeans brought to Europe
by Columbus *(see pp60–61)*.

The monastery was sacked
by Napoleon in 1808. It was
refounded by Franciscans a
century later. It is a major
centre of Catholicism, visited
by thousands of pilgrims.

Guided tours (in Spanish
only) begin in the museums
of illuminated manuscripts,
embroidered vestments and
fine art. They continue to the
choir and the magnificent
Baroque sacristy, nicknamed "the
Spanish Sistine Chapel", because
of Zurbarán's portraits of monks
hanging on the highly decorated
walls. For many, the chance to
touch or kiss the tiny Virgin's
dress in the *camarín* (chamber)
behind the altar is the highlight
of the tour. The 16th-century
Gothic cloister has two tiers of
horseshoe arches around an
ornate central pavilion. The
church, with a magnificent
16th-century iron grille partly
forged from the chains of freed
slaves, may be visited separately.

Environs
The surrounding Sierra de
las Villuercas and Los Ibores
sierras, where herbs were once
picked for the monastery pharmacy, have good woodland
walks. The road south also gives
access to the pasturelands of
La Serena, a vital breeding
ground for birds of the steppe
(see pp346–7), and the huge
reservoir of Cíjara, surrounded
by a game reserve.

Monasterio de Guadalupe, overlooking the town

For hotels and restaurants in this region see p571 and p597

⑨ Trujillo

Cáceres. 👥 9,600. 🚌 ℹ️ Plaza
Mayor, 927 32 26 77. 🗓 Thu. 🎭
Chíviri (Easter Sun), Feria del Queso
(weekend of 1 May).
🌐 **turismotrujillo.com**

When the Plaza Mayor of the
medieval hilltop town of Trujillo
is floodlit at night, it is one of the
most beautiful squares in Spain.
By day, there is much to visit,
including the Iglesia de Santa
María la Mayor, on one of the
town's winding streets, which
contains various sarcophagi.

At the top of the hill is an
11th-century **Islamic fortress**
with spectacular views over
the square, the town and the
surroundings. Trujillo was
the birthplace of several
conquistadors, most notably

Statue of Francisco Pizarro in Trujillo's
main square

Francisco Pizarro, who conquered
Peru (see p62), of whom there
is a statue in the main square.
His brother, Hernando Pizarro,
founded the Palacio del Marqués
de la Conquista, one of several
palaces and convents built
with New World wealth. It has
an elaborate corner window
with carved stone heads of
the Pizarro brothers and their
Inca wives. The beautiful 16th-
century **Palacio de Juan Pizarro
de Orellana** was built by
descendants of Francisco de
Orellana, the explorer of
Ecuador and the Amazon.

In late April or early May,
gourmets flock here for the
four-day cheese fair.

🏰 Islamic Fortress
Paseo Ruiz de Mendoza 8. **Open** daily.
🚫 🎫

🏰 Palacio de Juan Pizarro
de Orellana
Plaza de Don Juan Tena (access
via the convent). **Tel** 927 32 11 58.
Open 10am–dusk daily.

The Virgin of Guadalupe,
her face blackened by smoke
from smouldering lamps, is
worshipped by pilgrims from
around the world. She is kept
in the *camarín*, and dressed
up for feast days. On her lap
sits the infant Jesus.

**Gothic
cloister**

Embroidery museum

**Painting and
sculpture
museum**

Church

The chapterhouse
has 97 illuminated
manuscripts by the
monks of Guadalupe.

The sacristy
contains Zurbarán's
*Father Gonzalo de
Illescas at Work.*

⑩ Street-by-Street: Cáceres

After Alfonso IX of Leon conquered Cáceres in 1229, its growing prosperity as a free trade town attracted merchants, and later aristocracy, to settle here. They rivalled each other with stately homes and palaces fortified by watchtowers, most of which Isabel and Fernando, the reigning monarchs (see pp60–61), ordered to be demolished in 1476 to halt the continual jostling for power. Today's serene Renaissance town dates from the late 15th and 16th centuries, after which economic decline set in. Untouched by the wars of the 19th and 20th centuries, Cáceres became Spain's first listed heritage city in 1949.

★ Casa de los Golfines de Abajo
The ornamental façade of this 16th-century mansion displays the shield of one of the town's leading families, the Golfines.

Casa y Torre de Carvajal
This typical Renaissance mansion has a 13th-century round Arab tower and a peaceful garden with a patio.

PIAS DE ROCO

CALLE DE LA AMARGURA

CUESTA DEL MARQUÉS

CALLE OBRAS

PLAZA DE SANTA MARÍA

★ Iglesia de Santa María
Facing the Palacio Episcopal, this Gothic-Renaissance church has a beautiful cedarwood reredos and a 15th-century crucifix – the *Cristo Negro* (Black Christ).

PLAZA MAYOR

The Torre de Bujaco is 12th-century tower that visitors can climb for good views of Plaza Mayor

Arco de la Estrella
This low-arched gateway was built by Manuel Churriguera 1726. It leads through the city walls from the Plaza Mayor in the Old Town and is flanked a 15th-century watchtower.

| 0 metres | 50 |
| 0 yards | 50 |

Key

— Suggested route

Barrio de San Antonio
This quaint old Jewish quarter, with narrow streets of whitewashed houses restored to their original condition, takes its name from the nearby hermitage of St Anthony.

★ **Museo de Cáceres**
Housed in the Casa de las Veletas, this museum has contemporary art and archaeology from the region.

The Convento de San Pablo sells delicious *yemas* (candied egg yolks) made by the nuns.

Casa y Torre de las Cigüeñas
The slender, battlemented tower of the House of the Storks was allowed to remain after 1476 because of the owner's loyalty to Isabel. It is now owned by the army and not open to the public.

The Iglesia de San Mateo, built between the 14th and 17th centuries, is one of Cáceres' earliest churches.

Casa del Sol (Casa de los Solís)
The façade of this elegant Renaissance building, once home of the Solís family, is emblazoned with a sun *(sol)* motif.

For keys to symbols *see back flap*

⓫ Arroyo de la Luz

Cáceres. 🚹 6,300. 🚌 ⓘ Plaza de la Constitución 21, 927 27 04 37, Wed–Sun. 🛒 Thu. 🎭 Día de la Luz (Easter Mon), Fiestas (15 Aug). 🌐 **arroyodelaluz.es**

Arroyo de la Luz is home to one of the artistic masterpieces of Extremadura. Its Iglesia de la Asunción contains a spectacular altarpiece, completed in 1565, which incorporates 20 paintings by the mystical religious painter Luis de Morales.

Environs
Nearby, Los Barruecos Natural Park is home to Europe's largest white-stork colony (see pp346–7), their nests often built on top of gigantic granite stones. There are some good picnic spots in the surrounding countryside.

Alterpiece in the Iglesia de la Asunción, Arroyo de la Luz

⓬ Alcántara

Cáceres. 🚹 1,700. 🚌 ⓘ Avenida de Mérida 21, 927 39 08 65. 🛒 Tue. 🎭 Classic Drama Festival (Aug), San Pedro (18–19 Oct). 🌐 **turismoalcantara.es**

Alcantara has two important sights. One is the drystone Roman bridge, above the Tagus River, with its honorary arch and a temple. The other the restored Convento de San Benito. This was built as the headquarters of the Knights of the Order of Alcántara during the 16th century and was sacked by Napoleon. Its surviving treasures are in the Iglesia de Santa María de Almocovar.

The Roman bridge spanning the River Tagus at Alcántara

⓭ Valencia de Alcántara

Cáceres. 🚹 6,000. 🚌 ⓘ Calle de Hernán Cortés, 927 58 21 84. 🛒 Mon. 🎭 San Isidro (15 May), San Bartolomé (24 Aug). 🌐 **valenciadealcantara.net**

The Gothic quarter of this hilltop frontier town is given an elegant air by its fountains and orange trees. The Castillo de Piedrabuena, in nearby San Vicente de Alcántara, was built by the Knights of the Order of Alcántara. On the town's outskirts are more than 40 dolmens, or megalithic burial sites.

Environs
Alburquerque, to the southeast, is sited on a rocky outcrop with a panoramic view from the ramparts and keep of its castle. Below is the Old Town and the 15th-century Iglesia de Santa María del Mercado.

⓮ Mérida

Badajoz. 🚹 58,100. 🚌 🚌 ⓘ Calle José Álvarez Sáenz de Buruaga, 924 33 07 22. 🛒 Tue. 🎭 Easter Week, Classic Drama Festival (Jul–Aug), Feria (1–5 Sep). 🌐 **turismomerida.org**

Founded by Augustus in 25 BC, Augusta Emerita grew into the cultural and economic capital of Rome's westernmost province, Lusitania, but lost its eminence under the Moors. Though a small city, Mérida, the capital of Extremadura, has been named a UNESCO World Heritage site thanks to the large number of fine Roman monuments.

The best approach is from the west of town, via the modern suspension bridge over the Río Guadiana, bringing you to the original entrance of the Roman city and Arab fortress.

The city's centrepiece is the Teatro Romano (see pp54–5). One of the best-preserved Roman theatres anywhere, it is still used in summer for the city's drama festival and is part of a larger site with an amphitheatre (anfiteatro) and gardens. Nearby are the remains of a Roman house, the Casa del Anfiteatro, where there are underground galleries and large areas of well-preserved mosaics.

Opposite stands the stunning red-brick **Museo Nacional de Arte Romano**. The semicircular arches of its main hall are built to the same height as the city's Los Milagros aqueduct. Over three floors, the gallery exhibits ceramics, mosaics, coins and statuary. There is also an

Megalithic tomb on the outskirts of Valencia de Alcántara

Mérida's well-preserved Roman theatre, still used as a venue for classical drama

excavated stretch of the famous Via de la Plata Roman road. Near the museum are several other monuments, namely two villas with fine mosaics, and a racecourse.

A chapel in front of the 3rd-century Iglesia de Santa Eulalia is dedicated to the child saint who was martyred on this site in Roman times. Towards the centre of the town are the Templo de Diana (1st century AD), with tall, fluted columns, and the Arco de Trajano. The **Museo de Arte Visigodo** (Museum of Visigothic Art) is in the Convento de Santa Clara, off the main square. From the huge Puente Romano there is a good view of the massive walls of the Alcazaba, one of Spain's oldest Moorish buildings (AD 835), whose precinct includes towers, a cistern and Roman ruins. To the east stands the Casa del Mitreo, with its Pompeiian-style frescoes and fine mosaics.

The magnificent, ruined Los Milagros aqueduct, with its granite and brick arches, is off the N630 towards Cáceres.

Sculpture of Emperor Augustus

🏛 **Museo Nacional de Arte Romano**
Calle José Ramón Mélida. **Tel** 924 31 16 90. **Open** Tue–Sun. **Closed** some pub hols. 🎫 (free Sat pm & Sun am). ♿ 🌐 **mecd.gob.es/mnromano**

🏛 **Museo de Arte Visigodo**
Calle Sta Julia. **Tel** 924 31 01 16. **Open** Tue–Sun. **Closed** some public hols.

Mérida Town Centre

① Iglesia de Santa Eulalia
② Museo Nacional de Arte Romano
③ Casa del Anfiteatro
④ Anfiteatro
⑤ Teatro Romano
⑥ Casa del Mitreo
⑦ Alcazaba
⑧ Puente Romano
⑨ Museo de Arte Visigodo
⑩ Arco de Trajano
⑪ Templo de Diana

0 metres 250
0 yards 250

⓯ Badajoz

Badajoz. 🎈 152,500. ✈️ 🚃 🚌
ℹ️ Pasaje de San Juan, 924 22 49 81.
🚢 Tue & Sun. 🎭 Carnival (Feb/Mar).
🌐 **turismobadajoz.es**

Badajoz was a major centre under the Moors, but centuries of conflict robbed it of its former glories. Today, it is mostly known for its extravagant Carnival.

The Alcazaba houses the **Museo Arqueológico**, which has over 15,000 pieces from around the province, as far back as Palaeolithic times. The fortress overlooks colourful Plaza Alta, a former medieval market square. Dating from the 13th–18th centuries, the cathedral has a stunning tiled cloister. The MEIAC museum of contemporary Spanish and Latin American art is on Calle Museo (open Tue–Sun).

🏛️ Museo Arqueológico
Plaza José Álvarez Saez de Buruaga.
Tel 924 00 19 08. **Open** Tue–Sun.

⓰ Olivenza

Badajoz. 🎈 12,000. 🚌 ℹ️ Pl de Santa María del Castillo 15, 924 49 01 51. 🚢 Sat. 🎭 Muñecas de San Juan (23 Jun).

A Portuguese enclave until 1801, Olivenza has a lively vibe. Within the walled town are the medieval castle, housing the **Museo Etnográfico González Santana**, a museum of rural life, and three churches. Santa María del Castillo has a family tree of the Virgin Mary. Santa María Magdalena is a fine example of the 16th-century Portuguese Manueline style.

Interior of Santa María Magdalena church, Olivenza

The 16th-century Santa Casa de Misericordia has blue and white tiled friezes. In one, God offers Adam and Eve 18th-century coats to cover their nakedness.

Off the main square, the Casa Fuentes bakery sells *Técula Mécula* cake.

🏛️ Museo Etnográfico González Santana
Plaza de Santa María. **Tel** 924 49 02 22.
Open Tue–Sun. 🎫 ♿
🌐 **elmuseodeolivenza.com**

⓱ Cancho Roano

Zalamea de la Serena, EX114 (Carretera Zalamea-Quintana) km 3. **Tel** 629 23 52 79. **Open** daily (except Sun pm). **Closed** some public hols.

This sanctuary-palace, which is thought to have been built under the civilization of Tartessus *(see p53)*, was discovered in the 1960s. Excavations on this small site (begun in 1978) have revealed a moated temple that was rebuilt three times – many of the walls and slate floors are still intact. Each temple was constructed on a grander scale than the previous one and then burned in the face of invasion during the 6th century BC.

Most of the artifacts unearthed from the site are on display in the archaeological museum at Badajoz.

Environs
A Roman funereal monument stands next to the church in nearby Zalamea de la Serena. The town comes alive during the August fiestas, when the townsfolk act out the classic 17th-century play, *The Mayor of Zalamea*, by Calderón de la Barca *(see p38)*, which was supposedly based on a local character. Shops in the town also sell *torta de la Serena*, a strong, creamy cheese made of sheep's milk.

Remains of the Tartessan sanctuary at Cancho Roano

⓲ Zafra

Badajoz. 🎈 16,700. 🚃 🚌 ℹ️ Plaza de España 8, 924 55 10 36. 🚢 Sun & last Sat of month. 🎭 San Miguel (Sep/Oct). 🌐 **visitazafra.com**

At the heart of this graceful town, nicknamed "little Seville" because of its similarity to the capital of Andalucía, are two arcaded squares. The Plaza Grande, the larger of the two, near the Iglesia de la Candelaria, was built in the 15th century. The older square is Plaza Chica, which used to be the marketplace. On Calle Sevilla is the

The colourful tiled cloister in the cathedral of Badajoz

Altarpiece by Zurbarán in the Iglesia de la Candelaria at Zafra

15th-century Convento de Santa Clara. Nearby is the Alcázar de los Duques de Feria, now a parador with a patio of Herreriano style.

⑲ Jerez de los Caballeros

Badajoz. ⚐ 10,000. 🚌 ℹ️ Plaza de San Agustín 1, 924 73 03 72. 🛒 Wed. 🎉 Easter week, Feria del Jamón (May). 🌐 turismo.jerezdeloscaballeros.es

The hillside profile of Jerez, broken by three Baroque church towers, is one of Extremadura's most picturesque. This small town is also historically important – Vasco Núñez de Balboa, who discovered the Pacific, was born here. In the castle, now laid out as gardens, knights of the Order of Knights Templar were beheaded in the Torre Sangrienta (Bloody Tower) in 1312. The old quarters of the town grew up around three churches: San Bartolomé, its façade studded with glazed ceramics; San Miguel, whose brick tower dominates the Plaza de España; and Santa María de la Encarnación.

Environs
Fregenal de la Sierra, 25 km (16 miles) to the south, is an attractive old town with a bullring inside a 13th-century Templar castle, and the restored 16th-century convent of San Francisco. The Palace of the Condes de Torrepilares (C/ Iglesia de Santa Ana) is a superb example of civil architecture.

⑳ Llerena

Badajoz. ⚐ 6,000. 🚉 🚌 ℹ️ Calle Aurora 3, 924 87 05 51. 🛒 Thu. 🎉 Nuestra Señora de la Granada (1–15 Aug). 🌐 llerena.org

Extremadura's southeastern gateway to Andalucía, the town of Llerena is a mixture of Mudéjar and Baroque buildings. In the pretty square, lined with palm trees, stands the arcaded, whitewash-and-stone church of Nuestra Señora de la Granada, its sumptuous interior reflecting the town's former importance as a seat of the Inquisition (see p278). At one end of the square is a fountain designed by Zurbarán, who lived here for 15 years. Also worth seeing is the 16th-century Convento de Santa Clara, on a street leading out of the main square.

Environs
At Azuaga, 30 km (20 miles) to the east, is the Iglesia de la Consolación, containing Renaissance and Mudéjar tiles.

㉑ Tentudía

Badajoz. 🚌 Calera de León. ℹ️ Plaza de España 12, Calera de León, 924 584 084. Monasterio: **Open** Tue–Sun. 🎉 📷 (for groups). 🌐 turismoextremadura.com

Where the Sierra Morena runs into Andalucía, fortified towns and churches founded by the medieval military orders stand among the wooded hills of Tentudía. Here, on a hilltop, stands the tiny Monasterio de Tentudía. Founded in the 13th century by the Order of Santiago, the monastery contains a superb Mudéjar cloister, and reredos with Seville azulejos (tiles).

Calera de León, just 6 km (4 miles) north of Tentudía, has a Renaissance convent, also founded by the Order of Santiago, with a Gothic church and a cloister on two floors.

Bullring at Fregenal de la Sierra

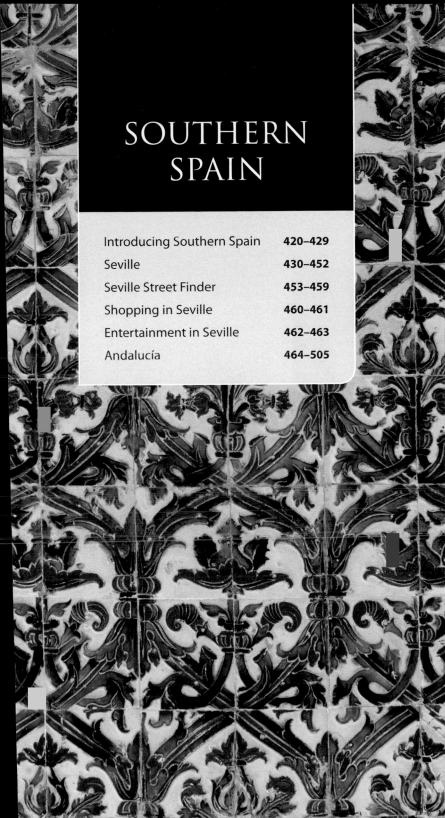

SOUTHERN SPAIN

Southern Spain at a Glance

The autonomous region of Andalucía dominates southern Spain, its landscape ranging from the deserts of Almería in the east, to the wetlands of Doñana National Park in the west; and from the snowcapped peaks of the Sierra Nevada to the beaches of the Costa del Sol. Three inland cities between them share the greatest of Spain's Moorish monuments: Granada, Córdoba and Seville, the capital, which stands on the banks of the Río Guadalquivir. Andalucía has many other historic towns as well as attractive, whitewashed villages, important nature reserves and the sherry-producing vineyards around Jerez de la Frontera.

Córdoba's Mezquita *(see pp486–7)* has a remarkable forest of arches in its interior and an exquisitely decorated mihrab (prayer niche) facing Mecca.

Seville *(see pp430–63)* is dotted with evidence of its Moorish heritage. The cathedral's bell tower was built as a minaret in 1198 and extended to include a belfry in the 16th century.

The Parque Nacional de Doñana *(see pp470–71)*, a large wetland protected area, is home to a vast array of wildlife including lynxes, flamingoes, eagles, deer and wild cattle.

Seville
Alcala de Guadaira
Huelva
Utrera
ANDALU
(see pp464–
Jerez de la Frontera
Cádiz
Medina Sidonia
Algeciras
Gib
Puente Nuevo

0 kilometres   50
0 miles   25

◄ Beautiful *azulejos*, Moorish ceramic tiles, at the Real Alcázar, Seville

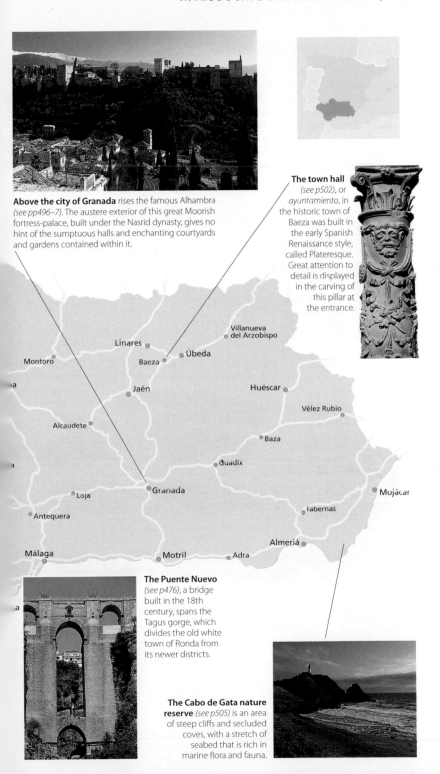

Above the city of Granada rises the famous Alhambra *(see pp496–7)*. The austere exterior of this great Moorish fortress-palace, built under the Nasrid dynasty, gives no hint of the sumptuous halls and enchanting courtyards and gardens contained within it.

The town hall *(see p502)*, or *ayuntamiento*, in the historic town of Baeza was built in the early Spanish Renaissance style, called Plateresque. Great attention to detail is displayed in the carving of this pillar at the entrance.

The Puente Nuevo *(see p476)*, a bridge built in the 18th century, spans the Tagus gorge, which divides the old white town of Ronda from its newer districts.

The Cabo de Gata nature reserve *(see p505)* is an area of steep cliffs and secluded coves, with a stretch of seabed that is rich in marine flora and fauna.

The Flavours of Southern Spain

Andalucía is vast, bordered on one side by the Mediterranean and on the other by the Atlantic. Inland are undulating hills and lofty mountains, endless olive groves and bright fields of sunflowers. The cuisine is as varied as the terrain, with a huge array of seafood, superb meat and game, and a harvest of sun-ripened fruit and vegetables. The *tapeo* (tapas-bar-hopping) is a regional institution and, around Granada, these morsels are often still served free with drinks. Along the Costa del Sol, and in the cities, new culinary skills and international influences have brought on a storm of trendy gastrobars, but in other areas traditional recipes are still the norm.

Olives and olive oil

Diners choosing from a selection at a tapas bar

Tapas

The *tapeo*, or tapas crawl, is an intrinsic part of Andalucían life. Each bar is usually known for a particular speciality: one might be well-known for its *croquetas* (croquettes made with a thick bechamel, usually filled with ham or cod), while another will serve exceptional hams, and yet another might make the best *albóndigas* (meatballs) in the neighbourhood. Tapas are often accompanied by a glass of sherry, or a beer *(una caña)*. Tapas were once free but that tradition has largely died out, except for in Granada where the tradition originated.

Seafood

It's not surprising, given its extensive coastline, that Southern Spain offers every imaginable variety of seafood, including cod, hake, prawns, crayfish, clams, razor clams, octopus, cuttlefish, sole and tuna. Almost every seaside resort will offer *pescaíto frito* (fried fish), originally a Malaga dish, made with the freshest catch of the day. In Cádiz, they are served appealingly in a paper cone, and in nearby Sanlúcar do not miss the sweet and juicy *langostinos* (king prawns).

Jamón ibérico bellota
Morcilla with onion
Morcilla with rice
Salchichón ibérico bellota
Chorizo rosario picante
Lom embucha

Selection of delicious Spanish *embutidos* (cured meats)

Regional Dishes and Specialities

Andalucía embodies many of the images most closely associated with Spain – the heady rhythms of flamenco, striking white villages and bullfighting. And tapas – in Andalucía, you can easily make a meal of these delectable treats, and most bars have an excellent range. Don't miss the mouthwatering hams from Jabugo and Trevélez which are famed throughout Spain, or the platters of freshly fried fish liberally doused with lemon juice. An ice-cold sherry (the word comes from Jerez, where most sherry is produced) is deliciously refreshing in the searing summer heat and is the most popular tipple at southern fiestas. While pork remains the most appreciated local meat, duck, beef and lamb are also favourites, subtly flavoured with aromatic bay leaves.

Pomegranates

Gazpacho This famous chilled soup is made with plump, ripe tomatoes, garlic and peppers.

Andalucían vegetable seller displaying fresh local produce

Meat and Game

Pork and beef are the most popular meats in Andalucía. Glossy black bulls (some raised for bullfighting but most for meat) are a common sight, and one of the most popular local dishes is *rabo de toro* (bull's tail)

Prawns and sardines on display at the fish market

The famous hams of Jabugo (in the southwest) and Trevélez (near Granada) are among the finest produced in Spain, and are made with free-range, black-footed pigs fed on a diet of acorns. All kinds of cured meats are made here, often to traditional recipes which have remained unchanged for centuries. In the wild inland Sierras, you will find an abundance of game in season, along with the traditional country staples of lamb and rabbit.

Fruit and Vegetables

The undulating Andalucían fields and hillsides are covered with olive groves, and the best oils are graded as carefully as fine wines. Olive oil is liberally used in *andaluz* cuisine, and the typical southern breakfast is toasted country bread topped with slices of tomato and drizzled with olive oil. The hot climate is perfect for fruit and vegetables. Favourites include oranges, their sweet-scented trees lining the streets, luscious peaches, papayas, persimmons and mangoes, as well as tomatoes, asparagus, aubergines (eggplants) and artichokes. The chilled tomato soup, *gazpacho*, is a classic, but *salmorejo*, which is thicker and topped with a sprinkling of chopped boiled eggs and ham, is even tastier.

On the Menu

Chocos con habas Cuttlefish is cooked with beans, white wine and plenty of bay leaves.

Pato a la Sevillana Succulent duck, cooked slowly with onion, leeks, carrots, bay leaf and a dash of sherry, this is a speciality of Seville.

Rabo de Toro An *andaluz* classic, made with chunks of bull's tail, slowly braised with vegetables, bay leaf and a dash of sherry until tender.

Salmorejo Cordobés A creamy tomato dip thickened with breadcrumbs.

Torta de Camarones Delicious fritters filled with tiny, whole shrimp.

Tortilla del Sacromonte A speciality of Granada: omelette with brains, kidney or other offal, peppers and peas.

Huevos a la Flamenca Eggs are baked in a terracotta dish with vegetables, ham and chorizo sausage.

Pescaíto Frito A seaside favourite, this is a platter of small fish tossed in batter and fried in olive oil.

Tocino de Cielo This simple but delicious dessert consists of creamy egg custard with a caramel syrup topping.

Wines of Southern Spain

Andalucía is a land of fortified wines, and the best of these is *jerez* (sherry). Andalucíans drink the light, dry fino and manzanilla styles of sherry as wines (they only have 15.5 per cent alcohol) – always chilled, and often as an accompaniment to tapas *(see pp578–9)*. The longer-aged, richer, yet still dry styles of amontillado and oloroso sherry go well with the cured *jamón serrano*. Other wines include fino, which may or may not be fortified, and Madeira-like Málaga.

Working the soil in Jerez

Wine Regions

The Jerez wine region covers the chalky downs between the towns of Jerez, Sanlúcar and El Puerto de Santa María. South of the Montilla-Moriles region are Málaga's vineyards, which have been reduced by urban development.

Tío Pepe is one of the finos of Jerez, which are noted for their bouquet of *flor* (yeast), pale colour and appetizing finish.

Montilla, softer in style than sherry, can make an excellent partner for Andalucía's regional cuisine.

Manzanilla is matured only in the town of Sanlúcar de Barrameda, which is situated where the Guadalquivir River meets the Atlantic Ocean. Like fino, it is bone dry, but has a distinctive salty tang.

Key

☐ Condado de Huelva

■ Jerez-Xérès-Sherry

☐ Montilla-Moriles

▨ Málaga

| 0 kilometres | 100 |
| 0 miles | 50 |

Key Facts about Wines of Southern Spain

Location and Climate
The Jerez region has one of the sunniest climates in Europe – summer heat tempered by ocean breezes. The best type of soil is white, chalky *albariza*. In Montilla it is more clayey.

Grape Varieties
The best dry sherry is produced from the Palomino grape. Pedro Ximénez is used for the sweeter styles and is the main grape in Montilla and Málaga. Moscatel is also grown in Málaga.

Good Producers
Condado de Huelva: Manuel Sauci Salas (Riodiel), A.Villarán (Pedro Ximénez Villarán). **Jerez:** Barbadillo (Solear), Blázquez (Carta Blanca), Caballero (Puerto), Garvey (San Patricio), González Byass (Alfonso, Tío Pepe), Hidalgo (La Gitana, Napoleón), Lustau, Osborne (Quinta), Pedro Domecq (La Ina), Sandeman. ***Montilla-Moriles:*** Alvear (C.B., Festival), Gracia Hermanos, Pérez Barquero, Tomás García. ***Málaga:*** Scholtz Hermanos, López Hermanos.

How Sherry is Made

Sherry is mixed from two principal grape varieties: Palomino, which makes a drier, more delicate sherry; and Pedro Ximénez, which is made into a fuller, sweeter type of sherry.

Grape-drying is only required for Pedro Ximénez grapes. They are laid on esparto mats to shrivel in the sun, concentrating the sugar.

Crusher and de-stemmer

Grape-picking takes place during the first three weeks in September. Palomino grapes are taken to the presses quickly to ensure freshness.

Grape-pressing and destalking, in cylindrical stainless-steel vats, is usually done at night to avoid the searing Andalucían heat.

Fermentation vat in steel

Flor, a yeast, may form on the exposed surface of young wine in the fermentation vat, preventing oxidization and adding a delicate taste. If *flor* develops, the wine is a fino.

Fortification is the addition of pure grape spirit, raising the level of alcohol from around 11 per cent by volume to around 18 per cent for olorosos, and 15.5 per cent for finos.

The *solera* system

The youngest *solera* contains new wine.

Sherry for bottling is taken from the oldest *solera* on the bottom row.

The finished product

The *solera* system assures that the qualities of a sherry remain constant. The wine from the youngest *solera* is mixed with the older in the barrels below and as a result takes on its character.

Moorish Architecture

The first significant period of Moorish architecture arrived with the Cordoban Caliphate. The Mezquita was extended lavishly during this period and possesses all the enduring features of the Moorish style: arches, stucco work and ornamental use of calligraphy. Later, the Almohads imported a purer Islamic style, as can be seen in La Giralda *(see pp442–3)*. The Nasrids built the superbly crafted Alhambra *(see pp496–7)* and the Mudéjares *(see p59)* used their skill to create beautiful Moorish-style buildings such as the Palacio Pedro I in Seville's Real Alcázar *(see pp446–7)*.

Reflections in water, combined with an overall play of light, were central to Moorish architecture.

Moorish domes were frequently unadorned on the outside. Inside, an intricate lattice of stone ribs supported the dome's weight. Like this one in the Mezquita *(see pp486–7)*, they were inlaid with multicoloured mosaics featuring stylized flowers.

Defensive walls

Moorish gardens were often arranged around gently rippling pools and channels.

Pre-Caliphal era 710–929	Caliphal era 929–1031	Almoravid and Almohad era 1091–1248	Nasrid era c.1238–1492
	1031–91 *Taifa* period *(see p58)*		**c.1350** Alhambra palace

700	800	900	1000	1100	1200	1300	1400

785 Mezquita in Córdoba begun

1184 La Giralda in Seville begun

936 Medina Azahara near Córdoba begun

c.1350 Palacio Pedro I

Mudéjar era, after c.1215

Azulejos *(see p444)*, glaze tiles, often adorned walls geometric patterns, as he in the Real Alcázar *(pp446*

Moorish Arches

The Moorish arch was developed from the horseshoe arch that the Visigoths used in the construction of churches. The Moors modified it and used it as the basis of great architectural endeavours, such as the Mezquita. Subsequent arches show more sophisticated ornamentation and the slow demise of the basic horseshoe shape.

Caliphal arch, Medina Azahara
(see p483)

Almohad arch, Real Alcázar (see pp446–7)

Mudéjar arch, Real Alcázar (see pp446–7)

Nasrid arch, the Alhambra (see pp496–7)

Moorish Palace

The palaces of the Moors were designed with gracious living, culture and learning in mind. The imaginary palace here shows how space, light, water and ornamentation were combined to harmonious effect.

Arcaded galleries provided shade around courtyards.

Clay tiles

Entrance halls were complex to confuse unwanted visitors.

Moorish baths made use of steam and hot water. Like Roman baths, they often had underfloor heating.

Water cooled the Moors' elegant courtyards and served a contemplative purpose, such as in the Patio de los Leones in the Alhambra (see p497).

Elaborate stucco work typifies the Nasrid style of architecture. The Sala de los Abencerrajes in the Alhambra (see p497) was built using only the simplest materials, but it is nevertheless widely regarded as one of the most outstanding monuments of the period of the Moorish occupation.

Flamenco, the Soul of Andalucía

More than just a dance, flamenco is a rousing artistic expression of the joys and sorrows of life. Although it has interpreters all over Spain and even the world, it is a uniquely Andalucían art form, traditionally performed by gypsies of the region. There are many styles of *cante* (song) from different parts of Andalucía, but no strict choreography – dancers improvise from basic movements, following the rhythm of the guitar and their feelings. Flamenco was neglected in the 1960s and 1970s, but had since seen a revival of serious interest in traditional styles and the development of exciting new forms.

Sevillanas, a folk dance favoured by Andalucíans and strongly influenced by flamenco, is the official dance of Seville's April Fair.

At a *tablao* (flamenco club) there will be at least four people on stage, including the hand-clapper.

The origins of flamenco are hard to trace. Gypsies may have been the main creators of the art, mixing their own Indian-influenced culture with existing Moorish and Andalucían folklore, and with Jewish and Christian music. There were gypsies in Andalucía by the early Middle Ages, but only in the 18th century did flamenco begin to develop into its present form.

The Spanish Guitar

The guitar has a major role in flamenco, traditionally accompanying the singer. The flamenco guitar developed from the modern classical guitar, which evolved in Spain in the 19th century. Flamenco guitars have a lighter, shallower construction and a thickened plate below the soundhole, used to tap rhythms. Today, flamenco guitarists often perform solo. One of the greatest, Paco de Lucía, began by accompanying singers and dancers, before making his debut as a soloist in 1968. His inventive style, which combines traditional playing with Latin, jazz and rock elements, has influenced many musicians outside the realm of flamenco, such as the group Ketama, who play flamenco-blues.

Classical guitar

Legendary guitarist Paco de Lucía

Singing is an integral part of flamenco and the singer often performs solo. Camarón de la Isla (1950–92), a gypsy born near Cádiz, was among the most famous contemporary *cantaores* (flamenco singers). He began as a singer of expressive *cante jondo* (literally, "deep song"), from which he developed his own distinctive style. He has inspired many singers.

Where to Enjoy Flamenco

Madrid has several good *tablaos*, flamenco venues (*see p325*). In Granada, Sacromonte's caves (*p495*) are an exciting location. In Seville, the Barrio de Santa Cruz (*pp438–47*) has good *tablaos*.

The **proud** yet graceful posture of the *bailaora* is suggestive of a restrained passion.

A harsh, vibrating voice is typical of the singer.

The *bailaora* (female dancer) is renowned for amazing footwork as well as intensive dance moments. Eva Yerbabuena and Sara Baras are both famous for their personal styles. Both lead their own acclaimed flamenco companies. Another flamenco star is Juana Amaya.

Traditional polka-dot dress

The *bailaor* (male dancer) plays a less important role than the *bailaora*. However, many have achieved fame, including Antonio Canales. He has introduced a new beat through his original foot movements.

The Flamenco Tablao

These days it is rare to come across spontaneous dancing at a tablao, but if dancers and singers are inspired, an impressive show usually results. Artists performing with duende *("magic spirit") will hear appreciative* olés *from the audience.*

Flamenco Rhythm

The unmistakable rhythm of flamenco is created by the guitar. Just as important, however, is the beat created by hand-clapping and by the dancer's feet in heeled shoes. The *bailaoras* may also beat a rhythm with castanets; Lucero Tena (born in 1938) became famous for her solos on castanets. Graceful hand movements are used to express the dancer's feelings of the moment – whether pain, sorrow, or happiness. Like the movements of the rest of the body, they are not choreographed, and the styles used vary from person to person.

Castanets made of wood

Flamenco hand movements

Introducing Seville

The capital of Andalucía is a compact city with a rich cultural heritage. Conveniently, many of its principal sights can be found within or very near the city centre, which is set on the east bank of the Río Guadalquivir. Most visitors head straight for the cathedral and La Giralda, Real Alcázar and Museo de Bellas Artes. Among other highly popular monuments are the beautiful Renaissance palace of Casa de Pilatos and Seville's bullring, the Plaza de Toros de la Maestranza. There are, however, many other churches, monuments and museums to discover, along with a wealth of excellent restaurants and atmospheric bars.

Museo de Bellas Artes *(see p436)* is Spain's second most important fine arts museum after the Prado in Madrid.

Iglesia de la Magdalena *(see p436)* is an impressive Baroque church containing countless murals, altarpieces and paintings.

Plaza de Toros de la Maestranza *(see p436),* a bullfighting landmark since its construction in 1761, is a fine example of late Spanish Baroque architecture. Its museum holds a collection of matador costumes, photographs and paintings dedicated to the tradition.

Torre del Oro *(see p437)* means "Tower of Gold", a name derived from the golden reflection the 13th-century structure casts on to the water. A thick chain used to stretch from the tower across to the other side of the river, stopping the entry of enemy ships. Today the Torre del Oro houses a naval museum.

CALLE ALFONSO

CALLE TORNEO

CALLE SAN PABLO

EL ARENAL
(See pp432–37)

CALLE ADRIANO

PASEO DE CRISTOBAL COLON

Guadalquivir

Seville

| 0 metres | | 300 |
| 0 yards | | 300 |

Casa de Pilatos *(see p444)* is an exquisite combination of Renaissance, Mudejar and Baroque architecture. The palace was commissioned by the first Marquis of Tarifa in 1529, inspired by the Renaissance architecture he had seen on a trip through Europe.

CALLE LARAÑA

CALL RECAREDO

CUESTA DEL ROSARIO

CALLE SIERPES

SANTA CRUZ
(See pp438–447)

CALLE SAN JOSE

AV. DE MÉNENDEZ PELAYO

A CONSTITUCIÓN

CALLE SAN FERNANDO

Cathedral and La Giralda *(see pp442–3)* stand at the heart of Seville. The cathedral was built in the 1400s over a 12th-century mosque, part of which still remains in the lower part of the city's emblematic bell tower, La Giralda.

Real Alcázar *(see pp446–7)* is an stunning palace built under Abd Al Roman III, with intricate plasterwork and Moorish tiles throughout.

Hospital de la Caridad *(see p437)* was constructed in the 15th century as a charity hospital and artists of the time, including Juan de Valdés Leal and Murillo, were commissioned to decorate the chapel with a clear message to the faithful.

EL ARENAL

Bounded by the Río Guadalquivir and guarded by the 13th-century Torre del Oro, El Arenal used to be a district of munitions stores and shipyards. Today this quarter is dominated by the dazzling white bullring, the Plaza de Toros de la Maestranza, where the Sevillians have been staging *corridas* for more than two centuries. The many bars and bodegas in the neighbouring streets are especially busy during the summer bullfighting season.

Once central to the city's life, the influence of the Guadalquivir declined as it silted up during the 17th century. By then El Arenal had become a notorious underworld haunt clinging to the city walls. The river was converted into a canal in the early 20th century but restored to its former navigable glory in time for Expo '92. The east bank was transformed into a tree-lined promenade with excellent views of Triana and La Isla de la Cartuja across the water.

The Hospital de la Caridad testifies to the city's continuing love affair with the Baroque. Its church is filled with famous paintings by Murillo, and the story of the Seville School is told in the immaculately restored Museo de Bellas Artes further north. The city's stunning collection of art includes great works by Zurbarán, Murillo and Valdés Leal.

Sights at a Glance

Historic Buildings
- ❸ Plaza de Toros de la Maestranza
- ❹ Hospital de la Caridad
- ❺ Torre del Oro

Museums
- ❶ Museo de Bellas Artes

Churches
- ❷ Iglesia de la Magdalena

See also Seville Street Finder
maps 1, 3, 5

0 metres 500
0 yards 500

◀ Stunning domed ceiling at the Museo de Bellas Artes, Seville

For keys to symbols *see back flap*

Street-by-Street: El Arenal

Once home to the port of Seville, El Arenal also housed the ammunition works and the artillery headquarters. Now its atmosphere is set by the city's bullring, the majestic Plaza de Toros de la Maestranza. El Arenal is a popular nightlife hub year-round, but during the bullfighting season *(see p436)* the area's bars and restaurants are especially packed. The riverfront is dominated by one of Seville's best-known monuments, the Moorish Torre del Oro, while the long, tree-lined promenade beside the Paseo de Cristóbal Colón is perfect for a slow, romantic walk along the Guadalquivir.

❸ ★ **Plaza de Toros de la Maestranza**
Seville's 18th-century bullring, one of Spain's oldest, has a Baroque façade in white and ochre.

CALLE DE ADRIANO

CALLE ANTONIA DÍAZ

PASEO DE CRISTÓBAL COLÓN

Carmen (see p451), sculpted in bronze, stands opposite the bullring.

Paseo Alcalde Marqués de Contadero

The Teatro de la Maestranza, a showpiece theatre and opera house, was opened in 1991. Home of the Orquesta Sinfónica de Sevilla, the theatre also features international opera and dance companies.

0 metres		75
0 yards		75

The Guadalquivir used to cause catastrophic inundations. Following floods in 1947, a barrage was constructed. Today, tourists enjoy peaceful boat trips, starting from the Torre del Oro.

El Buzo ("The Diver") is one of many traditional tapas bars and *freidurías* on or just off Calle Arfe. Nearby is Meson Cinco Jotas, a bar where *jamón ibérico* (*see p468*) is served.

Locator Map
See Seville Street Finder map 3

El Postigo is an arts and crafts market.

GARCÍA VINUESA

To the Cathedral

El Torno, in the secluded Plaza de Cabildo, sells sweets made in a convent.

ARFE

AVENIDA DE LA CONSTITUCIÓN

TOMÁS DE IBARRA

DOS DE MAYO

TEMPRADO

❹ ★ Hospital de la Caridad
The walls of this Baroque hospital church are hung with fine paintings by Bartolomé Esteban Murillo and Juan de Valdés Leal.

To Real Alcázar

Maestranza de Artillería

CALLE SANTANDER

Key

— Suggested route

❺ ★ Torre del Oro
Built in the 13th century to protect the port, this crenellated Moorish tower now houses a small maritime museum.

Madonna and Child in the Baroque Iglesia de la Magdalena

① Museo de Bellas Artes

Plaza del Museo 9. **Map** 1 B5. **Tel** 95 554 29 42. 🚌 C5, 6, 13, 14, 27, 32, 43. **Open** 9am–8pm Tue–Sat, 9am–3pm Sun & public hols. 🔲 (free for EU citizens) ✉ ♿ 🇼 **museos deandalucia.es**

The Convento de la Merced Calzada houses one of the best art museums in Spain. Completed in 1612 by Juan de Oviedo, the building is designed around three patios. The Patio Mayor is the largest of these, remodelled by the architect Leonardo de Figueroa in 1724. The convent church is notable for its Baroque domed ceiling, painted by Domingo Martínez.

San Jerónimo Penitente in the Museo de Bellas Artes

The museum's collection of Spanish art and sculpture, from the medieval to the modern, focuses on the work of Seville School artists. Among the star attractions is *La Servilleta*, a Virgin and Child (1665–8), which is said to be painted on a napkin *(servilleta)*. One of Murillo's most popular works, it may be seen in the restored convent church.

The boisterous *La Inmaculada* (1672) by Juan de Valdés Leal is in a gallery devoted to the artist's forceful religious paintings. Several fine works by Zurbarán include *San Hugo*

en el Refectorio (1655), which was painted for the monastery at La Cartuja *(see p452)*.

② Iglesia de la Magdalena

Calle San Pablo 10. **Map** 3 B1. **Tel** 95 422 96 03. 🚇 Plaza Nueva. 🚌 3, 21, 40, 41, 43, C5. **Open** hours vary, see website for details. 🕯 8–10:30am & 8:15pm Mon–Sat; 9am, 10:30am, noon & 8:15pm Sun, plus seasonal variations. 🇼 **rpmagdalena.org**

This immense Baroque church by Leonardo de Figueroa, completed in 1709, is gradually being restored to its former glory. In its southwest corner stands the Capilla de la Quinta Angustia, a Mudéjar chapel with three cupolas. This chapel survived from an earlier church where the great Seville School painter Bartolomé Murillo was baptized in 1618.

The font that was used for his baptism is now in the baptistry of the present building. The church's west front is topped by a belfry which is painted in vivid colours.

Among the religious works in the church are a painting by Francisco de Zurbarán, *St Dominic in Soria*, housed in the Capilla Sacramental (to the right of the south door), and frescoes by Lucas Valdés over the sanctuary. On the wall of the north transept there is a cautionary fresco of a medieval *auto-da-fé (see p278)*.

③ Plaza de Toros de la Maestranza

Paseo de Cristóbal Colón 12. **Map** 3 B2. **Tel** 954 21 03 15. 🚇 Puerta Jerez. 🚇 Archivo de Indias. 🚌 3, 21, 40, 41, C5. **Open** 9:30am–7pm daily (Apr–Oct: to 9pm). **Closed** Good Friday, 25 Dec, from 3pm bullfight days. 🔲 🇼 **realmaestranza.com**

Seville's famous bullring was built between 1761 and 1881 and holds up to 14,000 spectators. Guided tours of this immense building start from the main entrance on Paseo de Cristóbal Colón. On the west side is the Puerta del Príncipe (Prince's Gate), through which the triumphant matadors are carried aloft by admirers from the crowd.

Just beyond the *enfermería* (emergency hospital) is a museum of portraits, posters and costumes, including a purple cape painted by Pablo Picasso. The tour continues on to the chapel where matadors pray for success, and then to the stables where the horses of the *picadores* (lance-carrying horsemen) are kept.

The bullfighting season starts on Easter Sunday and continues intermittently until October. Most *corridas* take place on Sunday evenings. Tickets can be bought from the *taquilla* (booking office) at the bullring.

A few doors from the Plaza de Toros is the Teatro de la Maestranza. Seville's opera house, designed by Luis Marín de Terán and Aurelio de Pozo, opened in 1991. Fragments of ironwork from the 19th-century ammunition works that first occupied the site adorn the river façade.

Arcaded arena of the Plaza de Toros de la Maestranza, begun in 1761

Finis Gloriae Mundi by Juan de Valdés Leal in the Hospital de la Caridad

❹ Hospital de la Caridad

Calle Temprado 3. **Map** 3 B2. **Tel** 95 422 32 32. 🚇 🚌 Puerta Jerez. 🚌 3, 21, 40, 41, C4, C5. **Open** 9am–1:30pm, 3:30–7:30pm daily. 🅿 ✉

This charity hospital was founded in 1674 and it is still used today as a sanctuary for elderly and infirm people. In the gardens stands a statue of its benefactor, Miguel de Mañara, whose dissolute life before he joined a brotherhood is said to have inspired the story of Don Juan. The façade of the hospital church, with its whitewashed walls, reddish stonework and framed *azulejos*, provides a glorious example of Sevillian Baroque.

Inside are two square patios decorated with plants, 18th-century Dutch tiles, and fountains with Italian statues of Charity and Mercy. At their northern end a passage to the right leads to another patio, containing a 13th-century arch which survives from the city's shipyards.

Inside the church there are a number of original canvases by some of the leading painters of the 17th century, despite the fact that some of its greatest artworks were looted by Marshal Soult during the Napoleonic occupation of 1808–14 *(see p66)*. Directly above the entrance is the ghoulish *Finis Gloriae Mundi* (The End of the World's Glory) by Juan de Valdés Leal, and opposite hangs his morbid *In Ictu Oculi* (In the Blink of an Eye). Many of the other works that can be seen are by Murillo, including *St John of God Carrying a Sick Man* and portraits of the Child Jesus and *St John the Baptist as a Boy*.

❺ Torre del Oro

Paseo de Cristóbal Colón. **Map** 3 B2. **Tel** 95 422 24 19. 🚇 🚌 Puerta Jerez. 🚌 3, 6, 21, 40, 41, C3, C4. **Open** 9:30am–6:45pm Tue–Fri, 10:30am–6:45pm Sat & Sun. **Closed** Aug & Mon. 🅿 (free Tue & for EU citizens). ✉

In Moorish Seville the Tower of Gold formed part of the walled defences, linking up with the Real Alcázar *(see pp446–7)*. It was built as a defensive lookout in 1220, with a companion tower on the opposite bank. A metal chain stretched between them to prevent hostile ships from sailing upriver. The gold in its name may be the gilded *azulejos* that once clad its walls, or treasures from the Americas unloaded here, or the gold reflection it casts on the water. The tower has had many uses, such as a chapel and a prison. Now, as the Museo Marítimo, it exhibits maritime maps and antiques.

The Torre del Oro, built by the Almohads

Float in Holy Week procession

SANTA CRUZ

Seville's old Jewish quarter, the Barrio de Santa Cruz, is a warren of alleyways and patios that has long been the most picturesque corner of the city. Many of the best-known sights are located here: the cavernous Gothic cathedral with its landmark tower, La Giralda; the splendid Real Alcázar, with the royal palaces and lush gardens of Pedro I and Carlos V; and the Archivo de Indias, holding documents that tell of Spain's exploration and conquest of the Americas.

Spreading northeast from these great monuments is an enchanting maze of whitewashed streets. The Golden Age artist Bartolomé Esteban Murillo lived here in the 17th century, while his contemporary, Juan de Valdés Leal, decorated the Hospital de los Venerables with superb Baroque frescoes. Further north is one of Seville's favourite shopping streets, the Calle de las Sierpes. The market squares around it, such as the charming Plaza del Salvador, provided backdrops for some of the stories of Cervantes. Nearby, the ornate façades and interiors of the Ayuntamiento (town hall) and the Casa de Pilatos, a gem of Andalucían architecture, testify to the great wealth that flowed into the city from the New World during the 16th century, much of it spent on art.

Sights at a Glance

Historic Buildings
❷ Ayuntamiento
❹ Casa de Pilatos
❺ Hospital de los Venerables
❻ Archivo de Indias
❼ Real Alcázar pp446–7

Churches
❶ Seville Cathedral and La Giralda
pp442–3

Streets and Plazas
❸ Calle de las Sierpes

See also Seville Street Finder maps 1–6

| 0 metres | 400 |
| 0 yards | 400 |

◀ Seville's landmark bell tower, La Giralda, illuminated at dusk

For keys to symbols see back flap

Street-by-Street: Santa Cruz

The maze of narrow streets to the east of Seville
Cathedral and the Real Alcázar represents Seville at its
most romantic and compact. As well as the expected
souvenir shops, tapas bars and strolling guitarists,
there are plenty of picturesque alleys, hidden plazas
and flower-decked patios to reward the casual
wanderer. Once a Jewish ghetto, its restored
buildings, with characteristic window grilles, are
now a harmonious mix of upmarket residences and
tourist accommodation. Good bars and restaurants
make the area well worth an evening visit.

Plaza Virgen de los Reyes is often
lined by horse-drawn carriages. In
the centre of the square is an early
20th-century fountain by José Lafita.

Palacio Arzobispal,
the 18th-century
Archbishop's Palace,
is still used by
Seville's clergy.

**❶ ★ Cathedral and
La Giralda**
This huge Gothic
cathedral and its Moorish
bell tower are Seville's
most popular sights.

**Convento de la
Encarnación**

PLAZA
DEL
TRIUNFO

AVENIDA DE LA CONSTITUCIÓN

SANTO TOMÁS

MIGUEL MANARA

ROMERO M

MA

Plaza del Triunfo
has a Baroque column
celebrating the city's
survival of the great
earthquake of 1755.
In the centre is a
modern statue of
the Virgin Mary
(Immaculate
Conception).

❻ Archivo de Indias
Built in the 16th century as a merchants' exchange,
the Archive of the Indies now houses documents
relating to the Spanish colonization of the Americas.

For hotels and restaurants in this area see pp571–2 and pp597–8

Calle Mateos Gago is shaded by orange trees and filled with souvenir shops, cafés and tapas bars. Bar Giralda at No. 2, whose vaults are the remains of a Moorish bathhouse, is popular for its wide variety of tapas.

Locator Map
See Seville Street Finder maps 3, 4

Plaza Santa Cruz is adorned by an ornate iron cross from 1692.

❺ ★ Hospital de los Venerables
The 17th-century home for elderly priests has a splendidly restored Baroque church.

Callejón del Agua is a whitewashed alleyway offering glimpses into enchanting plant-filled patios. It is called "Water Street" because it was once a water conduit to the Real Alcázar.

| 0 metres | 50 |
| 0 yards | 50 |

❼ ★ Real Alcázar
Seville's Royal Palaces are a rewarding combination of exquisite Mudéjar (see pp446–7) craftsmanship, regal grandeur and landscaped gardens.

Key

— Suggested route

❶ Seville Cathedral and La Giralda

Seville's cathedral occupies the site of
a great mosque built by the Almohads
(*see p58*) in the late 12th century.
Based on the Koutoubia Mosque
of Marrakesh, La Giralda, along
with its bell tower and the Patio
de los Naranjos, are a legacy of
the original Moorish structure
here. Work on the Christian
cathedral, the largest in Europe, began
in 1401 and took just over a century to
complete. As well as enjoying its Gothic
immensity and the works of art in its
chapels and sacristy, visitors ascend the
ramped La Giralda for stunning city views.

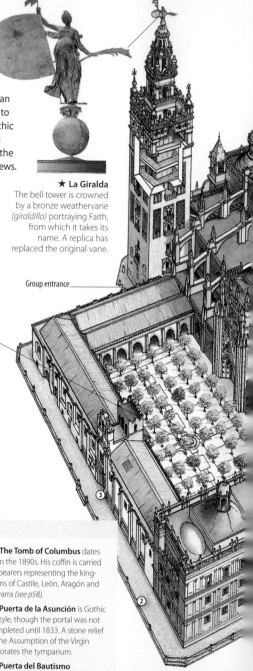

★ **La Giralda**
The bell tower is crowned
by a bronze weathervane
(*giraldillo*) portraying Faith,
from which it takes its
name. A replica has
replaced the original vane.

Group entrance

★ **Patio de los Naranjos**
In Moorish times worshippers
would wash their hands and feet
in the fountain under the orange
trees before praying.

KEY

① **Iglesia del Sagrario**, a large
17th-century chapel, is now used
as a parish church.

② **Roman pillars** brought from
Itálica (*see p482*) surround the
cathedral steps.

③ **Puerta del Perdón** (exit)

④ **The Sacristía Mayor** houses
many works of art, including
paintings by Murillo.

⑤ **The Tomb of Columbus** dates
from the 1890s. His coffin is carried
by bearers representing the kingdoms of Castile, León, Aragón and
Navarra (*see p58*).

⑥ **Puerta de la Asunción** is Gothic
in style, though the portal was not
completed until 1833. A stone relief
of the Assumption of the Virgin
decorates the tympanum.

⑦ **Puerta del Bautismo**

Retablo Mayor
Santa María de la Sede, the cathedral's patron saint, sits at the high altar below a water-fall of gold. The 44 gilded relief panels of the reredos were carved by Spanish and Flemish sculptors between 1482 and 1564.

VISITORS' CHECKLIST

Practical Information
Avenida de la Constitución.
Map 3 C2. **Tel** 954 56 57 43.
Cathedral & La Giralda: **Open**
11am–3:30pm Mon, 11am–5pm
Tue–Sat, 2:30–6:30pm Sun.
4:30–6pm Mon by appt.
Cathedral: summer: 8–9am;
winter: 8–10:30am. Capilla Mayor:
8am–2pm, 4–7pm.
catedraldesevilla.es

Transport
Puerta Jerez. Archivo de
Indias. C3, C4, C5, 5, 41.

Main entrance

★ **Capilla Mayor**
Monumental iron grilles forged in 1518–32 enclose the main chapel, which is dominated by the overwhelming Retablo Mayor.

The Rise of La Giralda

The tower was built as a minaret in 1198. In the 14th century the bronze spheres at its top were replaced by Christian symbols. A new belfry was planned in 1557, but built to a more ornate design by Hernán Ruiz in 1568.

| 1198 | 1400 | 1557 (plan) | 1568 |

Genoese fountain in the Mudéjar Patio Principal of the Casa de Pilatos

❷ Ayuntamiento

Plaza Nueva 1. **Map** 3 C1. **Tel** 955 47 12 32. 🚇 Plaza Nueva. **Open** tours 5pm & 7:30pm Mon–Thu. **Closed** Aug. 🎟️ 📷

Seville's City Hall stands between the Plaza de San Francisco, where *autos-da-fé* (public trials of heretics) were held, and the Plaza Nueva.

Building was completed between 1527 and 1534. The side bordering the Plaza de San Francisco is a fine example of ornate Plateresque style *(see p29)* favoured by the architect Diego de Riaño. The west front is Neo-Classical, built in 1891. Sculpted ceilings survive in the vestibule and the lower Casa Consistorial (Council Meeting Room), containing Velázquez's *Imposition of the Chasuble on St Ildefonso.* The upper Casa Consistorial has a dazzling coffered ceiling and paintings by Zurbarán and Valdés Leal.

❸ Calle de las Sierpes

Map 3 C1. 🚌 C5, 10, 11, 12, 13, 14, 27, 32, 40, 41, 43. Casa de la Condesa Lebrija. **Tel** 95 422 78 02. 🚇 Plaza Nueva. **Open** 10:30am–7:30pm Mon–Fri, 10am–2pm, 4–6pm Sat, 10am–2pm Sun; Jul & Aug: to 3pm Mon–Fri, to 2pm Sat. **Closed** Sun in Jul & Aug. 📷 🌐 palaciodelebrija.com

Seville's main shopping promenade, the "Street of the Snakes", runs north from Plaza de San Francisco. Long-established stores selling hats, fans and traditional *mantillas* (lace headdresses) stand alongside clothes and souvenir shops. The parallel streets of Cuna and Tetuán also offer some enjoyable window-shopping. Halfway up the road walking north, Calle Jovellanos to the left leads to the 17th-century Capillita de San José. Further on at the junction with Calle Pedro Caravaca is the Real Círculo de Labradores, a men's club founded in 1856.

Opposite – with its entrance in Calle Cuna – is a 15th-century private mansion, the Casa de la Condesa Lebrija. Treasures on display include a Roman mosaic from the ruins of nearby Itálica *(see p482)* and a collection of *azulejos.*

Right at the end of the street is La Campana, Seville's best-known *pastelería.*

❹ Casa de Pilatos

Plaza de Pilatos 1. **Map** 4 D1. **Tel** 95 422 52 98. 🚌 C3, C4, C5, 21, 24, 27. **Open** 9am–6pm daily (to 7pm Jul & Aug). 🎟️ 📷 first floor. 📷 🌐 **fundacionmedinaceli.org**

Enraptured by by the architectural and decorative wonders of High Renaissance Italy and the Holy Land, the first Marquis of Tarifa built the Casa de Pilatos. So called because it was thought to resemble Pontius Pilate's home in Jerusalem, today it is the residence of the Dukes of Medinaceli and is one of the finest palaces in Seville.

Visitors enter through a marble portal, commissioned by the Marquis in 1529 from Genoese craftsmen. Across the arcaded Apeadero (carriage yard) is the Patio Principal. This courtyard is essentially Mudéjar *(see p59)* in style and decorated with *azulejos* and intricate plasterwork. In its corners are three Roman statues, depicting Minerva, a dancing muse and Ceres, and a Greek statue of Athena, dating from the 5th century BC.

In its centre is a fountain that was imported from Genoa. To the right, through the Salón del Pretorio with its coffered ceiling and marquetry, is the Corredor de Zaquizamí. The antiquities

Azulejos

Colourful *azulejos*, glazed ceramic tiles, are a striking feature of Seville. The craft was introduced to Spain by the Moors, who created fantastic mosaics in sophisticated geometric patterns for palace walls – the word *azulejo* derives from the Arabic for "little stone". New techniques were introduced in the 16th century and later mass production extended their use to decorative signs, shop façades and advertising hoardings.

Azulejo billboard for Studebaker Motor Cars (1924), Calle Tetuán

Fresco by Juan de Valdés Leal in the Hospital de los Venerables

on display in adjacent rooms include a bas-relief of *Leda and the Swan* and two Roman reliefs commemorating the Battle of Actium of 31 BC.

Coming back to the Patio Principal, you turn right into the Salón de Descanso de los Jueces. Beyond is a rib-vaulted Gothic chapel, with Mudéjar plasterwork walls and ceiling. On the altar is a copy of a 4th-century sculpture in the Vatican, *The Good Shepherd*. Left through the Gabinete de Pilatos, with its small central fountain, is the Jardín Grande.

Returning once more to the main patio, behind the statue of Ceres, a tiled staircase leads to the upper floor. It is roofed with a wonderful *media naranja* (half-orange) cupola built in 1537. There are Mudéjar ceilings in some rooms, full of family portraits and antiques.

❺ Hospital de los Venerables

Plaza de los Venerables 8. **Map** 3 C2. **Tel** 95 456 26 96. 🚇 Archivo de Indias. **Open** 10am–6pm daily. **Closed** 1 Jan, Good Friday, 25 Dec. 🗓 (free 2–6pm Tue). ♿ 🖷

Set in the heart of the Barrio de Santa Cruz, this home for elderly priests was begun in 1675 and completed around 20 years later by Leonardo de Figueroa. It has now been restored as a cultural centre by FOCUS (Fundación Fondo de Cultura de Sevilla).

Stairs from the central, rose-coloured, sunken patio lead to the upper floors, which, along with the infirmary and cellar, are used as exhibition galleries.

The Hospital church, a show-case of Baroque splendours, has frescoes by both Juan de Valdés Leal and his son Lucas Valdés. Other highlights of the church include sculptures of St Peter and St Ferdinand by Pedro Roldán, flanking the east door; and *The Apotheosis of St Ferdinand* by Lucas Valdés, top centre in the reredos of the main altar. Its frieze (inscribed in Greek) advises to "Fear God and Honour the Priest".

In the sacristy, the ceiling has an effective trompe l'oeil depicting *The Triumph of the Cross* by Juan de Valdés Leal.

❻ Archivo de Indias

Avda de la Constitución. **Map** 3 C2. **Tel** 95 450 05 28. 🚇 🚌 C5, Puerta Jerez. 🚇 Archivo de Indias. **Open** 9:30am–5pm Mon–Sat (to 2pm mid-Jun–mid-Sep), 10am–2pm Sun and public hols. 🖷

The Archive of the Indies illustrates Seville's pre-eminent role in the colonization and exploitation of the New World. Built between 1584 and 1598 to designs by Juan de Herrera, co-architect of El Escorial *(see pp334–5)*, it was originally a *lonja* (exchange), where merchants traded. In 1785, Carlos III had all Spanish documents relating to the "Indies" collected under one roof. Among the archive's 86 million handwritten pages and 8,000 maps and drawings are letters from Columbus, Cortés and Cervantes, and the correspondence of Felipe II.

Upstairs, the library rooms contain displays of drawings, maps and facsimile documents.

Façade of the Archivo de Indias by Juan de Herrera

❼ Real Alcázar

In 1364 Pedro I ordered the construction of a royal residence within the palaces which had been built by the city's Almohad *(see p58)* rulers. Craftsmen from Granada and Toledo created a jewel box of Mudéjar patios and halls, the Palacio Pedro I, now at the heart of Seville's Real Alcázar. Later monarchs added their own distinguishing marks: Isabel I *(see p60)* dispatched navigators to the New World from her Casa de la Contratación, while Carlos I (the Holy Roman Emperor Charles V – *see p62*) had grandiose apartments built. More recently, in 2014, the Alcázar was used as a location for the hit TV show *Game of Thrones*.

Gardens of the Alcázar
Laid out with terraces, fountains and pavilions, these gardens provide a delightful refuge from the heat and bustle of Seville.

★ **Charles V Rooms**
Vast tapestries and lively 16th-century *azulejos* decorate the vaulted halls of the apartments and chapel of Charles V.

Plan of the Real Alcázar

The complex has been the home of Spanish kings for almost seven centuries. The palace's upper floor is used by the royal family today.

Key

 Area illustrated above

Gardens

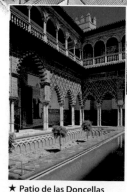

★ **Patio de las Doncellas**
The Patio of the Maidens boasts plasterwork by the top craftsmen of Granada.

★ Salón de Embajadores
Built in 1427, the dazzling dome of the Ambassadors' Hall is of carved and gilded, interlaced wood.

VISITORS' CHECKLIST

Practical Information
Patio de Banderas. **Map** 3 C2.
Tel 95 450 23 24. **Open** 9:30am–7pm daily (to 5pm Oct–Mar); night visits with theatre, check website (book in advance).
w alcazarsevilla.org

Transport
Puerta Jerez. C5.
Archivo de Indias.

Horseshoe Arches
Azulejos and complex plasterwork decorate the Ambassadors' Hall, which has three symmetrically arranged, ornate archways, each with three horseshoe arches.

Puerta del León (entrance)

Patio del Yeso
The Patio of Plaster, a garden featuring flowerbeds and a water channel, retains features of the earlier, 12th-century Almohad Alcázar.

KEY

① **Patio del Crucero** lies above the old baths.

② **Jardín de Troya**

③ **Patio de las Muñecas** (Patio of the Dolls) and its surrounding bedrooms formed the domestic heart of the palace. It derives its name from two tiny faces on one of its arches.

④ **Casa de la Contratación**

⑤ **The façade** of the Palacio Pedro I is a prime example of Mudéjar style.

⑥ **The Patio de la Montería** was where the court met before hunting expeditions.

FURTHER AFIELD

The north of Seville, La Macarena, is a characterful mix of decaying Baroque and Mudéjar churches, and old-style tapas bars. The place to visit here is the Basílica de la Macarena, a shrine to Seville's much-venerated Virgen de la Esperanza Macarena. Among the many convents and churches in the area, the Convento de Santa Paula offers a rare opportunity to peep behind the walls of an enclosed community.

The area south of the city is dominated by the extensive, leafy Parque María Luisa. A large part of the park originally formed the grounds of the Baroque Palacio de San Telmo. Many of the historic buildings in the park were erected for the Ibero-American Exposition of 1929. The grand five-star Hotel Alfonso XIII and the crescent-shaped Plaza de España are

the most striking legacies of this upsurge of Andalucían pride. Nearby is the Royal Tobacco Factory, forever associated with the fictional gypsy heroine Carmen, who toiled in its sultry halls. Today, it is part of the Universidad, Seville's university. There is more to see across the river from the city centre. With its cobbled streets and shops selling ceramics, the Triana quarter retains the feel of old Seville. In the 15th century a Carthusian monastery, the Monasterio de Santa María de las Cuevas, was built north of Triana. Columbus resided there and the area around it, the Isla de la Cartuja, was chosen as the site for Expo '92. Today the site is home mainly to offices but the Isla Mágica amusement park, Teatro Central and the Torre Sevilla, the tallest building in Andalucía, are also located here.

Sights at a Glance

Churches and Convents

1 Basílica de la Macarena
2 Convento de Santa Paula
3 Iglesia de San Pedro

Historic Buildings

5 Palacio de las Dueñas
6 Palacio de San Telmo
7 Universidad
10 Torre Sevilla
12 Cámara Oscura, Torre de Los Perdigones

Historic Areas

4 Metropol Parasol
8 Parque María Luisa
9 Triana
11 Isla de la Cartuja

St John the Baptist by Montañés in the Convento de Santa Paula

❶ Basílica de la Macarena

Calle Bécquer 1. **Map** 2 D3. **Tel** 954 90 18 00. 🚌 C1–5, 2, 10, 13, 14. **Open** 9am–2pm, 5–9pm daily (from 9:30am Sun). **Closed** Easter Fri. 🏛 (museum).

Built in 1949 by Gómez Millán, the Basílica de la Macarena is Neo-Baroque in style and was intended as a new home for the much-loved Virgen de la Esperanza Macarena. It backs on to the 13th-century Iglesia de San Gil, where the image was housed until a fire broke out in 1936.

The image of the Virgin, standing above the main altar amid waterfalls of gold and silver, has been attributed to Luisa Roldán (1656–1703), the most talented female artist of the Seville School.

The Virgin's magnificent processional gowns and jewels are held in the Treasury museum.

❷ Convento de Santa Paula

Calle Santa Paula 11. **Map** 2 E5. **Tel** 95 453 63 30. 🚌 C1, C2, C3, C4, C5, 10, 11. **Open** 10am–1pm Tue–Sun. 🏛 🎫

Founded in 1475, Santa Paula is a working convent and home to about 30 nuns. The museum consists of two galleries filled with religious artifacts and paintings. The nave of the convent church has an elaborate wooden roof, dating from 1623. Among the statues in the church

are St John the Evangelist and St John the Baptist, both the work of Juan Martínez Montañés.

❸ Iglesia de San Pedro

Pl San Pedro. **Map** 2 D5. **Tel** 954 21 68 58. 🚌 10, 11, 12, 15, 16, 20, 24, 27, 32, C5. **Open** 9am, 11am & 8pm Mon–Sat, 10am, 11am, noon, 1pm, 8pm Sun. 🏛

This church features a mix of architectural styles; Mudéjar elements survive in the lobed brickwork of its tower, which is surmounted by a Baroque *(see p29)* belfry, and the interior has a Mudéjar wooden ceiling. The vault of one of its chapels is decorated with exquisite geometric patterns of bricks. Diego Velázquez, the Golden Age painter *(see p36)*, was baptized in this church in 1599.

Behind the church, in Calle Doña María Coronel, cakes are sold from a revolving drum in the wall of the 14th-century Convento de Santa Inés.

❹ Metropol Parasol

Plaza de la Encarnación. **Map** 2 D5. 🚌 C5, 10, 11, 12, 15, 16, 20, 24, 27, 32. Observation deck & walkways: **Tel** 95 456 15 12. **Open** 10am–11pm daily (to 11:30pm Fri & Sat. 🏛 Museum: **Tel** 955 47 15 80. **Open** 10am–7:30pm Tue–Sun (to 1:30pm Sun & pub hols). 🏛 🎫 🌐 setasdesevilla.com

Known locally as *"Las Setas"* ("The Mushrooms"), this ultramodern structure with a latticed canopy was built from 2005–2011, and includes a museum, market, bars and restaurants. The main draw is the observation deck.

❺ Palacio de las Dueñas

Calle Dueñas 5. **Map** 2 D5. 🚌 C5, 10, 11, 12, 15, 16, 20, 24, 27, 32. **Tel** 954 21 48 28. **Open** 10am–5:15pm (Apr–Sep: to 7:15pm). **Closed** 1 & 6 Jan, 25 Dec. 🏛 (free after 4pm Mon).

Built in Renaissance style with Mudejar and Gothic influences, this 15th-century palace is the official Seville residence of the Dukes of Alba. Its courtyards

offer a peaceful oasis from the bustle of the streets. The house's grand rooms are filled with elegant period furniture, but there are also family photos and personal letters scattered about, plus a room dedicated to the history of the Feria de Abril.

❻ Palacio de San Telmo

Avenida de Roma. **Map** 3 C3. **Tel** 955 00 10 10. 🔲 🚇 Puerta de Jerez. 🚌 C3, C4, C5, 3, 5, 6, 41. 🕐 Thu, Sat & Sun by appt. 🏛 🎫

This imposing palace, named after the patron saint of navigators, was built in 1682 as a university to train ships' pilots,

❼ Parque María Luisa

Map 4 D4. 🔲 🚇 Prado de San Sebastián. Museo Arqueológico: **Tel** 955 12 06 32. **Open** 9am–7:30pm Tue–Sat (9am–2:30pm Jun–mid-Sep), 9am–2:30pm Sun. **Closed** 1 & 6 Jan, 1 May, 24, 25 & 31 Dec. 🏛 (free for EU citizens). 🏛 Museo de Artes y Costumbres Populares: **Tel** 955 54 29 51. **Open** as above. 🏛 🎫 🛗

Princess Maria Luisa donated part of the grounds of the Palacio de San Telmo to the city for this park in 1893. Landscaped by Jean

Plaza de España was built in a theatrical style by Aníbal González.

The Glorieta de Bécquer is an arbour with sculpted figures depicting the phases of love – a tribute to poet Gustavo Adolfo Bécquer.

navigators and high-ranking officers. In 1849 it became the residence of the Dukes of Monpensier and until 1893 its grounds included what is now Parque María Luisa. Today it is the presidential headquarters of the Junta de Andalucía (the regional government). The most striking feature of the Palacio de San Telmo is the exuberant Churrigueresque portal designed by Leonardo de Figueroa, and completed in 1734. Surrounding the Ionic columns are allegorical figures representing the Sciences and Arts.

Opposite is Seville's most famous hotel, the Alfonso XIII, dating from the 1920s. Non-residents are welcome to visit the bar and the restaurant.

❼ Universidad

Calle San Fernando 4. **Map** 3 C3. **Tel** 954 55 11 23. 🚇 Puerta de Jerez. 🚌 Puerta de Jerez or Prado de San Sebastian. 🚌 C1, C2, C3, C4, 5, 21, 22, 25, 26, 28, 29, 30, 31, 34, 37, 38. **Open** 8am–8:30pm Mon–Fri. **Closed** public hols. 🎫 (free, 11am Mon–Thu, except Aug). 🌐 **us.es**

The former Real Fábrica de Tabacos (Royal Tobacco Factory) is now part of Seville University. In the 19th century, three-quarters of Europe's cigars were manufactured here, rolled by 10,000 *cigarreras* (female cigar-makers) – the inspiration for French author Mérimée's *Carmen*.

Built in 1728–71, the factory complex is the third-largest building in Spain. The moat and

Baroque fountain in one of the patios in the Universidad

watchtowers are evidence of the importance given to protecting the king's lucrative tobacco monopoly.

Forestier, director of the Bois de Boulogne in Paris, the park was the leafy setting for the 1929 Ibero-American Exposition. The legacies of this extravaganza are the Plaza de España, decorated with regional scenes on ceramic tiles, and the Plaza de América, both the work of Aníbal González. On

the latter, in the Pabellón Mudéjar, the Museo de Artes y Costumbres Populares displays traditional Andalucían folk arts. The Neo-Renaissance Pabellón de las Bellas Artes houses the provincial Museo Arqueológico. Exhibits include statues and fragments found at Itálica (*see p482*).

Fuente de los Leones

Plaza de América

Museo Arqueológico

Pabellón Real

The Isleta de los Patos sits in a lake graced by ducks and swans.

Museo de Artes y Costumbres Populares

Decorative tiles at Centro Cerámica Triana, a museum dedicated to the arts of ceramics

⑨ Triana

Map 3 A2. 🚇 Plaza de Cuba, Parque de los Príncipes. 🚌 C1, C2, C3.

This close-knit area, named after the Roman Emperor Trajan, was once Seville's gypsy quarter. Triana remains a traditional working-class district, with compact, flower-filled streets. For centuries it has been famous for its potteries and associations with flamenco . Visit the museum dedicated to this fine craft at Centro Cerámica Triana (Calle Antillano Campos 14), formerly the factory of the Cerámica Santa Ana shop. Among other displays, you can admire tiles decorated by the famous Anibal Gonzalez, before seeing the kilns used (some dating from the 16th century), plus tools and materials.

A good way to approach Triana is across the Puente de Isabel II, leading to the Plaza del Altozano. The Museo de la Inquisición, in Castillo de San Jorge, is largely tasteful and avoids sensational images, concluding with a presentation on human rights today. Nearby is one of the characteristic streets of the area, the Calle Rodrigo de Triana, named after the Andalucían sailor who was the first to sight the shores of the New World on Columbus's voyage of 1492.

The Iglesia de Santa Ana, founded in the 13th century, is Triana's most popular church. In the baptistry is the Gypsy Font, believed to pass on the gift of flamenco song to the children of the faithful.

⑩ Torre Sevilla

Calle Gonzalo Jiménez de Quesada 2. **Map** 1 A5. 🚌 C1, C2, 6, 43.

Designed by the Argentine architect César Pelli, this 40-storey tower was the subject of much controversy while in its planning stages. Despite UNESCO voting against its construction, due to its obstruction of the skyline, the Torre Sevilla now presides over the Guadalquivir River, offering commanding panoramic views. It is the tallest building in Andalucía and will house a five-star hotel on the top 13 floors. The remaining floors will primarily be devoted to office space.

An adjacent shopping centre will host 80 shops, two supermarkets and 27 restaurants, with a garden roof.

⑪ Isla de la Cartuja

Map 1 B3. 🌐 caac.es 🚌 C1, C2. Monasterio de Santa María de las Cuevas: **Open** Tue–Sun. 🏛 ♿ Centro Andaluz de Arte Contemporáneo: **Tel** 95 503 70 70. **Open** Tue–Sun. 🏛 (free Tue for EU citizens). Isla Mágica: **Tel** 902 16 17 16. **Open** Apr: Sat & Sun; May: Thu, Sat & Sun; Jun & Jul: Tue–Sun; Aug–mid-Sep: daily; mid-Sep–Oct: Sat, Sun. **Closed** Nov–mid-Apr. 🏛 ♿ 🌐 islamagica.es

The site of Expo '92 (see pp72–3), this area has since been transformed into a sprawling complex of exhibition halls, museums and entertainment and leisure spaces.

The 15th-century Monasterio de Santa María de las Cuevas, inhabited by monks until 1836, now houses the Centro Andaluz de Arte Contemporáneo, which contains works by Andalucían artists, plus Spanish and international art. Free jazz jam sessions take place in the patio of the café on Sundays.

The centrepiece of Expo, the Lago de España, is part of the Isla Mágica theme park. This re-creates the journeys and exploits of the explorers who left Seville in the 16th century for the New World. Isla Mágica also has a water park, the Agua Mágica.

⑫ Cámara Oscura

Torre de los Perdigones, Calle Resolana. **Map** 2 D3. 🚌 C1, C2, C3, C4, C5, 2, 13, 14. **Tel** 679 09 10 73. **Open** noon–5pm Tue–Sun (closed when raining). 🏛

This huge camera obscura uses mirrors and magnifying lenses to display an image of the surrounding area. The Tower of Perdigones also offers scenic views of the city.

Main entrance of the Carthusian Monasterio de Santa María de las Cuevas, founded in 1400

SEVILLE STREET FINDER

The map references given with the sights described in the Seville section of the guide refer to the maps on the following pages. Map references are also given for Seville hotels *(see pp571–2)* and restaurants *(pp597–8)*. The schematic map below shows the area of Seville covered by the *Street Finder*. The symbols used for the sights and other features are listed in the key at the foot of the page.

0 kilometres 1
0 miles 0.5

Key

- Major sight
- Place of interest
- Other building
- Railway station
- Metro station
- Tram stop
- Bus station
- River bus boarding point

- *i* Tourist information
- Hospital with casualty unit
- Police station
- Church
- Convent or monastery
- = Railway line
- Pedestrianized street

Scale of Map Pages

0 metres 250
0 yards 250

SHOPPING IN SEVILLE

The shopping experience in Seville is influenced by its culture – bustling with energy until the moment the siesta arrives, then relaxing over lunch before the frenzy begins again. Seville has a good mix of well-known chain stores and independently owned gift shops, and the stores in this vibrant city are as colourful and diverse as the people themselves. The main shopping district winds through Calle Tetuán and Calle Sierpes, and flows on towards Plaza Nueva and over to Plaza Alfalfa, where you will find a fantastic range of goods – anything from the latest fashions to unique Spanish arts and crafts. Yet more diverse items can be found while strolling along Amor de Dios towards Alameda de Hercules, where there are many wonderful Moroccan, bohemian and artsy shops to explore.

Specialist Shops

The streets of Calle Cuna, Calle Francos and Calle Lineros are lined with shops that capture the flamenco spirit. **Lina Boutique** has impeccably styled, unique dresses as well as accessories. **Roberto Garrudo** sells flamenco dance shoes, while beautiful handmade shawls and intricate lace mantillas (veils) can be found at **Juan Foronda**. Handmade sombreros (hats), in addition to tasteful men's accessories, are available at **Maquedano**. For a fabulous range of leather goods and fashions, **El Caballo** is the place to shop.

To relive the spirit of Semana Santa (Easter Week), religious items can be bought at **Antigua Casa Rodríguez**.

At **Poster Félix** you can find historical posters from festivals and bullfights of years gone by, and other vintage Spanish collectibles.

An array of fans at Díaz, Calle Sierpes, Seville

Department Stores and Galerias

El Corte Inglés, Spain's national department store, has two main locations in the centre – Plaza Duque de la Victoria and Plaza Magdalena. The larger building at Plaza Duque offers clothes, shoes, sporting goods, cosmetics, a gourmet shop and a supermarket; the smaller building stocks music, books and art supplies. The outlet in Plaza Magdalena sells fine china, kitchenware and appliances. It also houses a supermarket and a DIY section. El Corte Inglés is open Monday to Saturday until 10pm.

Plaza de Armas is the only shopping centre in the heart of town, with shops, bars, restaurants, a nightclub, cinema and a supermarket. Nervion Plaza, the largest shopping hub close to the city centre (accessible by metro), is lined with shops, restaurants, bars and a cinema. A shopping mall is due to open at Torre Sevilla by the end of 2017. Shopping centres are open 10am–10pm Monday to Saturday.

Open-Air Markets

The lively and colourful open-air markets feature a dazzling display of unique wares and are a great way to spend a leisurely morning. Distinctive accessories and clothing can be found in the markets of Plaza Duque de la Victoria and Plaza Magdalena, open all day (weather permitting) Thursday to Saturday.

The markets at Plaza Encarnación, El Arenal, Plaza del Altozano, in Triana, and Calle Fería (open mornings, Monday to Saturday) offer local produce, fish, meat and cheese, while the Thursday market at Calle Fería specializes in bric-a-brac. On Sunday mornings, stamps, coins and other collectibles are traded in Plaza del Cabildo, and the painters' market in Plaza del Museo has displays of local art.

Stylish handmade *sombreros*

Antiques and Crafts

Antique shops are scattered throughout the city centre, mainly in Barrio Santa Cruz and Alfalfa. **Antigüedades el Museo** has classic Spanish and European furnishings and art, while handmade goods can be found at **El Postigo**, an arts and crafts centre. **Sevillarte** boasts unique ceramics and functional artwork with Andalucían influences. Seville's great ceramic tradition is visible in the Triana district, which still has several operating ceramic workshops. Ceramic shops can also be found along Calle Sierpes and Calle Tetuán.

Food and Wine

To bring home some of Seville's gastronomic specialities or to prepare a nice picnic, visit **Latas y Botellas**. The gourmet shop **El Corte Inglés** has exquisite luxuries for the discerning palate, as well as an ample wine cellar. For general groceries try the supermarket downstairs. Every area has several small convenience stores. For out-of-hours shopping, **SuperCor** is open 8am–2am daily.

Fashion

The shops of Calle Tetuán and Calle Sierpes bustle with an exciting range of the latest fashions. **Aurora Gaviño** has exclusive women's clothes and accessories in a range of styles – from flamenco to bridal wear. **Loewe** offers classic lines of clothing, luggage and accessories for both men and women, while **Zara** stocks all the latest high-street trends. **Adolfo Domínguez** offers high fashion for men, women and children. For unique and exotic accessories, head to the Alfalfa district, where several shops offer distinctive jewellery, handbags and other goods. **Esmeralda** has the biggest selection. For stylish baby clothes with Sevillian flair, head to **Larrana**.

The well-heeled of Seville shop at the vast array of shoe stores in the area as well as at the well-stocked "shoe street" of Calle Córdoba.

Books, Music and Souvenirs

Small bookshops are tucked into numerous corners of the city, but for the biggest selection of books in multiple

An art poster with a typical Sevillian flavour

languages, go to **Casa del Libro**. Music aficionados can find regional sounds of flamenco, Rock Andaluz and Semana Santa music, as well as international artists at **FNAC**, with its impressive collection of CDs, DVDs and books. Also, a large selection of musical instruments and equipment can be found at **Sevilla Musical**.

Typical souvenir shops are abundant along Avenida de la Constitución, Calle Mateos de Gago and all throughout Barrio Santa Cruz.

DIRECTORY

Specialist Shops

Antigua Casa Rodríguez
Calle Alcaiceria de la Loza 10. **Map** 3 C1, 6 D3.
Tel 954 21 24 27.

El Caballo
Calle Antonia Diaz 7.
Map 3 B2, 5 B4.
Tel 955 12 55 02.

Juan Foronda
Calle Sierpes 79. **Map** 3 C1, 5 C3. **Tel** 954 21 40 50.

Lina Boutique
Calle Lineros 17. **Map** 3 C1, 6 D3. **Tel** 954 21 24 23.

Maquedano
Calle Sierpes 40. **Map** 3 C1, 5 C3. **Tel** 954 56 47 71.

Poster Félix
Avenida de la Constitución 26. **Map** 3 C2.
Tel 954 218 026.

Roberto Garrudo
Calle Córdoba 9. **Map** 3 C1, 6 D3. **Tel** 954 21 84 19.

Department Stores and Galerias

El Corte Inglés
Plaza Duque de la Victoria 8, 13B. **Map** 1 C5, 5 C2.
Tel 954 59 70 00.
One of several branches.

Antiques and Crafts

Antigüedades el Museo
Plaza del Museo 4. **Map** 1 C5, 5 B2. **Tel** 954 56 01 28.

El Postigo
Calle Arfe s/n. **Map** 3 B2, 5 C4. **Tel** 954 56 00 13.

Sevillarte
Calle Sierpes 66. **Map** 3 C1, 5 C3. **Tel** 954 21 28 36

Food and Wine

Latas y Botellas
Calle Regina 14. **Map** 2 D5, 6 D1. **Tel** 954 29 31 22.

SuperCor
Avda Carlos V, 16.
Map 4 D3.

Fashion

Adolfo Domínguez
C/ Puente y Pellón 11. **Map** 3 C1, 6 D2. **Tel** 954 21 95 57.

Aurora Gaviño
Calle Álvarez Quintero 16.
Map 6 D3. **Tel** 954 22 54 94.

Esmeralda
Calle Alcaiceria de la Loza 26. **Map** 3 C1, 6 D3.
Tel 954 22 55 11.

Larrana
Calle Blanca de los Rios 4.
Map 3 C1, 6 D3.
Tel 954 21 52 80.

Loewe
Plaza Nueva 12. **Map** 3 B1, 5 C3. **Tel** 954 22 52 53.

Zara
Calle Rioja 10. **Map** 3 B1, 5 C2. **Tel** 954 21 10 58.

Books, Music and Souvenirs

Casa del Libro
C/ Velázquez 8. **Map** 3 C1, 5 C3. **Tel** 902 02 64 10.

FNAC
Avenida de la Constitución 8. **Map** 3 C1, 5 C4. **Tel** 902 10 06 32.

Sevilla Musical
Calle Cardinal Spinola 3.
Map 1 C5, 5 C1
Tel 954 91 57 55.

ENTERTAINMENT IN SEVILLE

Seville is universally famed as being a city of celebration and vitality, and this is reflected in its two spring festivals, Semana Santa and Feria de Abril *(see p437)*. In fact, the city has a year-round programme of interesting cultural events. The modern Teatro de la Maestranza and Teatro Lope de Vega, along with a number of independent venues, host a range of dance, music, theatre and arts festivals, while the world's most important flamenco festival, the Bienal de Flamenco, takes place in the city. Seville also has an enviable selection of night spots, from the quiet, more relaxed area surrounding the cathedral to the buzzing bars of Calle Betis and the Alfalfa district. For sports fans, a local derby between Real Betis and Sevilla FC is an absolute must-see.

Decorative tile commemorating Seville's Real Betis football club

Seasons and Tickets

In Seville, the arts season usually starts in September, lasting until June–July. From April to the end of the summer, the streets and open-air stages also host shows.

Two of the city's biggest events – the Bienal de Flamenco and the Bienal de Arte Contemporáneo – are biannual and take place in the autumn in even-numbered years.

Tickets for major sports events, opera, concerts and festivals should be booked in advance – details can be provided by the city's tourist information offices. Football matches are very popular, so buy these in advance too.

Entertainment Guides

A monthly events guide, *El Giraldillo* (www.giraldillo.es) covers film, music, theatre, clubs, art, sport, books, gay life, travel and much more. *La Teatral*, a bimonthly publication, focuses on theatre and dance.

Flamenco

Flamenco embraces a broad range of dancing, singing and musical styles. One venue with high-quality performances is **Los Gallos**. For something really authentic, go to **La Anselma** in the Triana quarter – the traditional home of the gypsy community. **La Carbonería** is an informal bar where free flamenco shows are often performed by amateur artists.

Promoting semi-professional local artists, **Casa de la Memoria** in the Santa Cruz district presents varied shows daily. As the venue is quite small, it is recommended you buy tickets in advance, and show up early to get a seat. In Calle Betis, there are bars where the public can watch and join in with *sevillanas*, a popular Andalucían folk dance.

The **Museo del Baile Flamenco** is a good place to learn about the origins of the dance and current developments, as well as see performances.

Music and Dance

The setting of Bizet's *Carmen*, Rossini's *The Barber of Seville* and Mozart's *Don Giovanni* and *Figaro*, Seville is a city of opera lovers. International opera companies perform at the elegant **Teatro de la Maestranza** starting in December and lasting until May. This theatre is home to the Real Orquesta Sinfónica de Sevilla, whose performances are highly regarded. The annual programme of the theatre also includes chamber and classical music seasons. **Teatro Lope de Vega** and **Conservatorio Superior de Música Manuel Castillo** are two other remarkable venues for classical music.

A live performance of flamenco at Los Gallos

Rosario Flores, the famous Andalucían singing star, performing at one of her concerts

The Maestranza and **Teatro Central** are the main venues hosting a wide range of national and international classical and contemporary dance performances.

Rock, Jazz and Blues

Few international rock stars make it to Seville, as Barcelona and Madrid tend to attract all the big names. However, large concerts are sometimes held at **Estadio Olímpico** or at **FIBES Palacio de Exposiciones y Congresos de Sevilla**. Some of Spain's most popular groups and singers in the pop genre, such as Manuel Carrasco, Merche and David Bisbal, are from Andalucía. **Café Naima**

and **Sala Malandar Luxuria**, have live music from local bands, including jazz, folk and rock, but the highlight of the jazz calendar in Seville has to be the International Jazz Festival, held in November at the Teatro Central.

Nightlife

The nightlife of Seville offers an endless array of possibilities. Calle Betis, along the Triana side of the river, has many bars, restaurants and clubs. Alameda de Hércules is one of the liveliest areas, with **Bar 1987** and **Café Central** as main bohemian hotspots. **Las Columnas** is a traditional tapas bar in Barrio de Santa Cruz district and **Bar Garlochi** is recommended for the first drink of the night. **La Terraza** at Eme Catedral Hotel is *the* place to see and be seen at (booking essential). The streets around Plaza de la Alfalfa overflow with youthful revellers, while young professionals gather in Calle Arfe, in the El Arenal district.

Frequented by Spanish celebrities, **Antique** in Isla de la Cartuja is the place to dance till dawn. In summer, their outdoor terrace boasts two pools and fashion shows.

Bullfighting

The Maestranza Bullring *(see p436)* is mythical among fans of bullfighting. Some of the most important bullfights in Spain are held here during the Feria de Abril. The season runs from April to October. It is advisable to book in advance if the matadors are famous, and also if you want a seat in the *sombra* (shade). Tickets are sold at the *taquilla* (box office) at the bullring.

Amusement Parks

Isla Mágica *(see p452)* re-creates the exploits of 16th-century New World explorers, with eight zones ranging from Mundo Maya to Amazonia, and from El Dorado to La Metrópolis de España. It is great fun for children of all ages. Visitors to the **Acuario de Sevilla** can see more than 400 marine species in their different habitats.

DIRECTORY

Flamenco

La Anselma
Calle Pages del Corro 49.
Map 3 A2, 5 A5.

La Carbonería
Calle Céspedes 21a.
Map 4 D1, 6 E3.
Tel 954 21 44 60.

Casa de la Memoria
Calle Cuna 6. **Map** 3 C1,
6 D2. **Tel** 954 56 06 70.
🔳 casadelamemoria.es

Los Gallos
Plaza Santa Cruz 11.
Map 4 D2, 6 E4.
Tel 954 21 69 81.
🔳 tablaolosgallos.com

Museo del Baile Flamenco
Calle Manuel Rojas Marcos
3. **Map** 3 C1, 6 D3. **Tel** 954
34 03 11. 🔳 museodel baileflamenco.com

Music and Dance

Conservatorio Superior de Música Manuel Castillo
Calle Baños 48. **Map** 1 C5,
5 B1. **Tel** 677 90 37 62.

Teatro Central
Av José Gálvez s/n, Isla
de la Cartuja. **Map** 1 C2.
Tel 955 54 21 55.

Teatro de la Maestranza
Paseo de Colón 22. **Map** 3
B2, 5 C5. **Tel** 954 22 33 44.

Teatro Lope de Vega
Avda María Luisa s/n. **Map**
3 C3. **Tel** 955 47 28 28.

Rock, Jazz and Blues

Café Naima
Calle Trajano 47. **Map** 1
C5, 5 C1. **Tel** 954 38 24 85.

Estadio Olímpico
Isla de la Cartuja, s/n.
Map 1 B1.

FIBES
Avenida Alcalde Luis
Uruñuela 1.
Tel 954 47 87 00.
🔳 fibes.es

Sala Malandar Luxuria
Avenida Torneo 43.
Map 1 B4.
Tel 954 37 01 88.

Nightlife

Antique
Matemáticos Rey Pastor y
Castro s/n. **Map** 1 B3.
Tel 954 46 22 07.

Bar 1987
Alameda de Hércules 93.
Map 2 D4.
Tel 672 66 44 55.

Bar Garlochi
Calle Boteros 26.
Map 3 C1, 6 E3.

Café Central
Plaza Alameda de
Hércules 64. **Map** 2 D4.
Tel 645 77 01 32.

Las Columnas
Calle Rodrigo Caro 1.
Map 3 C2, 6 E4.

La Terraza
Eme Catedral Hotel,
Calle Alemanes 27.
Map 3 C2, 6 D4.
Tel 954 56 00 00.

Amusement Parks

Acuario de Sevilla
Muelle de las Delicias,
Area Sur, Puerto de
Sevilla. **Map** 5 C5.
Tel 955 44 15 41.
🔳 acuariosevilla.es

ANDALUCÍA

Huelva · Cádiz · Málaga · Gibraltar · Sevilla
Córdoba · Granada · Almería · Jaén

Andalucía is where all Spain's stereotypes meet. Bullfights, beaches, flamenco, white villages, flashy fiestas, religious processions, tapas and sherry are all here in abundance. But each is part of a larger whole, which further lists great art and architecture, nature reserves, excellent cuisine and a charming, easy-going way of life.

The eight provinces of Andalucía, plus the British territory of Gibraltar, stretch across Southern Spain from the deserts of Almería to the Portuguese border. One of Spain's longest rivers, the Guadalquivir, bisects the region and the mainland's highest peaks can be found in the Sierra Nevada. Andalucía is linked to the central tableland by a pass, the Desfiladero de Despeñaperros.

Successive invaders left their mark on Andalucía. The Romans built cities in this southern province, which they called Baetica, among them Córdoba, its capital, the well-preserved Itálica near Seville, and Cástulo, once the largest city on the peninsula. It was in Andalucía that the Moors lingered longest and left their greatest buildings – Córdoba's Mezquita

and the splendid palace of the Alhambra in Granada. Inevitably, perhaps, the most visited places are the great cities and the busy Costa del Sol, with Gibraltar, a geographical and historical oddity, at its western end. But there are many attractions tucked into other corners of the region. Many of the sights of Huelva province, bordering Portugal, are associated with Christopher Columbus, who set sail from here in 1492. Film directors have put to good use the atmospheric landscapes of Almería's arid interior, which are reminiscent of the Wild West or Arabia. Discreetly concealed among the countless olive groves that cover Jaén province, but not to be missed, are Andalucía's two lovely Renaissance towns, Úbeda and Baeza.

The city of Jaén surrounded by olive groves, seen from the Castillo de Santa Catalina

◀ Pedestrians strolling on the seaside promenade in Marbella, Costa del Sol

Exploring Andalucía

Andalucía is Spain's most varied region and promises rewarding Spanish experiences, from exploring dramatic desert scenery at Tabernas and windsurfing on the Costa del Sol, to skiing in the Sierra Nevada and sherry tasting in Jerez. Of the many nature reserves, the vast, watery Doñana teems with birdlife, while Cazorla is a rugged limestone massif. Granada and Córdoba are unmissable for their Moorish heritage; Úbeda and Baeza are Renaissance gems; and Ronda is one of dozens of superb white towns.

Key

— Motorway
— Major road
— Secondary road
— Scenic route
— Main railway
— Minor railway
— International border
— Regional border
△ Summit

0 kilometres 25
0 miles 25

The smart marina at Sotogrande

For keys to symbols see back flap

Getting Around

Andalucía has a modern motorway network, with the principal NIV A4 (E5) from Madrid following the Guadalquivir Valley to Córdoba, Seville and Cádiz. The fast AVE train links Málaga, Seville and Córdoba with Madrid. Coaches cover most of the region. The main airports are Málaga, Seville, Jerez and Gibraltar.

View of the Alhambra palace
from the Albaicín, Granada

Sights at a Glance

The famed *jamón ibérico* hanging in a bar in Jabugo, Sierra de Aracena

❶ Sierra de Aracena

Huelva. 🚋 El Repilado. 🚌 Aracena.
i Calle Pozo de la Nieve s/n,
Aracena, 663 93 78 77. 🅰 Sat.

This wild mountain range is one of the most remote and least visited corners of Andalucía. On the hillside are the ruins of a Moorish fort. The hill is pitted with caverns and in one, the **Gruta de las Maravillas**, is a lake in a chamber hung with many stalactites.

The village of Jabugo is famed for its ham, *jamón ibérico*, or *pata negra (see p422)*.

Off the A471 are the giant opencast mines at Minas de Riotinto, where iron, copper and silver have been exploited since Phoenician times. The **Museo Minero** traces the history of the Rio Tinto Company.

🏞 Gruta de las Maravillas
Pozo de la Nieve. **Tel** 663 93 78 76
(for info about availability). **Open**
10am–1:30pm, 3–6pm. 🎦 🎟

🏛 Museo Minero
Plaza del Museo. **Tel** 959 59 00 25.
Open daily. **Closed** 1 & 6 Jan, 25 Dec.
🎦 ♿ 🎟 ⓦ **parqueminero deriotinto.es**

❷ Huelva

Huelva. 🏙 130,000. 🚋 🚌 *i* Calle Jesús Nazareno 21, 959 65 02 00.
🅰 Fri. 🎉 Las Columbinas (3 Aug).

Founded as Onuba by the Phoenicians, Huelva had its grandest days as a Roman port. It was almost wiped out in the great Lisbon earthquake of 1755. It is an industrial city today, sprawling around the quayside on the Río Odiel.

Columbus's departure for the New World *(see p60)* from Palos de la Frontera, across the Río Odiel estuary, is celebrated in the excellent **Museo Provincial**, which also charts the history of the Rio Tinto mines. To the east of the centre, the Barrio Reina Victoria is a bizarre example of English mock-Tudor suburban bungalows built by the Rio Tinto Company for its workers in the early 20th century. South of the town, at Punta del Sebo, the Monumento a Colón, a rather bleak statue of Columbus created by Gertrude Vanderbilt Whitney in 1929, dominates the Odiel estuary.

Bronze jug, Museo Provincial, Huelva

Environs
There are three resorts with sandy beaches near Huelva: Punta Umbria, on a promontory next to the bird-rich wetlands of the Marismas del Odiel; Isla Cristina, an important fishing port with excellent seafood restaurants; and Mazagón with miles of windswept dunes.

The hilly region east of Huelva known as El Condado produces many of Andalucía's finest wines, and Bollullos del Condado has the largest wine cooperative in the region. Niebla, nearby, has a Roman bridge. The town walls and 12th-century **Castillo de los Guzmanes** are both Moorish.

🏛 Museo Provincial
Alameda Sundheim 13. **Tel** 959 65
04 24. **Open** Tue–Sun. ♿

🏰 Castillo de los Guzmanes
Calle Campo Castillo, Niebla.
Tel 959 36 22 70. **Open** daily.

❸ Monasterio de la Rábida

Huelva. 🚌 from Huelva. **Tel** 959 35
04 11. **Open** Tue–Sun. ♿ 🎟 🎦

Four kilometres (2 miles) to the north of Palos de la Frontera is the Franciscan Monasterio de la Rábida, founded in the 15th century.

In 1491, a dejected Columbus sought refuge here after his plans to sail west to find the East Indies had been rejected by the Catholic Monarchs. Its prior, Juan Pérez, fatefully used his considerable influence as Queen Isabella's confessor to reverse the royal decision.

Inside, frescoes painted by Daniel Vásquez Díaz in 1930 glorify the explorer's life and discoveries. Also worth seeing are the Mudéjar cloisters, the flower-filled gardens and the beamed chapterhouse.

Frescoes depicting the life of Columbus at the Monasterio de la Rábida

❹ Palos de la Frontera

Huelva. 🏠 12,000. 🚌 ℹ️ Parque Botánico José Celestino Mutis Paraje de la Rábida, 959 49 46 64. 🏛️ Sat. 🎉 Santa María de la Rábida (3 & 16 Aug).

Columbus set sail for the New World on 3 August 1492 from Palos, the home town of his two captains, the brothers Martín and Vicente Pinzón. Martín's former home, the **Casa Museo de Martín Alonso Pinzón**, is now a small museum of exploration, and his statue stands in the main square.

The 15th-century Iglesia de San Jorge has a fine portal, through which Columbus left after hearing Mass before boarding the *Santa María*. The pier is now silted up.

Environs
In the beautiful white town of Moguer are treasures such as the 16th-century hermitage of Nuestra Señora de Montemayor, and the Neo-Classical town hall. The **Monasterio de Santa Clara** houses the Museo Diocesano de Arte Sacro and has a pretty cloister.

🏛️ **Casa Museo de Martín Alonso Pinzón**
Calle Colón 24. **Tel** 959 10 00 41. **Open** Mon–Fri. 🎉

⛪ **Monasterio de Santa Clara**
Plaza de las Monjas. **Tel** 959 37 01 07. **Open** Tue–Sun am. **Closed** public hols. 🎉 ⬜

❺ El Rocío

Huelva. 🏠 2,500. 🚌 ℹ️ Avenida de la Canaliega, 959 44 38 08. 🎉 Romería (May/Jun).

Bordering the Parque Nacional de Doñana *(see pp470–71)*, El Rocío is famous for its annual *romería*, which sees almost a million people converge on the village. Many of the pilgrims travel from distant parts of Spain, some on gaudily decorated oxcarts, to visit the Iglesia de Nuestra Señora del Rocío. A statue of the Virgin in the church is believed to have performed miraculous healings since 1280. Early on the Monday morning of the festival, men from Almonte fight to carry the statue in procession, and the crowd clambers onto the float to touch the image.

Crowds following the image of the Virgin at El Rocío

Andalucía's Fiestas

Carnival *(Feb/Mar)*, Cádiz. The whole city puts on fancy dress for one of Europe's largest and most colourful carnivals. Groups of singers practise for many months to perform ditties satirizing current fashions, celebrities and politicians.

Romería de la Virgen de la Cabeza *(last Sun in Apr)*, Andújar (Jaén). A mass pilgrimage to a lonely sanctuary in the Sierra Morena.

Día de la Cruz *(first week in May)*, Granada and Córdoba. Neighbourhood groups compete to create the most colourful crosses adorned with flowers on squares and street corners.

Córdoba Patio Fiesta *(mid-May)*. Flower-decked patios in old Córdoba are opened to the public with displays of flamenco.

El Rocío *(May/Jun)*. More than 70 brotherhoods of pilgrims arrive at the village of El Rocío to pay homage to the Virgen del Rocío.

Columbus Festival *(late Jul/early Aug)*, Huelva. This celebration of Columbus's voyage is dedicated to the native music and dance of a different Latin American country every year.

Exaltación al Río Guadalquivir *(mid-Aug)*, Sanlúcar de Barrameda (Cádiz). Horses are raced on the beach at the mouth of the Río Guadalquivir.

Iglesia de Nuestra Señora del Rocío, El Rocío

❻ Parque Nacional de Doñana

Doñana National Park is ranked among Europe's greatest wetlands. Together with its adjoining protected areas, the park covers in excess of 500 sq km (193 sq miles) of marshes and sand dunes. The area used to be a hunting ground *(coto)* belonging to the Dukes of Medina Sidonia. As the land was never suitable for human settlers, wildlife was able to flourish. In 1969, this large area became officially protected. In addition to a wealth of endemic species, thousands of migratory birds stop over in winter when the marshes become flooded again, after months of drought.

Shrub Vegetation
Backing the sand dunes is a thick carpet of lavender, rock rose and other low shrubs.

Prickly Juniper
This species of juniper *(Juniperus oxycedrus)* thrives in the wide dune belt, putting roots deep into the sand. The trees may get buried beneath the dunes.

Palacio del Acebrón

El Rocío

La Rocina

El Acebuche

Matalascañas

Palacio de Doñana

Laguna de Santa O.

Coastal Dunes
Softly rounded, white dunes, up to 30 m (100 ft) high, fringe the park's coastal edge. The dunes, ribbed by prevailing winds off the Atlantic, shift constantly.

Monte de Doñana, the wooded area behind the sand dunes, provides shelter for lynx, deer and boar.

The Interior
The number of visitors to the park's interior is strictly controlled to ensure minimal environmental impact. The only way to view the wildlife here is on officially guided day tours.

Key

◻ Marshes

◻ Dunes

••• Parque Nacional de Doñana

••• Parque Natural de Doñana

▬ Road

Deer
Fallow deer *(Dama dama)* and larger red deer *(Cervus elaphus)* roam the park. Stags engage in fierce contests in late summer as they prepare for breeding.

Wild cattle use the marshes as waterholes.

Imperial Eagle
The imperial eagle *(Aquila adalberti)* is one of Doñana's rarest birds.

Río Guadiamar

José Antonio Valverde
ℹ

Marisma de Hinojos

Marisma Gallega

Greater Flamingo
During the winter months, the salty lakes and marshes provide the beautiful, pink greater flamingo *(Phoenicopterus ruber)* with crustaceans, its main diet.

Río Guadalquivir

Sanlúcar de Barrameda
ℹ
Fábrica de Hielo

| 0 kilometres | 5 |
| 0 miles | 5 |

The Lynx's Last Refuge

The lynx is one of Europe's rarest mammals. In Doñana about 30 individual Spanish lynx *(Lynx pardellus)* have found a refuge. They have yellow-brown fur with dark brown spots and pointed ears with black tufts. Research is under way into this shy, nocturnal animal, which tends to stay hidden in scrub. It feeds mainly on rabbits and ducks, but might catch an unguarded fawn.

The elusive lynx, only glimpsed with patience

For keys to symbols *see back flap*

❼ Sanlúcar de Barrameda

Cádiz. 🔼 63,000. 🚌 ℹ️ Calle Calzada Duquesa Isabel s/n, 956 36 61 10. 🟢 Wed. 🐎 Exaltación al Río Guadalquivir and horse races (mid-Aug).

A fishing port at the mouth of the Río Guadalquivir, Sanlúcar is overlooked by a Moorish castle. This was the departure point for Columbus's third voyage in 1498 and also for Magellan's 1519 expedition to circumnavigate the globe.

Sanlúcar is best known for its light, dry manzanilla sherry made by, among other producers, **Bodegas Barbadillo**. Boats from the quay take visitors across the river to the Parque Nacional de Doñana *(see pp470–71)*.

Environs

Chipiona, along the coast, is a lively little resort town with an excellent beach. The walled town of Lebrija, inland, enjoys views over vineyards. Its Iglesia de Santa María de la Oliva is a reconsecrated 12th-century Almohad mosque.

🍷 Bodegas Barbadillo

Calle Luis de Eguilaz 11. **Tel** 956 38 55 21. **Open** Tue–Sat. 🐎 🎫 ♿

Entrance to the Barbadillo bodega in Sanlúcar de Barrameda

❽ Jerez de la Frontera

Cádiz. 🔼 190,000. ✈️ 🚉 🚌 ℹ️ Plaza del Arenal s/n, Edificio Los Arcos, 956 33 88 74. 🟢 Mon. 🐎 Grape Harvest (Sep).

Jerez is the capital of sherry production *(see pp424–5)* and many bodegas can be visited. Among the well-known are Pedro Domecq and González Byass.

The city is also famous for its **Real Escuela Andaluza de Arte Ecuestre**, an equestrian school with public displays on Tuesdays and Thursdays. On other days you may be able to watch the horses being trained. The **Palacio del Tiempo**, nearby, has one of the largest clock collections in Europe. On the Plaza de San Juan, the 18th-century **Palacio de Penmartín** houses the Centro Andaluz de Flamenco, where exhibitions give a good introduction to this music and dance tradition *(see pp428–9)*. The partially restored, 11th-century **Alcázar** encompasses a well-preserved mosque, now a church. Just to the north is the cathedral.

Environs

Not far from Jerez, the Monasterio de la Cartuja Santa María de la Defensión is considered one of the most beautiful in Spain. The port of El Puerto de Santa María has several **bodegas** that can be visited, including Osborne. The town also has a 13th-century castle and a large bullring.

🏛️ Real Escuela Andaluza de Arte Ecuestre

Duque de Abrantes. **Tel** 956 31 96 35 (by appt). **Open** Mon–Fri. 🐎 ♿ 🌐 realescuela.org

🏛️ Palacio del Tiempo

Calle Cervantes 3. **Tel** 956 18 21 00. **Open** Tue–Sun. 🐎 ♿

🏛️ Palacio de Penmartín

Plaza de San Juan 1. **Tel** 956 90 21 34. **Open** Mon–Fri. **Closed** public hols.

🏛️ Alcázar

Alameda Vieja. **Tel** 956 14 99 55. **Open** daily. **Closed** 1 & 6 Jan, 25 Dec. 🐎 ♿ 🎫

🍷 Sherry Bodegas

Open phone for tour times. 🐎 González Byass: Calle Manuel María González 12, Jerez. **Tel** 956 35 70 16. Pedro Domecq: Calle San Ildefonso 3, Jerez. **Tel** 956 15 15 00. Sandeman: C/ Pizarro 10, Jerez. **Tel** 675 64 71 77. Osborne: C/ de los Moros, Puerto de Santa María. **Tel** 956 86 91 00. Terry: C/ San Ildefonso 3, Jerez. **Tel** 956 15 15 00.

Real Escuela Andaluza de Arte Ecuestre, Jerez de la Frontera

● Cádiz

Jutting out of the Bay of Cádiz, and almost entirely surrounded by water, Cádiz lays claim to being Europe's oldest city. Legend names Hercules as its founder, although history credits the Phoenicians with establishing the town of Gadir in 1100 BC. Occupied by the Carthaginians, Romans and Moors in turn, the city also prospered after the Reconquest *(see pp58–9)* on wealth taken from the New World. In 1587 Sir Francis Drake sacked the city in the first of many British attacks in the war for world trade. In 1812 Cádiz briefly became Spain's capital when the nation's first constitution was declared here *(see p67)*.

VISITORS' CHECKLIST

Practical Information
Cádiz. 🅰 155,000. 🛈 Avenida José León de Carranza s/n, 956 28 56 01. 🚆 Mon. 🎭 Carnival (Feb/Mar). 🅦 cadizturismo.com

Transport
🚉 Plaza de Sevilla, **Tel** 902 24 05 05. 🚌 Plaza de la Hispanidad, **Tel** 956 80 70 59.

Exploring Cádiz
The joy of visiting Cádiz is to wander along the waterfront with its well-tended gardens and open squares before exploring the Old Town, which is full of narrow alleys busy with market and street life.

The pride of the city is its Carnival *(see p471)* – a riotous explosion of festivities, fancy dress, singing and drinking.

⛪ Catedral
Known as the Catedral Nueva (New Cathedral) and built on the site of an older one, this Baroque and Neo-Classical church, with its dome of golden-yellow tiles, is one of Spain's largest. In the crypt is the tomb of composer Manuel de Falla (1876–1946). The cathedral's treasures are stored in the Casa de la Contaduría, behind the cathedral.

🏛 Museo de Cádiz
Plaza de Mina. **Tel** 856 10 50 23. **Open** 9am–8pm Tue–Sat (to 3pm Jun–mid-Sep); 10am–3pm Sun & pub hols. ♿
The museum has archaeological exhibits charting the history of Cádiz and the largest art gallery in Andalucía, with works by Rubens, Zurbarán and Murillo. On the third floor is a collection of puppets made for village fiestas.

🏛 Torre Tavira
Calle Marqués del Real Tesoro 10. **Tel** 956 21 29 10. **Open** daily. **Closed** 1 Jan, 25 Dec. 📷 📸
The city's official watchtower in the 18th century has now been converted into a camera obscura, and offers great views.

⛪ Oratorio de San Felipe Neri
Calle Santa Inés s/n. **Tel** 956 80 70 18. **Open** 10:30am–2pm, 4:30–8pm (Jul & Aug: 5:30–8:30pm) Tue–Fri, 10:30am–2pm Sat, 10am–1pm (Jul & Aug: to noon) Sun.

In 1812, as Napoleon tightened his grip on Spain *(see pp66–7)*, a provisional government assembled at this 18th-century church to try to lay the foundations of Spain's first constitutional monarchy. The liberal constitution it declared was bold but ineffectual.

Roman marble statue from the 2nd century in the Museo de Cádiz

Cádiz Cathedral

The cupola was built between 1812 and 1838 by Juan Daura, the last in a long line of architects of this cathedral.

Baroque vaults

The presbytery altar was partly sponsored by Isabel II *(see p75)*.

Neo-Classical tower

Neo-Classical façade

Fishing boats at the resort of Zahara de los Atunes on the Costa de la Luz

❿ Costa de la Luz

Cádiz. 🚉 Cádiz. 🚌 Cádiz, Tarifa.
ℹ️ Paseo de la Alameda s/n, Tarifa,
956 68 09 93.

The Costa de la Luz (Coast of Light) between Cádiz and Tarifa, at Spain's southernmost tip, is an unspoiled, windswept stretch of coast characterized by strong, pure light – the source of its name. From the Sierra del Cabrito, to the west of Algeciras, it is often possible to see the outline of Tangier and the parched Moroccan landscape below the purple-tinged Rif mountains across the narrow Strait of Gibraltar.

Tarifa is named after an 8th-century Moorish commander, Tarif ben Maluk, who landed there with his forces during the Moorish conquest (see pp56–7). Later, Tarifa and its 10th-century castle were defended by the legendary hero Guzmán during a siege by the Moors in 1292.

Tarifa has since become the windsurfing capital of Europe. The breezes that blow on to this coast also drive the numerous wind turbines on the hills.

Off the N340 (E5), at the end of a long, narrow road which strikes out across a wilderness of cacti, sunflowers and lone cork trees, is Zahara de los Atunes, a modest holiday resort with a few hotels. Conil de la Frontera, to the west, is busier and more built up.

The English admiral Nelson defeated a Spanish and French fleet off Cabo de Trafalgar in 1805, but died in the battle.

⓬ A Tour Around the Pueblos Blancos

Instead of settling on Andalucía's plains, where they would have fallen prey to bandits, some Andalucíans chose to live in fortified hilltop towns and villages. These are known as *pueblos blancos* (white towns) because they are whitewashed in the Moorish tradition (see p30). They are working agricultural towns today, but touring them will reveal a host of references to the past.

② Ubrique
Nestling at the foot of the Sierra de Ubrique, this *pueblo* is known for its flourishing leather industry.

↑ Sevilla

← Cádiz, Jerez

A372

① Arcos de la Frontera

Embalse de Hurones

Charco de los Hurones

CA5221

0 kilometres   10
0 miles   5

⑨ Jimena de la Frontera
Set amid hills, where wild bulls graze among cork and olive trees, this town has a ruined Moorish castle.

CA503

La Sauceda

Key

▰▰ Tour route
══ Other roads

Tips for Drivers

Tour length: 205 km (127 miles).
Stopping-off points: There are places to stay and eat at all of these pueblos, but Ronda has the widest range of hotels and restaurants (see p601). Arcos has a parador (see p572).

⑧ Gaucín
From here there are unsurpassed vistas over the Mediterranean, the Atlantic, the Rock of Gibraltar and across the strait to the Rif mountains of North Africa.

⓫ Arcos de la Frontera

Cádiz. 🏠 30,000. 🚌 ℹ️ C/ Cuesta de Belén 5, 956 70 22 64. 🅿️ Fri. 🎭 Toro del Domingo de Resurrección (last day of Easter), Velada de Nuestra Señora de las Nieves (4–6 Aug), Semana Santa, Feria de San Miguel (end of Sep).

Although legend has it that a son of Noah founded Arcos, it is more probable that it was the Iberians. It gained the name Arcobriga in the Roman era and, under the Caliphate of Córdoba (see p56), became the Moorish stronghold of Medina Arkosh. It is an archetypal white town, with a labyrinthine old quarter.

On the Plaza de España, at the top of the town, are the parador (see p572) and the Iglesia de Santa María de la Asunción, a Late Gothic-Mudéjar building noted for its choir stalls and altarpiece. The huge, Gothic Iglesia de San Pedro, perched on the edge of a cliff formed by the Río Guadalete, is a striking building. Nearby is the **Palacio del Mayorazgo**, which has an ornate Renaissance façade. The **town hall** (ayuntamiento) has a fine Mudéjar ceiling.

Environs
In the 15th-century the Guzmán family was granted the dukedom of Medina Sidonia, a white west of Arcos de la Frontera. The area became one of the most important ducal seats in Spain. The Gothic Iglesia de Santa María la Coronada is the town's finest building. It contains a notable collection of Renaissance religious art.

🏛️ **Palacio del Mayorazgo**
Calle San Pedro 2. **Tel** 956 70 30 13.

Iglesia de Santa María de la Asunción in Arcos de la Frontera

(Casa de Cultura). **Open** 10am–2pm Mon–Fri. ♿

🏛️ **Ayuntamiento**
Plaza del Cabildo. **Tel** 956 70 49 50.
Open Mon–Fri. **Closed** public hols.

③ **Zahara de la Sierr**
Fanning out below a castle ruin, this fine pueblo blanco has been declared a national monument.

④ **Grazalema**
This village in the Sierra de Grazalema has the highest rainfall in Spain.

⑤ **Ronda la Vieja**
Significant remains of the Roman town of Acinipo, including a theatre, can be visited.

⑥ **Setenil**
Some of the streets of this unusual white town, which climbs up the sides of a gorge, are covered by rock overhangs. The gorge was carved out of volcanic tufa rock by the Río Trejo.

Ronda ⑦
(see pp476–7)

⑬ Street-by-Street: Ronda

One of the most spectacularly located cities in Spain, Ronda sits on a massive rocky outcrop, straddling a precipitous limestone cleft. Because of its impregnable position this town was one of the last Moorish bastions, finally falling to the Christians in 1485. On the south side perches a classic Moorish *pueblo blanco (see pp474–5)* of cobbled alleys, window grilles and dazzling whitewash – most historic sights are in this part of the town. Located in El Mercadillo, the newer town, is one of the oldest bullrings in Spain.

★ **Puente Nuevo**
An impressive feat of 18th-century civil engineering, the "New Bridge" over the 100-m- (330-ft-) deep Tajo gorge joins old and new Ronda.

Convento de Santo Domingo was the local headquarters of the Inquisition *(see p278)*.

To El Mercadillo, Plaza de Toros, parador and tourist information

Casa del Rey Moro
From this 18th-century mansion, built on the foundations of a Moorish palace, 365 steps lead down to the river.

Mirador El Campillo (viewpoint)

SANTO DOMINGO

CALLE ARMIÑÁN

TENORIO

PLAZA DEL CAMPILLO

★ **Palacio Mondragón**
Much of this palace was rebuilt following the Reconquest *(see pp58–9)*, but its arcaded patio is adorned with original Moorish mosaics and plasterwork.

| 0 metres | 75 |
| 0 yards | 75 |

Palacio del Marqués de Salvatierra
Bizarre images of biblical scenes and South American Indians embellish the façade of this palace, built in Renaissance style in the 18th century.

To Puente Viejo, Baños Árabes

MARQUÉS DE SALVATIERRA

Santa María la Mayor
A minaret and a Muslim prayer niche survive from the 13th-century mosque which once stood on the site of this church.

Minarete San Sebastián is a remnant of a 14th-century mosque.

CA2MEN

SCALERA

ARMIÑAN

PLAZA DUQUESA DE PARCENT

Ayuntamiento
The town hall was remodelled in the 20th century and incorporates parts of older buildings. It has a two-tier arcaded façade and Mudéjar ceiling.

Key

— Suggested route

Bullfighting at Ronda

Ronda's Plaza de Toros is the spiritual home of bullfighting. Inaugurated in 1785, it is one of the oldest, most important bullrings in Spain. In September, aficionados travel from all over the country for the singular atmosphere of the Corrida Goyesca and millions watch it on television. It is the dream of every aspiring matador to fight at Ronda. The classic Ronda style (more severe than the exuberant School of Seville) was developed by Pedro Romero. Born in 1754, he is widely considered to be the father of modern bullfighting.

Romero, who killed over 6,000 bulls

⑭ Algeciras

Cádiz. 🚊 200,000. 🚌 ℹ️ Paseo Río de la Miel s/n, 670 94 87 31. 🚌 Tue. 🎭 Feria Real (24 Jun–2 Jul).

From the industrial city of Algeciras, there are spectacular views of Gibraltar, 14 km (9 miles) away across its bay. The city is a major fishing port and Europe's main gateway for ferries to North Africa, especially Tangier and Spain's territories of Ceuta and Melilla.

⑮ Gibraltar

British Crown Colony. 🚊 35,000. 🚌 ℹ️ Duke of Kent House, Cathedral Square, (+35) 020 07 49 50. 🎭 Nat Day (10 Sep). 🌐 **visitgibraltar.gi**

The high, rocky headland of Gibraltar was signed over to Britain "in perpetuity" at the Treaty of Utrecht in 1713 (see p66). Today, about 4 million people stream across the border annually from La Línea de la Concepción in Spain.

Among the chief sights of Gibraltar are those testifying to its strategic military importance over the centuries. Halfway up the famous Rock are an 8th-century Moorish castle, whose **keep** was

St Michael's Cave, which served as a hospital during World War II

used as a prison until 2010, and 80 km (50 miles) of **siege tunnels** housing storerooms and barracks. **St Michael's Cave**, which served as a hospital during World War II, is now used for classical concerts.

The **Apes' Den**, near Europa Point, Gibraltar's southernmost tip, is home to the tailless apes. Legend says that the British will keep the Rock only as long as the apes remain there.

A cable car takes visitors to the Top of the Rock, at 450 m (1,475 ft). **Gibraltar Museum** charts the colony's history.

🏛️ **The Keep, Siege Tunnels, St Michael's Cave, Apes' Den**
Upper Rock Area. **Tel** (+35) 020 04 59 57. **Open** daily (except Siege Tunnels: Mon–Fri). **Closed** 1 Jan, 25 Dec. 🎫

🏛️ **Gibraltar Museum**
18 Bombhouse Lane.
Tel (+35) 020 07 42 89. **Open** Mon–Sat. **Closed** public hols. 🎫

The Costa del Sol

Thanks to its average of 300 days of sunshine a year and its varied coastline, the Costa del Sol, between Gibraltar and Málaga, offers a full range of beach-based holidays and water sports. Complementing the sophistication and luxury of Marbella are many other popular resorts aimed at the mass market. More than 30 of Europe's finest golf courses lie just inland.

Puerto Banús is Marbella's ostentatious marina. The expensive shops, restaurants and glittering nightlife reflect the wealth of its clientele.

Estepona's quiet evenings make it popular with families with young children. Behind the big hotels are old squares shaded by orange trees.

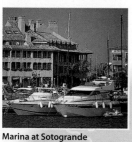

Marina at Sotogrande is an exclusive resort of luxury villas. The marina is fronted by good seafood restaurants.

San Pedro de Alcántara
Estepona   Atala
Ronda del Mar
Sabinillas
Punta de la Chullera
Rio Guadiaro
Sotogrande
Los Barrios   San Roque
Algeciras   Bahia de Algeciras   La Línea de la Concepción
GIBRALTAR (UK)
Gibraltar
Punta de Europa
Punta del Carnero
Tarifa

San Pedro de Alcántara is a quiet resort with a modern marina and smart holiday developments.

Yachts and motorboats in the exclusive marina of Marbella – the summer home of the international jet set

⑯ Marbella

Málaga. 🚹 120,000. 🚌 ℹ️ Glorieta de la Fontanilla, Paseo Marítimo, 952 76 87 60. 🚇 Mon. 🎪 San Bernabé (Jun). 🌐 **marbella.es**

Marbella is one of Europe's most exclusive holiday resorts, frequented by royalty and film stars. There are 24 beaches,

including Puerto Banus, Playa Rio Verde and Playa Nagueles. In winter, the major attraction is the golf. Among the delights of the old town, with its spotlessly clean alleys, squares, and smart shops and restaurants, is the Iglesia de Nuestra Señora de la Encarnación. The **Museo del**

Grabado Español Contemporáneo displays some of Pablo Picasso's least-known work.

🏛️ **Museo del Grabado Español Contemporáneo**
Calle Hospital Bazan. **Tel** 952 76 57 41. **Open** Mon–Sat. **Closed** public hols. 🚫

Marbella is the Costa del Sol's most stylish resort. The Playa de Don Carlos is considered the best of its 24 beaches.

El Chapparal
Málaga
El Palo
La Capellania
Rincón de la Victoria
Torremolinos
Benalmádena Costa
Torreblanca
Marbella
Fuengirola
Cabopino
Cala de Mijas
Punta de Calaburra

Rincón de la Victoria is an unspoiled family beach, famous for its spit-roasted sardines.

Torremolinos, a high-rise holiday metropolis, is less brash than it used to be. Huge sums have been spent on new squares, a promenade, green spaces, and improving the beach with millions of tonnes of golden sand.

Cabopino, on a not-too-crowded stretch of coast, has areas that include nudist and gay beaches.

Benalmádena Costa caters almost exclusively for package holidays. Behind the rather rocky beaches and very large marina is a plethora of tourist attractions.

Fuengirola still has an active fishing port – as these boxes of fresh fish suggest – although it is better known today as a package-holiday resort with a chiefly British clientele. It has a spectacular backdrop of steep, ochre mountains.

0 kilometres 10
0 miles 10

The main façade of Málaga's cathedral, consecrated in 1588

⑰ Málaga

Málaga. ✈ 650,000. ✈ 🚌 🚍 ⛴
🛈 Plaza de la Marina 11, 951 92 60
20. 🏠 Sun. 🎭 Carnival (Feb/Mar),
Feria (second Sat–third Sun of Aug).
ⓦ malagaturismo.com

Málaga, the second-largest city in Andalucía, is today a thriving port, just as it was in Phoenician times, and again under the Romans and then the Moors. It also flourished during the 19th century, when sweet Málaga wine (see p424) was one of Europe's most popular drinks – until phylloxera ravaged the area's vineyards in 1876.

The cathedral, begun in 1528 by Diego de Siloé, is a bizarre mix of styles. The half-built second tower, abandoned in 1765 when funds ran out, gave the cathedral its nickname: La Manquita ("the one-armed one").

Málaga's **Museo Picasso** displays works by the native artist, while the Casa Natal de Picasso, where the painter spent his early years, is now the Picasso Foundation. The **Centre Pompidou Málaga** has an impressive collection of modern and contemporary artworks.

Málaga's vast Alcazaba (see p57) was built between the 8th and 11th centuries. There is a partially excavated Roman amphitheatre by its entrance. Housed in the Palacio de la Aduana, the Museo de Málaga displays archaeological artifacts, including some from the site.

On the hill directly behind the Alcazaba are the ruins of the Castillo de Gibralfaro, a 14th-century Moorish castle.

Environs

In the hills to the north and east of Málaga is the Parque Natural de los Montes de Málaga. Wildlife, such as eagles and wild boars, thrive here amid the scent of lavender and wild herbs. Walkers can follow a number of scenic marked trails. Going north on the C345 you can also visit Ecomuseo Lagar de Torrijos, a preserved winery of the 1840s.

🏛 **Museo Picasso**
Calle San Agustín 8. **Tel** 952 12 76 00. **Open** Tue–Sun. **Closed** 1 Jan, 25 Dec. 🌐

🏛 **Centre Pompidou Málaga**
Pasaje Doctor Carillo Casaux s/n, Muelle Uno. **Tel** 951 92 62 00. **Open** Wed–Mon.

⑱ Garganta del Chorro

Málaga. 🚆 El Chorro. 🚍 Parque Ardeles. 🛈 Plaza Fuente de Arriba 15, El Chorro, 952 49 61 00.

Up the fertile Guadalhorce Valley, beyond the village of El Chorro, is one of the geographical wonders of Andalucía.

The Garganta del Chorro is an immense chasm, 180 m (590 ft) deep and in places only 10 m (30 ft) wide, cut by the river through a limestone mountain. Downstream, a hydroelectric plant detracts from the wildness of the place.

The Caminito del Rey is a catwalk clinging to the rock face which leads to a bridge across the gorge (visit www.caminito delrey.info to book access).

Environs

Álora, a classic white town (see pp474–5) with a ruined Moorish castle and an 18th-century church, lies 12 km (7 miles) down the valley.

Along the twisting MA441 from Álora is the village of Carratraca. In the 19th and early 20th centuries, Europe's highest society travelled here for the healing powers of the sulphurous springs. These days, Carratraca has a faded glory – water still gushes out at 700 litres (155 UK and 185 US gal) a minute and the outdoor baths remain open, but they are little used.

The Garganta del Chorro, rising high above the Guadalhorce River

Weathered limestone formations in El Torcal

⓳ El Torcal

Málaga. 🚉 Antequera. 🚌 Antequera.
ℹ️ Antequera, 952 70 25 05. Parque
Natural del Torcal: **Tel** 952 24 33 24.
Open 10am–5pm daily (to 7pm Apr–
Sep). 🌐 **torcaldeantequera.com**

A massive exposed hump of
limestone upland, which has
been slowly weathered into
bizarre rock formations and
caves, the Parque Natural del
Torcal is popular with hikers.
Marked trails lead from a
visitors' centre.

The park is also a pleasure
for natural historians, with fox
and weasel populations, and
colonies of eagles, hawks and
vultures, as well as rare plants
and flowers like wild orchids.

⓴ Antequera

Málaga. 🚹 42,000 🚉 🚌 ℹ️ Plaza
San Sebastián 7, 952 70 25 05. 🚍 Tue.
🎉 Ferias (end May & mid-Aug).
🌐 **antequera.es**

This busy market town was
strategically important first as
Roman Anticaria and later as
a Moorish border fortress
defending Granada.

Of its many churches, the
Iglesia de Nuestra Señora del
Carmen, with its vast Baroque
altarpiece, is not to be missed. At
the opposite end of the town is
the 19th-century **Plaza de Toros**,
with a museum of bullfighting.

The hilltop castle was built in
the 13th century on the site of
a Roman fort. Visitors can walk
round the castle walls by
approaching through the 16th-
century Arco de los Gigantes.

There are excellent views of
Antequera from the Torre del
Papabellotas on the best-
preserved part of the wall.

In the town below, the 18th-
century **Palacio de Nájera** is
the setting for the Municipal
Museum, the star exhibit of
which is a splendid Roman
bronze statue of a boy.

The massive dolmens, just
outside the town, are thought
to be the burial chambers of
tribal leaders and date from
around 2500–2000 BC.

Environs

Laguna de la Fuente de Piedra,
north of Antequera, teems with
bird life, including huge flocks of
flamingoes, which arrive to breed
after wintering in West Africa.
A road off the N334 leads to a
lakeside viewing point. There
is a visitors' centre in Fuente de
Piedra village. To the east, also off
the N334, is Archidona, with its
18th-century, octagonal Plaza

The triumphal, 16th-century Arco de los
Gigantes, Antequera

Ochavada built in French style,
but which also incorporates
traditional Andalucían features.

🎪 Plaza de Toros

Carretera de Sevilla. **Tel** 952 70 81 42.
Open Tue–Sun. Museo Taurino:
Open Sat, Sun, public hols.

🏛️ Palacio de Nájera

Coso Viejo. **Tel** 952 70 83 00.
Open Tue–Sun. 🎨

Palacio del Marqués de la Gomera, in
Osuna, completed in 1770

㉑ Osuna

Sevilla. 🚹 17,500. 🚉 🚌 ℹ️ Calle
Sevilla 37, 954 81 57 32. 🚍 Mon.
🎉 San Alcádio (17 Jan), Virgen de
la Consolación (8 Sep).

Osuna was once a key Roman
garrison town. It rose again to
prominence in the 16th century
under the Dukes of Osuna, who
wielded immense power. In
the 1530s they founded the
Colegiata de Santa María, a
grand church with a Baroque
reredos and paintings by José
de Ribera. This was followed in
1548 by the University, a rather
severe building with a beautiful
patio. Some fine mansions,
among them the Palacio del
Marqués de la Gomera, also
reflect the town's former glory.

Environs

To the east lies Estepa, whose
modern-day fame rests on
its biscuits – *polvorones* and
mantecados. The Iglesia del
Carmen has a black and white,
Baroque façade.

Tomb of Servilia in the Roman necropolis in Carmona

22 Carmona

Sevilla. 25,000. 🚌 ℹ️ Alcázar de la Puerta de Sevilla, 954 19 09 55. 🚇 Mon & Thu. 🎪 Feria (May), Fiestas Patronales (8–16 Sep). 🌐 turismo.carmona.org

Carmona is the first major town east of Seville, its old quarter built on a hill above the suburbs on the plain. Beyond the Puerta de Sevilla, a gateway in the Moorish city walls, is a dense cluster of mansions, Mudéjar churches, and winding streets.

The Plaza de San Fernando has a feeling of grandeur which is characterized by the Renaissance façade of the old **Ayuntamiento**. The present town hall, set just off the square, dates from the 18th century; in its courtyard are some Roman mosaics. Close by is the Iglesia de Santa María la Mayor. Built in the 15th century over a mosque, whose patio still survives, this is the finest of Carmona's churches.

Dominating the town are the ruins of the Alcázar del Rey Pedro, once a palace of Pedro I, known as Pedro the Cruel. Parts of it now form a parador (see p572).

Just outside Carmona is the **Necrópolis Romana**, the extensive remains of a Roman burial ground. A site museum displays some of the items found in the graves, including statues, glass and jewellery.

🏛️ **Ayuntamiento**
Calle Salvador 2. **Tel** 95 414 00 11. **Open** Mon–Fri. **Closed** public hols.

🏛️ **Necrópolis Romana**
Avenida Jorge Bonsor 9. **Tel** 600 14 36 32. **Open** Tue–Sun. **Closed** 1 Jan, 1 May & 25 Dec.

23 Itálica

Avda de Extremadura 2, Santiponce, Sevilla. **Tel** 955 12 38 47. 🚌 from Seville. **Open** 9am–2:30pm Sun & pub hols; also 9am–5:30pm Tue–Sat (Apr–mid-Jun: to 7:30pm, mid-Jun–mid-Sep: to 2:30pm). 🅿️

Itálica was founded in 206 BC by Scipio Africanus. One of the earliest Roman cities in Hispania (see pp54–5), it grew to become important in the 2nd and 3rd centuries AD. Emperor Hadrian, who was born in the city and reigned from AD 117–138, added marble temples and other grand buildings.

Roman mosaic from Itálica

Archaeologists have speculated that the changing course of the Río Guadalquivir may have led to Itálica's later demise during Moorish times.

Next to the vast but crumbling amphitheatre is a display of finds from the site. More treasures are displayed in the Museo Arqueológico in Seville (see p451).

Traces of Itálica's streets and the mosaic floors of some villas can be seen, but little remains of the city's temples or its baths, as most of the stone and marble has been plundered over the centuries. Some well-preserved Roman baths and a theatre can be seen in the village of Santiponce, just outside the site.

24 Sierra Morena

Sevilla & Córdoba. 🚉 Cazalla, Constantina. 🚌 Constantina, Cazalla. ℹ️ Constantina (Sevilla): 955 88 12 97; Cazalla (Sevilla): 954 88 35 62; Córdoba: 957 64 11 40; El Robledo: 955 88 95 93.

The Sierra Morena, clad in oak and pine woods, runs across the north of the provinces of Sevilla and Córdoba. It forms a natural frontier between Andalucía and the plains of neighbouring Extremadura and La Mancha. Smaller sierras (ranges of hills) within the Sierra Morena chain are also named individually.

Fuente Obejuna, north of Córdoba, was immortalized by Lope de Vega (see p294) in his play about an uprising in 1476 against a local overlord. The Iglesia de San Juan Bautista in Hinojosa del Duque is a vast church in both Gothic and Renaissance styles. Belalcázar is dominated by the huge tower of a ruined 15th-century castle. Storks nest on the church towers of the plateau of Valle de los Pedroches, to the east.

Cazalla de la Sierra, the main town of the sierra north of Seville, is popular with young Sevillanos at weekends. Liquor de Guindas, a concoction of cherry liqueur and aniseed, is produced here. Constantina, to the east, is more peaceful with superb views of the countryside.

A cow grazing in the pastures of the Sierra Morena north of Seville

㉕ Palma del Río

Córdoba. 🚹 19,400. 🚉 🚌 🚹 Plaza Mayor de Andalucía s/n, 957 64 43 70. 📅 Tue. 🎉 Ferias (19–21 May & 18–20 Aug). 🌐 **palmadelrio.es**

The Romans sited a strategic settlement here, on the road between Córdoba and Itálica, almost 2,000 years ago. The remains of the 12th-century city walls are a reminder of the town's frontier days under the Almohads (see p58). The Iglesia de la Asunción, a Baroque church, dates from the 18th century. The Monasterio de San Francisco is now a hotel (see p574), and guests can eat dinner in the 15th-century refectory of the Franciscan monks. Palma del Río is the home town of El Cordobés, one of

Bell tower, La Asunción

Spain's most famous matadors. His biography, Or I'll Dress You in Mourning, paints a vivid picture of life in the town and of the hardship which followed the end of the Civil War.

Environs

One of the most dramatic silhouettes in Southern Spain breaks the skyline of **Almodóvar del Río**. The Moorish castle – parts of it dating from the 8th century – stands on a hilltop overlooking the whitewashed town and fields of cotton.

🏰 **Castillo de Almodóvar del Río** **Tel** 957 63 40 55. **Open** daily. 🚫 **Closed** 1 Jan, 25 Dec.

㉖ Écija

Sevilla. 🚹 40,000. 🚌 🚹 Calle Elvira -A, Palacio de Benamejí, 955 90 29 33. 📅 Thu. 🎉 Feria (21–24 Sep). 🌐 **turismoecija.com**

Écija is nicknamed "the frying pan of Andalucía" owing to its famously torrid climate. In the searing heat, the palm trees on the Plaza de España provide blissful shade. An ideal place to sit and observe daily life passing by, this is also a spot for evening strolls.

Écija has 11 Baroque church steeples, many adorned with gleaming azulejos (see p444), and together they make a very impressive sight. The most florid of these is the Iglesia de Santa María, which overlooks the Plaza de España. The Iglesia de San Juan, with its exquisite, brightly coloured bell tower, is a very close rival.

Of the many mansions along Calle Emilio Castelar, the Baroque **Palacio de Peñaflor** is worth a visit. Its pink marble doorway is topped by twisted columns, while an attractive wrought-iron balcony runs along the whole front façade.

🏛 **Palacio de Peñaflor** Calle Emilio Castelar 26. **Tel** 954 83 02 73. **Closed** for refurbishment.

㉗ Medina Azahara

Córdoba. **Tel** 957 10 49 33. 🚌 Córdoba. **Open** 9am–8pm (to 3pm mid-Jun–mid-Sep, to 6pm mid-Sep–Mar) Tue–Sat; 9am–6pm Sun & public hols. 🅿

Just a few kilometres north of Córdoba lies this once glorious palace. Built in the 10th century for Caliph Abd al Rahman III, it is named after his favourite wife, Azahara. He spared no expense,

Detail of woodcarving in the main hall of Medina Azahara

employing more than 15,000 mules, 4,000 camels and 10,000 workers to bring building materials from as far as North Africa.

The palace is built on three levels and includes a mosque, the caliph's residence and fine gardens (see pp426–7). Marble, ebony, jasper and alabaster once adorned its many halls, and it is believed that shimmering pools of quicksilver added lustre.

The glory was short-lived. The palace was sacked by Berber invaders in 1010 and over subsequent centuries it was ransacked for its building materials. Now, the ruins give only glimpses of its former beauty – a Moorish main hall, for instance, decorated with marble carvings and a carved wood ceiling. The palace is currently being restored.

Trompe l'oeil on the ornate Baroque façade of the Palacio de Peñaflor, Écija

⑳ Street-by-Street: Córdoba

The heart of Córdoba is the old Jewish quarter, situated to the west of the Mezquita's towering walls. A walk around this area gives the sensation that little has changed since the 10th century, when this was one of the greatest cities in the Western world. Wrought ironwork decorates cobbled streets too narrow for cars, where silversmiths create fine jewellery in their workshops. Most of the chief sights are here, while modern city life takes place some blocks north, around the Plaza de Tendillas. To the east of this square is the Plaza de la Corredera, a 17th-century arcaded square with a daily market.

Sinagoga
Hebrew script covers this 14th-century synagogue. Spain's other synagogues are in Toledo, Madrid and Barcelona.

Capilla de San Bartolome
This small church was built in the Gothic-Mudéjar style. It is decorated with elaborate plasterwork and tiles.

Casa de Sefarad is a cultural centre with exhibits on Judeo-Spanish history in the heart of the old Jewish quarter.

★ Alcázar de los Reyes Cristianos
Water terraces fountains add to the tranquil atmosphere of the gardens belonging to the palace-fortress of the Catholic Monarchs *(see pp60–61)*, built in the 14th century.

| 0 metres | | 100 |
| 0 yards | | 100 |

Key

— Suggested route

The Callejón de las Flores brims with colourful geraniums, which contrast with the whitewashed walls of this alley, leading to a tiny square.

Palacio Episcopal

QUEBRADO

CORREGIDOR

Puerta del Puente

The Puente Romano spans the Río Guadalquivir. A museum on its southeast side explores the different cultures of medieval Córdoba.

TOR BOSCO
HERRERO
MAGISTRAL GONZÁLEZ FRANCÉS
DE TORRIJOS
MADOR DE LOS RÍOS
TERESA DE JORNET
RONDA DE ISASA

★ **Mezquita**
The mighty walls of the Great Mosque (*see pp486–7*) hide delicate arches, pillars and a dazzling *mihrab*.

Decorations on an early Christian sarcophagus, Museo Arqueológico

Exploring Córdoba

Córdoba lies on a sharp bend in the Río Guadalquivir, which is spanned by a Roman bridge linking the 14th-century Torre de la Calahorra and the old town. One of the most atmospheric squares in Andalucía is the Plaza de los Capuchinos. With its haunting stone calvary, it is particularly evocative when seen by moonlight.

🏛 Museo de Bellas Artes
Plaza del Potro 2. **Tel** 957 10 36 59. **Open** Tue–Sun.
Exhibits in a former charity hospital include sculptures by local artist Mateo Inurria (1867–1924) and works by Valdés Leal, Zurbarán and Murillo of the Seville School.

🏛 Museo Arqueológico
Plaza Jerónimo Páez 7. **Tel** 957 35 55 29. **Open** Tue–Sun. 🏛
Located in a Renaissance mansion, displays include the remains of a Roman theatre found beneath the building, Roman pottery and impressive finds from the Moorish era.

🏛 Palacio de Viana
Plaza Don Gome 2. **Tel** 957 49 67 41. **Open** Tue–Sun (am only Sun & public hols). 🏛 🏛
Furniture, tapestries, paintings and porcelain are displayed in the 17th-century former home of the Viana family.

🏛 Museo Romero de Torres
Plaza del Potro 1. **Tel** 957 47 03 56. **Open** Tue–Sun. 🏛 (free Fri).
Julio Romero de Torres (1874–1930), who was born in this house, captured the soul of Córdoba in his paintings.

Córdoba: the Mezquita

Córdoba's Great Mosque, dating back 12 centuries, embodied the power of Islam on the Iberian Peninsula. Abd al Rahman I *(see pp56–7)* built the original mosque between AD 785 and 787. The building evolved over the centuries, blending many architectural forms. In the 10th century al Hakam II made some of the most lavish additions, including the elaborate *mihrab* (prayer niche) and the *maqsura* (caliph's enclosure). During the 16th century a cathedral was built in the heart of the reconsecrated mosque, part of which was destroyed.

Patio de los Naranjos
Orange trees grow in the courtyard where the faithful washed before prayer.

KEY

① **Puerta de San Esteban** is set in a section of wall from an earlier Visigothic church.

② **The Puerta del Perdón** is a Mudéjar-style entrance gate, built during Christian rule in 1377. Penitents were pardoned here.

③ **Torre del Alminar**, a bell tower 93 m (305 ft) high, is built on the site of the original minaret. Steep steps lead to the top for a fine view of Córdoba.

④ **Capilla Mayor**

⑤ **The cathedral choir** has Churrigueresque stalls carved by Pedro Duque Cornejo in 1758.

⑥ **Capilla Real**

Expansion of the Mezquita

Abd al Rahman I built the original mosque. Extensions were added by Abd al Rahman II, al Hakam II and al Mansur.

Key to Additions

☐ Mosque of Abd al Rahman I
☐ Extension by Abd al Rahman II
☐ Extension by al Hakam II
☐ Extension by al Mansur
☐ Patio de los Naranjos

Cathedral
Part of the mosque was destroyed to accommodate the cathedral, started in 1523. Featuring an Italianate dome, it was designed chiefly by members of the Hernán Ruiz family.

VISITORS' CHECKLIST

Practical Information
Calle Torrijos 10. **Tel** 957 47 05 12.
Open 10am–7pm Mon–Sat,
8:30–11:30am, 3–7pm Sun &
pub hols (Nov–Feb: to 6pm
Mon–Sat, 8:30–11:30am,
3–6pm Sun & pub hols).
🕀 9:30am Mon–Sat; 11am,
noon & 1:30pm Sun & hols.

★ **Arches and Pillars**
More than 850 columns of granite, jasper and marble support the roof, creating a dazzling visual effect. Many were taken from Roman and Visigothic buildings.

★ **Mihrab**
This prayer niche, richly ornamented, held a gilt copy of the Koran. The worn flagstones indicate where pilgrims circled it seven times on their knees.

★ **Capilla de Villaviciosa**
The first Christian chapel was built in the mosque in 1371 by Mudéjar (see p59) craftsmen. Its multi-lobed arches are stunning.

Baroque statuary in the Fuente del Rey at Priego de Córdoba

㉙ Montilla

Córdoba. ⚑ 23,000. 🚏 🚉 ℹ Capitán Alonso de Vargas 3, 957 65 24 62. 🚌 Fri. 🎉 Grape Harvest (late Aug).

Montilla is the centre of an important wine region that produces an excellent smooth white fino *(see p424)*. Unlike sherry, it is not fortified with alcohol. Several bodegas, including **Alvear** and **Pérez Barquero**, will show visitors around by prior arrangement.

The Mudéjar Convento de Santa Clara dates from 1512. The town library and tourist office is in the Casa del Inca, so named because Garcilaso de la Vega, who wrote about the Incas, lived there in the 1500s.

Environs

Aguilar, 13 km (8 miles) to the south, has the unusual, eight-sided Plaza de San José (built in 1810) and several seigneurial houses.

Baena, 40 km (25 miles) to the west of Montilla, has been famous for its olive oil since Roman times. On the Plaza de la Constitución is the Casa del Monte, a mansion dating from the 18th century. At Easter thousands of costumed drummers take to the streets.

🏛 Bodega Alvear
Avda María Auxiliadora 1. **Tel** 957 65 01 00. **Open** Mon–Fri. 🕐 12:30pm.

🏛 Bodega Pérez Barquero
Avenida de Andalucía 27. **Tel** 957 65 05 00. **Open** Mon–Fri. **Closed** Aug.

㉚ Priego de Córdoba

Córdoba. ⚑ 23,000. 🚌 ℹ Plaza de la Constitución 3, 957 70 06 25. 🚌 Sat. 🎉 Feria Real (1–5 Sep). 🌐 turismodepriego.com

Priego de Cordóba's claim to be the capital of Cordoban Baroque is borne out by the dazzling work of carvers, ironworkers and gilders in the many houses, and especially churches, built with wealth generated by a prosperous 18th-century silk industry.

A restored Moorish fortress stands in the whitewashed medieval quarter, the Barrio de la Villa. Close by is the outstanding Iglesia de la Asunción, converted from Gothic to Baroque style by Jerónimo Sánchez de Rueda. Its pièce de résistance is the sacristy, created in 1784 by local artist Francisco Javier Pedrajas. The main altar is Plateresque *(see p29)*.

At midnight every Saturday the brotherhood of another Baroque church, the Iglesia de la Aurora, parades the streets singing songs in praise of the Virgin.

Silk merchants built many of the splendid mansions that follow the curve around the Calle del Río. At the street's end is the Baroque Fuente del Rey (The King's Fountain). The 139 spouts splash water into three basins adorned with a riot of statuary.

La Asunción, Priego de Córdoba

Environs

Zuheros, perched on a crag in the limestone hills northwest of Priego, is one of Andalucía's prettiest villages. Rute, to the southwest, is known for its *anís (see p581)*.

Alcalá la Real, in the lowlands east of Priego, is overlooked by the hilltop ruins of a castle and a church. There are two handsome Renaissance buildings on its central square: the Fuente de Carlos V and the Palacio Abacia.

㉛ Montefrío

Granada. ⚑ 7,000. 🚌 ℹ Plaza España 1, 958 33 60 04. 🚌 Mon. 🎉 Fiesta patronal (14–18 Aug).

The approach to Montefrío from the south offers wonderful views of tiled rooftops and pretty whitewashed houses. This archetypal Andalucían town is topped by the remains of its Moorish fortifications and the 16th-century Gothic Iglesia de la Villa. In the centre of town is the Neo-Classical Iglesia de la Encarnación, designed by Ventura Rodríguez (1717–85). The town is known for its chorizo, as well as its numerous stone crosses, thought to have been constructed in the 16th and 17th centuries.

Environs

Santa Fé was built by the Catholic Monarchs at the end of the 15th century. Their army

Barrels of Montilla, the sherry-like wine from the town of the same name

The castle overlooking the resort of Almuñécar on the Costa Tropical

camped here while laying siege to Granada, and this was the site of the formal surrender of the Moors in 1492 *(see pp60–61)*. A Moor's severed head, carved in stone, adorns the spire of the parish church.

Sited above a gorge, Alhama de Granada was named *Al hammu (hot springs)* by the Moors. Their baths, close to the spot where the hot water gushes from the ground just outside town, can be seen in the Hotel Balneario.

Loja, on the Río Genil, near Los Infiernos gorge, is known as "the city of water" because of its spring-fed fountains.

⓫ Nerja

Málaga. ⚇ 18,000. 🚌 *i* Calle Carmen 1, 952 52 15 31. 🚍 Sun. 🎭 Feria (9–12 Oct). **w** nerja.org

This well-established resort, built on a cliff above sandy coves, lies at the foot of the beautiful Sierra de Almijara. There are sweeping views up and down the coast from the rocky promontory known as El Balcón de Europa (the Balcony of Europe). Along it runs a promenade lined with cafés and restaurants.

East of the town are the **Cuevas de Nerja**, a series of vast caverns which were discovered in 1959. Wall paintings found here are believed to be about 20,000 years old. Only a few of the many cathedral-sized chambers are open to public view. One of these has been converted into an impressive auditorium which has a capacity of several hundred people.

Environs
In Vélez-Málaga, the ruins of the Fortaleza de Belén, a Moorish fortress, dominate the medieval Barrio de San Sebastián.

🐾 Cuevas de Nerja
Carretera de las Cuevas de Nerja. **Tel** 952 52 95 20. **Open** daily. **Closed** 1 Jan, 15 May. 🖼

㉝ Almuñécar

Granada. ⚇ 22,000. 🚌 *i* Avda Europa, 958 63 11 25. 🚍 Fri, 1st Sat of each month. 🎭 Virgen de la Antigua (15 Aug). **w** almunecar.info

Almuñécar lies on the Costa Tropical, so named because its climate allows the cultivation of exotic fruit. Inland, mountains

rise to more than 2,000 m (6,560 ft). The Phoenicians founded the first settlement here, called Sexi, and the Romans constructed an aqueduct, the remains of which can be seen today. Almuñécar is now a popular holiday resort.

Above the Old Town is the castle, built by the Moors and altered in the 1500s. Below it is the **Parque Ornitológico**, which has an aviary and botanic gardens. The **Museo Arqueológico Cueva de Siete Palacios** displays a variety of Phoenician artifacts.

Environs
The ancient white town of **Salobreña** is set amid fields of sugar cane. Narrow streets lead up a hill to a restored Arab castle with fine views of the Sierra Nevada *(see p491)*.

🦜 Parque Ornitológico
Plaza de Abderraman. **Tel** 958 63 56 17. **Open** daily.

🏛 Museo Arqueológico Cueva de Siete Palacios
Calle Cueva de Siete Palacios s/n. **Tel** 607 86 54 66. **Open** Tue–Sun. 🖼

🏰 Castillo de Salobreña
Calle Andrés Segovia. **Tel** 958 61 03 14. **Open** daily. **Closed** pub hols. 🖼 🎫

One of the succession of sandy coves that make up the resort of Nerja

The majestic peaks of the Sierra Nevada towering, in places, to over 3,000 m (9,800 ft) above sea level

㉞ Lanjarón

Granada. 🏔 24,000. 🚌 ℹ Avenida de Madrid s/n, 958 77 04 62. 🔄 Tue & Fri. 🎉 San Juan (24 Jun).

Scores of clear, snow-fed springs bubble from the slopes of the Sierra Nevada; their abundance at Lanjarón, on the southern side of this great range of mountains, has given the town a long history as a health spa. From June to October, visitors flock to take the waters for arthritic, dietary and nervous ailments. Bottled water from Lanjarón is sold all over the country.

A major festival begins on the night of 23 June and ends in an uproarious water battle in the early hours of 24 June, the Día de San Juan. Everyone in the streets gets doused.

The town is on the threshold of Las Alpujarras, a scenic upland area of dramatic landscapes, where steep, terraced hillsides and deep-cut valleys conceal remote, whitewashed villages. Roads to and from Lanjarón wind slowly and dizzily around the slopes.

㉟ A Tour of Las Alpujarras

The fertile, upland valleys of Las Alpujarras, clothed with chestnut, walnut and poplar trees, lie on the southern slopes of the Sierra Nevada. The architecture of the quaint white villages which cling to the hillsides – compact clusters of irregularly shaped houses with tall chimneys sprouting from flat, grey roofs – is unique in Spain. Local specialities are ham cured in the cold, dry air of Trevélez and brightly coloured, handwoven rugs.

④ Trevélez
Trevélez, in the shadow of Mulhacén, Spain's highest mountain, is famous for its cured ham.

② Poqueira Valley
Capileira, Bubión and Pampaneira are three villages typical of Las Alpujarras in this pretty river valley.

SIERRA

▲ *Mulhacén*
3,479 m
11,410 ft

Trevélez

④

A4132

Juvile

Poqueira

② ③ **Pórtugos**

Pitres

Guadalfeo

A348 A4130 A348#

*Lanjarón
Granada* ①

SIERRA DE LA

① Orgiva
This is the largest town of the region, with a Baroque church in the main street and a lively Thursday market.

③ Fuente Agria
People come to this spring to drink the iron-rich, naturally carbonated waters.

❸❻ Laujar de Andarax

Almería. 🅰 2,000. 🚌 ℹ️ Carretera AL-5402 Láujar–Berja, km 1, 950 51 41 49. 🗓 3 & 17 of each month. 🎉 San Vicente (22 Jan), San Marcos (25 Apr), Virgen de la Salud (19 Sep).

Laujar, in the arid foothills of the Sierra Nevada, looks southwards across the Andarax Valley towards the Sierra de Gádor.

Andarax was founded by one of the grandsons of Noah. In the 16th century, Abén Humeya, leader of the greatest Morisco rebellion *(see p63)*, made his base here. The revolt was crushed by Christian troops and Abén Humeya was killed by his own followers. Inside Laujar's 17th-century

Painting, Iglesia de la Encarnación

church, La Encarnación, is a statue of the Virgin by Alonso Cano. Next to the Baroque town hall *(ayuntamiento)* is a fountain inscribed with some lines written by Francisco Villespesa, a dramatist and poet who was born in Laujar in 1877: "Six fountains has my pueblo/He who drinks their waters/will never forget them/so heavenly is their taste."

El Nacimiento, a park to the east of Laujar, is a suitable place to have a picnic. You can accompany it with one of the area's hearty red wines. Ohanes, above the Andarax valley further to the east, is an attractive hill town of steep streets and whitewashed houses known for its crops of table grapes.

❸❼ Sierra Nevada

Granada. 🚌 from Granada. ℹ️ Plaza de Andalucía, Cetursa Sierra Nevada, 958 24 91 11. 🌐 sierranevada.es

Fourteen peaks more than 3,000 m (9,800 ft) high crown the Sierra Nevada. The snow lingers until July and begins falling again in late autumn. One of Europe's highest roads, the A395, runs past Solynieve, an expanding ski resort at 2,100 m (6,890 ft), and skirts the two highest peaks, Pico Veleta at 3,398 m (11,149 ft) and Mulhacén at 3,482 m (11,420 ft).

The Sierra's closeness to the Mediterranean and its altitude account for the great diversity of the indigenous flora and fauna found on its slopes – the latter including golden eagles and some rare butterflies.

There are several mountain refuges for the use of serious hikers and climbers.

---

⑥ Yegen
A plaque marks the house where Gerald Brenan, the author of *South from Granada*, lived in the 1920s.

↑ *Lacalahorra*

⑧ Puerto de la Ragua
This pass, which leads across the mountains to Guadix, is nearly 2,000 m (6,560 ft) high and is often snowbound in winter.

⑦ Válor
Abén Humeya, leader of a rebellion by Moriscos in the 16th century, was born here. A commemorative battle between Moors and Christians is staged each year in mid-September.

⑤ Cádiar
Free wine is traditionally on tap during the village's October fiesta.

Tips for Drivers

Tour length: 85 km (56 miles).
Stopping-off points: There are bars and restaurants in Orgiva, Capileira, Bubión *(see p599)* and Trevélez. Orgiva, Bubión and Trevélez have good hotels. Orgiva is the last petrol stop before Cádiar.

Key

🚌 Tour route
═ Other roads
▲ Mountain peak

0 kilometres   5
0 miles   5

A5402
Alcolea
AL4401
A4130
Macina
• *Yátor*   *Ugíjar* •   *Cherín*
A348#   *A348#*
Ugíjar
CONTRAVIESA

⑱ Granada

The guitarist Andrés Segovia (1893–1987) described Granada as a "place of dreams, where the Lord put the seed of music in my soul". It was first occupied by the Moors in the 8th century, and its golden period came during the rule of the Nasrid dynasty *(see pp58–9)* from 1238 to 1492, when artisans, merchants, scholars and scientists all contributed to the city's international reputation as a centre for culture. Under Christian rule, following its fall to the Catholic Monarchs in 1492 and the expulsion of the Moors *(see pp60–61)*, the city blossomed in Renaissance splendour. There was a period of decline in the 19th century, but Granada has been the subject of renewed interest and many efforts have been made to restore it to its past glory.

Entrance to the Moorish *mihrab* in the Palacio de la Madraza

Façade of Granada Cathedral

Exploring Granada

The old city centre around the cathedral is a maze of narrow one-way streets. It contains the Alcaicería – a reconstruction of a Moorish bazaar that burned down in 1843. Granada's two main squares are the Plaza Bib-Rambla, near the cathedral, and the Plaza Nueva. From the latter, Cuesta de Gomérez leads up to the city's two principal monuments: the Alhambra and the Generalife. On a hill opposite is the Albaicín district.

Churches well worth a visit are the Iglesia de San Juan de Dios, almost overwhelming in its wealth of Baroque decoration, and the Renaissance Iglesia de San Jerónimo.

🏛 Cathedral

Calle Gran Vía 5. **Tel** 958 22 29 59. **Open** daily. 🖼
On the orders of the Catholic Monarchs, work on the cathedral began in 1523 to plans in a Gothic style by Enrique de Egas. It continued under the Renaissance maestro, Diego de Siloé, who also designed the façade and the magnificent Capilla Mayor. Under its dome, 16th-century windows depict Juan del Campo's *The Passion*. The west front was designed by Alonso Cano, who was born in the city. His grave can be seen in the cathedral.

🏛 Capilla Real

Calle Oficios 3. **Tel** 958 22 92 39. **Open** daily. **Closed** Jan 1, Good Fri, Dec 25.
The Royal Chapel was built for the Catholic Monarchs between 1506 and 1521 by Enrique de Egas. A magnificent *reja* (grille) by Maestro Bartolomé de Jaén encloses the high altar and the Carrara marble figures of Fernando and Isabel, their daughter Juana la Loca (the Mad) and her husband Felipe el Hermoso (the Fair). Their coffins are in the crypt. In the sacristy there are art treasures, including paintings by Botticelli and Van der Weyden.

🏛 Palacio de la Madraza

Calle Oficios 14. **Tel** 958 99 63 50. **Open** 9am–2pm, 5–8pm Mon–Fri.
Originally an Arab university (now part of Granada University), this building later became the city hall. The façade is 18th century. The Moorish hall has a finely decorated *mihrab* (prayer niche).

🏛 Corral del Carbón

Calle Mariana Pineda. **Tel** 958 22 59 90. **Open** 10:30am–1:30pm, 5–8pm Mon–Fri, 10:30am–2pm Sat. **Closed** public hols.
A relic of the Moorish era, this galleried courtyard was a theatre in Christian times. Today it houses a cultural centre.

🏛 Casa de los Tiros

Calle Pavaneras 19. **Tel** 958 22 06 29. **Open** mid-Sep–May: 10am–8:30pm Tue–Sat, 10am–5pm Sun & pub hols; Jun–mid-Sep: 9am–3:30pm Tue–Sat, 10am–5pm Sun & pub hols. **Closed** 1 Jan, 1 May, 25 Dec.
Built in Mudéjar style in the 1500s, this palace owes its name

Grille by Maestro Bartolomé de Jaén enclosing the altar of the Capilla Real

Cupola in the sanctuary of the Monasterio de la Cartuja

to the muskets projecting
from its battlements (*tiro* means
"shot"). It originally belonged
to the family that was awarded
the Generalife after the fall
of Granada. Among their possessions was a sword that had
belonged to Boabdil. This is
carved on the façade, along with
statues of Mercury, Hercules
and Jason.

🏛️ Alhambra and Generalife
See pp496–8.

🏛️ El Bañuelo
Carrera del Darro 31. **Tel** 958 02 78
00. **Open** 10am–2pm Tue–Sat.
Closed public hols.

These columnated Arab baths
were built in the 11th century.

🏛️ Centro Cultural Caja Granada
Avenida de la Ciencia, 2. **Tel** 958 22 22
57. **Open** 8:30am–2pm Mon–Wed,
8:30am–2pm, 4:30–7pm Thu–Sat,
11am–2pm Sun, public hols. 📷
🌐 **memoriadeandalucia.com**

A cultural centre with a theatre,
restaurant and the superb
Memoria de Andalucia Museum.

🏛️ Monasterio de la Cartuja
Paseo de la Cartuja. **Tel** 958 16 19 32.
Open daily.

Founded in 1516 by Christian
warrior, El Gran Capitán, this
monastery outside Granada
has a dazzling cupola by Antonio
Palomino, and a Churrigueresque (*see p29*) sacristy by Luis
de Arévalo and Luis Caballo.

Granada City Centre

0 metres 250
0 yards 250

Street-by-Street: The Albaicín

This corner of the city, on the hillside opposite the Alhambra, is where one feels closest to Granada's Moorish ancestry. Now mostly pedestrianized, this was the site of the first fortress, built in the 13th century, along with more than 30 mosques. Most of the city's churches were built over their sites. Along the cobbled alleys stand *cármenes*, villas with Moorish decoration and gardens, secluded from the world by high walls. In the jasmine-scented air of evening, stroll up to the Mirador de San Nicolás for a magical view over the rooftops of the Alhambra glowing in the sunset.

Street in the Albaicín
Steep and sinuous, the Albaicín's streets are truly labyrinthine. Many street names start with *Cuesta*, meaning "slope".

Real Chancillería
Built in 1530 by the Catholic Monarchs, the Royal Chancery has a beautiful Renaissance façade.

Casa de los Pisa, also known as Museo San Juan de Dios, displays works of art – some depicting St John of God, who died here in 1550.

0 metres   50
0 yards   50

★ **Iglesia de Santa Ana**
Just north of Plaza Nueva stands this 16th-century brick church in Mudéjar style. It has an elegant Plateresque portal and, inside, a coffered ceiling.

★ Museo Arqueológico

The ornate Plateresque carvings on the museum's façade include this relief of two shields. They show heraldic devices of the Nasrid kings of Granada, who were defeated by the Catholic Monarchs in 1492 *(see pp60–61)*.

Key

— Suggested route

Carrera del Darro
The road along the Río Darro leads past crumbling bridges and the fine façades of ancient buildings, now all restored.

To Mirador de San Nicolás

To Sacromonte

The Convento de Santa Catalina was founded in 1521.

★ El Bañuelo
Star-shaped openings in the vaults let light into these well-preserved Moorish baths, which were built in the 11th century.

Sacromonte

Granada's gypsies formerly lived in the caves honeycombing this hillside. In the past, travellers would go there to enjoy spontaneous outbursts of flamenco. Today, virtually all the gypsies have moved away, but touristy flamenco shows of variable quality are still performed here in the evenings *(see pp428–9)*. Sitting at the very top of the hill is the Abadía del Sacromonte, a Benedictine monastery. The ashes of St Cecilio, Granada's patron saint, are kept inside.

Aerial view of the Abadía del Sacromonte

The Alhambra

A magical use of space, light, water and decoration characterizes this most sensual piece of architecture. It was built under Ismail I, Yusuf I and Muhammad V caliphs when the Nasrid dynasty *(see pp58–9)* ruled Granada. Seeking to belie an image of waning power, they created their idea of paradise on Earth. Modest materials were used (plaster, timber and tiles), but they were superbly worked. Although the Alhambra suffered pillage and decay, including an attempt by Napoleon's troops to blow it up, in recent times it has undergone extensive restoration and its delicate craftsmanship still dazzles the eye.

★ Salón de Embajadores
The ceiling of this sumptuous throne room, built from 1334 to 1354, represents the seven heavens of the Muslim cosmos.

★ Patio de Arrayanes
This pool, set amid myrtle hedges and graceful arcades, reflects light into the surrounding halls.

Entrance

KEY

① **Patio de Machuca**

② **Patio del Mexuar** was a council chamber where the reigning sultan listened to the petitions of his subjects and met with his ministers. It was completed in 1365.

③ **Sala de la Barca**

④ **Washington Irving's apartments**

⑤ **Jardín de Lindaraja**

⑥ **Baños Reales**

⑦ **Sala de las Dos Hermanas**, with its honeycomb dome, is regarded as the ultimate example of Spanish Islamic architecture.

⑧ **Sala de los Reyes**, a great banqueting hall, was used to hold extravagant parties and

sumptuous feasts. Beautiful ceiling paintings on leather, from the 14th century, depict tales of hunting and chivalry.

⑨ **Puerta de la Rawda**

⑩ **The Palace of Charles V** (1526) houses a collection of Spanish Islamic art, whose highlight is the Alhambra vase *(see p58)*.

Palacio del Partal
A pavilion with an arched portico and a tower is all that remains of this palace, the oldest building in the Alhambra.

VISITORS' CHECKLIST

Practical Information
Alhambra and Generalife. **Tel** 958 92 60 31. **Open** 8:30am–8pm daily (mid-Oct–mid-Mar: to 6pm daily). Arrive 1 hour before scheduled visit; allow 3 hours for visit. Night visits: Mar–Oct: 10–11:30pm Fri & Sat; Nov–Feb: 8–9:30pm Fri & Sat. 🎨 📷
W alhambra-patronato.es

Transport
🚌 2, C3, C4.

★ **Sala de los Abencerrajes**
This hall takes its name from a noble family, who were rivals of Boabdil *(see pp60–61)*. According to legend, he had them massacred while they attended a banquet here. The geometrical ceiling pattern was inspired by Pythagoras' theorem.

★ **Patio de los Leones**
The patio, which is lined by arcades supported by slender columns, has as a centrepiece the meticulously restored marble fountain with its 12 lions.

Plan of the Alhambra

To the Generalife

Main gate

The Alhambra complex includes the Palacios Nazaríes, the 13th-century Alcazaba, the 16th-century Palace of Charles V, and the Generalife *(see p498)*, which is located just off the map.

Key

- ■ Palacios Nazaríes (shown above)
- ■ Palace of Charles V
- ■ Alcazaba
- ■ Gardens
- ■ Iglesia de Santa Maria
- ■ Other buildings

Granada: Generalife

From the Alhambra's northern side, a footpath leads to the Generalife, the country estate of the Nasrid kings. Here, they could escape from palace intrigues and enjoy tranquillity high above the city, a little closer to heaven. The name Generalife, or Yannat al Arif, has various interpretations, perhaps the most pleasing being "the garden of lofty paradise". The gardens, begun in the 13th century, have been modified over the years. They originally contained orchards and pastures. The Generalife provides a magical setting for Granada's annual music and dance festival *(see p45)*.

The Patio de la Acequia is an enclosed Oriental garden built round a long central pool. Rows of water jets on either side make graceful arches above it.

Sala Regia

Jardines Altos (Upper Gardens)

The Escalera del Agua is a staircase with water flowing gently down it.

Entrance

The Patio de Polo was the courtyard where palace visitors, arriving on horseback, would tether their steeds.

The Patio de los Cipreses, otherwise known as the Patio de la Sultana, was the secret meeting place for Zoraya, wife of the Sultan Abu-l-Hasan, and her lover, the chief of the Abencerrajes.

The Patio del Generalife lies just before the entrance to the Generalife. The walk from the Alhambra to the Generalife gardens passes first through the Jardines Bajos (lower gardens), before crossing this Moorish patio with its characteristic geometric pool.

The forbidding exterior of the castle above La Calahorra

③⑨ Castillo de La Calahorra

La Calahorra, Granada. **Tel** 958 67 70 98. ⌷ Guadix. **Open** 10am–1pm, 4–6pm Wed. ⌷

Grim, immensely thick walls and stout, cylindrical corner towers protect the castle on a hill above the village of La Calahorra. Rodrigo de Mendoza, son of Cardinal Mendoza, had the castle built for his bride: the work was carried out between 1509 and 1512 by Italian architects and craftsmen. Inside is an ornate, arcaded Renaissance courtyard over two floors with pillars and a Carrara marble staircase.

④⓪ Guadix

Granada. ⛰ 20,100. ⌷ ⌷
i Avenida de la Constitución 15–18, 958 66 28 04. ⌷ Sat. ⌷ Fiesta & Feria (31 Aug–5 Sep). **W** guadix.es

The troglodyte quarter, with its 2,000 caves, is the town's most remarkable sight. The **Centro de Interpretación Cuevas de Guadix** and **Cueva Museo de Alfarería la Alcazaba** show how people live underground.

The cathedral was begun in 1594 and finished between 1701 and 1796. Relics of San Torcuato, who founded Spain's first Christian bishopric, are kept in the cathedral museum.

Near the Moorish Alcazaba is the fine Mudéjar-style Iglesia de Santiago.

🏛 **Centro de Interpretación Cuevas de Guadix**
Plaza de Ermita Nueva s/n. **Tel** 958 66 55 69. **Open** Mon–Sat. ⌷

🏛 **Cueva Museo de Alfarería la Alcazaba**
Calle San Miguel 57. **Tel** 958 66 47 67. **Open** daily. ⌷

④① Jaén

⛰ 115,000. ⌷ ⌷ **i** Calle Maestra 8, 953 31 32 81. ⌷ Thu. ⌷ Nuestra Señora de la Capilla (11 Jun), San Lucas (18 Oct), Romería de Santa Catalina (25 Nov). **W** turjaen.org

The Moors called Jaén *Geen* – meaning "way station of caravans" – because of its strategic site on the road beween Andalucía and Castile. Their hilltop fortress was rebuilt as the **Castillo de Santa Catalina** after it was captured by King Fernando III in 1246. Part of it is now a parador *(see p573)*.

Andrés de Vandelvira, who was responsible for many of Úbeda's fine buildings *(see pp500–501)*, designed Jaén's cathedral in the 16th century. Later additions include two 17th-century towers that now flank the west front.

An old mansion, the **Palacio Villardompardo**, houses a museum of arts and crafts, and also gives access to the Baños Árabes, the 11th-century baths of Ali, a Moorish chieftain. These have horseshoe arches, ceilings with star-shaped windows and two ceramic vats in which bathers once immersed themselves. Tucked away in an alley is the Capilla de San Andrés, a Mudéjar chapel founded in the

16th century by Gutiérrez González who, as treasurer to Pope Leo X, was endowed with privileges. A gilded iron screen by Maestro Bartolomé de Jaén is the highlight of the chapel.

The Real Monasterio de Santa Clara was founded in the 13th century and has a lovely cloister dating from the late 16th century. Its church, which has a coffered ceiling, contains a bamboo image of Christ made in Ecuador.

The **Museo Provincial** displays Roman mosaics and sculptures, and Iberian, Greek and Roman ceramics.

🏰 **Castillo de Santa Catalina**
Ctra al Castillo. **Tel** 953 12 07 33. **Open** daily. **Closed** 1 Jan, 24, 25 & 31 Dec.

🏛 **Palacio Villardompardo**
Plaza Santa Luisa de Marillac. **Tel** 953 24 80 68. **Open** Tue–Sun. **Closed** public hols.

🏛 **Museo Provincial**
Paseo de la Estación 29. **Tel** 953 10 13 66. **Open** Tue–Sun. **Closed** 1 Jan, 1 May, 25 Dec.

Horseshoe arches supporting the dome at the Baños Árabes, Jaén

Whitewashed cave dwellings in the troglodyte quarter of Guadix

Roman bridge spanning the Guadalquivir at Andújar

⓸ Andújar

Jaén. 🚉 40,000. 🚌 🚍 ℹ️ Pl Santa María. Torre del Reloj, 953 50 49 59. 🛒 Tue. 🎭 Romería (last Sun of Apr).

Andújar stands on the site of an Iberian town, Iliturgi, which was destroyed in the Punic Wars *(see p54)* by Scipio. The Romans built the 15-arched bridge spanning the Río Guadalquivir.

In the central square is the Gothic Iglesia de San Miguel, with paintings by Alonso Cano. The Iglesia de Santa María la Mayor has a Mudéjar tower. Inside it is El Greco's *Christ in the Garden of Olives* (c.1605). A pilgrimage to the nearby Santuario de la Virgen de la Cabeza takes place in April.

Environs

The Baños de la Encina fortress has 15 towers and ramparts built in AD 967. Further north, the road and railway between Madrid and Andalucía squeeze through a spectacular gorge in the eastern reaches of the Sierra Morena, the Desfiladero de Despeñaperros.

⓺ Cástulo

Jaén. Archaeological Ensemble: Crta Linares–Torreblascopedro (JV-3003) km 3.3. **Tel** 600 143 464. **Open** Tue–Sun. **Closed** 1 & 6 Jan, 24, 25 & 31 Dec. 🖼️ Monographic Museum of Cástulo: C/ General Echagüe 2, Linares. **Tel** 953 106 074. **Open** as above. 🌐 **juntade andalucia.es/cultura/museos/CACS**

Just outside Linares, the ancient city of Cástulo features relics from as far back as 3,000 BC, or the Neolithic period. However, most of its remains are a necropolis, an underground water storage system and residential quarters, including a synagogue – date from the Iberian and Roman civilizations. The Monographic Archaeo-logical Museum of Cástulo explores the history of the site through a series of exhibits.

⓸ Baeza

See pp502–3.

⓹ Úbeda

Jaén. 🚉 35,000. 🚍 ℹ️ Palacio Marqués de Contadero, Calle Baja del Marqués 4, 953 77 92 04. 🛒 Fri. 🎭 San Miguel (28 Sep). 🌐 **andalucia.org**

Úbeda, a UNESCO World Heritage Site, is a showcase of Renaissance magnificence, thanks to the patronage of some of Spain's most influential men of the 16th century, including such dignitaries as Juan Vázquez de Molina, who gave his name to

Úbeda City Centre

① Hospital de Santiago
② Museo Arqueológico
③ Iglesia de San Pablo
④ Capilla del Salvador
⑤ Parador de Úbeda
⑥ Palacio de las Cadenas
⑦ Santa María de los Reales Alcázares

0 metres 250
0 yards 250

For keys to symbols *see back flap*

◀ Castle against a backdrop of snowcapped mountains, Sierra Nevada

Úbeda's most historic square. The Old Town is contained within city walls that were first raised by the Moors in 852.

Created on the orders of the Bishop of Jaén around 1562, the colossal former **Hospital de Santiago** was designed by Andrés de Vandelvira, who refined the Spanish Renaissance style into its more austere characteristics. The façade is flanked by square towers, one topped with a blue-and-white-tiled spire. The **Museo Arqueológico** exhibits artifacts from Neolithic to Moorish times.

The Iglesia de San Pablo has a 13th-century apse and a beautiful 16th-century chapel by Vandelvira. It is surmounted by a Plateresque tower that was completed in 1537.

A monument to the poet and mystic St John of the Cross (1549–91) stands in the Plaza de Vázquez de Molina. The Capilla del Salvador, on the square, was designed in the 16th century as the personal chapel of Francisco de los Cobos, then secretary of state. Behind it stand Cobos' palace, with a Renaissance façade, and the Hospital de los Honrados Viejos (Hospital of the Honoured Elders), looking on to the Plaza de Santa Lucía. From here, the Redonda de Miradores follows the line of the city walls and offers views of the countryside.

Plaza Vázquez de Molina also holds Úbeda's parador. Built in the 16th century, but much

The Castillo de la Yedra, rising above the village of Cazorla

altered in the 17th, it was the residence of Fernando Ortega Salido, dean of Málaga and chaplain of the Capilla del Salvador.

Úbeda's town hall and tourist office occupy the Palacio de las Cadenas, a mansion built for Vázquez de Molina by Vandelvira. It gets its name from the iron chains (cadenas) once attached to the columns supporting the main doorway.

Also on the square are the church of Santa María de los Reales Alcázares, which dates mainly from the 13th century, and the Cárcel del Obispo (Bishop's Jail), where nuns who had been punished by the bishop were confined.

🏛 **Hospital de Santiago**
Calle Obispo Cobos. **Tel** 953 75 08 42. **Open** Mon–Sat (Aug: Mon–Fri)

🏛 **Museo Arqueológico**
Casa Mudéjar, Calle Cervantes 6. **Tel** 953 10 86 23. **Open** Tue–Sun. ♿

Cazorla's Wildlife

More than 100 bird species live in this nature reserve, some very rare, such as the golden eagle and the griffon vulture. Cazorla is the only habitat in Spain, apart from the Pyrenees, where the lammergeier lives. Mammals in the park include the otter – active at dawn and dusk – mouflon and wild boar, and a small remaining population of Spanish ibex. The red deer was reintroduced in 1952. Among the flora supported by the limestone geology is the indigenous *Viola cazorlensis*.

Wild boar foraging for roots, insects and small mammals

🌳 Parque Natural de Cazorla

Jaén. 🚌 Cazorla. 🛈 Plaza de Santa María, 953 71 01 02.

First-time visitors are amazed by the spectacular scenery of this 2150 sq km (830-sq-mile) nature reserve with thickly wooded mountains rising to peaks of 2,000 m (6,500 ft) and varied, abundant wildlife.

Access to the Parque Natural de Cazorla, Segura y Las Villas is via the town of Cazorla. Its imposing Moorish **Castillo de la Yedra** houses a folklore museum. A blues festival takes place in the town every July (see p45). From Cazorla, the road winds upwards beneath the ruins of the clifftop castle at La Iruela. After crossing a pass, it drops down to a cross-roads (El Empalme del Valle) in the valley of the Río Guadalquivir. Roads lead to the river's source and to the quiet modern parador.

The main road through the park follows the river. The information centre at Torre del Vinagre is 17 km (11 miles) from the crossroads.

Environs

There is a well-restored Moorish castle at Segura de la Sierra, 30 km (19 miles) from the reserve's northern edge. Below it is an unusual rock-hewn bullring.

🏰 **Castillo de la Yedra**
Tel 953 10 14 02. **Open** Tue–Sun. **Closed** 1 Jan, 17 Sep, 24, 25 & 31 Dec. 🎫 (free for EU citizens).

For hotels and restaurants in this region see pp572–4 and pp598–602

⑭ Street-by-Street: Baeza

Nestling amid the olive groves that characterize much of Jaén province, beautiful Baeza is a small town, unusually rich in Renaissance architecture. Called Beatia by the Romans and later the capital of a Moorish fiefdom, Baeza is portrayed as a "royal nest of hawks" on its coat of arms. It was conquered by Fernando III in 1226 – the first town in Andalucía to be definitively won back from the Moors – and was then settled by Castilian knights. An era of medieval splendour followed, reaching a climax in the 16th century, when Andrés de Vandelvira's splendid buildings were erected. The town was designated a UNESCO World Heritage Site in 2003.

★ **Palacio de Jabalquinto**
An Isabelline-style *(see p28)* façade, flanked by elaborate, rounded buttresses, fronts this splendid Gothic palace.

Key

Suggested route

Antigua Universidad
From 1542 until 1825, this Renaissance and Baroque building was one of Spain's first universities.

Torre de los Aliatares is a 1,000-year-old tower built by the Moors.

To Úbeda

PLAZA DE ESPANA

O. NARVAEZ

COMPAÑIA

PLAZA SANTA CRUZ

SAN FELIPE

BEATO AVILA

ROMAN

BARBACANA

MERCADERIAS

PASEO DE LA CONSTITUCIÓN

PASEO DE TUNDIDORES

GASPAR BECERRA

Ayuntamiento
Formerly a jail and a courthouse, the town hall is a dignified Plateresque structure *(see p29)*. The coats of arms of Felipe II, Juan de Borja and of the town of Baeza adorn its upper façade.

Casas Consistoriales Bajas

La Alhóndiga, the old corn exchange, has impressive triple-tier arches running along its front.

VISITORS' CHECKLIST

Practical Information
🖼 19,000. **Map** Jaén.
ℹ Plaza del Pópulo, 953 77 99
82. 🚍 Tue. 🎭 Semana Santa
(Easter), Feria (mid-Aug), Romería
de la Yedra (early Sep).

Transport
🚆 Linares-Baeza, 902 43 23 43.
🚌 Avenida Alcalde Puche Pardo,
953 74 24 53.

★ **Cathedral**
The impressive
cathedral was rebuilt
by Andrés de
Vandelvira in 1567.
The Capilla Sagrario
has a choir screen by
Bartolomé de Jaén.

PLAZA
SANTA
MARÍA

OBISPO MENGIBAR

SAN GIL

Fuente de Santa María
Architect-sculptor Ginés Martínez
of Baeza designed this fountain
in the form of a triumphal arch.
It was completed in 1564.

Antigua Carnicería
is the 16th-century
former slaughter-
house.

**Puerta de Jaén y Arco
de Villalar**
This gateway in the city
ramparts is adjoined by
an arch erected in 1521
to appease Carlos I (*see
p62*) after a rebellion.

| 0 metres | | 75 |
| 0 yards | | 75 |

To Jaén

★ **Plaza del Pópulo**
The Casa del Pópulo, a
fine Plateresque palace,
now the tourist office,
overlooks this square. In
its centre is the Fuente
de los Leones, a fountain
with an Ibero-Roman
statue flanked by lions.

For keys to symbols *see back flap*

Renaissance castle overlooking the village of Vélez Blanco

⓪ Vélez Blanco

Almería. 🚹 2,200. 🚌 Vélez Rubio.
ⓘ Avenida Marqués de los Vélez, 950 41 95 85. 🗓 Wed. 🎭 Cristo de la Yedra (second Sun of Aug).

The mighty Castillo de Vélez Blanco was built between 1506 and 1513 by the first Marquis de Los Vélez. The Renaissance interiors are now displayed in the Metropolitan Museum in New York, but there is a reconstruction of one of the patios.

Just outside, the **Cueva de los Letreros** contains paintings from c.4000 BC. One depicts the Indalo, a figure holding a rainbow and believed to be a deity with magical powers, now adopted as the symbol of Almería.

🏛 **Cueva de los Letreros**
Camino de la Cueva de los Letreros.
Tel 694 46 71 36. **Open** 4:30pm Wed, Sat, Sun & public hols (Jul & Aug: 7pm); book ahead. 🎫

⓪ Mojácar

Almería. 🚹 7,000. 🚌 ⓘ Plaza del Frontón 1, 950 61 50 25. 🗓 Wed, Sun.
🎭 Moors and Christians (second weekend of Jun), San Agustín (28 Aug). 🆆 **mojacar.es**

From a distance, Mojácar shimmers like the mirage of a Moorish citadel, its white houses cascading over a lofty ridge, 2 km (1 mile) inland from long, sandy beaches.

Following the Civil War *(see pp70–71)*, the village fell into ruin as most of its inhabitants emigrated, but in the 1960s it was discovered by tourists, which gave rise to a new era of prosperity. The old gateway in the walls still remains, but otherwise the village has been completely rebuilt, and holiday complexes have grown up along the nearby beaches. The coast south from Mojácar is among the least built up in Spain, with only small resorts and villages along its length.

⓪ Tabernas

Almería. 🚹 3,000. 🚌 ⓘ Carretera Nacional 340 km 464, 950 52 50 30.
🗓 Wed. 🎭 Virgen de las Angustias (11–15 Aug).

Tabernas is set in Europe's only desert. The town's Moorish fortress dominates the harsh surrounding scenery of cactus-dotted, rugged hills and dried-out riverbeds, which has provided the setting for many classic spaghetti westerns. Two film sets can be visited: **Mini-Hollywood** and **Fort**

Bravo Texas Hollywood, 1 km (1 mile) and 4 km (2 miles) from Tabernas respectively.

Not far from town is a solar energy research centre, where heliostats track the sun.

Environs
Sorbas sits on the edge of the chasm of the Río de Aguas. Its notable buildings are the 16th-century Iglesia de Santa María and a 17th-century mansion said to have been a summer retreat for the Duke of Alba.

Nearby is the karst scenery, honeycombed with hundreds of cave systems, of the Yesos de Sorbas nature reserve. Permission to explore them is required from Andalucía's environmental department.

🎬 **Mini-Hollywood**
Carretera N340. **Tel** 950 36 52 36.
Open daily (Sat & Sun Nov–Easter).
🎫 🆆 **oasysparquetematico.com**

🎬 **Fort Bravo Texas Hollywood**
Carretera N340, Tabernas. **Tel** 902 07 08 14. **Open** daily. 🎫 🆆 **fortbravo.es**

Desert landscape around Tabernas, reminiscent of the Wild West

Still from *For a Few Dollars More* by Sergio Leone

Spaghetti Westerns

Two Wild West towns lie off the N340 highway west of Tabernas. Here, visitors can re-enact classic film scenes or watch stuntmen performing bank hold-ups and saloon brawls. The *poblados del oeste* were built during the 1960s and early 1970s, when low costs and eternal sunshine made Almería the ideal location for spaghetti westerns. Sergio Leone, director of *The Good, the Bad and the Ugly*, built a ranch here and film sets sprang up in the desert. Local gypsies played Indians and Mexicans. The deserts and Arizona-style badlands are still used for television commercials and series, and by film directors such as Steven Spielberg.

The 10th-century Alcazaba, which dominates Almería's old town

⑩ Almería

Almería. 🚉 170,000. ✈ 🚌 🚆
Estación Intermodal. 🛈 Parque
Nicolás Salmerón, 950 17 52 20.
🏛 Tue, Fri & Sat. 🎪 Feria (last week
of Aug). 🖥 **turismoalmeria.com**

Almería's colossal **Alcazaba**,
dating from AD 995, is the largest
fortress built by the Moors in
Spain. The huge structure bears
witness to the city's Golden
Age, when it was an important
port under the Caliphate of
Córdoba (see pp56–7) exporting
brocade, silk and cotton.

During the Reconquest, the
Alcazaba withstood two major
sieges before eventually falling
to the armies of the Catholic
Monarchs (see pp60–61) in 1489.
The royal coat of arms can be
seen on the Torre del Homenaje,
built during their reign. The
Alcazaba also has a Mudéjar
chapel and gardens.

Adjacent to the Alcazaba is
the old fishermen's and gypsy
quarter of La Chanca, where
some families live in caves with
painted façades. This district is
poor, and it is unwise to walk
around here alone or at night.

Brightly coloured entrance to a gypsy cave
in La Chanca district

Berber pirates from North
Africa often raided Almería.
Consequently, the cathedral
looks almost like a castle, with
its four towers, thick walls and
small windows. The site was
originally a mosque. This was
converted into a church, but
in 1522 it was destroyed in
an earthquake. Work on the
present building began in 1524
under the direction of Diego de
Siloé, who designed the nave
and high altar in Gothic style.
The Renaissance façade and the
carved walnut choir stalls are by
Juan de Orea. Traces of Moorish
Almería's most important
mosque can be seen in the
Templo San Juan. The Plaza Vieja
is an attractive 17th-century
arcaded square. On one side is
the town hall (ayuntamiento),
with a cream and pink façade
(1899). In Calle Real, the Castillo
de Tabernas Museo del Aceite
de Oliva (tel 950 27 28 88)
illustrates the fine art of making
olive oil.

Environs
One of Europe's most important examples of a Copper Age
settlement is located at **Los
Millares**, near Gádor, 17 km
(11 miles) north of Almería.
As many as 2,000 people may
have occupied the site around
2500 BC.

🏰 Alcazaba
Calle Almanzor. **Tel** 950 80 10 08.
Open Tue–Sun. **Closed** 1 Jan, 25 Dec.
🖥 **museosdeandalucia.es**

🏛 Los Millares
Santa Fé de Mondújar. **Tel** 677 90 34
04. **Open** Wed–Sun. **Closed** 1 Jan,
6 Jan, 25 Dec.

⑪ Parque Natural de Cabo de Gata

Almería. 🚌 San José. 🛈 Centro de
Visitantes de las Amoladeras, Carretera
Alp-202 km 7 (Retamar-Pujaire), 950
16 04 35. **Open** daily.

Towering cliffs of volcanic
rock, sand dunes, salt flats and
secluded coves characterize the
290-sq-km (110-sq-mile) Parque
Natural de Cabo de Gata. Within
its confines are a few fishing
villages, and the small resort
of San José. A lighthouse stands
at the end of the cabo (cape),
which can be reached by road
from the village of Cabo de
Gata. The park includes a stretch
of seabed 2 km (1 mile) wide
and the marine flora and fauna
protected within it attract scuba
divers and snorkellers.

The dunes and saltpans
between the cape and the
Playa de San Miguel are a
habitat for thorny jujube trees.
Many migrating birds stop here,
and among the 170 or so bird
species recorded are flamingoes,
avocets, griffon vultures and
Dupont's larks.

Environs
Set amid citrus trees on the edge
of the Sierra de Alhamilla, Níjar's
fame stems from the pottery
and the handwoven jarapas –
blankets and rugs – that are
made here. The barren plain
between Níjar and the sea has
been brought under cultivation
using vast plastic greenhouses
to conserve the scarce water.

The dramatic, dark volcanic rocks at Cabo
de Gata, east of Almería

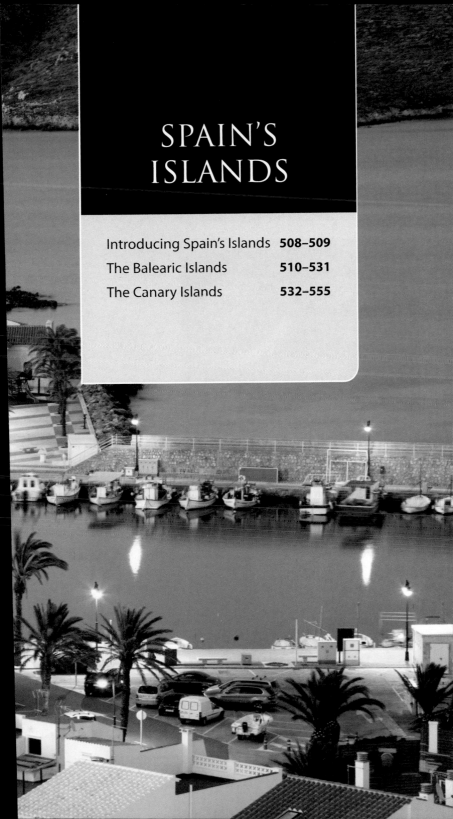

SPAIN'S ISLANDS

Introducing Spain's Islands

Spain's two groups of islands lie in separate seas – the Balearics in the Mediterranean and the Canaries in the Atlantic, off the African coast. Both are popular package-tour destinations blessed with warm climates, good beaches and clear waters. But each has more to offer than the high-rise hotels, fast-food restaurants and nightclubs that they are often associated with. The Balearics have charming villages, wooded hills, caves and prehistoric monuments, while the extraordinary volcanic landscapes of the Canaries are unlike any other part of Spain and are home to four of the country's national parks.

Ibiza *(see pp514–16)* is the liveliest of the Balearic Islands. Ibiza town and Sant Antoni are the main tourist centres, offering world-famous nightlife and excellent beaches.

Eivissa (Ibiza)

Ibiza

Formentera

CANARY ISLANDS
(see pp532–55)

Tenerife *(see pp538–43)*, the largest of the Canary Islands, is fertile in the north but arid in the south. The volcanic summit of Mount Teide dominates the island. Tenerife's beaches are black, but many have been improved with white sand imported from the Sahara Desert.

Santa Cruz de La Palma

La Palma

La Gomera *(see p537)* is best explored by car. The Torre del Conde tower is in the main town of San Sebastián.

La Gomera

San Sebastián de La Gomera

Santa Cruz de Tener

Tenerife

Los Cristianos

0 kilometres 50
0 miles 25

El Hierro Valverde

◀ Yachts moored in Fornell harbour, Menorca

Menorca

Menorca Mahón

t de Sóller

Alcúdia

Cala Ratjada

Mallorca

Palma

Manacor

ndratx

Santanyí

EARIC
ANDS
pp510–31)

In Menorca *(see pp526–31)* tourism has
developed more slowly than in Mallorca
and Ibiza, and the island has largely
avoided being over-commercialized.
Scattered across the countryside are the
ruins of unique Bronze Age buildings.

Mallorca *(see pp518–25)*
best known for its beaches,
has caves and other natural
features to explore. The most
spectacular of the island's
historic sights is the great
Gothic cathedral in Palma,
which rises above the boats
moored in the old harbour.

0 kilometres		50
0 miles		25

Lanzarote *(see p552–4)*
is the most attractive of
the Canary Islands, even
though the landscape is
strikingly bare. White
houses contrast starkly
with black volcanic
fields. The most dramatic
attraction is Timanfaya
National Park, including
the Montañas del Fuego.

Haría

Lanzarote

Arrecife

Playa Blanca

Corralejo

Puerto
del Rosario

Fuerteventura

Las Palmas
e Gran Canaria

Agaete

*Gran
Canaria*

lomas

Morro Jable

Gran Canaria *(see p546–9)* centres on a
symmetrical volcanic cone. The capital city
of Las Palmas has some interesting museums
and monuments. In contrast, the sprawling
Maspalomas, on the south coast, is the biggest
holiday resort in Spain.

THE BALEARIC ISLANDS

Ibiza · Formentera · Mallorca · Menorca

Chic resorts and attractive coves and beaches, combined with a climate which is hot but never uncomfortably so, have made tourism the mainstay of life along the coasts of the Balearic Islands. Inland, there is peace and quiet in abundance, and a great variety of sights to seek out: wooded hills, pretty villages, monasteries, country churches, caves and prehistoric monuments to name but a few.

Talaiotic ruins *(see p531)*, Roman settlements and medieval fortresses scattered across these islands are reminders of the waves of colonizers that have been drawn to the Balearics, strategically located at a crossroads in the Mediterranean. In the 13th century Catalan settlers brought their language, a dialect of which is widely spoken today.

Today, the islands can justifiably claim to cater for all tastes: from sunseekers on package holidays, for whom the larger resorts serve as brash fun factories, to jet-setters and film stars, who head for luxurious but discreet hideaways in the hills.

Tourism has been established the longest in Mallorca, the largest island, with Palma its beating heart. The green countryside of Menorca is dotted with prehistoric monuments, and the island's towns are full of noble, historic mansions. Ibiza has two distinct aspects: its coastline, which is notched by innumerable rocky coves, and the hilly interior, characterized by brilliant white farmhouses and robust churches. On small and relatively undeveloped Formentera, the pace of life is slow. The islets surrounding the four principal islands are largely uninhabited; one of them, Cabrera (off Mallorca), is a national park.

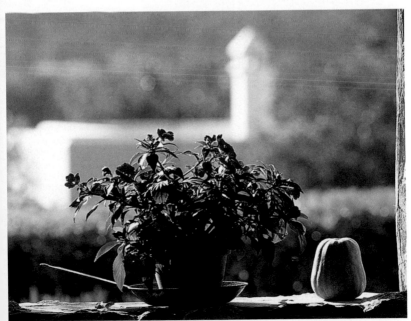

View through the window of one of Ibiza's traditional, whitewashed farmhouses

◀ The dazzling turquoise water at Cala Salada, Ibiza

Exploring the Balearics

Though the Balearic islands are often associated with high-density, inexpensive package tourism, they offer enough variety to satisfy everyone's tastes. For those unattracted by the bustle of the coastal resorts and their beautiful beaches, the countryside and the old towns of Palma, Ibiza, Maó and Ciutadella are relatively undisturbed. Mallorca is by far the most culturally rich of the Balearics, with its distinguished collection of modern and traditional galleries, and interesting museums. Menorca is strong on Neolithic remains and Neo-Colonial architecture, while Ibiza is for lovers of clear, painterly light and rustic peasant houses; it also has some of the wildest nightclubs in Europe. Formentera – for many, the most alluring island – has crystal water, white sand, a pure, parched landscape and total tranquillity.

Poblat des Pescadors in the tourist village of Binibeca

Early-morning mist on the waters of Port de Pollença in Mallorca

MALLORCA
VALLDEMOSSA
Estellencs
ANDRATX
Port d'Andratx
Palma Nova
PALMA
Badia
Pal

IBIZA
ELS AMUNTS
Sant Vicenç
SANT ANTONI
SANTA EULÀRIA
SANT JOSEP
Jesús
Sa Talaiassa
475m
IBIZA (EIVISSA)
Ses Salines
Sant Francesc
FORMENTERA
Cala Saona
Es Caló
Cap de Barbaria
Platja de Migjorn
Punta Roja

Getting Around

Nearly all foreign visitors to the Balearics arrive by plane – the no-frills airlines making it all the more popular. Mallorca, Menorca and Ibiza connect to major European cities as well as Madrid, Barcelona and Valencia. Several airlines fly to most other Spanish cities out of Son Sant Joan Airport in Palma. Another way of arriving is by boat from Barcelona, Valencia or Dénia. Between the islands there are regular ferry services, run by Transmediterranea, Balearia and Iscomar. Mallorca is the only island with rail services, which run between Palma and Inca (now extended to Sa Pobla and Manacor), and between Palma and Sóller. Roads vary from excellent to poor. The best way to get around is by car, except on Formentera, where cycling is best.

Sights at a Glance

A peaceful stroll on the sands of Ibiza's Sant Miquel beach

0 kilometres 25

0 miles 15

Key

- ━━ Motorway
- ━━ Major road
- ═══ Secondary road
- ━━ Scenic route
- ─── Minor railway
- △ Summit

The rocky coast around the Coves d'Artà in Mallorca

For keys to symbols *see back flap*

Ibiza

This small island, the nearest of the Balearics to the coast of Spain, was unknown and untouched by tourism until the 1960s, when it suddenly appeared in Europe's holiday brochures along with Benidorm and Torremolinos. There is still a curious, indefinable magic about Ibiza town (Eivissa) and the island has not lost its character. The countryside, particularly in the north, is a rural patchwork of groves of almonds, olives and figs, and wooded hills. Ibiza town, on the other hand, retains the air of a 1950s Spanish provincial borough. At once package-tour paradise, hippie hideout and glamour hot spot, this is one of the Mediterranean's mythical destinations.

An Ibizan shepherdess

The bustling harbour of the resort of Sant Antoni

❶ Sant Antoni

Baleares. 🄼 17,500. 🚌 🚢
ℹ️ Passeig de Ses Fonts, 971 34 33 63. 🎨 Sant Antoni (17 Jan), Sant Bartolomé (24 Aug). 🆆 **ibiza.travel**

Ibiza's second town, Sant Antoni was known by the Romans as Portus Magnus because of its large natural harbour. Formerly a tiny fishing village, it has turned into a sprawling and exuberant resort. Although it was once notoriously over-commercialized, the town has undergone a dramatic face-lift. Nevertheless, the 14th-century parish church of Sant Antoni is practically marooned in a sea of modern high-rise hotels.

To the north of Sant Antoni, on the road to Cala Salada, is the chapel of Santa Agnès, an unusual early Christian temple (not to be confused with the village of the same name). When this catacomb-like chapel was discovered, in 1907, it contained Moorish weapons and fragments of pottery.

❷ Sant Josep

Baleares. 🄼 13,500. ℹ️ Plaça Església s/n, 971 80 16 27. 🎨 Sant Josep (19 Mar). 🆆 **ibiza.travel**

The village of Sant Josep, the administrative centre of south-west Ibiza, lies in the shadow of Ibiza's highest mountain. At 475 m (1,560 ft), Sa Talaiassa offers a panorama of all Ibiza, including the islet of Es Vedrá, rising from the sea like a rough-cut pyramid. For the most

The salt lakes of Ses Salines, a haven for many bird species

accessible view of this enormous rock, take the coastal road to the sandy cove of Cala d'Hort, where there are a number of good restaurants and a quiet beach.

Environs
Before tourism, salt was Ibiza's main industry, most of it coming from the salt flats at Ses Salines in the southeast corner of the island. Mainland Spain is the chief consumer of this salt, but much goes to the Faroe Islands and Scandinavia for salting fish. Ses Salines is also an important refuge for birds, including the flamingo. Es Cavallet, 3 km (2 miles) east, is an unspoiled stretch of soft, white sand. The Phoenician village of Sa Caleta is a UNESCO World Heritage Site.

❸ Ibiza (Eivissa)

Baleares. 🄼 35,000. ✈️ 🚌 🚢
ℹ️ Plaza de la Catedral, 971 39 92 32. 🗓️ Mon–Sat. 🎨 San Juan Bautista (24 Jun), Fiestas Patronales (1–8 Aug). 🆆 **eivissa.es**

The old quarter of Ibiza town, known as Eivissa in Catalan, is a miniature citadel guarding the mouth of the almost circular bay. The Portal de ses Taules, a magnificent gateway in the north wall of the 16th-century fortifications, carries the finely carved coat of arms of the kingdom of Aragón, to which the Balearic Islands belonged in the Middle Ages *(see p231)*. Inside the walls is the 16th-century Església de Santo Domingo with its three red-tiled domes. The Baroque interior, with its barrel-vaulted ceiling and frescoed walls, has been restored to its former glory. Works of art by Erwin Bechtold, Barry Flanagan and other artists connected with Ibiza are on display in the **Museu d'Art Contemporani**, just inside the Portal de ses Taules. Crowning the whole Dalt Vila is the cathedral, a 13th-century Catalan Gothic building with 18th-century additions. The cathedral's Museu Diocesà houses assorted works of art.

Under the Carthaginians, the soil of Ibiza was considered holy. The citizens of Carthage deemed it an honour to be buried in the **Necrópolis Púnica del Puig des Molins**. Part of it can be visited by the public.

The crossroads village of Jesús, 3 km (2 miles) north, is worth a visit for its 16th-century church. Originally built as part

A backstreet in the Sa Penya district of Ibiza town

of a Franciscan monastery, it has a 16th-century altarpiece by Rodrigo de Osona the Younger.

🏛 **Museu d'Art Contemporani**
Ronda Narcís Puget s/n. **Tel** 971 30 27 23. **Open** Tue–Sun. **Closed** Mon & public hols. 🅿 ♿

🏛 **Necrópolis Púnica del Puig des Molins**
Via Romana 31. **Tel** 971 30 17 71. **Open** Tue–Sun. **Closed** Mon & public hols. 🆆 maef.es

❹ Els Amunts

Baleares. 🚌 Sant Miquel. 🅸 Els Amunts Interpretation Centre, Carretera Sant Llorenç s/n, Sant Joan de Labritja, 971 32 51 41.

Els Amunts is the local name for the uplands of northern Ibiza, which stretch from Sant Antoni on the west coast to Sant Vicenç in the northeast. Though hardly a mountain range – Es Fornàs is the highest point, at a mere

A view across the port towards Ibiza's upper town

450 m (1,480 ft) – the area's inaccessibility has kept it unspoiled. There are few special sights here, apart from the landscape: pine-clad hills sheltering fertile valleys whose rich red soil is planted with olive, almond and fig trees, and the occasional vineyard. Tourist enclaves are scarce, except for a handful of small resorts, such as Port de Sant Miquel, Portinatx and Sant Vicenç. Inland, villages like Sant Joan and Santa Agnès offer an insight into Ibiza's quiet, rural past.

The architectural high points of northern Ibiza are several beautiful white churches, like the one in Sant Miquel, which on Thursdays in summer, is host to a display of Ibizan folk dancing. Outside Sant Llorenç is the tranquil, fortified hamlet of Balàfia, with flat-roofed houses, tiny whitewashed alleys, and a watchtower that was used as a fortress during raids by the Turks.

Ibiza's Hottest Spots

Ibiza's reputation for extraordinary summer nightlife is largely justified. The main action takes place in the Calle de la Virgen in the old harbour district, with its bars, fashion boutiques and restaurants; and the mega-discos out of town – Privilege, Pachá, Amnesia, Es Paradis and, perhaps the wildest of them all, Space. Some of them close as late as 7am. (Most clubs close during winter.) Ibiza has long been a magnet for the rich and famous. Celebrities seem to be more elusive of late, but well-known faces can still be glimpsed dining in Heart Ibiza, being seen at Ocean Beach Club day or night, or soaking up the rays on the beach at Ses Salines.

Nightclubbers enjoying a bubble bath at Amnesia

The unspoiled coastline of Formentera, seen from La Mola

❺ Santa Eulària

Baleares. 🗺 36,000. 🚌 🚲 ℹ️ Carrer Mariano Riquer Wallis 4, 971 33 07 28. 🛒 Wed & Sat. 🎉 Fiesta (12 Feb), Cala Llonga (14–15 Aug).

The town of Santa Eulària des Riu (Santa Eulalia del Río), on the island's only river, has managed to hold on to its character more than many other Spanish resorts.

The 16th-century church, with its covered courtyard, and the surrounding old town were built on the top of a little hill, the Puig de Missa, because this site was more easily defended in times of war than the shore below.

Ajdacent to the church is the **Museo Etnológico de Ibiza y Formentera**, a folk museum housed in an Ibizan farmhouse. The exhibits (labelled in Catalan only) include traditional costumes, farming implements, toys and an olive press. A collection of photographs covering 50 years shows how Ibiza has changed.

The domed roof of Santa Eulària's 16th-century church

Two art and craft markets, Punta Arabí (Wed) and Las Dalias (Sat), held just outside town, feature hundreds of stalls.

🏛 Museo Etnológico de Ibiza y Formentera

Can Ros, Puig de Missa. **Tel** 971 33 28 45. **Open** Mon–Sat. **Closed** mid-Dec–mid-Jan. 🐾 🎥

❻ Formentera

Baleares. 🗺 10,700. 🚢 from Ibiza. ℹ️ Estación Marítima, Puerto de La Savina, 971 32 20 57. 🛒 Sun. 🎉 Fiesta Sant Jaume (25 Jul). 🌐 **formentera.es**

An hour's boat ride from Ibiza will bring you to this largely unspoiled island where waters are blue and way of life is slow.

From the small port of La Savina, where the boat docks, there are buses to other parts of the island, or you can hire a car, moped or bicycle from one of the shops nearby.

Sant Francesc Xavier, Formentera's tiny capital, is situated 3 km (2 miles) from La Savina. Most of the island's amenities are in this town, plus a pretty 18th-century church in the main square, and a folk museum.

From Sant Francesc, a bumpy minor road leads for 9 km (6 miles) southwards, ending at Cap de Barbaria, the site of an 18th-century defensive tower and a lighthouse.

Formentera is entirely flat, apart from the small plateau of La Mola, which takes up the whole eastern end of the island.

From the fishing port of Es Caló the road winds upwards past the Restaurante Es Mirador, with its panoramic view, to the village of Nostra Senyora del Pilar de la Mola on top of the plateau. About 3 km (2 miles) to the east is a lighthouse, Far de la Mola, sited on the highest point of the island. Nearby stands a monument to Jules Verne (1828–1905), who used Formentera for the setting of one of his novels, *Hector Servadac*.

Although there are many purple road signs indicating places of cultural interest on Formentera, most lead only to disappointment. But one sight well worth seeking out is the megalithic sepulchre of Ca Na Costa (2000 BC) near Sant Francesc, the only one of its kind in the Balearics. This monument, a circle of upright stone slabs, predates the Carthaginians *(see pp52–3)*.

However, the island's great strength is its landscape, which has a delicate beauty and some of the Mediterranean's last unspoiled shorelines. More than 60 per cent of the island's landscape is protected by law. The finest beaches are, arguably, Migjorn and Cala Sahona, southwest of Sant Francesc. Nearly all beaches have nudist areas.

Illetes and Llevant are two beautiful beaches on either side of a long sandy spit in the far north of the island. To the north, between Formentera and Ibiza, is the island of Espalmador, with its natural springs.

The Flavours of the Balearics

This quartet of beautiful islands, strategically positioned on ancient trading routes, has been fought over for thousands of years. Each occupying force – Arabs, Catalans, French and British among them – has left its mark and the local cuisine reflects this. Mediterranean seafood, particularly spectacular lobster and crayfish, remains the most prominent local ingredient, but the islands are also known for their delicious pastries and desserts, like the feather-light *ensaimada* from Mallorca and the typical Ibizan *flaó*. Cured meats (*embutits*) and traditionally made cheeses are also local specialities.

Locally grown oranges

Seafood from the Mediterranean in a Mallorcan fish market

Mallorca and Menorca

Seafood predominates in the Balearic islands. Menorca is renowned for *caldereta de llagosta* (spiny lobster stew), once a simple fishermen's dish but now an expensive delicacy. The classic Mallorcan dish is *pa amb oli*, a slice of toasted country bread rubbed with garlic and drizzled with local olive oil. Menorca's creamy garlic sauce *all i oli* is a delicious accompaniment to meat and seafood dishes, and the island also produces fine cheese, *formatge de Maó*.

Ibiza and Formentera

Seafood also reigns supreme on Ibiza and its quieter little sister, Formentera, especially in *calders* (stews) such as *borrida de rajada* (skate with potatoes, eggs and pastis), and *guisat de peix*. Pork is the staple meat. For a picnic, try *cocarrois*, pastries filled with meat, fish or vegetables and *formatjades*, soft-cheese-filled pastries flavoured with cinnamon. Delicious local desserts include *gató* (almond cake served with ice cream) and Ibizan *flaó*, made with creamy cheese and eggs, and flavoured with mint.

Cuscussó menorquin (bread pudding)

Flaó ibicenco

Gulletas de alaior (aniseed biscuits)

Ensaïmades

El gató (almond tart)

Formatjades

Appetizing selection of delicious Balearic pastries

Regional Dishes and Specialities

Fish and shellfish (particularly the revered local lobster) are omnipresent in the Balearics, particularly along the coast. Try them simply grilled to fully appreciate their freshness (many seaside restaurants have their own fishing boats), but you'll also find wonderful, slow-cooked stews which are bursting with flavour. The rugged inland regions provide mountain lamb and kid, along with pork, which is also used to make *embutits* including spicy Mallorcan *sobrassada* which is delicious with *pa amb oli*. The tourist industry hasn't killed off the long-standing farming tradition on the Balearics, which produce plentiful fruit and vegetables. Mallorca makes its own robust wines, particularly around the village of Binissalem, while Menorca, thanks to the long British occupation of the island, makes its own piquant gin.

All i oli

Tumbet de peix A fish pie, made with layers of firm white fish, peppers, aubergine (eggplant) and sliced boiled egg.

Mallorca

Mallorca is often likened to a continent rather than an island. Its varied nature never fails to astonish, whether you are looking for landscape, culture or just entertainment. No other European island has a wider range of scenery, from the fertile plains of central Mallorca to the almost alpine peaks of the Tramuntana. The island's mild climate and lovely beaches have made it one of Spain's foremost package tour destinations but there is a wealth of culture, too, evident in sights like Palma Cathedral *(see pp524–5)*. Mallorca's appeal lies also in its charm as a living, working island: the cereal and fruit crops of the central plains, and the vineyards around Binissalem are vital to the island's economy.

Terraced orange grove in the Sierra Tramuntana

❼ Andratx

Baleares. 🗻 10,500. 🚌 ℹ️ Avenida de la Cúria 1, 971 62 80 00. 🗓 Wed. 🎉 San Pedro (29 Jun).

This small town lies amid a valley of almond groves in the shadow of Puig de Galatzó, which rises to 1,026 m (3,366 ft). With its ochre and white shuttered houses and the old watchtowers perched high on a hill above the town, Andratx is a very pretty place.

The road southwest leads down to Port d'Andratx 5 km (3 miles) away. Here, in an almost totally enclosed bay, expensive yachts are moored in rows along the harbour and luxury holiday homes pepper the hillsides. In the past, Port d'Andratx's main role was as the fishing port and harbour for Andratx, but since the early 1960s it has gradually been transformed into an exclusive holiday resort for the rich and famous. When visiting Port d'Andratx, it is a good idea to leave all thoughts of the real Mallorca behind and simply enjoy it for what it is – a chic and affluent resort.

❽ La Granja

Carretera de Banyalbufar km 1.5, Esporles. **Tel** 971 61 00 32. 🚌 **Open** daily; Feb–Oct: horse dressage shows 3–4:25pm Wed & Fri. 🐎 ♿ **W** lagranja.net

La Granja is a private estate near the little country town of Esporles. Formerly a Cistercian convent, it is now the property of the Seguí family, who have opened their largely unspoiled 18th-century house to the public as a kind of living museum. Peacocks roam the gardens, salt cod and hams hang in the kitchen, *The Marriage of Figaro* plays in the ballroom, and the slight air of chaos just adds to the charm of the place.

❾ Valldemossa

Baleares. 🗻 2,000. 🚌 ℹ️ Avenida Palma 7, 971 61 20 19. 🗓 Sun. 🎉 Santa Catalina Thomás (28 Jul), San Bartolomé (24 Aug).

This pleasant mountain town is linked with George Sand, the French novelist who stayed here in the winter of 1838–9 and later wrote unflatteringly of the island in *Un Hiver à Majorque*. Dearer to Mallorcans is the Polish composer Frédéric Chopin (1810–49), who stayed with Sand at the **Real Cartuja de Jesús de Nazaret**. "Chopin's cell", off the monastery's main courtyard, is where a few of his works were written, and still houses the piano on which he composed.

Bust of Frédéric Chopin at Valldemossa

Nearby is a 17th-century pharmacy displaying outlandish medicinal preparations such as "powdered nails of the beast". In the cloisters is an art museum with works by Tàpies, Miró and the Mallorcan artist Juli Ramis (1909–90), and a series of Picasso illustrations, *The Burial of the Count of Orgaz*, inspired by the El Greco painting of the same name *(see p36)*.

🏛 **Real Cartuja de Jesús de Nazaret**

Plaça de la Cartuja de Valldemossa. **Tel** 971 61 29 86. **Open** daily. **Closed** 1 Jan, 25 Dec, Sun in Dec & Jan. 🐎 ♿ **W** cartujavalldemossa.com

A view across the harbour of Port d'Andratx

⑩ Alfàbia

Carretera de Sóller km 17. **Tel** 971 61 31 23. 🚌 **Closed** Sat pm & Sun, Dec. 🅿 🆆 **jardinesdealfabia.com**

Very few *possessiós* in Mallorca are open to the public, which makes Alfàbia worth visiting. The house and garden are an excellent example of a typical Mallorcan aristocratic estate and exude a Moorish atmosphere. Very little remains of the original 14th-century architecture, so it is well worth looking out for the Mudéjar inscription on the ceiling of the entrance hall and the Hispano-Arabic fountains and pergola. The garden is a sumptuous 19th-century creation, making imaginative use of shade and the play of water.

⑪ Sóller

Baleares. 🅰 9,100. 🚉 🚌 🅸 Plaza España 15, 971 63 80 08. 🚆 Sat. 🎪 Sa Fira & Es Firó (2nd week May).

Soller is a little town grown fat on the produce of its olive groves and orchards, which climb up the slopes of the Sierra Tramuntana. In the 19th century Sóller traded its oranges and wine for French goods, and the town retains a faintly Gallic, bourgeois feel.

One of Sóller's best-known features is its delightfully old-fashioned narrow-gauge railway, complete with quaint wooden carriages. The train departs from Palma and terminates in Sóller, at the station in the Plaça d'Espanya. From there, an antique tram travels to the fishing village of Port de Sóller, 5 km (3 miles) to the west.

Environs

From Sóller a road winds southwards along the spectacular west coast to Deià (Deyá). This village was once the home of Robert Graves (1895–1985), the English poet and novelist, who came to live here in 1929. His simple tombstone can be seen in the small cemetery. The **Museu Arqueològic**, curated by the archaeologist William Waldren, offers a glimpse into prehistoric Mallorca. Outside

Houses and trees crowded together on the hillside of Deià

the village is Son Marroig, the estate of Austrian Archduke Ludwig Salvator (1847–1915), who documented the Balearics in a series of books included in a display of his possessions.

🏛 Museu Arqueològic

Carrer Teix 4, Deià. **Tel** 971 63 90 01. **Open** Tue, Thu, Sun. 🗎

Statue of La Moreneta at the Santuari de Lluc

⑫ Santuari de Lluc

Lluc. 🚌 from Palma. **Tel** 971 87 15 25. **Open** Sun–Fri. 🅿 museum only. 🆆 **lluc.net**

High in the mountains of the Sierra Tramuntana, in the remote village of Lluc, is an institution regarded by many as the spiritual heart of Mallorca. The Santuari de Lluc was built mainly in the 17th and 18th centuries on the site of an ancient shrine. The monastery's Baroque church, with its imposing façade, contains the stone image of

La Moreneta, the Black Virgin of Lluc, supposedly found by a young shepherd boy on a nearby hilltop in the 13th century. The sanctuary is home to a children's choir, the Blauets, established in the 16th century. The kids sing the "Salve Regina" twice a day (see the website for times). Along the Camí dels Misteris, the paved walkway up to this hilltop, there are some bronze bas-reliefs by Pere Llimona. Just off the main Plaça dels Pelegrins are a café and bar, and a gift shop. The museum, on the first floor, includes Mallorcan paintings and medieval manuscripts. The monastery incorporates a guesthouse.

From Lluc, 13 km (8 miles) of tortuous road winds through the hills and descends towards the coast, ending at the beautiful rocky bay of Sa Calobra. From here, it is just 5 minutes' walk up the coast to the deep gorge of the Torrent de Pareis.

Sheer cliff face rising out of the sea at Sa Calobra

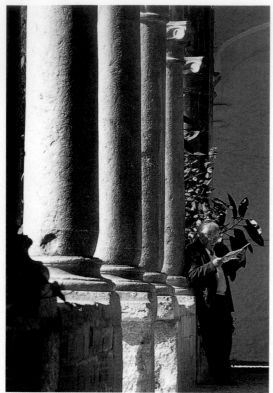

The cloisters of the Convent de Santo Domingo in Pollença

⑬ Pollença

Baleares. 🏛 16,200. 🚌 ℹ Carrer
Guillem Cifre de Colonya s/n, 971
53 50 77. 🛍 Sun. 🎭 Sant Antoni
(17 Jan), Patron Saint (2 Aug).

Although Pollença is one of
Mallorca's most popular tourist
spots, it still appears unspoiled.
The town, with its ochre-
coloured stone houses and
winding lanes, is picturesquely
sited on the edge of fertile
farmland. The Plaça Major, with its
bars frequented mainly by locals,
has an old-world atmosphere.

Pollença has fine churches,
including the 18th-century
Parròquia de Nostra Senyora dels
Àngels and the Convent de
Santo Domingo, containing the
Museu de Pollença, with its
displays of archaeology and art.
It also holds Pollença's Classical
Music Festival in the summer. A
chapel on the hilltop, El Calvari,
is reached either by road or a
long climb of 365 steps. On the

altar there is a Gothic Christ,
carved in wood. The nearby Port
de Pollença is an attractive resort
spread around a huge bay.

Environs
Alcúdia, 10 km (6 miles) to the
east, is surrounded by 14th-
century walls with two huge
gateways. Near the town centre
is the **Museu Monogràfic de
Pollentia**, exhibiting statues,
jewellery and other remains
found in the Roman settlement
of Pollentia, 2 km (1 mile) south
of Alcúdia.

🏛 **Museu de Pollença**
Carrer Guillem Cife de Colonya 33.
Tel 971 53 11 66. **Open** Tue–Sun. 🎫

🏛 **Museu Monogràfic
de Pollentia**
Carrer de Sant Jaume 30, Alcúdia.
Tel 971 54 70 04. **Open** Tue–Sun. 🎫

⑭ Palma

See pp522–5.

⑮ Puig de Randa

8 km (5 miles) northeast of Llucmajor.
🚌 to Llucmajor, then taxi.
ℹ Carrer Constitución 1, Llucmajor,
971 66 91 62.

In the middle of a fertile plain
called the *pla* rises a mini-
mountain 543 m (1,780 ft) high,
the Puig de Randa. It is said that
Mallorca's greatest son, the
14th-century theologian and
mystic Ramon Llull, came to a
hermitage on this mountain to
meditate and write his religious
treatise, *Ars Magna*. On the
way up Puig de Randa there
are two small monasteries, the
14th-century Santuari de Sant
Honorat and the Santuari de
Nostra Senyora de Gràcia. The
latter, built on a ledge under
an overhanging cliff, contains
a 13th-century chapel with fine
Valencian tiles inside.

On the mountaintop is the
Santuari de Cura, built to
commemorate Llull's time on
the *puig*, and largely devoted
to the study of his work. Its
central courtyard is built in the
typical beige stone of Mallorca.
A small museum, housed in a
16th-century former school
off the courtyard, contains
some of Llull's manuscripts.

The philosopher Ramon Llull

⑯ Capocorb Vell

Carretera Llucmajor–Cap Blanc (MA-
6014) km 23. **Tel** 971 18 01 55. 🚌 El
Arenal. **Open** 10am–5pm Fri–Wed.
🎫 🌐 talaiotscapocorbvell.com

Mallorca is not as rich in
megalithic remains as Menorca,
but this *talaiotic* village *(see
p531)* in the stony flatlands
of the southern coast is worth
seeing. The settlement, which

dates back to around 1000 BC, originally consisted of five *talaiots* (stone tower-like structures with timbered roofs) and another 28 smaller dwellings. Little is known about its inhabitants and the uses for some of the rooms inside the buildings, such as the tiny underground gallery. Too small for living in, this room may have been used to perform magic rituals.

Part of the charm of this place lies in its surroundings among fields of fruit trees and dry-stone walls, a setting that somehow complements the ruins. Apart from a snack bar nearby, the site remains mercifully undeveloped and relatively peaceful.

One of the *talaiots* of Capocorb Vell

⑰ Cabrera

Baleares. 🚢 from Colònia Sant Jordi. **ℹ** Carrer Gabriel Roca s/n, Colònia Sant Jordi, 971 65 60 73.

From the beaches of Es Trenc and Sa Ràpita, on the south coast of Mallorca, Cabrera looms on the horizon. The largest island in an archipelago of the same name, it lies 18 km (11 miles) from the most southerly point of Mallorca. Cabrera is home to several rare plants, reptiles and seabirds, such as Eleonora's falcon. The waters are important for marine life. All this has resulted in it being declared a national park *(see pp34–5)*. For centuries Cabrera was used as a military base and it has a small population. On it stand a 14th-century castle and a simple inn.

A street in Felanitx

⑱ Felanitx

Baleares. 🔼 17,300. 🚌 **ℹ** Avenida Cala Marçal, Portocolom, 971 82 60 84. 🕑 Sun. 🎉 Sant Joan Pelós (24 Jun).

This bustling agricultural town is the birthplace of Renaissance architect Guillem Sagrera (1380–1456) and the 20th century painter Miquel Barceló. Felanitx is visited mainly for three reasons: the imposing façade of the 13th-century church, the Esglesia de Sant Miquel; its *sobrassada de porc negre* (a spiced raw sausage made from the meat of the local black pig), and its lively religious fiestas including Sant Joan Pelos *(see p527)*.

About 5 km (3 miles) southeast is the Castell de Santueri, founded by the Moors but rebuilt in the 14th century by the kings of Aragón, who ruled Mallorca. Though a ruin, it is worth the detour for the views to the east and south from its vantage point, 400 m (1,300 ft) above the plain.

⑲ Coves del Drac

500 m (0.3 miles) south of Porto Cristo. 🚌 from Porto Cristo. **Tel** 971 82 07 53. **Open** daily. **Closed** 1 Jan, 25 Dec. 🎫 **ⓦ** cuevasdeldrach.com

Mallorca has numerous caves, ranging from mere holes in the ground to cathedral-like halls. The four vast chambers of the Coves del Drac are reached by a steep flight of steps. At the bottom is the beautifully lit cave, "Diana's Bath". Another chamber holds the underground lake, Martel, 29 m (95 ft) below ground level and 177 m (580 ft) long. Music fills the air of the cave, played from boats plying the lake. Equally dramatic are the two remaining caves, charmingly named "The Theatre of the Fairies" and "The Enchanted City".

Environs
The **Coves d'Hams** is so called because some of its stalactites are shaped like hooks – *hams* in Mallorcan. The caves are 500 m (1,640 ft) long and contain the "Sea of Venice", an underground lake on which musicians sail.

The entrance to the **Coves d'Artà**, near Capdepera, is 40 m (130 ft) above sea level and affords a wonderful view. The caves' main attraction is a stalagmite 22 m (72 ft) high.

🎫 **Coves d'Hams**
Carretera Manaçor–Porto Cristo, km 11.5. **Tel** 971 82 09 88. **Open** daily. **Closed** 1 Jan, 25 Dec. 🎫 **ⓦ** cuevas delshams.com

🎫 **Coves d'Artà**
Carretera Coves s/n, Canyamel. **Tel** 971 84 12 93. **Open** daily. **Closed** 1 Jan, 25 Dec. 🎫 **ⓦ** cuevasdearta.com

The dramatically lit stalactites of the Coves d'Artà

⑭ Street-by-Street: Palma

On an island whose name has become synonymous with mass tourism, Palma surprises with its cultural richness. Under the Moors it was a prosperous town of fountains and cool courtyards. After Jaime I had conquered it in 1229, he wrote, "It seemed to me the most beautiful city we had ever seen." Signs of Palma's past wealth are still evident in the sumptuous churches, grand public buildings and fine private mansions that crowd the old town. The hub of the city is the old-fashioned Passeig des Born, whose cafés invite you to try one of Mallorca's specialities, the ensaïmada, a spiral of pastry dusted with icing sugar.

Plaça del Marqués de Palmer

The CaixaForum, once the Gran Hotel, is now a cultural centre.

The Forn des Teatre is an old pastry shop noted for its ensaïmades and gató (almond cake).

Palau Reial de l'Almudaina
This palace belongs to the Spanish royal family and houses a museum, whose highlights include the chapel of Santa Ana, with its Romanesque portal, and the Gothic tinell or salon.

Key

— Suggested route

La Llotja is a beautiful 15th-century exchange with tall windows and delicate tracery.

PLAÇA REI JOAN CARLES

PASSEIG DES BORN

CARRER UNIO

CARRER JUAME II

CARRER DE PALAU REIAL

CARRER DE SANT PERE N

CARRER MIRADOR

AVINGUDA D ANTONI MAURA

To Castell de Bellver and Fundació Pilar i Joan Miró

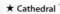
★ Cathedral
Built of golden limestone quarried from Santanyí, Palma's huge Gothic cathedral stands in a dramatic location near the waterfront.

Parc de la Mar

To Plaça Espanya, bus and train stations

| 0 metres | 100 |
| 0 yards | 100 |

VISITORS' CHECKLIST

Practical Information
Baleares. 🚹 380,000. ℹ️ Plaça Reina 2, 971 17 39 90. 🚆 Sat. 🎭 San Sebastián (20 Jan). 🌐 **info mallorca.net** Museu de Mallorca: **Tel** 971 17 78 38. **Open** 10am–6pm Mon–Fri, 11am–2pm Sat. Banys Àrabs: **Open** daily. 🏛️ Palau de l'Almudaina: **Open** Tue–Sun. 🏛️

Transport
✈️ 9 km (6 miles) east. 🚉 Plaça Espanya, 971 75 20 51. 🚌 Plaça Espanya, Calle Eusebi Estada, 971 17 77 77. ⛴️ Muelle de Peraires, 971 70 73 00 (Transmediterranea).

The circular walls of Palma's Gothic Castell de Bellver

🏰 Castell de Bellver
Carrer Camilo José Cela 17. **Tel** 971 73 50 65. **Open** Tue–Sun. 🏛️
About 5 km (3 miles) from the city centre, 113 m (370 ft) above sea level, is Palma's Gothic castle. Commissioned by Jaime II during the short-lived Kingdom of Mallorca (1276–1349) as a summer residence, it soon after became a prison until 1915. Today the castle frequently hosts concerts and plays.

🏰 Fundació Pilar i Joan Miró
Carrer Joan de Saridakis 29. **Tel** 971 70 14 20. **Open** mid-May–mid-Sep: 10am–7pm Tue–Sat; mid-Sep–mid-May: 10am–6pm Tue–Sat; 10am–3pm Sun all year, 🏛️ (free Sat). ♿ 📷 🌐 **miro.palmademallorca.es**

When Joan Miró died in 1983, his wife converted his former studio and gardens into an art centre. The building – "the Alabaster Fortress" – was designed by Navarrese architect Rafael Moneo. It incorporates Miró's original studio (complete with unfinished paintings), a permanent collection, a shop, a library and an auditorium.

🐠 Palma Aquarium
Carrer Manuela de los Herreros i Sorá 21. **Tel** 902 70 29 02. **Open** daily. 🏛️ 🌐 **palmaaquarium.com**

Located a 15-minute drive from the city centre, this aquarium is home to a range of flora and fauna from the Mediterranean Sea and the Indian, Atlantic and Pacific oceans. Visitors can see recreated ecosystems featuring 700 species and 5 million litres of seawater.

★ Basílica de Sant Francesc
The church and cloister of St Francis are in a refined Gothic style with a Baroque altarpiece and rose window.

SANT ALONSO

The Museu Diocesà, housed in the Bishop's Palace, has a collection of religious treasures.

Museu de Mallorca
The museum has displays on local history, art and architecture, including this statue of an ancient warrior.

CARRER DALT MURADA

Banys Àrabs
The 10th-century baths, with their well-preserved arches, are a remnant of the Balearic Islands' Moorish culture.

Palma Cathedral

According to legend, when Jaime I of Aragón was caught in a storm on his way to conquer Mallorca in 1229, he vowed that if God led him to safety he would build a great church in his honour. In the following years the old mosque of Medina Mayurqa was torn down and architect Guillem Sagrera (1380–1456) drew up plans for a new cathedral. The last stone was added in 1587, and in subsequent years the cathedral has been rebuilt, notably early last century when parts of the interior were remodelled by Antoni Gaudí *(see pp144–5)*. Today Palma Cathedral, or Sa Seu, as Mallorcans call it, is one of the most breathtaking buildings in Spain, combining vast scale with typically Gothic elegance *(see p28)*.

Bell Tower
This robust tower was built in 1389 and houses nine bells, the largest of which is known as N'Eloi, meaning "praise".

Palma Cathedral
One of the best-sited cathedrals anywhere, it is spectacularly poised high on the sea wall, above what was once Palma's harbour.

KEY

① **Portal Major**

② **19th-century tower**

③ **Flying buttresses**

④ **Cathedral Museum** contains one of the highlights of the beautifully displayed collection in the Old Chapterhouse, a 15th-century reliquary of the True Cross which is encrusted with jewels and precious metals.

⑤ **The Great Organ** was built with a Neo-Gothic case in 1795, and restored in 1993 by Gabriel Blancafort.

⑥ **The Capella Reial**, or Royal Chapel, was redesigned by Antoni Gaudí between 1904 and 1914.

⑦ **Choir stalls**

⑧ **Portal del Mirador**

Entrance to cathedral museum

★ Great Rose Window
The largest of seven rose windows looks down from above the High Altar like a gigantic eye. Built in 1370 with stained glass added in the 16th century, the window has a diameter of over 11 m (36 ft).

Capella de la Trinitat
This tiny chapel was built in 1329 as the mausoleum of Jaime II and III of Aragón. It contains their alabaster tombs.

Bishop's Throne
Built in 1269 and made of Carrara marble, the chair is embedded in a Gothic vaulted niche.

Nave
The magnificent ceiling, 44 m (144 ft) high, is held up by 14 slender pillars. At over 19 m (62 ft) wide, it is one of the broadest naves in the world.

★ Baldachino
Gaudí's bizarre wrought-iron canopy above the altar incorporates lamps, tapestries and a multicoloured crucifix.

Menorca

Menorca is set apart from the rest of the country in many ways, not least of which its distance from the mainland. The coastline of Menorca is, arguably, more unspoiled than in any other part of Spain. Its countryside remains largely green and pleasant with cows roaming the meadows. The old towns of Maó – the island's capital – and Ciutadella are filled with noble, historic buildings and beautiful squares. Menorca also has abundant reminders of its more distant history: the island boasts a spectacular hoard of Bronze Age stone structures, which provide an invaluable insight into its prehistoric past. The Menorcans are often more inclined to drink the locally brewed gin (ginebra) than the wine which is favoured elsewhere in Spain.

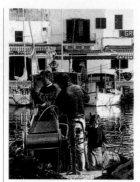

Fishermen mending their nets in Ciutadella's harbour

The peaceful seafront of Ciutadella at twilight

⑳ Ciutadella

Baleares. 🗺 28,600. 🚌 🚢 🅸 Plaça des Born, 971 48 41 55. 🏪 Fri & Sat. 🎉 Sant Joan (23–24 Jun).
🌐 illesbalears.es

The key date in the history of Ciutadella is 1558. In that year the Turks, under Barbarossa, entered and decimated the city, consigning 3,495 of its citizens to the slave markets of Constantinople. Of Ciutadella's main public buildings, only the fine Catalan Gothic Església Catedral de Menorca managed to survive this fearsome onslaught in more or less its original condition, only later to be stripped of all its paintings, ornaments and other treasures by Republican extremists during the Civil War.

The nearby Plaça des Born was built as a parade ground for Moorish troops, and from 1558 was gradually rebuilt in

Renaissance style. Today it is one of Spain's most impressive squares, containing pleasant cafés and bordered by shady palm trees. At the centre of the Plaça d'es Born is an obelisk which commemorates the "Any de sa Desgràcia" (Year of

The historic Plaça des Born in the centre of Ciutadella

Misfortune), when the Turks invaded the city. Around the square are the Gothic-style town hall (ajuntament), the late 19th-century Teatre Municipal d'es Born, and a series of aristocratic mansions with Italianesque façades, the grandest of which is the early 19th-century Palau de Torre-Saura. From the northern end of the square there is a fine view over the small harbour.

If you walk up the Carrer Major d'es Born past the cathedral, you come to Ses Voltes, an alley lined on both sides by whitewashed arches. Turn right along the Carrer del Seminari for the Baroque Església dels Socors and the **Museu Diocesà** with its displays of ecclesiastical paraphernalia. In the narrow streets of the old town there are many impressive palaces, including the early 19th-century **Palau Salort**, on the Carrer Major d'es Born, which is closed to the public, though its exterior can be admired. The Art Nouveau market (1895), its ironwork painted in municipal dark green, stands nearby.

The peace of Ciutadella is disturbed every June by the Festa de Sant Joan, a spectacular ritual of horsemanship. During the festival the local gin (ginebra) is drunk copiously and the city grinds to a halt.

🏛 **Museu Diocesà**
Carrer del Seminari 7. **Tel** 971 48 12 97.
Open May–Oct: Tue–Sat. 🖼 🅱 🎟

🏛 **Palau Salort**
Carrer Major d'es Born 9. **Closed** to the public.

㉑ Ferreries

Baleares. 🏔 4,600. 🚌 ℹ Town Hall:
Carrer Sant Bartomeu 55, 971 37 30
03. 🛒 Tue, Fri, Sat. 🎎 Sant Bartomeu
(23–25 Aug).

Ferreries lies between Mercadal
and Ciutadella and sprang up
when a road was built to
connect the two towns. Today
Ferreries is an attractive village of
white houses, built against the
slope of a hill. The simple church,
Sant Bartomeu, dates from 1770.

The bay of Santa Galdana,
10 km (6 miles) to the south, is
even prettier. You can take a
pleasant walk from the beach
inland through the fertile riverbed of Barranc d'Algendar.

Courtyard in the Santuari del Toro

㉒ Es Mercadal

Baleares. 🏔 5,000. 🚌 ℹ Town Hall:
Carrer Major 16, 971 37 50 02. 🛒 Sun.
🎎 Sant Martí (third Sun of Jul).

Es Mercadal is a small country
town – one of the three, with
Alaior and Ferreries, that are
strung out along the main road
from Maó to Ciutadella. The

town is unremarkable in itself,
but within reach of it are three
places of interest.

El Toro, 3 km (2 miles) to
the east, is Menorca's highest
mountain, at 350 m (1,150 ft).
It is also the spiritual heart of
the island and at its summit is
the Santuari del Toro, built in
1670, which is run by nuns.

About 10 km (6 miles) north of
Es Mercadal, the fishing village
of Fornells transforms itself
every summer into an outpost
of St Tropez. In the harbour,
smart yachts jostle with fishing
boats, and the local jet-set crowd
into the Bar Palma. Fornells'
main culinary speciality is the
caldereta de llagosta (lobster
casserole), but the quality
varies and prices can be high.

The road-cum-dirt track to the
Cap de Cavalleria, 13 km (8 miles)
north of Es Mercadal, passes
through one of the Balearics'
finest landscapes. Cavalleria is a
rocky promontory, whipped by
the tramontana wind from the
north. It juts out into a choppy
sea which, in winter, looks more
like the North Atlantic than the
Mediterranean. At the western
edge of the peninsula are the
remains of Sanisera, a Phoenician
village mentioned by Pliny in the
1st century AD. The road leads
to a headland, with a lighthouse
and cliffs 90 m (295 ft) high,
where peregrine falcons, sea
eagles and kites ride the wind.

Further west along the coast
is a string of fine, unspoiled
beaches, though with difficult
access: Cala Pregonda, Cala del
Pilar and La Vall d'Algaiarens are
three of the most beautiful.

Horse rearing in the
fiesta of Sant Lluís

The Balearic
Islands' Fiestas

Sant Antoni Abat (*16–17 Jan*),
Mallorca. This fiesta is celebrated with parades and the
blessing of animals all over
Mallorca and in Sant Antoni
in Ibiza.

Sant Joan (*24 Jun*), Ciutadella
(Menorca). The horse plays
a major part in Menorca's
festivals. In the streets and
squares of Ciutadella on
24 June, the Day of St John
the Baptist, elegantly dressed
riders put their horses
through ritualized medieval
manoeuvres. The fiesta
reaches a climax when the
horses rear up on their hind
legs and the jubilant crowds
swarm around them trying
to hold them up with their
hands. Similarly, the annual
fiesta in Sant Lluís, which
takes place at the end of
August, sees many of the
locals taking to the streets
on horseback.

Sant Joan Pelós (*24 Jun*),
Felanitx (Mallorca). As part of
this fiesta, a man is dressed in
sheepskins to represent John
the Baptist.

Romeria de Sant Marçal (*30
Jun*), Sa Cabeneta (Mallorca).
A feature of this fiesta is a
market selling *siurells*, primitive
Mallorcan whistles.

Our Lady of the Sea (*16 Jul*),
Formentera. The island's
main fiesta honours the
Virgen del Carmen, patroness
of fishermen, with a flotilla
of fishing boats.

A quiet stretch of beach at Santa Galdana

The steep hillside of Maó running up from the harbour

㉓ Maó

Baleares. 🏛 28,000. ✈ 🚌 ⛴
ℹ Plaza Constitución 22, 971 36 37 90.
🏪 Tue, Sat. 🎉 Festa de Sant Antoni
(17 Jan), Festes de Gràcia (7–8 Sep).

The quietly elegant town of Maó has lent its Spanish name, Mahón, to mayonnaise. It was occupied by the British three times during the 18th century. The legacy of past colonial rule can be seen in sober Georgian town houses, with their dark green shutters and sash windows.

Maó's harbour is one of the finest in the Mediterranean. Taking the street leading from the port to the upper town, the S-shaped Costa de Ses Voltes, you come to the 18th-century Església del Carme, a former Carmelite church whose cool white cloister now houses an attractive fruit and vegetable market. Behind the market is the **Col·lecció Hernández Sanz y Hernández Mora**, which houses Menorcan art and antiques. The nearby Plaça Constitució is overlooked by the church of Santa Maria, which has a huge organ. Next door is the town hall (ajuntament) with its Neo-Classical façade, into which is mounted the famous clock donated by Sir Richard Kane (1660–1736), the first British governor of Menorca.

Located at the end of the Carrer Isabel II is the Església de Sant Francesc, with an intriguing Romanesque doorway and Baroque façade. The church houses the refurbished Museu de Menorca, which is open daily except Monday. Two minutes' walk south of here will take you to Maó's main square, the Plaça de S'Esplanada, behind which is the **Ateneu de Maó**, a centre of Menorca-related culture and learning. Inside are collections of local ceramics and maps, and a library. It is advisable to obtain permission before looking around. On the north side of the harbour is a mansion known as Sant Antoni or the Golden Farm. As Maó's finest example of Palladian architecture, it has an arched façade, painted plum red, with white arches, in the traditional Menorcan style. Nelson, the British admiral, is thought to have stayed here. The house has a collection of Nelson memorabilia and a fine library but is closed to the public.

🏛 **Col·lecció Hernández Sanz y Hernández Mora**
Carrer Anuncivay 2. **Tel** 971 35 65 23.
Open 10am–1:30pm daily (also 6–8pm Mon–Sat).

🏛 **Ateneu de Maó**
Carrer Rovellada de Dalt 25. **Tel** 971 36 05 53. **Closed** Sun, public hols.

㉔ Cales Coves

Baleares. 🚌 Sant Climent, then 25 mins walk. **Tel** Maó, 971 36 37 90.

On either side of a pretty bay can be found Cales Coves – the site of Neolithic dwellings of up to 9 m (30 ft) in length, hollowed out of the rock face. The caves, thought to have been inhabited since prehistoric times, are today occupied by a community of people seeking an alternative lifestyle. Some of the caves have front doors, chimneys and even butane cookers.

About 8 km (5 miles) west, along the coast, lies Binibeca, a tourist village built in a style sympathetic to old Menorca. The jumble of white houses and tiny streets of the Poblat de Pescadors, an imitation fishing village, have the look of the genuine article.

Modern sculpture outside one of the dwellings at Cales Coves

◀ Yachts and pleasure boats at Cales Coves, Menorca

Ancient Menorca

Menorca is exceptionally rich in prehistoric remains – the island has been described as an immense open-air museum. The majority of the sites are the work of the "talayot" people who lived between 2000 BC and 1000 BC and are named after the *talaiots* or huge stone towers that characterize the Menorcan landscape. There are hundreds of these Bronze Age villages and structures dotted around the island. Usually open to the public and free of charge, these sites provide an invaluable insight into the ancient inhabitants of the Balearics.

Huge *talaiot* amid the settlement of Trepucó

Different Structures

The ancient stone structures scattered around the countryside of Menorca and, to a lesser extent, Mallorca can be placed into three main categories: taulas, talaiots *and* navetas.

 Taulas are two slabs of rock, one placed on top of the other, in a "T" formation. Suggestions as to their possible function range from a sacrificial altar to a roof support.

 Talaiots are circular or square buildings that may have been used as meeting places and dwellings.

 Navetas are shaped like upturned boats and apparently had a dual role as dwellings and burial quarters. At least ten of these remain in Menorca.

Spectacular *taula* at Talatí de Dalt, standing 3 m (10 ft) high

Menorca has an estimated 1,600 megalithic sites, and the most interesting of these are shown here. *Talayot* remains are found all over the island, usually in rural settings, though most are in the flatter and more fertile south.

Cala Morell
Fornells
Ciutadella
Naveta d'es Tudons · Torrellafuda · Ferreries · Es Mercadal
Torretrencada
Alaior
Torralba d'en Salord
Torre d'en Gaumés · Talatí de Dalt · Maó
Trepucó
Sant Lluís

0 kilometres 10
0 miles 5

THE CANARY ISLANDS

La Palma · El Hierro · La Gomera · Tenerife
Gran Canaria · Fuerteventura · Lanzarote

Poised on the edge of the tropics west of Morocco, the Canaries enjoy a generous supply of sunshine, pleasantly tempered by the trade winds. Their scenery ranges from lava deserts to primeval forests and from sand dunes to volcanic peaks. The old towns on the main islands, meanwhile, have colonial centres that make for pleasant exploration.

Seven islands and half a dozen islets make up the Canary archipelago. They are the tips of hundreds of volcanoes that first erupted from the seabed 14 million years ago. Teneguía on La Palma last erupted in 1971.

In the 14th and 15th centuries, when navigators discovered the islands and claimed them for Spain, they were inhabited by the Guanches, who practised a stone culture. Sadly, little evidence of them remains.

Today the islands are divided into two provinces. The four western isles, making up the province of Santa Cruz de Tenerife, are all mountainous; Tenerife's colossal dormant volcano, Mount Teide, casts the world's biggest sea-shadow. La Palma, El Hierro and La Gomera, where Columbus stayed on his voyages, are all small, unspoiled islands, and make for refreshing respite away from Tenerife's mass tourism.

The eastern islands belong to the province of Las Palmas. Forested Gran Canaria is the biggest and its capital, Las Palmas de Gran Canaria, is a colonial town. Lanzarote, by contrast, is flat, with lunar landscapes, while Fuerteventura has long, pristine beaches.

Protected area of sand dunes at Maspalomas, next to the busy Playa del Inglés, Gran Canaria

◄ Picturesque view of the stretch of golden sand at Playa de Las Teresitas, Tenerife

Exploring the Western Canary Islands

Tenerife has the widest range of holiday attractions of any of the Canary Islands. The province of Santa Cruz de Tenerife also includes the three tiny westerly islands of La Palma, La Gomera and El Hierro, which are beautiful and yet often overlooked by tourists. Gradually, more visitors are discovering these peaceful, green havens. If you enjoy walking, wildlife and mountain scenery, visit one of these hideaways. All three islands have comfortable hotels, including paradors. But, compared with Gran Canaria and the eastern islands, there are fewer sandy beaches here, and little organized entertainment or sightseeing.

Las Teresitas artificial beach, Santa Cruz de Tenerife

Sights at a Glance

1. La Palma
2. El Hierro
3. La Gomera
4. Los Cristianos
5. *Parque Nacional del Teide* pp542–3
6. Puerto de la Cruz
7. La Orotava
8. Candelaria
9. La Laguna
10. Montes de Anaga
11. Santa Cruz de Tenerife

Roque Bonanza on the rocky east coast of El Hierro

Key

═══ Motorway

▬▬▬ Major road

═══ Secondary road

▬▬▬ Scenic route

△ Summit

Terraced hillside, maximizing cultivation in the lush green Valle Gran Rey, on the island of La Gomera

0 kilometres 25
0 miles 10

TENERIFE

MONTES DE ANAGA

LA LAGUNA
Tacoronte

Playa de Las Teresitas

SANTA CRUZ DE TENERIFE

El Rosario

PUERTO DE LA CRUZ

Buenavista del Norte
Garachico
LA OROTAVA

Punta de Teno

CANDELARIA

Güimar

Pico del Teide
3718m

PARQUE NACIONAL DEL TEIDE

Parador de Cañadas del Teide

Guia

Punta de Abona

Vilaflor

Adeje
Granadilla de Abona

Sebastián

Playa de las Américas
Arona

El Médano

LOS CRISTIANOS

Punta de la Rasca
Costa del Silencio
Punta Roja

The wild landscape of Punta de Teno in western Tenerife

Getting Around

From mainland Spain there are flights *(see p626)* and ferries *(see p627)* to the Canary Islands. Transport to the small islands is mainly from Tenerife. La Gomera is easily reached by ferry or hydrofoil from Los Cristianos, or by plane from Gran Canaria or Tenerife. Airports on La Palma and El Hierro are served by regular flights from Tenerife's northern airport of Los Rodeos. Unless you take an organized coach trip, a car is essential to see the island scenery. Roads are improving, but great care is needed for mountain driving.

❶ La Palma

Santa Cruz de Tenerife. 🏛 80,000.
✈ 🚢 Santa Cruz de la Palma.
ℹ Plaza de la Constitución s/n, Santa
Cruz de la Palma, 922 41 21 06.
W visitlapalma.es

Reaching an altitude of 2,426 m
(7,959 ft) on a land base of less
than 706 sq km (280 sq miles),
La Palma is the world's steepest
island. It lies on the northwestern
tip of the archipelago and has
a cool, moist climate and lush
vegetation. The mountainous
interior is covered with forests
of pine, laurel and giant fern.

The centre of the island is
dominated by the Caldera de
Taburiente, a volcano's massive
crater, more than 8 km (5 miles)
wide. National park status
(see pp34–5) is an indication
of its botanical and geological
importance. The International
Astrophysics Observatory crowns
the summit. A couple of roads
traverse La Palma's dizzy heights,

The Parque Nacional de la Caldera de Taburiente, La Palma

offering spectacular views of
the craters of La Cumbrecita
and Roque de los Muchachos.

Santa Cruz de la Palma, the
island's main town and port,
is an elegant place of old
houses with balconies, some
fine churches and several 16th-
century buildings. In the
cobbled street behind the seafront, Calle O'Daly (named after
an Irish banana trader), are the
Iglesia El Salvador, boasting a
Mudéjar coffered ceiling, and
the town hall (ayuntamiento),
which is housed in a cardinal's
palace. A full-sized cement
replica of the Santa María,
Columbus's flagship, stands at
the end of the Plaza Alameda.

The tortuous mountain road
southwest of Santa Cruz winds
over Las Cumbres mountains
via Breña Alta to El Paso in the
centre of the island. A relatively
sizable community, the village
is known for its silk production
and hand-rolled cigars.

Pastel façades and delicate wooden
balconies in Santa Cruz, La Palma

Among the almond terraces
and vineyards of southern La
Palma, solidified lava from the
Teneguía volcano is a reminder
of its recent activity (see p555).

Craters on El Hierro, Spain's most
western territory

❷ El Hierro

Santa Cruz de Tenerife. 🏛 10,500.
✈ 🚢 Puerto de la Estaca. ℹ Calle
Doctor Quintero 4, Valverde, 922 55
03 02. **W** elhierro.travel

Due to a dearth of sandy
beaches, El Hierro has escaped
tourist invasions. Instead it has
caught the attention of
naturalists, with its hilly landscape and unusual fauna and
flora. El Hierro is the smallest of
the Canaries, and the furthest
west; it is the last place in Spain
where the sun sets.

Valverde, the island's capital;
stands inland at 600 m (2,000 ft)
above sea level. Canary pines
and peculiarly twisted juniper
trees cover El Hierro's mountainous interior, best seen from

La Gomera's Whistle Language

The problems of communication posed
by La Gomera's rugged terrain produced
an unusual language, known as El Silbo.
This system of piercing whistles probably
developed because its sounds carry across
the great distances from one valley to
the next. Its origins are mysterious,
but it was allegedly invented by the
Guanches (see p551). Few young
Gomerans have any use for El Silbo
today, and the language would probably
be dead if it were not for the demonstrations of it still held for interested visitors
at the parador, and in the restaurant at
Las Rosas.

El Silbo practised on
La Gomera

the many footpaths and scenic viewpoints along the roads. A ridge of woodland, curving east–west across the island, marks the edge of a volcano. The crater forms a fertile depression known as El Golfo.

In the far west is the Ermita de los Reyes, a place of pilgrimage and the starting point of the island's biggest fiesta, held in July every four years.

The turquoise seas off the south coast are popular with skin-divers, who base themselves in the small fishing village of La Restinga.

❸ La Gomera

Santa Cruz de Tenerife. 🄼 21,400. ✈ 🚢 🛈 Calle Real 32, San Seba stián de la Gomera, 922 14 15 12. 🅦 lagomera.travel

La Gomera is the most accessible of the smaller western islands, only 40 minutes by hydrofoil from Los Cristianos on Tenerife (90 minutes by ferry), or by plane from Tenerife or Gran Canaria. Many come to La Gomera for a day only, taking a coach trip. Others hire a car and explore on their own: a scenic but exhausting drive for a single day as the terrain is intensely buckled, and the central plateau is deeply scored by dramatic ravines. Driving across these gorges involves negotiating countless dizzying hairpin bends.

The best way to enjoy the island is to stay a while and explore it at leisure, preferably doing some walking. On a

Terraced hillsides in the fertile Valle Gran Rey, La Gomera

fine day, La Gomera's scenery is glorious. Rock pinnacles jut above steep slopes studded with ferns while terraced hillsides glow with palms and flowering creepers. The best section, the Parque Nacional de Garajonay, is a UNESCO World Heritage Site.

San Sebastián, La Gomera's main town and ferry terminal, is situated on the east coast, a scattering of white buildings around a small beach. Among its sights are some places associated with Columbus (*see pp62–3*), who topped up his water supplies here before

setting out on his adventurous voyages. A well in the customs house bears the grand words "With this water America was baptized". According to legend he also prayed in the Iglesia de la Asunción, and stayed at a local house.

Beyond the arid hills to the south lies Playa de Santiago, the island's only real resort, which has a grey pebble beach. Valle Gran Rey, in the far west, is a fertile valley of palms and staircase terraces. These days it is colonized by foreigners attempting alternative lifestyles. In the north, tiny roads weave a tortuous course around several pretty villages, plunging at intervals to small, stony beaches. Las Rosas is a popular stop-off for coach parties, who can enjoy the visitors' centre and a restaurant with a panoramic view.

The road towards the coast from Las Rosas leads through the town of Vallehermoso, dwarfed by the huge Roque de Cano, which is an impressive mass of solidified lava. Just off the north coast stands Los Órganos, a fascinating rock formation of crystallized basalt columns resembling the pipes of an organ.

Juniper trees on El Hierro, twisted and bent by the wind

Tenerife

In the language of its aboriginal Guanche inhabitants Tenerife means "Snowy Mountain", a tribute to its most striking geographical feature, the dormant volcano of Mount Teide, Spain's highest peak. The largest of the Canary Islands, Tenerife is a roughly triangular landmass rising steeply on all sides towards the cloud-capped summit that divides it into two distinct climatic zones: damp and lushly vegetated in the north, sunny and arid in the south. Tenerife offers a more varied range of attractions than any of the other Canary Islands, including its spectacular volcanic scenery, water sports and a vibrant atmosphere after dark. Its beaches, however, have unenticing black sand and are rather poor for swimming. The main resorts are crowded with high-rise hotels and apartments, offering nightlife but little peace and quiet.

Bananas in northern Tenerife

❹ Los Cristianos

Santa Cruz de Tenerife. 🌄 60,000. 🚌 📶 ℹ Paseo Playa de las Vistas 1, 922 78 70 11. 🚢 Sun. 🎭 Fiesta del Carmen (first Sun of Sep). 🗎 **webtenerife.com**

The old fishing village of Los Cristianos, on Tenerife's south coast, has grown into a town spreading out along the foot of barren hills. Ferries and hydrofoils make regular trips from its little port to La Gomera and El Hierro *(see pp536–7)*.

To the north lies the modern expanse of Playa de las Américas, Tenerife's largest development. It offers visitors a cheerful, relaxed, undemanding cocktail of sun and fun.

A brief sortie inland leads to the much older town of Adeje and to the Barranco del Infierno, a wild gorge with an attractive waterfall (2 hours' round walk from Adeje).

Along the coast to the east, the Costa del Silencio is a pleasant contrast to most of

the other large resorts, with its bungalow developments surrounding fishing villages. Los Abrigos has lively fish restaurants lining its harbour.

Further east, El Médano shelters below an ancient volcanic cone. Its two beaches are popular with windsurfers.

❺ Parque Nacional del Teide

See pp542–3.

❻ Puerto de la Cruz

Santa Cruz de Tenerife. 🌄 27,500. 🚌 ℹ Calle Puerto Viejo 13, 922 38 87 77. 🚢 Sat. 🎭 Carnival (Feb–Mar), Fiesta del Carmen (second Sun of Jul). 🗎 **webtenerife.com**

Puerto de la Cruz, the oldest resort in the Canaries, first came to prominence in 1706, when a volcanic eruption obliterated Tenerife's main port of Garachico. Puerto de la Cruz took its place,

later becoming popular with genteel English convalescents. The town's older buildings give it much of its present character.

The beautiful Complejo Costa Martiánez, designed by the Lanzarote architect César Manrique *(see p552)*, compensates for a lack of good beaches with its seawater pools, palms and fountains. Other attractions include the tropical gardens of **Loro Parque**, where visitors can also see parrots and dolphins.

Outside town, the **Jardín de Orquídeas** is the oldest garden in Tenerife, and has a large orchid collection. Icod de los Vinos, a short drive west, has a spectacular ancient dragon tree.

🦜 **Loro Parque**
Avenida Loro Parque. **Tel** 922 37 38 41. **Open** daily. 🎭 🗎 **loroparque.com**

🌸 **Jardín de Orquídeas**
Camino Sitio Litre s/n. **Tel** 922 38 24 17. **Open** daily. 🎭
🗎 **jardindeorquideas.com**

The landscaped Lago Martiánez lido, Puerto de la Cruz

The Dragon Tree

The Canary Islands have many unusual plants, but the dragon tree (*Dracaena draco*) is one of the strangest. This primitive creature looks a little like a giant cactus, with swollen branches that sprout multiple tufts of spiky leaves. When cut, the trunk exudes a reddish sap once believed to have magical and medicinal properties. Dragon trees form no annual rings, so their age is a mystery. Some are thought to be hundreds of years old. The most venerable surviving specimen can be seen at Icod de los Vinos.

---

❼ La Orotava

Santa Cruz de Tenerife. 🖼 40,000.
🚌 ℹ️ Calle Calvario 4, 922 32 30 41.
🎭 Carnival (Feb/Mar), Corpus Christi
(May/Jun), Romería San Isidoro
Labrador (Jun). 🅆 **webtenerife.com**

A short distance from Puerto
de la Cruz, in the fertile hills
above the Orotava Valley, La
Orotava makes a popular
excursion. The old part of this
historic town clusters around
the large Iglesia de Nuestra
Señora de la Concepción. This
domed Baroque building with
twin towers was built in the late
18th century to replace an
earlier church that was destroyed in earthquakes at the
beginning of that century.

In the surrounding streets
and squares are many old
churches, convents and grand
houses with elaborate wooden
balconies. Casa de los Balcones
and Casa del Turista, on Calle San
Francisco, sell handicrafts and
regional food products.

Nuestra Señora de la Candelaria, patron
saint of the Canary Islands

❽ Candelaria

Santa Cruz de Tenerife. 🖼 17,000. 🚌
ℹ️ Avenida de la Constitución 7, 922
03 22 30. 🚍 Sat, Sun. 🎭 Nuestra
Señora de la Candelaria (14–15 Aug).
🅆 **webtenerife.com**

This coastal town is famous for
its shrine to Nuestra Señora de la
Candelaria, the Canary Islands'
patron saint, whose image is
surrounded by flowers and
candles in a modern church in
the main square. Supposedly
washed ashore in pagan times,

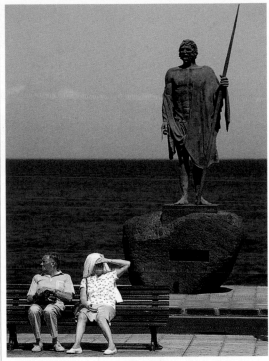

Statue of a Guanche chief on the seafront of Candelaria

this gaudy Virgin was venerated
before Christianity reached
the island. In 1826 a tidal wave
returned her to the sea, but a
replica draws pilgrims to worship
here every August. Outside,
stone effigies of Guanche chiefs
line the sea wall.

❾ La Laguna

Santa Cruz de Tenerife. 🖼 141,000.
🚌 ℹ️ Calle de la Carrera 7, 922 63
11 94. 🚍 daily. 🎭 San Benito (15 Jul),
Santísimo Cristo de la Laguna (14 Sep).
🅆 **webtenerife.com**

A bustling university town,
La Laguna is the second-largest
settlement on Tenerife and a
UNESCO World Heritage Site.

Its old quarter, best explored
on foot, has many historic
buildings and good museums.
Most of the sights lie between
the bell-towered Iglesia de
Nuestra Señora de la Concepción
(1502), and the Plaza del
Adelantado, on which stand the
town hall, a convent and the
Palacio de Nava.

❿ Montes de Anaga

Santa Cruz de Tenerife. 🚌 Santa Cruz
de Tenerife, La Laguna.

The rugged mountains north of
Santa Cruz are kept lush by a
cool, wet climate. They abound
with a range of birds and plants,
including cacti, laurels and tree
heathers. Walking the trails is
very popular, and maps showing many of the best paths are
available from the tourist office.
A steep road with marker posts
climbs up from the village of
San Andrés by the beautiful but
artificial beach of Las Teresitas.
On clear days there are splendid
vistas along the paths, especially
from the viewpoints of Pico del
Inglés and Bailadero.

Winding down through the
laurel forests of Monte de las
Mercedes and the valley of
Tejina, you will first come to
the town of Valle de Guerra,
where there is an ethnographic
museum. Next, you will reach
Tacoronte, with its interesting
churches and a bodega, where
you can sample local wines.

The Canary Islands' Fiestas

Carnival *(Feb/Mar)*, Santa Cruz de Tenerife. One of Europe's biggest carnivals, this grand street party is a lavish spectacle of extravagant costumes and Latin American dance music to rival that of Rio de Janeiro. For years under the Franco regime, Carnival was suppressed for its irreverent frivolity. It begins with the election of a queen of the festivities and builds up to a climax on Shrove Tuesday, when there is a large procession. The "funeral" of an enormous mock sardine takes place on Ash Wednesday. Carnival is also celebrated on the islands of Lanzarote and Gran Canaria.

Revellers in Carnival outfits on Tenerife

Corpus Christi *(May/Jun)*, La Orotava (Tenerife). The streets of the town are filled with flower carpets in striking patterns, while the Plaza del Ayuntamiento is covered in copies of works of art, formed from coloured volcanic sands.
La Bajada de la Virgen de las Nieves *(Jul, every five years: 2020, 2025)* Santa Cruz de La Palma.
Romería de la Virgen de la Candelaria *(15 Aug)*, Candelaria (Tenerife). Pilgrims come here in their thousands to venerate the Canary Islands' patroness.
Fiesta del Charco *(7–11 Sep)*, San Nicolás de Tolentino (Gran Canaria). People leap into a large saltwater pond to catch mullet.

Large ships moored at the busy port of Santa Cruz de Tenerife

⓫ Santa Cruz de Tenerife

Santa Cruz de Tenerife. 🏔 220,000. 🚢
🚌 ℹ️ Plaza de España, 922 28 12 87.
🗓 Sun. 🎭 Carnival (Feb/Mar), Día de la Cruz (3 May). 🅦 **webtenerife.com**

Tenerife's capital city is an important regional port, with a deep-water harbour suitable for large ships. Its most attractive beach, Las Teresitas, lies 7 km (4 miles) to the north. It was created by importing millions of tonnes of Saharan sand and building a protective reef just offshore. Shaded by palms, backed by mountains and so far devoid of concrete hotel developments, the result improves on anything nature has bestowed on Tenerife.

Santa Cruz boasts many handsome historic buildings. The hub of the town is around the Plaza de España, near the harbour. Just off it is the Calle de Castillo, the main shopping street. Its two most noteworthy churches are the Iglesia de Nuestra Señora de la Concepción, with parts dating from 1500, and Baroque Iglesia de San Francisco.

Particularly interesting is the **Museo de la Naturaleza y el Hombre**, in the Palacio Insular, where Guanche mummies grin in glass cases. Inside the museum you can also see the cannon which is alleged to have removed the arm of the British admiral Nelson during an unsuccessful raid on the city in the late 18th century.

Other attractions include the **Museo de Bellas Artes**, which features old masters as well as modern works, and the **TEA – Tenerife Espacio de las Artes**, which hosts temporary art and photography exhibitions. Contemporary sculptures adorn the Parque Municipal García Sanabria, a pleasant park with shady paths, laid out in 1926.

At the Mercado de Nuestra Señora de África, outside stalls sell domestic goods, while those inside offer an eclectic mix of regional produce spices and cut flowers. Santa Cruz is especially worth a visit during its flamboyant carnival.

🏛 **Museo de la Naturaleza y el Hombre**
Calle Fuentes Morales 1. **Tel** 922 53 58 16. **Open** daily. 🚼 &

🏛 **Museo de Bellas Artes**
Calle José Murphy 12.
Tel 922 24 43 58. **Open** Tue–Sun.

🏛 **Tenerife Espacio de las Artes**
Avda de San Sebastián 10. **Open** Tue–Sun. 🅦 **teatenerife.es**

The artificial beach of Las Teresitas in Santa Cruz

The Flavours of the Canary Islands

The exotic fruits and vegetables that grow in the subtropical climate of the Canaries, along with the unusual fish that are caught in local waters, have led to a cuisine very different from that of the Iberian Peninsula. From the original inhabitants, the Guanche, culinary traditions survive in local staples like *gofio* (maize meal). Over the centuries, Spanish, Portuguese and North African influences have been incorporated into the local cuisine, but the underlying theme is always one of simplicity and a reliance on ultra-fresh local produce. All kinds of unusual delicacies are available, from sweet-fleshed parrotfish to succulent tropical fruits.

Maize (corn)

Fish straight from the ocean, being dried in the sun to preserve them

Seafood and Meat

The Canaries offer an incredible array of seafood, with varieties unknown on the Spanish mainland. Delicacies like *lapas* (limpets) are around only for a few months during the summer, and are usually served simply grilled (*a la plancha*). Other unusual varieties include wreckfish, damselfish, dentex and parrotfish. These, along with more common varieties, are usually fried, baked in a salt crust or dried in the sun.

Meats include standard Iberian favourites like pork, kid and beef, but they are often prepared according to ancient Guanche traditions.

Fruit and Vegetables

The mild, stable Canarian climate is perfect for growing luscious tropical fruits (the most famous crop of the islands being bananas). Exotic vegetables thrive, too, as well as potatoes and tomatoes, which were introduced here 500 years ago from the newly discovered Americas. The islands boast varieties of potato unknown elsewhere, and these feature in the local favourite *papas arrugadas* ("wrinkly potatoes"), which are made by boiling potatoes in their skins in very salty water – sometimes seawater.

Dates · Bananas · Pineapple · Papayas (paw paw) · Mangoes · Guavas

Mouthwatering fresh fruits from the Canary Islands

Canarian Dishes and Specialities

The Greeks named the Canaries "the fortunate islands", and they are certainly blessed in terms of the freshness and abundance of the local produce. What ever you choose to eat, you can be sure of encoutering a bowl of the ubiquitous *mojo* sauce. This aromatic Canarian creation accompanies almost every dish, and appears in countless versions: the main ones are red *picón*, which is spiced up with pepper and paprika, and green *verde*, with parsley and coriander. The Canarian staple, *gofio* (roasted maize meal), is served for breakfast and used in local dishes such as *gofio de almendras*, a rich almond dessert. The islands are also known for delicious pastries like the honey-drizzled *bienmesabes* (meaning "tastes good to me") and traditional cheeses.

Almonds

Sopa de pescados tinerfeña
This Tenerife fish soup of sea bass and potatoes is scented with saffron and cumin.

❺ Parque Nacional del Teide

Towering over Tenerife, Mount Teide, surrounded by a wild volcanic landscape, is an awesome sight. 180,000 years ago a much larger adjacent cone collapsed, leaving behind the devastation of Las Cañadas, a 16-km- (10-mile-) wide caldera, and the smaller volcano, Teide, on its northern edge. Today volcanic material forms a wilderness of weathered, mineral-tinted rocks, ash beds and lava streams. A single road crosses the plateau of Las Cañadas, passing a parador, cable car station, and visitors' centre. Follow the marked paths for unforgettable views of this unique, protected area.

Volcanic Landscapes
The eight-minute cable-car ride leaves you 160 m (525 ft) short of Teide's summit. Authorization must be given to climb up to the summit.

Los Roques de García
These flamboyantly shaped lava rocks near the parador are some of the most photographed in the whole park. The rocks of Los Azulejos, nearby, glitter blue-green because of the copper deposits within them.

Pico del Teide
3,718 m ②

Pico Viejo
3,135 m ①

La Rambleta
3,555 m

↖ *Chío*

⚟ **Mirador de Chío**

Roques de García

C823

Mirador d La Rulet

Mirador de la Ruleta

Llano de Ucanca

Mirador de Boca Tauce

Vilaflor ↓

C821

Key

═══ Road

▬▬▬ Track

▬ ▬ Footpath

0 kilometres	2
0 miles	1

KEY

① **Pico Viejo**, a volcanic cone also known as Montaña Chahorra, last erupted in the 18th century.

② **Pico del Teide**, which is still volcanically active, is Spain's highest summit.

③ **At the Visitors' Centre**, a video film and exhibition chart the origins of the park.

Wild Flowers

The inhospitable badlands of Las Cañadas are inhabited by some rare and beautiful plants. Many of these are unique to the Canary Islands. Most striking is the tall *Echium wildprettii*, a kind of viper's bugloss, whose red flowers reach 3 m (10 ft) in early summer. Other common plants include Teide broom, the Teide daisy, and a unique species of violet. The best time of year for flower-spotting is May to June. Displays housed in the visitors' centre will help identify them. Don't take any plants away with you: all vegetation within the park is strictly protected and must not be uprooted or picked.

La Caldera de Las Cañadas

A rim of fractured crags forms a pie-crust edge to the sides of this enormous caldera – a wide volcanic crater (*see p555*). Now collapsed and intensely eroded, the perimeter of the caldera measures 45 km (28 miles).

Las Cañadas

The flat expanses of the seven *cañadas* (small sandy plateaus) were created by the collapse of ancient craters. Several colourful plants have managed to colonize this dusty, barren wasteland.

Parador

A mountain lodge, the Parador de Cañadas del Teide is set in surreal scenery, and makes an excellent base for those who want to explore the park thoroughly over the course of multiple days.

Canary mustard *(Descurainia bourgeauana)*

Teide wallflower *(Erysimum scoparium)*

Teide violet *(Viola cheiranthifolia)*

Teide viper's bugloss *(Echium wildpretii)*

Exploring the Eastern Canary Islands

The Eastern Province of the Canary Islands – Las Palmas – comprises the islands of Gran Canaria, Lanzarote and Fuerteventura. All feature unusual and spectacular scenery, plenty of sunshine and excellent sandy beaches, but each has a very different atmosphere. Gran Canaria boasts the only really large town, Las Palmas de Gran Canaria, which is also the administrative centre for the eastern islands. It also offers the biggest resort, Maspalomas, with its Playa del Inglés, which has a package-holiday feel. As a contrast, the white beaches of Fuerteventura have been left fairly undeveloped and it is still possible to find privacy among their sand dunes. Lanzarote has fine beaches, too, while its interior is dominated by a volcanic landscape which makes for great excursions.

Corralejo's beach, in the north of Fuerteventura

The marina at Puerto Rico, in southern Gran Canaria

Getting Around

Most people travel from mainland Spain to the eastern islands by air *(see p626)*. The alternative is a long sea crossing from Cádiz *(see p627)*. There are flights between all the islands, mainly from Gran Canaria. There are also regular inter-island ferries. Taxis and public transport are fine within resorts, but expensive over long distances. Cars can be hired on all the islands, usually at airports or ferry terminals. The main roads are well surfaced and fast on the flatter sections, though traffic in Gran Canaria can be heavy in places. A four-wheel drive Jeep is advisable to reach some remoter beaches.

Cenobio de Valerón ○
Gáldar ○
AGAETE ⑮ Arucas ⑰ **LAS PALMAS DE GRAN CANARIA**
Firgas ○
Teror ○
CRUZ ⑯ **TAFIRA**
DE TEJEDA ⑱ *Vega de San Mateo*
San Nicolás ○ *Telde*
de Tolentino *Roque Nublo* ○ *Pico de las Nieves 1949m*
Mogán ○ ○ *Santa Lucía*
PUERTO DE ⑫ *Agüimes*
MOGÁN
⑬ **PUERTO RICO**
⑭ **MASPALOMAS**

GRAN CANARIA

Key

━━ Motorway
━━ Major road
══ Secondary road
━━ Scenic route
△ Summit

Sights at a Glance

Volcanoes of Montañas de Fuego in Parque Nacional de Timanfaya, Lanzarote

Gran Canaria

Gran Canaria is the most popular of the Canary Islands, with over 3 million holiday-makers visiting it each year. The island offers a surprising range of scenery, climate, resorts and attractions within its compact bounds. Winding roads follow the steep, ruggedly beautiful terrain which rises to a symmetrical cone at the centre of the island. Las Palmas, Gran Canaria's capital and port, is the largest city in the Canaries, and Maspalomas/Playa del Inglés, in the south, is one of the biggest resorts in Spain. Both tourist meccas are packed with high-rise hotels and villa complexes, but not far away there is some marvellous scenery to discover.

Holiday-makers on the golden sands of Puerto Rico beach

⓬ Puerto de Mogán

Las Palmas. 🚐 1,500. 🅸 Centro Comercial de Puerto Rico, Fase 2, Puerto Rico, 928 56 11 38. 🚢 Fri. 🎎 Virgen del Carmen (Jul). 🆆 grancanaria.com

Situated at the end of the verdant valley of Mogán, this is one of Gran Canaria's most appealing developments – an idyll to many visitors after the brash Playa del Inglés. Based around a small fishing port, it consists of a village-like complex of pretty, white, creeper-covered houses and a similarly designed hotel built around a marina. Boutiques, bars and restaurants add an ambience without any of the accompanying rowdiness.

The sandy beach, sheltered between the cliffs, is scarcely big enough for all visitors; a car is recommended to reach more facilities at Maspalomas. Ferries provide a leisurely way to get to nearby resorts.

Sun-worshippers in Puerto Rico

⓭ Puerto Rico

Las Palmas. 🚐 1,800. 🅸 Centro Comercial de Puerto Rico, Fase 2, 928 56 11 38. 🎎 María de Auxiliadora (May), San Antonio (13 Jun), Carmen (16 Jul).

The barren cliffs west of Maspalomas now sprout apartment complexes at every turn. Puerto Rico is an over-developed resort, but has one of the more attractive beaches on the island, a firm crescent of imported sand supplemented by lidos and excellent water-sports facilities. It is a great place to learn sailing, diving and windsurfing, or just to soak up the ultraviolet – Puerto Rico enjoys the best sunshine record in the whole of Spain.

⓮ Maspalomas

Las Palmas. 🚐 33,000. ✈ 🅸 Centro Comercial Anexo II 20, Playa del Inglés, 928 76 84 09. 🚢 Wed & Sat. 🎎 Santiago (25 Jul), San Bartolomé (24 Aug). 🆆 grancanaria.com

When the motorway from Las Palmas Airport first tips you into this bewildering mega-resort, it seems like a homogeneous blur, but gradually three separate communities emerge. San Agustín, the furthest east, is sedate compared with the others. It has a series of beaches of dark sand, attractively sheltered by low cliffs and landscaped promenades, and a casino.

The next exit off the coastal highway leads to Playa del Inglés, the largest and liveliest resort, a triangle of land jutting into a huge belt of golden sand. Developed from the end of the 1950s, the area is built up with giant blocks of flats linked by a maze of roads. Many hotels lack sea views, though most have spacious grounds with swimming pools. At night the area pulsates

Floral arches decorating a street of apartments in Puerto de Mogán

with bright disco lights and flashing neon. There are more than 300 restaurants and over 50 nightclubs.

West of Playa del Inglés the beach undulates into the Dunas de Maspalomas. A pleasant contrast to the hectic surrounding resorts, these dunes form a protected nature reserve. Their western edge (marked by a lighthouse) is occupied by a cluster of luxury hotels. Just behind the dunes lies a golf course encircled by bungalow estates.

Everything is laid on for the package holiday: water sports, excursions, fast food, as well as go-karts, camel safaris and funfairs. Best of these include **Palmitos Park**, with exotic birds in subtropical gardens, and **Sioux City**, a fun-packed Western theme park.

🏞 **Palmitos Park**
Barranco de los Palmitos. **Tel** 928 79 70 70. **Open** daily. 🚻 ♿
W palmitospark.es

🏞 **Sioux City**
Cañón del Águila. **Tel** 928 76 25 73. **Open** Tue–Sun. 🚻 ♿
W siouxcitypark.es

⓯ Agaete

Las Palmas 🚌 5,600. 🚉 Avenida Senora de las Nieves 1, 928 55 43 82. 🎉 Fiesta de las Nieves (5 Aug).
W agaete.es

The cloudier northern side of the island is far greener and lusher than the arid south, and banana plantations take up most of the coastal slopes. Agaete, on the northwest coast,

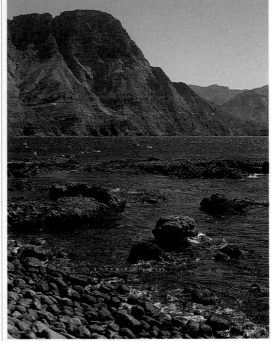

The rocky shore and steep cliffs of the northeast coast near Agaete

a pretty scatter of white houses around a striking rocky bay, is growing into a small resort. Every August, Agaete holds the Fiesta de la Rama, a Guanche *(see p551)* rainmaking ritual which dates from long before the arrival of the Spanish. An animated procession of villagers bearing green branches heads from the hills above the town down to the coast and into the sea. The villagers beat the water to summon the rain.

The Ermita de las Nieves contains a 16th-century Flemish triptych and model sailing ships. Close by is the **Huerto de las Flores**, a botanical garden.

Environs

A brief detour inland up along the Barranco de Agaete takes you through a fertile valley of papaya, mango and citrus trees. North of Agaete are the towns of Guía and Gáldar. Though there is little to see here, both parish churches do contain examples of the religious statuary of the celebrated 18th-century sculptor, José Luján Pérez.

Nearby, towards the north coast, lies the Cenobio de Valerón. One of the most dramatic of the local Guanche sights, this cliff-face is pock-marked with nearly 300 caves beneath a basalt arch. These are believed to have been hideaways for Guanche priest-esses, communal grain stores and refuges from attack.

🏛 **Huerto de las Flores**
Calle Huertas. **Tel** 680 70 02 01. **Open** Tue–Sat. 🚻 ♿ 📷

Miles of wind-sculptured sand: the dunes at Maspalomas

⓰ Tafira

Las Palmas. 🏘 23,000. 🚌 ℹ️ C/ Triana 93, Las Palmas, 928 21 96 00. 🎉 San Francisco (Oct). **W** **grancanaria.com**

The hills southwest of Las Palmas have long been desirable residential locations. A colonial air still wafts around Tafira's patrician villas. The **Jardín Canario**, a botanical garden founded in 1952, is the main reason for a visit. Plants from all of the Canary Islands can be studied in their own, re-created habitats.

Near La Atalaya lies one of Gran Canaria's most impressive natural sights – the Caldera de la Bandama. This is a volcanic crater 1,000 m (3,300 ft) wide, best seen from the Mirador de Bandama where you gaze down into the green depression about 200 m (660 ft) deep. Some of the inhabited caves in the Barranco de Guayadeque, a valley of red rocks to the south, were dug in the late 15th century. A few of them have electricity.

🪴 **Jardín Canario**
Carretera de Dragonal, km 7, Tafira.
Tel 928 21 95 80. **Open** daily.
Closed 1 Jan, Good Fri, 25 Dec.
&♿ **W** **jardincanario.org**

⓱ Las Palmas de Gran Canaria

Las Palmas. 🏘 378,000. 🚌 ⛴ ℹ️ C/ Triana 93, 928 21 96 00. 🎉 Carnival (Feb/Mar). **W** **grancanaria.com**

Las Palmas is the largest city in the Canary Islands. A bustling seaport and industrial city, it sees 1,000 ships docking each month.

Palm trees in a natural setting in the Jardín Canario, Tafira

Las Palmas has faded somewhat from the days when wealthy convalescents flocked here in winter and glamorous liners called in on transatlantic voyages. But it remains a vibrant place to visit.

Las Palmas is a sprawling city built around an isthmus. The modern commercial shipping area, Puerto de la Luz, takes up the eastern side of the isthmus, which leads to the former island of La Isleta, a sailors' and military quarter. On the other side of the isthmus is the crowded Playa de las Canteras, a 3-km- (2-mile-) long stretch of golden beach. The promenade behind has been built up with bars, restaurants and hotels.

The town centre stretches along the coast from the isthmus. For a scenic tour, begin in the Parque Santa Catalina, near the port. This is a popular, shady square of cafés and newspaper kiosks. In the leafy residential quarter of Ciudad Jardín are

the Parque Doramas and the traditional casino hotel of Santa Catalina.

The Pueblo Canario is a tourist enclave where visitors can watch folk dancing, and browse in the craft shops and the small art gallery. All this can be viewed from above by walking uphill towards the Altavista district and the Paseo Cornisa.

At the end of town is the Barrio Vegueta, an atmospheric quarter which dates back to the Spanish conquest. At its heart stands the Catedral de Santa Ana, begun in 1500. The adjacent **Museo Diocesano de Arte Sacro** contains works of religious art. The square in front is guarded by Canarian dogs in bronze.

Nearby, the **Casa de Colón** is a 15th-century governor's residence where Columbus stayed. A museum dedicated to his voyages displays charts, models and diary extracts.

Early history can be seen in the **Museo Canario**, which contains Guanche mummies, skulls, pottery and jewellery.

Bronze dog at Plaza Santa Ana

🏛 **Museo Diocesano de Arte Sacro**
Calle Espíritu Santo 20.
Tel 928 31 49 89. **Open** Mon–Sat. 🖼

🏠 **Casa de Colón**
Calle Colón 1. **Tel** 928 31 23 73. **Open** daily. **Closed** 1 Jan, 24, 25 & 31 Dec. 🖼

🏛 **Museo Canario**
Calle Doctor Verneau 2. **Tel** 928 33 68 00. **Open** daily. **Closed** 1 Jan, 25 Dec.
🖼 📷 **W** **elmuseocanario.com**

The Casa de Colón museum, Las Palmas, dedicated to Columbus

For hotels and restaurants in this region see p575 and pp604–5

⑱ Tour of Cruz de Tejeda

Gran Canaria's mountainous interior makes for an ideal day tour, from any part of the island. Choose a fine day or the views may be obscured. The route from Maspalomas leads through dry ravines of bare rock and cacti, becoming more fertile with altitude. Roads near the central highlands snake steeply through shattered, tawny crags, past caves and pretty villages to panoramic viewpoints from which you can see Mount Teide *(see pp542–3)* on Tenerife. On the north side, the slopes are much lusher, growing citrus fruits and eucalyptus trees.

White farmhouses en route to Teror

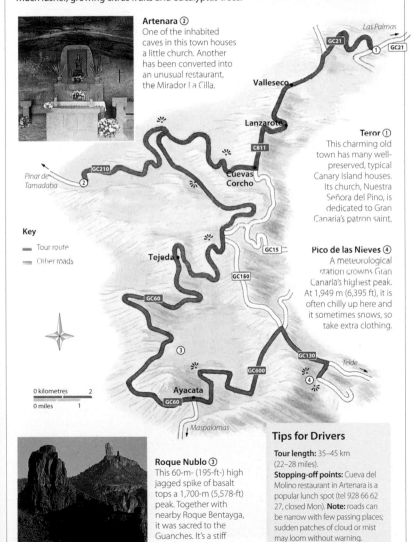

Artenara ②
One of the inhabited caves in this town houses a little church. Another has been converted into an unusual restaurant, the Mirador La Cilla.

Teror ①
This charming old town has many well-preserved, typical Canary Island houses. Its church, Nuestra Señora del Pino, is dedicated to Gran Canaria's patron saint.

Pico de las Nieves ④
A meteorological station crowns Gran Canaria's highest peak. At 1,949 m (6,395 ft), it is often chilly up here and it sometimes snows, so take extra clothing.

Roque Nublo ③
This 60-m- (195-ft-) high jagged spike of basalt tops a 1,700-m (5,578-ft) peak. Together with nearby Roque Bentayga, it was sacred to the Guanches. It's a stiff climb to the summit.

Key
━━━ Tour route
━━━ Other roads

0 kilometres 2
0 miles 1

Tips for Drivers

Tour length: 35–45 km (22–28 miles).
Stopping-off points: Cueva del Molino restaurant in Artenara is a popular lunch spot (tel 928 66 62 27, closed Mon). **Note:** roads can be narrow with few passing places; sudden patches of cloud or mist may loom without warning.

For keys to symbols *see back flap*

Fuerteventura

Lying just 100 km (60 miles) off the Atlantic coast of Morocco, leaf-shaped Fuerteventura is continually battered by coastal winds – no doubt why every summer the island hosts the Windsurfing & Kiteboarding World Cup. It is the second largest of the Canary Islands after Tenerife, and the most sparsely populated: its 69,500 inhabitants are outnumbered by goats. The island used to be densely wooded, but European settlers cut down the timber for ship-building; the dry climate (so dry, water has to be shipped over from the mainland) and the goats have since reduced the vegetation to parched scrub. The only significant revenue is tourism, with visitors having more than 150 splendid beaches to choose from. The island is popular with water-sports fans and naturists alike.

A herd of goats near the airport on Fuerteventura

⑲ Península de Jandía

Las Palmas. 🚌 Costa Calma, Morro Jable. 🚢 (jetfoil) from Gran Canaria. 🛈 Centro Comercial Cosmo, Bajo, 928 54 07 76.

Excellent beaches of pale sand fringe the Jandía Peninsula in the south of Fuerteventura. A string of *urbanizaciones* (residential developments) now takes up much of the peninsula's sheltered east coast (Sotavento).

Costa Calma, a burgeoning cluster of modern complexes, offers the most interesting beaches with long stretches of fine sand interrupted by low cliffs and coves. Morro Jable, a fishing village now swamped by new developments, lies at the southern end of a vast, glittering strand. Beyond Morro Jable, the access road dwindles away into a potholed track leading towards the lonely lighthouse at Punta de Jandía.

Expanses of deserted sand, accessible only by four-wheel drive vehicle, line the westerly, windward coast (Barlovento) – too exposed for all but the hardiest beach-lovers. Some of the island's best subtropical marine life can be found in this area, however, making it popular with skin divers.

From 1938 to the early 1960s, Jandía belonged to a German entrepreneur and was out of bounds to locals. Even today, rumours of spies, submarines and secret Nazi bases still circulate.

⑳ Betancuria

Las Palmas. 🚹 740. 🚌 🛈 Calle Juan de Bethancourt 6, 928 87 80 92. 🎉 San Buenaventura (14 Jul), Romería de La Peña (3rd Sat of Sep).

Inland, rugged peaks of extinct volcanoes, separated by wide plains, present a scene of austere grandeur. Scattered, stark villages and obsolete windmills occupy the lowlands, which are occasionally fertile enough to nurture a few crops or palm trees. Beyond, devoid of vegetation, the hills form stark outlines. From a distance they appear brown and grey, but up close the rocks glow with an astonishing range of mauves,

The gilded interior of the Iglesia Santa María in Betancuria

pinks and ochres. The richness of colour in this interior wilderness is at its most striking at sunset.

Betancuria, built in a valley surrounded by mountains in the centre of the island, is named after Jean de Béthencourt, Fuerteventura's 15th-century conqueror, who moved his capital inland to thwart pirates. Nestling in the mountains, this peaceful oasis is now the island's prettiest village. The Iglesia de Santa María contains gilded altars, decorated beams and sacred relics. The **Museo Arqueológico** houses many local artifacts.

Environs

To the south, the village of Pájara boasts a 17th-century church with a curiously decorated doorway. Its design of serpents and strange beasts is believed to be of Aztec influence. Inside, the twin aisles both contain statues: one of a radiant Madonna and Child in white and silver, the other a Virgen de los Dolores in black.

La Oliva, to the north, was the site of the Spanish military headquarters until the 19th-century. The Casa de los Coroneles (House of the Colonels) is a faded yellow mansion with a grand façade and hundreds of windows. Inside it has coffered ceilings. The fortified church and the arts centre displaying works of Canary Island artists are also worth a visit.

🏛 **Museo Arqueológico**
Calle Roberto Roldán. **Tel** 928 85 14 00. **Open** Tue–Sat. 🅿 ♿

㉑ Caleta de Fuste

Las Palmas. 🗻 1,600. 🚌 ℹ️ Calle Juan Ramón Soto Morales 10, El Castillo, 928 16 32 86. 🚢 Sat. 🎉 Día del Carmen (16 Jul), Nuestra Señora de Antigua (8 Sep).

South of Puerto del Rosario about halfway down the eastern coast, lies Caleta de Fuste. The attractive low-rise, self-catering holiday centres surround a horseshoe bay of soft, gently shelving sand. The largest complex, El Castillo, takes its name from an 18th-century watchtower situated by the harbour.

There are many water-sports facilities, including diving and windsurfing schools, as well as the Pueblo Majorero, an attractive "village" of shops and restaurants around a central plaza near the beach. These features make Caleta de Fuste one of Fuerteventura's most relaxed and pleasant resorts.

Fishing boats on a beach on the Isla de Lobos, near Corralejo

㉒ Puerto del Rosario

Las Palmas. 🗻 16,500. 🚢 🚌 🚌 ℹ️ Avenida Marítima s/n, 928 85 01 10. 🎉 El Rosario (7 Oct). 🌐 **turismo-puertodelrosario.org**

Fuerteventura's administrative capital was founded in 1797. Originally known as Puerto de Cabras (Goats' Harbour), after a nearby gorge that was once used for watering goats, it was rechristened to smarten up its image in 1957. The only large port on Fuerteventura, Puerto del Rosario is the base for inter-island ferries and a busy fishing industry. The town is also enlivened by the presence of the Spanish army, which occupies large barracks once used by the Spanish Foreign Legion.

㉓ Corralejo

Las Palmas. 🗻 7,200. 🚌 ℹ️ Avenida Marítima 16, 928 86 62 35. 🚢 Mon & Fri. 🎉 Día del Carmen (16 Jul). 🌐 **corralejograndesplayas.com**

This much-expanded fishing village is now (together with the Jandía Peninsula) one of the island's two most important resorts. Its main attraction is a belt of glorious sand dunes stretching to the south, resembling the Sahara in places, and protected as a nature reserve – a designation that arrived too late to prevent the construction of two hotels right on the beach.

The rest of the resort, mostly consisting of apartments and hotels, spills out from the town centre. The port area is lively, with busy fish restaurants and an efficient 40-minute ferry service to Lanzarote.

Offshore is the tiny Isla de Lobos, named after the once abundant monk seals (*lobos marinos*). Today, scuba divers, snorkellers, sport fishers and surfers claim the clear waters. Glass-bottomed cruise boats take less adventurous excursionists to the island for barbecues and swimming trips.

The Guanches

When Europeans first arrived in the Canary Islands in the late 14th century, they discovered a tall, white-skinned race, who lived in caves and later in small settlements around the edges of barren lava fields. Guanche was the name of one tribe on Tenerife, but it came to be used as the European name for all the indigenous tribes on the islands, and it is the one that has remained. The origins of the Guanches are still unclear, but it is probable that they arrived on the islands in the 1st or 2nd century BC from Berber North Africa. Within 100 years of European arrival the Guanches had been subdued and virtually exterminated by the ruthless conquistadors. Very few traces of their culture remain today.

Reminders of the Guanches can be seen in many places in the Canaries. Specimens of their mummified dead, as well as baskets and stone and bone artifacts, are on display in several museums and there are statues of chiefs in Candelaria (*see p539*) on Tenerife.

Guanche bowl for preparing *gofio (see p541)*

A Guanche basket

Lanzarote

The easternmost and fourth largest of the Canary Islands is virtually treeless and relies on desalination plants for some of its water. Yet many visitors consider Lanzarote the most attractive of all the islands for the vivid shapes and contrasting colours of its volcanic landscapes. Despite low rainfall, carefully tended crops flourish in its black volcanic soil. Locals pride themselves on the way their island has been preserved from the worst effects of tourism; there are no garish billboards, overhead cables or high-rise buildings. Its present-day image owes much to the artist César Manrique. Touring the spectacular volcanic Timanfaya National Park is a favourite trip.

Wind turbines harnessing Lanzarote's winds for power

㉔ Playa Blanca

Las Palmas. ⛰ 4,500. 🚍 ⛴ 🛈 Calle Varadero 3, 928 51 90 18. 🎉 Nuestra Señora del Carmen (16 Jul).
🌐 **turismolanzarote.com**

The fishing village origins of this resort are readily apparent around its harbour. Although it has expanded in recent years, Playa Blanca remains an agreeably

Las Coloradas beach near Playa Blanca in southern Lanzarote

family-oriented place with some character. It has plenty of cafés and restaurants, shops and bars, and several large hotels. However, the buildings are well dispersed and the resort is rarely noisy at night. Visitors converge here not for nightlife or contrived entertainment, but for relaxing beach holidays. There are one or two good stretches of sand near to the town, but the most enticing lie hidden around the rocky headlands to the east, where

the clear, warm sea laps into rocky coves, and clothes seem superfluous. Playa de Papagayo is the best known of these, but a diligent search will probably gain you one all to yourself. A four-wheel-drive vehicle is advisable to negotiate the narrow, unsurfaced roads which lead to these beaches.

The underwater **Museo Atlántico** combines art and conservation. Jason deCaires Taylor's dramatic installations act as an artificial reef, and visitors share the statues with banks of sardines and octopuses.

🏛 **Museo Atlántico**
Puerto Marina Rubicón, Calle el Berrugo 2. **Tel** 928 51 73 88. **Open** 10am–5pm Mon–Fri (diving: to 4pm).
📷 🌐 **cactlanzarote.com/cact/ museo-atlantico/**

㉕ Parque Nacional de Timanfaya

Las Palmas Yaiza. 🛈 Carretera LZ–67, km 11.5, Mancha Blanca, 928 11 80 42. **Open** daily. 📷

From 1730 to 1736, a series of volcanic eruptions took place on Lanzarote. Eleven villages were buried in lava, which eventually spread over 200 sq km (77 sq miles) of Lanzarote's most fertile land. Miraculously, no one was killed, though many islanders emigrated.

Today, the volcanoes that once devastated Lanzarote provide one of its most lucrative and enigmatic attractions, aptly known as the Montañas del

César Manrique (1919–92)

Local hero César Manrique trained as a painter, and spent time in mainland Spain and New York before returning to Lanzarote in 1968. He campaigned for traditional and environmentally friendly development on the island for the remaining part of his life, setting strict building height limits and colour requirements. Dozens of tourist sites throughout the Canaries benefited from his talents and enthusiasm.

César Manrique in 1992

For hotels and restaurants in this region see p575 and pp604–5

The dramatic volcanic landscape of the Parque Nacional de Timanfaya

Fuego (Fire Mountains). They are part of the Parque Nacional de Timanfaya, established in 1974 to protect a fascinating and important geological record. The entrance to the park lies just north of the small village of Yaiza. Here you can pause and take a 15-minute camel ride up the volcanic slopes for wonderful views across the park. Afterwards, you pay the entrance fee and drive through haunting scenery of dark, barren lava cinders topped by brooding red-black volcano cones. Finally, you will reach Islote de Hilario. You can park at El Diablo panoramic restaurant. From here, buses take visitors for exhilarating 30-minute tours of the desolate, lunar-like landscapes.

Afterwards, back at Islote de Hilario, guides will provide graphic demonstrations that this volcano is not extinct, but only dormant – brushwood pushed into a crevice bursts instantly into a ball of flame, while water poured into a sunken pipe shoots out in a scorching jet of steam.

The road from Yaiza to the coast leads to the Salinas de Janubio, where salt is extracted from the sea. At Los Hervideros the rough coast can create spectacular seas and further north, at El Golfo, is an eerie emerald-coloured lagoon.

㉖ Puerto del Carmen

Las Palmas. 🏔 13,700. 🚌 🚢
ℹ️ Avenida de la Playa, 928 51 33 51.
🎭 Nuestra Señora del Carmen (16 Jul). 🟥 turismolanzarote.com

More than 60 per cent of Lanzarote's tourists stay in this resort, which stretches several kilometres along the seafront. The coastal road carves its way through a solid slab of holiday infrastructure, which is pleasantly designed and unoppressive, and offers easy access to a long golden beach, Playa Blanca, which in places is very wide. Another beach nearby is Playa de los Pocillos. To the north is the quaint village of Tías and A Casa José Saramago, the house-cum-museum where the Nobel Prize-winning writer (1922–2010) lived his last 18 years in exile after the Portu-guese government deemed his work religiously offensive.

㉗ Arrecife

Las Palmas. 🏔 46,900. ✈️ 🚌
ℹ️ Calle Triana 38, 928 81 17 62.
🎭 San Ginés (25 Aug).
🟥 turismolanzarote.com

Arrecife, with its modern buildings and lively streets, is the commercial and administrative centre of the island. Despite its modern trappings, the capital retains much of its old charm, with palm-lined promenades, a fine beach and two small forts. **Castillo San Gabriel** offers lovely views from a mezzanine, accessed via a stone walkway over the sea, crossing the Puente de Bolas. It also houses the Museo de Historia de Arrecife. The 18th-century **Castillo de San José** is now a museum of contemporary art and was renovated faithfully to the original interior by César Manrique. One of his paintings is on display here.

🏠 **Castillo San Gabriel**
Puerto de Naos. **Tel** 928 80 28 84.
Open 9am–1pm Mon–Fri.

🏠 **Castillo de San José**
Puerto de Naos. **Tel** 928 81 23 21.
Open daily. **Closed** 1 Jan, 25 Dec.

㉘ Costa Teguise

10 km (6 miles) north of Arrecife.
🚌 ℹ️ Avenida Islas Canarias, Junto Pueblo Marinero, 928 59 25 42.
🟥 turismolanzarote.com

This resort, largely financed by a mining conglomerate, has transformed the arid, low-lying terrain north of Arrecife into an extensive cluster of time-share accommodation, leisure clubs and luxury hotels. The contrast between old town Teguise (see p554), Lanzarote's former capital, and the exclusive Costa Teguise is striking. Fake greenery and suburban lamps line boulevards amid barren ashlands. White villas line a series of small sandy beaches. The high level of investment has succeeded in attracting jet-set clientele. King Juan Carlos also has a villa here.

Umbrellas on the beach, Puerto del Carmen

Iglesia de San Miguel on the main square in Teguise

㉙ Teguise

Las Palmas. 🏔 12,300. 🚌 ℹ️ Plaza de la Constitución, 928 84 53 98. 🚍 Sun. 🎭 Día del Carmen (16 Jul), Las Nieves (5 Aug). 🌐 **turismolanzarote.com**

Teguise, the island's capital until 1852, is a well-kept, old-fashioned town with wide, cobbled streets and patrician houses grouped around the Iglesia de San Miguel. Visit on a Sunday, when there is a handicrafts market and folk dancing. Outside Teguise, in the castle of Santa Bárbara is the **Museo de la Piratería**, which tells the story of the pirates who passed through here.

Environs
To see more of inland Lanzarote, follow the central road south of Teguise, through the strange farmland of La Geria. Black volcanic ash has been scooped into protective, crescent-shaped pits which trap moisture to enable vines and other crops to flourish. Mozaga, one of the main villages in the area, is a major centre of wine production.

On the roadside near Mozaga is the *Monumento al Campesino*, Manrique's *(see p552)* striking modern sculpture dedicated to Lanzarote's farmers.

Between Teguise and Arrecife is the **Fundación César Manrique**. The former home of the artist incorporates five lava caves, some of his own work and his contemporary art collection.

🏛 **Museo de la Piratería**
Montaña de Guanapay. **Tel** 928 84 50 01. **Open** daily. **Closed** 1 & 6 Jan, 25 Dec. 🚗 🌐 **museodelapirateria.com**

🏛 **Fundación César Manrique**
Taro de Tahíche. **Tel** 928 84 31 38. **Open** daily. **Closed** 1 Jan. 🚗
🌐 **fcmanrique.org**

㉚ Haría

Las Palmas. 🏔 4,000. 🚌 ℹ️ Plaza de la Constitución 1, 928 83 52 51. 🚍 Sat. 🎭 San Juan (24 Jun). 🌐 **turismolanzarote.com**

Palm trees and white, cube-shaped houses distinguish this picturesque village. It acts as a gateway to excursions round the northern tip of the island. The road to the north gives memorable views over exposed cliffs, and the 609-m- (2,000-ft-) high Monte Corona.

Environs
From Manrique's **Mirador del Río** you can see La Graciosa, and the northernmost of the Canary Islands, Alegranza. Orzola is a delightful fishing village providing fish lunches as well as boat trips to La Graciosa. To the south are the Mala prickly pear plantations, where cochineal (crimson dye) is extracted from the insects which feed on the

plants. Nearby is the **Jardín de Cactus**, a well-stocked cactus garden with a smart restaurant, again designed by Manrique.

🗼 **Mirador del Río**
Haría. **Tel** 928 52 65 48. **Open** daily. 🚗
🌵 **Jardín de Cactus**
Guatiza. **Tel** 928 52 93 97. **Open** daily. 🚗

Landscaped pool on top of the caves of Jameos del Agua

㉛ Jameos del Agua

Las Palmas. **Tel** 928 84 80 20. **Open** daily. 🚗

An eruption of the Monte Corona volcano formed the Jameos del Agua lava caves on Lanzarote's northeast coast. In 1965–8, these were landscaped by César Manrique into an imaginative subterranean complex containing a restaurant, night-club, a swimming pool edged by palm trees, and gardens of oleander and cacti. Steps lead to a shallow seawater lagoon where a rare species of blind white crab, unique to Lanzarote, glows softly in the dim light. An exhibition on volcanology and Canarian flora and fauna also deserves a look. Folk-dancing evenings are regularly held in this unusual setting.

Environs
Another popular attraction is the nearby **Cueva de los Verdes**, a tube of solidified lava stretching 6 km (4 miles) underground. Guided tours of the caves are available.

🕳 **Cueva de los Verdes**
Haría. **Tel** 928 84 84 84. **Open** daily. 🚗

Volcanic ash swept into crescent-shaped pits for farming, La Geria

Volcanic Islands

The volcanic activity which formed the Canary Islands has created a variety of scenery, from distinctive lava formations to enormous volcanoes crowned by huge, gaping craters. The islands are all at different stages in their evolution. Tenerife, Lanzarote, El Hierro and La Palma are still volcanically active; dramatic displays of flames and steam can be seen in Lanzarote's Montañas de Fuego *(see p552)*. The last eruption was on La Palma in 1971.

Origin of the Islands

The Canaries are situated above faults in the earth's crust, which is always thinner under the oceans than under the continents. When magma (molten rock) rises through these cracks, volcanoes are formed.

Atlantic Ocean — Transform fault — Atlas Fault — Canary Islands — Thin oceanic crust — Upper mantle — Dense lower mantle — Thick continental crust — Africa — Continental mantle between crust and earth's core

Evolution of the Canary Islands

Fissures — Feeder dykes — Basalt lava flows — Crust — Mantle — Magma chamber

1 **Lanzarote, El Hierro and La Palma** are wide, gently sloping shield volcanoes standing on the sea floor. All of them are composed of basalt formed by a hot, dense magma. The flexible crust is pressed down by the weight of the islands.

Caldera — Shallow magma chamber

2 **An explosive eruption** can empty the magma chamber, leaving the roof unsupported. This collapses under the weight of the volcano above to form a depression, or caldera, such as Las Cañadas on Tenerife. There are thick lava flows during this stage of the island's evolution.

Sea level — Exposed solidified magma chamber

3 **If eruptions cease**, a volcano will be eroded by the action of the sea, and by wind and rain. Gran Canaria's main volcano is in the early stages of erosion, while the volcano on Fuerteventura has already been deeply eroded, exposing chambers of solidified magma.

Rope lava near La Restinga, El Hierro *(see pp536–7)*

Pico Viejo crater, next to Mount Teide, Tenerife *(see p542)*

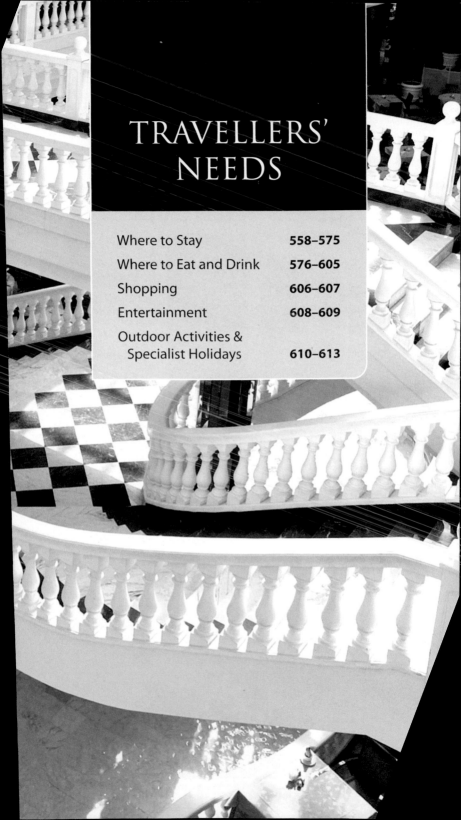

TRAVELLERS' NEEDS

WHERE TO STAY

Luxury hotels set in medieval castles, mansions converted into youth hostels, designer B&Bs in the heart of buzzing cities – there is a huge range of places to stay in Spain. The country has some 10,000 establishments and over one and a half million beds to choose from; it's no wonder that tourism sustain's Spain's economy. Suites in once-royal palaces are at the top of the scale and then there are luxury beach hotels on the Costa del Sol and in the Balearic and the Canary Islands. Visitors can stay on remote farms, or in old, self-catered villas. For budget travel there are pensions, family-run *casas rurales*, guesthouses and camp sites, as well as refuges with stunning views for mountaineers. Some of the best hotels in all these categories and in every style and price range are listed on pages 562–75.

Entrance to Taberna del Alabardero in Seville *(see p571)*

Hotel Grading and Facilities

Spain's hotels are classified into categories and awarded stars by the regional tourist authorities. Hotels (indicated by an H on a plaque near the door) have one to five stars. *Hostales* (Hs) and *pensiones* (P) are cheaper than hotels, offer fewer comforts, and have one to three stars. A *pensión* that is not good enough to be awarded a star is known as a *casa de huéspedes* (guesthouse).

Spain's star-rating system reflects the range of facilities available rather than the quality of service. Most hotels have air-conditioning, and many provide amenities like internet access or restaurant offering local fare. ~~o~~st hotel restaurants are open ~~n~~on-residents. *Hotel-residencias* ~~~~and *hostal-residencias* (HsR) ~~~~t have dining rooms, but ~~~~erve breakfast. Among ~~~~argest hotel chains are ~~~~**tels International**, ~~~~and **NH-Hotels**. Tour ~~~~ften book rooms ~~~~ger hotel groups.

Paradors

Paradors are government-run hotels, classified from three to five stars. Spain's first parador opened in the Sierra de Gredos in 1928; there is now a wide network of over 90, on the mainland and the Canary Islands. Most, and certainly the most historic, are located in the centre and the north of the mainland. The best are in former royal hunting lodges, castles, monasteries and other monuments; some modern paradors have been purpose-built, often in spectacular scenery or in towns of historic interest.

A parador is not necessarily the best hotel in town, but it can be counted on to deliver a high level of comfort and service. Each is furnished in its own individual style, and has a restaurant offering regional cuisine. They are generally well signposted.

If you plan to tour in high season or to stay in the smaller paradors, be sure to reserve in advance. The paradors may be booked through the **Central de Reservas** or through London agent **Keytel International**.

Prices

Spanish law requires all hotels to display their prices behind the reception and in each room. As a rule, the higher a hotel's star rating, the more you pay. Rates for a double room can be as little as €35–50 a night for a one-star *hostal*; a five-star hotel will cost more than €275 a night, but a room price higher than €350 a night is rare, especially outside Madrid or Barcelona.

Prices usually vary according to room, region and season. A suite or a room with a view, a balcony or other special feature may cost more than average. Rural and suburban hotels tend to be less expensive than those in the city centre. All the prices on pages 562–75 are based on mid- or high-season rates. High season covers July and August, Easter and the Christmas period, but in some areas it runs from April to October. In the Canary Islands the winter is high season.

A parador within a modern extension of a medieval castle

and-white floor and sweeping staircase at a luxury hotel in Tenerife

Many of Spain's city hotels charge especially inflated rates for their rooms during major fiestas such as the April Fair in Seville (see p435), Los Sanfermines in Pamplona (see p136), Carnival in Santa Cruz de Tenerife (see p540) and Easter Week (see p42) – and major trade fairs.

Most hotels quote prices per room and meal prices or per person without including VAT (IVA), which is 10 per cent off the mainland and 5 per cent on the Canary Islands.

Stylish lounge area at Hotel Arts, Barcelona (see p565)

Booking and Check-in

During the off-season period, especially in rural or small towns, there is no real need to book ahead; but if you plan to travel in high season, you should reserve a room in advance. You will need to reserve if you want a special room: one with a double bed (twin beds are the norm); on the ground floor; away from a noisy main road; or a room with a view.

The resort hotels often close from autumn to spring. It is advisable to check ahead that your preferred hotels will be open at that time of year.

You will normally be asked for your credit card details when you book a room. A deposit of 20–25 per cent may be requested if you book during a peak period or for a stay of more than a few nights. Send it by credit card or giro in Spain

and by credit card or banker's draft from outside the country. If you have to cancel, do so at least a week before the booking date or you may lose all or some of the deposit.

In most cases hotels will honour a booking only until 8pm unless business is poor. If you are delayed, call the hotel to assure them you are coming and to tell them when to expect you.

When you check in to a hotel you will be asked for your passport or identity card to comply with Spanish police regulations. It will normally be returned to you promptly as soon as your details have been copied.

You are expected to check out of your room by noon on the last day of your stay, or to pay for another night.

Paying

Most hotels accept major credit cards. In some large, busy hotels you may be asked for an authorization hold on your credit card until you check out. Make sure this is cancelled when you pay your bill.

Personal and travellers' cheques are not accepted in almost all Spanish hotels, even if backed by a cheque guarantee card or drawn on a Spanish bank. Many people pay cash, and in some cheap hotels this may be the only mode of payment accepted.

Tipping hotel staff such as porters and cleaners is left to the discretion of the guests.

View over the palm-lined pool of a Lanzarote hotel, with the beach beyond

Casas Rurales

The owners of some casas rurales (country houses) accept a few visitors, usually in high season. They are most numerous in Asturias, Navarra, Aragón and Cataluña (where they are called cases de pagès). They are also becoming common in Galicia and Cantabria (where they are called casonas), and in Andalucía.

Casas rurales range from manor houses to small, isolated farms. Some offer bed and breakfast; some an evening meal or full board; and others are self-catering. Do not expect hotel service or lots of facilities. You may, however, be given a friendly welcome and good home cooking, all at an affordable price. You can book casas rurales directly or through regional associations, such as **RAAR** in Andalucía, **Ruralia** in Asturias, **Turismo Verde** in Huesca, Aragón, **Ruralverd** in Catalonia and **AGATUR** (Asociación Gallega de Turismo Rural) in Galicia.

Agroturisme Biniatram in Menorca, offering rooms in converted farm

Self-catering and B&Bs

Villas and holiday flats let by the week are plentiful along the coasts, and on the rise in the cities. In the countryside there are many *casas rurales* (farm and village houses) for rent by the day. For information about the *casas rurales* and bookings, contact their regional organizations *(see p559)*. In the UK, **Villas 4 You** acts as an agent for owners of holiday houses and flats in Spain, as does **International Lodging Corporation** in the US. There are more options in the travel sections of UK Sunday newspapers. Tour operators offer a range of self-catering accommodation.

The prices for self-catering accommodation vary according to the location, the property and the season. A four-person villa with a pool can cost under €350 for a week if it is inland and €1,200 a week or more if it is on the coast.

An apartment hotel (known as a *villa turística* in Andalucía) is another option. Half hotel, half holiday flat, it gives guests a choice between self-catering (all rooms have a kitchen) or eating in the hotel restaurant. Holiday villages are similar, often catering for specialist interests. One example is the village of Ainsa, in the mountain sports region of Aragón *(see p567)*, which offers a mix of camping and hostel accommodation, with restaurants and bars.

Although B&Bs are arguably not as popular in Spain as they are elsewhere in Europe, there are a number of guesthouse

Camping site close to the beach, in Miami Platja, Catalonia

options that are great for independent travellers. **HolidayLetting**, **HomeAway** and **Airbnb** all offer excellent websites for researching such options.

Youth Hostels and Mountain Refuges

To use the network of *albergues juveniles* (youth hostels) in Spain you need to show a YHA (Youth Hostel Association) card from your country or an international card, which you can buy from any hostel. Here, the prices per person for bed and breakfast are lower than hotel prices.

Youth hostels can be booked directly or via the **Red Española de Albergues Juveniles** (Spanish Network of Youth Hostels). Despite the name, there is no age limit.

Mountaineers heading for the more remote areas may use the *refugios* (refuges) – shelters with a dormitory, cooking facilities and heating. Some are huts with a few bunks; others are houses with up to 50 beds.

The *refugios* are marked on large-scale maps of mountain areas and national parks and administered by the regional mountaineering associations. The **Federación Española de Deportes de Montaña y Escalada** (FEDME) and the local tourist offices can supply their addresses.

Camp Sites

There are nearly 1,200 camp sites in Spain. Most are on the coasts, but some are also outside major cities, and in the popular countryside and mountain areas. Most have electricity and running water; some also have laundrettes, playgrounds, restaurants, shops or a pool. **Glamping Hub** offers a more upscale camping experience, with unparalleled access to nature. There is a variety of unique accommodation to choose from, including luxury treehouses, retro-style caravans, yurts, caves, tepees, eco-friendly domes, luxury tents and cabins all over Spain.

It is a good idea to carry a camping carnet with you. This can be used instead of a passport to check in at sites and it covers you for third-party insurance. Carnets are issued in the UK by the AA, RAC and the **Camping and Caravanning Club**.

Every year, the *Guía Oficial de Campings* is published by Turespaña. More details are also available from the **Federación Española de Empresarios de Campings y Parques de Vacaciones**. In Spain, camping is only permitted on official sites.

le on the edge of Cazorla nature reserve, Jaén

Monasteries and Convents

If you have a taste for peace and austerity you may enjoy a night in one of Spain's 150 religious houses where guests are welcome. Most belong to the Benedictine and the Cistercian orders. Room prices are inexpensive. They are not hotels, however; you have to book ahead by writing or by phone; and few have private telephones or televisions. The guests may be asked to tidy their rooms, observe the same strict mealtimes as the monks or nuns and to help with the washing up. Some convents admit only women and some monasteries only men.

Travellers with Disabilities

Hotel managers will advise on access for people in wheelchairs, and the staff will help, but few hotels are well equipped for disabled guests, although some of the youth hostels are. **COCEMFE** (the Confederación Coordinadora Estatal de Minusválidos Físicos de España) runs a hotel in Madrid for disabled people's groups. It also advises on hotels for guests with special needs. Accessible holidays can be booked through **Can Be Done**, which has a list of accommodation on the coast and Islands, including resorts and self-catering apartments.

Further Information

Turespaña (Spanish Tourist Office) has a useful website, which has a very comprehensive database of hotels, hostals, pensions and other accommodation in Spain. Bookings can be made via the website as well.

Recommended Hotels

The hotels listed on pages 562–75 cover a range of themes and price ranges. Hotels in the **luxury** category offer first-class amenities, excellent service and plush surrounds, while **boutique** establishments are usually small and independently run, with

Wrought-iron gates adorn the entrance to Hotel Alma, Barcelona

high-end design elements. **Historic** hotels promise a characterful stay in a building of note, and places listed under **Rooms with a view** boast stunning settings. Finally, **B&Bs** are guesthouses or inns, often with a hearty breakfast supplied.

Certain entries, marked as DK Choice, offer something extra special. They may be set in beautiful surroundings, a historic palace or in a converted farmhouse where you're treated like a member of the family. Common to all is a second-to-none quality of service and atmosphere.

DIRECTORY

Hotel Grading & Facilities

Grupo Riu
Tel 902 40 05 02.
w riu.com

Meliá Hotels International
Tel 91 276 47 47.
w melia.com

NH-Hoteles
Tel 91 398 44 38.
w nh-hotels.com

Paradors

Central de Reservas
José Abascal 2, 28003
Madrid. Tel 902 54 79 79.
w parador.es

Keytel International
w keytel.co.uk

Casa Rurales

AGATUR
Recinto Ferial, Apdo 26,
Silleda, 36540, Pontevedra.
Tel 986 57 70 00.
w agatur.org

RAAR
Sagunto 8, 04004,
Almería. Tel 902 44 22 33.
w raar.es

Ruralia
Calle Centro de Empresas,
oficina 3, 33500, Llanes
(Asturias).
Tel 902 10 70 70.
w ruralia.com

Ruralverd
Calle del Pí 11, Principal 8,
08002, Barcelona.
Tel 93 304 37 74.
w ruralverd.es

Turismo Verde
Calle Miguel Servet 12,
22002, Huesca. Tel 902 29
41 41, or 974 24 09 41.
w turismoverde.es

Self-catering and B&Bs

Airbnb
w airbnb.com

HolidayLettings
w holidaylettings.com

HomeAway
w homeaway.com

International Lodging Corporation
w ilcweb.com

Villas 4 You
Tel 0800 074 0122.
w villas4you.co.uk

Youth Hostels & Mountain Refuges

Federación Española de Deportes de Montaña y Escalada
Tel 93 426 42 67.
w fedme.es

Red Española de Albergues Juveniles
Tel 91 308 46 75.
w reaj.com

Camp Sites

Camping and Caravanning Club
Tel 024 7647 5426 in UK.
w campingand
caravanningclub.co.uk

Federación Española de Empresarios de Campings y Parques de Vacaciones
C/ Orense 32, entreplanta,
28020, Madrid.
Tel 914 48 12 34.
w fedcamping.com

Glamping Hub
w glampinghub.com

Travellers with Disabilities

Can Be Done
Congress House, 14 Lyon
Road, Harrow HA1 2EN,
UK. Tel 020 8907 2400.
w canbedone.co.uk

COCEMFE
C/ Luis Cabrera 63, 28002,
Madrid. Tel 917 44 36 00.
w cocemfe.es

Further Information

Turespaña
Tel 0207 317 2011 in UK.
Tel 212 265 8822 in US.
w spain.info

Where to Stay

Galicia

A CORUÑA: Hotel Melia Maria Pita €
Rooms with a View
Avenida Pedro Barrié de la Maza 1, 15003
Tel *981 20 50 00*
W melia.com
A family-friendly hotel with good service, kids' clubs and family suites. Beachfront location.

A CORUÑA: Hotel Hespería Finisterre €€
Luxury
Paseo del Parrote 2–4, 15001
Tel *981 20 54 00*
W hesperia.com
Harbour views and five-star facilities. An excellent base for exploring the area.

A GUARDA: Hotel Convento de San Benito €
Historic
Plaza San Benito s/n, 36780
Tel *986 61 11 66*
W hotelsanbenito.es
Delightful hotel set in a restored medieval convent with sea views. All the rooms are decorated with antiques, and guests can enjoy the collection of ancient books and manuscripts in the library. There is also a small museum.

BAIONA: Parador de Baiona €€
Historic
Rua Arquitecto Jesus Valverde, 36300
Tel *986 35 50 00*
W parador.es
This walled medieval fortress, not far from the Old Town, boasts a spectacular location, surrounded by the sea on three sides.

CAMBADOS: Parador de Cambados €€
Historic
Paseo Calzada s/n, 36630
Tel *986 54 22 50*
W parador.es
This elegant 17th-century mansion is a great base for exploring the lush landscapes of the Rías Baixas.

LUGO: Hotel Rústico Vila do Val €
Boutique
Praza Santa María 2, 27770, Ferreira do Valadouro
Tel *982 57 16 53*
W hotelviladoval.com
This charming, rustic hotel tucked away 20 minutes from the coast makes an excellent base for exploring the local surroundings.

OURENSE: Monasterio de Santo Estevo €
Historic
Monasterio de Santo Estevo s/n, 32162
Tel *988 01 01 10*
W parador.es
Modern comfort in a beautiful medieval parador set in a former monastery. The surrounding hills are ideal for hiking.

PONTEVEDRA: Balneario de Mondariz €€
Luxury
Avenida Enrique Peinador s/n, 36890
Tel *986 65 61 56*
W balneariomondariz.es
Housed in a traditional stone building, this hotel has a justly famous spa, plus kids' activities and a golf course. The hotel has always been a favourite with artists and politicians.

RIBADEO: Hotel Rolle €
Historic
Calle Ingeniero Schulz 9, 27700
Tel *982 12 06 70*
W hotelrolle.com
Set in an 18th-century town house, this hotel has charming, rustic rooms and friendly service.

SANTIAGO DE COMPOSTELA: San Miguel Hotel Gastronómico €
Rooms with a View
Praza de San Miguel dos Agros 9, 15704
Tel *981 55 57 79*
W sanmiguelsantiago.com
Views of the Old Town, chic rooms and an excellent restaurant are among the draws at this hotel, which offers a good combination of old and new. There is also a beautiful courtyard garden.

Monasterio de Santo Estevo in Ourense, boasting spectacular views

SANTIAGO DE COMPOSTELA: San Francisco Hotel Monumento €€
Historic
Campillo San Francisco 3, 15705
Tel *981 58 16 34*
W sanfranciscohm.com
Stylish, modern hotel set in a historic monastery. Indoor swimming pool and hot tub.

SANXENXO: Hotel Carlos I Silgar €€
Luxury
Calle Vigo s/n, 36960
Tel *986 72 70 36*
W hotelcarlos.es
Spa facilities, spacious rooms, a seafront location and impeccable service draw guests to this hotel in the centre of Sanxenxo.

DK Choice

VIGO: Gran Hotel Nagari €€
Boutique
Praza de Compostela 21, 36201
Tel *986 21 11 11*
W granhotelnagari.com
An extremely chic and luxurious hotel, with spacious, beautifully decorated rooms and all modern amenities. The spa offers a plethora of treatments to relax and indulge the senses.

Asturias and Cantabria

CABRANES: Hostería de Torazo €€€
Luxury
Plaza de la Sienra 1, Torazo, 33535
Tel *985 89 80 99*
W hosteriadetorazo.com
Modern hotel with a plush spa, comfortable rooms and a good restaurant. Set in a pretty, traditional village.

CANGAS DE ONÍS: Parador de Cangas de Onís €
Historic
Villanueva de Cangas, 33550
Tel *985 84 94 02*
W parador.es
There are beautiful views at this stunning 8th-century monastery on the banks of the River Sella.

COLUNGA: Palacio de Libardón €
Historic
Lugar Barrio de Arriba 197, 33325
Tel 605 81 63 87
w palaciodelibardon.com
A restored *palacio* with excellent
food and great mountain views.
Each room has a different décor.

**CUDILLERO: Hotel Casona
Selgas** €
Historic
Avenida Selgas s/n, 33154
Tel 985 59 05 48
w hotelcasonaselgas.com
A small, family-run hotel in a
traditional Asturian building
along the Pilgrim's Route, with
superb service and helpful hosts.

DK Choice

**FUENTE DÉ: Parador de
Fuente Dé** €
Historic
Barrio Espinama s/n, 39588
Tel 942 73 66 51
w parador.es
This parador has all the usual
high standards and amenities,
but it's the truly spectacular
setting, surrounded by the
mountains of the Picos de
Europa, that sets it apart. Explore
or simply marvel at the views.

GIJÓN: Hotel Hernán Cortes €
Historic
Fernandez Vallin 5, 33205
Tel 985 34 60 00
w hotelhernancortes.es
Comfortable rooms in a historic
casino building. Central location
near the beach, bars and shops.

**LLANES: Hotel Rural
Cuartamenteru** €
Rooms with a View
Barrio Anteji s/n, Poo de Llanes, 33509
Tel 985 40 32 76
w cuartamenteru.com
This hotel in a tranquil setting
near the beach boasts lovely
mountain views. Open Mar–Oct.

MIESES: Posada el Bosque €
Boutique
*Crta Monastero de Santo.
Toribio, 39586*
Tel 942 73 01 27
w posadaelbosque.com
This charming mountain hotel
with stunning views is the ideal
spot for a romantic getaway.

**OVIEDO: Castillo del Bosque
La Zoreda** €€
Luxury
*Bosque de La Zoreda s/n, 33170,
La Manjoya*
Tel 985 96 33 33
w castillodelbosquedelazoreda.com

Designer minimalism at Hotel Miró, Bilbao

Five-star luxury hotel housed in
a fabulous 20th-century palace
surrounded by beautiful gardens.

PECHÓN: Hotel Tinas €€
Boutique
Barrio Quintana 64, 39594
Tel 942 71 73 36
w tinasdepechon.com
The *Tinas* is a contemporary,
stylish hotel close to the beach.
All rooms have kitchenettes.

**RIBADESELLA: Hotel Villa
Rosario I** €€
Historic
Dionisio Ruizsánchez 6, 33560
Tel 985 86 00 90
w hotelvillarosario.com
Renovated palace on the seafront
at Ribadesella. Sea and mountain
views, and excellent facilities.

**SAN VICENTE DE LA BARQUERA:
Hotel Villa de San Vicente** €
Rooms with a View
Calle Fuente Nueva 1, 39540
Tel 942 71 21 38
w hotelvsvicente.com
Clean, cosy and quiet rooms in a
superb location, overlooking the
sea. Lovely views of the castle.

**SANTANDER: Hostal
Jardin Secreto** €
B&B
Calle Cardenal Cisneros 37, 39007
Tel 942 07 07 14
w jardinsecretosantander.com
Simple, tastefully decorated rooms,
with a garden on the terrace.

**SANTILLANA DEL MAR:
Hotel Casa del Marqués** €€
Historic
Calle del Cantón 26, 39330
Tel 942 81 88 88
w hotelcasadelmarques.com
Once home to the first Marqués
of Santillana del Mar, this 500-
year-old building is now a hotel.

The Basque Country, Navarra and La Rioja

**ANGUIANO: Abadía
de Valvanera** €
Historic
*Crta LR-435, km 24.6,
Monasterio de Valvanera*
Tel 941 37 70 44
w abadiavalvanera.com
Simple, understated rooms in an
old Benedictine abbey in the
beautiful Sierra de la Demanda.

BERA: Hotel Churrut €
Historic
Plaza de los Fueros 2, 31780
Tel 948 62 55 40
w hotelchurrut.com
A converted, restored 17th-
century home. Cosy and stylish.
Excellent restaurant.

BILBAO: Hotel Carlton €€
Historic
Plaza de Federico Moyúa 2, 48009
Tel 944 16 22 00
w hotelcarlton.es
This elegant 1926 hotel is a
city landmark. Rooms are
decorated in classical style.

BILBAO: Hotel Miró €€
Boutique
Alameda Mazarredo 77, 48009
Tel 946 61 18 80
w mirohotelbilbao.com
Designed by Antonio Miró, this
minimalist luxury hotel is close
to the Guggenheim Museum.

**BRIÑAS: Hospedería Señorío
de Briñas** €
Historic
Calle Señorío de Briñas 5, 2
Tel 941 30 42 24
w hotelesconencanto
A historic palace amid
wine country. Come
visits to the family-

For more information on types of

DONAMARÍA: Donmaria'ko Benta €
Inn
Barrio Ventas 4, 31750
Tel *948 45 07 08*
W donamariako.com
Family-run place in a 19th-century stone building with a traditional restaurant and garden views.

DK Choice
ELCIEGO: Hotel Marqés de Riscal €€€
Boutique
Calle Torrea 1, 01340
Tel *945 18 08 80*
W hotel-marquesderiscal.com
This stunning hotel combines avant-garde design with an unbeatable location in the heart of the Basque wine country. Indulge in grape-based spa treatments, relax on the rooftop lounge or take a winery tour.

GETARIA: Hotel Rural Gaintza €
B&B
Calle San Prudentzio Auzoa 26, 20808
Tel *943 14 00 32*
W txakoligaintza.com
Elegant, contemporary rooms in an old farmhouse with views of beautiful vineyards.

HARO: Los Agustinos €€
Historic
San Agustín 2, 26200
Tel *941 31 13 08*
W hotellosagustinos.com
This hotel was originally founded in 1373 as a convent. The rooms are set around impressive cloisters topped with a glass ceiling.

HONDARRIBIA: Parador de Hondarribia €€€
Historic
Plaza de Armas 14, 20280
Tel *943 64 55 00*
W parador.es
A 10th-century castle featuring original artifacts, courtyards and terraces. Impressive views as well.

LAGUARDIA: Hospedería Los Parajes €€
Boutique
Calle Mayor 46–48, 01300
Tel *945 62 11 30*
W hospederiadelosparajes.com
This 15th-century stylish hotel features a spa with *hammam*. Each room is uniquely decorated.

LEKEITIO: Hotel Zubieta €€
Historic
Atea s/n, 48280
Tel *946 84 30 30*
W hotelzubieta.com
A 17th-century country house on the outskirts of the town. Pretty rooms overlook the gardens.

LOGROÑO: Hotel Calle Mayor €
Historic
Marqués de San Nicolás 71, 26001
Tel *941 23 23 68*
W hotelcallemayor.com
A former 16th-century mansion, this urban hotel blends modern design within historic walls.

MUNDAKA: Atalaya Hotel €
B&B
Itxaropen Kalea 1, 48360
Tel *946 17 70 00*
W atalayahotel.es
Rooms with garden or sea views. A prime location for surfers and sun-worshippers.

OLITE: Parador de Olite €
Historic
Plaza de Teobaldos 2, 31390
Tel *948 74 00 00*
W parador.es
Set in a majestic 15th-century castle, this parador is a national monument. Classical interiors.

PAMPLONA: Pamplona Catedral Hotel €
Boutique
Calle Dos de Mayo 4, 31001
Tel *948 22 66 88*
W pamplonacatedralhotel.com
Designer rooms in a former convent by the cathedral, right in the historic centre. The hotel also features a trendy bar.

PAMPLONA: Gran Hotel La Perla €€€
Historic
Plaza del Castillo 1, 31001
Tel *948 22 30 00*
W granhotellaperla.com
Rooms have historical themes at this hotel, Ernest Hemingway's favourite Pamplona haunt.

RONCESVALLES: Hotel Roncesvalles €
Historic
Mayor s/n, 31650
Tel *948 76 01 05*
W hotelroncesvalles.com
Once a medieval hospital, this chic hotel now hosts many pilgrims of the Camino de Santiago.

SAN SEBASTIÁN: Aida €
B&B
Calle Iztueta 9, 20001
Tel *943 32 78 00*
W pensionesconencanto.com
In a charming old building, this guesthouse has cosy rooms and studios with kitchenettes.

SAN SEBASTIÁN: Hotel Maria Cristina €€€
Luxury
Paseo República Argentina 4, 20004
Tel *943 43 76 00*
W hotel-mariacristina.com
A five-star hotel decorated in *belle époque* style and known for its excellent service. River views.

SANTO DOMINGO DE LA CALZADA: Parador de Santo Domingo €
Historic
Plaza del Santo 3, 26250
Tel *941 34 03 00*
W parador.es
Dating from the 12th century, this parador was once a hospital for pilgrims on the Camino.

VITORIA: La Casa de los Arquillos €
Historic
Calle de Los Arquillos 1–2, 01001
Tel *945 15 12 59*
W lacasadelosarquillos.com
This 18th-century building was once a tailor's workshop. The rooms are bright and airy.

Barcelona
Old Town
Bonic Barcelona €
B&B **Map** 5 A3
Josep Anselm Clavé 9, 08002
Tel *626 05 34 34*
W bonic-barcelona.com
A charming little B&B in the Gothic Quarter, with delightful staff and thoughtful extras.

...on at Hotel Marqés de Riscal in Elciego

see page 562

Hotel Banys Orientals   €
Boutique   **Map** 5 B3
Carrer Argenteria 37, 08003
Tel *932 68 84 60*
w hotelbanysorientals.com
Stylish accommodation in a restored historic building, with a choice of rooms or suites.

Duquesa de Cardona   €€
Boutique   **Map** 5 A3
Passeig Colom 12, 08002
Tel *932 68 90 90*
w hduquesadecardona.com
Understated, classic hotel with a sublime roof terrace overlooking the yachts in the Port Vell.

Hotel Barcelona Catedral   €€
Boutique   **Map** 5 A2
Carrer Capellans 4, 08002
Tel *933 04 22 55*
w barcelonacatedral.com
Elegant rooms, and a panoramic roof terrace with a plunge pool. Efficient service.

Hotel España   €€
Historic   **Map** 2 F3
Sant Pau 9–11, 08001
Tel *935 50 00 00*
w hotelespanya.com
A restored 1859 gem with a great restaurant and bar containing murals by Domènech i Montaner (of Palau de la Música fame).

Hotel Yurbban   €€
Boutique   **Map** 5 B1
Carrer Trafalgar 30, 08010
Tel *932 68 07 27*
w yurbban.com
Chic, designer rooms, plus a rooftop sundeck and plunge pool. Guests enjoy complimentary wine and cheese at the daily "wine o'clock" sessions.

> ### DK Choice
>
> ### Hotel Mercer   €€€
> Luxury   **Map** 5 B3
> *Carrer Lledó 7, 08002*
> **Tel** *933 10 74 80*
> w mercerbarcelona.com
> Exclusive and intimate, this hotel occupies a sumptuous historic mansion which incorporates a section of ancient Roman walls. Behind the old façade is a sleek, contemporary interior as well as a roof terrace with plunge pool.

Hotel Neri   €€€
Boutique   **Map** 5 A2
Sant Sever 5, 08002
Tel *933 04 06 55*
w hotelneri.com
This enchanting hideaway is located in an 18th-century palace with a superb restaurant.

The stylish rooftop terrace with plunge pool at Hotel Mercer, Barcelona

Ohla   €€€
Luxury   **Map** 5 B1
Via Laietana 49, 08003
Tel *933 41 50 50*
w ohlahotel.com
A flamboyant five-star option, the Ohla boasts a sundeck and plunge pool, plus a stylish and upmarket tapas bar.

Eixample

Hostal L'Antic Espai   €
B&B   **Map** 3 B5
Gran Via 660, 08010
Tel *933 04 19 45*
Quirky and decorated with antiques, this B&B has simple rooms. Breakfast is served on the flower-filled terrace.

Hotel Actual   €€
Boutique   **Map** 3 B3
Rosselló 238, 08008
Tel *935 52 05 50*
w hotelactual.com
Stay in comfortable, minimalist rooms with a monochromatic decor. Great value for the location.

Hotel Jazz   €€
Boutique
Pelai 3, 08001
Tel *935 52 96 96*
w hoteljazz.com
The Jazz offers spacious, modern rooms, a rooftop sundeck with a plunge pool, and attentive service. Great value for money.

> ### DK Choice
>
> ### Alma   €€€
> Boutique   **Map** 3 B4
> *Mallorca 271, 08008*
> **Tel** *932 16 44 90*
> w almabarcelona.com
> The elegant Alma is famed for its excellent service. It offers chic, minimalist rooms and a lovely secret courtyard and roof terrace. Enjoy amenities such as the spa and pool.

Hotel Omm   €€€
Luxury   **Map** 3 B3
Rosselló 265, 08008
Tel *934 45 40 00*
w hotelomm.es
Modern, ultra-trendy hotel in an award-winning contemporary building with a restaurant overseen by the Roca brothers, plus club and spa.

Mandarin Oriental Hotel   €€€
Luxury   **Map** 3 A4
Passeig de Gràcia 38–40, 08007
Tel *931 51 88 88*
w mandarinoriental.com
Plush five-star hotel with white-and-gold interiors and a superb Michelin-starred restaurant.

Further Afield

ABaC   €€€
Luxury
Avinguda Tibidabo 1, 08022
Tel *933 19 66 00*
w abacbarcelona.com
Ultra-chic hotel with a garden, attached to a restaurant with two Michelin stars.

> ### DK Choice
>
> ### Hotel Arts   €€€
> Luxury   **Map** 6 E4
> *Carrer de la Marina 19–21, 08005*
> **Tel** *932 21 10 00*
> w hotelartsbarcelona.com
> A stunning hotel in a glass sky-scraper right on the beach. Outstanding amenities include a 42nd-floor spa with panoramic views, a wide selection of top-quality restaurants and bars and a fabulous collection of contemporary art. Excellent service.

Catalonia

BEGUR: Hotel Aiguaclara   €€
Boutique
Sant Miquel 2, 17255
Tel *972 62 29 05*
w hotelaiguaclara.com
Set in a beautiful village, the Aiguaclara has just a handful of enchanting rooms, a garden, cosy nooks for reading and relaxing, and an excellent restaurant.

BORREDÀ: El Querol Vell   €€
Historic
Carrer Manresa 75, 08619
Tel *938 23 98 10*
w elquerolvell.com
Set in beautiful countryside, this farmhouse has charming rooms, plus a garden and a restaurant.

For more information on types of hotels *see page 5*

Sleek, contemporary exterior of Ciutat de Girona, Girona

CADAQUÉS: Hotel Llané Petit €
Boutique
Platja Llane Petit s/n, 17488
Tel *972 25 10 20*
W llanepetit.com
Charming beachfront option on the edge of town, with crisp blue-and-white rooms.

CARDONA: Hotel Bremon €€
Historic
Cambres 15, 08261
Tel *938 68 49 02*
W hotelbremon.com
An elegantly converted convent, this hotel has stylish rooms and apartments. Cosy restaurant.

DELTEBRE: Delta Hotel €
B&B
Avinguda del Canal, Camí de la Illeta s/n, 43580
Tel *977 48 00 46*
W deltahotel.net
Charming family-run rural hotel; a great base for exploring the beautiful Ebro Delta.

FIGUERES: Hotel Duran €€
Historic
Lausaca 5, 17600
Tel *972 50 12 50*
W hotelduran.com
A hotel with comfortable rooms and a restaurant that was once frequented by Salvador Dalí.

GIRONA: Ciutat de Girona €
Boutique
Nord 2, 17001
Tel *972 48 30 38*
W hotelciutatdegirona.com
This stylish, modern hotel offers a choice of rooms and apartments, a wellness centre and a restaurant.

GRANOLLERS: Fonda Europa €€
Historic
Anselm Clavé 1, 08402
Tel *938 70 03 12*
W hotelfondaeuropa.com
A classic, long-established inn with fine rooms and a smart restaurant serving Catalan cuisine.

LLAFRANC: El Far de Sant Sebastià €€
Boutique
Muntanya de Sant Sebastià, 17211
Tel *972 30 16 39*
W hotelelfar.com
A romantic hotel on a clifftop overlooking the coast, the El Far also has a fine restaurant.

LLORET DE MAR: Sant Pere del Bosc Hotel & Spa €€€
Luxury
Paratge Sant Pere del Bosc s/n, 17310
Tel *972 36 16 36*
W santperedelboschotel.com
Lavish suites and a spectacular spa in a Modernist villa 5 km (3 miles) from the beaches.

MONTBLANC: Fonda Cal Blasi €
Historic
Carrer Alenyá 11, 43400
Tel *977 86 13 36*
W santperedelboschotel.com
A cosy hotel in a 19th-century building with rustically decorated rooms and a restaurant serving local specialities.

MONTSENY: Hotel Can Cuch €€
Historic
Can Cuch de Muntanya 35, 08445
Tel *931 03 39 80*
W hotelcancuch.com
Stunning *masia* (farmhouse) in the hills with exquisite guest-rooms and expansive views.

MONTSERRAT: Abat Cisneros €€
Historic
Plaça de Montserrat s/n, 08199
Tel *938 77 77 01*
Located next to the basilica, this hotel has comfortable rooms, and it offers hearty Catalan cuisine in the restaurant.

OLOT: Les Cols Pavelons €€
Luxury
Avinguda de les Cols 2, 17800
Tel *699 813 817*
W lescolspavellons.com
Stunning hotel with glassy cube pavilions in the garden, and an award-winning restaurant.

DK Choice

PLATJA D'ARO: Silken Park Hotel San Jorge €€
Boutique
Avenida Andorra 28, 17250
Tel *972 65 23 11*
W hoteles-silken.com
Friendly and relaxed, this elegant hotel in a fine clifftop location on the Costa Brava has pleasant rooms with balconies overlook-ing the sea. Steps lead down the cliff to a perfect little cove fringed with rocks and pine trees.

SANTA CRISTINA D'ARO: Mas Tapiolas €€€
Boutique
Carretera C65, km 7, Veinat de Solius s/n, 17246
Tel *932 83 70 17*
W hotelmastapiolas.es
Mas Tapiolas is a gorgeous hotel set in a beautiful 18th-century farmhouse a short drive from the beaches. Lovely gardens and a fine restaurant.

SITGES: Hotel Galeon €
Boutique
Sant Francesc 46, 08870
Tel *938 94 13 79*
W hotelsitges.com
Amenities at this friendly, classic hotel with cosy rooms, many with terraces, include a small pool shaded by palm trees in the garden.

TARRAGONA: Hotel Pigal €
B&B
Carrer Cardenal Cervantes 6, 43004
Tel *977 50 68 18*
W hotelpigal.com
Stay in immaculate, simply furnished rooms in a central location. This little hotel prides itself on its friendly service.

TORRENT: Mas de Torrent Hotel & Spa €€€
Historic
Afueras de Torrent, 17123
Tel *902 55 03 21*
W hotelmastorrent.com
Refined rooms, good service and an excellent restaurant are to be found in this *masia* (farmhouse).

TOSSA DE MAR: Hotel Cap d'Or €
B&B
Passeig del Mar 1, 17320
Tel *972 34 00 81*
W hotelcapdor.com
This small, whitewashed hotel is set in an 18th-century building right on the seafront.

Plush furnishings at Mas de Torrent Hotel & Spa, Torrent

VIC: Parador de Vic-Sau €€
Boutique
Paraje el Bac de Sau. Crta de
Tavèrnoles, Bv 5213, km 10, 08500
Tel *938 12 23 23*
This modern parador has an idyllic
setting in woods overlooking a
lake. Lovely grounds and pool.

VIELHA: Hotel El Ciervo €€
Historic
Plaça de Sant Orenc 3, 25530
Tel *973 64 01 65*
W hotelelciervo.net
Family-run hotel with rustically
decorated rooms and a lounge
with a roaring fire in winter.

Country-cottage style at Barosse B&B, Barós

Aragón

AINSA: Los Siete Reyes €
Boutique
Plaza Mayor s/n, 22330
Tel *974 50 06 81*
W lossietereyes.com
Rooms at this hotel in a historic
mansion have views of either
Ainsa's old square or the Pyrenees.

ALQUEZAR: Casa Alodia €
Boutique
C/San Gregorio; C/Arrabal s/n, 22145
Tel *626 35 18 16*
W casa-alodia.com
This hotel has two buildings: San
Gregorio's suits families, Arrabal is
good for a romantic break.

BARÓS: Barosse €
B&B
Calle Estiras 4, 22712
Tel *974 36 05 82*
W barosse.com
This enchanting stone-built B&B
offers five beautiful rooms and a
daily-changing evening menu.

DK Choice

CALACEITE: Hotel Cresol €
Inn
Calle Santa Bárbara 16, 44610
Tel *609 90 81 90*
W hotelcresol.com
This inn is a beautifully converted
olive mill. In the rooms,
contemporary artworks and
traditional furniture provide a
perfect balance between the
ancient and the modern.

FUENTESPALDA:
Mas de la Serra €€
Inn
Mas de la Serra, 44587
Tel *976 36 90 98*
W masdelaserra.com
A remote, renovated farmhouse
surrounded by acres of almond
trees. Glorious views.

MIRAMBEL: Las Moradas
del Temple €€
Boutique
Calle Agustín Pastor 15, 44141
Tel *964 17 82 70*
W lasmoradasdeltemple.es
A romantic hotel with four-poster
beds, set in a charming stone inn
in Mirambel's historic centre.

SALLENT DE GALLEGO:
Hotel Valle de Izas €
Boutique
Calle Francia 26, 22640
Tel *974 48 85 08*
W hotelvalledeizas.com
Traditionally decorated wooden
rooms give this village hotel near
Formigal ski resort a homely feel.

ZARAGOZA: Hotel Sauce €
Boutique
Calle Espoz y Mina 33, 50003
Tel *976 20 50 50*
W hotelsauce.com
This central hotel offers tastefully
designed rooms and breakfasts
featuring home-made cakes.

Valencia and Murcia

ALICANTE: Amerigo €
Boutique
Calle Rafael Altamira 7, 03002
Tel *965 14 65 70*
W hospes.es
Facilities at this old Dominican
convent converted into a stylish
hotel include a spa, pool, bar
and restaurant. Pets allowed.

BOCAIRENT: Hotel L'Estació €
Historic
Parc de l'Estació s/n, 46880
Tel *962 35 00 00*
W hotelestacio.com
A warm welcome awaits at this
gorgeous country inn converted
from a 19th-century train station.
It is set in beautiful parkland, so
peace and quiet are guaranteed.

CALPE: Gran Hotel Sol y Mar €
Luxury
Calle Benidorm 3, 03710
Tel *965 87 50 55*
W granhotelsolymar.com
This charming, modern hotel is
close to both town and beach.
Spa on site. Over 16s only.

CARTAGENA: La Manga Club
Principe Felipe €€
Luxury
La Manga Club, 30389
Tel *968 17 55 77*
W lamangaclub.com
This exclusive Spanish-village-
style hotel is popular with
celebrities. It has a spa, sports
facilities and entertainment.

DÉNIA: Rosa €
Boutique
Calle Congre 3, Las Marinas 03700
Tel *965 78 15 73*
W hotelrosadenia.com
This Mediterranean-style mansion
set in beautiful gardens has
comfortable, modern bedrooms.

ELX: Hotel Huerto del Cura €
Inn
Porto de la Morera 14, 03203
Tel *966 61 00 11*
W hotelhuertodelcura.com
A lush palm tree oasis with
bungalow accommodation and
a pool. Some rooms have wood-
beamed ceilings; all are tastefully
decorated in neutral colours.

DK Choice

FORTUNA: Balneario Lea
Historic
Calle Balneario, 30630
Tel *902 44 44 10*
W leana.es
Renowned as Murci
hotel – it was foun
this atmospheric
conjures up a u
the past, with M

Stylish decor at Hostal Gala, Madrid

LA VILA JOÍOSA:
Hotel Montiboli €€
Luxury
Partida Montiboli, 03570
Tel *965 89 02 50*
W montiboli.com
Facilities at this clifftop hotel with spectacular sea views include two outdoor pools, a spa and a gourmet restaurant.

MURCIA: Arco de San Juan €
Historic
Plaza de Ceballos 10, 30003
Tel *968 21 04 55*
W arcosanjuan.com
Next to Murcia's cathedral, this beautifully converted palace has spacious rooms and a blend of old and new furnishing styles.

ORIHUELA: Hotel Palacio Tudemir €
Luxury/Boutique
Calle Afonso XIII 1, 03330
Tel *966 73 80 10*
W hotelpalaciotudemir.com
In the historic centre of Orihuela, this lovingly restored 18th-century palace features a spa and a gourmet restaurant.

PENÍSCOLA: Hostería del Mar €€
Historic
Avinguda Papa Luna 18, 12598
Tel *964 48 06 00*
W hosteriadelmar.net
Beachfront hotel with free Wi-Fi and a garden with a seasonal outdoor pool. Most rooms have ~onies. Minimum stay of seven ~s with half board in summer.

~CIA: Hostal Venecia €

~yuntamiento 3, 46002
~2 67
~ecia.com
~l in the heart of
~unctional modern
~ith balconies
~square, free
~e service.
~ible.

~age 562

VALENCIA: SH Inglés Boutique €
Boutique
Calle Marqués de Dos Aguas 6, 46002
Tel *963 94 02 51*
W inglesboutique.com
This tastefully furnished 18th-century palace offers affordable rooms and excellent facilities.

VILAFAMÉS: El Jardin Vertical €€
Historic
Carrer Nou 15, 12192
Tel *964 32 99 38*
W eljardinvertical.com
Refurbished 17th-century red-stone house in a hilltop village, amid olive and almond groves. Perfect for a relaxing holiday.

XÀBIA: Hotel Javea €
Boutique
Carrer Pío X 5, 03730
Tel *965 79 54 61*
W hotel-javea.com
A charming hotel with simple, stylish rooms and wonderful port views. Panoramic views from the restaurant.

XÀTIVA: Hostería Mont Sant €
Historic
Subida al Castillo de Xàtiva s/n, 46800
Tel *962 27 50 81*
W mont-sant.com
Beautifully restored, this convent in citrus-filled gardens features a spa and a restaurant. Ideal for those seeking peace and quiet.

Madrid
Old Madrid

Abracadabra €
B&B **Map** 3 C4
Calle Bailén 39, 28005
Tel *911 30 18 51*
W abracadabrasuites.com
A warm, beautifully refurbished guesthouse in the centre of Madrid. Hardwood floors, neutral shades and Moroccan touches add charm to the rooms.

DK Choice

Hostal Gala €
Boutique **Map** 4 E1
Costanilla de los Angeles 15, 28013
Tel *915 41 96 92*
W hostalgala.com
An excellent choice in the city centre, this hostel has affordable yet stylish rooms and apartments, many with balconies overlooking a delightful square. Warm, friendly service and extras such as power showers make this place stand out.

Hotel Plaza Mayor €
Historic **Map** 4 E3
Calle Atocha 2, 28012
Tel *913 60 06 06*
W h-plazamayor.com
Stay in smart, modern rooms with parquet flooring and bare stone walls at this 19th-century town house near Plaza Mayor.

Mayerling Hotel €
Boutique **Map** 4 F3
Calle del Conde Ramanones 6, 28012
Tel *914 20 15 80*
W mayerlinghotel.com
A designer hotel with minimalist, but comfortable, rooms. Free Wi-Fi and wheelchair accessible.

Posada del León de Oro €
Historic **Map** 4 E3
Calle Cava Baja 12, 28005
Tel *911 19 14 94*
W posadadelleondeoro.com
A 19th-century inn and restaurant with stylish rooms arranged around a traditional courtyard.

Hotel Liabeny €€
Boutique **Map** 4 F1
Calle de la Salud 3, 28013
Tel *915 31 90 00*
W liabeny.es
Central hotel offering amenities such as a gym, sauna, restaurant and free Wi-Fi. Very good value.

Casa de Madrid €€€
Luxury **Map** 4 D2
Calle Arrieta 2 (2nd floor), 28013
Tel *915 59 57 91*
W casademadrid.com
Exquisite central guesthouse with a handful of antique-furnished rooms and all modern comforts.

Bourbon Madrid

Hotel One Shot Prado 23 €€
Boutique **Map** 7 B3
Calle del Prado 23, 28014
Tel *914 20 40 01*
W hoteloneshotprado23.com
Chic rooms – some with balconies, and all with hardwood floors and free Wi-Fi – in this unique hotel.

Hotel Único €€
Boutique **Map** 6 E3
Calle Claudio Coello 67, 28001
Tel *917 81 01 73*
☑ unicohotelmadrid.com
An enchanting hotel with stylish
rooms and a Michelin-starred
restaurant. Attentive service.

Me Madrid Reina Victoria €€
Luxury **Map** 7 A3
Plaza de Santa Ana 14, 28012
Tel *912 76 47 47*
☑ memadrid.com
In a trendy location, this hotel
has stunning rooms and suites,
a rooftop bar and a restaurant.

Hotel Hospes Puerta Alcalá €€€
Boutique **Map** 8 D1
Plaza de la Independencia 3, 28001
Tel *914 32 29 11*
☑ hospes.com
Beautiful rooms, a fabulous spa
and a gourmet restaurant in this
19th-century converted mansion
in front of the Parque del Retiro.

DK Choice

Hotel Ritz by Belmond €€€
Luxury **Map** 7 C2
Plaza de la Lealtad 5, 28014
Tel *917 01 67 67*
☑ mandarinoriental.com/
ritzmadrid
This opulent *belle-époque*-style
gem set in gardens right next
to the Prado boasts a gilded
interior and the rarefied air of
another century. Elegant
informal attire is requested in
the hotel's public areas. Excellent
service and a splendid bar where
luminaries like Dalí and Lorca
once held court.

Further Afield

Artrip Hotel €€
Boutique **Map** 7 A5
Calle Valencia 11, 28012
Tel *915 39 32 82*
☑ artriphotel.com
Modern hotel with exposed
brick walls, high ceilings and
sleek, spacious rooms.

Clement Barajas Hotel €€
Boutique
Avenida General 43, 28042
Tel *917 46 03 30*
☑ clementhoteles.com
This hotel has bright rooms.
Convenient for Barajas Airport,
with a regular shuttle service.

Silken Puerta América €€€
Luxury
Avenida de América 41, 28002
Tel *917 44 54 00*
☑ hoteles-silken.com

Each floor of this spectacular
hotel was designed by a different
celebrity architect. The top-floor
bar has superb views over Madrid.

Madrid Province

CHINCHÓN:
Condesa de Chinchón €
Boutique
Calle de los Huertos 26, 28370
Tel *918 93 54 00*
☑ condesadechinchon.com
Beautiful little hotel with modern
rooms and an excellent restaurant.
Conveniently located for Madrid.

SAN LORENZO DE EL ESCORIAL:
Hotel Posada Don Jaime €
Historic
Calle San Anton 24, 28200
Tel *918 96 52 18*
☑ posadadonjaime.es
Traditionally decorated rooms,
a lovely, plant-filled terrace and a
seasonal plunge pool.

Castilla y León

AMPUDIA: Casa del Abad €
Boutique
*Plaza Francisco Martín Gromaz 12,
34191*
Tel *979 76 80 08*
☑ casadelabad.com
Formerly an abbey, this iconic
17th-century building still retains
many of its original features.

ÁVILA: Hostel Puerta
del Alcázar €
B&B
Calle San Segundo 38, 05001
Tel *920 21 10 74*
☑ puertadelalcazar.com
In front of the city walls, this hotel
has a restaurant and a terrace
with views over the cathedral.

Lavish interiors of the sitting area
at the Hotel Ritz by Belmond

ÁVILA: Palacio de los Velada €€
Historic
Plaza de la Catedral 10, 05001
Tel *920 25 51 00*
☑ veladahoteles.com
Refurbished 16th-century palace
located close to the cathedral.
Excellent restaurant, El Tostado.

BURGOHONDO: Posada
Real El Linar del Zaire €
Boutique
Carretera Avila-Casavieja 42B, 05113
Tel *920 28 40 91*
☑ ellinardelzaire.com
A great base for exploring the Valle
del Alberche. Nearby activities
include canoeing and golf.

BURGOS: Torre Berrueza €
Boutique
*Calle Nuño Rasura 5, 09560,
Espinosa de los Monteros*
Tel *610 34 23 04*
☑ torreberrueza.es
Housed in a 12th-century stone
tower, this hotel has a restaurant
serving traditional dishes.

BURGOS: NH Collection
Palacio de Burgos €€€
Historic
Calle de la Merced 13, 09002
Tel *947 47 99 00*
☑ nh-collection.com/es/hotel/nh-
collection-palacio-de-burgos
This centrally located, 16th-
century inn has exquisite rooms
and a lovely gourmet restaurant.

CANDELADA: El Mirlo Blanco €
B&B
*Carretera Candelada a Madrigal de
la Vera, km 2, 1, 05480*
Tel *902 10 40 00*
☑ el-mirlo-blanco.com
A rural hideaway with sauna and
Jacuzzi, plus massages, set amid
abundant countryside.

CIRCO DE GREDOS: Refugio
Laguna Grande €
B&B
Laguna de Gredos s/n, 05634
Tel *920 20 75 76*
☑ refugiolagunagrandede
gredos.es
This refuge offers basic dormitory
accommodation. The spectacular
mountain views make up for the
spartan environment.

LEÓN: NH Collection
Plaza Mayor €
Luxury
Plaza Mayor 15–17, 24003
Tel *987 34 43 57*
☑ nh-hotels.com
An ancient setting – in an 18th-
century building on the main
square – meets modern design
at this hotel with comfortable
rooms and an elegant restaurant.

For more information on types of hotels *see page*

LUYEGO: Hosteria Camino €
Boutique
Calle Nuestra Señora de los
Remedios 25, 24717
Tel *987 60 17 57*
W hosteriacamino.com
Each room is named after a
constellation at this charming
hotel on the Camino de Santiago.

MEDINACELI: Hotel Medina
Salim €
Boutique
Calle Barranco 15, 42240
Tel *975 32 69 74*
W hotelmedinasalim.com
A modern building incorporating
the town's old walls. Great views
and a spa (not included in rates).

PEDRAZA: Hospedería de
Santo Domingo €
Inn
Calle Matadero 3, 40172
Tel *921 50 99 71*
W hospederiadesantodomingo.com
This hotel in the Jewish Quarter
offers superb views of the Sierra
de Guadarrama and the aqueduct.

PONFERRADA: Hotel Aroi
Bierzo Plaza €
Boutique
Plaza del Ayuntamiento 4, 24001
Tel *987 40 90 01*
W aroihoteles.com
Well-equipped rooms and two
cosy restaurants serving regional
fare. Ideal for exploring El Bierzo.

PUEBLA DE SANABRIA:
Posada de las Misas €
Boutique
Plaza Mayor 13, 49300
Tel *980 62 03 58*
W posadadelasmisas.com
Beautiful views from this well-
located hotel. Guests have access
to the library and galleries.

DK Choice

SALAMANCA: Hotel Rector €€
Boutique
Paseo Rector Esperabé 10, 37008
Tel *923 21 84 82*
W hotelrector.com
Formerly the mansion of a
distinguished local family, this
refined hotel oozes elegance
but with a personal touch. The
rooms are cleaned twice daily.

SALAMANCA: NH Puerto
de la Catedral €€
Luxury
Plaza Juan XXIII 5, 37008
Tel *923 28 08 29*
W nh-hotels.com
This elegant chain hotel in the
historic quarter offers well-
appointed, contemporary rooms.

Entrance to one of the elegant and spotless
rooms at Hotel Rector, Salamanca

SANTA MARÍA DE MAVE:
El Convento de Mave €
Historic
Calle Monasterio s/n, 34402
Tel *979 12 36 11*
W elconventodemave.com
This 12th-century monastery has
had a 21st-century makeover. Bike
rental available, plus workshops.

SEGOVIA: Hotel Don Felipe €
Historic
Calle de Daoiz 7, 40001
Tel *921 46 60 95*
W hoteldonfelipe.es
Set in a mansion, this serene
hotel offers modern facilities
and has a peaceful garden.

SOMAÉN: Posada Real de
Santa Quiteria €€
Historic
Barrio Alto 8, 42257
Tel *975 32 03 93*
W posadasantaquiteria.com
Rooms are beautifully decorated
at this enchanting country inn.

SORIA: Hotel Solar de Tejada €
Boutique
Calle Claustrilla 1, 42002
Tel *975 23 00 53*
W hosteriasolardetejada.es
Located in the heart of town,
this hotel offers individually
decorated rooms and free Wi-Fi.

TOLBANOS: Molino de
los Gamusinos €€
Boutique
Camino del Molino s/n, 05289
Tel *920 22 77 14*
W losgamusinos.com
This secluded hotel is an ideal
retreat from where you can
explore the area.

VALLADOLID: Meliá Recoletos €
Boutique
Calle Acera de Recoletos 13, 47004
Tel *902 14 44 40*
W melia.com

Refreshingly quiet chain hotel
situated in the heart of the city.
Free Wi-Fi and a garden terrace.

ZAMORA: Parador de Zamora €€
Luxury
Plaza de Viriato 5, 49001
Tel *980 51 44 97*
W parador.es
Suits of armour and tapestries
adorn the interior at this parador
set in a medieval palace.

Castilla-La Mancha

ALARCÓN: Parador de Alarcón €€€
Luxury
Avda Amigos de los Castillos 3, 16214
Tel *969 33 03 15*
W parador.es
A medieval castle from the
8th century, perched on a cliff.
Stunning views of the Júcar river.

ALBACETE: Hotel Santa Isabel €€
Luxury
Avenida Gregorio Arcos s/n, 02007
Tel *967 26 46 80*
W hotelsantaisabelalbacete.com
Stunning modern hotel with a
vintage car collection in the
garage. Free Wi-Fi.

ALMADÉN: Plaza de Toros
de Almadén €
Historic
Plaza Waldo Ferrer s/n,13400
Tel *926 26 43 33*
W hotelplazadetoros.com
Enjoy comfortable, rustic and
individually decorated rooms at
this hotel in a former bull ring.

ALMAGRO: Hotel Casa
Grande Almagro €
Boutique
Calle Federico Relimpio 10, 13270
Tel *671 49 62 88*
W casagrandealmagro.com
A 16th-century property, close
to Plaza Mayor and the famous
medieval theatre.

ALMONACID DE TOLEDO:
Villa Nazules €
Luxury
Crta Almonacid a Chueca s/n, 45190
Tel *925 59 03 80*
W villanazules.com
Villa Nazules is a four-star hotel
boasting an excellent spa and
wellness facilities.

CUENCA: Convento del Giraldo €
Historic
Calle San Pedro 12, 16001
Tel *969 23 27 00*
W hotelconventodelgiraldo.com
This historic, charming building
fuses 17th-century character with
comforting modern touches.

CUENCA: Parador de Cuenca €€
Historic
Subida San Pablo s/n, 16001
Tel *969 23 23 20*
🅦 parador.es
Housed in a former monastery
in the Hoz del Huécar gorge,
near Cuenca's hanging houses.

DK Choice

**SIGÜENZA: Molino de
Alcuneza** €€
Historic
Crta Alboreca, km 0.5, 19264
Tel *949 39 15 01*
🅦 molinodealcuneza.com
This idyllic hotel is located
close to the medieval city of
Sigüenza. The building dates
from the 14th century and once
served as a mill. The modern
spa includes a *hammam*.

**TALAVERA DE LA REINA:
Be Live City Center Talavera** €
Boutique
Avenida de Toledo s/n, 45600
Tel *925 72 72 00*
🅦 belivehotels.com
Central, four-star hotel with bright,
elegant rooms with expansive
views over the city.

TOLEDO: Hotel Santa Isabel €
Boutique
Calle Santa Isabel 24, 45002
Tel *925 25 31 20*
🅦 hotelsantaisabeltoledo.es
In the 14th-century abode of a
local noble, this hotel has a roof
terrace with views over the city.

TOLEDO: Parador de Toledo €€
Luxury
Cerro del Emperador s/n, 45002
Tel *925 22 18 50*
🅦 parador.es
A vast establishment set on the
hillside with excellent views.
Superb restaurant and a pool.

VALDEPEÑAS: Veracruz Plaza €
Boutique
Plaza Veracruz s/n, 13300
Tel *926 31 30 00*
🅦 hotelveracruzplaza.com
Indulge at the amazing spa –
with steam room, a Turkish
bath and treatments – at this
modern hotel.

**VILLANUEVA DE LOS INFANTES:
La Morada de Juan de Vargas** €
Boutique
Calle Cervantes 3, 13320
Tel *926 36 17 69*
🅦 lamoradadevargas.com
Rooms are individually decorated
at this charming establishment
in a 16th-century building. The
hotel is close to the main square.

YESTE: Balneario de Tus €
Historic
Crta Yeste-Tus, km 13, 02485
Tel *967 43 68 17*
🅦 balneariodetus.com
A spa destination since Roman
times. Contemporary treatments
include hot mud wraps.

Extremadura

ALANGE: Gran Hotel Aqualange €
Rooms with a View
Paseo de las Huertas 3, 06840
Tel *924 36 56 08*
🅦 balneariodealange.com
Unwind at this grand spa hotel
next to the thermal Roman baths.
Closed Nov–mid-Mar.

**BADAJOZ: NH Gran Hotel
Casino de Extremadura** €€
Luxury
Adolfo Diaz Ambrona 11, 06006
Tel *924 28 44 02*
🅦 nh-hotels.com
Ultramodern hotel in a quiet
area by the river, with a spa and
a classy restaurant with views.

**CÁCERES: Sercotel
Extremadura Hotel** €€
Luxury
Avda Virgen de Guadalupe 28, 10001
Tel *927 62 96 39*
🅦 extremadurahotel.com
Enjoy the peaceful surroundings
at this hotel near the city centre.
Free Wi-Fi, pool and a restaurant.

**JARANDILLA DE LA VERA:
Parador de Jarandilla
de la Vera** €€
Historic
Avenida García Prieto 1, 10450
Tel *927 56 01 17*
🅦 parador.es
This 14th-century palace, once
the home of Charles V, has simple
rooms. Ideal for visiting Yuste.

MÉRIDA: Hotel Adealba €
Boutique
Romero Leal 18, 06800
Tel *924 38 83 08*
🅦 hoteladealba.com

Bright, modern hotel in a 19th-
century town house within
walking distance of the Roman
sights. Spa and restaurant.

**TRUJILLO: Eurostars Palacio
de Santa Marta** €
Historic
Ballesteros 6, 10200
Tel *927 65 91 90*
🅦 eurostarshotels.com
A 16th-century palace blending
traditional features with modern
comforts. Many rooms have
views of the square or the castle.

DK Choice

**ZAFRA: Casa Palacio
Conde de La Corte** €€
Boutique
Plaza del Pilar Redondo 2, 06300
Tel *924 56 33 11*
🅦 vivedespacio.com/
condedelacorte
This 19th-century palace, the
former residence of the sixth
Count Corte of Berrona, has
been restored to represent the
grandeur of that era. The decor
incorporates period features
with modern amenities.

Seville

El Arenal

Hispano Luz Confort €
B&B **Map** 3 C2
Calle Miguel Mañara 4, 41004
Tel *955 63 80 79*
🅦 hotelhispanoluzsevilla.com
Rooms are comfortable and
cheery at this hostel in a historic
building next to the Real Alcázar.
Rooftop terrace, free Wi-Fi.

Taberna del Alabardero €€
Historic **Map** 5 B3
Calle Zaragoza 20, 41001
Tel *954 50 27 21*
🅦 tabernadelalabardero.es
All rooms have hydromassage
baths, and there is a restaurant
serving Andalucían cuisine. Free
Wi-Fi in the communal areas.

The warm-toned central courtyard of Taberna del Alabardero, Seville

For more information on types of hotels *see p.*

Santa Cruz

DK Choice

Casa Numero Siete €€
Boutique **Map** 6 E3
Calle Virgenes 7, 41004
Tel *954 22 15 81*
🆆 casanumero7.com
Discover luxury in a 19th-century
mansion in the heart of Seville's
evocative Old Quarter. The decor
at this small but immaculate
guesthouse includes antiques
and family heirlooms. Relax in
the elegant lounge and enjoy
the discreet but friendly service.

Alfonso XIII €€€
Historic **Map** 3 C3
Calle San Fernando 2, 41004
Tel *954 91 70 00*
🆆 hotel-alfonsoxiii-seville.com
This spectacular hotel combines
Mudejar architecture with
modern comforts. Work out in
the fitness centre, relax in the
sauna or the seasonal outdoor
swimming pool, or enjoy a
cocktail on the terrace.

Las Casas del Rey de Baeza €€€
Boutique **Map** 6 E2
Plaza Jesús de la Redención 2, 41003
Tel *954 56 14 96*
🆆 hospes.com
Stylish hotel with chic bedrooms
and Colonial-style furniture. Lovely
rooftop pool, plus an open-air
patio and spa.

EME Catedral Hotel €€€
Luxury **Map** 6 D4
Calle Alemanes 27, 41004
Tel *954 56 00 00*
🆆 emecatedralhotel.com
Four great restaurants, a cocktail
bar, a rooftop pool and a terrace
with fabulous views are among
the attractions at his central
hotel with a spa.

Further Afield

Patio de la Alameda €
B&B **Map** 2 D4
Alameda de Hercules 56, 41002
Tel *954 90 49 99*
🆆 patiodelaalameda.com
This hotel offers mosaic-tiled
bathrooms and Baroque mirrors
in rooms set around three
courtyards. The rooftop terrace
has a chill-out bar with views of
the historic surroundings. Free
Wi-Fi in the communal areas.

Casa Sacristia de Santa Ana €€
Historic **Map** 2 D4
Alameda de Hercules 22, 41002
Tel *954 91 57 22*
🆆 hotelsacristia.com

This hotel is housed within a
beautifully restored 18th-century
sacristy. Rooms, decorated with
period furniture, feature wooden
or marble floors. Fine restaurant
and free Wi-Fi.

Andalucía

ARACENA: Finca Buen Vino €€
B&B
Carretera N433, km 95, 21208
Tel *959 12 40 34*
🆆 fincabuenvino.com
Established hilltop guesthouse
offering spacious, individually
furnished rooms and self-
catering cottages. Famed for its
cuisine and cookery courses.

**ARCOS DE LA FRONTERA:
Casa Grande** €
Historic
Calle Maldonaldo 10, 11360
Tel *956 70 39 30*
🆆 lacasagrande.net
A gleaming whitewashed 18th-
century mansion with splendid
views of the Andalucían country-
side. Family rooms available.
Good breakfast spread.

**ARCOS DE LA FRONTERA:
Parador de Arcos
de la Frontera** €€
Historic
Plaza del Cabildo, 11630
Tel *956 70 05 00*
🆆 parador.es
Stay in spacious rooms, some
with a Jacuzzi, in a converted
magistrate's mansion with a
beautiful inner courtyard and
fabulous views from the terrace.
The restaurant serves gluten-free
and vegetarian options.

CÁDIZ: Hotel Playa Victoria €€
Boutique
*Glorieta Ingeniero La Cierva 4,
11010*
Tel *956 20 51 00*
🆆 palafoxhoteles.com

Ecofriendly hotel with avant-garde
interior furnishings. Seasonal
outdoor pool (open Jun–Sep)
and direct access to the beach.

CAÑOS DE MECA: La Breña €€
Boutique
Avenida Trafalgar 4, 11149
Tel *956 43 73 68*
🆆 hotelbrena.com
Spacious, shabby-chic rooms,
some with sea views, and a
charming terrace overlooking the
ocean. Seasonal outdoor pool.

DK Choice

**CARMONA: Parador
de Carmona** €€
Luxury
Calle Alcazar s/n, 41410
Tel *954 14 10 10*
🆆 parador.es
Originally a Moorish fortress,
this parador has a stunning
hilltop location and majestic
interiors decorated with
tapestries and antiques. The
rooms are comfortable and
stylish. Relax in the outdoor
swimming pool (seasonal).
Warm and friendly service.

**CASTELLAR DE LA FRONTERA:
Casa Convento La Almoraima** €
Historic
*Carretera Algeciras-Ronda s/n, Finca
la Almoraima, 11350*
Tel *956 69 30 50*
🆆 laalmoraimahotel.com
A former monastery turned into
a modern hotel, with a seasonal
outdoor pool and free Wi-Fi.

CAZORLA: Molino la Farraga €
Historic
Camino de la Hoz, 23470
Tel *953 72 12 49*
🆆 molinolafarraga.com
A restored 200-year-old mill set
in tranquil gardens. The property
includes a small farm, a botanical
garden and a vegetable patch
for guests to enjoy.

View from the roof terrace at Casa Grande, Arcos de la Frontera

CAZORLA: Parador de Cazorla €
Luxury
Calle Sierra de Cazorla s/n, 23470
Tel *953 72 70 75*
🅆 parador.es
Vintage parador in the heart of the pine-forested Parque Natural de Cazorla. There is a gallery of mounted animals in the lobby. Closed Jan–mid-Feb.

CÓRDOBA: Hotel Maestre €
Inn
Calle Romero Barros 4–6, 17003
Tel *957 47 24 10*
🅆 hotelmaestre.com
A classic hotel with a flower-filled patio. Simple rooms and self-catering apartments on offer. Free Wi-Fi.

CÓRDOBA: Hospes Palacio de Bailio €€€
Boutique
Calle Ramirez de las Casas Deza 10–12, 14001
Tel *957 49 89 93*
🅆 hospes.com
Magnificently restored 17th-century palace with elegant furnishings and beautiful gardens. Amenities include a spa, outdoor pool and free Wi-Fi.

GIBRALTAR: Rock Hotel €€
Historic
Europa Road 3, 30339
Tel *956 77 30 00*
🅆 rockhotelgibraltar.com
A 70-year-old cliffside Colonial-style hotel with a nostalgic aura and stately guest rooms. Free Wi-Fi; wheelchair accessible.

GRANADA: Posada del Toro €
Inn
Elvira 25, 18010
Tel *958 22 73 33*
🅆 posadadeltoro.com
Renovated 19th-century inn blending old charm and modern comforts. Wi-Fi in all rooms. In the historic centre, right on the edge of the Albaicín.

GRANADA: Parador de Granada €€€
Luxury
Calle Real de la Alhambra, 18009
Tel *958 22 12 40*
🅆 parador.es
This parador enjoys an incomparable location inside the grounds of the Alhambra Palace. Elegantly appointed rooms.

GRAZALEMA: Hotel Fuerte Grazalema €
Inn
Baldio de los Alamillos, Carretera A372, km 53, 11610
Tel *956 13 30 00*
🅆 fuertehoteles.com

A wood-panelled ceiling and bed canopy in a room at La Bobadilla, Loja

A comfortable rural hotel inside the Grazalema Nature Reserve, with good children's facilities. Ideal for outdoor types.

JAÉN: Parador de Jaén €€
Historic
Castillo de Santa Catalina s/n, 23002
Tel *953 23 00 00*
🅆 parador.es
Hilltop parador set in a renovated 18th-century castle with Arabic-style rooms. Panoramic views, seasonal outdoor pool and lush gardens. Free Wi-Fi.

LOJA: La Bobadilla €€€
Luxury
Carretera Salinas–Villanueva de Tapia (A-333), km 65.5, Finca Bobadillo, 18300
Tel *958 32 18 61*
🅆 barcelolabobadilla.com
All rooms and suites in this plush hotel have a unique decor. Facilities include outdoor and indoor pools, a spa and a fitness room, as well as numerous activities. Free Wi-Fi.

MÁLAGA: Salles Hotel €€
Luxury
Calle Marmoles 6, 29007
Tel *952 07 02 16*
🅆 salleshotel.com
In the heart of Málaga, this well-appointed hotel has a seasonal rooftop pool, plus free Wi-Fi and family rooms.

MARBELLA: Marbella Club Hotel €€€
Luxury
Bulevar Príncipe Alfonso von Hohenlohe, 29600
Tel *952 82 22 11*
🅆 marbellaclub.com
Deluxe beachside hotel with lush gardens, pools, world-class golf course and spa. The Kids' Club has a music room, dance studio and other forms of entertainment.

MAZAGÓN: Parador de Mazagón €€
Luxury
Carretera San Juan-Matalascañas, km 30, 21120
Tel *959 53 63 00*
🅆 parador.es
Comfortable parador set amid pinewoods in a stunning location overlooking a pristine Atlantic beach. Indoor and outdoor pools.

MIJAS: Hotel Hacienda Puerta del Sol €
Luxury
Crta Fuengirola-Mijas, km 4, 29650
Tel *952 48 64 00*
🅆 hhpuertadelsol.es
Stylish hotel with tennis courts, gym and open-air pools. Family rooms and free Wi-Fi.

MONACHIL: La Almunia del Valle €€
Boutique
Camino de la Umbria, 18193
Tel *958 30 80 10*
🅆 laalmuniadelvalle.com
Small and friendly retreat high in the Sierra Nevada. Pretty gardens and an open-air pool.

NERJA: El Carabeo €
Boutique
Calle Hernando de Carabeo 34, 29780
Tel *952 52 54 44*
🅆 hotelcarabeo.com
All the suites here have private terraces overlooking the garden and sea. Book-filled lounge, plus a restaurant and seasonal pool.

OJEN: Posada del Angel €
Inn
Calle Mesones 21, 29610
Tel *952 88 18 08*
🅆 laposadadelangel.net
A charming hotel with Moorish touches and lovely terraces. Each room is individually decorated. Seasonal outdoor pool.

ORGIVA: Taray Botánico €
Rooms with a View
Crta A348 Tablete-Abuñol, 18400
Tel *958 78 45 25*
🅆 hoteltaray.com
Whitewashed rural hotel with an olive- and orange-filled garden. Facilities available for guests with disabilities, plus seasonal pools.

PALMA DEL RIO: Monasterio de San Francisco €
Historic
Avenida del Pio XII 35, 14700
Tel *957 71 01 83*
🅆 intergrouphoteles.com
A romantic hotel in a 15th-century monastery with lovely gardens and an inner courtyard. Rooms are simple but spacious. Restaurant and outdoor pool.

For more information on types of hotels *see page 561*

Spectacular old-world setting at Belmond La Residencia in Deiá, Mallorca

PECHINA: Hotel Balneario de Sierra de Alhamilla €
Historic
Calle Los Baños s/n, 04259
Tel *950 31 74 13*
W balneariosierraalhamilla.es
Well-restored 18th-century spa hotel that has a thermal pool with underwater jets. Lovely courtyards.

PRIEGO DE CÓRDOBA:
Casa Olea €
Inn
Crta CO-231/CO-7204, Zamoranos
Tel *696 74 82 09*
W casaolea.com
A traditional Andalucían *cortijo* (farmhouse) with luxurious bedding and underfloor heating. Wonderful views from the pool, garden and terrace. Lounge with fireplace in winter. Free Wi-Fi.

PUERTO DE SANTA MARIA:
Monasterio de San Miguel €
Historic
Calle Virgen de los Milagros 27, 11500
Tel *956 54 04 40*
W monasteriosanmiguelhotel.com
This former Capuchin monastery offers simple rooms, spacious gardens and lush public areas for contemplation, plus a large pool.

SAN JOSÉ: Cortijo el Sotillo €€
Historic
Carretera San Jose, 04118
Tel *950 61 11 00*
W cortijoelsotillo.es
Relaxed 18th-century farmhouse in the Cabo de Gata natural park. Good restaurant and outdoor pool.

SANLUCAR LA MAYOR:
Exe Gran Hotel Solucar €
Inn
Carretera Nac. Sevilla–Huelva A472 s/n, Sanlucar la Mayor, 41800
Tel *955 70 34 08*
W exegranhotelsolucar.com
Airy rooms with basic amenities. Guests can enjoy breakfast at the lovely poolside courtyard.

TARIFA: Hurricane Hotel €€
Boutique
Carretera N-340, km 78, 11380
Tel *956 68 49 19*
W hotelhurricane.com
Laid-back Moorish-style hotel with lush gardens, two pools, a gym, sauna and massage facilities.

ÚBEDA: Zenit El Postigo €
Inn
Calle El Postigo 5, 23400
Tel *953 75 00 00*
W elpostigo.zenithoteles.com
Comfortable modern hostelry with amenities including a cosy winter fireplace and summer pool.

VEJER DE LA FRONTERA:
La Casa del Califa €€
Boutique
Plaza de España 16, 11150
Tel *956 44 77 30*
W califavejer.com
Wander through a labyrinth of alcoves and passageways to find cozy sitting rooms, a games room and a terrace with fabulous views.

The Balearic Islands

FORMENTERA, ES CALÓ:
Hotel Entre Pinos €€€
B&B
Carretera La Mola, km 12.3, 07872
Tel *971 32 70 19*
W hotelentrepinos.es
A relaxed, family-run hotel near two stunning beaches. Outdoor pool and spa services available.

FORMENTERA, LA SAVINA:
Hostal La Savina €
B&B
Avinguda Mediterranea 20–40, 07870
Tel *971 32 22 79*
W hostal-lasavina.com
Charming family-run hotel on the beach, with simple, whitewashed rooms, many with sea views.

IBIZA, IBIZA CITY:
Mirador de Dalt Vila €€€
Historic
Plaça Espanya 4, 07800
Tel *971 30 30 45*
W hotelmiradoribiza.com
Sumptuous 19th-century palace with elegant rooms and a small pool, plus an excellent restaurant.

IBIZA, PORTINATX:
Sandos El Greco €€
Luxury
Cala Portinatx s/n, 07810
Tel *971 32 05 70*
W sandos.com
All-inclusive, adults-only resort with a great location in Portinatx Bay. Amenities include a water park, pool and buffet restaurant.

IBIZA, SANT JOAN DE LABRITJA:
The Giri Residence €€€
Boutique
Carrer Principal 3–5, 07810
Tel *971 33 33 45*
W thegiri.com
A fashionable getaway combining Moroccan interiors with a relaxed ambience. Closed Nov–Apr.

MALLORCA, DEIÁ:
Belmond La Residencia €€€
Luxury
Son Canals s/n, 07179
Tel *971 63 90 11*
W belmond.com
A renowned art hotel in two ancient manors, with a sculpture garden. Closed Nov–Mar.

MALLORCA, PALMA:
Hotel Feliz €€
Boutique
Avinguda Joan Miró 74, 07015
Tel *971 28 88 47*
W hotelfeliz.com
This bright hotel by the harbour has tasteful rooms, a roof terrace with a hot tub and a restaurant.

MALLORCA, POLLENÇA:
Hotel Posada de Lluc €
Boutique
Roser Vell 11, 07460
Tel *971 53 52 20*
W posadalluc.com
Rooms in this old building feature original stone walls and beamed ceilings. Bike rental available.

DK Choice

MALLORCA, POLLENÇA:
Son Brull €€€
Boutique
Carretera Palma–Pollença PM 220, km 49.8, 07460
Tel *971 53 53 53*
W sonbrull.com
A family-run spa-hotel in an old farmstead, Son Brull is surrounded by nature. Each of the rooms is tastefully decorated with subtle Mallorcan touches. Excellent restaurant.

MALLORCA, PORTIXOL:
Portixol €€€
Boutique
Calle Sirena, 07006
Tel *971 27 18 00*
W portixol.com
One of the island's most stylish hotels. Chic rooms, many with a terrace, plus pool and restaurant.

MENORCA, CALA MORELL:
Agroturisme Biniatram €
B&B
Carretera Cala Morell, km 1, 07760
Tel *971 38 31 13*
W biniatram.com

This peaceful farmhouse boasts inviting rooms and well-equipped apartments, along with a pool.

MENORCA, ES CASTELL:
Sant Joan de Binissaida   €€€
Boutique
Camí de Binissaida 108, 07720
Tel *971 35 55 98*
🔲 binissaida.com
An idyllic rural hotel in an 18th-century farmhouse, with vast grounds, a pool and a restaurant.

MENORCA, MAHÓN:
Hostal La Isla   €€
B&B
Santa Caterina 4, 07701
Tel *971 36 64 92*
🔲 hostal-laisla.com
This family-run guesthouse offers comfortable rooms and packed lunches on request. Great value.

The Canary Islands

EL HIERRO, SABINOSA:
Balneario Pozo de la Salud   €
Rooms with a View
El Pozo de la Salud s/n, 38911
Tel *922 55 95 61*
Relax with the sound of the sea at this hotel with sleek, modern rooms, a spa and outdoor pool.

EL HIERRO, VALVERDE:
Parador de El Hierro   €
Luxury
Las Playas 15, 38910
Tel *922 55 80 36*
🔲 parador.es
A tranquil, modern hotel with a garden featuring palms. Ask for a room with a sea view. Hot tub, outdoor pool and a fitness centre.

FUERTEVENTURA, CORRALEJO:
Gran Hotel Atlantis
Bahia Real   €€€
Luxury
Avenida Grandes Playas s/n, 35660
Tel *928 53 71 53*
🔲 bahiarealresort.com
Five-star hotel right on the sea-front, with stunning views, two pools set in lush gardens, six restaurants and a spa.

FUERTEVENTURA, VILLAVERDE:
Hotel Rural Mahoh   €
B&B
Sitio de Juan Bello, 35660
Tel *928 86 80 50*
🔲 mahoh.com
Housed in a 19th-century country manor fashioned out of volcanic stone and wood, surrounded by gardens. Pool and equestrian school, plus a games room with a large multilingual library. Buffet breakfast included.

DK Choice
GRAN CANARIA, ARGUINEGUÍN:
Radisson Blu Resort   €€€
Luxury
Barranco de la Verga s/n, 35120
Tel *928 15 06 06*
🔲 radissonblu.com
Located on the top of a cliff, this is one of Gran Canaria's most stylish hotels. Enjoy sweeping views of the Atlantic from the rooms, restaurants and pools. Relax on the beaches nearby or in the on-site bijou spa.

GRAN CANARIA, MARZAGÁN:
Hotel El Mondalón   €
Boutique
Carretera de los Hoyos, GC–801 1800pk, 35017
Tel *928 35 57 58*
🔲 hotelruralmondalon.es
This countryside hotel features a games room, heated outdoor pool with a waterfall and a children's play area.

LA GOMERA, PLAYA DE SANTIAGO: Jardín Tecina   €€
Luxury
Lomada de Tecina s/n, 38811
Tel *922 14 58 50*
🔲 jardin-tecina.com
Close to the airport, the Jardín Tecina has a large garden, pool and fitness centre. Each room has a private terrace with a view.

LA GOMERA, SAN SEBASTIÁN:
Parador de la Gomera   €€
Luxury
Lomo de la Horca s/n, 38800
Tel *922 87 11 00*
🔲 parador.es
Traditional Canarian building, with an outdoor pool and stunning views of neighbouring Tenerife, including Mount Teide.

LA PALMA, BREÑA BAJA:
Hacienda San Jorge   €
Boutique
Playa de Los Cancajos 22, 38712
Tel *922 18 10 66*
🔲 hsanjorge.com

Take a dip on Los Cancajos' black-sand beach or in the hotel's seawater pool, shaped like a lake. All rooms are self-catering.

LA PALMA, TAZACORTE:
Hotel Hacienda de Abajo   €€
Boutique
Calle Miguel de Unamuno 11, 38770
Tel *922 40 60 00*
🔲 hotelhaciendadeabajo.com
An opulent, antiques-filled 17th-century sugar estate. Most rooms have a balcony, terrace or garden.

LANZAROTE, ARRIETA:
Finca de Arrieta   €
Boutique
Diseminado Arrieta 1, 35542
Tel *928 82 67 20*
🔲 lanzaroteretreats.com
Quirky eco retreat powered by clean energy. Villas and yurts feature all modern comforts.

LANZAROTE, COSTA TEGUISE:
Sands Beach Resort   €
Rooms with a View
Avenida Islas Canarias 18, 35508
Tel *928 59 58 20*
🔲 sandsbeach.eu
Self-catering apartments with a resort full of amenities and a spa. Full entertainment programme, as well as a Kids' Club.

TENERIFE, GARACHICO:
Hotel San Roque   €€
Historic
Calle Esteban de Ponte 32, 38450
Tel *922 13 34 35*
🔲 hotelsanroque.com
A lovingly restored 18th-century manor house offering elegant rooms with Charles Rennie Mackintosh furniture.

TENERIFE, PUERTO DE LA CRUZ:
Hotel Botanico   €€
Luxury
Avenida Richard J. Yeoward 1, 38400
Tel *922 38 14 00*
🔲 hotelbotanico.com
A plush five-star hotel with a range of suites, restaurants and leisure facilities. Or simply lose yourself and all track of time in the Oriental Spa Garden.

Agroturisme Biniatram's stunning pool and

For more

WHERE TO EAT AND DRINK

One of the joys of eating out in Spain is the sheer sociability of the Spanish. Family and friends, often with children in tow, can be seen eating out from early in the day until after midnight. The country's food has a highly regional bias and traditional restaurants will typically serve dishes based on local produce. Spain also has its fair share of top-quality gourmet restaurants, notably in the Basque Country. The restaurants listed on pages 582–605 have been selected for their food and conviviality. Pages 578–81 illustrate some of the best tapas and drinks on offer; and the book's five regional sections include features on each area's unique food and wines.

An elaborately decorated bar, with a variety of drinks on offer, Barcelona

Restaurants and Bars

The cheapest and quickest places to eat are the bars and cafés that serve tapas. However, not all bars serve food. This is especially true of pubs, which are more about drinking and socializing. Family-run *bar-restaurantes*, *ventas*, *posadas*, *mesones* and *fondas* – all old words for the different types of inns – serve inexpensive, sit-down meals. *Chiringuitos* are ̶achside bars that open only ̶̶ng the summer season.

̶̶ restaurants close one day ̶̶ome for lunch or dinner ̶̶ost for an annual ̶̶ from the tourist ̶̶ close on some ̶̶Always call the ̶̶ check.

̶̶ain

Many work places allow their staff to have a break for breakfast between 10 and 11am, which is why cafés are often busy mid-morning. This meal may consist of a savoury snack, such as a *bocadillo* (sandwich) with sausage, ham or cheese, a thick slice of *tortilla de patatas* (potato omelette) or a *churro* (fried batter stick). Fruit juice, coffee or beer are the usual accompaniments.

During the week, people take a break for *la comida* (lunch) at about 2pm. This is the main meal of the day. From about 1pm at weekends, people will stop in the bars for a beer or a *copa* (glass) of wine with tapas. This tradition is called *irse de cañas* (*caña* is a type of beer). The cafés, *salones de té* (tearooms) and *pastelerías* (pastry shops) fill up by about 5:30 or 6pm for *la merienda* (tea) of sandwiches, pastries or cakes, with coffee, tea or juice. By 9pm, bars are crowded with people having tapas with sherry, wine

Decorative lamp in a bar

or beer. In Spain *la cena* (dinner or supper) begins at about 9 or 10pm. Restaurants sometimes begin their evening service earlier for tourists. In summer, however, Spanish families and groups of friends often do not sit down to eat until as late as midnight. At weekend lunchtimes, especially in summer, you may find that restaurants are filled by large and noisy family gatherings.

How to Dress

A jacket and tie are rarely required, but the Spanish dress smartly, especially for city restaurants. Day dress is casual in beach resorts, but shorts are frowned upon in the evenings.

Reading the Menu

Aside from tapas, perhaps the cheapest eating options in Spanish restaurants are the *platos combinados* (meat or fish with vegetables and, usually, chips) and the fixed-price *menú*

Designer tapas bar in Barcelona

Dining alfresco at tables on a café terrace

del día. A *plato combinado* is only offered by cheaper establishments. Most restaurants offer an inexpensive, fixed-price *menú del día* at lunchtime, normally of three courses, but with little choice. Some restaurants offer a *menú de degustación* consisting of a choice of six or seven of the head chef's special dishes.

The Spanish word for menu is *la carta*. It starts with *sopas* (soups), *ensaladas* (salads), *entremeses* (hors d'oeuvres), *huevos y tortillas* (eggs and omelettes) and *verduras y legumbres* (vegetable dishes).

Main courses are *pescados y mariscos* (fish and shellfish) and *carnes y aves* (meat and poultry). Daily specials are chalked on a board or clipped to menus. Paella and other rice dishes may be served as the first course. A useful rule is to follow rice with meat, or start with serrano ham or salad and then follow with a paella.

Desserts are called *postres* in Spanish. These can include fruit, *natillas* (custard) and *flan* (crème caramel). Gourmet restaurants have more creative choices.

In big cities such as Madrid there's an increasing number of good vegetarian restaurants. Most menus have at least one vegetable or egg dish. A good number of places welcome children.

Wine Choices

Dry fino wines go with shellfish, serrano ham, olives, soups and most first courses. Main courses are usually accompanied by wines from Ribera del Duero, Rioja, Navarra or Penedès. A bar might serve wines from Valdepeñas or the local vineyards. Oloroso wines *(see p581)* are often ordered as a digestif.

Prices and Paying

If you order from *la carta* in a restaurant, your bill can soar way above the price of the *menú del día*, especially if you order pricey items such as fresh seafood, fish or *jamon ibérico (see p422)*. If there is an expensive fish such as sole or swordfish on the menu at a bargain price, it will be frozen. Sea bass and shellfish such as large prawns, lobster and crab, are priced by weight as a rule. The price ranges given in this guide apply to the regular menu, but if you have tapas it is usually cheaper.

La cuenta (the bill) includes service and perhaps a small cover charge. Prices on menus do not always include VAT (IVA), so 10 per cent may be added to the total bill. The Spanish hardly ever tip restaurant waiters more than 5 per cent, often just rounding up the bill.

Cheques are never used in Spain. The major credit cards and international direct debit cards are accepted in most restaurants, but sometimes not in smaller places like tapas bars, cafés or *bodegas*.

Smoking

Smoking is banned inside all bars and restaurants. However, it is permitted on outside terraces.

Wheelchair Access

New restaurants are designed for wheelchairs, but phone in advance to check on access to tables and toilets.

Recommended Restaurants

The restaurants in this guide have been selected for a variety of criteria including good food, service and location. They range from down-to-earth tapas bars to coastal places specializing in seafood and inland locales featuring country fare, to sophisticated establishments with tasting menus prepared by leading chefs. Places serving Modern Spanish food offer contemporary versions of traditional classics, whereas places we have decribed as Traditional Spanish serve more conventional fare, such as stews and fish dishes.

Any entry highlighted as DK Choice offers something that distinguishes it from the masses, be it a celebrity chef, sensational food, unusual location or unique menu.

Extensive choice of wine on show at a restaurant in Santander

Choosing Tapas

Tapas, sometimes called *pinchos*, are small snacks that originated in Andalucía in the 19th century to accompany sherry. Stemming from a bartender's practice of covering a glass with a saucer or *tapa* (cover) to keep out flies, the custom progressed to a chunk of cheese or bread being used, and then to a few olives being placed on a platter to accompany a drink. Once free of charge, tapas are usually paid for nowadays (except in cities like Granada and León) and a selection makes a delicious light meal. Choose from cold meats to elaborately prepared hot dishes of meat, seafood or vegetables.

Mixed green olives

Patatas bravas is a piquant dish of fried potatoes with a spicy red sauce.

Albóndigas (meatballs) are a hearty *tapa*, often served with a spicy tomato sauce.

Almendras fritas are fried, salted almonds.

Banderillas are canapés skewered on toothpicks. The entire canapé should be eaten at once.

Calamares fritos are squid rings and tentacles which have been dusted with flour before being deep-fried in olive oil. They are usually served garnished with a piece of lemon.

Jamón serrano is salt-cured ham dried in mountain *(serrano)* air.

On the Tapas Bar

Almejas Clams

Berberechos Steamed cockles

Berenjenas al horno Roasted aubergines (eggplants)

Boquerones Anchovies

Boquerones al natural Fresh anchovies in garlic and olive oil

Buñuelos de bacalao Salted cod fritters

Butifarra Catalonian sausage

Calabacín rebozado Battered courgettes (zucchini) (Catalan)

Calamares a la romana Fried squid rings

Callos Tripe

Caracoles Snails

Champiñones al ajillo Mushrooms fried in white wine with garlic

Chistorra Spicy sausage

Chopitos Cuttlefish fried in batter

Chorizo al vino Chorizo sausage cooked in red wine

Chorizo diablo Chorizo served flamed with brandy

Costillas Spare ribs

Criadillas Bulls' testicles

Croquetas Croquettes of ham, seafood, chicken or vegetables

Empanada Pastry filled with tomato, onion and meat or fish

Ensaladilla rusa Potatoes, carrots, red peppers, peas, olives, boiled egg, tuna and mayonnaise

Gambas al pil pil Spicy, garlicky fried king prawns (shrimp)

Longaniza roja Spicy red pork sausage from Aragón (*Longaniza blanca* is paler and less spicy)

Magro Pork in a paprika and tomato sauce

Tapas Bars

Even a small village will have at least one bar where the locals go to enjoy drinks, tapas and conversation with friends. On Sundays and holidays, favourite places are packed with whole families enjoying the fare. In larger towns it is customary to move from bar to bar, sampling the specialities of each. A *tapa* is a single serving, whereas a *ración* is similar to an entrée-sized portion. Tapas are usually eaten standing or perching on a stool at the bar rather that sitting at a table, for which a surcharge is usually made.

Diners make their choice at a busy tapas bar

Chorizo, a popular sausage flavoured with paprika and garlic, may be eaten cold or fried and served hot.

Salpicón de mariscos is a luxurious cold salad of assorted fresh seafood in a zesty vinaigrette.

Gambas a la plancha is a simple but flavourful dish of grilled prawns (shrimp).

Tortilla española is the ubiquitous Spanish omelette of onion and potato bound with egg.

Queso manchego is a sheep's-milk cheese from La Mancha.

Pollo al ajillo consists of small pieces of chicken (often wings) sauted and then simmered with a garlic sauce.

Manitas de cerdo Pig's trotters

Mejillones Mussels

Morcilla Black (blood) pudding

Muslitos del mar Crab-meat croquettes, on a claw skewer

Navajas Grilled razor-shells

Orejas de cerdo Pig's ears

Pa amb tomàquet Bread rubbed with olive oil and tomatoes (Catalan)

Pan de ajo Garlic bread

Patatas a lo pobre Potato chunks sautéd with onions and red and green peppers

Patatas alioli Potato chunks in a garlic mayonnaise

Pescadito fritos Small fried fish

Pimientos de padrón Small green peppers which are occasionally hot

Pimientos rellenos Stuffed peppers

Pinchos morunos Pork skewers

Pisto Thick ratatouille of diced tomato, onion and courgette

Pulpitos Baby octopus

Rabo de toro Oxtail

Revueltos Scrambled eggs with shrimp, cod or vegetables

Sepia a la plancha Grilled cuttlefish

Sesos Brains, usually lamb or calf

Surtido de Ibéricos Assortment of cold cuts/charcuterie

Tabla de quesos A range of Spanish cheeses

Tortilla riojana Ham, sausage and red pepper omelette

Tostas Bread with various toppings such as tuna or Brie

Verdura a la plancha Grilled vegetables

What to Drink in Spain

Spain is one of the world's largest wine-producing countries and many fine wines are made here, particularly reds in La Rioja and sherry in Andalucía. Many other beverages – alcoholic and non-alcoholic – are served in bars and cafés, which provide an important focus for life in Spain. The Spanish are also great coffee drinkers. In the summer, a tempting range of cooling drinks is on offer, in addition to beer, which is always available. Brandy and a variety of liqueurs, such as *anís*, are drunk as apéritifs and *digestifs*, as is chilled pale gold fino sherry.

Customers enjoying a drink at a terrace café in Seville

Hot chocolate

A plate of *churros* (batter sticks)

Café con leche

Camomile   Lime flower

Hot Drinks

Café con leche is a large half-and-half measure of milk and espresso coffee; *café cortado* is an espresso with a splash of milk; *café solo* is a black coffee. Hot chocolate is also popular and is often served with *churros* (batter sticks). Herbal teas include *manzanilla* (camomile) and *tila* (lime flower).

Cold Drinks

In most Spanish towns and cities it is safe to drink the tap water, but people generally prefer to buy bottled mineral water, either still *(sin gas)* or sparkling *(con gas)*. Besides soft drinks, a variety of other thirst-quenching summer beverages is available, including *horchata (see p257)*, a sweet, milky drink made from ground *chufas* (earth almonds). Another popular refreshing drink is *leche merengada* (lemon and cinnamon flavoured milk ice cream). *Gaseosa*, fizzy lemonade, can be drunk either on its own or as a mixer, usually with wine. *Zumo de naranja natural* (freshly squeezed orange juice) is an excellent thirst quencher.

Sparkling and still mineral water

Horchata, made from *chufas*

Spanish Wine

Wine has been produced in Spain since pre-Roman times and there is a great variety on offer today, including famous types such as Rioja. The key standard for the industry is the *Denominación de Origen* (DO) classification, a guarantee of a wine's origin and quality. *Vino de la Tierra* is a classification of wines below that of DO in which over 60 per cent of the grapes come from a specified region. ..no de Mesa, the lowest category, covers ..ic unclassified wines. For more detailed ..rmation on Spain's principal wine-..ucing regions, refer to the following ... Northern Spain *(see pp82–3)*, Eastern ...ee pp206–7), Central Spain *(see ...*), and Southern Spain *(see pp424–5)*.

Penedès white wine   Rioja red wine   Sparkling wine (*cava*)

Spirits and Liqueurs

Spanish brandy, which comes mainly from the sherry bodegas in Jerez, is known as *coñac*. Most bodegas produce at least three different labels and price ranges. Magno is a good middle-shelf brandy; top-shelf labels are Cardenal Mendoza and Duque de Alba. *Anís*, which is flavoured with aniseed, is popular. *Pacharán*, made from sloes, is sweet and also tastes of aniseed. Licor 43 is a vanilla liqueur. Ponche is brandy that has been aged and flavoured with herbs.

Anís *Pacharán* Licor 43 Ponche

Sherry and Vermouth

Two brands of fino sherry

Sherry, or *fino*, is produced in bodegas in Jerez de la Frontera (Andalucía) and in nearby towns El Puerto de Santa María and Sanlúcar de Barrameda *(see pp424–5)*. Similar kinds of wine are produced in Montilla near Córdoba. Pale fino is dry and light and excellent as an apéritif, while amber amontillado (aged fino) has a strong, earthy taste and oloroso is full-bodied and ruddy. Vermouth, or *vermut*, is fast becoming a staple on Spanish drinks menus, with vermouth bars appearing in a number of cities.

Beer

Most Spanish beer *(cerveza)* is bottled lager, although you can almost always find it on draught. Popular brands include Moritz, Alhambra, San Miguel, Cruzcampo, Mahou and Estrella. In Barcelona a glass of beer is called *una caña*; in Madrid, *un tercio*. Alcohol-free lager *(cerveza sin alcohol)* is available.

Bottled beers

Red wine and lemonade

Mixed Drinks

Popular with tourists, sangria is a refreshing mixture of red wine, *gaseosa* (lemonade) and other ingredients including chopped fruit and sugar. Spaniards tend to drink wine diluted with lemonade, or *vino con gaseosa*, also known as *tinto de verano* in the south. Another favourite drink is *Agua de Valencia*, a refreshing blend of *cava* (sparkling wine) and orange juice. Gin and tonic is a popular drink across Spain.

Sangria

How to Read a Wine Label

If you know what to look for, the label will provide a key to the wine's flavour and quality. It will bear the name of the wine and its producer or bodega, its vintage if there is one, and show its *Denominación de Origen* (DO) if applicable. Wines labelled *joven* are recent vintages and the least expensive, while *crianza* and *reserva* wines are aged a minimum of three years – part of that time in oak casks – and therefore more expensive. Table wine *(vino de mesa)*, the lowest quality, may be *tinto* (red), *blanco* (white) or *rosado* (rosé). *Cava* is a sparkling wine made by the *méthode champenoise* in specified areas of origin.

Brand name

Company's crest

Capacity of the bottle

Estate-bottled rather than cooperative

The wine's *Denominación de Origen*

The vintage

Symbol for region

Where to Eat and Drink

Galicia

A CORUÑA: Cúrcuma €
Tapas
Marconi 4, 15002
Tel *646 14 66 42* **Closed** *Mon, Sun*
This small, popular tapas bar is a great-value option. Creative fare and friendly staff. Book ahead.

A CORUÑA: Restaurante Comer y Picar €
Tapas
Calle Comandante Fontanes 1, 15003
Tel *981 28 52 20* **Closed** *Mon & Sun dinner*
Family-run place next to Riazor beach. *Zamburiñas* (scallops) and *pulpo* (octopus) are specialities.

A CORUÑA: Domus €€
Modern Spanish
Calle Ángel Rebollo s/n, 15002
Tel *981 20 11 36* **Closed** *Mon, Tue dinner, Wed & Sun*
An architectural gem with spectacular sea views. Modern Spanish fare, with friendly service.

A CORUÑA: Taberna Gaioso €€
Fine Dining
Plaza España 15, 15001
Tel *981 21 33 55* **Closed** *Sun pm; Mon*
The sophisticated dining room and *bodega* perfectly match the cuisine. Tapas and à la carte menu.

BAIONA: Tapería San Xoán €
Tapas
Rúa San Xoan 19, 36300 (Pontevedra)
Tel *628 89 62 40* **Closed** *Tue*
Excellent, varied tapas served in a stone-built bar-restaurant. Good-value and a lively atmosphere.

BETANZOS: La Taberna 1931 €
Traditional Spanish
Travesía Progreso 6, 15300
Tel *981 97 05 13* **Closed** *Tue*

Fine dining and wine in the elegant Yayo Daporta, Cambados

Home-cooked Galician food and craft beer in a central location. The house speciality is tortilla.

BETANZOS: Vega Comer y Picar €
Traditional Spanish
Calle los Angeles 3, 15300
Tel *981 77 32 54*
Quality local fare. Go for the tortilla – the town's signature dish – and enjoy it either at the bar or in the restaurant area.

DK Choice

CAMBADOS: Yayo Daporta €€€
Fine Dining
Calle del Hospital 7, 36630
Tel *986 52 60 62* **Closed** *Mon, Sun dinner, 14–28 Nov*
Haute cuisine served in an elegant, intimate atmosphere in a 16th-century building. Faultless, innovative cooking underpinned by the finest, freshest ingredients, and accompanied by a selection of wines that guests pick themselves from the bodega. A well-deserved Michelin star holder.

CEDEIRA: Vila Vella Cedeira €€
Traditional Spanish
Paseo Arriba da Ponte 19, 15350
Tel *981 48 07 64* **Closed** *Mon*
Choose between a variety of *pintxos* in the tapas bar or the superb seafood in the dining room at this convivial restaurant.

FISTERRA: O Centelo €€
Seafood
Avenida del Puerto s/n, 15155
Tel *981 74 04 52*
Enjoy fresh seafood while taking in wonderful views over the port, especially at sunset. There is also an inexpensive tapas bar on the ground floor.

LUGO: Taberna do Labrego €
Traditional Spanish
Camino Real 32, 27372, Pacios-Begonte
Tel *982 39 82 62* **Closed** *Mon*
This hidden gem offers great-value Gallegan cuisine in a quaint setting. Also noted for its excellent gin and tonics.

LUGO: Paprica €€
Mediterranean
Calle Noreas 10, 27001
Tel *982 25 58 24* **Closed** *Sun pm; Mon*
This intimate restaurant is decorated in an attractive, modern style. Innovative food at surprisingly competitive prices.

Price Guide
Prices are based on a three-course evening meal for one including a half bottle of house wine, service and taxes.

€ up to €40
€€ €40 to €55
€€€ over €55

MALPICA: As Garzas €€€
Fine Dining
Porto Barizo, 15113
Tel *981 72 17 65*
A modern take on traditional Spanish cuisine earned As Garzas its Michelin star. Huge windows showcase its beach-front setting.

O GROVE: Marisquerias Solaina €€€
Seafood
Avenida Beiramar s/n, 36980
Tel *986 73 34 04*
Top-quality seafood. Match it with a glass of white wine for the perfect accompaniment.

ORTIGUEIRA: Club Naútico €€
Mediterranean
Puerto Deportivo s/n, 15330
Tel *681 05 46 37* **Closed** *Mon*
Delicious seafood served in smart surroundings overlooking the marina. Good, inexpensive tapas as well.

OURENSE: A Taberna €
Traditional Spanish
Calle Julio Prieto 32, 32005
Tel *988 24 33 32* **Closed** *Mon*
This delightfully old-fashioned restaurant serves excellent, home-cooked local cuisine. It has a gourmet shop, too.

OURENSE: La Table €
French
Plaza de la Capela 29, O Pereiro de Aguiar, 32710
Tel *988 25 96 77* **Closed** *Mon*
Small, but top-quality restaurant serving tasty French dishes. Impeccable service.

PONTEVEDRA: Restaurante Mare e Monti €
Italian
Rúa Eduardo Pondal 8, 36003
Tel *886 21 48 94* **Closed** *Mon*
Lovely Italian restaurant. Stone-baked pizzas and traditional pastas feature on the menu.

RIBADEO: Casa Villaronta €
Seafood
Calle de San Francisco 9, 27700
Tel *982 12 86 09*
Casa Villaronta – reputed to serve the best *pulpo* (octopus) in the world – is always busy.

SAN SALVADOR DE POIO:
Casa Solla €€€
Fine Dining
Avenida de Sineiro 7, 36005
Tel *986 87 28 84* **Closed** *Mon,
Thu & Sun dinner; mid-Dec–early
Jan; Semana Santa*
One of the best restaurants in
Spain. Innovative cooking in a
remote setting.

**SANTA COMBA: Fogón Retiro
da Costiña** €€€
Fine Dining
Avenida de Santiago 12, 15840
Tel *981 88 02 44*
Traditional fare elevated to haute
cuisine status by a creative chef.
The bodega provides perfect
accompaniments to superb meals.

**SANTIAGO DE COMPOSTELA:
Abastos 2.0** €
Modern Spanish
*Plaza de Abastos s/n, Casetas 13–18,
15704*
Tel *654 01 59 37* **Closed** *Mon, Sun*
An appealing contemporary
approach to traditional cuisine
using fresh, local produce.

**SANTIAGO DE COMPOSTELA:
O Dezaseis** €
Tapas
Calle de San Pedro 16, 15703
Tel *981 57 76 33* **Closed** *Sun*
A stylish, rustically decorated bar
serving a choice of traditional
and creative tapas, plus a fan-
tastic set lunch *(menú del día)*.

**SANTIAGO DE COMPOSTELA:
O Gato Negro** €
Seafood
Rúa Raíña s/n, 15702
Tel *981 58 31 05* **Closed** *Sun pm; Mon*
Quintessentially authentic
sea-food bar and restaurant.
Excellent tapas and main dishes.

**SANTIAGO DE COMPOSTELA:
Casa Marcelo** €€
Fusion
Rúa Hortas 1, 15705
Tel *981 55 85 80* **Closed** *Mon, Sun*
Watch the chef preparing Asian-
fusion delights in the open kitchen
at this charming restaurant.

**SANXENXO: La Taberna
de Rotilio** €€
Traditional Spanish
Avenida del Puerto 7–9, 36960
Tel *986 72 02 00* **Closed** *Mon, Sun
dinner, Nov–mid-Mar*
All the regional classics in generous portions and creatively
presented. Friendly service.

VERÍN: Casa Zapatillas €
Traditional Spanish
Avenida Luis Espada 34, 32600
Tel *988 41 07 29*

Impeccable style at El Corral del Indianu, Arriondas

Classic Spanish cuisine, great
tapas and a phenomenal selection of Galician wines make this
traditional eatery a local favourite.

VIGO: Tapas Areal €
Tapas
Calle de México 36, 36204
Tel *986 41 86 43*
Varied selection of tapas at this
popular spot. Leave room for a
home-made dessert.

VIGO: La Trastienda del Cuatro €
Modern Spanish
Pablo Morillo 4, 36201
Tel *986 11 58 81*
The creative menu here combines
tradition with modernity. Fine
selection of wines. Good service.

VIVEIRO: Restaurante Nito €€€
Traditional Spanish
Hotel Ego, Playa de Area 1, 27850
Tel *982 56 09 87*
Located in Hotel Ego, this lovely
spot combines great seafood
with glorious views.

Asturias and
Cantabria

**AMPUERO: Restaurante
Solana** €€
Fine dining
La Bien Aparecida No 11, 39849
Tel *942 67 67 18* **Closed** *Mon,
Sun dinner, 15 days in Nov*
Michelin-starred hilltop restau-
rant. Worth the journey for its
creative cuisine and great views.

**ARRIONDAS: El Corral
del Indianu** €€
Modern Spanish
Avenida de Europa 14, 33540
Tel *985 84 10 72* **Closed** *Thu*
Elaborate cooking with the finest
ingredients has earned chef José
Antonio Campoviejo a Michelin
star at this chic restaurant. The *menú
de degustación* has 12 courses.

DK Choice

**ARRIONDAS: Casa
Marcial** €€€
Fine Dining
La Salgar 10, Parres, 33540
Tel *985 84 09 91* **Closed** *Mon*
Set in the rolling countryside,
Casa Marcial was the childhood
home of renowned chef Nacho
Manzano and is now host to
his inspired cooking and two
Michelin stars. The menu offers
modern twists on Spanish
classics complemented by an
impressive wine list – all served
in elegant surroundings.

**CANGAS DE ONÍS:
Sidrería Los Ramos** €
Traditional Spanish
La Venta s/n, 33550
Tel *608 14 59 97* **Closed** *Jan–Feb*
Delicious, regional home-cooked
food. A solid choice, always pop-
ular with the locals.

**CASTRO URDIALES:
La Arboleda** €
Seafood
Calle Ardigales 48, 39700
Tel *942 87 19 93*
In addition to local fish and
seafood, La Arboleda also serves
quality meats. Reservation
recommended. Friendly staff.

CUDILLERO: Bar Casa Julio €
Traditional Spanish
Plaza de la Marina 7, 33150
Tel *617 43 82 54*
Good-quality food, especially fish
and seafood, in this cosy eatery
highly recommended by locals.

GIJÓN: Sidrería La Galana €
Tapas
Plaza Mayor 10, 33201
Tel *985 17 24 29*
Boasting a great location on the
bustling Plaza Mayor in the Old
Town, La Galana offers superb
tapas and a vibrant atmosphere.

For more information on types of restaurants *see page 577*

GIJÓN: Ciudadela €€
Mediterranean
Calle Capua 7, 33202
Tel *985 34 77 32*   **Closed** *Sun dinner; Mon*
The dishes from the constantly changing menu of this inviting restaurant are served with style. The two dining areas include a romantic, candlelit grotto.

LAREDO: La Marina Company €
Seafood
Calle Zamanillo, 39770
Tel *942 60 63 35*
Simple, well-executed traditional fare with excellent-value set menu options. In the Old Town.

The dining area located by the sea at Annua, San Vicente de la Barquera

LASTRES: El Barrigón de Bertín €€
Fine Dining
Calle San Jose, 33330
Tel *985 85 04 45*   **Closed** *Tue*
Multi-award-winning chef with an haute cuisine take on classic Asturian cooking. Uses the finest and freshest local ingredients.

LLANES: Sidrería El Rubiu €
Traditional Spanish
Lugar Vidiago, s/n, 33597
Tel *985 41 14 18*
Stone-built restaurant serving hearty Asturian food. The *fabada* (bean stew) is a must-try.

NOJA: Restaurante Sambal €€
Fine Dining
Calle el Arenal, 39180
Tel *942 63 15 31*   **Closed** *Sun–Thu dinner in winter*
Gourmet dining accompanied by fine views. Terrace for good weather. Excellent wine list.

NOREÑA: Sidrería Casa El Sastre €
Traditional Spanish
Calle de Fray Ramon 27, 33180
Tel *985 74 12 52*   **Closed** *Mon*
Home-cooked regional fare and delicious desserts. Wash it all down with a local cider.

OVIEDO: Taberna Salcedo €
Traditional Spanish
Bermúdez de Castro 38, 33011
Tel *984 28 37 49*
Growing increasingly popular among locals, this place offers a mainly traditional menu, with the occasional modern dish. Good wine selection, too.

OVIEDO: Casa Fermín €€€
Fine Dining
Calle de San Francisco 8, 33003
Tel *985 21 64 52*   **Closed** *Sun*
Casa Fermín has a well-deserved reputation for excellence, and the high prices reflect the quality. Modern decor.

POTES: Casa Cayo €
Traditional Spanish
Calle Cantabra, 6, 39570
Tel *942 73 01 50*
Hearty, regional fare. Perfect after a day's hiking in the mountains. The restaurant has a cellar with good-quality wines.

RIBADESELLA: Restaurante Güeyu Mar €€€
Seafood
Playa de Vega 84, 33560
Tel *985 86 08 63*
The terrace of this fine restaurant specializing in grilled fish and seafood overlooks Vega beach.

SAN VICENTE DE LA BARQUERA: Annua €€€
Fine Dining
Paseo de la Barquera s/n, 39540
Tel *942 71 50 50*   **Closed** *Mon*
Michelin-starred restaurant with breathtaking views over the sea. Impeccable cooking, creative menus and a superb wine list.

SANTA EULALIA DE OSCOS: Mesón La Cerca €
Traditional Spanish
La Cerca, 33776
Tel *985 62 60 41*
Located in a quaint building with outdoor tables under a *horreo* (stilted grain store). Famous for the empanadas.

SANTANDER: Marcello €
Italian
Calle Floranes 29, 39010
Tel *942 37 30 07*   **Closed** *Mon*
This authentic Italian restaurant serves a wide range of traditional food. Enjoy excellent service and a relaxed atmosphere.

SANTANDER: La Bombi €€
Traditional Spanish
Calle de Casimiro Sáinz 15, 39003
Tel *942 21 30 28*
Brilliantly executed northern Spanish food in a beautifully decorated dining room.

SANTANDER: Cañadio €€
Tapas
Calle de Gómez Oreña, 15, 39003
Tel *942 31 41 49*   **Closed** *Sun*
This long-established restaurant, with a branch in Madrid, is a classy joint. Excellent, varied tapas in a fun atmosphere.

SANTANDER: El Marucho €€
Seafood
Calle de Tetuán 21, 39004,
Tel *942 27 30 07*   **Closed** *Tue*
Bite into fresh fish and seafood at this simple, rustic bar-restaurant. Lively atmosphere and a good-value option.

SANTILLANA DEL MAR: Los Blasones €
Traditional Spanish
Plaza de la Gandara, 8, 39330
Tel *942 81 80 70*   **Closed** *Thu in winter; Nov–Mar*
Authentic regional cuisine with an emphasis on local ingredients. Charming, rustic vibe.

SANTILLANA DEL MAR: Casa Uzquiza €
Traditional Spanish
Calle del Escultor Jesús Otero 5, 39330
Tel *942 84 03 56*   **Closed** *Mon*
Enjoy tasty local cuisine in the stone-walled dining room, or out on the pretty terrace in summer.

SOMO: La Alberuca €
Traditional Spanish
Calle Jorganes 1, 39140
Tel *942 51 05 04*
Recommended by locals, this small restaurant offers the best-quality produce in the area.

VILLAVICIOSA: El Verano €€
Seafood
Calle Agüero 3, 33300
Tel *985 89 24 65*
This appealingly unpretentious restaurant in the tiny hamlet of Agüero, about 8 km (5 miles) from Villaviciosa, serves some of the finest seafood in Asturias.

Key to Price Guide *see page 582*

The Basque Country, Navarra & La Rioja

AOIZ: Beti Jai €
Traditional Navarran
Santa Águeda 2, 31430
Tel *948 33 60 52* **Closed** *Sun dinner*
Set in a Basque rural hotel. Serves classic Navarran fare, but with new culinary twists and flavours.

CINTRUÉNIGO: Maher €€
Fine Dining
Ribera 19, 31592
Tel *948 81 11 50* **Closed** *Sun dinner; Mon; mid-Dec–mid-Jan*
Time-honoured recipes are given a contemporary twist at this elegant restaurant, using seasonal products sourced from Ribera.

ESTELLA: Navarra €€
Traditional Navarran
Calle Gustavo de Maeztu, 31200
Tel *948 55 00 40* **Closed** *Sun dinner; Mon; Jan*
Set in an old Navarran house decked out in medieval decor. Specialities include lamb and stuffed asparagus.

EZCARAY: El Rincón del Vino €
Traditional Riojan
Calle Jesús Nazareno 2, 26280
Tel *941 35 43 75* **Closed** *winter: Mon–Thu dinner, Sep–Jun: Wed*
Suckling lamb and other grilled specialities at the weekend. The adjacent wine shop has thousands of Riojan labels.

EZCARAY: El Portal de Echaurren €€
Modern Riojan
Calle Padre José García 19, 26280
Tel *941 35 40 47* **Closed** *Sun dinner; Mar–Jul: Mon & Tue*
The first restaurant in La Rioja's history to receive a Michelin star. Run alongside a gastronomic hotel. Delicious seafood.

HARO: Las Duelas €
Modern Riojan
San Agustín 2, 26200
Tel *941 30 44 63*

Set in a monastery, Las Duelas offers a wide variety of Riojan dishes. Flawless balance between traditional and creative cuisine.

LOGROÑO: Bar Soriano €
Tapas
Travesía del Laurel 2, 26001
Tel *941 22 88 07* **Closed** *Wed*
Each tapas bar has a different speciality on this popular street: here you'll find succulent *champis* (button mushrooms), served *pintxo*-style on French bread.

LOGROÑO: Mesón Egües €
Traditional Riojan
Campa 3, 26005
Tel *941 22 86 03* **Closed** *Sun*
Uses the highest-quality ingredients to create simple but hearty grilled dishes. Try the braised oxtail and *chuleta* (chop).

OLITE: Casa Zanito €€
Traditional Navarran
Rua Mayor 16, 31390
Tel *948 74 00 02* **Closed** *Mon & Tue; 18 Dec–24 Jan*
A charming hotel-restaurant located in medieval Olite. Go for the fixed-price Menú Labrit.

PAMPLONA: Ansoleaga 33 €
Fine Dining
Florencio de Ansoleaga 33, 31001
Tel *948 04 48 60*
Nibble on Navarran food while admiring the views of the old town from the dining room.

PAMPLONA: Café Bar Gaucho €
Pintxos
Calle de Espoz y Mina 7, 31002
Tel *948 22 50 73*
This small, buzzing place is one of Pamplona's best pintxo bars, with a huge variety of flavoursome dishes. Cash only.

PAMPLONA: Europa €€
Fine Dining
Espoz y Mina 11, 31002
Tel *948 22 18 00* **Closed** *Sun*
Situated in Hotel Europa in the heart of town. Try the chocolate mousse with orange confit.

SAN SEBASTIÁN: La Fábrica €
Modern Basque
Calle Puerto 17, 20003
Tel *943 43 21 10*
In the old town near the harbour, this restaurant is housed in a former brewery. One of their specialities is sea bass.

SAN SEBASTIÁN: Zeruko €
Pintxos
Pescadería 10 (Old Town)
Tel *943 42 34 51* **Closed** *Mon*
Whipping up creative *pintxos*, trendy Zeruko is a hugely popular destination in San Sebastián's "pintxo-crawl" scene.

DK Choice

SAN SEBASTIÁN: Akelarre €€€
Modern Basque
Padre Orkolaga 56, 20008
Tel *943 31 12 09* **Closed** *Sun dinner, Mon; Jan–Jun: Tue; Feb & early Oct*
One of Spain's most highly regarded restaurants, Akelarre offers inventive Basque cuisine rooted in tradition. The dining room's sweeping views of the Atlantic set the perfect stage for an unforgettable meal. Order the *menú de degustación* to sample the best of the season.

SAN SEBASTIÁN: Arzak €€€
Modern Basque
Alcalde José Elosegui 273, 20015
Tel *943 278 465/34 943 285 593*
Closed *Sun & Mon; mid-Jun–early Jul*
Dine at this iconic Basque eatery by living legend Juan Mari Arzak and his daughter Elena. With three Michelin stars, Arzak has a "laboratory of flavours" next door, where alchemists experiment with more than 1,000 ingredients.

SAN VICENTE DE LA SONSIERRA: Casa Toni €
Traditional Riojan
Zumalacárregui 27, 26338
Tel *941 33 40 01* **Closed** *Tue–Thu & Sun dinner; Mon; 2 wks Jul & Sep*
Traditional Riojan food with a modern twist. Go for the special, four-course Menú el Rocio for €25.

SANTO DOMINGO DE LA CALZADA: Los Caballeros €
Traditional Riojan
Calle Mayor 58, 26250
Tel *941 34 27 89* **Closed** *Sun dinner*
Cod is the speciality at this restaurant located in a historic building next to the cathedral, but there is a wide-ranging regional menu, too. Rustic decor.

Views of the Atlantic from Akelarre's dining room, San Sebastián

For more information on types of restaurants *see page 577*

TAFALLA: Túbal €€€
Traditional Navarran
Plaza de Navarra 4, 31300
Tel *948 70 08 52* **Closed** *Sun & Tue–Thu dinner; Mon*
Vegetables from the restaurant's own garden feature prominently on the menu. Tables on balconies overlook the square.

TUDELA: Restaurante 33 €
Fine Dining
Calle Pablo Sarasate 7, 31500
Tel *948 82 76 06* **Closed** *Sun–Wed dinner*
The food is big on flavour at this award-winning establishment. Most products are from the restaurant's own garden.

URDÁNIZ: El Molino de Urdániz €€€
Fine Dining
Crta Francia por Zubiri (Na-135) km 16.5, 31698
Tel *948 30 41 09* **Closed** *Mon; Tue, Wed & Sun dinner*
A rustic stone-built house serving dishes that combine traditional food from the Pyrenees with cutting-edge execution and complex flavours.

VIANA: Borgia €€
Fine Dining
Calle Serapio Urra, 1 31230
Tel *948 64 57 81*
Modern decor and authentic food of the highest quality. Borgia specializes in steaks – try the beef cheek with blood-orange sauce.

VITORIA: El Clarete €
Modern Basque
Cercas Bajas 18, 01001
Tel *945 26 38 74* **Closed** *Mon–Wed dinner; Sun*
Food deeply rooted in Basque tradition with an innovative twist. Go for the *marmitako* (tuna stew) with lobster or suckling pig with a mango cream. Great tapas bar as well.

VITORIA: Zaldiaran €€€
Modern Basque
Avenida Gasteiz 21, 01008
Tel *945 13 48 22* **Closed** *Tue*
Zaldiaran is regarded as Vitoria's best restaurant. Relish creative fare made with elaborate techniques and flavours.

Barcelona

Old Town

La Báscula €
Vegetarian **Map** 5 C3
Flassaders 30, 08003
Tel *933 19 98 66*

A charming café in a renovated old chocolate factory serving vegetarian and vegan dishes, plus great cakes and pastries.

Bodega la Plata €
Tapas **Map** 5 A3
Mercé 28, 08002
Tel *933 15 10 09*
A miniature, old-fashioned bodega serving wine straight from the barrel along with a small selection of tapas. The freshly fried sardines are a huge hit.

DK Choice

Café de L'Acadèmia €
Modern Catalan **Map** 5 B3
Lledó 1, Plaça Sant Just, 08002
Tel *933 19 82 53* **Closed** *Sat & Sun; 3 wks Aug*
A long-established favourite, Café de L'Acadèmia serves fresh, modern Catalan cuisine in a brick-lined dining room and out on a candlelit terrace overlooking an enchanting Gothic square. The menu changes regularly according to what is freshly available on the market.

Can Culleretes €
Traditional Catalan **Map** 5 A3
Quintana 5, 08002
Tel *933 17 30 22* **Closed** *Mon, Sun dinner*
Barcelona's oldest restaurant, Can Culleretes is great for classics such as *botifarra amb seques* (country sausage with beans) and seafood stew.

Kaiku €
Mediterranean **Map** 5 B3
Plaça del Mar 1, 08003
Tel *932 21 90 82* **Closed** *Mon, Sun dinner; Aug; winter: dinner*

Old-world charm meets new-world tapas at Suculent, Barcelona

Deceptively simple-looking, serving fantastic dishes prepared with smoked rice and home-grown vegetables. Opt for the dessert platter to taste a range.

Lo de Flor €
Mediterranean **Map** 2 E2
Carretes 18, 08001
Tel *934 42 38 53* **Closed** *lunch; Tue; 2 wks Aug*
Romantic, rustic restaurant with minimalist decor. Short but well-chosen wine list.

Mam i Teca €
Modern Catalan **Map** 2 F2
Carrer de la Lluna 4, 08001
Tel *934 41 33 35* **Closed** *Tue, Sat lunch*
Tiny, welcoming space serving simple but exquisite dishes using mainly organic Catalan produce.

La Paradeta €
Seafood **Map** 5 C3
Comercial 7, 08009
Tel *932 68 19 39* **Closed** *Mon*
Fish and chips, Barcelona-style. Choose your fish and watch it being cooked. No reservations.

Quimet i Quimet €
Tapas Bar **Map** 2 D3
Poeta Cabanyes 25, 08004
Tel *934 42 31 42* **Closed** *Sun, Sat dinner; Aug*
A tiny, bottle-lined tapas bar with delicious cheeses, canapés and other treats. Standing room only.

Senyor Parellada €
Mediterranean **Map** 5 B3
Argenteria 37, 08003
Tel *933 10 50 94*
Elegant yet relaxed restaurant for modern fare in a handsome 19th-century town house.

DK Choice

Suculent €
Tapas **Map** 2 F3
Rambla del Raval 43, 08001
Tel *934 43 65 79* **Closed** *Mon; Sun dinner*
This pretty old bodega has been reinvented as a trendy gastro bar by a trio of celebrity chefs, while retaining its original essence. It offers a range of creative tapas, cheese and cured meats platters, plus more substantial fare such as lamb chops and rice dishes.

Teresa Carles €
Vegetarian **Map** 5 A1
Carrer de Jovellanos 2, 08001
Tel *933 17 18 29*
This elegant family-run place with wooden interiors is one of the city's best vegetarian restaurants.

Key to Price Guide *see page 582*

Dos Palillos' colourful decor matches its inventive menu, Barcelona

Zim

Tapas   €   **Map** 5 B2
Carrer Daqueria 20, 08002
Tel 934 12 65 48   **Closed** lunch
Miniature bar serving wines by the glass along with simple tapas, with a focus on fine Catalan cheeses.

Gravin

Italian   €€   **Map** 5 B3
Rera Palau 3–5, 08003
Tel 932 68 46 28   **Closed** Mon & Tue lunch
Sophisticated Italian food from the Puglia region in an elegant dining room with exposed brick walls and tiled floors.

La Mar Salada

Mediterranean   €€   **Map** 5 B5
Passeig Joan Borbó 58–59, 08003
Tel 932 21 10 15   **Closed** Tue
Bright and modern setting, with a fantastic set lunch. Great for seafood lovers with dishes such as cod pilpil with honey and spinach.

Pla

Fusion   €€   **Map** 5 A3
Bellafila 5, 08002
Tel 934 12 65 52   **Closed** lunch
Hidden down a narrow street, this reliably good option offers deftly prepared fusion cuisine.

Dos Palillos

Tapas   €€€   **Map** 2 F2
Elisabets 9, 08001
Tel 933 04 05 13   **Closed** Sun & Mon; Tue & Wed lunch
Ultra-chic yet relaxed tapas bar with a Michelin star, serving spectacular Asian fusion tapas.

Koy Shunka

Japanese   €€€   **Map** 5 B3
Carrer Copons 7, 08002
Tel 934 12 79 39   **Closed** Mon; Sun dinner; Aug
A Michelin star supports its claim to being the best Japanese restaurant in the city, with an adventurous menu.

Eixample

Bar Calders

Café   €   **Map** 2 D2
Parlament 25, 08015
Tel 933 29 93 49
A pretty terrace, perfect for a vermut (vermouth) and delicious tapas, hummus and salads. Named after Catalan writer Pere Calders.

Bardeni

Modern Catalan   €€   **Map** 3 C4
València 454, 08013
Chef Dani Lechuga prepares phenomenal tapas for the dedicated carnivore, with dishes such as steak tartare and black pudding croquetas.

Boca Grande

Seafood   €€   **Map** 3 A3
Passatge de la Concepció 12, 08003
Tel 934 67 51 49
This trendy restaurant dishes out delicious fresh seafood in spectacular surroundings. It also has a lovely terrace, oyster bar, winery and cocktail bar.

Fábrica Moritz

Tapas   €€   **Map** 2 E1
Ronda de Sant Antoni 41, 08011
Tel 934 26 00 50
A huge bar and restaurant in a sumptuous, beautifully renovated Modernista building.

Ikibana

Fusion   €€   **Map** 2 D2
Avinguda del Paral.lel 148, 08015
Tel 934 24 46 48
A striking interior and Japanese-Brazilian fusion cuisine make Ikibana one of Barcelona's most stylish restaurants.

Petit Comitè

Modern Catalan   €€   **Map** 3 A3
Passatge de la Concepció 13, 08008
Tel 936 33 76 27   **Closed** Mon
Contemporary decor and food by lauded chef Nandu Jubany make this a popular uptown option.

Tapas 24

Tapas   €€   **Map** 3 A5
Diputació 269, 08007
Tel 934 88 09 77   **Closed** Sun
Inventive selection of everyday to fantastic creative tapas by the chef Carles Abellan.

Tickets

Tapas   €€   **Map** 1 C2
Avinguda Paral·lel 164, 08015
Closed lunch (except Sat); Mon & Sun
Imaginative tapas and a funfair-themed interior in this restaurant. You can only book online at www.ticketsbar.es.

DK Choice

La Xalada

Mediterranean   €€   **Map** 2 D2
Carrer del Parlament 1, 08013
Tel 936 76 03 30   **Closed** Mon & Tue; Wed lunch
One of the trendiest eateries on Carrer del Parlament, La Xalada serves delectable Catalan cuisine, prepared with a deft, modern touch and the very best seasonal produce. There are a few tables out on the small terrace, or you can eat in the delightfully retro interior, with gilded columns and artfully mismatched furnishings and china.

Moments

Modern Catalan   €€€   **Map** 3 A5
Passeig de Gràcia 38–40, 08007
Tel 931 51 87 81   **Closed** Sun & Mon
Chef Raül Balam has earned two Michelin stars for his inventive takes on Catalan cuisine at this sophisticated hotel restaurant.

Further Afield

Casa de Tapes Cañota

Tapas   €   **Map** 1 B2
Lleida 7, 08004
Tel 933 25 91 71   **Closed** Mon, Sun dinner; mid-Aug–early Sep
This big and bustling joint serves gourmet tapas such as succulent beef with garlic.

DK Choice

Gut

Mediterranean   €   **Map** 3 B2
Carrer del Perill 13, Gràcia, 08012
Tel 931 86 63 60
Arrive early for a seat at this charming restaurant, where tasty, healthy food, including vegetarian and gluten-free options, is prepared daily with market-fresh ingredients. Also, don't miss the delicious, home-made cakes.

For more information on types of restaurants see page 577

Cafè Godot €€
Mediterranean Map 3 B2
C/ de Sant Domènec 19, Gràcia, 08012
Tel *933 68 20 36*
Stylish modern café serving
bistro-style food with a
contemporary twist, including
a great brunch on weekends.

Kuai Momos €€
Tapas Map 3 B2
Carrer Martínez de la Rosa 71, Gràcia, 08012
Tel *932 18 53 27* **Closed** *Sun*
A chic, lively restaurant serving
Asian tapas such as *gyoza*
(Japanese dumplings), salads,
curries and rice dishes.

Wagokoro €€
Japanese Map 3 A1
Regàs 35, 08006
Tel *935 01 93 40* **Closed** *Sun–Tue; 1 wk Aug*
Outstanding, authentic
Japanese food is served in this
simple dining room run by a
warm and welcoming Catalan-
Japanese couple.

ABaC €€€
Modern Catalan
Ave Tibidabo 1, 08022
Tel *933 19 66 00* **Closed** *Sun & Mon*
Exceptional cuisine from chef
Jordi Cruz, who, in 2004, became
the youngest Spanish chef to
earn a Michelin star at just 25. His
creations at ABaC have earned
two of the coveted gongs.

Botafumeiro €€€
Seafood Map 3 A2
Gran de Gràcia 81, 08012
Tel *932 18 42 30*
A large, traditional restaurant
with white-aproned waiters
bearing ultra-fresh seafood
platters to the crowded tables
at this popular local.

Catalonia

ANGLÈS: Aliança 1916 €€
Modern Catalan
Carrer Jacint Verdaguer 3, 17160
Tel *972 42 01 56* **Closed** *Mon; Sun, Tue & Wed lunch*
Set in a colourful century-old
villa, this multifunctional space
serves as a café, tapas bar and
(excellent) restaurant.

ARTIES: Casa Irene €€
Traditional Catalan
Carrer Major 3, 25599
Tel *973 64 43 64* **Closed** *Mon*
This elegant restaurant, offering
quality fare, resides in a stone-
built traditional house; perfect
after a day on the ski slopes.

Tables with a picturesque view at El Motel, Figueres

BANYOLES: Ca L'Arpa €€€
Modern Catalan
Passeig Industria 5, 17820
Tel *972 57 23 53* **Closed** *Mon, Tue lunch, Sun dinner*
Part of a chic hotel, this restaurant
specializing in modern Catalan
cuisine can be found in Banyoles'
charming historic quarter.

BEGUR: Fonda Caner €€
Traditional Catalan
Pi i Ralló 10, 17255
Tel *972 62 23 91* **Closed** *Nov–Mar*
A traditional restaurant, with lots
of old-fashioned charm, tucked
away in Begur's old quarter.
Organic and seasonal cuisine.

BEGUR: Restaurant Rostei €€
Mediterranean
Concepció Pi 8, 17255
Tel *972 62 42 15* **Closed** *Sun–Thu, Fri & Sat lunch in winter; Mon, Tue–Sat lunch in summer*
A romantic restaurant in Begur's
historic quarter, Restaurant Rostei
serves delicious seafood and
fantastic desserts.

BESALÚ: Cúria Reial €€
Traditional Catalan
Plaça de la Llibertat 14, 17850
Tel *972 59 02 63* **Closed** *Tue*
Traditional Catalan cuisine served
under stone vaults. Try the duck
with foie gras.

CADAQUÉS: Compartir €€€
Modern Catalan
Riera Sant Vicenç s/n, 17488
Tel *972 25 84 82*
A trio of Catalunya's top chefs offer
highly imaginative dishes such as
sardines marinated in orange,
olives and mint, or asparagus
served with a piquant foam.

CALDES D'ESTRAC: Marola €€
Seafood
Passeig dels Anglesos 6, 08393
Tel *937 91 32 00* **Closed** *Tue; Sun, Mon, Wed & Thu dinner*

A modest yet charming spot with
a beachfront setting – perfect for
fresh seafood and paella.

CAMBRILS: Can Bosch €€€
Seafood
Rambla Jaume I 19, 43850
Tel *977 36 00 19* **Closed** *Mon, Sun dinner; late Dec–Jan*
There is delectable seafood to
be had here, overlooking the
port at Cambrils. The restaurant
has held a coveted Michelin star
since 1984.

ESCUNHAU: El Niu €€
Traditional Catalan
Deth Pònt 1, 25539
Tel *973 64 14 06* **Closed** *Sun dinner; late Jun–late Jul*
Traditional mountain inn with
a roaring fireplace. The menu
features tasty grilled meats. The
dining room has a hunting-
inspired decor.

FIGUERES: El Motel €€€
Traditional Catalan
Avinguda Salvador Dalí 170, 17600
Tel *972 50 05 62*
This elegant restaurant enjoys
a reputation for serving fine
regional cuisine. It also has an
extensive wine list.

GARRAF: La Cúpula €€
Seafood
Platja de Garraf, 08871
Tel *936 32 00 15* **Closed** *Mon & Tue; Sun, Wed & Thu dinner*
With a splendid clifftop setting,
La Cúpula is a perfect place for
a seafood lunch.

GIRONA: Divinum €€
Tapas
Albereda 7, 17004
Tel *872 08 02 18* **Closed** *Sun; Mon dinner*
Divinum is an elegant,
contemporary tapas restaurant
with an excellent wine list to
accompany the petite dishes.

DK Choice

**GIRONA: El Celler
de Can Roca** €€€
Modern Catalan
Carrer de Can Sunyer 48, 17007
Tel *972 22 21 57* **Closed** *Sun &
Mon; 1 wk Aug; Easter*
This temple to molecular
gastronomy boasts three
Michelin stars. It is run by the
three Roca brothers: Joan is
head chef, Jordi is dessert chef
and Josep is the sommelier.
Expect innovative dishes such
as oysters with champagne and
caramelized olives served on a
bonsai tree. You must reserve
11 months in advance.

**HORTA DE SANT JOAN:
Mas del Cigarrer** €
Traditional Catalan
*Crta Horta de Sant Joan a Bot s/n,
43596*
Tel *977 43 51 53* **Closed** *mid-Sep–
June; Sun & Mon, Tue–Thu dinner*
Famous for *calçots* (barbecued
leek-like vegetable) and cargolades
(feasts of *calçots* and wild snails).

L'AMETLLA DE MAR: L'Alguer €€
Seafood
Trafalgar 21, 43860
Tel *977 45 61 24* **Closed** *Mon;
mid-Dec–mid Jan*
Fresh seafood served in a dining
room with door-to-ceiling glass
windows, right on the seafront.

**L'ESPLUGA DE FRANCOLÍ:
Hostal del Senglar** €€
Traditional Catalan
Plaça Montserrat Canals 1, 43440
Tel *977 87 04 11* **Closed** *Mon*
This place has an excellent
reputation for flame-grilled
meats and hearty country dishes.

LLAGOSTERA: Els Tinars €€€
Modern Catalan
Crta de Sant Feliu a Girona, km 7, 17240
Tel *972 83 06 26* **Closed** *Mon, Sun
dinner*
First-rate contemporary cuisine
with a focus on seasonal local
produce. Good value set menus.

LLEIDA: L'Estel de la Mercè €€
Modern Catalan
Carrer Cardenal Cisneros 30, 25002
Tel *973 28 80 08* **Closed** *Mon,
Sun dinner*
A bright hotel-restaurant serving
fresh, contemporary Catalan
cuisine. A gastro tapas bar, too.

PERALADA: Cal Sagristà €€
Traditional Catalan
Rodona 2, 17491
Tel *972 53 83 01* **Closed** *Tue, Mon
dinner; 3 wks Feb & Nov*

Fresh, delicious Catalan cuisine
in a charmingly restored old
convent; save room for dessert.

RIPOLL: Reccapolis €€
Traditional Catalan
Crta de Sant Joan 68, 17500
Tel *972 70 21 06* **Closed** *Wed, Sun–
Thu dinner; mid-Aug–mid-Sep*
Comforting country favourites in
a handsome century-old house;
excellent set lunch.

ROSES: Rafa's €€
Seafood
Carrer Sant Sebastià 56, 17480
Tel *972 25 40 03* **Closed** *Sun, Mon;
Dec–mid-Jan*
Informal, convivial and hugely
popular seafood restaurant with
expertly cooked fish.

ROSES: Els Brancs €€€
Modern Catalan
Av. de José Díaz Pacheco 26, 17480
Tel *972 25 62 00* **Closed** *lunch; Mon;
Oct–Mar*
An award-winning gastronomic
restaurant serving creative
Catalan cuisine. Amazing terrace
over the cliff, perfect for sunset
views of Roses Bay.

**SANT CARLES DE LA RÀPITA:
Miami Can Pons** €€
Seafood
Passeig Marítim 18–20, 43540
Tel *977 / 4 05 51* **Closed** *Sun*
Classic seafront restaurant in
the Hotel Miami Mar. Attentive
service and excellent value.

**SANT FELIU DE GUÍXOLS:
Cau Del Pescador** €€
Seafood
Carrer Sant Doménec 11, 17220
Tel *972 32 40 52* **Closed** *Mon; Tue
in winter*
A smart restaurant in an old
fisherman's cottage. Sample the
justly famed *suquet* (seafood stew).

The white-on-blonde, luxurious dining
room at El Celler de Can Roca, Girona

**SANT FELIU DE GUÍXOLS:
Villa Más** €€€
Traditional Catalan
Passeig de Sant Pol 95, 17220
Tel *972 82 25 26* **Closed** *Mon except
Jun–Aug; early Dec–early Jan*
Enchanting 19th-century villa
overlooking the Sant Pol beach.
Outstanding Catalan cuisine and
a fine selection of wines.

**SANT FRUITÓS DE BAGES:
L'Ó** €€€
Modern Catalan
Camí de Sant Benet de Bages, 08272
Tel *938 75 94 29* **Closed** *Mon–Wed,
Sun dinner*
Minimalist dining room in a
medieval monastery. Inventive
Catalan cuisine by Michelin-
starred chef Jordi Llobet.

**SANT JOAN DE LES ABADESSES:
La Teuleria** €€
Traditional Catalan
Carretera C 38, km 1 5, 17860
Tel *972 72 05 07* **Closed** *Wed; Sun
dinner; last wk Aug*
An elegant restaurant offering
such regional dishes as roasted
lamb from the Ripollès area. Very
good-value gastronomic menu.

**SANT POL DE MAR:
Sant Pau** €€€
Modern Catalan
Carrer Nou 10, 08395
Tel *937 60 06 62* **Closed** *Sun & Mon;
Thu lunch, 3 wks May & Nov*
Carme Ruscalleda, one of the
world's best chefs, works her
magic here at one of Spain's
finest restaurants.

**SANT SADURNÍ D'ANOIA:
La Cava d'en Sergi** €€
Modern Catalan
Carrer de València 17, 08770
Tel *938 91 16 16* **Closed** *Mon,
Sun dinner (all day last Sun of the
month); 3 wks Aug*
Stylish restaurant serving
modernized Catalan classics with
a wonderful range of local wines.

**SANTA CRISTINA D'ARO:
Can Roquet** €€
Mediterranean
*Plaça de l'Església, Romanyà de la
Selva, 17246*
Tel *972 83 30 81*
Tasty modern French and Catalan
cuisine, and a lovely terrace
overlooking fields and woods.

SITGES: Cinnamon €
Fusion
Passeig de Pujades 2, Vallpineda, 08750
Tel *938 94 71 66* **Closed** *Mon & Tue;
Wed, Thu & Sun dinner*
Delicious Asian fusion cuisine
in a lovely old farmhouse. Hosts
DJ sessions and other events.

For more information on types of restaurants *see page 577*

SITGES: El Pou €
Tapas
Sant Pau 5, 08770
Tel *931 28 99 21* **Closed** *Tue; Mon,
Wed & Thu lunch in winter*
In the old centre, this relaxed
restaurant offers a great selection
of classic and modern tapas.

TARRAGONA: La Cuineta €
Mediterranean
Baixada del Patriarca 2, 43003
Tel *977 22 61 01* **Closed** *lunch; Sun*
This delightful little restaurant in
the historic quarter of Tarragona
serves fresh Mediterranean dishes.
It also offers a great-value lunch
menu for €15.

TARRAGONA: Aq €€
Modern Catalan
Carrer Les Coques 7, 43003
Tel *977 21 59 54* **Closed** *Sun & Mon*
Exciting contemporary cuisine by
chef Ana Ruiz is served up in this
smart dining room. The lunch
menu is great value.

TARRAGONA: Sol-Ric €€
Mediterranean
Avenida Via Augusta 227, 43007
Tel *977 23 20 32* **Closed** *Mon;
Sun dinner*
Savour divine seafood and other
regional fare in an elegant setting
with a great summer terrace.

TARRAGONA: Les Coques €€€
Traditional Catalan
Carrer Sant Llorenç 15, 43003
Tel *977 22 83 00* **Closed** *Sun*
A long-established favourite in
the old city serving sophisticated
regional dishes.

VALLGORGUINA: Can Barrina €€
Traditional Catalan
Crta de Palautordera E, 08469
Tel *938 47 30 65*
This beautiful country hotel and
restaurant in Montseny Natural

Outdoor seating at Restaurant Canteré
in Hecho

Park offers delicious Catalan
food, splendid views and a
charming terrace.

VIC: D. O. Vic €€
Modern Catalan
Sant Miquel de Sants 16, 08500
Tel *938 83 23 96* **Closed** *Mon &
Sun; 2 wks Aug*
Small, minimalist restaurant
serving outstanding Catalan
cuisine with a creative touch.

Aragón

**AÍNSA: Restaurante Bodegón
de Mallacán** €
Regional Spanish
Plaza Mayor 6, 22330
Tel *974 50 09 77*
Hotel Posada Real's restaurant
offers a taste of medieval times.
The wild boar marinated in red
wine is a must-try.

AÍNSA: Callizo €€
Modern Spanish
Plaza Mayor, 22330
Tel *974 50 03 85*
Refined, beautifully presented
and imaginative cuisine served
in this elegant restaurant on the
main square.

**ALBARRACÍN: Rincón del
Chorro** €
Regional Spanish
Calle Chorro 15, 44100
Tel *978 71 01 12* **Closed** *Mon, Sun
dinner; winter: Mon–Thu & Fri–
Sun dinner*
Mega portions are piled high on
your plate at this Albarracín
staple. Oxtail stew is a popular
choice to get your teeth into.

**ANCILES: Restaurante
Ansils** €
Regional Spanish
Calle General Ferraz 6, 22469
Tel *974 55 11 50* **Closed** *Mon–Fri
lunch in winter*
Nestled in a picturesque Pyrenees
village, this place specializes in
local Valle de Benasque cuisine.

**CATALAYUD: Mesón de
La Dolores** €
Regional Spanish
Calle Sancho y Gil 4, 50300
Tel *976 88 90 55*
This traditionally decorated
hotel-restaurant prepares classic
fare with a contemporary touch.

DARACO: Restaurante Ruejo €
Modern Spanish
Calle Mayor 88, 50360
Tel *976 54 50 71*
This classy restaurant serves up
an inventive menu featuring,

among other specialities,
octopus salad and cheese and
honey ice cream.

ESQUEDES: Venta del Sotón €€
Regional Spanish
*Carretera A-132 Huesca-Puente la
Reina km 14, 22810*
Tel *974 27 02 41* **Closed** *Tue lunch
(Jul–Oct), Sun–Wed dinner; Mon;
3wks in Nov*
Sample the tasting menu at this
ivy-clad, slate-roofed establish-
ment. The large circular chimney
is typical of Pyrenean properties.

FRAGA: +Billauba €€
Regional Spanish
Avenida de Aragón 41E, 22520
Tel *974 47 41 67* **Closed** *Sun; Mon–
Thu dinner; 1 wk Jan, 2 wks Aug*
Every season marks a new menu
at +Billauba, with dishes crafted
from freshly sourced ingredients.

**GRAUS: Restaurante
El Criticón** €
Traditional Spanish
*Hotel Palacio del Obispo, Plaza
Coreche, 222430*
Tel *974 54 59 00* **Closed** *Sun–Thu
dinner*
A temple to classic Spanish food
named for a book by Baltasar
Gracían, who lived in Graus.

HECHO: Restaurante Canteré €
Modern Spanish
Calle Aire 1, 22720
Tel *974 37 52 14* **Closed** *Sun–Thu
dinner; Wed*
Enjoy the popular bar, located
at ground level, before moving
up to this cutting-edge
restaurant with thematic
seasonal menus.

DK Choice

HUESCA: El Origen €
Modern Spanish
Plaza de la Justicia 4, 22001
Tel *974 22 97 45*
Old meets new at this central
Huesca spot, which, although
committed to Aragonese
cuisine, whips up some delightful dishes from across the
country. Opt for the fixed-price
tasting menu. Vegetarians are
well catered for here. There is a
children's playground to keep
the kids amused as well.

JACA: La Tasca de Ana €
Tapas
Calle Ramiro I 3, 22700
Tel *974 36 47 26* **Closed** *2 wks May &
Sep; winter: Mon–Fri lunch*
Efficient waiters serve a variety of
tapas treats at this reasonably
priced bar.

Contemporary, sleek dining room at Saboya 21, Tarazona

SOS DEL REY CATÓLICO:
La Cocina del Principal €€
Traditional Spanish
Calle Fernando El Católico 13, 50680
Tel 948 88 83 48 **Closed** Mon
Fresh, locally sourced fruit
and vegetables are used at this
establishment, located in the
centre of the medieval village.

TARAZONA: Saboya 21 €€
Traditional Spanish
Calle Marrodán 34, 50500
Tel 976 64 35 15 **Closed** Sat–Thu
dinner; Mon
Light, bright dining room boasts
a menu to match its decor. Local
meat, seafood and vegetable
dishes on offer.

TERUEL: Restaurante Yain €
Traditional Spanish
Plaza de la Judería 9, 44001
Tel 978 62 40 76 **Closed** Mon & Sun;
Tue–Thu dinner
Located in the town's Jewish
quarter, this establishment prides
itself on the excellence of its
sommellier. It takes its name from
the Hebrew word for wine.

TERUEL: Restaurante Rufino €€
Traditional Spanish
Calle Ronda Ambeles 36, 44001
Tel 978 60 55 26 **Closed** Sun &
Mon dinner
This small, stylish restaurant
specializing in truffles draws
large crowds.

ZARAGOZA: Palomeque €
Tapas
Calle Agustín Palomeque 11, 50004
Tel 976 21 40 82 **Closed** Sun
Come here for tapas in the
morning and more substantial
meals during lunch and dinner.
Presentation is sheer artistry.

ZARAGOZA: La Rinconada
de Lorenzo €€
Modern Spanish
Calle La Salle 3, 50006
Tel 976 55 51 08 **Closed** Sun dinner

Award-winning tapas and choice
traditional recipes at this long-
established local favourite.

ZARAGOZA: El Chalet €€€
Modern Spanish
Calle Santa Teresa de Jesús 25, 50006
Tel 976 56 91 04 **Closed** Mon,
Sun dinner
This two floor converted villa,
just around the corner from Real
Zaragoza's home ground, has a
striking glass canopy. Tasty,
creatively presented dishes.

Valencia and Murcia

ALICANTE. Rincón Gallego €
Seafood
Plaza del Ayuntamiento 7, 03002
Tel 965 14 00 14 **Closed** Mon
Galician restaurant serving tapas
and regional dishes such as pulpo
a la gallega (steamed octopus)
and percebes (goose barnacles).

BENIMANTELL: L'Obrer €
Traditional Spanish
Crta de Alcoi 25, 03516
Tel 965 88 50 88 **Closed** Sun;
dinner (except Fri & Sat in Aug)
Elegant restaurant with charming
decor serving classic Spanish and
Mediterranean fare, including
grilled meats.

CARAVACA DE LA CRUZ:
El Casón de los Reyes €
Traditional Spanish
Crta Granada 11, 30400
Tel 968 72 22 47
A welcoming place with tasty
tapas, meals featuring local recipes
and a great-value set lunch.

FORCALL: Mesón de la Villa €
Traditional Spanish
Plaza Mayor 8, 12310
Tel 964 17 11 25 **Closed** Mon
Vaulted restaurant in 16th-century
cellars below the town hall. Great-
value Mediterranean dishes.

LORCA: Paredes €
Traditional Spanish
Calle de Granada 588, 30817
Tel 626 27 77 25 **Closed** Tue–Thu
dinner, Sun
Small, welcoming restaurant
serving tasty Spanish cuisine.
Good meat and seafood dishes.

DK Choice

MORELLA: Casa Roque €
Fusion
Calle Cuesta de San Juan 1, 12300
Tel 964 16 03 36 **Closed** Tue–Thu
& Sun dinner; Mon (except Aug)
This popular eating spot is
located in an old stone mansion
high in the wild Mestrat region
of inland Castellón. The eclectic
range of dishes includes such
gastronomic delights as steak
with truffles in puff pastry. With
a superb menú de degustación
and a good-value menu of
the day.

ONDARA: Casa Pepa €€€
Traditional Spanish
Partida de Pamís 7–30, 03760
Tel 965 76 66 06 **Closed** Tue & Sun
dinner; Mon; Jul & Aug
Enjoy Michelin-star food in a
pleasant old mansion amid orange
and olive trees. Expect well-
executed, sophisticated dishes.

VALENCIA: L'Estimat €€
Seafood
Passeig de Neptú 16, Playa de las
Arenas
Tel 963 71 10 18 **Closed** Tue;
Mon & Sun dinner
Perhaps the best seafood spot on
the entire Valencia beachfront.
Wide selection of set menus and
an excellent à la carte choice.

VALENCIA: La Salita €€
Modern Spanish
Calle Séneca 12, 46021
Tel 963 81 75 16
Well-presented contemporary
cuisine from top chef Begoña
Rodrigo, who changes the menu
every fortnight in order to feature
the best seasonal produce.

Madrid
Old Madrid

La Bola €
Traditional Spanish **Map** 4 D1
Calle de la Bola 5, 28013
Tel 915 47 69 30
Cocido (stew) cooked in a charcoal
grill has been served here in
traditional clay pots since 1870.
Classic Castilian dishes served in
an old-fashioned atmosphere.

Bright and quirky interior at Delic, Madrid

Casa Lucas   €
Modern Spanish   Map 4 E3
Calle Cava Baja 30, 28005
Tel *913 65 08 04* **Closed** *Wed lunch*
Cosy wine bar serving top-quality
tapas. Try the tuna tataki with
onion, soy sauce and apple
compote. Booking recommended.

Casa Revuelta   €
Tapas   Map 4 E3
*Calle Latoneros 3 (off Plaza Puerta
Cerrada), 28005*
Tel *915 21 45 16* **Closed** *Sun dinner;
Mon*
This long-established classic
boasts a colourfully tiled interior
and serves tasty local dishes,
including salt cod fritters and
callos a la madrileña (tripe).

La Ciudad Invisible   €
Café   Map 4 E1
Costanilla de los Ángeles 7, 28013
Tel *915 42 25 40*
Do a spot of reading at this stylish
yet relaxed travel book-shop and
café-bar. It offers a variety of light
meals, tapas and wine, and regularly
features changing art exhibitions.

DK Choice

Delic   €
Café   Map 3 C3
Costanilla de San Andrés 14, 28005
Tel *913 64 54 50* **Closed** *Mon*
A hip favourite on a charming
square, Delic is perfect for a lazy
breakfast or a tasty light lunch –
try the leek tart or the Japanese
dumplings. With wonderful
tarts, muffins and brownies, it
is also a great stop for tea and
cakes in the afternoons. Later
on, come for cocktails and
occasional live music.

Emma y Julia   €
Italian   Map 4 E3
Calle Cava Baja 19, 28005
Tel *913 66 10 23* **Closed** *Tue lunch;
Mon*

Actors, artists and even the royal
family are regulars at this popular
restaurant that had the first gluten-
free menu in the city. Serves
some of the best pizzas, too.

La Gastroteca de Santiago   €
Modern Spanish   Map 4 D2
Plaza de Santiago 1, 28013
Tel *915 48 07 07*
This place has elaborate dishes
and an excellent wine list. Be sure
to leave space for the artisanal
desserts. Fancy atmosphere,
charming terrace.

Naïa   €
Modern Spanish   Map 4 D3
Plaza de la Paja 3, 28005
Tel *913 66 27 83*   **Closed** *Mon*
This chic but relaxed bistro in the
heart of Old Madrid is popular with
the boho actor and artist type.

El Abrazo de Vergara   €€
Modern Spanish   Map 4 D2
Calle Vergara 10, 28013
Tel *915 42 00 62* **Closed** *Sun dinner;
Mon*
Diners at this sleek restaurant
enjoy a range of gourmet tapas
and traditional Mediterranean
dishes with an innovative twist.

Casa Jacinto   €€
Traditional Madrileño   Map 4 D1
Calle Reloj 20, 28013
Tel *915 42 67 25* **Closed** *Sun dinner;
Mon*
Hidden behind a humble
exterior, Casa Jacinto serves the
best *cocido* (local stew) in town.
Be sure to try their home-made
desserts. Good wine list, too.

Casa Lucio   €€
Traditional Spanish   Map 4 E3
Calle Cava Baja 35, 28005
Tel *913 65 32 52*
Since 1974, Lucio's *huevos
estrellados* (slummed eggs) have
been a speciality of this eatery
serving quality fare in a traditional
setting. Long list of Spanish wines.

Julián de Tolosa   €€
Spanish   Map 4 D3
Calle Cava Baja 18, 28005
Tel *913 65 82 10* **Closed** *Sun dinner*
A handsome restaurant with
exposed brick walls, famous
for its huge, succulent steaks
cooked on a charcoal brazier.
The menu also features a number
of Basque specialities.

Botín   €€€
Traditional Madrileño   Map 4 E3
Calle Cuchilleros 17, 28005
Tel *913 66 42 17*
Listed by the *Guinness Book of
Records* as the world's oldest
restaurant, Botín is set in a series
of rustic interconnected dining
rooms and is justly lauded for
its superb *cochinillo* (roast
suckling pig).

Dstage   €€€
Fine Dining   Map 5 B5
Calle Regueros 8, 28004
Tel *917 02 15 86*
Highly acclaimed chef Diego
Guerrero has garnered a string
of awards for his stunning
cuisine. There is a choice of
degustation menus, each with
around 12 artistically presented
and ever-evolving courses.

La Terraza del Casino   €€€
Modern Spanish   Map 7 A2
Calle Alcalá 15, 28014
Tel *915 32 12 75* **Closed** *Mon, Sun*
Dazzling decor and a stunning
terrace are matched by
impressive adventurous fare
by an award-winning chef.

Bourbon Madrid

**Café del Círculo de
Bellas Artes**   €
Café   Map 7 B2
Calle Marqués de Casa Riera 2, 28014
Tel *913 60 54 00*
This airy Art Deco café is
located in a beautiful cultural
centre, and is worth coming for
everything from coffee to a tasty
lunch, to evening cocktails.

Café Gijón   €
Café   Map 6 D5
Calle Paseo de Recoletos 21, 28004
Tel *915 21 54 25*
One of Madrid's famous literary
cafés, established in 1887, Gijón
serves classic dishes with a
modern twist in a wood-panelled
room or on the large terrace.

La Casa del Abuelo   €
Tapas   Map 7 A2
Calle Victoria 12, 28012
Tel *910 00 01 33*
La Casa del Abuelo (Grandfather's
House) has been in the hands of

the same family for a century, and the family specializes in delicious prawns served with a local sweet wine and a range of tasty tapas.

Cien Llaves €
Traditional Spanish   **Map** 7 C1
C/ Paseo de Recoletos 2, 28001
Tel 915 77 59 55   **Closed** Mon & Tue dinner; Sun
Located in the old kitchens of the Palacio de Linares. The terrace, a unique outdoor setting in downtown Madrid, has a magical atmosphere, surrounded by greenery.

Lateral Gastrobar €
Tapas   **Map** 7 A3
Plaza de Santa Ana 12, 28012
Tel 914 20 15 82
One of Madrid's best terraces, the Lateral offers a variety of pintxos, which use quality products and merge traditional and avant-garde recipes.

Ainhoa €€
Basque   **Map** 5 C5
Calle Bárbara de Braganza 12, 28004
Tel 913 08 27 26   **Closed** Sun & Mon dinner; Aug
Specializing in classic Basque cuisine, this restaurant, close to the Paseo de Recoletos, offers a delicious experience. Good-value midweek dinner menu.

Bar Tomate €€
Mediterranean   **Map** 5 C4
Calle Fernando el Santo 26, 28010
Tel 917 02 38 70
A fashionable spot for market fresh dishes like tuna tartare with guacamole or hake with olives and tomatoes. The airy, loft-style interior has big wooden tables, perfect for groups.

Estado Puro €€
Tapas   **Map** 7 A3
Plaza Cánovas del Castillo 4,, 28012
Tel 917 79 30 36
Super-stylish, with gourmet tapas by celebrated chef Paco Roncero, who takes classic recipes such as buñuelos de bacalao (cod puffs) and reinvents them brilliantly.

Taberna del Chato €€
Tapas   **Map** 4 F3
Calle Cruz 35, 28012
Tel 915 23 16 29   **Closed** Mon–Fri lunch
Exquisite wines and beautifully presented gourmet tapas – from ham croquettes to nidos de langostinos (langoustine nests) – have made this restaurant a firm local favourite.

Palacio Cibeles €€€
Modern Spanish   **Map** 7 C1
Plaza Cibeles 1, 6th floor, 28014
Tel 915 23 14 54
The spectacular, Neo-Gothic former post office building houses a modern restaurant on the 6th floor, with fabulous views complementing its contemporary cuisine.

Further Afield

Bodegas La Ardosa €
Tapas   **Map** 5 A5
Calle Colón 13, 28004
Tel 915 21 49 79
An old-fashioned tapas bar where you can enjoy salmorejo cordobés (a thicker version of gazpacho) and other staples.

Naif Madrid €
International   **Map** 5 A5
Calle San Joaquín 16, 28004
Tel 910 07 20 71
A boho chic, loft-style restaurant with tasty gourmet burgers, fancy sandwiches and inspired salads. Good for lunch, afternoon coffee and cake, and evening cocktails.

La Pescadería €
Modern Spanish   **Map** 4 F1
Calle de la Ballesta 32, 28004
Tel 915 23 90 51
Try the salmon tartar, baby cuttle-fish and tuna belly millefeuille at this restaurant with a fancy yet friendly atmosphere.

Le Patron €€
International   **Map** 2 F5
Calle del Barco 27, 28004
Tel 91 70 46 811   **Closed** Sun dinner; Mon
In the Malasaña area of Madrid, this restaurant offers an interesting mix of traditional

French cuisine and tapas-style Spanish dishes. The light-filled interior with mismatched furniture is decorated with framed posters.

La Tasquita de Enfrente €€
Modern Spanish   **Map** 4 F1
Calle Ballesta 6, 28004
Tel 915 32 54 49
There's no menu here: you'll be offered a selection based what-ever was freshest at the market. What you can be sure of is authentic Spanish recipes given a modern twist using locally sourced produce. The wines are selected for you that best pair with each dish.

Santceloni €€€
Modern Spanish
Paseo de la Castellana 57, 28046
Tel 912 10 88 40
The late great chef Santi Santamaria is mourned, but his legacy lives on in this spectacular and award winning restaurant. Classic Spanish dishes are reinter-preted with flair and imagination. Impeccable service and presentation.

Madrid Province

ALCALÁ DE HENARES:
Hostería del Estudiante €€
Traditional Spanish
Calle Colegios 3, 28801
Tel 918 88 03 30   **Closed** Sun dinner; Mon & Tue
The regional delicacies served at this 16th century converted residence have become an institution. Try the famous migas (fried breadcrumbs with garlic) and duelos y quebrantos (traditional Manchegan dish with scrambled eggs, chorizo and bacon).

DK Choice

ARANJUEZ:
Casa José €€€
Modern Spanish
Calle Abastos 32
Tel 918 91 14 88
Casa José is an enchanting restaurant, in a beautifully restored mansion, with sophisticated dishes like leek with broccoli foam and sea anemone, or marinated grouper. Local produce is used wherever possible, and the extensive wine list features more than 250 labels, including interesting boutique wines.

Wooden tables and chairs at Bar Tomate, a bright, airy option in Madrid

For more information on types of restaurants see page 577

CHINCHON:
Mesón Cuevas del Vino €
Traditional Spanish
Calle Benito Hortelano 13, 28370
Tel *918 94 02 06* **Closed** *Sun dinner*
A 17th-century mill, now a
rustically decorated restaurant,
Mesón Cuevas del Vino is
a good bet for classic dishes like
lamb chops.

EL ESCORIAL:
Montia €
Modern Spanish
Calle Calvario 4, 28200
Tel *911 33 69 88* **Closed** *Mon*
This Michelin-starred restaurant
serves creative dishes made
using organic regional products.

NAVACERRADA: El Rumba €
Modern Spanish
Plaza del Doctor Gereda 1, 28491
Tel *918 56 04 05* **Closed** *Sun, Wed &*
Thu dinner; Mon & Tue
El Rumba does wonderful
charcoal-grilled local meats, and
a sprinkling of modern dishes like
scallops with citrus and *salmorejo*.

SAN LORENZO DE EL ESCORIAL:
Casa Zaca €€
Traditional Spanish
Calle Embajadores 6, San Ildefonso,
28200
Tel *921 47 00 87* **Closed** *Tue–Fri*
dinner; Mon
A former coaching inn now
boasts the town's most elegant
restaurant, featuring classic fare,
such as *cocido* (chickpea stew),
callos (beef tripe stew) and a
delicious lamb stew.

TOLEDO: La Abadía €
Traditional Spanish
Plaza de San Nicolas 3, 45002
Tel *925 25 11 40*
Enjoy seasonal tapas in a 16th-
century setting. Wash the food
down with a beer from their
extensive international selection.

TOLEDO: Adolfo €€€
Modern Spanish
Calle Hombre de Palo 7, 45001
Tel *925 22 73 21*
Dine under a splendid
artesanado ceiling at Adolfo,
where sophisticated versions
of Toledano dishes are
accompanied by excellent wines.

Castilla y León

AMPUDIA: El Arambol
de Casa del Abad €
Traditional Spanish
Plaza Francisco Martín Gromaz 12,
34191
Tel *979 76 80 08*

Tuck in to substantial dishes like
a medieval friar in the old cellar
and winepress of San Miguel de
Ampudia's residence.

ARANDA DE DUERO:
Mesón El Pastor €
Regional Spanish
Plaza de la Virgencilla 11, 09400
Tel *947 50 04 28* **Closed** *Tue lunch*
A prominent wood-burning
brick oven takes pride of place,
where the regional speciality
lechazo asado (roasted milk-fed-
only lamb) is prepared.

ARÉVALO: Asador Siboney €
Regional Spanish
Calle Figones 4, 05200
Tel *920 30 15 23* **Closed** *dinner*
This is one fancy grill housed in
a colonial mansion with many
works of art. Their signature dish
is *cochinillo* (piglet).

ASTORGA: Las Termas €
Regional Spanish
Calle Santiago 1, 24700
Tel *987 60 22 12* **Closed** *Mon*
Suitable for those with big
appetites, because the portions
are generous. The rare *cocido*
maragato (local stew with
cabbage, chickpeas and seven
different meats) is a speciality.

ATAPUERCA: Comosapiens €
Regional Spanish
Camino de Santiago 24–26, 09199
Tel *947 43 05 01* **Closed** *Wed*
This refurbished straw loft has
a menu that brings Castilian-
Leonese tradition up to speed.

ÁVILA: Alcaravea €
Regional Spanish
Plaza Catedral 15, 05001
Tel *920 22 66 00* **Closed** *Sun dinner*
The menu here features local
staples that have been passed
down over the years.

Mesón Cuevas del Vino in Chinchon, for
classic fare in a rustic setting

BENAVENTE: El Ermitaño €
Regional Spanish
Crta Benavente–León km 1.2, 49600
Tel *980 63 22 13* **Closed** *Mon*
You'll struggle to tell the colour
of the crockery at this Michelin-
starred restaurant, as portions are
generous to overflowing.

BURGOS: Cardamomo
Vegetariano €
Vegetarian
Calle Jesús María Ordoño 3, 09004
Tel *947 05 21 52* **Closed** *Mon & Sun*
Burgos may be famous for its
cheese, but the menu at this
central spot is virtually vegan.

BURGOS: La Favorita €
Pinchos
Calle Avellanos 8, 09003
Tel *947 20 59 49*
Delve into tasty snacks at this
urban tavern. Plenty of
vegetarian-friendly options.

CANEDO: Prada a Tope-Palacio
de Canedo €
Regional Spanish
Calle La Iglesia s/n, 24546
Tel *987 56 33 66*
Hearty fare for the hungry
includes chorizo sausages
marinated in wine.

CARRIÓN DE LOS CONDES:
La Corte €€
Regional Spanish
Calle Santa María 36, 34120
Tel *979 88 01 38* **Closed** *Fri (except*
Aug); mid-Oct–mid-Apr
Refuel while walking the Camino
de Santiago at this hostel rest-
aurant, specializing in filling
Castilian cuisine. Open for
breakfast, lunch and dinner.

COVARRUBIAS: Casa Galin €
Regional Spanish
Plaza Doña Urraca 4, 09346
Tel *974 40 65 52* **Closed** *Tue, Sun*
dinner
Indulge in Castilian-style fare
here, with salty *sopa castellana*
(garlic soup) and the classic *olla*
podrida (a pork and bean stew).

EL BURGO DE OSMA:
Virrey Palafox €
Traditional Spanish
Calle Universidad 7, 42300
Tel *975 34 13 11* **Closed** *Mon & Sun*
This elegant hotel restaurant
boasts suckling roast piglet as
its signature dish.

GUIJUELO: El Pernil Ibérico €
Traditional Spanish
Calle Chinarral 62, 37770
Tel *923 58 14 02*
Enjoy excellent cold meats at
this tavern. If you don't leave full
enough, you can buy them, too.

Key to Price Guide *see page 582*

Elegant place settings at El Rincon de Antonio, Zamora

LEÓN: La Gitana €
Regional Spanish
Calle de las Carnicerías 7, 24003
Tel *987 21 51 71* **Closed** *Thu*
In the pedestrianized Húmedo neighbourhood, La Gitana is a relaxed place – you can use bread to mop up your plate.

LEÓN: Cocinandos €€
Modern Spanish
Calle Campanillas 1, 24008
Tel *987 07 13 78* **Closed** *Mon & Sun*
Marrying style with substance, this Michelin-starred gem offers a sophisticated take on traditional Castilian recipes.

LEÓN: Delirios €€
Modern Spanish
Calle Ave María 2, 24007
Tel *987 23 76 99* **Closed** *Mon & Sun dinner (all day Sun in summer)*
This central restaurant, located just around the corner from the cathedral, is a temple to modern gastronomy. Innovative cuisine, emphasizing the use of local products.

PALENCIA: Asador La Encina €
Regional Spanish
Calle de Casañe 2, 34002
Tel *979 71 09 36*
Famous for its *tortilla de patata* (Spanish omelette), this modern grill does the simple things well.

PALENCIA: La Traserilla €€
Regional Spanish
Calle de San Marcos 12, 34001
Tel *979 74 54 21*
Also known as Casa de Comidas (House of Food), the old exterior contrasts with the modern decor. Big on meat and vegetables.

SALAMANCA: La Cocina de Toño €
Modern Spanish
Calle de la Gran Via 20, 37001
Tel *923 26 39 77* **Closed** *Sun dinner; Mon*

Michelin-starred establishment doing Nouveau Castilian cuisine with a Basque twist.

SALAMANCA: iPan iVino €
Tapas
Calle Felipe Espino 10, 37002
Tel *923 26 86 77*
Colourful wine bar with creative tapas and probably the best wine menu in the city.

SALAMANCA: Zazu Bistro €€
Mediterranean
Plaza de la Libertad 8, 37002
Tel *923 26 16 90*
This stylish restaurant pays tribute to Mediterranean cuisine with nods to classic French and Italian recipes. Wine list to match.

SEGOVIA: El Bernardino €
Traditional Spanish
Calle Cervantes 2, 40001
Tel *921 46 24 77*
Updated Castillian cuisine with traditional roots, served up in a graceful town house. The town's star dish, roast suckling pig, is the house speciality.

SEGOVIA: Cueva de San Esteban €
Traditional Spanish
Calle de Valdeláguila 15, 40001
Tel *921 46 09 82*
The *jamón* hanging from the ceiling gives you an idea how traditional this restaurant is.

SEGOVIA: Restaurante José María €€
Regional Spanish
Calle Cronista Lecea 11, 40001
Tel *921 46 11 11*
Chef José María Ruiz Benito combines Segovian staples with the latest gastronomic fashions.

SIGUENZA: El Doncel €€
Modern Spanish
Paseo de la Alameda 3
Tel *949 39 00 01*

A beautiful 18th-century mansion provides a sublime setting for exciting contemporary cuisine. Extensive wine list.

SORIA: Baluarte €
Modern Spanish
Calle Caballeros 14, 42002
Tel *975 21 36 58*
Enjoy a fine gastronomic experience during the mushroom and black truffle season at this Michelin-starred restaurant.

TORDESILLAS: Bar-Restaurante Figón €
Traditional Spanish
Plaza Pepe Zorita 22, 47100
Tel *983 77 13 98* **Closed** *Wed dinner*
Octopus salad is a popular dish at this laid-back local. A greater menu selection than elsewhere.

VALLADOLID: La Parrilla de San Lorenzo €
Traditional Spanish
Calle Pedro Niño 1, 47001
Tel *983 33 50 88*
Located in the basement of a monastery, this grill is a treasure trove of antiques. The menu is just as traditional with family recipes handed down through generations.

DK Choice

ZAMORA: El Rincón de Antonio €€
Regional Spanish
C/ de la Rúa de los Francos 6, 49001
Tel *980 53 53 70*
Housed in a 19th-century mansion in medieval Zamora, the kitchen utilizes local products to recreate the food of Zamora of old. There are bite-sized tapas offerings at the bar. Choose from a cellar offering 800 different vintages, along with cava, liqueurs and spirits.

Castilla-La Mancha

DK Choice

ALBACETE: Álvarez €
Regional Spanish
Calle Carmen 42, 02005
Tel *967 21 82 69*
If you grew up in Castilla-La Mancha, a meal here would be a nostalgic experience. For this is food Mama used to make. There are croquettes of various stuffings, *gazpacho manchego* (meat-based stew) and *cordero asado* (roast lamb). Desserts include a ricotta and almond flan.

For more information on types of restaurants *see page 577*

ALBACETE: Nuestro Bar €
Regional Spanish
Calle Alcalde Conangla 102, 02002
Tel *967 24 33 73*
Part bar, part restaurant, part
museum. Traditional agricultural
equipment and antique cooking
utensils adorn the walls.

**ALBACETE: Restaurante
Don Gil** €€
Modern Spanish
Calle Baños 2, 02004
Tel *967 23 97 85* **Closed** *Mon*
Located alongside the Mercado
de Villacerrada, this is where
Albacete's in crowd come to eat.

ALCOCER: Casa Goyo €
Regional Spanish
Calle Mayor 44, 19125
Tel *949 35 50 03* **Closed** *Mon*
Hostal España's in-house
restaurant is a rustic affair. Make
sure you go with an appetite
because the portions are huge.

ALMAGRO: El Corregidor €
Regional Spanish
Calle de Jerónimo Ceballos 2, 13270
Tel *926 86 06 48*
Housed in an 18th-century
palace, there are different dining
rooms that surround a traditional
patio. Classic Manchegan cuisine.

**CIUDAD REAL:
Pago del Vicario** €€
Traditional Spanish
*Carretera Ciudad Real–Porzuna,
km 16, 13196*
Tel *926 66 60 27*
Overlooking the barrel room and
the vineyard, this place offers a
fusion cuisine. The Manchegan
roast lamb goes superbly with
the wines from one of the best
wine cellars of the region.

CUENCA: Raff €
Tapas
Calle Federico García Lorca 3, 16004
Tel *969 69 08 55*

The stylish, contemporary
ambience in this restaurant is in
contrast to the traditional tapas
and *raciónes* on offer.

CUENCA: El Secreto €
Regional Spanish
Calle Alfonso VIII, 81, 16001
Tel *678 61 13 01* **Closed** *Tue dinner;
Wed*
Feast off the à la carte menu
or share the mouthwatering
tapas. Special set menus
for vegetarians.

CUENCA: Figón de Huécar €€
Spanish
Calle Julián Romero 6, 16001
Tel *696 24 00 62* **Closed** *Mon*
The erstwhile family residence of
a famous local singer enjoys spec-
tacular views over the Huécar
Gorge. Its terrace is beautifully lit
up at night.

**GUADALAJARA:
Amparito Roca** €€
Modern Spanish
Calle de Toledo 19, 19002
Tel *949 21 46 39* **Closed** *Sun dinner*
Tiled floor, wooden walls and a
flower on every table makes
eating at this experimental
restaurant feel like an event.

ILLESCAS: El Bohío €€€
Modern Spanish
Avenida Castilla-La Mancha 81, 45200
Tel *925 51 11 26*
Chef Pepe Rodríguez has been
awarded a Michelin star for the
traditional yet inventive menu
at El Bohío.

**MARCHAMALO: Restaurante
Las Llaves** €€
Modern Spanish
Plaza Mayor 16, 19180
Tel *949 25 04 85* **Closed** *Mon*
Pass through the grand portal
of a 16th-century building to
discover a suitably elegant interior.
Foie gras features on the menu.

OCAÑA: Restaurante Palio €€
Regional Spanish
Calle Mayor 12, 45300
Tel *925 13 00 45* **Closed** *Sun–Wed
dinner*
This restaurant prides itself on its
attention to detail – its home-
made bread uses stone-ground
organic flour.

OROPESA: Tierra €€€
Modern Spanish
Calle de la Oropesa 9, 45572
Tel *925 45 75 34*
Enjoy gourmet fare in this Michelin-
starred restaurant in the luxurious
Hotel Valdepalacios. Its name,
meaning "land", refers to the area's
richness of culture, agriculture
and cuisine. Warm atmosphere.

**SAN PEDRO: Restaurante
Montecristo** €
Regional Spanish
*Paseo de la Libertad, 14, 03360
(Albacete)*
Tel *967 36 44 55* **Closed** *Tue*
Red meat and fresh fish
dominate the menu at this
established riverside restaurant.

**TALAVERA DE LA REINA:
Taberna Mingote** €
Tapas
Plaza Federico García Lorca 5, 45600
Tel *925 82 56 33*
Small tables give this tavern a
lively atmosphere, even when
it's not packed. Tapas options
change during the week.

**TALAVERA DE LA REINA:
Penalty** €€
Seafood
Calle de la Cabeza del Moro 5, 45600
Tel *925 81 53 44* **Closed** *Mon*
Ensuring the highest quality of
ingredients, Penalty imports its
fish and shellfish from Galicia,
one of Spain's most noted areas
for seafood.

**TARANCÓN: Restaurante
Hospedería, Finca La Estacada** €€
Regional Spanish
Carretera Nnal 400 km 103, 16400
Tel *969 32 71 88*
Housed in a luxury complex which
includes a hotel, spa and vineyard,
this restaurant offers excellent
views of the vines which produce
its highly regarded wines.

TOLEDO: Casa Aurelio €
Regional Spanish
Plaza del Ayuntamiento 8, 45002
Tel *925 22 77 16* **Closed** *Tue*
Dishes to make your mouth
water at this Toledo institution
include the delectable *crêpe de
bacalao con crema de cigala* and
pâté de sardinas (cod crepe with
lobster cream and sardine pâté).

The elegant Restaurante Hospedería, Finca La Estacada, Tarancón

Key to Price Guide *see page 582*

TOLEDO: Madre Tierra €
Vegetarian
Bajada de la Tripería 2, 45001
Tel *925 22 35 71*   Closed *Tue, Mon dinner*
Enjoy the fruits (and vegetables) of Mother Earth at Toledo's first vegetarian restaurant, complemented with extensive tea and wine lists.

TOLEDO: Restaurante Locum €€
Regional Spanish
Calle de Locum 6, 45001
Tel *925 22 32 35*   Closed *Tue*
A short walk from Toledo's cathedral you'll find a traditional restaurant featuring the likes of *rabo del toro* (stewed bull tail).

TOLEDO: Adolfo €€€
Modern Spanish
Calle del Hombre de Palo 7, 45001
Tel *925 22 73 21*   Closed *Sun dinner*
The pleasant roof terrace offers panoramic views of the city below. Wine is sourced from the restaurant's private vineyard.

VALDEPEÑAS: La Fonda de Alberto €
Modern Spanish
Calle del Cristo 67, 13300
Tel *926 31 61 76*   Closed *Mon*
Cold soups and salads are the highlights of summer menus while hearty red meat dishes feature in winter. Along with a wine list 300+ strong.

VALDEPEÑAS: Venta del Comendador de la Villa de Valdepeñas €
Regional Spanish
Calle de Bernardo Balbuena 2, 13300
Tel *926 31 22 26*
Food like grandmother used to make: fine breads with thyme, rosemary and mint flavours. Good, central location.

Extremadura

ALANGE: Meson Trinidad €
Regional Spanish
Encomienda 51, 06840
Tel *924 36 50 66*   Closed *Tue*
This family-run inn serves authentic local dishes in a friendly atmosphere with spectacular views of the castle.

CÁCERES: El Figón de Eustaquio €
Regional Spanish
Plaza de San Juan 12–14, 10003
Tel *927 24 43 62*   Closed *1–15 Jul*
In the heart of the historic centre, this long-standing and resolutely old-fashioned restaurant has been preparing tasty dishes since 1947. Their speciality is game.

CÁCERES: Torre de Sande €€
Modern Spanish
Calle de los Condes 3, 10003
Tel *927 21 11 47*   Closed *Mon, Tue*
On the historic main square, this modern restaurant offers a wide range of tapas and à la carte dishes based on local recipes.

CÁCERES: Atrio €€€
Regional Spanish
Plaza de San Mateo 1, 10003
Tel *927 24 29 28*
One of the finest restaurants in Spain, with two Michelin stars, Atrio serves modern cuisine with sterling service.

GUADALUPE: Hospedería del Real Monasterio €
Regional Spanish
Plaza de Juan Carlos I s/n, 10140
Tel *927 36 70 00*
Located in a Plateresque cloister and run by Franciscans, this place is popular for its traditional roasted lamb.

MERIDA: Ilunion Merida Palace €
Regional Spanish
Plaza España 19, 06800
Tel *924 38 38 00*
This restaurant, in a 16th-century palace-cum-hotel, offers elegant dining in relaxed surroundings.

TRUJILLO: Corral del Rey €
Regional Spanish
Plazuela Corral del Rey 2 (Plaza Mayor), 10200
Tel *927 32 30 71*   Closed *winter: Sun & Wed dinner; summer: all day Sun*
Specializing in roasted meat and fish with an extensive wine & cigar menu. Off the main square.

TRUJILLO: La Troya €
Regional Spanish
Plaza Mayor 10, 10200
Tel *927 32 13 64*
On the main square, this 16th-century *mesón* serves typical Spanish cuisine in hearty portions – the lamb stew is recommended.

ZAFRA: Parador €
Regional Spanish
Plaza Corazon de Maria 7, 06300
Tel *924 55 45 40*
Soak up the surroundings at this 15th-century castle while tasting tapas or dining from the à la carte menu.

ZAFRA: Ramirez €
Regional Spanish
Avenida San Miguel 18, 06300 Zafra
Tel *924 55 51 38*
Lively lunchtime or relaxed evening dining in this centrally located diner which offers an extensive range of local cuisine and informal tapas.

The warm red-and-white coloured interior of Restaurante Palio, Ocaña

Seville

El Arenal

Bodeguita Casablanca €
Tapas   Map 3 C2
Calle Adolfo Rodriguez Jurado 12, 41002
Tel *954 22 41 14*   Closed *Sun, Sat dinner*
Family-run tapas bar with a no-frills decor of tiles and barrel tables. Popular with locals.

La Brunilda Tapas €
Tapas   Map 3 B1
Calle Galera 5, 41001
Tel *954 22 04 81*   Closed *Sun dinner*
Bright, modern bar with excellent tapas, such as succulent ox sirloin with thyme potatoes and chicken breast with polenta and wild mushrooms.

Santa Cruz

Casa Plácido €
Tapas   Map 6 E4
Mesón del Moro 5, 41004
Tel *954 56 39 71*   Closed *Thu*
Diminutive tapas bar in heart of the old quarter. Traditional decor of tiles and bullfight posters, plus hanging hams. Fino from the barrel. Excellent tortillas.

DK Choice

La Quinta Braseria €
Modern Spanish   Map 6 E2
Plaza Padre Jeronimo de Cordoba 11, 41003
Tel *954 60 00 16*   Closed *Sun dinner; Mon*
Dine at this elegant restaurant with attentive service and excellent choices. Start with the *croquetas de pollo y trufa negra* (chicken and black truffle croquettes) or the tartare, followed by one of their juicy grilled meat selections. Reservations suggested.

Casa Robles   €€
Traditional Spanish   **Map** 3 C1
Calle Alvarez Quintero 58, 41001
Tel *954 56 32 72*
This prize-winning eating spot
boasts a stunning decor of
paintings, statues and coloured
tiles. On the menu is a great fish
and shellfish selection, plus
delectable home-made desserts.
Diners enjoy cathedral views
from the restaurant terrace and
the best wine list in Seville.

Doña Elvira   €€
Traditional Spanish   **Map** 3 C2
Plaza de Doña Elvira 6, 41004
Tel *954 22 73 88*
The legendary Don Juan has
links with this traditional Sevillan
restaurant. You can dine indoors
or al fresco, on the open-air
terrace. Known for its innovative
salads, paella and rice dishes,
seafood and meat.

Further Afield

Bar Antojo   €
Fusion   **Map** 1 C3
Calatrava 44, 41002
Tel *955 42 53 37*
A unique bar with mismatched
furniture, bookshelves and a
relaxed atmosphere, Bar Antojo
offers creative takes on regional
comfort food, with a bit of international fusion thrown in for
good measure.

Con Tenedor   €
Mediterranean   **Map** 2 E4
Calle San Luis 50, 41003
Tel *954 91 63 33*
A top-value spot with friendly
service, Con Tenedor serves up
dishes made from fresh market
produce. It also hosts art
exhibitions and live music on
Tuesday evenings.

Abades Triana seafood restaurant in Seville

Eslava   €
Seafood   **Map** 1 C4
Calle Eslava 3, 41002
Tel *954 90 65 68*   **Closed** *Mon;
Sun dinner*
Simple, unadorned eating spot
featuring creative Andalucían
cuisine. First-rate seafood and
salads and inventive choice of
tapas. Hugely popular.

Mesón Guadalquivir   €
Traditional Spanish   **Map** 4 E3
Calle Camilo José Cela 1, 41018
Tel *954 92 41 39*   **Closed** *Sun*
High-standard, reasonably priced
Andalucían cuisine in a chic-
yet-traditional city favourite.
Exceptional *chipiron a la plancha*
(freshly grilled squid) and home-
made lemon sorbet.

Torre de los Perdigones   €
Fusion   **Map** 2 D3
Calle Resolana s/n, 41009
Tel *954 90 93 53*
Restaurant set next to the tower,
amid parklands. Dishes include
arroz marinero (rice with seafood)
and *merluza al cava con langostinos*
(hake in a sparkling-wine sauce
with langoustines). Summer
terrace with live music.

> ### DK Choice
>
> **Vega 10**   €
> Fusion   **Map** 3 B3
> *Rosario Vega 10, 41011*
> **Tel** *955 23 77 48*   **Closed** *Sun*
> Vega 10 offers creative dishes
> that change according to
> season, using fresh, high-quality
> ingredients. The tapas menu
> changes daily as well. Also
> boasts a good wine selection.

Abades Triana   €€€
Seafood   **Map** 3 B3
Calle Betis 69, 41010
Tel *954 28 64 59*

Fabulous riverside establishment
with stunning vierws. Windowed
El Cubo section has "floating
glass" floor. Superb international
and Mediterranean cuisine. Also
exquisite tasting menus.

Andalucía

ALGECIRAS: La Cabaña   €
Traditional Spanish
Avenida Agua Marina 5, 11203
Tel *956 66 73 79*   **Closed** *Mon*
Warm, traditional restaurant with
indoor and terrace dining.
Offerings include Galician style
octopus and charcoal-grilled
sirloin steaks.

ALGECIRAS: Maridaje   €
Tapas
Calle Buen Aire 9, 11201
Tel *646 48 64 08*   **Closed** *Sun*
Sleek restaurant serving tasty,
large tapas. Try the *surtido de atun*,
a plate of tuna prepared in various
ways. Good selection of wines. No
reservations accepted, so get here
early before the queues start.

ALMERÍA: Casa Sevilla   €
Seafood
Calle Rueda López s/n, 04004
Tel *950 27 29 12*   **Closed** *Sun*
Sociable family restaurant serving
fresh seafood dishes. Go for the
*tempura de bacalao sobre arroz
meloso de hongos* (cod tempura
on a bed of creamy mushroom
rice). Monthly wine tastings.

**ALMERÍA: Rincón de
Juan Pedro**   €
Traditional Spanish
Calle Federico Castro 2, 04003
Tel *950 27 81 67*
Almeria town tapas favourite
with larger *raciónes* for the extra-
hungry. Serves pungent hams,
chorizos and cheeses, plus local
specialities like *trigo a la cortijera*
(wheat berry and sausage stew).

ALMERÍA: Club de Mar   €€
Seafood
Playa de Almadrabillas 1, 04007
Tel *950 23 50 48*   **Closed** *Tue*
Stylish restaurant in Almeria's
prestigious yacht club. Seafront
terrace. Renowned for its
bouillabaisse and fried fish platters.

ALMERÍA: Valentin   €€
Seafood
Calle Tenor Iribarne 19, 04001
Tel *950 26 44 75*   **Closed** *Mon; Sep*
This popular *marisquería* (restau-
rant specializing in shellfish)
has been given a nod by the
Michelin Guide. Everything is
market-fresh.

DK Choice

**ALMONTE: Aires de Doñana
(La Choza del Rocío)** €
Traditional Spanish
Avenida de la Canaliega 1
Tel *959 44 22 89* **Closed** *Mon*
This converted *choza* (large
thatched hut) is typical of the
Doñana park in which it's located.
Beautifully decorated, it enjoys
splendid terrace views across
woods and waterways. The
creative Andalucían cuisine
offers specialities like *revuelto
marismeño* (scrambled eggs
with local herbs).

ALMONTE: El Tamborilero €
Traditional Spanish
Calle Unamuno 15, 21730
Tel *959 40 69 55* **Closed** *Sun,
1 15 Jul*
Former bodega with traditional
decor. The chef invites you into
the kitchen to choose from their
selections of the day.

ALMUÑECAR: El Chaleco €
French
Avenida de la Costa del Sol, 37, 18690
Tel *958 63 24 02* **Closed** *Sun dinner;
Mon*
Welcoming restaurant with a
good range of meat, fish and
poultry dishes. For excellent
value, try one of their taster's
menus. Good selection of wine
and home-made desserts.

**ANTEQUERA: Caserío de
San Benito** €
Traditional Spanish
*Autovía A-45, Salida 86, Dirección
Málaga–Córdoba s/n, 29200*
Tel *952 111 103* **Closed** *Fri dinner;
Sat*
A great place to stop along the
motorway, this charming old
cortijo has an eclectic collection
of antiques in its patio. Dine on
the terrace – or, when it's cold,
cozy up by the fireplace in one
of their dining rooms. Regional
food is prepared with care.

BAEZA: Casa Juanito €€
Traditional Spanish
*Avenida del Alcalde Puché Pardo 57,
23440*
Tel *953 74 00 40*
Olive oil-based dishes at this cosy
family-run place in a historical
town include *cabrito con habas*
(young goat with broad beans).
Divine home-made desserts.

**BAEZA: Palacio de Gallego
Restaurante & Boutique** €€
Traditional Spanish
Calle Santa Catalina 5, 23440
Tel *667 76 01 84* **Closed** *Tue*

Appetizing tapas at El Molino de la
Romera, Carmona

Set in the peaceful courtyard of a
historic building close to the
Cathedral, the Palacio de Gallego
offers a fine selection of meats
and fish, grilled while you watch.
The wine list spans all regions
of Spain. Be sure to leave room
for dessert!

BENALMÁDENA: La Fuente €
Traditional Spanish
Plaza de España 9, 29639
Tel *952 56 94 66* **Closed** *Tue–Sun
lunch; Mon*
Charming restaurant with tables
on the square. Try the king
prawns in a mild chilli, ginger
and coriander butter with rice.

BUBIÓN: Teide €
Traditional Spanish
Calle Carretera s/n, 18412
Tel *958 76 30 37* **Closed** *2nd half
Jun*
At this pleasant stone-built restaurant in an Alpujarran village,
the simple menu includes such
dishes as *migas* (fried breadcrumbs with garlic) and *choto
asado* (roast kid).

CÁDIZ: Balandro €
Seafood
Alameda Apodaca 22, 11004
Tel *956 22 09 92*
Restaurant in converted 18th-
century mansion overlooking
the bay. Superb seafood, plus a
good selection of meat dishes.

**CÁDIZ: Freiduría Cervecería
Las Flores** €
Seafood
Plaza Topete 4, 11001
Tel *956 22 61 12*
Down-to-earth restaurant
specializing in shellfish and
fried fish platters. You can watch
as your choice is cooked on
the spot.

CÁDIZ: Ventorillo del Chato €
Seafood
Vía Augusta Julia, 11011
Tel *956 25 00 25* **Closed** *Sun dinner
(except Aug)*
This 18th-century seaside inn
specializes in fresh fish. Try the
corvino al vapor (steamed sea
bass) or the *pasta negra fresca
y frutos del mar* (fresh black
pasta with seafood)

CARBONERAS: El Cabo €€
Seafood
Paseo Marítimo 67, 04140
Tel *950 13 06 24* **Closed** *Mon*
This friendly beachside restaurant
close to Cabo de Gata National
Park produces imaginative
seafood dishes, such as squid
stuffed with spinach and nuts.

CARMONA: Goya €
Traditional Spanish
Calle Prim 2, 41410
Tel *954 14 30 60*
Typical Sevillian establishment
off the city's main square. Try
the baked lamb. The tapas bar
has good tortillas.

**CARMONA: El Molino
de la Romera** €
Traditional Spanish
Calle Sor Angela de la Cruz 8, 41410
Tel *954 14 20 00* **Closed** *Mon*
Converted from a 15th-century
Moorish olive oil mill and granary,
this evocative place serves
quality regional dishes, such as
succulent venison in red wine.

**CARMONA: Parador Alcázar
del Rey Don Pedro** €
Traditional Spanish
Calle del Alcázar s/n, 41410
Tel *954 14 10 10*
Stylish, traditional parador
restaurant with a Moorish patio
and a vaulted, antique-furnished
dining room.

CAZORLA: Meson Leandro €
Traditional Spanish
Calle Hoz 3, 23470
Tel *953 72 06 32* **Closed** *Wed,
2nd half Jun*
Michelin-recommended
restaurant in a lovely Jaén
village bordering a National
Park. Meson Leandro is famed
for its *carne a la piedra* (stone-
baked meat dishes).

CÓRDOBA: Horno San Luis €
Modern Spanish
Calle Cardenal Gonzalez, 14003
Tel *665 05 37 83*
Two-storey restaurant with lots
of romantic nooks and dining
rooms. Don't let the seemingly
simple menu fool you – the
cuisine is anything but typical!

For more information on types of restaurants *see page 577*

CÓRDOBA: Regadera €
Traditional Spanish
Ronda Isasa 10, 14003
Tel *957 10 14 00* **Closed** *Mon*
Just steps from the riverfront,
Regadera has a fresh appeal and
excellent-value menu of the day.

CÓRDOBA: San Miguel €
Traditional Spanish
Plaza San Miguel 1, 14002
Tel *957 47 01 66* **Closed** *Sun*
Sterling family-run spot.
Specialities include Iberian cured
meats, *pisto* (ratatouille) and
manitas de cerdo (pig's trotters).

CÓRDOBA: La Almudaina €€
Traditional Spanish
Campo Santo de los Mártires 1, 14004
Tel *957 47 43 42* **Closed** *Sun dinner*
Located in a former bishop's
palace. Dishes include the ever-
present *salmorejo* (thick *gazpacho*)
and *solomillo al foie* (pork sirloin
with foie gras).

**CÓRDOBA: Casa Pepe de
la Judería** €€
Traditional Spanish
Calle Romero 1, 14003
Tel *957 20 07 44* **Closed** *Sun*
Enduring favourite since
1928. Dine indoors or on the
flower-filled patio, and savour
the traditional Córdoban dish
flamenquin (pork loin rolled with
Iberian ham, then breaded and
deep fried).

EL ROCIO: Restaurante Toruño €
Traditional Spanish
Plaza Acebuchal 22, 21750
Tel *959 44 24 22*
Inviting restaurant with lovely
terrace and excellent views. Try
one of the rice dishes.

FUENGIROLA: Vegetalia €
Vegetarian
*Calle Santa Isabel 8, Los Boliches
29640*
Tel *952 58 60 31* **Closed** *Sun,
Jul–Aug*
Finnish-owned restaurant with
a self-service lunchtime buffet.
Delicious home-made desserts.

GERENA: Casa Salvi Tapas €
Tapas
Miguel de Cervantes 46, 41860
Tel *955 78 32 72*
Don't let the traditional decor
fool you: there is a vast, creative
selection of tapas and plates,
excellent grilled meats, seafood
and seasonal game.

GIBRALTAR: The Waterfront €
International
*Queensway Quay, Units 4/5 Ragged
Staff Wharf, Marina Bay*
Tel *350 2004 5666* **Closed** *Tue*

Picturesque views from the Rib Room,
Gibraltar

A romantic spot with lovely
sunset views. The menu includes
Cajun chicken, fish and veggie
dishes. Thursday is steak night,
with various cuts on offer.

GIBRALTAR: Rib Room €€€
Traditional Spanish
Rock Hotel, Europa Road
Tel *350 2007 3000*
Iconic restaurant in one of
Gibraltar's most distinguished
hotels, serving modern British
cuisine with Iberian and
Moroccan influences.

**GRANADA: Antigua Bodega
Castañeda** €
Traditional Spanish
Calle Elvira 5, 18010
Tel *958 22 97 06*
Archetypal tapas bar with barrels,
beams and colourful tiles. Feast
on Trevélez mountain ham, squid
and sardines and enjoy a chilled
fino on the side.

**GRANADA: Carmen del
San Miguel** €
Traditional Spanish
Plaza Torres Bermejas 3, 18009
Tel *958 22 67 23* **Closed** *Sun dinner;
all day Sun in summer*
Attractive restaurant overlooking
the Alhambra, with traditional
dishes, such as rabbit and quail.

GRANADA: Chikito €
Traditional Spanish
Plaza del Campillo 9, 18009
Tel *958 22 33 64* **Closed** *Wed*
Attractive tapas bar-restaurant.
Try their delicious broad beans
with ham or be brave and dig
into the *tortilla Sacromonte* –
omelette with marrow, brains,
herbs and bull's testicles!

Key to Price Guide *see page 582*

DK Choice

**GRANADA: Mirador de
Morayma** €
Traditional Spanish
C/ Pianista Gracia Carrillo 2, 18010
Tel *958 22 82 90* **Closed** *Sun
dinner*
Few restaurants offer such a
winning combination of idyllic
setting and quality cuisine.
Located beside the secluded
patio of a private house inside
the Albaicin, it enjoys superb
city views. The authentic
Andaluz food includes fresh
remojón (salad with salt cod,
olives and orange) and *salmorejo*
(thicker version of *gazpacho*).

GRANADA: Ruta del Veleta €
Fusion
*Crta Sierra Nevada 136, km 5, 4,
Cenes de la Vega, 18190*
Tel *958 48 61 34* **Closed** *Sun dinner*
Popular regional eating spot on
the old road to Sierra Nevada.
Alpujarran decor and hearty
dishes like roast kid. Seasonal
game and good seafood choice.

HUELVA: Azabache €
Traditional Spanish
Calle Vazquez Lopez 22, 21001
Tel *959 25 75 28* **Closed** *Sat dinner;
Sun*
The varied menu, based on top-
quality ingredients, includes
traditional dishes, plus innovative
versions of local fare. Excellent
seafood and good options for
vegetarians, too. Ample wine list.

JABUGO: Meson Cinco Jotas €
Traditional Spanish
Crta San Juan del Puerto, 21290
Tel *959 12 10 71* **Closed** *Mon*
Unpretentious restaurant in the
birthplace of Spain's greatest
jamón. Home-cured *Jabugo* and
cod with prawns and olives are
among the best dishes.

JAÉN: Taberna Don Sancho €
Traditional Spanish
Avenida de Andalucia 17, 23005
Tel *953 26 40 21*
Friendly, lively tavern with
imaginative versions of
traditional dishes. Ask for the
delicious cod with blueberries.

JAÉN: Casa Antonio €€
Traditional Spanish
Calle Fermín Palma 3, 23008
Tel *953 27 02 62* **Closed** *Mon; Sun
dinner; Aug*
Elegant restaurant with modern
decor and contemporary spins
on traditional dishes. The menu
changes regularly, but *cochinillo*
(suckling pig) features regularly.

JEREZ DE LA FRONTERA:
Reino de Leon Gastrobar €
Fusion
Calle Latorre 8, 11402
Tel *956 32 29 15*
Chic restaurant with dishes such as *torpedoes de gambones* (crispy prawns served with a sweet chili sauce) and *holjadre de solomillo de cerdo* (pastry-wrapped pork loin with a pink peppercorn sauce).

LA LINEA: La Marina €
Seafood
Paseo Maritimo, La Atunara s/n, 11300
Tel *956 17 15 31* **Closed** *Mon*
Large seaside eating spot with nautical decor. Great views of bay and Gibraltar. Delicious *chirlas marineras* (clams).

LA RINCONADA: El Pela €
Traditional Spanish
Plaza de Rodriguez Montes 2, 41300
Tel *954 79 77 03* **Closed** *Wed*
Down-to-earth Sevillan restaurant. Try the *arroz negro* (black rice). Breakfast is served with *pan prieto de la Algaba* (local speciality bread).

LOS BARRIOS:
Mesón El Copo €€
Seafood
C/ La Almadraba 2 (Palmones), 11369
Tel *956 67 77 10* **Closed** *Sun*
Top beachside seafood eating spot. Try the fresh local *urta* (sea bream) and *gallineta* (Atlantic red fish). Good home-made desserts.

MÁLAGA: Antigua Casa
de la Guardia €
Traditional Spanish
Alameda Principal 18, 29015
Tel *952 21 46 80* **Closed** *Sun*
Vintage 19th-century wine cellar and bar on Málaga's central avenue. Their speciality tipple is dark, rich Pedro Ximénez wine served directly from the barrel.

MÁLAGA: Café de Paris €
Fusion
Calle Velez Málaga s/n, 29016
Tel *952 22 50 43* **Closed** *Mon dinner; Sun*
Stylish restaurant serving modern Spanish-Mediterranean dishes including black truffles and *arroz au parmesan* (parmesan rice). Superb *menú de degustación*.

MÁLAGA: Mesón Cortijo
de Pepe €
Traditional Spanish
Plaza de la Merced 2, 29012
Tel *952 22 40 71* **Closed** *Tue*
Popular Andalucían tapas bar in emblematic square adjoining Picasso's birthplace. Good calamari and prawn dishes.

DK Choice

MÁLAGA: El Tintero II €
Seafood
Playa del Dedo s/n (El Palo), 29018
Tel *952 20 68 26*
This is without doubt the noisiest restaurant on the Costa del Sol, but don't let that put you off. Its beachside location, sweeping views across the bay and magnificent choice of fish dishes more than compensate. There's no menu. You simply point at the dish you want as waiters vociferously pass by announcing them. Except for lobster they're all more or less the same price. Staff count the plates when you're done to calculate your bill.

MÁLAGA: Mesón Astorga €€
Traditional Spanish
Calle Gerona 11, 29006
Tel *952 34 25 63* **Closed** *Sun*
This classical Malagueno restaurant serves dishes prepared from fresh market produce. Try the fried aubergine with sugar-cane honey.

MARBELLA: Altamirano €
Seafood
Plaza Altamirano 3, 29601
Tel *952 82 49 32* **Closed** *Wed, early Jan–mid-Feb*
Good-value family restaurant with garden for alfresco dining. Specialities range from *fritura malagueno* (fried fish platter) to *besugo a la brasa* (barbecued sea bream).

MARBELLA: Paco Jiménez €€€
Fine Dining
Plaza de Naranjos 11, 29601
Tel *952 77 36 10* **Closed** *lunch; Mon*
Book a table on the balcony overlooking the orange tree-lined Plaza de Naranjos, and enjoy an array of seafood and meat dishes. Excellent service contributes to making this an unforgettable dining experience.

MARBELLA: Skina €€€
Fusion
Calle Aduar 12, 29601
Tel *952 76 52 77* **Closed** *Sun, Mon, early Dec, early Jan–early Feb*
Chic, intimate, old town eating spot with eclectic fusion of dishes from rabbit terrine to sole with artichokes and tomato. Superlative tasting menu.

ORGIVA: Teteria Baraka €
Moroccan
Calle Estacion 12, 18400
Tel *958 78 58 94* **Closed** *Thu dinner*
With a warm and welcoming atmosphere, this restaurant and tea house offers lots of vegetarian options and a variety of delicious fresh juices. It is a popular hangout for the local hippy community. Halal meat; no alcohol served.

OSUNA: El Mesón del Duque €
Traditional Spanish
Plaza de la Duquesa 1, 41640
Tel *954 81 28 45* **Closed** *Wed*
This fine establishment with a terrace overlooking a church serves up a good and extensive choice of Andalucían specialities, including home-made meatballs.

OSUNA: Doña Guadalupe €€
Traditional Spanish
Plaza de Guadalupe 6–8, 41640
Tel *954 81 05 58* **Closed** *Sat, Sun; 2 wks Aug*
Family-run restaurant with outdoor terrace dining. Classic regional fare includes *faisan con arroz* (pheasant and wild rice).

PALMA DEL RIO: El Refectorio
(Monasterio de San
Francisco) €
Traditional Spanish
Avenida Pío XII 35, 14700
Tel *957 71 01 83*
Dine out in the atmospheric old rectory of a converted 15th-century monastery. Traditional dishes include game in winter. In summer, dining on the candlelit patio is a must.

Traditional tapas restaurant, Chikito, in Granada *(see p600)*

For more information on types of restaurants *see page 577*

PUERTO DE SANTA MARIA:
Pantalán G €€
Seafood
Avenida de la Libertad s/n, Puerto Sherry, 11500
Tel *956 87 18 65* **Closed** *Sun dinner*
Portside restaurant offering a delectable assortment of fish and seafood, but also meat. There is a good selection of vegetables as well, plus an extensive wine list.

RONDA: Pedro Romero €
Traditional Spanish
Calle Virgen de la Paz 18, 29400
Tel *952 87 11 10*
Named after a 17th-century matador, this restaurant serves excellent *rabo de toro* (braised bull's tail) and *perdiz con alubias* (partridge with kidney beans).

RONDA: Tragatapas €
Traditional Spanish
Calle Nueva 4, 29400
Tel *952 87 72 09*
Cosy unassuming locale in the town centre, with inventive tapas like asparagus and goat's cheese, marinated salmon and sautéed mushrooms. Excellent value.

RONDA: Puerta
Grande Ronda €€
Traditional Spanish
Calle Nueva 10, 29400
Tel *952 87 92 00* **Closed** *dinner; Tue*
A restaurant serving Andalucían dishes, some with innovative interpretations. Try one of the paellas, or the venison loin in a raspberry and blackberry sauce.

ROQUETAS DE MAR:
Alejandro €€€
Seafood
Avenida Antonio Machado 32, 04740
Tel *950 32 24 08* **Closed** *Mon; Sun dinner*
Boasting a Michelin star, this ultra-smart establishment specializes in exquisite seafood fusion dishes. Splash out on the *degustación con marisco* (tasting menu with shellfish).

SANLÚCAR DE BARRAMEDA:
Casa Bigote €
Seafood
Calle Pórtico Bajo de Guía 10, 11540
Tel *956 36 26 96* **Closed** *Sun*
Set beside the Gudalquivir estuary, Casa Bigote is a largely traditional marine restaurant serving fresh seafood and regional hams. Exceptional *lomo de atún* (tuna steak) and *langostinos* (king prawns).

TORREMOLINOS: Frutos €
Traditional Spanish
Avenida de la Riviera 80, 29620
Tel *952 38 15 40* **Closed** *Sun dinner*

One of the grand old Costa del Sol restaurants, Frutos serves first-rate traditional dishes like *judiones a la Granja* (Castilian-style white beans), roast suckling pig and fresh fish. Make sure to visit the well-stocked basement wine cellar.

TORREMOLINOS:
Nuevo Lanjarón €
Traditional Spanish
Calle Europa 10, 29620
Tel *952 38 87 74* **Closed** *Mon*
Probably the best-value restaurant on the Costa del Sol. Located in a neat white-and-ochre building in Torremolinos' old Calvario quarter, it offers a variety of set menus that include well-prepared fish and meat dishes. Try the *estofado de ternera* (veal stew) followed by home-made flan. Wonderful service.

TORREMOLINOS:
Yate El Cordobés €
Seafood
Paseo Maritimo s/n (Bajondillo), 29620
Tel *952 38 49 56* **Closed** *lunch (Feb & Dec)*
Located right on Bajondillo Beach, the local seafood dishes at Yate El Cordobés range from *espetos de sardinas* (charcoal cooked fresh sardines) to *mero en adobo* (grouper marinated in vinegar) and home-spun desserts.

DK Choice

ÚBEDA: Parador
Condestable Dávalos €
Traditional
Plaza Vázquez de Molina, 23400
Tel *953 75 03 45*
If you want to dine out in style in Úbeda, then don't miss this magnificent, sumptuous restaurant located in the old quarter's grand 16th-century parador. The setting is historic, the decor traditional and the atmosphere homely. Its wealth of gourmet offerings include an outstanding cold *ajo blanco* (garlic and almond soup) and mouthwatering game, such as stewed kid with pine nuts.

ÚBEDA: El Seco €
Traditional Spanish
Calle Corazon de Jesus 8, 23400
Tel *953 79 14 52*
A family-run restaurant in Úbeda, El Seco has a cosy dining room. Its home-cooked dishes include *bacalao* El Seco (cod in cream sauce) and *paletilla de cordero al horno* (oven-baked shoulder of lamb).

Beachfront dining at Yate El Cordobes in Torremolinos

VERA: Terrazza Carmona €
Traditional Spanish
Calle del Mar 1, 04620
Tel *950 39 07 60* **Closed** *Mon*
Award-winning roadside restaurant specializing in regional dishes like wild boar with olives. Indulge in a *tarta borracha* (drunken tart!) for dessert.

The Balearic Islands

DK Choice

FORMENTERA, CALÓ DE
SANT AGUSTI: Es Calo €€
Seafood
C/ Vicari Joan Mari 14, Es Calo de Sant Agusti
Tel *971 32 73 11* **Closed** *Nov–Mar*
Es Calo offers seafront dining with the freshest fish, seafood, paellas and meat dishes. Try the *arroz con bogavante* (rice with lobster) or the *chuletón de ternera a la piedra* (stone-cooked jumbo steak for two). Save room for the home-made desserts.

FORMENTERA, EL PILAR DE LA
MOLA: Pequeña Isla €
Regional Spanish
Avenida El Pilar, 101 El Pilar de la Mola
Tel *971 32 70 68* **Closed** *Nov–Apr*
In the hilltop village of La Mola, the menu at Pequeña Isla includes local dishes such as fish stew and roasted lamb.

FORMENTERA, SAN FERRAN:
Blue Bar €
Café
Carretera San Ferran–La Mola, km 7.8, Platja Migjorn, 07871
Tel *666 75 81 90* **Closed** *Dec–Feb*

One of the original 1960s hippie beach bars, Blue Bar on Formentera serves decent salads, pasta dishes, fish and vegetarian options.

IBIZA, IBIZA TOWN:
Sa Nansa €€
Seafood
Avenida 8 de Agosto 27, 07800
Tel *971 31 87 50*   **Closed** *Mon; Sun dinner*
Sa Nansa offers simply the best seafood, whether it is grilled, stewed or included in one of their fabulously tasty rice or noodle dishes.

IBIZA, IBIZA TOWN:
El Olivo Mio €€€
French
Pza de Vila 7–9, 07800
Tel *971 30 06 80*   **Closed** *Mon; mid-Oct–mid-Apr*
The menu at the popular El Olivo Mio restaurant in fashionable Dalt Vila is Ibizan-French with a *nueva cocina* edge. Get a table on the trendy terrace.

IBIZA, SAN ANTONIO:
Villa Mercedes €€€
Mediterranean
Passeig de la Mar, Puerto de San Antonio
Tel *971 34 85 43*   **Closed** *Sun–Thu dinner; Jan & Feb*
Villa Mercedes is a romantic restaurant with a lovely garden terrace and Moroccan-themed chill-out lounge. Live music and performances daily.

IBIZA, SAN CARLOS:
Anita's Bar €
Tapas
Lugar Barri San Carlos s/n, 07850
Tel *971 33 50 90*   **Closed** *Mon*
An institution, Anita's has played a major role in Ibiza's counterculture, and it remains a favourite. It features memorable wall art.

DK Choice

IBIZA, SAN LORENZO:
La Paloma €
Mediterranean
Carrer Can Pou 4, 07812
Tel *971 32 55 43*   **Closed** *dinner*
A labour of love undertaken by two families, La Paloma is a postcard-pretty garden restaurant that serves home-made dishes using organic, local ingredients. Situated in a renovated finca and surrounded by fruit orchards, a small range of delicious Italian-inspired dishes are served with genuine care.

IBIZA, SANT CARLES:
El Bigotes €
Seafood
Cala Mastella. Sant Carles, 07850
Tel *650 79 76 33*   **Closed** *dinner; Nov–Mar*
Perched on a crystalline cove, El Bigotes serves fresh fish in a simple rustic outdoor setting. There are two sittings: at noon for grilled fish and 2pm for seafood stew and rice.

DK Choice

MALLORCA, LLOSETA:
Santi Taura €€
Regional Spanish
Carrer Joan Carles I 48, 07360
Tel *656 73 82 14*   **Closed** *Mon lunch; Tue; Sun dinner*
Local chef Santi Taura reinterprets old recipes from the islands in this smart restaurant in Lloseta. Tasting menus are accompanied by an oration of the history and culture of what's on your plate.

MALLORCA, PALMA:
Café L'Antiquari €
Tapas
Carrer Arabi 5, 07003
Tel *871 57 23 13*   **Closed** *Sun*
A relaxed neighbourhood place with quirky decor and a friendly hippie vibe. Good brunches.

MALLORCA, PALMA:
Club Nautico Cala Gamba €
Seafood
Passeig Cala Gamba s/n, 07007
Tel *971 26 23 72*   **Closed** *Mon*
The decor is nautical, with large windows overlooking the marina. The menu is weighted towards locally caught fish.

MALLORCA, PALMA:
Gran Café Cappuccino €
Café
Carrer de Sant Miquel, 53, 07002
Tel *971 71 97 64*   **Closed** *Sun*
This is a stylish spot for morning coffee, light lunches and evening drinks in the heart of Palma.

MALLORCA, PALMA: Forn de Sant Joan €€
Mediterranean
Carrer Sant Joan 4, 07012
Tel *971 72 84 22*
One of Palma's best creative restaurants, set in an old bakery. Try the roasted suckling pig with apple compote and caramelized apples, but be sure to leave room for the sumptuous desserts.

DK Choice

MALLORCA, PALMA:
Marc Fosh €€€
Modern
Carrer de la Missió 7A, 07003
Tel *971 72 01 14*   **Closed** *Sun*
British chef Marc Fosh has garnered a well-deserved reputation as one of the island's finest chefs. This restaurant, inside the hip Convent de la Missió hotel, is where he shows off his artistry. His original cuisine delights without being too challenging.

MALLORCA, PORTIXOL:
C'an Punta €
Greek
C/ Vicari Joaquim Fuster 105, 07006
Tel *971 27 43 34*   **Closed** *Tue*
Located on the waterfront, this delightful place dishes out fresh Greek-inspired salads and tapas. Relaxed atmosphere.

The upmarket Marc Fosh in Palma, Mallorca

For more information on types of restaurants *see page 577*

MALLORCA, PORTIXOL:
Fibonacci Pan €
Café
C/ Vicario Joaquin Fuster 95, 07006
Tel *971 24 99 61*
This Scandinavian-style bakery
serves appetizing sandwiches,
moist cakes, flaky croissants, and
invigorating salads and soups.

MENORCA, ALAIOR: Es Forn
de Torre Soli Nou €
Grill
Urb. Torre Solí Nou, 07730
Tel *971 37 28 98*
Focusing on meat and poultry *a
la brasa* (barbecued), the best
tables are on the breezy terrace.

MENORCA, CIUTADELLA:
Es Tastet €
Mediterranean
Carrer Carnisseria 9, 07760
Tel *971 38 47 97* **Closed** *Sun lunch*
A great little owner-run place
that serves breakfast and tapas,
as well as pasta and fish dishes,
all using fresh market produce.

MENORCA, CIUTADELLA:
Cas Ferrer de Sa Font €€
Regional Spanish
Carrer del Portal de la Font 16, 07760
Tel *971 48 07 84* **Closed** *Apr, May,
Sep & Oct: Mon, Sun dinner; Jun–
Aug: Sun lunch; Nov–Mar*
Laid out in three rooms of an
imposing 17th-century town
mansion, Cas Ferrer serves a
small but good selection of
traditional island dishes.

MENORCA, ES CASTELL:
Son Granot €
Regional Spanish
Carretera Sant Felip, 07720
Tel *971 35 55 55* **Closed** *Sun (mid-
Jul–mid-Sep)*
Located on a hilltop, and part of
a rural hotel, Son Granot serves

Place settings at Son Granot in Es
Castell, Menorca

Key to Price Guide *see page 582*

traditional Menorcan cuisine.
Highlights include suckling pig
confit with braised melon.

MENORCA, FERRERIES:
Meson El Gallo €
Regional Spanish
*Crta Cala Santa Galdana, km 1.5,
07750*
Tel *971 37 30 39* **Closed** *Mon;
Nov–May*
The signature dish here is rooster
(*el gallo*) paella. It's also famed for
its steaks with Mallorcan cheese,
as well as a range of meats and
several types of *tortilla* (omelette).

DK Choice

MENORCA, MAHÓN:
Ses Forquilles €
Tapas
Rovellada de Dalt 20, 07703
Tel *971 35 27 11* **Closed** *Mon;
Sun in winter*
An inviting crowd-pleaser.
Creative gourmet tapas and
entrées made with the finest of
local produce. Tapas bar on
ground floor; restaurant above.

MENORCA, SA MESQUIDA:
Cap Roig €€
Seafood
Carretera Sa Mesquida 13, 07701
Tel *971 18 83 83* **Closed** *Mon;
mid-Oct–Easter*
Named after the star of its menu,
Cap Roig ("scorpion fish") is
highly recommended for its
caldereta de llagosta (lobster stew).

The Canary Islands

EL HIERRO, LA RESTINGA:
Restaurante El Refugio €
Seafood
Calle La Lapa 2, 38911
Tel *922 55 70 29* **Closed** *Mon*
This family restaurant in a rural
hotel has a rustic ambience. It
defines its cuisine as *de la barca al
plato* (from the boat to the plate).

EL HIERRO, VALVERDE:
La Mirada Profunda €
Modern Spanish
Calle Santiago 25, 38900
Tel *922 55 17 87* **Closed** *Mon dinner*
A taste of Barcelona's avant-garde,
flavour-rich gastronomy. The
wine list includes local vintages.

EL HIERRO, VALVERDE:
Tasca El Secreto €
Tapas
Calle Quintero Ramos 2, 38900
Tel *922 55 06 58* **Closed** *Sun*
Colourful restaurant with a
charming vintage style, boasting

a mix of traditional and modern
cuisine. Try the menu of the day
for excellent value.

FUERTEVENTURA, EL COTILLO:
La Vaca Azul €
Seafood
Calle Requena 9, 35660
Tel *928 53 86 85*
The famous Blue Cow is more
surf than turf, with the Atlantic
Ocean providing the majority of
the star ingredients on your
plate. The terrace offers stunning
views of the bay.

FUERTEVENTURA, MORRO DE
JABLE: La Laja €
Seafood
Avda Tomás Grau Gurrea 1, 35625
Tel *928 54 20 54*
Fresh fish doesn't come much
fresher than at this coastal
restaurant with a fabulous
beachfront terrace. Rice and
pasta dishes will suit vegetarians.

GRAN CANARIA, ARTENARA:
Restaurante Mirador La Cilla €
Regional
Camino de La Cilla 9, 35350
Tel *609 16 39 44*
A tunnel leads to a sun terrace –
offering panoramic views of
the surrounding mountains –
where you can linger over
Canarian regional specialities.

GRAN CANARIA, BAÑADEROS:
Restaurante Terraza El Puertillo €
Seafood
*Paseo Marítimo El Puertillo 12,
35414*
Tel *928 62 75 37*
The Hormigas make you feel part
of the family at their beachside
restaurant. They do a great paella,
as well as fresh fish.

GRAN CANARIA, EL
MADRONAL: Casa Martell €
Regional
*Carretera del Centro Km 18.2,
35308*
Tel *928 64 24 83*
There are specialities of the
house to enjoy but you won't
find them on any menu.
Home-grown organic vegetables
feature heavily.

GRAN CANARIA, LAS PALMAS:
Samsara €
Fusion
*CC La Charca, Avenida del Oasis 30,
35100*
Tel *928 14 27 36* **Closed** *Mon*
Stylish place which prepares
traditional Spanish ingredients
such as *solomillo* (sirloin) and
cordero (lamb) with exotic
spices and sauces, such as
curry and teriyaki.

GRAN CANARIA, LAS PALMAS:
Tres Jolie Las Palmas €
Italian
Calle Mendizabal, 24 Vegueta, 35100
Tel *928 96 50 86* **Closed** *Mon–Wed dinner; Sun*
Authentic Italian cuisine in the heart of Las Palmas. Good variety of pasta, meat, fish and vegetarian choices with very attentive service. The daily menu is fantastic value.

DK Choice

LA GOMERA, LAS HAYAS:
Restaurante La Montaña-
Casa Efigenia €
Vegetarian
Crta Las Hayas–Arure, Las Hayas, 38869
Tel *922 80 42 48*
Outside, eucalyptus trees guard the entrance to this celebrated hamlet restaurant, part of a rural accommodation complex. Inside, matriarch Efigenia traditionally spoonfeeds you your first taste of the restaurant's only main course, a hearty vegetable stew served with gofio (roasted maize). The freshest salads and almogrote (a cheesy dip) are perfect accompaniments.

LA GOMERA, SAN SEBASTIÁN DE LA GOMERA: Restaurante
El Charcón €€
Regional Spanish
Playa de la Cueva, 38800
Tel *922 14 18 98* **Closed** *Sun & Mon*
Freshly caught fish and seafood are the main focus at this pleasant restaurant housed in a natural cave. As well as fish, they utilize market-fresh vegetables in their meal preparation.

LA PALMA, FUENCALIENTE:
La Casa del Volcan €
Regional Spanish
Calle de los Volcanes 23, 38740
Tel *922 44 44 27* **Closed** *Mon*
Local cheese, goat and rabbit are some of the fixtures on the menu at this traditional restaurant, which specializes in Canarian food.

LA PALMA, GARAFIA:
Restaurante Briesta €
Traditional Spanish
Carretera General Las Tricias, km 6, 38787
Tel *922 40 02 10* **Closed** *Tue, Wed*
This charming family-run restaurant features a tree growing through it and a fireplace for chilly winter days. It serves a good variety of meat, including lamb and rabbit.

Tables on the terrace at El Rincón de Juan Carlos, Tenerife

LA PALMA, SANTA CRUZ DE LA PALMA: Restaurante Parrilla
Las Nieves €
Regional Spanish
Plaza de las Nieves 2, 38700
Tel *922 41 66 00*
Go local in an establishment where tourists are conspicuous by their absence. A daily menu offers a taste of authentic Canarian cuisine.

LANZAROTE, LA GERIA:
Bodega El Chupadero €
Regional Spanish
La Geria 3, 35570
Tel *928 17 31 15* **Closed** *Mon*
Simple, hearty fare can be had at this rustic restaurant attached to a bodega in Lanzarote's volcanic wine region. Cash only.

LANZAROTE, NAZARET:
Lagomar €
Modern Spanish
Calle Los Loros 2, 35539
Tel *928 84 56 65* **Closed** *lunch; Mon*
Lagomar is housed in a stunning property, built into the cliffs. Creative dishes include pork steak over sweet potato parmentier and paprika sauce.

LANZAROTE, TEGUISE:
La Cantina €
Tapas
Calle León y Castillo 8, 35530
Tel *928 84 55 36*
Located in picturesque Teguise, which was once the island's capital, this is a restaurant specializing in tapas which also includes an art gallery and deli on its premises.

LANZAROTE, TIMANFAYA:
Restaurante El Diablo €
Regional Spanish
Parque Nacional de Timanfaya, Charco Prieto, s/n, 35560
Tel *928 84 00 56* **Closed** *dinner*

Brace yourself for a truly unique dining experience at El Diablo: the food is grilled directly over a live volcanic crater, which billows out sulphuric steam.

TENERIFE, COSTA ADEJE:
El Molino Blanco €€
International
Avenida Austria 5, 38660
Tel *922 79 62 82*
A meat-heavy menu, though vegetarians will be pleased with the good selection of salads and vegetable dishes. The place transforms into a music venue after sunset.

TENERIFE, EL SAUZAL:
Terrazas del Sauzal €€
International
Pasaje Sierva de Dios 9, 38360
Tel *922 57 14 91* **Closed** *Mon, Tue*
It boasts an international menu, but eating here is really about the 10,000 sq m of surrounding gardens that makes for a picturesque setting.

TENERIFE, LOS GIGANTES:
El Rincón de Juan Carlos €€€
Modern Spanish
Acantilado de Los Gigantes, Pasaje Jacaranda, 2, 38683
Tel *922 86 80 40* **Closed** *Sun, Mon*
Juan Carlos Padron is Tenerife's only celebrity chef. He works with his brother Jonathan, a renowned pastry chef. Their tasting menus are inspired. Outstanding food, excellent wine and service to match.

TENERIFE, PUERTO DE LA CRUZ:
Tambo €
Seafood
Calle Añaterve 1, Punta Brava, 38400
Tel *922 37 62 62* **Closed** *Sun*
Seafood dominates the menu at Tambo, with the mussels and squid particularly recommended.

For more information on types of restaurants *see page 577*

SHOPPING IN SPAIN

Spain has a thriving shopping culture, with many unique, family-run boutiques as well as reliable chain stores and big department stores. Good buys include leather, fashion, wine and ceramics, though these days it is possible to find anything you are looking for, from traditional gifts to designer clothes. Spain has its own rules of etiquette when it comes to shopping. In small shops, most merchandise is behind the counter, and the clerk will retrieve whatever you need, making for a time-consuming, but friendly, way to shop. It is polite to greet the shop owner and fellow shoppers with a "buenos días" or "buenas tardes" as you enter, and to say "adiós" as you leave.

Fresh produce in a market in Pollença (Mallorca)

Opening Hours

Most shops in Spain, barring some supermarkets or department stores, close at midday. Small shops are usually open Monday to Saturday (10am–2pm and 5–8pm). Service-related shops, such as dry cleaners, tend to open an hour earlier and close an hour later. Nearly all shops are closed on Sunday and holidays, except during the Christmas season and sales.

Payment Methods

Cash is still the payment of choice in Spain. Cheques are rarely accepted, and credit cards may not be accepted in small shops or markets. Even in large stores, there may be a minimum purchase required for credit card users.
ATMs are widely available throughout the country, even in small towns, so getting cash should not be a problem.

VAT

Value added tax (VAT), known as *IVA* in Spanish, is included in the price of nearly everything in Spain. However, non-EU residents are eligible for a VAT refund *(see p616)*. If you buy goods worth a total of €90.15 or more, request a VAT refund form from the shopkeeper, then get it stamped at a Spanish customs office before you check your bags in at the airport. Present the stamped form at an affiliated bank or office in the airport, or mail it for the refund to be credited to your credit card.

Sales

Spain's twice-annual *rebajas* (sales) are a fantastic opportunity to find good deals on everything from shoes and clothes to linens, electronics and household goods. Most stores offer a reduction of 50 per cent or more.
The first *rebajas* of the year begin on 7 January and continue until mid-February. Summer *rebajas* start on 1 July each year and last until the end of August.

In addition to these two *rebajas* periods, shops can also offer sales at any time of year.

Markets

A visit to a Spanish market is a great lesson in local culture. Every town, large or small, has at least one fresh market, known as *mercadillo*, where you can buy local produce, Spanish cheeses and sausages and other foods.
Markets in the cities follow regular store opening hours, but in smaller towns they may only be open in the morning, or on certain days of the week.
Speciality markets for antiques, arts and crafts are popular in Spain, as are the *rastros* (flea markets). These are usually open only at weekends, though the times vary across markets and towns.
The country's most celebrated market is El Rastro *(see p306)*, a massive flea market in Madrid, which has been running for many generations. It is frequented by locals and tourists alike. Watch out for pickpockets.

Display of hand-painted ceramics in Toledo

Shopping in Barcelona pp190–93; in Madrid pp320–23; in Seville pp460–61

Regional Products

Spain has a strong artisan heritage, and the best places to buy authentic traditional items are the artisan markets and speciality shops. All over Spain, you'll find great pottery and ceramics. Spain's pottery is sturdy and colourful and each region puts its own spin on the traditional forms. Andalucía, El Bisbal in Catalonia, Paterna and Manises near Valencia and Talavera de la Reina in Castilla-La Mancha are the main centres for ceramic production.

Leather goods are another traditional craft. Reasonably priced shoes, wallets and accessories are available almost everywhere.

In Toledo, filigree metalwork and swords are sold on almost every street corner. Other sought-after products include guitars, traditional fans, Lladró porcelain figures and lacework.

A Madrid branch of the fashionable Camper shoe store

Food and Drink

Basketware, sold in all parts of Spain

Spain is second only to Italy in wine production, and Spanish wine is rated to be of the best value in Europe. Major wine regions are Penedès (reds, whites and cava), Priorat (reds), Rías Baixas (whites), Ribera del Duero (reds), Rioja (reds) and Toro (whites). Sherry and vermouth are also popular Spanish drinks.

A gourmet's paradise, Spain is great for food shopping. Olives and olive oil are always a good buy. Prominent olive-growing areas include Andalucía, Aragón and southern Catalonia. Seville produces marmalade from the countless orange trees that line its streets. You can also buy Spain's famous *Jamón Ibérico* (Iberian cured ham), or one of the many region-specific sausages such as Catalan *butifarra* and Castilian *morcilla*.

Gourmet chocolate shops can frequently be found in cities. Escribà in Barcelona has a good reputation for producing exquisite confectionery.

One-Stop Shopping

Small family-run shops are quaint, but when you're in a hurry department stores and one-stop shops are more convenient. Spain's most famous department store, El Corte Inglés, is found in every major city in Spain, sometimes with multiple branches. This megastore sells everything from clothes and sports goods, to furniture and food. Other one-stop shops include hypermarkets such as Carrefour (the Walmart of Europe), Alcampo and Hipercor. American-style malls, called *centros comerciales* in Spain, are gaining popularity and can be found on the outskirts of most large cities.

Fashion

Spain has a long textile history, so it's no surprise to find good-quality clothing here. In large cities such as Madrid and Barcelona, you'll find boutiques of major Spanish labels, including Antonio Miro, Lydia Delgado, Josep Font, Adolfo Dominguez and Loewe. Spanish fashion may not be on par with Paris or Milan yet, but designers here are increasingly gaining a reputation for quality and originality. Spanish-owned chains such as Zara, Mango and Massimo Dutti are known around the world for their affordable, cutting-edge fashion.

Mallorca is a good place to buy shoes, home to Spain's most famous shoe company, Camper. Along with branded shoes, *espadrilles* (traditional Spanish rope soled shoes) are a good informal option.

Size Chart

Women's dresses, coats and skirts

European	36	38	40	42	44	46	48
British	8	10	12	14	16	18	20
American	4	6	8	10	12	14	16

Women's shoes

European	36	37	38	39	40	41
British	3	4	5	6	7	8
American	5	6	7	8	9	10

Men's suits

European	44	46	48	50	52	54	56	58 (size)
British	34	36	38	40	42	44	46	48 (inches)
American	34	36	38	40	42	44	46	48 (inches)

Men's shirts (collar size)

European	36	38	39	41	42	43	44	45 (cm)
British	14	15	15½	16	16½	17	17½	18 (inches)
American	14	15	15½	16	16½	17	17½	18 (inches)

Men's shoes

European	39	40	41	42	43	44	45	46
British	6	7	7½	8	9	10	11	12
American	7	7½	8	8½	9½	10½	11	11½

ENTERTAINMENT IN SPAIN

Spain is famous for its vibrant, colourful culture – wherever you are, there is usually a fiesta going on somewhere nearby, or some impromptu celebration taking place in the street. So, while there's usually no need to seek out formal entertainment, those who do want to plan a day or night out will find plenty of choice, ranging from raucous cabarets and gripping sporting matches, to live flamenco and highbrow cultural events. Although Madrid, Barcelona and, to a lesser extent, Seville have the widest selection of programmes, the other regional capitals are not far behind. The coastal resorts also witness a lot of action in the summer months. Regular annual events in various parts of Spain are detailed on pages 42–3.

Preparing for a dressage display at the equestrian school in Jerez

Traditional Music and Dance

Spain's rich musical heritage is marked by typical regional instruments, musical styles and dance forms. The *txistu*, a small wind instrument is typical to the Basque Country, Galicia and Asturias lilt to the notes of the *gaita* (bagpipes), while Valencia is proud of its countless brass bands.

Andalucía is the home of flamenco, while Aragón's rhythm comes from the hop-step of its folk dance, *jota*. In Catalonia, the famous *sardana* (see p229) is accompanied by a *flabiol* (flute), *tabal* (drum) and *gralla* (a type of oboe).

Jazz, Rock and Pop

Television talent shows tend to dominate the Spanish pop industry, but many creative bands fail to get international recognition only because they sing in Spanish. At the cultural crossroads of southern Europe, the Spanish music scene is also enriched by influences from South America and Africa.

The Benicassim festival in July and the Sonar festival in June in Barcelona are the preferred live events for those in search of new music. An international blues festival is held every July in Cazorla *(see p45)*, with big international jazz artists playing in small town stadiums and even bullrings.

The Spanish music channel RNE 3 broadcasts an eclectic selection of Spanish as well as international music.

Flamenco

Flamenco *(see pp428–9)* is a traditional art form that combines song, music and dance. Infused with sensuality and emotion, it originated in Andalucía but is performed all over Spain. It is a highly varied musical form, and acts can range from spontaneous performances in gypsy patios to international spectacles in major concert halls.

Shows are often adapted to tourists' tastes. To see and hear flamenco that even purists admire, try the smaller venues or catch a performance during an Andalucían fiesta, particularly in the provinces of Seville and Jerez.

Córdoba hosts the National Flamenco Competition in November every third year. The next two are being held in 2019 and 2022.

Classical Music, Opera and Ballet

Opera, classical music and ballet are performed in all the major cities in concert halls. The best-known venues include the Auditorio Nacional de Música and Teatro Real in Madrid *(see p326)*, Palau de la Música in Valencia *(see p256)*, Teatro de la Maestranza in Seville *(see p462)* and Gran Teatre del Liceu and L'Auditori *(see p195)* in Barcelona.

For a more unusual concert setting, look out for performances in Spain's spectacular caves, such as those found in Nerja *(see p489)*, Drac *(see p521)* and the Cuevas of Canelobre

Palau de la Música, Valencia

Entertainment in Barcelona pp194–9; in Madrid pp324–9; in Seville pp462–3

View of the stage area at the beautifully preserved Roman theatre in Mérida, Extremadura

near Alicante. Sacred music can still be heard in some of Spain's monasteries. Montserrat *(see pp222–3)* is famous for its all-boy choir. In Leyre monastery *(see p139)*, the Gregorian plainchant is performed during Mass.

Theatre

Spain has a great repertoire of classical theatre and, although most performances are in Spanish, it may be worth going to a show for the venue alone.

Corral de Comedias in Almagro *(see p403)* is a perfectly preserved 17th-century Golden Age theatre. Mérida's stunning Roman theatre *(see pp58–9 and pp414–5)* serves as the splendid backdrop for an annual summer festival of classical theatre.

Cinema

Spain's thriving film scene has certainly gained international exposure. The country makes around 100 feature films a year with directors such as Pedro Almodóvar and Alejandro Amenábar.

Most foreign-language films are dubbed in Spanish, but select cinemas in university cities and areas with a number of foreign residents show films in their original language. San Sebastián hosts an acclaimed international film festival *(see p127)* in September, and the Sitges Film Festival takes place in October.

The open-air summer cinemas in some coastal resorts are an experience in themselves, but do remember to carry a mosquito repellent.

Nightlife

Spain's prodigious nightlife starts later than in most other countries, with 11pm considered an early start for most revellers. The idea is to spend the first part of the evening in pubs or *bares de copas*: sparsely decorated drinking dens, usually with loud music blaring. Then people move on to the nightclubs, often located out of town, where the noise will not bother anyone.

You can enjoy a floorshow while dining out at coastal package-holiday resorts such as Lloret del Mar on the Costa Brava, Maspalomas on Gran Canaria, Torremolinos on the Costa del Sol and Benidorm on the Costa Blanca.

Spectator Sports

Football is Spain's favourite sport and is centred on the battle between the two top teams, Real Madrid and Barcelona. Other teams with large followings include Real Betis from Seville, Deportivo La Coruña, FC Valencia and Atlético de Madrid. Cycling, tennis, basketball and golf are also popular.

Bullfighting

Although controversial, bullfighting is one of Spain's most recognized sporting events *(see pp40–41)*. Visitors can watch a bullfight in one of the large, traditional arenas in Madrid *(see p310)* and Seville *(see p436)*, or in Valencia, Bilbao and Zaragoza. All bullfights start at around 5pm. Tickets should be bought directly at the venue. Bullfighting is banned in Catalonia.

Entertainment for Children

Spain's big theme parks are Port Aventura, on the Costa Daurada *(see p228)*, Terra Mítica, outside Benidorm *(see p264)*, and Parque Warner, in Madrid. Other amusements suitable for kids include the cowboys of Mini-Hollywood *(see p504)* and the dancing horses of Jerez *(see p472)*.

Rollercoaster ride at Port Aventura on the Costa Daurada

OUTDOOR ACTIVITIES & SPECIALIST HOLIDAYS

Spain is one of Europe's most geographically varied countries, with mountain ranges, woodlands and river deltas suitable for scenic tours and sports holidays. The options are endless and include sailing on the Mediterranean or surfing in the Atlantic, mountain climbing in the Pyrenees or rambling through the plains of Castille, snow skiing in the Sierra Nevada or water-skiing off the coast of Mallorca. Weekend or week-long activity-led holidays, featuring everything from yoga to horse riding, are gaining popularity in Spain. To focus on just one activity, sign up for a specialist holiday. Local tourist offices can provide information on outdoor activities.

Walking and Trekking

Spain offers exciting choices for a challenging week-long trek through the Pyrenees, or a gentle walk along the coast. Look out for the wide, well-marked GR (*Grandes Recorridos* meaning "long-distance") trails, which crisscross Spain. Though most people usually choose to walk only a small portion of each GR trail, long-distance trekkers use them to traverse all the way across the country.

Nearly 8 per cent of Spain's total terrain is protected parkland, and the countless natural parks and 15 large national parks are the most popular and attractive hiking options. Some of the best parks for walking include Aragón's Parque Nacional de Ordesa *(see pp236– 7)*, Catalunya's Parque Nacional d'Aigüestortes *(see p215)*, and Asturias' Parque Nacional de los Picos de Europa *(see pp112– 13)*. For details about trails in the parks, contact the **Environment Ministry of Spain**.

For information on other trails, contact the **Federación Española de Deportes de Montaña y Escalada**.

Air Sports

The best way to take in Spain's landscape is to view it from above. Options for thrilling aerial views include hot-air ballooning, skydiving, paragliding and hang-gliding. One of the well-known hot-air balloon companies is **Globus Kon-Tiki**, which began flying in rural Catalonia and now covers the whole country. **Glovento Sur** operates in Southern Spain. Standard rides start from €165 per person, depending on the trip's length.

For those who have forever been fascinated by the birds' ability to fly, paragliding and hang-gliding are two excellent options. The **Real Federación Aeronáutica Española** can provide information on schools and outfitters across Spain. Contact them for further details.

When it comes to a real thrill, nothing surpasses skydiving. Reputable companies offering skydiving courses or tandem jumps include **Skydive Empuriabrava** in Catalonia and **Skydive Lillo** near Toledo. Expect a single tandem jump (a jump made while attached to a qualified instructor) to cost between €220 and €320.

Water Sports

Spain is virtually surrounded by water, so it is little surprise that sailing is popular here. The country's most celebrated yacht ports are those of upscale resorts including Palma and Marbella, and in 2007 and 2010 the port of Valencia hosted the prestigious America's Cup sailing tournament. Mooring a private yacht or sailboat in a top-notch marina is expensive and often impossible. A much easier alternative is to rent a sailboat by the day or week, or to sign up for a half- or full-day sailing excursion. Most other seaside towns also have small recreational ports offering sailboats and yacht charters which can be rented by providing a sailing licence. For details, contact the **Real Federación Española de Vela**.

Scuba diving is available up and down the coast of Spain and on nearly all the islands. However, the best places for underwater exploration are around the Canary Islands. Just off the island of El Hierro are the warm, calm waters of the Mar de las Calmas, which is full of colourful coral and

Paragliding above the Vall d'Aran in the eastern Pyrenees

Whitewater rafting in the Spanish Pyrenees

dozens of marine species. In the Mediterranean, head to the Balearic Islands or to the Illes Medes, seven tiny islets off the Costa Brava that are home to some of the most diverse marine life in all the Mediterranean. The local Illes Medes information office, **Estació Nàutica**, will provide detailed information about area outfitters.

Surfing and windsurfing are other popular sports. On mainland Spain the best places for either kind of surfing are the Basque coast (especially towns such as Zarautz and Mundaka) and Tarifa, which is also good for kitesurfing, on the Costa de la Luz. In the Canary Islands, try Lanzarote or Fuerteventura for surfing and El Médano (Tenerife) for windsurfing. El Médano's **Surf Center Playa Sur** has information.

Sea kayaking is becoming very popular and kayak rental

Windsurfing near Tarifa, on Southern Spain's Costa de la Luz

is now available in many Mediterranean resort towns. Since rentals are cheap and little prior experience is necessary, kayaking is a great option for boating novices who might want to spend some time out on the water.

Adventure Sports

Since Spain is Europe's second-most-mountainous country after Switzerland, mountain climbing is a natural sport here. Head to the Aragón Pyrenees or the Catalan Pyrenees for a wide range of challenging rock faces. Other popular spots include the mountain of Montserrat in Catalonia, the Parque Natural de los Cañones y Sierra de Guara in Aragón, the Sierra Nevada in Andalucía and the Picos de Europa in Asturias. For more information, contact the **Federación Española de Deportes de Montaña y Escalada**.

If mere mountain climbing doesn't sound interesting enough, go for *barranquismo* (canyoning), a thrilling adventure sport that lets you explore canyons, cliffs and rivers with a combination of hiking, climbing, rappelling and swimming.

The undisputed capital of canyoning is Parque Natural de la Sierra y los Cañones de Guara, a park and natural area in central Aragón that is home to dozens of "wet" and "dry" canyons. Outfitters such as **Camping Lecina**

provide wetsuits and experienced guides – a must for novices – for €45 per person. Most services and lodging are in, or near, the pretty town of Alquezar.

Another fun way to explore rivers is whitewater rafting. Although Spain is not known for its raging rivers, there are a few places where some white water can be found. Head for the rivers: Noguera Pallaresa in Catalunya, the Carasa in Asturias or the Miño in Galicia. Late spring and early summer are the best times for rafting, since run-off from melted snow ensures a good deal of water and big rapids.

Climbing a sheer rock face in the Parque Nacional de Ordesa, Aragón

Fishing

Deep-sea fishing excursions are offered all along Spain's coasts. Fishing in the Mediterranean or the Atlantic is unregulated except for marine reserves and some parks. Trout fishing in lakes and streams is possible; some of the best trout rivers are in Asturias, Rioja and Castilla y León. It is challenging to fish in the narrow, tree-lined streams of the Pyrenees.

It is essential to acquire a seasonal or a daily permit specifying if the fishing area is *sin muerte* (catch and release). Bring your own equipment, as only a few companies offer guided trips. For details on fishing sites and regulations, contact **Federación Española de Pesca y Casting**.

Cycling

Road biking and mountain biking are both popular in Spain. Helmets are recommended while cycling, especially on highways, where extreme caution should be exercised. Drivers here are not accustomed to sharing the road and accidents on highways are not uncommon. The **Real Federación Española de Ciclismo** will provide useful information as well as advice on how to plan a safe cycling excursion.

Mountain bikers will find plenty of trails to keep them busy pedalling in Spain. Several walking paths are also suitable for mountain biking, which are referred to as "BTT" (Bici Todo Terreno or all-terrain bikes; www.centrosbtt.es). Throughout Catalunya, Centros BTT are set up to inform bikers about trails and conditions. In other regions, where this service is not available, trail information and maps can be found at tourist offices.

For young or inexperienced cyclers, *vias verdes* (rail trails) are a fantastic option. These flat, long-distance trails follow the paths of discontinued rail lines, ideal for those who want lovely views without making an effort. Many *vias verdes* cut through historic towns, making interesting pit stops along the way. The **Fundación de los Ferrocarriles Españoles** has detailed information about routes.

Golf

Golf is popular throughout Spain, though most courses can be found near the coasts and coastal resort areas. There are too many important golfing areas to highlight just one; the **Real Federación Española de Golf** has detailed information on all the courses. Some of the golf courses offer activities for non-golfers as well. For year-round golf, head to the island of Tenerife, where nearly a dozen courses, including the beautifully situated **Golf Las Américas**, are huddled in the southern corner of the island.

Skiing and Winter Sports

Spain's mountainous terrain makes it an excellent place for skiing, and resorts here are often cheaper than those in the Alps or other places in Europe. The top ski resorts are the Sierra Nevada in Granada and Baqueira-Beret, in the Pyrenean Val d'Aran. It is also possible to ski in the Sierra de Guadarrama, just north of Madrid, and in a handful of other high-altitude areas. Details are available through the **Real Federación Española de Deportes de Invierno**. Visit www.atudem.es for more information (in Spanish) about ski resorts.

Birdwatching

Spain's mild climate attracts a huge variety of fowl year-round. In winter, one can observe birds native to northern Europe; in spring, native Mediterranean species come to nest. There are numerous natural parks working to conserve Spain's diverse bird population. The top bird-watching site is Extremadura's Parque Nacional Monfragüe, where big birds of prey can be seen swooping and hunting. Other excellent places to observe birds in their natural habitat are Andalucía's Parque Nacional de Doñana, Guadalquivir Delta and Laguna de Fuente de Piedra, and Delta de l'Ebre in southern Catalonia.

Spas

Health and wellness spas, or *balnearios*, are nothing new in Spain. As far back as Roman times residents here were enjoying the healthy benefits of mineral-rich waters along the Mediterranean or in the interior. Day spas offering a range of beauty and therapeutic treatments are popular as well, especially in cities and resorts. The **Asociación Nacional de Estaciones Termales** website (National Association of Thermal Resorts) has details on reputable spas throughout the country.

Naturism

Specially designated nudist, or naturist, beaches are not hard to find in Spain. Contact the various coastal tourist offices for details of nudist beaches. Alternatively, log on to the official website of the **Federación Española de Naturismo (FEN)**, which has a comprehensive list.

Specialist Holidays

A weekend or week-long specialist holiday provides the luxury of practising a favourite hobby, or probably learning a new one.

Food and wine holidays are more popular than ever in Spain, with its varied cuisine and excellent wines. A growing number of companies – many of them owned by expat British – have opened in recent years, offering everything from tours of well-known wine regions to the chance to harvest grapes or olives. For upscale, made-to-order tours of wine regions all over Spain, contact the Madrid-based company **Cellar Tours**. For daily cooking classes and an in-depth look at local Spanish cuisines and customs, try a cooking holiday like those offered by the Priorat-based **Catacurian** or the Málaga-based **Cooking Holiday Spain**.

The scenic landscapes of Spain are a wonderful inspiration to indulge the artistic temperament. A painting holiday offers the chance to escape to the quiet countryside and paint. Companies including **Authentic Adventures** offer multi-day holidays for artists of all levels. Holidays include instruction with an experienced painter as well as practising independently. Sculpture or drawing classes are often available too.

Activity-focused holidays are a great option as well. Spain's pleasant weather is particularly favourable for walking, biking, water-skiing or horseback riding. The holiday company **On Foot in Spain** offers a variety of walking holidays in Northern

Spain, while **Switchbacks Mountain Bike Vacations** has cycling holidays for all levels in Andalucía. For water-sports enthusiasts, **Xtreme Gene** specializes in water skiing holidays. Those interested in dance can try **Club Dance**, a London-based company offering dancing holidays. **Fantasia Adventure Holidays** specializes in horseback riding holidays in Southern Spain. To relax, a yoga holiday may be ideal. There are some great alternatives for getting away from the stress of daily life, such as **Kaliyoga**, which offers yoga instruction in a pristine setting. A healthy menu and ample free time for hiking or meditating add to the general feel-good factor of a yoga holiday.

A specialist holiday is also a great opportunity to learn Spanish. Language holidays are available in many parts of Spain, where the Spanish language can be learned in the best way possible – by immersing oneself completely in the country's culture. Language holidays provide the chance to observe the Spanish way of life from close quarters, for an extended period of time. The **Instituto Cervantes** has information on schools and classes across Spain.

DIRECTORY

Walking and Trekking

Environment Ministry of Spain
Pl Infanta Isabel I, Madrid.
Tel 915 97 65 77.
W mma.es

Federación Española de Deportes de Montaña y Escalada
Calle Floridablanca 84, Barcelona. **Tel** 934 26 42 67. W fedme.es

Air Sports

Globus Kon-Tiki
Aeródrom Odena – Igualada, Barcelona.
Tel 93 515 60 60.
W globuskontiki.com

Glovento Sur
Placeta Nevot 4 1°A, Granada. **Tel** 958 29 03 16. W gloventosur.com

Real Federación Aeronáutica Española
Calle Arlabán 7, 3a Planta, Oficinas 38–39, Madrid.
Tel 915 08 29 50.
W rfae.es

Skydive Empuriabrava
Sector Aeroclub s/n, Empuriabrava, Costa Brava, Catalonia.
Tel 972 45 01 11.
W skydive empuriabrava.com

Skydive Lillo
Aeródromo Don Quijote, Lillo. **Tel** 902 36 62 09.
W skydivelillo.com

Water Sports

Estació Náutica
Calle de la Platja 10–12, L'Estartit. **Tel** 972 75 06 99.
W enestartit.com

Real Federación Española de Vela
Calle Luis de Salazar 9, Madrid. **Tel** 915 19 50 08.
W rfev.es

Surf Center Playa Sur
El Médano, Tenerife.
Tel 922 17 66 88. W surf center.el-medano.com

Adventure Sports

Camping Lecina
Lecina, Sierra de Guara.
Tel 974 31 03 86.
W campinglecina.com

Federación Española de Deportes de Montaña y Escalada
See Walking and Trekking.

Fishing

Federación Española de Pesca y Casting
Madrid. **Tel** 915 32 83 52.
W fepyc.es

Cycling

Fundación de los Ferrocarriles Españoles
W viasverdes.com

Real Federación Española de Ciclismo
Madrid. **Tel** 915 40 08 41.
W rfec.com

Golf

Golf Las Américas
Playa de las Américas, Tenerife. **Tel** 922 75 20 05.
W golflasamericas.com

Real Federación Española de Golf
Arroyo del Monte 5, Madrid. **Tel** 915 55 26 82.
W rfegolf.es

Skiing and Winter Sports

Real Federación Española de Deportes de Invierno
Tel 913 76 99 30.
W rfedi.es

Spas

Asociación Nacional de Estaciones Termales
Tel 902 11 76 27
W balnearios.org

Naturism

Federación Española de Naturismo (FEN)
W naturismo.org

Specialist Holidays

Authentic Adventures
Tel 00 44 (0)1453 823328.
W authentic adventures.co.uk

Catacurian
Gratallops 43737, Tarragona. **Tel** 977 82 50 85. W catacurian.com

Cellar Tours
Calle Zurbano 45, 1°, Madrid. **Tel** 911 43 65 53.
W cellartours.com

Club Dance Holidays
42 South Molton Street, London (UK).
Tel 00 44 (0)20 7099 4816.
W clubdanceholidays. com

Cooking Holiday Spain
Urb. Torremar, C/ Roma 9, Benalmadena, Málaga.
Tel 637 80 27 43.
W cookingholiday spain.com

Fantasia Adventure Holidays
Calle Luis Braille P21–3A, Barbate, Cadiz.
Tel 610 94 36 85.
W fantasiaadventure holidays.com

Instituto Cervantes
Calle Alcalá 49, Madrid.
Tel 914 36 76 00.
W cervantes.es

Kallyoga
Orgiva, Granada.
Tel 858 99 58 90 or 00 44 (0)20 8123 6946 (UK).
W kaliyoga.com

On Foot in Spain
Ribeira, A Coruña.
Tel 686 99 40 62.
W onfootinspain.com

Switchbacks Mountain Bike Vacations
Barrio La Ermita s/n, Bubion, Granada.
Tel 660 62 33 05.
W switch-backs.com

Xtreme Gene
Xtreme Gene Watersports Complex, Embalse de la Breña, 14720 Almodovar del Río. **Tel** 957 05 70 10.
W xtreme-gene.com

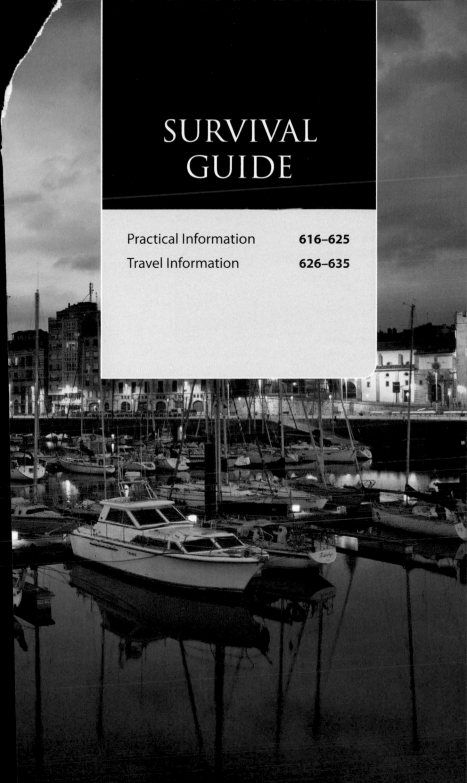

SURVIVAL GUIDE

PRACTICAL INFORMATION

Spain has a highly developed and diverse tourist industry that caters to a wide variety of travellers – from eco-friendly backpacking and cultural visits to some of Europe's most impressive heritage sites, to sunseeking at resorts for all ages and budgets. Information on

accommodation, restaurants and leisure activities can be found at the *oficinas de turismo* in all major towns. In addition, Spanish people are naturally open and welcoming to outsiders, so the best information often comes from the locals themselves.

Relaxing on a sandy Spanish beach in summer

When to Go

August is traditionally Spain's main holiday month. Many businesses close for the entire month, and traffic is very heavy at the beginning and end of this period. At any time of year, try to find out in advance if your visit coincides with local *fiestas* – although these are exciting attractions, they often entail widespread closures and high prices.

Visas and Passports

Spain is part of the Schengen Agreement, which establishes a common border for various countries in the European Union. Visitors from other participating countries will not be asked for identification upon arrival. However, it is recommended that you carry identification in any case. In addition, it is a legal requirement to carry identification at all times. A valid passport must be shown upon arrival from a non-Schengen country, including the UK.

Visas are not required for citizens of EU countries, Iceland, Norway and Switzerland. A list of entry requirements, available from Spanish embassies, specifies more than 40 other

countries, including the USA, Canada, Australia, New Zealand and Japan, whose nationals do not need to apply for a visa if they are visiting Spain for a period of up to 90 days. Those who are planning longer visits than this may apply to the *Gobierno Civil* (a form of local government office) for an extension. You will also need to provide proof of employment or proof of sufficient funds to support yourself during a longer stay. All visitors from countries other than those listed above are legally required to obtain a visa before travelling to Spain.

Student visas are available from the country of origin and give the holder permission to stay until the end of their course.

If you are intending to stay for a long time, it is recommended that you contact your nearest Spanish embassy several months in advance.

Tax-free goods sign

Travel Safety Advice

Visitors can get up-to-date travel safety information from the **Foreign and Commonwealth Office** in the UK, **State Department** in the US and the **Department of Foreign Affairs and Trade** in Australia.

Tax-Free Goods Information

Non-EU residents can claim back *IVA* (VAT) on single items worth over €90.15 bought in shops displaying a "Tax Free for Tourists" sign. Food, drink, tobacco, cars, motorbikes and medicines are exempt from this. You pay the full price and ask the sales assistant for a *formulario* (tax-exemption form). On leaving Spain, before you check your bags, ask customs officials to stamp your *formulario*; this must be done within three months of the purchase. You should then receive the refund, either by mail or alternatively from some banks and bureaux de change at the airport (La Caixa bank in Barcelona; and Global Refund at Terminals 1 and 4 of Madrid Airport), either in cash or as a refund to your credit card.

Tourist Information

All major cities and towns have *oficinas de turismo*. They will provide tourists with town.

OFICINA DE TURISMO *i*

Spanish tourist office sign, featuring the distinctive "i" logo plans, information about the locality, and details of activities and events. Several large cities abroad have a Spanish National Tourist Office; you can also visit www.spain.info, the official website of the Spanish Tourist Board

Social Etiquette

The Spanish often talk to people they do not know. Men shake hands meeting, and it is customary for men to greet women with a kiss on each cheek – even when first introduced. Friends and family members embrace or kiss upon meeting. You may be asked to cover legs and shoulders to enter churches and other monuments.

A bilingual Basque/Castilian reserved parking sign

Language

The main language of Spain, *Castellano* (Castilian), is spoken by almost everyone throughout the country. There are three main regional languages: Catalan, spoken in Catalonia; *Gallego* (Galician) in Galicia; and *Euskara* (Basque) in the Basque Country. Variants of Catalan are spoken in the Valencia region and also in the Balearic Islands. Learning a few courtesy phrases in Catalan can be a good way to win over the locals in these areas.

Places that deal with tourists – hotels, information offices, restaurants – usually employ people who speak English.

Admission Prices

Admission fees are charged for most museums and monuments, and prices vary within different regions, and depending on the importance of the sight. Some public museums are free on Sundays. Most museums have free admission coinciding with national or regional holidays. Check the individual museums' websites for more detailed information.

Opening Hours

Most museums in Spain close on Sunday afternoon and all day Monday. It is wise to check opening times in advance, since they can vary depending on the time of year. Many museums often close from 2pm to 5pm; some reopen from 5pm to 8pm. Churches may follow these hours, or they may only be open to the public for services.

In some smaller towns in Spain, it is not uncommon for churches, castles and other sights popular with tourists to be kept locked. The key, which is available to visitors on request, will be lodged with a caretaker in a neighbouring house, in the town hall or, sometimes, kept for safekeeping at the local bar.

Taxes and Tipping

Spain does not have a big tipping culture. There is no need to tip taxi drivers, and waiters are only tipped if they go the extra mile or if they are having to deal with a large group of diners. A small service charge is generally added to restaurant bills, particularly in tapas bars. A tip of 5 or 10 per cent, depending on the level of service and the overall price of the meal, is the norm in restaurants. VAT of 10 per cent is added to the bill, but this is often included in the price of the dishes (this must be stipulated on the menu). VAT of 10 per cent is also added to the hotel bill at the end of your stay.

Travellers with Disabilities

Spain offers a number of options for travellers with special needs. The national association for the disabled, the Confederación Coordinadora Estatal de Minusválidos Físicos de España (COCEMFE), publishes useful guides to facilities in Spain and will help plan a holiday to suit individual needs *(see p561)*.

If you need metro maps and other informative leaflets in Braille, these are available from the Spanish national organization for the blind, the Organización Nacional de Ciegos (ONCE). You will find that tourist offices and the social services departments of town halls are worth investigating as they can also provide useful up-to-date information on local conditions and facilities suitable for disabled travellers.

Travel Xperience is a travel agency based in Andorra, specializing in travel for people with reduced mobility. The UK-based Tourism For All (www.tourismforall.org.uk) offers information on facilities for the disabled in a selection of Spanish resorts. The Society for the Advancement of Travel for the Handicapped (SATH) publishes similar information on a number of destinations for travellers from the US.

COCEMFE logo

Conversion Chart

Imperial to metric
1 inch = 2.54 centimetres
1 foot = 30 centimetres
1 mile = 1.6 kilometres
1 ounce = 28 grams
1 pound = 454 grams
1 pint = 0.6 litre
1 gallon = 4.6 litres

Metric to imperial
1 millimetre = 0.04 inch
1 centimetre = 0.4 inch
1 metre = 3 feet 3 inches
1 kilometre = 0.6 mile
1 gram = 0.04 ounce
1 kilogram = 2.2 pounds
1 litre = 1.8 pints

Children catching small fish with nets, Cala Gracio, Ibiza

Travelling with Children

Spain is a famously child-friendly country, and travellers with kids will find that their offspring are usually welcome in bars, restaurants and hotels.

It is recommended that you take a few sensible precautions when travelling with children, especially in the summer months. Avoid being out and about in the hottest hours of the day (noon–3pm); apply sunscreen with a high protection factor on your children's skin regularly and liberally; always ensure they wear a sunhat with a wide brim; and take frequent breaks for refreshments. Visit www.travelforkids.com for a list of travel agents specializing in child-friendly family holidays.

All large hospitals in Spain provide a paediatrics service, and pharmacy attendants are trained to provide basic treatment for minor health complaints. Visit www.spain-expat.com/spain/information/doctors_in_spain for a list of English-speaking doctors. All public health-care facilities have access to interpreters, whether in person or via the phone.

Tiled street sign

Senior Travellers

There are plenty of options for both leisurely and more active holidays for senior travellers in Spain.

Health spas have become increasingly popular throughout the country, and they combine relaxation with specific treatments using thermal waters (www.balnearios.org). Walking tours suitable for senior travellers can be found along the country's network of green paths (www.viasverdes.com).

It is always worth enquiring about senior discounts as some of the larger hotels offer special rates.

LGBTQ Travellers

Attitudes to the LGBT community vary greatly between urban and rural areas in Spain. All major cities have thriving gay scenes, with Madrid and Barcelona boasting gay-friendly areas of town (Chueca and "Gayxample") with hotels, restaurants and services aimed at LGBT travellers. The Federación Estatal de Lesbianas, Gays, Transexuales y Bisexuales (FELGTB) (www.felgtb.org) provides information for travellers online and at its local offices in most Spanish towns.

The Gay Pride parades (www.cogam.org) have become major events and are a good place to meet people. A law allowing homosexual couples to marry, adopt children and enjoy the same rights as heterosexuals was passed in June 2005.

Travelling on a Budget

Travellers looking for budget accommodation should keep an eye out for the sign Hostal or Pensión, which indicates clean and comfortable rooms at a fraction of the cost of a hotel (see also www.hostelworld.com). Most restaurants in Spain offer a menú del día – three courses with wine for as little as €10, and tapas can be another cheap and filling option (they even come free with drinks in some areas).

The Spanish train service is relatively cheap (see pp628–9). Prices can vary on popular lines (for example, the Barcelona–Madrid) depending on the type and speed of train, so check in advance (www.renfe.es). The cheapest, and sometimes the quickest, way to get around is on the excellent network of coaches. Different companies serve different regions, so check timetables and prices online (www.alsa.es) or at the tourist office before travelling. Hitchhiking is not common in Spain, and you should avoid hitchhiking alone.

The best and cheapest spectacles in Spain are often found on the streets, especially during the fiesta mayor of the various regions and cities, which often include processions and dancing (see pp42–3).

Hostal sign indicating budget accommodation

Student Information

Holders of the International Student Identity Card (ISIC) are entitled to various benefits in Spain, such as discounted accommodation and travel fares as well as reduced entrance charges to museums, galleries and other attractions.

Information for student travellers from overseas is available from national student organizations and, in Spain, from INJUVE (www.injuve.es). Turismo, Intercambios y Viajes Educativos (TIVE) (www.madrid.org/inforjoven)offers specialist travel services for students in the Madrid area.

ISIC student card

Spanish Time

Spain is one hour ahead of Greenwich Mean Time (GMT) and, in summer, of British Summer Time (BST). The Canary Islands are on GMT in winter and an hour ahead in summer.

La madrugada refers to the small hours. *Mañana* (morning) lasts until about 2pm and *mediodía* (midday) is the part of the day from about 1pm to 4pm. *La tarde* is the afternoon (until about 9pm) and *la noche* the evening (9pm onwards).

Electrical Adaptors

Spain's electricity supply is 220 volts. Plugs have two round pins. A three-tier standard travel converter enables you to use appliances from abroad. Most hotels can lend you an adaptor. If you come from the USA, make sure that your electrical equipment works at this voltage.

Responsible Travel

After several decades of rapid construction that saw much of the country's coastline buried under concrete, Spain has taken big steps to encourage a more sustainable approach to tourism. A series of laws prohibits any construction up to 100 m (328 ft) from the coastline. Tourism, an important source of income, has also become more strictly regulated.

Casas rurales, private country homes that cater to small groups of tourists in a welcoming family atmosphere, offer a perfect option for green travel. Visit www.ecoturismorural.com for more details. The Blue Flag Programme, owned and run by the non-profit Foundation for Environmental Education (FEE), lists 550 beaches and 97 marinas in Spain that comply with their strict environmental criteria. Spain has a delicate ecosystem and several areas that are still barely developed for travellers – take extra care when visiting these spots.

Visitors to Spain can encourage sustainable tourism by using locally owned shops and businesses. Cities are legally obliged to have markets in each district. Elsewhere, go to family-owned shops or buy products at source: most towns have weekend food markets that draw local farmers.

Students enjoy reduced admission fees to many museums and galleries

DIRECTORY

Embassies

Australia (consulate)
Level 24, St Martin's Tower, 31 Market St, Sydney NSW 2000. **Tel** 29 261 2433.

United Kingdom
Torre Espacio, Paseo de la Castellana 259D, 28046 Madrid. **Tel** 91 714 63 00. **w** gov.uk/government/world.spain.es

United States
Calle Serrano 75, 28006 Madrid. **Tel** 91 587 22 00. **w** madrid.usembassy.gov

Travel Safety

Australia Department of Foreign Affairs and Trade
w smartraveller.gov.au

UK Foreign and Commonwealth Office
w gov.uk/foreign-travel-advice

US Department of State
w travel.state.gov/

Spanish Tourist Offices

Barcelona
Plaça de Catalunya 17, 08002 Barcelona. **Tel** 93 285 38 34. **w** barcelonaturisme.com

Madrid
Plaza Mayor 27 (Casa de la Panadería), 28012 Madrid. **Tel** 91 578 78 10. **w** esmadrid.com

Seville
Plaza San Francisco 19, Edif. Laredo, 41004 Seville. **Tel** 955 471 232. **w** visitasevilla.es

United Kingdom
6th Floor, 64 North Row, London W1K 7DE. **Tel** 00 44 (0)20 7317 2011. **w** spain.info

United States
60 East 42nd St, Suite 5300 New York NY 10165. **Tel** 00 1 (212) 265 8822. **w** spain.info

Disabled Travel

Travel Xperience
Tel 911 87 59 40.
w travel-xperience.com

Personal Security and Health

As in most European countries, it is sensible to be vigilant and particularly in cities. The country is generally safe, but certain parts are subject to petty crime so follow the usual advice. Carry cards and money in a belt, and never leave anything visible in your car. Taking out medical insurance cover is advisable, but pharmacists are good sources of assistance for minor health problems. If you lose your documents, contact the local police first to make a claim, then your consulate. Emergency phone numbers vary *(see box opposite)*.

Spanish Police

There are three types of police in Spain. The *Guardia Civil* (National Guard) police mainly rural areas. Their uniform is olive green, but there are local and regional variations. They impose fines for traffic offences outside the cities and police the borders.

The *Policía Nacional*, who mainly wear a blue uniform, operate in towns with a population of more than 30,000. They have been replaced with a regional force, the *Ertzaintza*, in the Basque Country, and with the *Mossos d'Esquadra* in Catalonia. These can be recognized by their respective red and blue berets.

The *Policía Local*, also called *Policía Municipal* or *Guardia Urbana*, dress in blue. They operate independently in each town and also have a separate branch for city traffic control. All three services will direct you to the relevant authority in the event of an incident requiring police help.

Personal Security and Property

Violent crime is rare in Spain, but visitors should avoid walking alone in poorly lit areas. Wear bags and cameras across your body, not on your shoulder.

Holiday insurance is there to protect you financially from the loss or theft of your property, but it is always best to take obvious precautions.

What to Be Aware Of

Be aware of street scams in large cities, including unexpected offers to help with bags, to clean stains off your clothes or to participate in impromptu football games. Never leave a bag or handbag unattended anywhere, and do not place your purse or handbag on the tabletop in a café. Take particular care at markets, tourist sights and stations. Be especially careful of pickpockets when getting on or off a crowded train or metro.

The moment you discover a loss or theft, report it to the local police station. To claim insurance you must do this immediately, since many companies give you only 24 hours. Ask for a *denuncia* (written statement), which you need to make a claim. If your passport is stolen, or if you lose it, report it to your consulate, too.

While tourists remain targets for petty crime in Spanish cities, remember that it is common for Spanish people to approach you and strike up a conversation, and you should not let normal precautions stop you from interacting with the locals.

Men occasionally make complimentary remarks *(piropos)* to women in public, particularly in the street. This is an old custom and is not intended to be intimidating.

Sign identifying a *Cruz Roja* (Red Cross) emergency treatment centre

In an Emergency

The nationwide number to use in case of an emergency (police, ambulance, fire) is 112. Local emergency numbers are listed in telephone directories under *Servicios de Urgencia*; they appear on tourist maps and leaflets, too.

For emergency medical treatment, call the emergency services or an ambulance, or go straight to the nearest hospital casualty department *(Urgencias)*.

Visit www.jointcommission. org for a list of hospitals vetted by the US-based NGO Joint Commission.

Pharmacies

Spanish pharmacists have wide responsibilities. They can advise and, in some cases, prescribe

Guardia Civil

Policía Nacional

Policía Local

without consulting a doctor. In a non-emergency, a *farmacéutico* is a good option. It is easy to find one who speaks English.

The *farmacia* sign is a green or red illuminated cross. Those open at night are listed in the windows of all the local pharmacies. Note that *perfumerías* sell toiletries only.

Spanish pharmacy sign

Medical Treatment

In general, the Spanish health system is modern and efficient, and it can be relied on for emergency treatment. There are two kinds of hospitals in Spain: public hospitals *(públicos)* and private clinics *(clínicas privadas)*. For emergency treatment, go straight to *Urgencias* at any hospital; for less serious problems, head to a *Centro de Atención Primaria* or *Ambulatorio* and ask for the *médico de urgencias*.

If you have private health insurance, you can go to a private clinic for normal medical complaints.

Legal Assistance

Some insurance policies cover legal costs, for instance after an accident. If you are in need of assistance and are not covered, telephone your nearest consulate. The *Colegio de Abogados* (lawyers' association) of the nearest city can also advise you on where to obtain legal advice or representation locally.

If you need an interpreter, consult the local *Páginas Amarillas* (Yellow Pages) under *Traductores* or *Intérpretes*. Only *Traductores – Interpretes Jurados* (Sworn Translators – Interpreters) are qualified to translate legal and official documents. Visit exteriores.gob.es to find one.

Travel and Health Insurance

All EU nationals are entitled to short-term free emergency health-care cover. To claim, you must obtain the European Health Insurance Card (EHIC) from the UK Department of Health or a post office before you travel. The card gives you free health cover at all public Spanish hospitals. It comes with a booklet explaining exactly what health care you are entitled to and how to claim. You may have to pay and claim the money back later. Not all treatments are covered, so for more peace of mind, arrange medical cover in advance.

There is a wide range of medical insurance available to travellers to Spain. Shop around before deciding because prices vary greatly, as do the levels of cover offered, with some including aspects like emergency travel back home or the cost of relatives joining you. Many credit cards also offer limited health insurance for their users.

Public Conveniences

Public pay-toilets are rare in Spain. Try department stores, or bars and restaurants where you are a customer. You may have to ask for a key (la llave), and it is best to bring your own tissues. There are also toilets at service stations on motorways. Toilets are most commonly known as *los servicios*.

Outdoor Hazards

Every summer Spain is prey to forest fires fanned by winds and fuelled by bone-dry vegetation. Be sensitive to fire hazards and use car ashtrays. Broken glass can also start a fire, so take your empty bottles away with you.

Patrol car of the *Policía Nacional*, Spain's main urban police force

Policía Local patrol car, mainly seen in small towns

Emergency ambulance in Madrid

The sign *coto de caza* in woodland areas identifies a hunting reserve where you must follow the country codes. *Toro bravo* means "fighting bull" – do not approach. A *camino particular* sign indicates a private driveway. Do not approach dogs that are protecting country properties.

If you are climbing or hill-walking, make sure that you are properly equipped and let someone know when you expect to return.

DIRECTORY

Emergency Numbers

Emergency: all services
Tel 112 (nationwide).

Policía Nacional
Tel 091 (nationwide).

Fire Brigade
(Bomberos)
Tel 112 (in most major cities).

Ambulance
Tel 112 (061 in some regions). For other cities' emergency services, consult the local telephone directory.

Banking and Local Currency

You can enter Spain with any amount of money, but if you intend to export more than €10,000, you should declare it. Travellers' cheques may be exchanged at banks, *oficinas de cambio de moneda* (foreign currency exchanges), some hotels and some shops. Banks generally offer the best exchange rates. The cheapest exchange may be offered on your credit or direct debit card, which you can use in ATMs displaying the appropriate sign.

A 24-hour ATM

Banking Hours

Spanish banks are beginning to extend their opening times, but expect extended hours only at large central branches in the big cities.

Banks are open from 8am to 2pm during the week. Some open until 1pm on Saturdays. All close on Saturdays in July and August; in some areas, they also close on Saturdays from May to September.

Changing Money

Most banks have a foreign exchange desk with the sign *Cambio* or *Extranjero*, which will accept travellers' cheques and cash. Always take your passport as identification to effect any transaction.

You can draw up to €300 on major credit cards at a bank. It is worth mentioning your travel plans to your bank and credit card company before you go away, so that your card is not blocked by their fraud prevention system.

Bureaux de change, with the sign *Cambio de Moneda* or "Change", may state that they charge no commission, but their exchange rates are invariably less favourable than those found at banks. One benefit is that they are often open outside normal banking hours. They are usually located in popular tourist areas, as well as at airports and mainline rail stations. *Cajas de Ahorro* (savings banks) also exchange money. They open from 8:30am to 2pm on weekdays and also on Thursday afternoons from 4:30pm to 7:45pm.

Cheques and Cards

The use of travellers' cheques is declining and it is not always easy to find places to cash the cheques. Banks also need 24 hours' notice to cash cheques larger than €3,000.

Prepaid VISA and MasterCard credit cards are a convenient way to pay, as are Travel Money Cards. These cards work like debit cards. They are available in several currencies from most banks, and can be reloaded through their websites.

The most widely accepted cards are **VISA**, and **MasterCard**, although **American Express** is also used. The major banks will allow cash withdrawals on credit cards. All ATMs accept most foreign cards, and they will often give you a choice of several languages, including English. Most, however, only operate with cards that have an electronic chip. Also, the level of commission charged on your withdrawal will depend on your own bank, and some credit cards may charge an additional fee.

When you pay with a card, cashiers pass it through a card-reading machine and you usually need to provide a PIN number. In shops you will always be asked for additional photo ID. Make sure you have an original identification document on hand (photocopies will rarely do), and note that a driver's licence is not an accepted form of ID in Spain.

As with the rest of Europe, cards are not always accepted in smaller bars and restaurants, so take some cash with you.

ATMs

If your card is linked to your home bank account, you can use it with your PIN to withdraw money from ATMs. All take VISA and MasterCard.

When you enter your PIN, instructions are displayed in English, French, German and Spanish. Many dispensers are inside buildings and to gain access you will have to run your card through a door-entry system.

Cards with the Cirrus and Maestro logos can also be widely used to withdraw money from cash machines.

BBVA

Logo for BBVA, the Banco Bilbao Vizcaya Argentaria

The Euro

Spain was one of the 12 countries adopting the euro in 2002, with its original currency, the peseta, phased out in the course of the same year.

EU countries using the euro as sole official currency are known as the Eurozone. Several EU members have opted out of joining this common currency.

Euro notes are identical throughout the Eurozone countries, each one including designs of fictional architectural structures and monuments. The coins, however, have one identical side (the value side), and one side with an image unique to each country. Both notes and coins are exchangeable in each of the participating euro countries.

Banknotes

Euro banknotes, each a different colour and size, come in seven denominations. The €5 note (grey in colour) is the smallest, followed by the €10 note (pink), €20 note (blue), €50 note (orange), €100 note (green), €200 note (yellow) and €500 note (purple).

€5

€10

€20

€50

€100

€200

€500

5 cents

2 cents

1 cent

€2

€1

50 cents

20 cents

10 cents

Coins

The euro has eight coin denominations: €2 and €1 (silver and gold); 50 cents, 20 cents and 10 cents (gold); and 5 cents, 2 cents and 1 cent (bronze).

Communications and Media

The telecommunications company Movistar dominates the industry in Spain, but companies like Orange, Yoigo and Vodafone also compete for the mobile-phone market. Despite the popularity of mobile phones, public telephones are still easy to find; most require simply a phone card. The postal service, Correos, is identified by a blue crown logo on a yellow background. Correos offices allow you to send registered post and they sell stamps, though most people buy them from *estancos* (tobacconists).

Telephoning in Spain

When calling from a fixed line, there are four charge bands for international calls: EU countries; non-EU countries and North-west Africa; North and South America; and the rest of the world. International calls can be quite expensive, especially when made from a hotel, which may add a surcharge. Though now harder to find, a call from a phone booth, or *cabina*, costs 35 per cent more than from a private phone, though using phone-cards, available at tobacconists, supermarkets and newsstands, gives much cheaper rates. Most reverse-charge calls must be made through the operator. When telephoning Spain from abroad, first dial the international code for Spain (34) followed by the area code.

Mobile Phones

In 2017, the EU ended roaming charges meaning European visitors travelling within the continent (including Iceland, Norway and Liechtenstein) can use their data abroad without incurring charges, making it

The logo of Spain's main telecom company

cheaper and easier to use your phone abroad than ever before.

If you are visiting from outside of the EU, and you're planning to make a lot of calls, the best option is to buy a Spanish top-up SIM card, or a handset with a top-up SIM card, at a department store or specialist phone shop. The most popular providers in Spain are Movistar and Vodafone; each have their own shops with experts who can give you advice. For a simple handset, plus SIM card (allowing free incoming calls in Spain), expect to pay in the region of €50–€60.

To add more credit to your phone card, purchase a scratch card from shops and supermarkets. Alternatively, you can do it automatically with your credit card by dialling a number from your phone – check with your service provider. Mobile phone top-ups are also available at most ATMs.

Internet and Email

Wireless hot spots are available in all airports, hotels and conference centres throughout Spain, although the majority are not free. Credit can be bought online with a major credit card.

The number of Internet cafés *(cibercafés)* in most cities and resorts is dwindling. *Locutorios* (privately owned call centres) often provide cheap Internet access. Also, free Internet access can be found in public libraries, some public areas (such as Madrid's Plaza Mayor), universities and most restaurants, bars and cafés offering Wi-Fi service.

Newspapers and Magazines

Newsagents in tourist-oriented town centres often stock periodicals in languages other than Spanish. The English-language daily newspapers available on publication day are the *International Herald Tribune*, the *Financial Times*, the *Guardian International* and the *Sun*, which is printed in the south of Spain.

A selection of Spanish newspapers

Useful Spanish Dialling Codes

- When calling within a city, within a province, or to call another province, dial the entire number. The province is indicated by the initial digits: Barcelona numbers, for example, start with 93; Girona with 972; and Tarragona 977.
- To make an international call, dial 00, then dial the country code, the area code and the number.
- Country codes are: UK 44; Eire 353; France 33; USA and Canada 1; Australia 61; New Zealand 64. It may be necessary to omit the initial digit of the destination's area code.

- For operator/directory service, dial 11888.
- For international directories, dial 11825.
- To make a reverse-charge (collect) call to the UK only, dial 900 961 682. Inexpensive international calls can be made in *locutorios*, or call centres. These can be found in most cities and towns. Cheap phone cards can also be purchased there.
- To report technical faults, dial 1002 (Movistar only).
- For the speaking clock and for a wake-up call, dial 1212 (from Movistar landlines only).

Several other English-language and European titles are also on the stands, but usually only the day after publication. The most widely read Spanish papers are *El País*, *El Mundo*, *ABC*, *La Razón* and *La Vanguardia* (in Catalonia).

Popular weekly news magazines such as *Time*, *Newsweek* and *The Economist* are readily available throughout the country.

Weekly listings magazines for local arts, entertainment and events are published in Barcelona *(see p194)*, Madrid *(see p324)* and Seville *(see p460)*. Several other Spanish cities also have their own listings magazines.

A number of foreign-language periodicals are published by expatriates in Madrid and in the country's other main tourist areas. Some examples in English include *Metropolitan* in Barcelona, *Sur* on the Costa del Sol, the *Costa Blanca News* and the *Mallorca Daily Bulletin*.

Television and Radio

Televisión Española, Spain's state television company, broadcasts on two channels, TVE1 and TVE2, which run 24 hours a day.

Several of the *comunidades* have their own publicly owned television channels, which broadcast in the language of the region. In addition, there are a few national television stations: Antena 3, Tele-5 (Telecinco), La Sexta and Cuatro.

Digital TV in Spain is offered by two companies, Canal+ and Imagenio. This provides access to dozens of local channels and the possibility of watching programmes in their original language or with subtitles.

Radio is very popular throughout Spain and there are a number of English-language radio stations based mainly in the south, including Talk Radio Europe, which is the largest network, (88.2 FM, 88.9 FM, 105.1 FM, 92.7 FM, 103.9 FM and 104.6 FM)

and Wave96FM (96 FM) from Malagá on the Costa del Sol. All of these stations can also be listened to online and are a good source of local and international news in English.

Postal Service

Correos is Spain's postal service. Mail sent within the same city usually takes a day to arrive. Deliveries between cities take two to three days. Urgent or important post can be sent

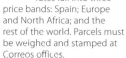

Spanish postbox

by *urgente* (express) or *certificado* (registered) mail. For fast delivery, use the Correos Postal Express Service or a private courier.

Post can be registered, and telegrams sent from all Correos offices. However, it is much easier to buy stamps from an *estanco* (tobacconist). Postal rates fall into three price bands: Spain; Europe and North Africa; and the rest of the world. Parcels must be weighed and stamped at Correos offices.

The main Correos offices open 8:30am–9:30pm Monday to Friday and 9:30am–1pm on Saturday; outside the cities they close by 1–2pm on weekdays

Letters sent from a post office usually arrive more quickly than if posted in a postbox *(buzón)*. In cities, postboxes are yellow pillar boxes; elsewhere they are small, wall-mounted postboxes. *Poste restante* letters should be addressed care of the *Lista de*

Correos and the town, and collected from main offices.

To send and receive money by post, ask for a *giro postal*.

Addresses

In Spanish addresses, the house number follows the name of the street. The floor of a block of flats comes after a hyphen. Therefore 4-2° means a flat on the second floor of number four. All postcodes in Spain have five digits, the first two being the province number.

Local Government

Spain is one of Europe's most decentralized states. Many powers have been devolved to the 17 regions, also known as *comunidades autónomas*, which have their own elected parliaments. These regions have varying degrees of independence from Madrid, with the Basques and Catalans enjoying the most autonomy. The *comunidades* provide some services – such as the promotion of tourism, plus education and health – that were once carried out by the central government.

The country is subdivided into 50 provinces and two autonomous cities (Ceuta and Melilla), each with its *diputación* (council). The affairs of each of the Balearic and Canary Islands are run by an island council.

Every town is administered by an *ayuntamiento* (town council – the word also means "town hall"), which is then supervised by an elected *alcalde* (mayor) and a team of councillors.

Murcia's town hall *(ayuntamiento or casa consistorial)*

TRAVEL INFORMATION

Spain has invested heavily in its transport infrastructure since 2005, creating new motorways and high-speed rail networks to connect much of the country. Madrid Airport is an important international travel hub, and new terminals at Malaga and Barcelona Airports have been built to cater for the huge influx of passengers. Intercity rail services are reliable and efficient, but coaches are a faster and more frequent option between smaller towns. In much of rural Spain, public transport is limited, and a car is the most practical option for getting about. Spain boasts some beautiful back roads to hidden areas of the country. Ferries connect mainland Spain with the UK, Italy, North Africa and the Balearic and Canary islands.

Green Travel

Public transport in larger cities has adopted a green focus, and most buses now run on clean fuel. Services are generally excellent, and reasonably priced. With the opening of the long-awaited Madrid–Barcelona high-speed rail link (the AVE), Spain now boasts one of Europe's best railway infrastructures. There are plans for added links to the Basque region and Galicia, and from Northern Spain into France. Prices on the AVE vary depending on the days you want to travel, and they are much lower if you buy your tickets online.

Some areas of Spain are still best accessed by road. Car users should consider renting hybrid vehicles, now available from major car rental firms. Local and environmentally friendly bus services reach most areas.

Aircraft at Ibiza's airport

Arriving by Air

Spain is served by most international airlines and many budget airlines. Its national carrier **Iberia** offers flights from most European capitals. **British Airways** flies to Madrid and Barcelona, as do US airlines **Delta**, **United** and **American Airlines**. Iberia has a wide-ranging service from the USA.

International Airports

The most regular international services operate from Madrid and Barcelona. Palma de Mallorca, Tenerife Sur, Las Palmas de Gran Canaria, Ibiza, Málaga, Lanzarote, Alicante, Fuerteventura and Menorca handle a lot of tourists, especially in the summer.

Tickets and Fares

Air fares vary by season and demand. Special deals, particularly for city breaks, often run in winter. Look out for Iberia's reduced fares and for low-cost carriers, such as **easyJet** and **Ryanair** (UK). **Vueling** offers low-cost flights from Spain to other European countries.

Airport	ℹ Information	Distance to City Centre	Taxi Fare to City Centre	Public Transport Time to City Centre
Alicante (Alacant)	902 40 47 04	10 km (6 miles)	€28	Bus: 20 mins
Barcelona	902 40 47 04	14 km (9 miles)	€35	Rail: 35 mins Bus: 25 mins
Bilbao	902 40 47 04	12 km (7 miles)	€26	Bus: 30 mins
Madrid	902 40 47 04	16 km (10 miles)	€35	Bus: 20 mins Metro: 30–40 mins
Málaga	902 40 47 04	8 km (5 miles)	€24	Rail: 15 mins Bus: 20 mins
Palma de Mallorca	902 40 47 04	9 km (5.5 miles)	€25	Bus: 15 mins
Las Palmas de Gran Canaria	902 40 47 04	18 km (11 miles)	€31	Bus: 60 mins
Santiago de Compostela	902 40 47 04	10 km (6 miles)	€28	Bus: 20–30 mins
Seville	902 40 47 04	10 km (6 miles)	€22–€30	Bus: 25–30 mins
Tenerife Sur – Reina Sofía	902 40 47 04	64 km (40 miles) to Santa Cruz	€80	Bus: 60 mins
Valencia	902 40 47 04	9 km (5.5 miles)	€20–€25	Bus: 20 or 60 mins

The departures concourse at Seville Airport

Internal Flights

In the past, the majority of domestic flights were operated by Iberia, but now there are other main carriers, such as **Air Europa** and Vueling. The most frequent shuttle service is the Puente Aéreo, run between Barcelona and Madrid by Iberia every 15 minutes at peak times, and half-hourly or hourly at other times. The flight generally takes 50 minutes. Vueling and Air Europa services between Madrid and the regional capitals are not as frequent as the Puente Aéreo, but they are usually cheaper; book early to take advantage of lower fares. Flights between the Canary Islands are operated by **Binter**. Some flights from domestic airports are billed as international flights and stop over at major Spanish cities en route.

Acciona
Trasmediterránea logo

Arriving by Sea

Ferries connect the Spanish mainland to the Balearic and Canary islands, and to North Africa, Italy and the UK. All the important routes are served by car ferries. Always make an advance booking, especially in summer.

Three routes link Spain with the UK. **Brittany Ferries** sails between Plymouth in the UK and Santander in Cantabria. There are also routes linking Portsmouth with Santander, and Portsmouth with Bilbao in the Basque Country. The crossings take over 24 hours. Each ship has cabins, chairs to sleep on, restaurants, cafés and cinemas. The Italian

Grimaldi Lines has overnight journeys to Rome, Livorno and Sardinia.

Ferries to the Islands

Frequent crossings run from Barcelona and Valencia to the three main Balearic islands. **Acciona Trasmediterránea** ferries take from four hours (using the fast ferry from Barcelona) to eight hours. The same company also operates frequent inter-island services, while small operators take day-trippers (passengers only) from Ibiza to Formentera. **Balearia** also sails to the Balearic Islands from Barcelona and Valencia.

Acciona Trasmediterránea operates a weekly service from Cádiz to the main ports of the Canary Islands, which normally takes 32 hours. Car ferries link the various islands. There are also passengers-only services between the islands of Gran Canaria, Tenerife and Fuerteventura, and between Tenerife and La Gomera.

Ferries to the islands have cabins, cafés, restaurants, bars, shops, cinemas, pools and sunbathing decks. They also have facilities for people with special needs. Entertainment is provided on mainland crossings to the Canary Islands.

Ferries to Africa

Acciona Trasmediterránea has daily services to the Spanish territories in North Africa: from Málaga and Almería to Melilla, and from Algeciras to Ceuta, as well as from Algeciras and Tarifa to Tangier. Balearia also sails to Ceuta and Tangier from Algeciras. It maybe worth checking the website for up-to-date offers.

Balearia car ferry sailing to the Balearic Islands

Travelling by Train

The Spanish state railway, RENFE (*Red Nacional de Ferrocarriles Españoles*), operates a service that is continually improving, particularly between cities. The fastest intercity services are called TALGO and AVE – these names are acronyms for the high-speed luxury trains that run on these routes. *Largo recorrido* (long-distance) and *regionales y cercanías* (regional and local) trains are notoriously slow, many stopping at every station on the way. They are much cheaper than the high-speed trains, but journey times can be hours longer.

Arriving by Train

There are several routes to Spain from France. The main western route runs from Paris through Hendaye in the Pyrenees to San Sebastián. The eastern route from Paris runs via Cerbère and Port Bou to Barcelona. The trains from London, Brussels, Amsterdam, Geneva, Zurich and Milan all reach Barcelona via Cerbère. At Cerbère there are also connections with the TALGO and the long-distance services to Valencia, Alicante, Girona and Murcia. If you book a sleeper on the TALGO from Paris, you travel to your destination without having to change trains. There are direct trains to Madrid and Barcelona from Paris, and to Barcelona from Milan, Geneva and Zurich.

Exploring by Train

Spain offers many options for train travellers. The introduction of high-speed services has made it possible to travel the long distances between the main cities extremely quickly. Ticket prices compare favourably with the cost of high-speed train fares in many other countries in Europe. Efficient high-speed AVE rail services link Madrid with Seville in two and a half hours, and with Barcelona in three hours. The AVE from Madrid to Zaragoza takes one and a half hours; to Málaga two hours and 40 minutes; and to Valladolid only 50 minutes. AVE routes also link Barcelona with

AVE high-speed trains at Estación de Santa Justa in Seville

Seville and with Málaga – both trips take five and a half hours.

The *largo recorrido* (long-distance) trains are so much slower that you usually need to travel overnight. You can choose between a *cochecama* (a compartment with two or four *camas*, or beds) or a *litera*, one of six seats in a compartment that converts into a bunk bed. You reserve these when booking and pay a supplement. Book at least a month in advance. *Regionales y cercanías* (the regional and local services) are frequent and cheap.

In Madrid the major stations for regional and long-distance trains are Atocha and Chamartín. The AVE runs from Atocha, and the TALGO from both. Sants and Passeig de Gràcia are Barcelona's two main stations. In Seville Santa Justa is the only

Logo for the high-speed rail service AVE

DIRECTORY

National Enquiries and Reservations

Luxury Train Club
Benwell House, Preston,
Chippenham, Wiltshire SN15 4DX,
UK. **Tel** 00 44124 989 0205.
ⓦ **luxurytrainclub.com**

RENFE
Tel 902 32 03 20; for information on disabled access call 902 24 05 05. ⓦ **renfe.es**

Regional Railways

ET
Tel 902 54 32 10.
ⓦ **euskotren.es**

FGC
Tel 900 90 15 15.
ⓦ **fgc.net**

FGV
Tel 961 92 40 00.
ⓦ **fgv.es**

station for regional and international services. Major train terminals pass luggage through scanners; allow extra time for this.

Fares

Fares for rail travel in Spain are structured according to the speed and quality of the service. Tickets for the TALGO and AVE trains cost the most.

Interrail tickets for people under 26 and Eurail tickets for non-EU residents are available from major travel agencies in Europe and from **RENFE** ticket offices in Spain. Always take proof of your identity when booking.

Holidays onboard Spain's luxury train (*see opposite*) are expensive but offer high standards of comfort.

Regional Railways

Three of the *comunidades autónomas* have regional rail companies. Catalonia and Valencia each has its own *Ferrocarrils de la Generalitat* – respectively, the **FGC** and the

Spain's Principal RENFE Network

Spain's rail network operates a wide variety of services. Consult a RENFE brochure or train timetable before buying your ticket.

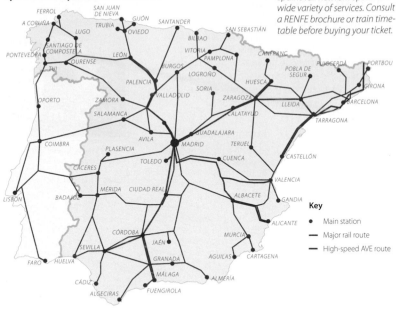

Key

● Main station
— Major rail route
— High-speed AVE route

FGV; and the Basque Country has the **ET** (*Eusko Trenbideak*).

Tickets for Spain's luxury train, similar to the Orient Express, can be obtained from travel agents. El Transcantábrico, run by the **Luxury Train Club**, travels the 1,000 km (620 miles) of Spain's north coast between San Sebastián and Santiago de Compostela. Passengers travel in style for eight days in 14 restored period carriages that were all built between 1900 and 1930.

The regional tourist offices publicize unusual rail services in their local areas, such as the narrow-gauge lines to Inca and Sóller in Mallorca *(see p519)*.

Booking Tickets

Tickets for TALGO, AVE and any other *largo recorrido* travel may be bought at any of the major railway stations from the *taquilla* (ticket office). They are also sold by all travel agents in Spain, who will charge a commission. RENFE tickets are sometimes sold by travel agents in other countries. Telephone reservations may be made directly to all RENFE ticket offices with a credit card. Tickets can also

Ticket machine for local and regional lines

be bought via the RENFE website, which has some cheaper fares, and printed out.

Tickets for local and regional services are purchased from the station *taquilla*. In larger stations, they can be bought from ticket machines. Tickets for *cercanías* (local services) cannot be reserved. For a one-way journey, ask for *ida*, and for a return, ask for *ida y vuelta*. Return tickets are cheaper.

Timetables

RENFE timetables change in May and October each year. Your travel agent will be able to provide the correct times for your train journey. Timetables can also be accessed in English via the RENFE website. In Spain, timetables are available from RENFE offices. Most come as leaflets and are broken down into the various types of journey: intercity, *largo recorrido* and *regionales*. *Cercanías* timetables are posted on boards at local railway stations.

Atocha, one of Madrid's largest mainline railway stations

Travelling by Road

Spain's fastest roads are its *autopistas*. They are normally dual carriageways and are subsidized by *peajes* (tolls). *Autovías* are similar but have no tolls. The *carretera nacional* is the countrywide network of main roads or highways with the prefix N. Smaller minor roads are generally less well kept, but they are often a more leisurely and enjoyable way to see rural areas of Spain.

Cambio de sentido (slip road) 300 m (330 yards) ahead

Arriving by Car

Many people drive to Spain via the French motorways. The most direct routes across the Pyrenees, using the motorways, pass through Hendaye on the western flank and Port Bou in the east. Other, rather more tortuous routes may be used, from Toulouse through the Vall d'Aran, for instance. From the UK, there are car ferries from Plymouth to Santander and from Portsmouth to Santander and Bilbao in northern Spain *(see p627)*.

What to Take

A Green Card from your motor insurance company is needed in order to extend your comprehensive cover to Spain. The RAC, AA and Europ Assistance have rescue and recovery policies with European cover. Spanish law requires you to carry your vehicle's registration document, a valid insurance certificate and your driving licence at all times. You must always be able to show a passport or a national identity card as ID. You must also display a sticker on the back of the car showing its country of registration. The headlights of right-hand drive vehicles need to be adjusted or deflected. Stickers for this are available at ferry ports and on ferries. You risk on-the-spot fines if you do not carry a red warning triangle and a reflective jacket. In winter, carry chains if you intend to drive in mountain areas. In summer, take drinking water when travelling in remote areas.

Buying Petrol

In Spain *gasolina* (petrol) and *gasoil* (diesel) are priced by the litre. *Gasolina sin plomo* (unleaded petrol) is available everywhere. All three cost more at the *autopista* service stations. Self-service stations, where you fill up yourself, are common. Modern petrol pumps in Spain are sometimes operated by credit card. You should run your card through the machine, press the buttons to indicate the amount of petrol you want in euros, and then serve yourself.

You must wait for service if there are attendants at the station. They will ask *¿cuánto?* (how much?); you should reply *lleno* (fill the tank), or specify an amount in euros: *diez euros, por favor*. If you do use your credit card to pay at a motorway service station, you will be asked to show your passport or another form of identification. Gibraltar and Andorra have tax-free, cheap petrol, so it is worth filling up before entering Spain.

Speed limit 50 km/h (31 mph)

Pedestrian crossing sign

Rules of the Road

Most traffic regulations and warnings to motorists are represented on signs by easily recognized symbols. However, a few road rules and signs may be unfamiliar to some drivers from other countries.

To turn left at a busy junction or across oncoming traffic, you may have to turn right first and cross a main road, often by way of traffic lights, a bridge or an underpass. If you are accidentally going the wrong way on a motorway or a main road with a solid white line, you can turn round at a sign for a *cambio de sentido*. At crossings, give way to the right unless a sign indicates otherwise. You must wear seat belts in both front and rear seats.

Oncoming drivers may flash their headlights to mean "you go", "danger", "your lights are on unnecessarily" or "speed trap ahead".

A filling station run by a leading chain with branches throughout Spain

peed Limits and Fines

Speed limits for cars without trailers on the roads in Spain are as follows:
• 120 km/h (75 mph) on *autopistas* (toll motorways);
• 100 km/h (62 mph) on *autovías* (non-toll motorways);
• 90 km/h (56 mph) on *carreteras nacionales* (main roads) and *carreteras comarcales* (secondary roads);
• 50 km/h (31 mph) in built-up areas.

Speeding fines are imposed on the spot and are determined by the speed at which you are driving; fines range from €6.50 to €12 per kilometre over the limit. Fines for other traffic offences (such as turning the wrong way into a one-way street) depend on the severity of the offence and often on the whim of the police officer.

Tests for drink-driving and fines for drivers over the blood alcohol legal limit, which is 25 mg per ml, are now imposed frequently throughout the country. If driving, it is best not to drink any alcohol at all.

Motorways

Spain has more than 2,900 km (1,800 miles) of *autopistas*, and many more are planned. These are generally toll roads and can be expensive to use. You can establish whether a motorway is toll-free by the letters that prefix the number of the road: A = free motorway, AP = toll motorway.

The long-distance tolls are calculated per kilometre, and the rate varies from region to region. Among the busiest and most expensive are the AP7 along the south coast from Barcelona to Alicante and the AP68 Bilbao–Zaragoza *autopista*.

There are service stations every 40 km (25 miles) or so along the *autopistas*, and they are marked by a blue and white parking sign (P) or a sign indicating the services available. As you approach a service station, a sign will indicate the distance to the next one and will also list its services. Most will have a petrol station, toilets, a shop and a café.

Driving through the Sierra Nevada along one of Europe's highest roads

Emergency telephones occur every 2 km (1.2 miles) along the *autopistas*.

Using Autopista Tolls

If you are travelling on an *autopista*, you pick up a ticket from a tollbooth *(peaje)* as you drive on to it and give it up at a booth as you exit. Your toll will be calculated according to the distance you have covered. Over some short stretches of motorways near the cities a fixed price is charged.

Tolls can be paid either in cash or by credit card. You must join one of three channels at the *peaje* leading to different booths. Do not drive into *telepago*, a credit system for which a chip on your windscreen is required. *Tarjetas* has machines for you to pay by credit card, while in *manual* an attendant will take your ticket and your money.

PEAJE TOLL

Autopista toll booths ahead

Other Roads

Carreteras nacionales, Spain's main roads, have black-and-white signs and are designated N (*Nacional*) plus a number. Those with Roman numerals (NIII) start at the Puerta del Sol in Madrid. The distance from the Kilometre Zero mark in the Puerta del Sol *(see p276)* appears on kilometre markers. Those with ordinary numbers (N6) have kilometre markers giving the distance from the provincial capital. Some *carreteras nacionales* are dual carriageways, but most are single-lane roads and can be slow. They tend to be least busy from 2pm to 5pm.

Autovías are roads built in recent years to motorway standard to replace N roads. They have blue signs similar to *autopista* signs. Because they have no tolls, they are busier than *autopistas*.

Carreteras comarcales, secondary roads, have a number preceded by the letter C. Other minor roads have numbers preceded by letters representing the name of the province, such as the LE1313 in Lleida. In winter, watch out for signs indicating whether a mountain pass ahead is open *(abierto)* or closed *(cerrado)*.

The *peaje manual* channel, with attendant

Car Hire

The most popular car-hire companies in Spain are **Europcar**, **Avis** and **Hertz**. All have offices at airports and major train stations, as well as in the larger cities.

In addition to the international car-hire companies, there is a growing number of low-cost hire firms like **Enterprise**, **easyCar**, **pepecar** and **hispacar**, although you may need to pick up your car some distance from the airport.

You can often get the best deals by booking in advance online. There are also fly-drive and other package deals including car hire available. Fly-drive, an option for two or more travellers, can be arranged by travel agents and tour operators.

If you wish to hire a car locally for around a week or less, you will be able to arrange it with a local travel agent. A car for hire is called a *coche de alquiler*.

For chauffeur-driven cars in Spain, Avis offers deals from major cities. Car-hire prices and conditions vary according to the region and locality.

Some of the leading car-hire companies operating in Spain

Maps

Fold-out road maps can be obtained at airports, on the ferries and from tourist offices. The Spanish Ministry of Transport publishes a comprehensive road map in book form, the *Mapa Oficial de Carreteras*. The oil company Repsol publishes the **Guía Repsol**, a road map and restaurant guide conveniently in one book and also available for iPhone and iPad. **Michelin** publishes a useful series of maps (440–448, with orange

City taxis queuing for fares outside an airport

covers) at a scale of 1:400,000 (1 cm:4 km), sold at bookshops and petrol stations. Websites www.guiarepsol.com and www.viamichelin.com allow you to plan your route, providing information on roads, weather and toll fees.

A series of more detailed maps at 1:200,000 for cycling and walking is published by Plaza y Janés. Military maps at scales of 1:50,000 and 1:100,000 are available from **Stanfords** in London and from some local and specialist bookshops in Spain, such as **Altaïr** in Barcelona. Tourist offices usually have free street maps.

You can find detailed street maps of central Barcelona on *pp184–9*, of Madrid on *pp312–19* and of Seville on *pp454–9* of this guide.

Parking

The arrival of resident-only parking schemes means that street parking is increasingly hard to come by in major cities.

As a rule, you may not park where the pavement edge is painted yellow or where a "no parking" sign is displayed. Occasionally there is a "no parking" sign on both sides of a city street, one saying "1–15" and the other "16–30". This means that you can park on one side of the street only for the fortnight indicated on the sign.

In the cities, non-metered on-street parking is rare, but there are blue pay-and-display parking spaces. To use them, buy a ticket from the machine and display it on the inside

No parking at any time of day

of your windscreen. The cost averages about €1–€3 per hour. You can usually park for up to two hours. Major cities have many underground car parks. You collect a ticket when you enter and either pay the attendant as you drive out, or pay at a machine which returns your ticket so you can deposit it in another machine at the exit.

Taxis

Every city and/or region has its own taxi design and tariffs, but all taxis will display a green light if they are free. All are metered; when you set off, a minimum fee will be shown. In smaller villages, the taxi may be a resident driving an unmetered private car – ask at your hotel or in a shop for the number of a recommended local driver.

Road Conditions and Weather Forecasts

For recorded road and traffic information, call the national toll-free number for **Información de Tráfico de Carreteras**. This service is in Spanish only. Ask at your hotel reception if you need a translation. The RAC offers route-planning services tailored to individual requirements; these may include current road conditions. The weather information service, **Agencia Estatal de Metereología**, gives forecasts for each region, as well as the national and international weather. It also gives details on maritime and mountain conditions.

Arriving by Coach

Often the cheapest way to reach and travel around Spain is by coach. **Eurolines** operates various routes throughout Europe and runs daily services to Barcelona. Check out the website for available offers.

Coaches from the UK depart from London Victoria Coach Station. Tickets may be bought from **National Express**, the sister company of Eurolines, or travel agents. The journey takes about 24 hours.

Alsa, a regional coach service

Travelling Around Spain by Coach

There is no Spanish national coach company, but private regional companies operate routes around the country. The largest coach company is **Alsa**, which runs in all regions and has routes and services that cover most of the country. Other companies operate in

Cycling

Cycling is popular in Spain, and there are bicycles for hire in most tourist spots. However, there are few cycle lanes outside the cities. Bicycles may be carried on *cercanías* trains after 2pm on Fridays until the last train on Sunday night; on any *regional* train with a goods compartment; and

Cycle touring, a popular holiday activity

on all long-distance overnight trains. If you need to take your bicycle long-distance at other times, check it in an hour before the train departs. You may have to send it as luggage and pay a baggage charge based on its weight. It might not travel with you, so you will have to collect it when it arrives.

particular regions – Alsina Graells, for instance, covers most of the south and east of Spain. Tickets and information for long-distance travel are available at all main coach stations as well as from travel agents, but note that it is not always possible to book tickets in advance.

In Madrid the biggest coach stations are Estación Sur and Intercambiador de Autobuses. Always check which coach station your bus is due to leave from when you purchase your ticket.

Indicators for Seville's circular bus routes

Local Buses

Local bus routes and timetables are posted at bus termini and stops. You pay on the bus or buy a card with preloaded trips called an *abono* from *estancos* (tobacconists).

DIRECTORY

Car Hire

Avis
Tel 0808 284 0014 in UK.
Tel 902 18 08 54 in Spain.
W avisworld.com
W avis.es

easyCar
W easycar.com

Enterprise
W enterprise.co.uk

Europcar
Tel 0871 384 1087 in UK.
Tel 902 50 30 10 in Spain.
W europcar.co.uk
W europcar.es

Hertz
Tel 0207 026 00 77 in UK.
Tel 91 749 77 78 in Spain.
W hertz.co.uk
W hertz.es

hispacar
W hispacar.com

pepecar
W pepecar.com

Maps

Altaïr
Gran Vía 616, 08007
Barcelona.
Tel 93 342 71 71.

Guía Repsol
W guiarepsol.com

Michelin
W viamichelin.es

Stanfords
12–14 Long Acre,
London WC2E 9LP.
Tel 020 7836 1321.
W stanfords.co.uk

Weather Forecasts

Agencia Estatal de Meteorología
W aemet.es

Traffic and Road Conditions

Información de Tráfico de Carreteras
Tel 011 from a landline.
W dgt.es/es/el-trafico

Coach Operators

Alsa
Tel 902 42 22 42.
W alsa.es

Eurolines
Tel 08717 81 81 77 in UK.
Tel 902 40 50 40 in Spain.
W eurolines.com

National Express
W nationalexpress.com

Coach Stations

Barcelona
Estació del Nord, Calle Ali
Bei 80. **Tel** 902 26 06 06.
W barcelonanord.com

Madrid
Estación Sur, Calle
Méndez Álvaro 83.
Tel 91 468 42 00.
W estacionauto
busesmadrid.com
Intercambiador de
Autobuses, Avenida de
América 9.

Seville
Estación Plaza de Armas,
Calle Cristo de la Expiración.
Tel 955 03 86 65.
W autobusesplaza
dearmas.es

Getting Around Cities

Sightseeing and getting around in Spain's cities is best done on foot and by public transport – try to avoid driving a car into the city centres. Barcelona, Valencia and Madrid all have efficient underground (metro) systems, as well as overground railways that link up with the suburbs and airports. Madrid also has a metro service from the airport to the city. Good city maps are available from tourist offices, or they can be printed out from the Internet. Municipal websites (www.bcn.cat for Barcelona; www.madrid.es for Madrid; www.valencia.es for Valencia; and www.sevilla.org for Seville) provide up-to-the-minute information in English on travelling in the cities.

Walking on Las Ramblas, Barcelona

Metro

The best way to see Barcelona over a couple of days is to buy a T10 ticket. Once you validate a T10, you can make 10 combined journeys on the metro, buses, trams and local trains for 75 minutes. The more expensive T-2Dies gives you unlimited transport for two days until the end of service. The Barcelona metro run by **Metro de Barcelona** is open from 5am to midnight Sundays to Thursdays, until 2am on Fridays and for 24 hours every Saturday.

Metro de Madrid is the third-oldest system in Europe (1919) after London and Paris. Its 13 lines serve the whole city and are divided into various zones depending on different areas of the city and surrounding area. You can buy a single ticket for Zona A or a ten-journey ticket; this allows travel on both metro and buses. Tourist tickets providing between one and seven days' unlimited travel can be purchased at train stations or at the airport. The metro runs every day from 6am to 1:30am.

The **Metro de Valencia**, operated by Ferrocarrils de la Generalitat Valenciana (FGV), is best used to get to and from the beach, since it does not go near the town centre. It also tends to skip other important destinations, such as the City of Arts and Sciences. The metro will also get you to many places around Valencia, beyond the city centre. A metro ticket to any station within the city limits is the same price.

Metro de Sevilla's first line opened in 2009, linking the centre with the city's outlying suburbs, and as such it is of relatively little relevance to visitors – these areas contain little of interest for tourists. Three more lines are planned in the coming years.

Buses and Trams

Buses in Spain can sometimes follow an erratic timetable and many do not run after 10pm, although there are some night buses.

In Barcelona the T10 and T-2Dies tickets are valid on buses and trams, on the metro and on trains to the airport.

Bus, tram and metro tickets in Madrid, including tourist tickets, are interchangeable. If you do not have a ticket, you can pay the driver directly. Most buses run from 6am until 11:30pm. Night buses (called *buhos*) run less frequently and always pass by the Plaza de Cibeles. The price is the same as for day tickets.

Valencia has a good bus network, and buses are the preferred way of travelling for locals. If you are out and about a lot during the day, get a ten-journey *bono* (voucher). You can view a map of the routes on the EMT website (www.emtvalencia.es). The tram runs from the Pont de Fusta (Wooden Bridge), near the Serrano Towers, around the city and to the beaches at Las Arenas and La Malvarrosa.

Buses are the easiest and cheapest way to get around Seville and to the main sights. The bus network is comprised of circular (C-1, C-2, C-3, C-4, C-5 buses) and line routes (north, south, east and west).

Trains

If you are heading out of Barcelona to nearby beaches or mountains, you can take a train from Plaça Catalunya, Passeig de Gràcia, Estació de França or Estació de Sants. The local overland train services are run by **Ferrocarrils de la Generalitat de Catalunya (FGC)** and the main line trains are run by RENFE *(see p628)*. T10 and T-2Dies tickets can also be used on local trains within the city area.

One of Barcelona's taxis

Madrid bus

Madrid's rail system is comfortable, economical and efficient. The 13 lines all leave from or pass through Atocha station, and trains run daily from 6am until midnight every 15–30 minutes. **Consorcio Regional de Transportes de Madrid** provide helpful information on routes, fares and tourist tickets.

Taxis

Barcelona's distinctive yellow-and-black taxi cabs can be relied upon for a good and reasonably priced service, although it is rare to find a driver who speaks English. The meter begins running with a set fee and will rise every kilometre. Be aware that the tariff rises at night and on Saturdays, Sundays and public holidays. There are supplements added to your taxi fare when arriving at or leaving the airport, port or train station; for each piece of luggage; and also after 10pm on Fridays, Saturdays and holidays.

The taxis in Madrid are white with a diagonal red band on the front doors. A lit green light on top of the taxi indicates that it is available. Finding a taxi in the downtown area of Madrid is relatively simple and should take only a few minutes. The taxi meter starts its fare with a flat fee, the *bajada de bandera* (lowering of the flag). After that, the meter runs according to the distance covered, the urban area, the day of the week (higher fares apply on holidays) and the pick-up point (there are higher fares for pick-ups in bus stations, train stations and the airport). The night fare is always higher than the day fare. All additional fares should be indicated on informational signs on the back windows. There is an extra charge for pick-ups and drop-offs at Barajas Airport, but there is no extra charge for luggage.

Taxis are a good option for short journeys in Valencia. There is a minimum fee during the day and fares are higher at night; extra fees apply for trips to the airport.

Seville's taxis provide a viable way of getting into town, although much of the city centre is difficult to access by car because of heavy traffic, especially during the Feria de Abril or Semana Santa *fiestas*. As elsewhere, the tariff is higher for journeys at night.

Walking

Barcelona is an excellent city to explore on foot. The Old Town (Ciutat Vella), near the port and up to the Plaza Catalunya, consists of narrow medieval streets and winding alleyways. It is easy to get lost in this area, and care should be taken here at night. Las Ramblas is one of the world's most famous walkways and offers a vibrant slice of Mediterranean street life. The Eixample area is also good for walking, with large boulevards in a grid pattern. If you need to get your bearings, simply ask a local which direction is *mar* (sea, to the south) and which is *montaña* (mountain, to the north).

Distances are considerable in Madrid, and it is advisable to combine walking with public transport to make more efficient use of your time in the city. The most popular areas to visit on foot are those around the emblematic Plaza Mayor and the city's most famous park, El Retiro, which is also near the most well-known museums.

Most sights in the centre of Seville are best reached on foot. The popular Barrio Santa Cruz should be visited with a map. During late spring and the summer, shade is highly prized. In summer months the city government stretches tarpaulins across the buildings in the centre so that many of the streets are in the shade.

Cycling

Cycling tours are a popular way of seeing Barcelona, and its cycle lanes provide safe access to most of the city. Visit www.bikerentalbarcelona. com or contact the tourist office to hire bikes.

For those wishing to explore Madrid, www.bravobike.com offer a wide variety of city bicycle tours, some of which include the surrounding areas.

There are many cycle lanes in Valencia, and cycling tours provide a great way of seeing all the major sights. More information can be found at www.doyoubike.com.

Seville is home to Sevici, a fleet of bicycles that can be hired on subscription. Visit www.sevici.es for details. (For more on cycling *see p633*.)

(For more on cycling *see p633*.)

DIRECTORY

Metro

Metro de Barcelona
Tel 902 07 50 27.
w tmb.cat

Metro de Madrid
Tel 902 44 44 03.
w metromadrid.es

Metro de Valencia
Tel 900 46 10 46.
w metrovalencia.es

Metro de Sevilla
Tel 902 36 49 85.
w metro-sevilla.es

Public transport

FGC (Barcelona)
Tel 900 90 15 15.
w fgc.net

Consorcio Regional de Transportes de Madrid
Tel 915 80 42 60, or 012 from Madrid.
w ctm-madrid.es

General Index

Acknowledgments

Dorling Kindersley would like to thank the following people whose contributions and assistance made preparation of this book possible.

Main Contributors

John Ardagh is a journalist and writer, and the author of several books on modern Europe.

David Baird, resident in Andalucía from 1971 to 1995, is the author of *Inside Andalucía*.

Vicky Hayward, a writer, journalist and editor, lives in Madrid, and has travelled extensively in Spain.

Adam Hopkins is an indefatigable travel writer and author of *Spanish Journeys: A Portrait of Spain*.

Lindsay Hunt has travelled widely and has contributed to several Eyewitness Travel Guides.

Nick Inman writes regularly on Spain for books and magazines.

Paul Richardson is the author of *Not Part of the Package*, a book on Ibiza, where he lives.

Martin Symington is a regular contributor to the *Daily Telegraph*. He also worked on the *Eyewitness Travel Guide to Great Britain*.

Nigel Tisdall, contributor to the *Eyewitness Travel Guide to France*, is the author of the *Insight Pocket Guide to Seville*.

Roger Williams has contributed to Insight Guides on Barcelona and Catalonia, and was the main contributor to the *Eyewitness Travel Guide to Provence*.

Additional Contributors

Mary Jane Aladren, Sarah Andrews, Pepita Aris, Emma Dent Coad, Rebecca Doulton, Harry Eyres, Josefina Fernández, Anne Hersh, Nick Rider, Mercedes Ruiz Ochoa, David Stone, Clara Villanueva, Christopher Woodward, Patricia Wright.

Additional Illustrations

Arcana Studio, Richard Bonson, Louise Boulton, Martine Collings, Brian Craker, Jared Gilbey (Kevin Jones Associates), Paul Guest, Steven Gyapay, Claire Littlejohn.

Additional Photography

David Cannon, Tina Chambers, Geoff Dann, Phillip Dowell, Mike Dunning, Lydia Evans, Neil Fletcher, Steve Gorton, Heidi Grassley, Frank Greenaway, Derek Hall, Colin Keates, Alan Keohane, Dave King, Cyril Laubsouer, Neil Mersh, Ella Milroy, D Murray, Ian Naylor, Ian O'Leary, Stephen Oliver, Alex Robinson, Rough Guides/Ian Aitken, Rough Guides/Demetrio Carrasco, J Selves, Rodney Shackell, Colin Sinclair, Tony Souter, Mathew Ward, P Wojcik.

Cartography

Lovell Johns Ltd (Oxford), ERA-Maptec Ltd.

Revisions Team

Sam Atkinson, Pilar Ayerbe, Hansa Babra, Rosemary Bailey, Vicky Barber, Teresa Barea, Claire Baranowski, Cristina Barrallo, Fran Bastida, Lynette McCurdy Bastida, Jill Benjamin, Marta Bescos, Vandana Bhagra, Sonal Bhatt, Julie Bond, Chris Branfield, Gretta Britton, Daniel Campi, Adriana Canal, Paula Canal (Word on Spain), Maria Victoria Cano, Lola Carbonell, Peter Casterton, Elspeth Collier, Carey Combe, Irene Corchado Resmella, Jonathan Cox, Martin Cropper, Neha Dhingra, Linda Doyle, Nicola Erdpresser, Bernat Fiol, Emer FitzGerald, Anna Freiberger, Rhiannon Furbear, Mary-Ann Gallagher, Candela García Sanchez-Herrera, Aruna Ghose, Elena González, Lydia Halliday, Des Hemsley, Matthew Hirtes, Tim Hollis, Claire Jones, Juliet Kenny, Sumita Khatwani, Priya Kukadia, Priyanka Kumar, Rahul Kumar, Michael Lake, Erika Lang, Maite Lantaron, Jude Ledger, Rebecca Lister, Shobhna Iyer, Hayley Maher, Sarah Martin, Lynnette McCurdy Bastida, Alison McGill, Caroline Mead, Sam Merrell, Kate Molan, Jane Oliver, Simon Oon, Mary Ormandy, Mike Osborn, Malcolm Parchment, Helen Partington, Susie Peachey, Elizabeth Pitt, Pollyanna Poulter, Anna Pirie, Tom Prentice, Rada Radojlic, Mani Ramaswamy, Lucy Ratcliffe, Erin Richards, Lucy Richards, Ellen Root, Sands Publishing Solutions, Sue Sharp, Lucy Sienkowska, Neil Simpson, Rituraj Singh, Sadie Smith, Peter Stone, Anna Streiffert, Leah Tether, Helen Townsend, Suzanne Wales, Jennifer Walker, Catherine Waring, Andy Wilkinson, Hugo Wilkinson, Robert Zonenblick.

Proofreader

Huw Hennessy, Nikky Twyman, Stewart J Wild.

Indexer

Helen Peters.

Special Assistance

Dorling Kindersley would like to thank the regional and local tourist offices, *ayuntamientos*, shops, hotels, restaurants and other organizations in Spain for their invaluable help. Particular thanks also to Dr Giray Ablay (University of Bristol); María Eugenia Alonso and María Dolores Delgado Peña (Museo Thyssen-Bornemisza); Ramón Álvarez (Consejería de Educación y Cultura, Castilla y León); Señor Ballesteros (Santiago de Compostela Tourist Office); Carmen Brieva, Javier Campos and Luis Esteruelas (Spanish Embassy, London); Javier Caballero Arranz; Fernando Cañada López; The Club Taurino of London; Consejería de Turismo, Castilla-La Mancha; Consejería de Turismo and Consejería de Cultura, Junta de Extremadura; Mònica Colomer and Montse Planas (Barcelona Tourist Office); Mario José Docal and Carmen Cardona (Patronato de Turismo, Lanzarote); Edilesa; Klaus Ehrlich; Juan Fernández, Lola Moreno and others at *El País-Aguilar*; Belén Galán (Centro de Arte Reina Sofía); Amparo Garrido; Adolfo Díaz Gómez (Albacete Tourist Office); Professor Nigel Glendinning (Queen Mary and Westfield College, University of London); Pedro Hernández; Insituto de Cervantes, London; Victor Jolín (SOTUR); Joaquim Juan Cabanilles (Servicio de Investigación Prehistórica, Valencia); Richard Kelly; Mark Little (*Lookout* Magazine); Carmen López de Tejada and Inma Felipe (Spanish National Tourist Office, London); Caterine López and Ana Roig Mundi (ITVA); Julia López de la Torre (Patrimonio Nacional, Madrid); Lovell Johns Ltd (Oxford); Josefina Maestre (Ministerio de Agricultura, Pesca y Alimentación); Juan Malavia García and Antonio Abarca (Cuenca Tourist Office); Mario (Promoción Turismo, Tenerife); Janet Mendel; Javier Morata (Acanto Arquitectura y Urbanismo. Madrid); Juan Carlos Murillo; Sonia Ortega and Bettina Krücken (Spain Gourmetour); Royal Society for the Protection of Birds (UK); Alícia Ribas Sos; Katusa Salazar-Sandoval (Fomento de Turismo, Ibiza); María Ángeles Sánchez and Marcos; Ana Sarrieri (Departamento de Comercio, Consumo y Turismo, Gobierno Vasco); Klaas Schenk; María José Sevilla (Foods From Spain); The Sherry Institute of Spain (London); Anna Skidmore (Fomento de

Turismo, Mallorca); Philip Sweeney; Rupert Thomas; Mercedes Trujillo and Antonio Cruz Caballero (Patronato de Turismo, Gran Canaria); Gerardo Uarte (Gobierno de Navarra); Fermín Unzue (Dirección General de Turismo, Cantabria); Puri Villanueva.

Artwork Reference
Sr Joan Bassegoda, Catedral Gaudí (Barcelona); José Luis Mosquera Muller (Mérida); Jorge Palazón, Paisajes Españoles (Madrid).

Photography Permissions
The Publisher would like to thank the following for their kind assistance and permission to photograph at their establishments: © Patrimonio Nacional, Madrid; Palacio de la Almudaina, Palma de Mallorca; El Escorial, Madrid; La Granja de San Ildefonso; Convento de Santa Clara, Tordesillas; Las Huelgas Reales, Burgos; Palacio Real, Madrid; Monasterio de las Descalzas; Bananera "El Guanche S.L."; Museo Arqueológico de Tenerife-OACIMC del Excmo, Cavildo Insular de Tenerife; Asociación de Encajeras de Acebo-Cáceres; Museo de Arte Abstracto Español, Cuenca; Fundación Juan March; Pepita Alia Lagartera; Museo Naval de Madrid; © Catedral de Zamora; Museo de Burgos; Claustro San Juan de Duero, Museo Numantino, Soria; San Telmo Museoa Donostia-San Sebastián; Hotel de la Reconquista, Oviedo; Catedral de Jaca; Museo de Cera, Barcelona; Museu D'Història de la Ciutat, Barcelona; © Capitol Catedral de Lleida; Jardí Botànic Marimurtra, Estació Internacional de Biologia Mediterrània, Girona; Museo Arqueológico Sagunto (Teatro Romano-Castillo); Museo Municipal y Ermita de San Antonio de la Florida, Madrid. Also all the other churches, museums, hotels, restaurants, shops, galleries and sights too numerous to thank individually.

Picture Credits
Key: a=above; b=below/bottom; c=centre; f=far; l=left; r=right; t=top.

Works of art have been published with the permission of the following copyright holders: *Dona i Ocell* Joan Miró © Succession Miró/ADAGP, Paris & DACS, London 2011 180tl; *Guernica* Pablo Ruiz Picasso 1937 © Succession Picasso/DACS, London 2011 303crb; *Morning* George Kolbe © DACS London 2011 174tr, 177tl; *Peine de los Vientos* Eduardo Chillida © DACS, London 2011 126b; Various works by Joaquín Sorolla © DACS, London 2011 309tr; *Rainy Taxi* Salvador Dalí © Kingdom of Spain, Gala - Salvador Dalí Foundation, DACS, London 2011 219tr; *Tapestry of the Foundation* Joan Miró 1975 © Succession Miró/ADAGP, Paris & DACS, London 175crb; *Three Gypsy Boys* © Joan Rebull 1976 148bl.

The publisher would like to thank the following individuals, companies and picture libraries for their kind permission to reproduce their photographs:

123RF.com: Maaike Bolhuis e v Bunschoten 430tr; byvalet 56cl; David Herraez 52clb; jarp5 40-41c; jorisvo 359bl; joserpizarro 447bl; Carlos Soler Martinez 359br; photoerick 236bc; Luciano de la Rosa 43tr; Alvaro German Vilela 376tr; Andrii Zhezhera 58bl, 60bl; **6 6 TOROS:** 41cb.

Abades Triana: 598bl; **AISA Archivo Iconografico, Barcelona:** Museo Nacional del Teatro *Poster for "Yerma"* (FG Lorca) Juan Antonio Morales y José Caballero © DACS, London 2011 39tr;

Agroturismo Biniatram: 559br, 575bc; **Akelarre:** 585bl; **AKG, London:** 71cr; **Alamy Images:** age fotostock 54clb, 191tr; Antiqua Print Gallery 41bl, 428cl; The Art Archive 8-9; ART Collection 371tc; Paul Hardy Carter 204cla; Michelle Chaplow 462bl; China Span/Keren Su 338-9; Chronicle 395br; Ian Dagnall 15br; Expuesto/Nicholas Randall 608br; Mike Finn-Kelcey 629c; Kevin Foy 191br; Granger Historical Picture Archive 53br; Dennis Hallinan 37cra; Robert Harding Picture Library 423cl, 608cla; Peter Horree 37bc; Eric James 137t; paulbourdice 517cla; Photo 12 71tl; PjrTravel 625c; Prisma Bildagentur AG 178; Profimedia. CZ s.r.o. 541cla; Alex Segre 81tl, 579tr; Richard Sowley 673cr; Peter Titmuss 205tl; travelstock44 158bl; Lucas Vallecillos 325br; Renaud Visage 422cla; Washington Imaging 621cra; Ken Welsh 602tr, 619bl; **Alsa Group S.L.L.C:** 633cl; **Annua:** 584tr; **ARCAID:** Paul Raftery 124bl; **The Art Archive:** Museo del Prado Madrid/Dagli Orti (A) *St Cecilia Patron Saint of Music* Nicolas Poussin (1594–1665) 299cr; **AWL Images:** Hemis 472bl.

Balearia: 627bl; **Bar Tomate:** 593bc; **Barosse:** 567tr; **Belmond Ltd.:** 569bc; **La Bobadilla:** 573tc; **Bridgeman Art Library:** *St Dominic Enthroned as Abbot* Bartolomé Bermejo 298cla; Index/ Museo del Prado, Madrid *Auto-da-fé in the Plaza Mayor* Francisco Rizi 278tc; Musée des Beaux-Artes, Berne *Colossus of Rhodes* Salvador Dalí 1954 © Kingdom of Spain, Gala – Salvador Dalí Foundation, DACS, London 2011 37tr; Museo del Prado, Madrid *Charles IV and his Family* Francisco de Goya y Lucientes 37cb, *The Adoration of the Shepherds* El Greco 296clb, *The Annunciation* Fra Angelico 297br, *The Clothed Maja* Francisco de Goya y Lucientes 297cra, *The Naked Maja* Francisco de Goya y Lucientes 297cr, *The Three Graces* Peter Paul Rubens 297br, *The Martyrdom of St Philip* José de Ribera 296cl; Museo Picasso, Barcelona *Las Meninas, Infanta Margarita* Pablo Ruiz Picasso 1957 © Succession Picasso/DACS, London 2011 36ca; **Bridgeman Images:** Spain: Berber general Tariq ibn Ziyad, Muslim conqueror of southern Spain in 711 / Pictures from History 57cb; **Michael Busselle:** 211r, 213b, 214t.

Café Gijón: 324br; **Camper Store,** Madrid: 607tr; **Casa Grande:** 572br; **El Celler de Can Roca:** 589bc; **Centro de Arte Reina Sofía:** *Bertsolaris* Zubiaurre © DACS, London 2011 129clb, *Paisaje de Cadaqués* Salvador Dalí 1923 © Kingdom of Spain, Gala – Salvador Dalí Foundation, DACS, London 2011 302cb, *Accidente* Ponce de León 302bl, *Toki-Egin (Homenaje a San Juan de la Cruz)* Eduardo Chillida 1952 © DACS, London 2011 303bl; **Cephas:** Mick Rock 33bl, 46tc, 82tr, 206tr, 206cla, 344tr, 425cr, 0; Roy Stedall-Humphryes 424tr, 425tr; **Chikito:** 601br; **Cinc Sentits:** 576br; **Ciutat de Girona:** 566tl; **Grupo Codorniu:** 207tl; **Bruce Coleman:** Dee Conway: 429ca, 429cr; **Comerç 24:** 603br; **Corbis:** Owen Franken 81c, 205c, 342cl, 343c, 423tl; Hemis/Hughes Herve 230; Michael Jenner 260–61; Jean-Pierre Lescourret 12tr; Massimo Listri 13b; Claude Medale 127bc; Caroline Penn 343tl; Jose Fuste Raga 12bl, 14b, 378–9; Robert Harding World Imagery/Marco Cristofori 2–3; Splash News/LOTE 27c; Rudy Sulgan 272; Westend61/Mel Stuart 506–7; **El Corral del Indianu:** 583tr **Giancarlo Costa:** 41bc; **Cover:** Genin Andrada 44bl, 47bl; Austin Catalan 72bl; Juan Echeverria 35cra, 45br, 549bl; Pepe Franco 190cla; Quim Llenas 129cra, 321tl; Matías Nieto 47cr; F J Rodríguez 129bl; **Cuidad de las Artes y las Ciencas (CACSA):** Javier Yaya Tur 257t; **Cocomfe:** 617b.

J D Dallet: 73tr, 468tl, 605br; **Delic:** 592tl; **Depositphotos Inc:** FelixHerencias 409bc; vampy1 516t; **El Deseo:** Pedro Almodóvar

309bc; **Dorling Kindersley:** Dreamstime / Lianem 414tc, Natural History Museum, London / Frank Greenaway 214bl, The University of Aberdeen / Gary Ombler 53tc; **Dos Palillos:** 587tr; **Dreamstime.com:** Alexsalcedo 126br; Alfonsodetomas 56bl, 367bc, 411tc, 427bl; Americanspirit 36–37c; Anasife 408tl; Birdiegal717 346bl; David Blazquez 425cl; Botond 350; Natalia Bratslavsky 57tl; Yuriy Brykaylo 76–77, 431cr; Wessel Cirkel 144clb; Davidmartyn 104; Digicomphoto 209cra; Deymos 14tr; Elenaphotos 256bl; Eng101 84crb; Maria Luisa Lopez Estivill 535t; Evgeniy_p 175tl; Iakov Filimonov 25b, 136cl, 165crb, 268–269, 609t; Carmen Gabriela Filip 368br; Gabriel García 353tr; Gkmf10 61br; Roberto Atencia Gutierrez 374bc; H368k742 209cla; Hergon 347bc; Imagin.gr Photography 4cb; Isselee 34c; Ivansmuk 144bl; Silvia Blaszczyszyn Jakiello 440bl; Kiko Jiménez 44cr; Joserpizarro 485tr; García Juan 347cl, 611bl; Tetyana Kochneva 553tl; Stelios Kyriakides 467tr; Lunamarina 34br, 59cra, 237cra; Marcelusw 346cl; Marlee 210; Matthi 16tr; Mcxas 32cla; Mikelane45 209crb, 347tl; Milosk50 64bl; Monysasi 30bl; Luciano Mortula 140–41; Juan Moyano 10bl, 532; Nanisub 79bl; Alexander Nikiforov 508bl; Sean Pavone 430br; Kostya Pazyuk 346br; William Perry 59bl; Pigprox 40tr, 430clb; Plotnikov 215br; Alexander Potapov 84cla; Alvaro Trabazo Rivas 40cl; Tiberiu Sahlean 214clb; Pere Sanz 27t; Jozef Sedmak 36hr 427br, 430cla, 431tl; Tomas Sereda 330; Slava296 556–7; Jose I. Soto 88, 495bl; Olaf Speier 208tr; Sandra Standbridge 214cl; Studiobarcelona 276tl; Svetlana195 39cr; Tinamou 64cla; Aleksandar Todorovic 484cl; Travelpeter 5cra; Tupungato 58clb; Typhoonski 560tr; T.w. Van Urk 33tr; Maarten Van De Ven 34cr; Maria Vazquez 275tl; Venemama 501tr; Alvaro German Vilela 32tr; Liqiang Wang 347cb; Whiskybottle 209bl; Robert Zehetmayer 304.

Edex: 55tl, **Edilesa:** 356b; **Elephant Club:** 576cr, **Paco Elvira:** 34crb; **EMI:** Hispavox 380bc; **Equipo 28** 429tl; **L'Estartit Tourist Board:** 221c; **ET Archive:** 56br; **Europa Press:** 73ca; **Mary Evans Picture Library:** 60cla, 67bl, 278bl, 477br; **Eye Ubiquitous:** James Davis Travel Photography 25tl, 222br

Firo Foto: 161cr; 537tr; **Flamencocool:** Seville, 461tr; **Grupo Freixenet:** 207tr; **Fundación César Manrique:** 552br; **Fundación Colección Thyssen-Bornemisza:** *Madonna of Humility* Fra Angelico 181tc, *La Virgen del Árbol* Petrus Christus 292tr, *Mata Mua* Paul Gauguin 1892 293br, *Harlequin with a Mirror* Pablo Ruiz Picasso 1923 © Succession Picasso/DACS, London 2011 292bl, *Hotel Room* © Edward Hopper 1931 292cla, *Portrait of Baron H H Thyssen-Bornemisza* © Lucian Freud 1981–82 292br, *Venus y Cupido* Peter Paul Rubens (after 1629) 293tl, *Santa Casilda* Francisco de Zurbarán 1640–1645 293cr, *Autumn Landscape in Oldenburg* Karl Schmidt-Rottluff 1907 © DACS, London 2011 293bl; **Fundació Joan Miró, Barcelona:** *Flama en l'Espai i Dona Nua* Joan Miró 1932 © Succession Miró/ADAGP, Paris and DACS, London, 2011 176tl.

Getty Images: Gonzalo Azumendi 404, 614–15; Baloulumix/ Julien Fourniol 448; California CPA 200–1; Alan Copson 418–19; DEA / C. SAPPA 473cra; DEA / G. DAGLI ORTI 50, 55tl, 59bc; DEA / G. NIMATALLAH 53clb; DEA / SALMER 207bc; DEA / W. BUSS 58-59c; DEA PICTURE LIBRARY 36clb, 36bl; R Duran (rduranmerino@gmail.com) 436; Krzysztof Dydynski 286; Michele Falzone 510; Florilegius 40bc, 40br, 41br; Heritage Images 58cla, 63tl, 63cb, 299tc, 299bl; Iconica/Don Klumpp

618tl; Domingo Leiva 382; I. Lizarraga 118; Peter Macdiarmid 73br; Conor MacNeill 146; marck from belgium 172; Stephen Munday 46cr; PHAS 52cla, 58cb; Photo 12 62cl; Meinrad Riedo 246; Ferran Traite Soler 162; Stringer / AFP 41c; Stringer / RAFA RIVAS 428br; Stringer / Wang Zhao 26tl; Visions of Our Land 166–7; Ken Welsh 462, 498–9; Terry Williams 616cla; zzafrankha – foodholic telling stories about food 528–9; **Godo Foto:** 224bl, 225tr, 229t, 253b, 259t, 337bl; **Ronald Grant Archive:** *For a Few Dollars More* © United Artists 504bl; © **FMGB Guggenheim Bilbao Museoa**. Erica Barahona Ede. All rights reserved. Partial or total reproduction is prohibited 124tr, *The Matter of Time* Richard Serra © ARS, NY and DACS, London 2011 124br, 125t.

Robert Harding Picture Library: 145cra, 164cla, 176br, 253tl, 307tl, 515br, Jose Lucas 431br, Lucas Vallecillos 495br; Nigel Blythe 23b, 153cr; Bob Cousins 30clb; Robert Frerck 469tr; James Strachan 284tl; **María Victoria Hernández:** 537bl; **Hostal Gala, Madrid:** 568tl; **Hotel Alma:** 561tr; **Hotel Arts Barcelona:** 559cl; **Hotel Marqes de Riscal:** 564bl; **Hotel Mercer:** 565tc; **Hotel Miró:** 563tr; **Hotel Rector:** 570tl.

The Image Bank, London: Incafo: J A Fernández & C De Noriega 79bl, 129br; Juan Carlos Muñoz 400b, 501bl; A Ortega 34bl; **Index:** 52c, 52b, 53cr, 53crb, 58cra, 60hr (d), 63tr, *Los Moriscos Suplicando al Rey Felipe III* 65cr, 68–9, 69bc, 71cb, *Carlos I* 74tc, 74clb, 75br; Bridgeman, London 62cra; CCJ 27hr: *Garrote Vil* José Gutiérrez Solana 1931 © DACS, London 2011 69clb(d); Galería del Ateneo, Madrid *Lucio Anneo Seneca* Villodas 54cl; Galeria Illustres Catalonia, Barcelona *Joan Prim I Prats* J Cusachs 67cra(d); Image *José Zorilla* 39cb; Instituto Valencia de Don Juan, Madrid *Carlos V* Simón Bening 63crb; Iranzo 60cra; Mithra 56clb, 62br(d), Museo de América, Madrid *Indio Yumbo y Frutas Tropicales* 63cra; Museo Lázaro Galdiano, Madrid *Lope de Vega* Anonymous 38tr; *Félix Lope de Vega* Francisco Pacheco 64br(d); Museo Municipal, Madrid *Fiesta en la Plaza Mayor de Madrid* Juan de la Corte 65tl; Museo del Prado, Madrid *Ascensión de un Globo Montgolfier en Madrid* Antonio Carnicero 66ca(d), *José Moreño Conde de Floridablanca* Francisco de Goya 66br(d), *Flota del Rey Carlos III de España* A Joli 67tl(d); National Maritime Museum, Greenwich *Batallu de Trafalgar* Chalmers 66clb; A Noé 60cb; Palacio del Senado, Madrid *Alfonso X "El Sabio"* Matías Moreno 38b(d), *Rendición de Granada* Francisco Pradilla 60–1(d); Patrimonio Nacional 55br; Private Collection, Madrid *Pedro Calderón de la Barca* Antonio de Pereda 65bl(d); Real Academia de Bellas Artes de San Fernando, Madrid *San Diego de Alcalá Dando de Comer a los Pobres* Bartolomé Esteban Murillo 65cra(d), *Fernando VII* Francisco de Goya 75tl(d), *Isabel II* 75tc, *Self-Portrait* Francisco de Goya 243b; A Tovy 73crb; **Nick Inman:** 208bc, 257tr, 624tr, 629b; **Institut Turístic Valenciá:** 249br; **iStockphoto.com:** MarioGuti 635tl; Sloot 237crb.

César Justel: 357bc.

Anthony King: 295tl.

Life File Photographic: 221c; Emma Lee 145cra, 633tr; **Andrzej Lisowski:** 626c; **Neil Lukas:** 470cb, 470bl.

Magnum: S Franklin 72cb; Jean Gaumy 73tl; **MARKA,** Milan: Sergio Pitamitz 158tl; Imagen Mas, Leon: 359tr; **Miguel Torres,**

SA: 207c; **John Miller:** 509clb, 533b, 542cl, 547bl, 552cla, 553br; **Mas de Torrent Hotel & Spa:** 566br; **Meson Cuevas Del Vino:** 594bc; **El Molino de la Romera:** 599tc; **El Motel – Hotel Empordà:** 588tl; **Museo Arqueológic de Barcelona:** 175c; **Museo Arqueológico de Villena:** 52–3; **Museo Arqueológico Nacional:** 300tl; **Museo Nacional Centro de Arte Reina Sofía:** 70–71c, 302tc, 303tc; **Museu de Ciencies Naturals de Barcelona:** 159tc; **Museo Nacional del Prado:** El Jardín de las Delicias 296bl; **Museu Picasso,** Barcelona: Auto Retrato Pablo Ruiz Picasso 1899–1900 © Succession Picasso/DACS, London 2011 157bl.

Natural Science Photos: Nigel Charles 112tl; **naturepl.com:** Jose Luis GOMEZ de FRANCISCO 35c; Jose B. Ruiz 84bl; **Naturpress:** Oriol Alamany 35bl; J L Calvo & J R Montero 347crb; José Luis Grande 471bc; Walter Kwaternik 34clb, 35crb, 346cra, 347cra; Francisco Márquez 469crb, 420bl; Aurelio Martín 35br; José A Martínez 84tr, 211b, 346clb, 346crb; © **National Maritime Museum:** 62–3; **Network:** Bilderberg/W Kunz 425tl; **NHPA:** Laurie Campbell 84cra; Stephen Dalton 85clb; Vicente García Canseco 35cla, 471ca; Manfred Daneggar 84br, 85br.

Omega Foto: 114tl; Manuel Pinilla 46bl.

José M Pérez de Ayala: 34cr, 470tr, 470cla, 471tl, 471ca; **The Photographers Library:** 527tr; **Pictures Colour Library:** 26b, 34tr, 262b, 420cl; **PRISMA:** 68cla, 68bl, 69crb, 70cla, 70clb, 71tr, 101tr, 144br, 243c, 254cl, 325tl, 465b, 520crb, 534clb, 536cl, 543clb, 543bc, 543br, 543bl, 547tr, 555bl, 555br; Franco Aguiar 75tr; El Ingenioso Hidalgo Don Quixote de la Mancha 1605 Ricardo Balaca 399br; Domènech & Azpil

iqueta 122tl; Albert Heras 190br; Marcel Jaquet 534clb, 545b; Hans Lohr 489br; Los Niños de la Concha Bartolomé Esteban Murillo 37bl(d); Museo de Arte Moderno, Barcelona Pío Baroja Ramón Casas 68cb(d); Museo de Bellas Artes, Bilbao Condesa Mathieu de Noailles Ignacio Zuloaga y Zubaleta © DACS, London 2011 122bl; Museo de Bellas Artes, Zaragoza Príncipe de Viana José Moreno Carbonero 134b (d); Mateu 195cr; Palacio del Senado, Madrid Alfonso XIII Aquino © DACS, London 2011 75crb; Patrimonio Nacional Palacio de Riofrío, Segovia: 68bc; Auto Retrato Pablo Ruiz Picasso 1907 © Succession Picasso/DACS, London 2011 69ca; Real Academia de Bellas Artes de San Fernando, Madrid Las Bodas de Camacho José Moreno Carbonero 39tl(d), Procession of the Flagellants Francisco de Goya 278br(d); **Pure Espana:** Port Aventura 609br.

Irene Corchado Resmella: 406bl, 407tr; **Restaurant Canteré:** 590bl; **Restaurante Hospedería, Finca la Estacada:** 596bl; **Restaurante Palio:** 597tr; **Rex Features:** Sipa Press 219cb; **Rex Shutterstock:** Agencia EFE 72cla, Epa / Toni Albir 39br; **Rib Room:** 600tc; **El Rincon de Antonio:** 595tl; **El Rincon de Juan**

Carlos: 605tr; © **Royal Museum of Scotland:** Michel Zabé 51t; José Lucas Ruiz: 44br, 462cl.

Saboya 21: 591tl; **María Ángeles Sánchez:** 42tr, 43bl, 47tl, 83t, 102tl, 294cla, 308bl, 391c, 409tr, 536tr, 536cr, 536bc, 540cl, 551tr; **El Serbal:** 577br; **Simply Fosh:** 603tr; **Son Granot:** 604bc; **Spanish Tourist Board:** 259c; **Spectrum Colour Library:** 144tr; **STA Travel Group:** 619ca; **Stockphotos:** Madrid: Campillo 611tl; Heinz Hebeisen 45bl; Mikael Helsing 610bl; Javier Sánchez 336tl; **Suculent:** 586bc; **James Strachan:** 295bc, 306tr, 306c, 308tr; **Tony Stone Worldwide:** Doug Armand 24bl; Jon Bradley 320bl; Robert Everts 444cra; **Superstock:** age fotostock 145crb; age fotostock / Heinz-Dieter Falkenstein 65bc; Album / Documenta 69tl; Album / Joseph Martin 64-65c, 74tr, 74cr, 74crb, 74bc, 298bl; Album / Oronoz 51b, 57cr, 59tl, 61tl, 61tr, 61cb, 63c, 64clb, 65crb, 66bl, 71bc, 75bl, 86-87tc, 294tr, 302cla, 309c; age fotostock / Massimo Pizzotti 282–3, 306bl; Album / Prisma 69tr; Peter Barritt 285cra; Bridgeman Art Library 298tr; DeAgostini 62clb, 66cl; Fine Art Images 66–67c; Iberfoto 57bc, 59c, 67br, 70br, 128br, 296tr; LatitudeStock 22; Pixtal 80cl; Science and Society / FLO 74cla, Universal Images Group 55cb, Westend61 / David Santiago Garcia 611cr, World History Archive 116tl.

Taberna del Alabardero: 558cl, 571br; **Telefónica:** 624ca.

Denominación de Origen Utiel-Requena: 207cb.

Vinas del Vero, S.A: 206cra; **Vinos de Jumilla:** 207bc; **Visions of Andalucía:** Michelle Chaplow 428–9; J D Dallet 401tr; **VU:** Christina García Rodero 24c, 42bl, 43cr, 372cl, 437cr.

Werner Forman Archive: National Maritime Museum, Greenwich 56cr; **Alan Williams:** 82bl; **Peter Wilson:** 340cr, 474b, 475cr, 481tl, 487tl.

Yayo Daporta: 582bl.

Front endpaper: All special photography except **Corbis:** Hemis/Hughes Herve rtc; **Dreamstime.com:** Davidmartyn Ltr; Iakov Filimonov Lc, Botond Lca; Marlee rtr; Luciano Mortula Rca; Juan Moyano Rcb; Jose I. Soto ltl; Gonzalo Azumendi lcl; Michele Falzone rcrb; Domingo Leiva lbl; I. Lizarraga Rtl; Meinrad Riedo rbl; Ken Welsh lbr..

Cover: Front and Spine: **4Corners:** Riccardo Spila. Back: **Dreamstime.com:** Sean Pavone.

All other images © Dorling Kindersley.
For further information see www.DKimages.com

Special Editions of DK Travel Guides

DK Travel Guides can be purchased in bulk quantities at discounted prices for use in promotions or as premiums. We are also able to offer special editions and personalized jackets, corporate imprints, and excerpts from all of our books, tailored specifically to meet your own needs.

To find out more, please contact:
in the United States **specialsales@dk.com**
in the UK **travelspecialsales@uk.dk.com**
in Canada DK Special Sales at **general@ tourmaline.ca**
in Australia **penguincorporatesales@ penguinrandomhouse.com.au**

Phrase Book

In an Emergency

Help!	¡Socorro!	soh-**koh**-roh
Stop!	¡Pare!	**pah**-reh
Call a doctor!	¡Llame a un médico!	yah-meh ah oon meh-dee-koh
Call an ambulance!	¡Llame a una ambulancia!	yah-meh ah oonah ahm-boo-**lahn**-thee-ah
Call the police!	¡Llame a la policía!	yah-meh ah lah poh-lee-**thee**-ah
Call the fire brigade!	¡Llame a los bomberos!	yah-meh ah lohs bohm-**beh**-rohs
Where is the nearest telephone?	¿Dónde está el teléfono más próximo?	dohn-deh ehs-**tah** ehl teh-**leh**-foh-noh mahs prohx-ee-moh
Where is the nearest hospital?	¿Dónde está el hospital más próximo?	dohn-deh ehs-**tah** ehl ohs-pee-**tahl** mahs prohx-ee-moh

Communication Essentials

Yes	Sí	see
No	No	noh
Please	Por favor	pohr fah-**vohr**
Thank you	Gracias	**grah**-thee-ahs
Excuse me	Perdone	pehr-**doh**-neh
Hello	Hola	**oh**-lah
Goodbye	Adiós	ah-dee-**ohs**
Goodnight	Buenas noches	bweh-nahs **noh** chehs
Morning	La mañana	lah mah-**nyah**-nah
Afternoon	La tarde	lah **tahr**-deh
Evening	La tarde	lah **tahr**-deh
Yesterday	Ayer	ah-**yehr**
Today	Hoy	oy
Tomorrow	Mañana	mah-**nyah**-nah
Here	Aquí	ah-**kee**
There	Allí	ah-**yee**
What?	¿Qué?	keh
When?	¿Cuándo?	**kwahn**-doh
Why?	¿Por qué?	pohr-**keh**
Where?	¿Dónde?	**dohn**-deh

Useful Phrases

How are you?	¿Cómo está usted?	koh-moh ehs-**tah** oos-**tehd**
Very well, thank you.	Muy bien, gracias.	mwee bee-**ehn grah**-thee-ahs
Pleased to meet you.	Encantado de conocerle.	ehn-kahn-**tah**-doh deh koh-noh-**thehr**-leh
See you soon.	Hasta pronto.	ahs-tah **prohn**-toh
That's fine.	Está bien.	ehs-**tah** bee-**ehn**
Where is/are ...?	¿Dónde está/están ...?	**dohn**-deh ehs-**tah**/ehs-**tahn**
How far is it to ...?	Cuántos metros/ kilómetros hay de aquí a ...?	**kwahn**-tohs meh-trohs/kee-**loh**-meh-trohs **eye** deh ah-**kee** ah
Which way to ...?	¿Por dónde se va a ...?	pohr **dohn**-deh seh **bah** ah
Do you speak English?	¿Habla inglés?	**ah**-blah een-**glehs**
I don't understand	No comprendo	noh kohm-**prehn**-doh
Could you speak more slowly, please?	¿Puede hablar más despacio, por favor?	pweh-deh ah-**blahr** mahs dehs-pah-thee-oh pohr fah-**vohr**
I'm sorry.	Lo siento.	loh see-**ehn**-toh

Useful Words

big	grande	**grahn**-deh
small	pequeño	peh-**keh**-nyoh
hot	caliente	kah-lee-**ehn**-teh
cold	frío	**free**-oh
good	bueno	**bweh**-noh
bad	malo	**mah**-loh
enough	bastante	bahs-**tahn**-the
well	bien	bee-**ehn**
open	abierto	ah-bee-**ehr**-toh
closed	cerrado	thehr-**rah**-doh
left	izquierda	eeth-key-**ehr**-dah
right	derecha	deh-reh-chah
straight on	todo recto	toh-doh **rehk**-toh
near	cerca	**thehr**-kah
far	lejos	**leh**-hohs
up	arriba	ah-**ree**-bah
down	abajo	ah-**bah**-hoh
early	temprano	tehm-**prah**-noh
late	tarde	**tahr**-deh
entrance	entrada	ehn-**trah**-dah
exit	salida	sah-**lee**-dah
toilet	lavabos, servicios	lah-**vah**-bohs sehr-**bee**-thee-ohs
more	más	mahs
less	menos	**meh**-nohs

Shopping

How much does this cost?	¿Cuánto cuesta esto?	**kwahn**-toh **kwehs**-tah ehs-toh
I would like ...	Me gustaría ...	meh goos-ta-**ree**-ah
Do you have...?	¿Tienen...?	tee-**yeh**-nehn
I'm just looking, thank you.	Sólo estoy mirando, gracias.	soh-loh ehs-**toy** mee-**rahn**-doh **grah**-thee-ahs
Do you take credit cards?	¿Aceptan tarjetas de crédito?	ah-**thehp**-tahn tahr-**heh**-tahs deh **kreh**-dee-toh
What time do you open?	¿A qué hora abren?	ah **keh** oh-rah **ah**-brehn
What time do you close?	¿A qué hora cierran?	ah keh oh-rah thee-**ehr**-rahn
This one.	Este.	**ehs**-the
That one.	Ese.	**eh**-she
expensive	caro	**kahr**-oh
cheap	barato	bah-**rah**-toh
size, clothes	talla	**tah**-yah
size, shoes	número	**noo**-mehr-oh
white	blanco	**blahn**-koh
black	negro	**neh**-groh
red	rojo	**roh**-hoh
yellow	amarillo	ah-mah-**ree**-yoh
green	verde	**behr**-deh
blue	azul	ah-**thool**
antiques shop	la tienda de antigüedades	lah tee-**ehn**-dah deh ahn-tee-gweh-**dah**-dehs
bakery	la panadería	lah pah-nah-deh-**ree**-ah
bank	el banco	ehl **bahn**-koh
book shop	la librería	lah lee-breh-**ree**-ah
butcher's	la carnicería	lah kahr-nee-theh-**ree**-ah
cake shop	la pastelería	lah pahs-teh-leh-**ree**-ah
chemist's	la farmacia	lah fahr-**mah**-thee-ah
fishmonger's	la pescadería	lah pehs-kah-deh-**ree**-ah
greengrocer's grocer's	la frutería la tienda de comestibles	lah froo-teh-**ree**-ah lah tee-**yehn**-dah deh koh-mehs-**tee**-blehs
hairdresser's	la peluquería	lah peh-loo-keh-**ree**-ah
market	el mercado	ehl mehr-**kah**-doh
newsagent's	el kiosko de prensa	ehl kee-**ohs**-koh deh **prehn**-sah
post office	la oficina de correos	lah oh-fee-**thee**-nah deh kohr-**reh**-ohs
shoe shop	la zapatería	lah thah-pah-teh-**ree**-ah
supermarket	el supermercado	ehl soo-pehr-mehr-**kah**-doh
tobacconist	el estanco	ehl ehs-**tahn**-koh
travel agency	la agencia de viajes	lah ah-**hehn**-thee-ah deh bee-**ah**-hehs

Sightseeing

art gallery	el museo de arte	ehl moo-**seh**-oh deh **ahr**-the
cathedral	la catedral	lah kah-teh-**drahl**
church	la iglesia la basílica	lah ee-**gleh**-see-ah lah bah-**see**-lee-kah
garden	el jardín	ehl hahr-**deen**
library	la biblioteca	lah bee-blee-oh-**teh**-kah
museum	el museo	ehl moo-**seh**-oh
tourist information office	la oficina de turismo	lah oh-fee-**thee**-nah deh too-**rees**-moh
town hall	el ayuntamiento	ehl ah-yoon-tah-mee-**ehn**-toh
closed for holiday	cerrado por vacaciones	thehr-**rah**-doh pohr bah-kah-thee-**oh**-nehs
bus station	la estación de autobuses	lah ehs-tah-thee-**ohn** deh owtoh-**boo**-sehs
railway station	la estación de trenes	lah ehs-tah-thee-**ohn** deh **treh**-nehs

Staying in a Hotel

Do you have a vacant room?	¿Tienen una habitación libre?	tee-**eh**-nehn oo-nah ah-bee-tah-thee-**ohn lee**-breh
double room	habitación doble	ah-bee-tah-thee-**ohn doh**-bleh
with double bed	con cama de matrimonio	kohn kah-mah deh mah-tree-**moh**-nee-oh
twin room	habitación con dos camas	ah-bee-tah-thee-**ohn** kohn dohs **kah**-mahs
single room	habitación individual	ah-bee-tah-thee-**ohn** een-dee-vee-doo-**ahl**
room with a bath	habitación con baño	ah-bee-tah-thee-**ohn** kohn **bah**-nyoh
shower	ducha	**doo**-chah
porter	el botones	ehl boh-**toh**-nehs
key	la llave	lah **yah**-veh
I have a reservation.	Tengo una habitación reservada.	tehn-goh **oo**-na ah-bee-tah-thee-**ohn** reh-sehr-**bah**-dah

Eating Out

Have you got a table for …?	¿Tienen mesa para …?	tee-**eh**-nehn meh-sah pah-**rah**
I want to reserve a table.	Quiero reservar una mesa.	kee-eh-roh reh-sehr-**bahr** oo-nah **meh**-sah
The bill, please.	La cuenta, por favor.	lah **kwehn**-tah pohr fah-**vohr**
I am a vegetarian	Soy vegetariano/a	soy beh-heh-tah-ree-**ah**-no/na
waitress/ waiter	camarera/ camarero	kah-mah-**reh**-rah/ kah-mah-**reh**-roh
menu	la carta	lah **kahr**-tah
fixed-price menu	menú del día	meh-**noo** dehl **dee**-ah
wine list	la carta de vinos	lah **kahr**-tah deh **bee**-nohs
glass	un vaso	oon **bah**-soh
bottle	una botella	oo-nah boh-**teh**-yah
knife	un cuchillo	oon koo-**chee**-yoh
fork	un tenedor	oon teh-neh-**dohr**
spoon	una cuchara	oo-nah koo-**chah**-rah
breakfast	el desayuno	ehl deh-sah-**yoo**-noh
lunch	la comida/ el almuerzo	lah koh-**mee**-dah/ ehl ahl-**mwehr**-thoh
dinner	la cena	lah **theh**-nah
main course	el primer plato	ehl pree-**mehr plah**-toh
starters	los entrantes	lohs ehn-tran-tehs
dish of the day	el plato del día	ehl **plah**-toh dehl **dee**-ah
coffee	el café	ehl kah-**feh**
rare	poco hecho	**poh**-koh **eh**-choh
medium	medio hecho	**meh**-dee-oh **eh**-choh
well done	muy hecho	mwee **eh**-choh

Menu Decoder

asado	ah-**sah**-doh	roast
el aceite	ah-**thee-eh**-teh	oil
las aceitunas	ah-theh-**toon**-ahs	olives
el agua mineral	ah-gwa mee-neh-**rahl**	mineral water
sin gas/con gas	seen gas/kohn gas	still/sparkling
el ajo	**ah**-hoh	garlic
el arroz	ahr-**rohth**	rice
el azúcar	ah-**thoo**-kahr	sugar
la carne	**kahr**-neh	meat
la cebolla	theh-**boh**-yah	onion
la cerveza	thehr-**beh**-thah	beer
el cerdo	**therh**-doh	pork
el chocolate	choh-koh-**lah**-teh	chocolate
el chorizo	choh-**ree**-thoh	chorizo
el cordero	kohr-**deh**-roh	lamb
el fiambre	fee-**ahm**-breh	cold meat
frito	**free**-toh	fried
la fruta	**froo**-tah	fruit
los frutos secos	froo-tohs seh-kohs	nuts
las gambas	**gahm**-bahs	prawns
el helado	eh-**lah**-doh	ice cream
al horno	ahl **ohr**-noh	baked
el huevo	oo-**eh**-voh	egg
el jamón serrano	hah-**mohn** sehr-**rah**-noh	cured ham
el jerez	heh-**rehz**	sherry

la langosta	lahn-**gohs**-tah	lobster
la leche	**leh**-cheh	milk
el limón	lee-**mohn**	lemon
la limonada	lee-moh-**nah**-dah	lemonade
la mantequilla	mahn-teh-**kee**-yah	butter
la manzana	mahn-**thah**-nah	apple
los mariscos	mah-**rees**-kohs	seafood
la menestra	meh-**nehs**-trah	vegetable stew
la naranja	nah-**rahn**-hah	orange
el pan	pahn	bread
el pastel	pahs-**tehl**	cake
las patatas	pah-**tah**-tahs	potatoes
el pescado	pehs-**kah**-doh	fish
la pimienta	pee-mee-**yehn**-tah	pepper
el plátano	**plah**-tah-noh	banana
el pollo	**poh**-yoh	chicken
el postre	**pohs**-treh	dessert
el queso	**keh**-soh	cheese
la sal	sahl	salt
las salchichas	sahl-**chee**-chahs	sausages
la salsa	**sahl**-sah	sauce
seco	**seh**-koh	dry
el solomillo	soh-loh-**mee**-yoh	sirloin
la sopa	**soh**-pah	soup
la tarta	**tahr**-tah	pie/cake
el té	teh	tea
la ternera	tehr-**neh**-rah	beef
las tostadas	tohs-**tah**-dahs	toast
el vinagre	bee-nah-greh	vinegar
el vino blanco	**bee**-noh **blahn**-koh	white wine
el vino rosado	**bee**-noh roh-**sah**-doh	rosé wine
el vino tinto	**bee**-noh **teen**-toh	red wine

Numbers

0	cero	**theh**-roh
1	uno	**oo**-noh
2	dos	dohs
3	tres	trehs
4	cuatro	**kwa**-troh
5	cinco	**theen**-koh
6	seis	says
7	siete	see-**eh**-the
8	ocho	**oh**-choh
9	nueve	**nweh**-veh
10	diez	dee-**ehth**
11	once	**ohn**-theh
12	doce	**doh**-theh
13	trece	**treh**-theh
14	catorce	kah-**tohr**-theh
15	quince	**keen**-theh
16	dieciséis	dee-eh-thee-**seh-ees**
17	diecisiete	dee-eh-thee-see-**eh**-the
18	dieciocho	dee-eh-thee-**oh**-choh
19	diecinueve	dee-eh-thee-**nweh**-veh
20	veinte	**beh**-een-the
21	veintiuno	beh-een-tee-**oo**-noh
22	veintidós	beh-een-tee-**dohs**
30	treinta	**treh**-een-tah
31	treinta y uno	treh-een-tah ee **oo**-noh
40	cuarenta	kwah-**rehn**-tah
50	cincuenta	theen-**kwehn**-tah
60	sesenta	seh-**sehn**-tah
70	setenta	seh-**tehn**-tah
80	ochenta	oh-**chehn**-tah
90	noventa	noh-**vehn**-tah
100	cien	**thee-ehn**
101	ciento uno	thee-**ehn**-toh oo-noh
102	ciento dos	thee-**ehn**-toh dohs
200	doscientos	dohs-thee-**ehn**-tohs
500	quinientos	khee-nee-**ehn**-tohs
700	setecientos	seh-teh-thee-**ehn**-tohs
900	novecientos	noh-veh-thee-**ehn**-tohs
1,000	mil	meel
1,001	mil uno	meel **oo**-noh

Time

one minute	un minuto	oon mee-**noo**-toh
one hour	una hora	**oo**-na **oh**-rah
half an hour	media hora	**meh**-dee-a **oh**-rah
Monday	lunes	**loo**-nehs
Tuesday	martes	**mahr**-tehs
Wednesday	miércoles	mee-**ehr**-koh-lehs
Thursday	jueves	hoo-**weh**-vehs
Friday	viernes	bee-**ehr**-nehs
Saturday	sábado	**sah**-bah-doh
Sunday	domingo	doh-**meen**-goh